THE OUTER LIMITS OF EUROPEAN UNION LAW

A commonly expressed view is that the citizens and the Member States are destined to be overcome by the European Union. There is a sense that the Union of today is not what was intended to be created or acceded to by the Member States or its citizens. *The Outer Limits of European Union Law* brings together a diverse group of legal scholars to consider aspects of EU substantive, constitutional and procedural law in a manner highlighting the many senses in which the Union is, or can be, limited. The contributors reveal not only the strengths of the various limits but also, and more crucially, the weakness of the limits, thereby demonstrating that the prospect of being overcome may be a genuine risk to be guarded against. By considering general themes (eg legitimacy) and core subject areas (eg policing, free movement of goods, remedies) the book reveals the various techniques used by the Court of Justice, Community institutions and the Member States to define and modify the limits of the European Union and European Union law.

The Outer Limits of European Union Law

Edited by

Catherine Barnard

and

Okeoghene Odudu

• HART •
PUBLISHING

OXFORD AND PORTLAND, OREGON
2009

Published in North America (US and Canada) by
Hart Publishing
c/o International Specialized Book Services
920 NE 58th Avenue, Suite 300
Portland, OR 97213–3786
USA
Tel: +1 503 287 3093 or toll-free: (1) 800 944 6190
Fax: +1 503 280 8832
E-mail: orders@isbs.com
Website: http://www.isbs.com

Hart Publishing, 16C Worcester Place, OX1 2JW
Telephone: +44 (0)1865 517530 Fax: +44 (0)1865 510710
E-mail: mail@hartpub.co.uk
Website: http://www.hartpub.co.uk

British Library Cataloguing in Publication Data
Data Available

ISBN: 978-1-84113-860-2

Typeset by Columns Design Ltd, Reading
Printed and bound in Great Britain by
TJ International Ltd, Padstow, Cornwall

Contents

List of Contributors

Catherine Barnard is Professor of EU and Employment Law, University of Cambridge, Fellow of Trinity College, Jean Monnet Chair of EU Law, Co-director of Centre for European Law Studies

Alan Dashwood is Professor of European Law, Fellow of Sidney Sussex College, University of Cambridge

Micahel Dougan is Professor of Law, University of Liverpool

Herwig Hofmann is Professor of European Law, University of Luxembourg

Assimakis Komninos is Associate, White & Case LLP, Brussels; Visiting Lecturer, IREA—Université Paul Cézanne Aix-Marseille III, Aix-en-Provence and University College London

Panos Koutrakos is Professor of Law, University of Bristol

Konrad Lachmayer is a Lecturer and post-doctorate researcher at the University of Vienna, Austria

Renato Nazzini is a Reader in Law, University of Southampton

Niamh Nic Shuibhne is a Reader in EC Law, University of Edinburgh

Okeoghene Odudu is Herchel Smith Lecturer in Law, University of Cambridge, Fellow of Emmanuel College and Assistant Director of the Centre for European Legal Studies

Jo Shaw is Salvesen Chair of European Institutions, Europa Institute, School of Law, University of Edinburgh

Eleanor Spaventa is a Reader in Law, University of Durham

Alina Tryfonidou is Lecturer in Law, University of Leicester

Angela Ward is a Barrister, Law Library, Dublin

Stephen Weatherill is Jacques Delors' Professor of Law, Somerville College, University of Oxford

1

Outer Limits of European Union Law: Introduction

CATHERINE BARNARD AND OKEOGHENE ODUDU*

I THE PROBLEM AND THE PROJECT

THE EUROPEAN UNION (EU) is constantly accused of invading the nooks and crannies of national life. In 1974 Lord Denning famously compared what is now EU law to 'an incoming tide' that 'cannot be held back'.[1] By 1990 he considered EU law had become 'a tidal wave bringing down our sea walls and flowing inland over our fields and houses—to the dismay of all'.[2] The fears of this constant encroachment can be seen in the claims of the no-campaigners in the Irish referendum on the Lisbon Treaty that ratification would put at risk national rules on abortion, Irish neutrality and the death penalty.[3] The Irish 'no' provides a concrete example of the deeply-felt sense that the incoming tide of EU law cannot be prevented from overtopping the barriers and defences that (once) protected national systems. More generally, citizens lament the erosion of national sovereignty in areas such as policing, border control and national security; they feel too much politically sensitive decision-making occurs at EU level.[4]

* Thanks to Angus Johnston who commented on this while nursing a very broken ankle.

[1] *HP Bulmer Ltd v J Bollinger SA (No 2)* [1974] Ch 401, at 418–19.

[2] Denning, *Introduction to The European Court of Justice: Judges or Policy Makers?* (London, Bruges Group, 1990) at 7–8

[3] http://www.no2lisbon.ie/; http://www.voteno.ie/; http://www.libertas.org/content/view/293/139/. Cf http://www.fiannafail.ie/article.phpx?topic=151&id=9081&nav=Local%20Item and http://www.euractiv.com/en/future-eu/interview-collective-remorse-ireland/article-174099.

[4] M Höpner and A Schäfer (2007) 'A new phase of European Integration: Organized Capitalisms in Post-Ricardian Europe' MPifG Discussion Paper 07/4 Max-Planck-Institut für Gesellschaftsforschung, Köln.

Concurrent with the claim that the EU does too much, is a claim that the EU does not do enough. As the 2001 Laeken Declaration recognises,[5] citizens demand that the EU be empowered to do 'something' about key issues such as terrorism, immigration, employment and the environment. But when the EU does act, expectations—often raised by the EU itself—are not fulfilled. For example, at the Lisbon summit in March 2000[6] the Union set itself the (over-ambitious) strategic goal of becoming the most competitive and dynamic knowledge-based economy in the world by 2010, capable of sustainable economic growth with more and better jobs and greater social cohesion.[7] In particular, the Lisbon and subsequently Stockholm European Councils set the EU the objective of reaching an overall employment rate of 70 per cent, an employment rate of over 60 per cent for women, and an employment rate among older men and women (55–64) of 50 per cent.[8] Only the employment rate for women shows any sign of being met by the 2010 deadline.[9] One of the explanations for the EU's failure to achieve these targets is the absence of clear competence for it to act in such sensitive areas. Instead, it is reliant on the Member States to deliver, at a time when the economy in the EU (and across the world) is suffering from historic levels of financial instability and a slowdown in the US and other major economies.[10] So, although the EU sends messages that it has the capacity to solve problems, solutions may well involve matters beyond the EU's control. It therefore sets itself up for a fall.

Returning to Lord Denning's observations in the introduction, is it true that the citizens and the Member States are being overcome by an incoming tide? If not, what has held the tide back? What limits the EU? These questions were addressed at a seminar hosted by the Centre for European Legal Studies at Cambridge in September 2007 and this volume presents the various responses of the participants. The contributors consider the question of outer limits of EU law from a number of perspectives. By considering general themes (for example legitimacy) and core subject

[5] 'Citizens often hold expectations of the European Union that are not always fulfilled. And vice versa—they sometimes have the impression that the Union takes on too much in areas where its involvement is not always essential. Thus the important thing is to clarify, simplify and adjust the division of competence between the Union and the Member States in the light of the new challenges facing the Union. This can lead both to restoring tasks to the Member States and to assigning new missions to the Union, or to the extension of existing powers, while constantly bearing in mind the equality of the Member States and their mutual solidarity.' http://www.ena.lu/laeken_declaration_future_european_union_15_december_2001-020003970.html.

[6] Presidency Conclusions, 24 March 2000.

[7] Para 5.

[8] Stockholm European Council, 23 and 24 March 2001, para 9.

[9] 'Renewed social agenda: Opportunities, Access and Solidarity in 21st Century Europe': COM(2008) 412, 13.

[10] COM(2007) 803.

areas (for example policing, free movement of goods and remedies) the book reveals the various techniques used by the Court of Justice, Community institutions, and Member States to define and modify the outer limits of the EU and EU law.

II THE IDENTIFIED LIMITS

It has always been clear that there are limits to the scope and field of application of EU law. This goes to the heart of the legitimacy of the EU project. The question is what are those limits and where do the outer limits actually lie?[11] Even in a single state identifying the limits of public power can be a difficult exercise. A federal system adds the complexity of knowing which part of the public sphere is properly authorised to exercise that power, and identifying the limits imposed in the division of competence between the central and local levels. For those interested in the EU this analytical task is made yet more complex by the *sui generis* nature of the Community and the Union and the very fluidity of those limits: for example, in one period criminal law matters or national security appear to fall wholly outside the scope of EC law and go to the core of national sovereignty; gradually Community law begins to encroach even upon these fields.

At the most fundamental level the need to identify limits flows from the idea that all democratic systems impose limits on the exercise of public power. In the context of the EU, it has long been known that the Union is not a self-authenticating entity. Instead, the EU is limited to exercising the powers conferred upon it by the Member States. This is made clear at a formal level in Article 5(1) EC, which provides that '[t]he Community shall act within the limits of the powers conferred upon it by this Treaty and of the objectives assigned to it therein'. This attempt to define the limits of the Community's competence creates the presumption that all which is not conferred remains with the Member States. The Lisbon Treaty makes this point expressly: Article 4(1) TEU-L provides that in accordance with

[11] See Anthony Arnull 'The Incoming Tide: Responding to Marshall' [1986] *PL* 383–99, Dawn Oliver 'Fishing on the incoming tide' (1991) *MLR* 54(3), 442–51; Andrew Geddes 'The incoming tide: the impact of EEC law: Part 1' *NLJ* 1991, 141 (6522), 1330,1337; Andrew Geddes 'The incoming tide: the impact of EEC law: Part 2' *NLJ* 1991, 141(6523), 1386–7; Stefanie Grant 'The incoming tide' *NLJ* 1992, 142 (6565), 1167–8, 1174; Oliver Hyams 'The incoming tide' *NLJ* 1994, 144(6634), 152,154; Dashwood 'The Limits of European Community Powers' (1996) 21 *ELRev* , 113–28; Dashwood 'States in the European Union' (1998) 23 *ELRev* , 201–216; Adrian Toutoungi 'Intel v Via: holding back the tide of compulsory licensing?' *European Intellectual Property Review* 2002, 24(11), 548–53; Seamus Burns 'An incoming tide' *NLJ* 2008, 158 (7303), 44–6 and; W van Gerven, 'The invader invaded or the need to uncover general principles common to the laws of the Member States', in GC Rodríguez Iglesias (ed), *Mélanges en hommage à Fernand Schockweiler* (Baden-Baden, Nomas 1999), 593, at 598.

Article 5, competences not conferred upon the Union in the Treaties remain with the Member States. Article 5(1) TEU-L states 'The limits of Union competences are governed by the principle of conferral'. 'Conferral' is defined in Article 5(2) TEU-L as the Union acting 'only within the limits of the competences conferred upon it by the Member States in the Treaties to attain the objectives set out therein'. For good measure it adds 'Competences not conferred upon the Union in the Treaties remain with the Member States'.

In terms of legislative competence to act, the EC Treaty contains an (ever-larger) number of Treaty provisions which provide the basis for Community action. These bases are currently scattered across the Treaty. By contrast, the Lisbon Treaty provides a streamlined catalogue of competences in Title I of the Treaty on the Functioning of the EU.[12] Some of the legal bases in the current EC Treaty identify specific areas for Community action (for example Article 175 on the environment and Article 47 on the mutual recognition of diplomas); others (notably Articles 95 and 308) are much less specific. Some of the more recently introduced legal bases are more careful in circumscribing Community competence to act. For example, Article 149, introduced at Maastricht, provides that the Community 'shall contribute to the development of quality education' but by 'encouraging cooperation between Member States and, if necessary, by supporting and supplementing their action, while fully respecting the responsibility of the Member States for the content of teaching and the organisation of education systems and their cultural and linguistic diversity'. By contrast, other provisions expressly articulate what the EC does not have the power to do. For example, Article 137(5) provides that the provisions of Article 137 'shall not apply to pay, the right of association, the right to strike or the right to impose lock-outs'. While this provision has led to some debate as to whether the Community has no competence at all in these areas or merely no competence under Article 137 (but may still enact legislation under, for example, Article 308), the provision does send out a strong message that these areas are very much a matter for the Member States.

However, even when Member States retain competence, the exercise of that competence is still subject to the ceiling of the EC Treaty, in particular the four freedoms.[13] The significance of this can be seen in *Viking*[14] where the Court ruled that collective action regulated by national law fell in principle

[12] M Dougan, 'The Treaty of Lisbon 2007: Winning Minds, Not Hearts' (2008) 45 *Common Market Law Review* 617.

[13] See also, in the field of taxation, Case C-80/94 *Wielockx* [1995] ECR I-2493, para 16; Case C-319/02 *Manninen* [2004] ECR I-7477, para 19 and in the field of healthcare See eg Case C–158/96, *Kohll v Union des caisses de maladie* [1998] ECR I–1931, paras 17–19.

[14] Case C–438/05, *Viking Line ABP v The International transport Workers' Federation, the Finnish Seaman's Union* [2007] ECR I-10779.

'within the scope of Article 43',[15] dismissing the argument that because Article 137(5) excluded Community competence in respect of the right to strike, strike action as a whole fell outside the scope of Community law.[16] Furthermore, in a remarkable process of bootstrapping, the European Court of Justice (ECJ) has been willing to use expressly limited Community competence to justify removing limits on the application of the Treaty provisions on the four freedoms it itself had identified. For example, in *Grzelczyk*'[17] the Court pointed to Article 149 EC to justify reversing its earlier approach in *Brown*[18] that assistance given to students for maintenance and training fell outside the scope of the EC Treaty for the purposes of Article 12 EC.[19] The Court said in *Grzelczyk* that 'There is nothing in the amended text of the Treaty to suggest that students who are citizens of the Union, when they move to another Member State to study there, lose the rights which the Treaty confers on citizens of the Union',[20] including the principle of non-discrimination.[21]

Viking and *Grzelczyk* provide good examples of what some might see as competence creep. They demonstrate how, what looks like carefully delimited Community competence, gets blurred in the interpretation of other Treaty provisions. *Grzelczyk* also shows the power of the Treaty provisions on citizenship to erode Member States' sovereign power to control and regulate their own social security systems.[22]

So far we have concentrated on the most obvious and visible limit to the Community's competence: its capacity to legislate in defined areas only. This means that, in principle, all other areas are left to the Member States. But this is not the only way that the Treaty creates space for Member States to act. Another obvious example is the derogations from the four freedoms (such as public policy, public security and public health). These have been supplemented by the mandatory—or public interest—requirements developed by the Court. In addition, Article 296 contains (a rather narrowly tailored) protection of Member States' national security interests. However, as chapter 12 by Barnard and chapter 13 by Koutrakos indicate, the Court has generally insisted on an increasingly narrow reading of these provisions.

[15] Para 37.

[16] Paras 39–41. See also Case C-341/05, *Laval un Partneri Ltd v Svenska Byggnadsarbetareförbundet* [2007] ECR I-11767, para 88. For a further example, see Article 295 'This Treaty shall in no way prejudice the rules in Member States governing the system of property ownership'. This provision is however, read subject to Articles 28 and 30 in the field on intellectual property rights: Case 24/67 *Parke Davis* [1968] ECR 55, 72

[17] Case C-184/99 *Rudy Grzelczyk v Centre public d'aide sociale d'Ottignies Louvain-la-Neuve* [2001] ECR I-6193, para 35.

[18] Case 197/86 *Brown v Secretary of State for Scotland* [1988] ECR 3205.

[19] Para 18.

[20] Para 35.

[21] Para 36.

[22] These points are elaborated further by Nic Shiubhne in ch 8.

Barnard argues that the derogations/mandatory requirements appear to give States considerable room for manoeuvre and an obvious way of preserving national regulatory autonomy. However, a study of cases decided in 1984, 1994 and 2004 reveals that increasingly the Court is saying that, on the facts of a particular case, the Member State has failed to make out a justification or, if it has made out a justification, the steps taken do not comply with the principles of proportionality, fundamental rights, effective judicial protection and legal certainty. This has marked a significant shift in the balance of power between the EU and the Member States.

Koutrakos also tells a story of growing scrutiny by the Court of the use of the Article 296 security derogation by the Member States. He notes that Article 296 was long considered to put the defence industries entirely beyond the reach of EU law. Their function of organising national defence was deemed to place them at the core of national sovereignty, a space much removed from the incrementally developing purview of Community law. However, recent developments, particularly in the case law of the Court, as well as the need to restructure national defence industries following the end of the cold war, have questioned this assumption, highlighted its flaws and gradually placed defence industries at the centre of an increasingly multilayered legislative and political dialogue at EU level.

As we have seen, the Court is a key player in the debates about the outer limits of Community law. Cases such as *Viking* and *Grzelczyk* illustrate one way in which the Court appears to have *expanded* the scope of application of Community law. In contrast, there are examples of the Court drawing a line in the sand and identifying the outer limits of the Treaty's power of negative intervention. *Keck*[23] is perhaps the most famous illustration of this. As is well known, the Court ruled that non-discriminatory national measures restricting or prohibiting certain selling arrangements do not breach Article 28. As Spaventa shows in chapter 11, this is not the only technique the Court has employed. In particular, it has used the doctrine of 'effect too uncertain and indirect', sometimes referred to as the 'remoteness' test, pursuant to which when there is no causal connection between the alleged barrier and intra-Community trade, the Treaty does not apply. In a related vein, the Court has also argued in *Deliège*[24] that while selection rules for participating in an international sports competition inevitably had the effect of limiting the number of participants in a tournament, such a limitation was inherent in the conduct of high-level international sports events. These cases suggest that while the Court has the tools with which to exercise self-restraint, it does not consistently apply them.

[23] Joined Cases C-267–8/91 *Keck and Mithouard* [1993] ECR I–6097.

[24] Joined Cases C-51/96 and C-191/97 *Deliège v Ligue Francophone de Judo et Disciplines Associés* [2000] ECR I–2549, para 64.

The Court has other more well-established techniques for limiting the application of Community law. In particular, it has, in Nic Shuibhne's words, employed legal or interpretative limits, representing the boundaries prescribed by the 'wording and general scheme'[25] of both the Treaty and legal interpretations of the Treaty. So, Community law is engaged only if there is an 'economic activity' at stake.[26] The need for economic activity limits Community law and preserves for Member States a greater degree of autonomy over that which can be said to be non-economic. However, as with most limits, the 'economic activity' threshold is not what it seems. Odudu demonstrates in chapter 10 that the Treaty does not contain a single definition of the term and that Treaty provisions seemingly limited to economic activity may also be applied to non-economic activity. This again provides a good illustration of the potential blurring of the edges of EC competence.

A further threshold is the requirement that Community law is engaged only if there is a transnational situation: wholly internal rules are not caught by Community law. Tryfonidou demonstrates in chapter 9 that, over time, the Court has taken different approaches to the wholly internal rule but the various approaches have generated problems, in particular the failure to reflect the economic realities of a case. She argues that situations that, on the face of it, do not involve an inter-state element, can, nonetheless, have a substantially negative impact on inter-state trade.

So far we have focused on a fairly narrow legal approach to the question of the limits of EU law. There are of course, other limits: in particular the territorial limits of the EU (that is the borders of the now 27 states) and the personal limits of the EU (for example most of the Community law rules on free movement do not apply to third country nationals). It is in this context that Shaw's contribution in chapter 5 offers a different perspective on the outer limits debate. Through a case study on political participation in the new Member States, particularly the Baltic states and Slovenia, Shaw demonstrates how enlargement prompts us to examine the concept of 'outer limits' anew. She starts with the obvious but important point that enlargement has shifted the geographic outer limits of the EU and has extended the reach of EU Law: enlargement has increased the number of people who can benefit from EC law, people who were previously third

[25] Borrowing from Case 26/62 *Van Gend en Loos v Nederlandse Administratie der Belastingen* [1963] ECR 1.

[26] Case T-313/02 *David Meca-Medina and Igor Majcen v Commission* [2004] ECR II-3291, paras 37 and 41; Case C-519/04 P *David Meca-Medina and Igor Majcen v Commission* [2006] ECR I-6991, paras. 22 and 25, AG Opinion para. 18; Case C-309/99 *JCJ Wouters and others v Algemene Raad van de Nederlandse Orde van Advocaten* [2002] ECR I-1577, para 57; C-369/04 *Hutchison 3G UK Ltd and Others v Commissioners of Customs and Excise* [2007] ECR-I 5247, para 28; and Cases C-284/04 *T-Mobile Austria GmbH and Others v Republik Österreich* [2007] ECR-I 5189, para 34.

country nationals, and the number of places in which Community law can be relied on.

However, she also points out that although this is the formal legal position, in fact the complex make up of these new states, largely due to the presence of substantial populations of non-nationals following the break-up of former states (the Soviet Union and Yugoslavia), has resulted in minorities not holding national citizenship of the host state and thus not benefitting from EU rights. Moreover, in Estonia, Latvia and Lithuania high barriers, including strict language tests, often prevent resident non-nationals gaining national citizenship. These are practical limits preventing a large number of individuals from having access to Community law.

III HAS THE UNION STRAYED BEYOND THE LIMITS AND, IF SO, HOW?

While it is clear that there are limits to EU law, there is also evidence that the Community and the Union stray beyond those limits. Eurosceptics cry foul. Europhiles are more benign: they recognise that the EU must stay within the limits laid down as part of the process of legitimising the endeavour but they also realise that the EU's legitimacy is under threat if it fails to deliver. Thus the EU must be able to function effectively and, at times, this requires a generous interpretation of rules which are themselves open textured. Take, for example, the Community's competence to legislate. As Weatherill points out in chapter 2, Article 5 EC is not supported by clear and easily monitored rules. The legal bases, most notably Articles 95 and 308, are broad and ambiguous. Dashwood notes in chapter 3 that the fuzziness of those limits can be (and have been) exploited by the legislature, especially in the pre-Maastricht era when Article 308 was used to extend Community competence into fields that were not logically connected with the common market project. This, he argues, is no longer acceptable. He says that there remains a role for Article 308 in allowing powers specifically attributed to the Community institutions by the EC Treaty to be supplemented, where this is demonstrably necessary to ensure the attainment of the objective for which the power in question was conferred. However, that role has become ever more limited, as specific legal bases have proliferated.

His view appears to be supported by the Court. On two well-known occasions—*Tobacco Advertising*[27] and *Opinion 2/94*[28]—the ECJ put its foot down and said that the legislation exceeded the scope of Community competence. But, as Weatherill shows, these cases are the exception rather

[27] Case C-376/98 *Germany v EP and Council (Tobacco Advertising)* [2000] ECR I-8419.
[28] *Opinion 2/94* [1996] ECR I-1759.

than the rule and the Court's stance is now more concerned with 'competence-enhancing' than 'competence-restricting'.[29] Furthermore, as Ward demonstrates in chapter 14, the Court's strict door-keeper function of the *locus standi* rules under Article 230(4) means that many potential challenges to the legality of Community action are kept out of the Courts. And even if parties overcome the hurdle of *locus,* the Court's scrutiny of Community measures is generally light, especially in so far as challenges based on subsidiarity are concerned.[30] Power and the exercise of power become increasingly centralised.

Hofmann offers a different perspective in chapter 4: crafting effective limits is problematic precisely because Union power is multi-level. Community legislation is implemented through an intense cooperation of administrative actors from both the EU and the Member States. He considers subsidiarity not to have failed but instead to underpin new forms of governance, so that subsidiarity influences how Union power is exercised (though cooperative networks) rather than rather than placing a limit on Union power as such. Shaw also emphasises that because governance is multi-level there is no clear separation between what the EU and Member States do. She highlights 'the extent to which the different sites and levels at which rights are granted under EU law and national law are increasingly becoming intermingled and indistinguishable'. In the case of EU political citizenship at least, and very probably in other areas such as employment policy which is based on extensive use of the Open Method of Coordination (OMC) toolkit, it becomes increasingly difficult to identify the outer limits of EU intervention with any degree of certainty and such blurring of lines of separation are hard for the Court to police.

Lachmeyer's chapter contains a case study of this very blurring of roles and responsibilities. He takes the subject of policing—traditionally considered to lie at the core of state sovereignty—and demonstrates how, given the increasingly transnational nature of crime and the need to combat terrorism, the EU has assumed a greater coordinating role, albeit a role that has been hampered by a lack of competence even under the third pillar. This has led to the use of a wide range of alternative strategies to overcome some of these Treaty limitations (for example international cooperation in the Prüm Treaty which subsequently became a third pillar

[29] See, dealing particularly with the Art 95 case law, D Wyatt, 'Community competence to regulate the internal market' Oxford Legal Studies Research Paper 9/2007, http://papers.ssrn.com/sol3/papers.cfm?abstract_id=997863; also M Seidel, 'Präventive Rechtsangleichung im Bereich des Gemeinsamen Marktes' [2006] *Europarecht* 26.

[30] Case C-103/01 *Commission v Germany* [2003] ECR I-5369 para 47; Cases C-154/04 and C-155/04 *Alliance for Natural Health* [2005] ECR I-6451 paras 99–108. *Cf* eg G Davies, 'Subsidiarity: the wrong idea, in the wrong place, at the wrong time' (2006) 43 *Common Market Law Review* 63.

measure, transnational mutual cooperation, transnational and supranational data exchange, coordination by and initiative taking by Europol, participation by Europol in joint investigation teams, and through shared competences of the EU regarding the external dimension of internal security measures (Passenger Name Record PNR Data Exchange)). These developments have helped to redefine the contours of the outer limits of Union law but inevitably, given the almost total absence of Community competence, have left little room for ECJ involvement.

One of the most dramatic ways in which Community law has intervened in the nooks and crannies of daily national life is through the application of the four freedoms. We have already seen, in cases such as *Viking* and *Grzelczyk,* that limits on the *Community's* competence to legislate do not prevent the Treaty provisions on free movement constraining *Member State* legislative or other activity. However, the Court's intervention goes beyond this. In particular, it has pushed the frontiers of Community intervention by generally moving, at least in the field of free movement of persons, services and capital, from the discrimination model (which preserves national regulatory autonomy so long as the rule does not discriminate either directly or indirectly), to the market access restrictions approach which does far more damage to national regulatory autonomy.[31] As Barnard notes, when combined with a robust reading of the derogations/justifications the application of the market access test marks a significant shift in power away from the Member States.

This move has caused concern. For example, in *Caixa-Bank*[32] Advocate General Tizzano expressed profound misgivings about the 'rather broad concept of restriction' in the case law covering all 'national measures *liable* to hinder *or make less attractive the exercise of fundamental freedoms* guaranteed by the Treaty'.[33] He said that such a broad approach to the 'restrictions' allows economic operators, both national and foreign, to abuse the Treaty to oppose any national measure that, solely because it regulated the conditions for pursuing an economic activity, could in the final analysis narrow profit margins and hence reduce the attractiveness of pursuing that particular economic activity.[34]

Yet, the Court has carried on regardless. In chapter 7 Dougan presents a case study of the remarkable impact of the market access approach on

[31] Case C-76/90 *Säger* [1991] ECR I–4221, para 12.

[32] Case C-442/02 *Caixa-Bank v Ministère de l'Économie, des Finances and de l'industrie* [2004] ECR I-8961.

[33] Para 39, emphasis in the original, criticising, in particular, Case C-255/97 *Pfeiffer Grosshandel* [1999] ECR I-2835.

[34] Para 62. The Court itself acknowledged this in Case C-290/04 *FKP Skorpio* [2006] ECR I-9461, para 46 'the application of the host Member State's national rules to providers of services is liable to prohibit, impede or render less attractive the provision of services to the extent that it involves expense and additional administrative and economic burdens'.

national social welfare systems 'a field which, only a few years ago, most people assumed lay truly at the outer limit of the Treaty'. His particular focus is to show how the EU ensures that a state's obligations to its own citizens no longer stop at the border to its territory. He notes that these developments have occurred despite the existence of Community legislation (Regulation 1408/71 and Regulation 883/2004) which appears to give greater autonomy to the Member States. He notes that at times the Court treats Regulation 1408/71 and the primary Treaty provisions as parallel legal regimes, each capable of applying independently to the same dispute, and each capable of producing a different final outcome, though without amounting to a direct clash of norms. At other times the Court treats primary Treaty rules as hierarchically superior to Regulation 1408/71, so that treatment consistent with the coordination regime provided by Regulation 1408/71 does not per se shield the Member State from judicial scrutiny under the market access approach for having infringed the Union citizen's right to free movement provided by the Treaty. However, the Court then permits the provisions of Regulation 1408/71 to act as the primary framework for judicial review during the subsequent process of objective justification, so that compliance with Community secondary legislation creates at least a strong presumption in favour of upholding the national territorial restrictions. Dougan sees the extension of Community Treaty intervention as legitimate in so far as it is to the benefit of the citizen. However, he argues that the Union must exercise 'sensitivity and restraint of its theoretical power, precisely in an area able to illuminate, in a most unflattering light, the Union's perilously fragile mandate to act'.

The Court would justify its intervention into such diverse fields as social welfare and defence on the grounds of effectiveness. This has also been the driving principle behind its extensive activity in the field of national remedies. Nazzini focuses on the principle of effectiveness and how this has been used by the Court to develop remedies for breach of Community competition law. He argues that the traditional understanding of the doctrine of national procedural autonomy—the bulwark against EC erosion of national rules on remedies—has imposed artificial limits on the development of Community law rights and limits (such as the refusal of the Court in the *Manfredi*[35] case to address the definition of the concept of 'causal relationship'). He also argues that the Court of Justice often uses the term 'effectiveness' ambiguously to cover both the principle of full effectiveness of Community law and the principle of effective judicial protection. While regarding the principles as closely linked and often pointing in the same direction, he considers them conceptually distinct: the

[35] Joined cases C-295/04 to C-298/04, *Vincenzo Manfredi et al v Lloyd Adriatico Assicurazioni SpA et al* [2006] ECR I-6619.

principle of effective judicial protection presupposes the existence of a right while the principle of full effectiveness of Community law may be the legal basis of the right.

Komninos adopts a more benign view of the Court of Justice in the field of remedies. He takes the case of competition law to offer 'a first paradigm of a more active role of Community law in the field of remedies in horizontal relationships between private parties and thus of a corresponding retreat of national remedial/procedural autonomy'. This judicial development paved the way for Community legislative action. He argues that competition law is by no means the only area of law which is ripe for such a remarkable development; developments in competition law have to be seen as a step in the long process of ensuring homogeneity and consistency in the broad area of Community law remedies, while ensuring full access to courts for individuals.

Ward argues that the Court's activism in respect of national remedies contrasts unfavourably with its minimal intervention in the field of Community remedies. She argues that the crafting, in the original EEC Treaty, of express remedies and procedures to challenge the legality of EEC measures has had a limiting effect on the development of the rules on, for example *locus*, while the silence of the foundation treaties on national sanctions and procedures has led to a body of case law that has 'grown like Topsy', and places no clear limits on the extent to which Member State law, including constitutional law, must fall under the imperatives of *effet utile*. She also argues that the case law on Member State remedies and procedural rules goes beyond the minimum limits set by Articles 6(1) and 13 of the European Convention on Human Rights, while the scheme for challenging the legality of EU measures quite possibly fails to measure up to them.

Effectiveness is not the only interpretative technique used by the Court to circumvent the textual limits on EU power. It has been particularly creative in its use of general principles of law. *Mangold*[36] provides a good example of this. The Court ruled that the principle of non-discrimination on grounds of age was to be regarded as a general principle of Community law,[37] the observance of which could not be made conditional on the expiry of the transposition date of the Framework Directive. Most strikingly, the Court indicated that general principles of law could be directly effective and enforceable in the national courts.[38] As Nic Shiubhne's demonstrates in chapter 8, the use of general principles of law, notably

[36] Case C-144/04 *Mangold v Rudiger Helm*, [2005] ECR I-9981. Although now cf C-427/06 *Bartsch v Bosch und Siemens Hausgeräte (BSH) Altersfürsorge GmbH*, judgment of 23 September 2008.

[37] Para 75.

[38] Para 77.

proportionality, in the field of citizenship has also significantly curtailed the limitations to citizens' rights. She argues that while this interpretative method could well have evolved for the Residence Directives independently, the application of a primary Treaty right moves 'things onto a different and normatively higher plane, perhaps best described as a constitutional one'. That understanding helps us to rationalise why proportionate economic insufficiency or not fully comprehensive medical insurance might mark the outer limits of free movement law as traditionally understood, but not those of EU citizenship.

The other technique used for expanding the limits of EU law is by eroding the limits the Court itself has recognised. As Nic Shuibhne shows, the Court has circumvented the wholly internal limitation by looking at past movement,[39] future (including potential) movement,[40] the movement of others,[41] movement deliberately undertaken so that Community rights could be invoked[42] and even the notion of 'passport movement' (that is where holding a passport from one State is in itself a sufficient trigger for Community rights to be attached to a situation involving one of the other States).[43]

Occasionally the Court simply ignores the textual limits. One of the best known examples is the variation of the position of the European Parliament under what was Article 173 EEC. In *Les Verts*[44] the Court said the Parliament had the right to be sued and in *Chernobyl*[45] the right to sue, at least to protect its own prerogatives. This development was endorsed by the Heads of State when the Treaty was amended to reflect this. In the very different context of policing Lachmeyer also notes the extent to which the

[39] Case C-370/90 *R v Immigration Appeal Tribunal and Singh, Ex p Secretary of State for the Home Department* [1992] ECR I-4265 (establishment); Case C-224/98 *D'Hoop v Office national de l'emploi* [2002] ECR I-6191 (citizenship).

[40] Although the Court rejected the possibility that purely hypothetical movement could be used to invoke the protection of citizenship (Case C-299/95 *Kremzow v Austria* [1997] ECR I-2629), other decisions protect an as-yet-to-be exercised right to move eg Case C-148/02 *Garcia Avello v Belgium* [2003] ECR I-11613, para 36 in particular (citizenship), on the inconvenience 'liable to be caused' by different States' rules on surnames). See Advocate General Sharpston's Opinion in Case C-212/06 *Government of the French Community and Walloon Government v Flemish Community*, judgment of 1 April 2008; Opinion delivered on 28 June 2007, see from para 64ff.

[41] Case C-255/99 *Humer* [2002] I-1205 (movement of the worker's dependent child); Case C-403/03 *Schempp v Finanzamt München V* [2005] ECR I-6421 (movement of the EU citizen's former spouse, see paras 21–2 in particular).

[42] It is a well established principle that deliberately taking advantage of Community rights by moving with that express intent does not constitute an abuse of Community law (see for example, Case C-109/01 *Secretary of State for the Home Department v Akrich* [2003] ECR I-9607, paras 55–7, free movement of workers).

[43] Case C-138/02 *Collins v Secretary of State for Work and Pensions* [2004] ECR I-2703; Case C-200/02 *Zhu and Chen v Secretary of State for the Home Department* [2004] ECR I-9925.

[44] Case 216/83 *Les Verts v Commission and Council* [1984] ECR 3325.

[45] Case C-70/88 *Parliament v Council* [1990] ECR I-2041.

Lisbon Treaty would mark a crucial shift from international coordination of policing to the integration of policing into the shared competences of the EU. However, it could be argued that the possibility of making such Treaty amendments creates an incentive on the actors to push at the boundaries of limits laid down by the Treaties.

IV WHAT ARE THE CONSEQUENCES OF GOING BEYOND THE LIMITS AND WHAT CAN BE DONE?

While one consequence of exceeding the limits of Community law is to have that step endorsed by Treaty amendment, more generally exceeding the limits means that legitimacy of the EU is harmed. However, as we have already suggested, the question of legitimacy is a complex one. As Weatherill puts it, legitimacy is damaged if the EU acts within the limits (because the EU is unable to deliver); legitimacy is damaged if the EU does a poor job (which will occur if the EU is institutionally or constitutionally ill equipped); and legitimacy is damaged if the Court fails to keep the institutions with the limits. The action can be illegitimate in two senses: *formally* illegitimate (ultra vires) or *socially* illegitimate, in that public opinion of the Union diminishes, as demonstrated by 'no' votes in the various referenda. He therefore argues that the EU should be kept within the limits through 'better competence monitoring' or 'competence control.' For him, there is a particular need to (i) clarify (but not necessarily simplify) and reorganise the Treaty rules governing competence and (ii) improve the system for monitoring the existence and exercise of competence by using national Parliaments.

Hofmann sees a more intensive proportionality review as having the potential to provide the main limit. When reviewing limitations of the exercise of power—both legislative and administrative in nature—proportionality review is currently undertaken with differing intensity in different contexts: measures of a more administrative nature are submitted to a stricter level of review from the point of view of the proportionality principle than cases of measures of a more legislative nature. The principle must be used to analyse whether the forum for decision-making is appropriate and to review the substance of specific measures. However, as Ward makes clear, *locus standi* rights are required in order that individuals' interests are protected by any type of review.

Perhaps it is through the adoption of legislation that judicial creativity is to be curtailed. This gives Member States the ability to protect their interests by participation and engagement with the EU and its institutions; However, as Nic Shuibhne notes the adoption of the Citizens' Rights Directive 2004/38 and as Dougan shows the existence of Regulation

1408/71, have not withstood the onslaught from the combined effect of citizenship rights and the market access test under the four freedoms.

V CONCLUSIONS

There are clearly limits to the scope of EU law but, as with an onion, peeling back the layers reveals ever more complexity to answer the deceptively simple question: what are the outer limits of EU law? We can still say that there are things that the EU does not do and ought not do: it does not have a police force or an army, it does not provide social welfare, education or health care. Nor does the EU have the competence to do any of these things. However the EU, and the Court in particular, is prepared to control the exercise of these powers by the Member States where national rules affect free movement. As the health care cases demonstrate, this inevitably has an impact on the shape of provision by the national systems.[46] It is in this context that some of the allegations of competence creep are most pronounced. And it is here that the EU must tread most carefully since the legitimacy of the EU is at its most precarious.

For those interested in deliberative democracy,[47] the constant contestation over the outer limits of EU law is a sign of a healthy, vibrant democratic process. The problem is that the debate about the outer limits of EU law is often ill-informed, as was demonstrated by much of the 'no' campaign literature leading up to the Irish referendum. A catalogue of competences, as the Lisbon Treaty provides, would offer a comfort blanket to sceptics and show that there are supposed to be limits to EU law. However, as the chapters in this book demonstrate any prescribed limits are not as fixed as would first appear.[48] This is not necessarily such a bad thing: rigidity can lead to a lack of flexibility and a lack of responsiveness.

Lord Denning obviously lamented the 'tidal wave' of EC law bringing down our sea walls. What he failed to appreciate is that much of national law is 'Community' law, particularly due to the principle of mutual

[46] See, eg, Cases C-368/98 *Vanbraekel v ANMC* [2001] ECR I-5363 and C-157/99 *Geraets-Smits and Peerbooms* [2001] ECR I-5473, Case C-385/99 *VG Müller-Fauré v Onderlinge Waarborgmaatschappij oz Zorgverzekeringen UA* and *EEM van Riet v Onderlinge Waarborgmaatschappij oz Zorgverzekeringen UA*, [2003] ECR I-4509.

[47] See, eg, J Cohen and C Sabel, 'Directly-deliberative polyarchy' (1997) 3 *European Law Journal* 313.

[48] For example, criminalisation being beyond the reach of the first pillar: Case C-176/03 *Commission v Council* [2005] ECR I-7879 on which see C Tobler, 'Annotation' (2006) 43 *Common Market Law Review* 835; E Herlin Karnell, 'Recent Developments in the Area of European Criminal Law' (2007) 14 *Maastricht Journal of European and Comparative Law* 1; H Labayle, 'L'Ouverture de la Jarre de Pandore, réflexions sur la compétence de la Communauté en matiere pénale' (2006) 42 *Cahiers de Droit Europeen* 382. *Cf* Case C-440/05 *Commission v Council* [2007] ECR I-9097.

recognition of national standards and an increasing use of OMC techniques and other new methods of governance. National law and Union law are more often in lockstep than opposition and this makes the determination of outer limits a more complicated exercise than would first appear.

2

Competence and Legitimacy

STEPHEN WEATHERILL*

I INTRODUCTION

THE OBSERVATIONS CONTAINED in this paper are based on an assumption that the legitimacy of the European Union is damaged if it trespasses beyond the sphere of the competences attributed to it by its founding treaties; and moreover that its legitimacy is damaged if it exercises competences attributed to it in a manner that unnecessarily interferes with the competences that remain in the hands of the Member States. This phenomenon of what can conveniently be labelled 'competence creep' engages harm to both the EU's *formal* and its *social* legitimacy. Adherence to the *formal* rule stipulated by Article 5(1) EC is undermined by such trends, while *social* acceptance of the EU is diminished where it is seen to stretch to act in spheres where popular acceptance of its legitimate role is weak and where, worse still, it may do a poor job because it is institutionally and/or constitutionally ill-equipped to do what it pretends to do.

Probably this starting-point is not controversial nor even particularly interesting. Furthermore it also obviously insouciantly begs some pressing questions, such as what is an 'unnecessary' interference with Member State competences, and who decides. It is slightly more intriguing to reflect on just why it is so relatively recently that the connection between competence creep and imperilled legitimacy has become a topic for active debate. What, however, is a good deal more interesting —and challenging and forward-looking too—is what we can do and should do to address the

* This paper was originally presented at the seminar on *The Outer Limits of EU Law* held in Sidney Sussex College, Cambridge in September 2007. I have also tested parts of it in early 2008 in Oxford, as part of the lecture series on *Governing the Globe? Foundations of Governance in a Globalized World* organised by Andrew Hurrell, in Edinburgh as the JDB Mitchell Memorial Lecture and in Exeter as the Lasok Lecture, and I thank all those who commented on it on these occasions. I need especially to thank Anand Menon for his insights. It is, however, solely my fault if the arguments fail to persuade or seem otherwise flawed. I have here largely retained the style of an oral presentation.

problems caused by this competence creep and the consequent impugned legitimacy of the EU. This invites reflection on recent institutional practice (in both judicial and political/legislative fora) and on the treaty reforms proposed in the Treaty establishing a Constitution and now found, in adjusted form, in the Treaty of Lisbon.

In this vein this paper represents an attempt to bring together more closely work that I have done in recent years on *competence*[1]; and (with Anand Menon) on *legitimacy*.[2] It the quest for 'Better Competence Monitoring' that occupies me most, from a perspective that tries to place in context just why 'competence' matters in tracking EU law and policymaking.

I here present a case to the effect that the current problems are in some respects exaggerated, and in other respects they are typically addressed without appreciation of the wider context. Some proposed solutions to the problems of competence creep and associated phenomena would, I think, cause more harm than good even if they are well-intentioned. So improved 'competence control' is necessary, but only according to a prescription which takes full account of the several ways in which the EU currently makes a beneficial contribution to achieving legitimate forms of governance in Europe. If my preferred solutions are modest, it is because I think modest and incremental development is the best way forward. In part this is because I simply do not accept that the EU deserves much of the criticism it regularly receives, in particular for its alleged deficiencies in democratic character. In part it is because I believe the EU fails to attract praise for many of its virtues, in particular those associated with its capacity to improve the performance of its Member States.

II THE PROBLEM SUMMARISED

The core of the 'competence problem' lies in the gap between the purity of the assertion of limited competence contained in Article 5(1) EC, on the one hand, and the practical operation of the pattern of legal bases scattered elsewhere throughout the Treaty combined with the prevailing institutional culture in the EU, on the other.

[1] S Weatherill, 'Competence creep and competence control' (2004) 23 *Yearbook of European Law* 1; S Weatherill, 'Better competence monitoring' (2005) 30 *EL Rev* 23.

[2] A Menon and S Weatherill, 'Legitimacy, Accountability and Delegation in the European Union' in A Arnull and D Wincott (eds), *Accountability and Legitimacy in the European Union* (Oxford, Oxford University Press, 2002); A Menon and S Weatherill, 'Transnational Sources of Legitimacy in a Globalizing World: how the European Union rescues its States' (forthcoming in *West European Politics*).

The Treaty contains an 'archipelago' of legal bases which authorise the making of legislation.[3] They are the product of incremental Treaty revision, they vary in scope and intensity and they are scattered throughout the EC Treaty from Article 12 (adoption of rules designed to prohibit discrimination on grounds of nationality) all the way through to the odd bunch of provisions found in Part Six of the Treaty, *General and Final Provisions*. Some are used frequently, some hardly at all. So Article 5(1) provides a neat and clear instruction to respect the limits imposed by the Treaty. But tracking what those limits actually *are* is very hard work. Moreover the Treaty does not declare particular sectors to be off-limits to the EC; nor does it reserve particular functions to the Member States. Article 5(1)'s reference to 'limits' is not supported by clear and easily monitored rules.

Some of the legal bases in the Treaty, two in particular, are very broad, even ambiguous, with the result that it is hard to advance specifically *constitutional* objections to proposed legislative initiatives. Articles 95 and 308 are the main culprits, for the reason that they and they alone were picked out as the EC Treaty's problem children in the Laeken Declaration. They have limits—in short, a tie to market-making under Article 95 and a tie to the EC's objectives under Article 308—but these are limits that lack precision. They have long been exploited for the making of wide-ranging legislation that is not easily connected to the objectives of the EC Treaty, but which, crucially in practice, is not easily shown *not* to be connected to those (broad, vague) objectives.[4] So for every *Tobacco Advertising* finding legislative use of Article 95 invalid[5] and for every *Opinion on Accession to the ECHR* finding use of Article 308 invalid[6] there are heaps of examples of legislative action based on Articles 95 and/or 308 in fields such as consumer protection and environmental protection where political will was strong but constitutional authority, though uncertain, typically assumed and left unchallenged.[7] And even in cases of challenge, the Court is sometimes remarkably generous in its view of the reach of the EC Treaty. A string of measures based on Article 95 has escaped annulment since *Tobacco Advertising* on the basis of the Court's finding that they were *likely* to prevent the emergence of obstacles caused by diverse national laws[8], a threshold of validity which is so lacking in precision and

[3] I take the metaphor from Lamberto Dini, CONV 123/02 19 June 2002 p 6.

[4] For a survey of practice under Art 308 see R Schütze, 'Organized Change towards an Ever Closer Union: Article 308 EC and the Limits to the Community's Legislative Competence' (2003) 22 *Yearbook of European Law* 79.

[5] Case C-376/98 *Germany v Parliament and Council* [2000] ECR I-8419.

[6] Opinion 2/94 [1994] ECR I-1759.

[7] See, eg, S Weatherill, *EU Consumer Law and Policy* (Cheltenham, Edward Elgar, 2005) ch 3; J Jans and H Vedder, *European Environmental Law* 3rd edn (Groningen, Europa, 2008) ch 2.

[8] For example, para 38 of Case C-380/03 *Germany v Parliament and Council* [2006] ECR I-11573.

predictability that, even after making due allowance for the vague and ambiguous textual materials gifted to the Court by the Treaty, one may readily regard the Court's stance as now more concerned with 'competence-enhancing' than 'competence-restricting'.[9] And the Court's view of the EC's competence to adopt measures relevant to criminal law in order to make fully effective the EC's rules on environmental protection is dramatic enough in its own right as an assertion of the primacy of the EC pillar over the non-EC EU[10] but all the more extraordinary as a new motor of competence creep when one reflects that this logic cannot easily be confined solely to environmental matters but rather seems to permit the development of a species of EC criminal law wherever (and however) that is judged necessary to make other policies 'effective'.[11] This hints at the use of Article 95 to make a harmonised criminal law. Moreover a broadly conceived programme of harmonisation itself tends to spill over in so far as the Court chooses to adopt a *communautaire* approach to matters not within the explicit material scope of the legislative measure. Its interventions into national civil procedure via the consumer law Directives offer good illustrations of these trends.[12] Public procurement too offers a rich field of inquiry.[13] Legislative competence creep may be accompanied by judicial competence creep. It may nourish it.

Rules governing the *exercise* of an attributed competence are found in Articles 5(2) and 5(3) EC: subsidiarity and proportionality. Logically these fall for consideration only once an attributed legislative competence has been identified, which explains why the Court in *Tobacco Advertising*, having found no such competence, simply ignored matters of subsidiarity and proportionality. As a general observation there is little here that is operationally useful in checking the scope of legislative ambition. From an economic perspective subsidiarity might conceivably help to focus attention on the need for a proper accounting of the costs and benefits of

[9] See, dealing particularly with the Art 95 case law, D Wyatt, 'Community competence to regulate the internal market' Oxford Legal Studies Research Paper 9/2007, http://papers.ssrn.com/sol3/papers.cfm?abstract_id=997863; also M Seidel, 'Präventive Rechtsangleichung im Bereich des Gemeinsamen Marktes' [2006] *Europarecht* 26.

[10] Case C-176/03 *Commission v Council* [2005] ECR I-7879 on which see C Tobler, 'Annotation' (2006) 43 *CML Rev* 835; E Herlin-Karnell. 'Recent Developments in the Area of European Criminal Law' (2007) 14 *Maastricht Journal of European and Comparative Law* 1; H Labayle, 'L'Ouverture de la Jarre de Pandore, réflexions sur la compétence de la Communauté en matiere pénale' (2006) 42 *Cahiers de Droit Europeen* 382.

[11] *Cf* Case C-440/05 *Commission v Council* judgment of 23 October 2007.

[12] For example, Case C-168/05 *Mostaza Claro v Centro Móvil Milenium* [2006] ECR I-10421, concerning Directive 93/13 on unfair terms. That the Court's energetic approach is specific to the consumer context is made clear in Joined Cases C-22/05 to C-225/05 *van der Weerd et al* judgment of 7 June 2007, paras 39–40.

[13] For example, Case C-230/02 *Grossmann Air Service* [2004] ECR I-1829; Case C-315/01 *GAT* [2003] ECR I-6351; Case C-327/00 *Santex SpA* [2003] ECR I-1877.

choosing between centralised rules and local autonomy[14] but this serves to highlight the fact that subsidiarity's role is promoting the asking of the right sort of questions rather than providing definitive answers. In itself it is deficient in the necessary vigour to act as an operationally useful controlling mechanism.[15] It is easy to add the label of 'compliance with subsidiarity' to a measure's Preamble, but it is rare to see any serious engagement with what is at stake in making that judgement. The same is lamentably true of policy statements, which too often pay mere lip-service to the rigours of subsidiarity. So for example, as part of the drive against money laundering the Council in 2006 adopted a 'third pillar' Framework Decision, 2006/783 on the application of the principle of mutual recognition to confiscation orders.[16] In Recital [9] it is stated that cooperation between Member States presupposes confidence that decisions to be recognised and executed 'will always be taken in compliance with the principles of legality, subsidiarity and proportionality'. But nowhere else in the 20 page text is subsidiarity even mentioned. For the Court too, subsidiarity is no basis for intensive review of legislative choices. In *R v Secretary of State ex parte BAT and Imperial Tobacco*[17] The challenged Directive was found to fall within the permitted (post-*Tobacco Advertising*) scope of Article 95 and therefore it complied with Article 5(1) EC. It was accordingly in principle susceptible to review for compliance with the principle of subsidiarity in Article 5(2), but the Court then adopted an approach which makes it hard to imagine circumstances in which a harmonisation measure will be found to violate the demands of subsidiarity. The Directive's objective is to eliminate the barriers raised by the differences between State laws. This objective cannot be sufficiently achieved by the Member States individually—indeed it is the variety of approaches taken that causes the problem! The Court concluded therefore that the matter called for action at Community level. It appears that the Court has deftly sustained subsidiarity as a legal principle on paper while conceding much in practice to legislative discretion. Once it is determined that a competence to establish common rules exists, the political decision to exercise that competence seems *in practice* immune from judicial subversion. One may readily sympathise with the Court's anxiety to avoid judicial second-guessing of political judgements[18] but the consequence is that the validity of Community acts is highly unlikely to be set aside in the

[14] See eg J Pelkmans, 'Subsidiarity between Law and Economics' College of Europe Research Papers in Law 1/2005.

[15] *Cf* eg G Davies, 'Subsidiarity: the wrong idea, in the wrong place, at the wrong time' (2006) 43 *CML Rev* 63.

[16] [2006] OJ L328/59.

[17] Case C-491/01 [2002] ECR I-11543.

[18] In fact the Court has neatly reached a conclusion which reflects Lord Mackenzie Stuart's apprehension about the role of subsidiarity as a principle applied by the Court: see

name of subsidiarity.[19] And Article 5(3)—proportionality—betrays a similar, if slightly milder, judicial anxiety to avoid usurpation of the legislative role.[20]

As a general observation the current system governing the scope of EC competence is founded on an assumption of *ex ante* restraint by the political institutions and *ex post* review by the Community judicature. In principle an act should not be adopted if it trespasses beyond the scope of the mandate conferred by the Treaty. Nor should a competence, even if established as attributed by the Treaty, be exercised if that would conflict with the principles of subsidiarity and/or proportionality. And if the rules are infringed the act is susceptible to annulment by the Court. But 'institutional incestousness' prevails in the EU. Each of these institutions may—in different ways, at different times, to differing degrees—tend to be in favour of EU-level action at the expense of national action. And not necessarily for bad reasons: the Treaty itself attributes broad and ambiguous powers to the EC so policing the limits is inevitably difficult, and not necessarily to be taken as revealing a pro-*communautaire* bias. But there is a general impression that there is a greater readiness to exploit an opportunity to legislate than to reflect on whether action should not be taken at all. The EU has an institutional momentum in favour of legislation. There is competence creep and there is the associated phenomenon of legislative creep too. Of course, States also suffer from this malaise but the anxieties about legitimacy are different in the EU context.

Once again the core problem is a structural weakness which places few brakes on the motors of 'creeping competence' supplied by the Treaty text itself and by the institutional set-up of the EU. The risk is that the EU does too much—and does it poorly. That slippage tends to damage its legitimacy in both a formal and a social sense.

III THE PROBLEM EXAGGERATED

It is necessary to assess the gravity of this set of problems associated with the phenomenon of competence creep. Article 5(1) EC promises national political actors and processes so that when deciding whether to ratify an agreed Treaty revision, they can control which areas of activity they choose to transfer to the EU, and on what terms—they can ring-fence the scope of the transfer. That is not how it works in practice—and the whole structure

European Institute of Public Administration, *Subsidiarity: The Challenge of Change* (Proceedings of the Jacques Delors Colloquium, EIPA, Maastricht, 1991).

[19] See similarly Case C-103/01 *Commission v Germany* [2003] ECR I-5369 para 47; Cases C-154/04 & C-155/04 *Alliance for Natural Health* [2005] ECR I-6451 paras 99–108,

[20] See generally T Tridimas, *The General Principles of EC Law* (Oxford, Oxford University Press, 1999), ch 3.

of the Treaties and of the EU's institutional architecture is such that it *cannot* work like that in practice. Clearly there is a risk of a backlash against the EC's perceived illegitimate pretensions. National political elites, liable to be outvoted in ever wider fields at EC level, are likely to react negatively; so too are national Parliaments and constitutional courts, and, perhaps in the long term most alarming of all, citizens are likely to suffer alienation from the complexity that flows from incremental drift in the growth of multi-level governance. The conditions for resistance to the EU's claims to authority are ripe. The Treaty of Nice's Declaration on the Future of the Union and the Laeken Declaration recognised this, and the matter was aired regularly at the Convention on the Future of Europe, where attention to the matter of competence control occupied much time.[21] The EU is accordingly commonly accused of invading the nooks and crannies of national life.

There is, however, a tendency to exaggerate the scope of competence creep. Let it first be noticed that the Treaty itself is loaded in favour of a broad approach to the scope of competence. Article 5(1) EC is neat and clear—respect the limits imposed by the Treaty. But, as explained, tracking what those limits are is very hard work. The Treaty does not seek to establish solid walls separating State from EU functions. It is accordingly hard to devise objections of a *constitutional* nature, transcending mere political disagreement about the virtues of a particular proposed measure, especially those advanced under the broadest of the provisions of the Treaty authorising legislative action, Articles 95 and 308. But that is the nature of the Treaty.

Moreover, although the EC possesses a competence in a number of areas it is commonly the case that EC action is not designed to suppress State action. The type of action which the EU may take may be limited; the scope of residual national competence may be considerable (though unfortunately often ill-defined).[22] For example, EC action in the fields of culture and public health is defined by Articles 151 and 152 EC respectively as supplementary to State action. Harmonisation of laws pursuant to these provisions is explicitly excluded. Articles 176, 137 and 153 EC, governing competence to legislate in the fields of environmental protection, social policy and consumer protection respectively, stipulate that national measures that are stricter than the agreed Community standard are permitted. So just because the EC is competent to act in a particular area

[21] See Weatherill, 'Competence creep and competence control' above n 1.

[22] *Cf* R Schütze, 'Supremacy without Pre-Emption? The very slowly emergent doctrine of Community pre-emption' (2006) 43 *CML Rev* 1023; R Schütze, 'Co-operative federalism constitutionalised: the emergence of complementary competences in the EC legal order' (2006) 31 *EL Rev* 167; R Schütze, 'Dual federalism constitutionalised: the emergence of exclusive competences in the EC legal order' (2007) 32 *EL Rev* 3; F de Cecco, 'Room to Move? Minimum Harmonisation and Fundamental Rights'(2006) 43 *CML Rev* 9.

does not mean that State action in that area is excluded. In fact, exclusive EC competence is very much the exception not the rule.

Moreover, the reality of the scope of EC competence is that in some areas it is not legislative at all. Commonly the achievement of economic integration collides with Member States' powers to act in realms where the Community is not competent to act as a substitute legislator. Social security is a common example,[23] taxation is another,[24] sport too,[25] and even the maintenance of public order and the safeguarding of internal security have been revealed as matters of national competence that are nevertheless reviewable in so far as their pursuit impedes cross-border trade.[26] Free movement law prevents States (and sometimes private actors too) acting in the absence of justification for chosen practices that impede cross-border trade. The Community cannot go further than this: it cannot mandate the ground rules for the organisation of the activity in question, although plainly EC law circumscribes the scope of sovereign State choices. The Court thereby assumes an important role in developing an EC policy of sorts in areas—health care, sport and so on—where the Treaty offers little policy guidance. And it is in that process of justification that the Court is called on to recognise the particular features of each industry—to develop a policy that is more than just trading freedom. But public and private actors retain important spheres of autonomy even though they are certainly operating within the field of application of Community law.

More fundamentally still, in the rush to hail and fear the over-mighty EU there is a risk of concentrating on what the EU *can* do and ignoring what the EU *cannot* do. The EU does not have a police force or an army; it does not have tax-raising powers; it does not determine the shape of systems of social welfare or of education or of health care.[27] The site of primary responsibility for hugely important areas of deep political saliency to the peoples of Europe remain at national level. Quite properly so, from the perspective of those who doubt the EU is able to bear the load of responsibility for such politically contested policy areas.[28] And, one may conclude, there is simply no need for injecting more aggressive patterns of accountability and representation. This, of course, is not an uncontested point of view. Other scholars find a much greater degree of politically sensitive decision-making to be occurring at EU

[23] *Cf* eg Case C-512/03 *JEJ Blankaert* [2005] ECR I-7685; Case C-372/04 *Ex p Watts* [2006] ECR I-4325.

[24] *Cf* eg Case C-446/03 *Marks and Spencer v Halsey* [2005] ECR I-10837.

[25] For example, Case C-415/93 *Bosman* [1995] ECR I-4921; Case C-519/04 P *Meca-Medina and Majcen v Commission* [2006] ECR I-6991.

[26] Case C-265/95 *Commission v France* [1997] ECR I-6959.

[27] See in particular in this vein A Moravcsik, 'The European Constitutional Compromise and the neofunctionalist legacy' (2005) 12 *Journal of European Public Policy* 349.

[28] For example, G Majone, 'Europe's Democratic Deficit: The Question of Standards' (1998) 4 *European Law Journal* 5.

level, even in the heartland of the economically bountiful project of market integration where, even if one accepts the basic narrative of enhanced efficiency, gains are demonstrably spread unevenly across Europe and where the project to make an internal market also involves a degree of assumption of policy-making responsibilities at EU level involving sensitive policy choices.[29] Other policies, especially of a redistributive character, are still more susceptible to harsh contestation. Here it is argued that the EU's activities have become so heavily politicised that the (relative) absence of input legitimacy—the attenuated form of parliamentary oversight found in the EU when compared with the Member States—can no longer be tolerated. The issue here is how far can EU competence legitimately stretch under the guise of technical collective problem-solving—'output legitimacy'—in an interdependent world. From this springs, for example, advocacy of an elected Commission, or at least an elected Commission President, accountable to, perhaps, the European Parliament.

Some go further. Some draw from this a case in favour of a much more aggressive 'democratisation' of the EU's modus operandi according to an argument which doubts that the autonomy which is foundationally characteristic of the supranational method can plausibly sustain such contestation and that legitimacy requires more overt systems of accountability. There are links here back to the case for EU 'Statehood' famously advanced by Judge Mancini—and equally famously contemporaneously contested by Joseph Weiler.[30] A recent contribution which I think belongs in this vein, albeit written by political scientists not lawyers, is written by Follesdal and Hix under the title 'Why There is a Democratic Deficit in the EU: A Response to Majone and Moravcsik'.[31] I agree with the need to take seriously the issue of legitimacy in the EU (but not just *of* the EU) but confess doubts whether suggestions that political contestation at EU level is a means to reconcile citizens to its legitimate role in matters of economic governance are correct. It may indeed be counter-productive in that distaste for an over-mighty EU would increase. Absent a European *demos*, importing representative majoritarian practices that have a (modestly) successful track record at state level would aggravate legitimation problems, not cure them.[32]

[29] Of an increasingly politicised nature, according to M Höpner and A Schäfer (2007). 'A new phase of European Integration: Organized Capitalisms in Post-Ricardian Europe' MPifG Discussion Paper 07/4 Max-Planck-Institut für Gesellschaftsforschung, Köln.

[30] G Mancini, 'Europe: the Case for Statehood' (1998) 4 *European Law Journal* 29; J Weiler, 'Europe: the Case against the Case for Statehood' (1998) 4 *European Law Journal* 43.

[31] *European Governance Papers* 2005/2 available at http://www.connex-network.org/eurogov/.

[32] For (what I think is) a similarly motivated anxiety, see P Magnette, 'How can one be European? Reflections on the Pillars of European Civic Identity' (2007) 13 *European Law Journal* 664.

Just *how* serious one reckons this to be probably depends on one's sense of how much really is being done at EU level, rather than at State level, which requires or at least deserves a degree of political contestation. As a minimum, one can concede that the incrementally developed allocation of tasks between the EU and its Member States may not follow a wholly rational model.[33] The more one is persuaded that the EU really is engaged in deeply controversial political choices the more one feels uncomfortable with the benevolence of the core narrative of output legitimacy achieved through establishing autonomous 'supranational' institutions. This, for sure, is a major debate and one's self-positioning within it affects the degree of equanimity one displays in the face of competence creep. Remember too, that a negative portrayal of the EU is commonly presented by national politicians who are (rationally) induced to exploit the popular misunderstanding of its nature and purpose to shift blame for unpopular decisions onto the EU while, where possible, claiming credit for decisions and policies that really belong to the EU or, at least, could not be taken or advanced withoutit. As a (very) general set of observations, I have some doubts as to whether the level of politicisation requiring statist models of accountability is quite as high as claimed; I have grave doubts whether 'democratisation' is the way to go; and I am anxious that the EU's credentials as problem-solver and as a means to 'tame' the corruptive excesses of nationally biased political processes is not only being neglected here but may indeed be undermined. That is, injecting greater 'input legitimacy' at EU level robs it of 'output legitimacy', to the detriment of the Member States' own plausible claims to be strengthening their own legitimacy through participation in the EU system.

This suggests an argument that competence creep is part of the game. There are good reasons why parts of the EU can function successfully only provided that they enjoy a degree of autonomy from the Member States. In this vein the independence of the Commission and the Court are most conspicuously required in order to provide an environment within which commitments can be extracted and enforced on a credible long-term reciprocal basis. The EU, as an incomplete contract, could not function without institutions that enjoy a degree of distance from political elites within the Member States. Although it is true that the State scores better than the EU when measured against the normal (state-inspired) expectations of 'democracy'—there is accountability and voting, whereas in the EU, at least in the supranational institutions, most prominently the Court and the Commission, there is not—democracy is only part of the story of political legitimacy, which also demands that those exercising political

[33] *Cf* eg A Alesina, I Angeloni and L Schuknecht, 'What does the European Union Do?', (2005) 123(3) *Public Choice* 275.

power are able to achieve a high degree of effectiveness in meeting the expectations of the governed citizens: 'output legitimacy'. States may be rather poor at solving some problems which can be much more successfully dealt with by the EU. This perspective connects with broader notions that the EU's core function is to 'tame' states, economically but also politically.[34] States are not so easily assumed to be democratic or legitimate.[35] In this sense the phenomenon of competence creep is one of the prices paid for establishing autonomous institutions at EU level—they need flexibility to be able to adapt to their mission, and they may on occasion go too far by expanding influence in a way that might undermine the discharge of State functions for no adequate compensating benefit[36] (although of course it is by no means the Court and the Commission alone which have conspired to amplify the scope of the EU's influence). In this sense competence creep is loaded into the model that leads to fulfilment of the task of finding solutions to common problems. Aggressive curtailment of the condition of autonomy that generates competence creep and the risk of illegitimate action would in turn tend to impair the flexibility needed for effective problem-solving through the EU.[37]

IV THE PROBLEM ADDRESSED

If, as has been argued, the problem is exaggerated, and largely presentational, and if aggressive adjustment, maximising control of institutional autonomy in the EU at the expense of its effectiveness, might generate more costs than benefits, then that conditions the way forward. It cautions against radical change but it does make a case for trying to craft a system that is less easily misunderstood, and less easily misrepresented—a system that curtails the damagingly illegitimate excesses of competence creep without undermining the effective and flexible exploitation of the EU

[34] Familiar enough as a theme in eg N MacCormick, *Questioning Sovereignty* (Oxford, Oxford University Press, 1999); J Weiler, *The Constitution of Europe* (Cambridge, Cambridge University Press, 1999).

[35] See the work of Christian Joerges, eg 'What is left of the European Economic Constitution?' (2005) 30 *EL Rev* 461 and '"Deliberative Political Processes" Revisited: what have we learned about the Legitimacy of Supranational Decision-Making?' (2006) 44 *Journal of Common Market Studies* 779, and of Miguel Maduro, eg in 'The importance of being called a constitution: constitutional authority and the authority of constitutionalism' (2005) 3 *International Journal of Constitutional Law* 332.

[36] For a recent detailed inquiry into practice see V Schmidt, *Democracy in Europe: the EU and National Polities* (Oxford, Oxford University Press, 2006). Criticism in this vein of the Court requires another set of benchmarks again, of course—but see eg C Newdick, 'Citizenship, Free Movement and Health Care: Cementing Individual Rights by Corroding Social Solidarity' (2006) 43 *CML Rev* 1645; N Nic Shuibhne, 'Annotation of Case C-76/05 *Schwarz*, Case C-318/05 *Commission v Germany*, Cases C-11/06 & C-12/06 *Morgan, Bucher*' (2008) 45 *CML Rev* 771.

[37] As in fact was explicitly foreseen in the Laeken Declaration.

system as an arena for problem-solving. So, shorn of exaggeration, what are the problems? They are principally the ill-organised structure of the Treaty; the place of Articles 95 and 308; and 'institutional incestuousness', which may involve not only the legislative institutions but also on occasion the Court's troublingly broad reading of the scope of EC competence.

This leaves me favourably disposed to a model which retains flexibility in the application of EC law across the wide range of areas to which the Treaty is relevant. It leaves me favourably disposed to a model which avoids seeking to inject (national) politics-as-usual into the EC's lifestyle and which shuns deeper 'democratisation'. It leaves me receptive to the idea that the Court can do a marginally better job but, given the political sensitivity of what is at stake coupled to the unavoidably flexible nature of some of the competence-conferring provisions in the Treaty, convinced that there are dangers in expecting too much of the Court. And my underlying assumption is that we need to measure the claims to legitimacy of the EU by examining the strengths and weaknesses of both the EU and the Member States, and that the problem-solving capacity of the EU, as a source of legitimacy, depends on institutional autonomy and a degree of risk of competence creep which is endemic.

In this vein, although it was always quite hard to get excited about the Treaty establishing a Constitution, the agreed but ultimately rejected provisions governing competence were, I think, generally helpful. The solution proposed by the Convention on the Future of Europe, and endorsed by the Heads of State and Government in 2004, was composed of two parts. First, the agreed text sought to clarify (but not necessarily simplify) and reorganise the Treaty rules governing competence. Secondly, it freshened the system for monitoring the existence and exercise of competence by bringing in new actors from outwith the uncritical EU family—most of all, national Parliaments were to be invested with the responsibility to stop creep according to a new *ex ante* monitoring system, the 'early warning system' and the so-called yellow card procedure. So, it was intended that the rules should be clearer, making misperceptions less excusable and their application easier. And, in the shape of national Parliaments, an extra and previously excluded new monitor would be introduced into aspects of the 'competence debate'—one which moreover had a real incentive to look critically at centralising tendencies promoted by the EU lawmaking process given its political marginalisation consequent on such rhythms.

The Reform Treaty unveiled in the summer of 2007 included strong traces of the Treaty establishing a Constitution's chosen pattern, and this is now visible in the agreed text of the Lisbon Treaty.[38]

[38] [2007] OJ C/306.

In the Lisbon Treaty there is an abiding concern to clarify more aggressively that the Member States are the source of the competences which are conferred on the Union. This is visible in the addition to paragraph 1 of Article 1 EU. Moreover, the Treaty broadcasts the point that competences not conferred on the Union rest with the Member States. This is visible in what will become Articles 4 and 5 EU, once the Lisbon Treaty enters into force. This is not new as a matter of law, but the explicit hammering home of these points in the Treaty reflects the political desire to emphasise still further the limited nature of the EU's powers and functions.

The EC Treaty is to be renamed the Treaty on the Functioning of the European Union (TFEU) by the Lisbon Treaty. A new Title (Title I) on *Categories and areas of Union competence* reflects the persisting ambition to provide a more transparent and better organised catalogue than the current 'archipelago'.[39] The three main types of competence attributed to the EU which were foreseen by the Treaty establishing a Constitution endure in the Lisbon Treaty—exclusive, shared and supporting. And lists are provided which connect particular activities to particular types of competence. This is, as a minimum, an easier read than anything to be found in the current EC Treaty. Moreover, by systematically connecting types of competence to particular areas of activity, it moves us beyond the incremental growth of case law dealing with these tricky but very important issues. There is here (as elsewhere) clearly life after death for the Treaty establishing a Constitution, in the sense that the Lisbon Treaty has persisted with the basic intent and structure first unveiled by Giscard d'Estaing in 2003 and agreed by the Heads of State and Government in 2004. Equally, the small number of 'new' legal bases foreseen by that text are absorbed in the Lisbon Treaty (for example on sport, energy and so on). However, the Treaty establishing a Constitution would have brought the successor to Article 308 into this early part of the Treaty. The Lisbon Treaty does not. It simply amends Article 308, and makes explicit that it may not apply to matters falling within the Common Foreign and Security Policy, but leaves it where it is, renumbered as Article 352 and lurking in its hard to spot location towards the end of the EC Treaty, now to be renamed the TFEU.

Under the Lisbon Treaty national Parliaments are to exercise the essence of the newly granted responsibilities which were already mapped out in the ill-fated Treaty establishing a Constitution. Article 5 EU concerns monitoring of subsidiarity. And an adjustment to Article 308 EC (which becomes Article 352 TFEU) requires the Commission to draw the attention of national Parliaments to legislative proposals adopted under this base using the procedures referred to in the context of subsidiarity. Again, this is in essence to

[39] Above n 3.

preserve the model agreed in the Treaty establishing a Constitution. For the very first time national Parliaments enjoy a direct right of participation in the EU lawmaking process, albeit that this involvement is focused on two particular manifestations of the sin of competence creep, the place of the subsidiarity principle and the use of Article 308 as a base for legislation.

A new Article 12 EU, located in Title II on *Provisions on Democratic Principles*, deals with the role of national Parliaments. They shall 'contribute actively to the good functioning of the Union'. The means envisaged to bring this about cover: receiving information from the Union's institutions and having draft legislative acts forwarded to them in accordance with the Protocol; and ensuring respect for the subsidiarity principle in line with the procedure set out in the Protocol; plus several other activities which I do not consider here because they are not directly relevant to issues of competence.

The Protocol on the role of national Parliaments deals with the distribution of information to national Parliaments; the submission of a reasoned opinion in cases of suspected violation of the subsidiarity principle; an eight week (this is extended from six weeks, as provided for in the Treaty establishing a Constitution) standstill period designed to give national Parliaments a real, practical opportunity to intervene, applicable in all but urgent cases.

The Protocol on subsidiarity and proportionality absorbs this procedure in Article 6. Then in Article 7 it puts flesh on the bones. The essence is unchanged from the Treaty establishing a Constitution's model. The vigour of the procedure is however enhanced. Where reasoned opinions on non-compliance with subsidiarity represent at least one third of all the votes allocated to national Parliaments, the draft must be reviewed. The Commission may then maintain, amend or withdraw the draft, giving reasons for this. Where reasoned opinions on non-compliance with subsidiarity represent a simple majority of votes cast by national parliaments,[40] then the Commission must review the proposal and, if it decides to maintain it, it must itself present a reasoned opinion dealing with its view why the proposal complies with the subsidiarity principle. These opinions are then made available to the Union legislator and shall be considered in the manner set out in Article 7(3) of the Protocol. This constitutes a more elaborate version of the consequences should the Commission choose to maintain its proposal in the face of objections registered by national Parliaments than had been planned under the Treaty establishing a Constitution. Plainly the aim is to maximise the opportunity for dialogue and for the voice of the national Parliaments to be heard effectively.

[40] Do they have to raise the *same* objection(s)? This is left open, as it was in the Treaty establishing a Constitution.

So, in the matter of national parliamentary involvement, the Lisbon Treaty envisages a slightly deeper intrusion than was foreseen by the Treaty establishing a Constitution—eight, not six weeks standstill and an elaborated requirement of a formal Commission response in some circumstances where objections are raised. I doubt this tweaking will make much difference but it may induce richer dialogue, and it is possibly a slight improvement. But basically the Lisbon Treaty adheres to the model proposed by the Convention on the Future of Europe and adopted in the Treaty establishing a Constitution.

The planned procedure is in detail imperfect, in my view.[41] The Treaty establishing a Constitution's early warning procedure should have covered the functional successor to Article 95, and not only the functional successor to Article 308. Both are twinned in the Laeken Declaration as problem cases from the perspective of competence creep and they should stay twinned in the new procedure. But the Lisbon Treaty confirms this unfortunate error. In addition, the national Parliaments should be able to raise objections pertinent to proportionality, not only subsidiarity. The two principles are closely related and in some respects they overlap (for example, in judging the appropriate intensity of action) and to include one but not the other risks triggering unhelpful demarcation disputes. The Treaty establishing a Constitution got this wrong, and this is repeated in the Lisbon Treaty.

But, those points of detail aside, I am basically in favour of this model as one that seeks to adjust the current pattern's presentation and in a smallish way its substance but which accepts the basic structure of the EU as sound, while seeking to promote more dialogue about whether particular proposals are valid or well-intentioned.[42] In particular I oppose procedures that would be more interventionist, several of which were aired at the Convention on the Future of Europe.[43] So, 'hard lists' governing competence were correctly rejected in the subsequently agreed Treaties. One could envisage different models of 'hard lists', involving, for example, exhaustive and tightly defined lists of the areas in which the Union is competent to act or identification of areas off-limits to the Union and therefore remaining within the exclusive competence of the Member States.[44] One might

[41] See Weatherill, 'Competence creep and competence control' above n 1.

[42] In similar vein, V Constantinesco, 'Les compétences et le principe de subsidiarité' (2005) 41 *Revue Trimistrielle de Droit Europeen* 305. For helpful examination of the model proposed in the Treaty establishing a Constitution see House of Lords EU Committee 'Strengthening national parliamentary scrutiny of the EU—the Constitution's subsidiarity early warning mechanism': http://www.publications.parliament.uk/pa/ld200405/ldselect/ldeucom/101/10102.htm.

[43] *Cf* Weatherill 'Better competence monitoring' (n 1above).

[44] For example, CONV 47/02 15 May 2002 reports that 'a minority' requested the replacement of the existing system by a 'catalogue' of Union powers; and a 'minority' favoured a list of powers reserved to the Member States. For an attempt see the *Freiburg*

advocate the deletion of Articles 95 and/or 308 as the principal problem cases in the corrosion of competence creep. One might seek to equip national Parliaments with a veto, a red card rather than the yellow card which they are handed under the agreed Treaty. One might envisage sterner judicial control of adopted or even proposed legislation, perhaps involving a freshly minted 'court of competence', comprising members drawn from not only the EU but also national judiciaries. The basic aim, whichever particular model is promoted, is to block competence creep and to confine the EU to an agenda which can be reliably identified in advance; and to ensure the whistle can be blown quickly and uncontroversially if the boundary is crossed. The problem is that this will impose significant costs measured in inflexibility. It will diminish the EU's capacity to act effectively in order to address (the rather wide range of) objectives assigned to it by its Treaty. A hard list would set up antagonisms and rigidities that would cause damage worse than the cure, in particular because the imposition of an inflexible division between Union and State competences is likely to harm the EU's capacity to fulfil its mission by denying it an adaptable and efficiently-functioning system of governance that properly implicates several levels. Moreover, it is very hard to see how a rule could feasibly be devised that would shelter State autonomy from not only EC legislative action but also the Treaty provisions governing the internal market and competition policy. Or at least any such rule would have major costs measured in the suppression of the basic pro-competitive, pro-integrative thrust of the core of internal market law. Areas of truly exclusive State competence are few and, were it otherwise, the achievement of the core economic objectives of the Treaty would be gravely imperilled. Put another way, many provisions of the EC Treaty are broad, functionally-driven and perhaps vague, but for good reason. The call for a hard list, like the call for a red card rather than a yellow card to be granted to national Parliaments, is driven by neglect of the virtues of EC law's influence on national choices and is dominated by the perceived vices. It is an unbalanced remedy. And it would, by fracturing the EU's problem-solving flexibility, weaken its principal source of legitimacy. Similarly the establishment of a new competence-specific judicial tribunal would not simply set up tense jurisdictional demarcation disputes, it would deal a mortal blow to the existing Court's credibility.[45] Crucially, competence and legitimacy work together—

draft, CONV 495/03. *Cf* eg L Hoffmann and J Shaw, 'Constitutionalism and Federalism in the Future of Europe debate: the German Dimension' *Federal Trust Paper* 03/04, February 2004.

[45] It is however possible that use of the new *ex ante* monitoring system will provide the basis for a slightly more intensive *ex post* control by the Court, see D Wyatt, 'Could a yellow card for National Parliaments strengthen judicial as well as political policing of subsidiarity?' (2006) 2 *Croatian Yearbook of European Law and Policy* 1.

just as trespass beyond the limits of attributed competence strains legitimacy, so too unduly confined competence undermines legitimacy by diminishing the EU's problem-solving capacity.

I should make clear that I do not believe the involvement of national Parliaments will revolutionise the culture of EU lawmaking. It is a plan that is based on the assumption that neither the Council nor the European Parliament is reliable in protecting national political cultures from encroachment by the EU, even if both institutions have their roots in direct democracy practised at national level. Indeed the Council is notoriously an arena in which national executives may exploit the EU tier of governance to evade national Parliamentary control and/or to circumvent blockages to policy reform at national level—and then blame the EU for tying national hands that have in fact been willingly so tied. The European Parliament is directly elected, but rarely consequent on campaigns infused by European, rather than national, debates and its relative invisibility insulates it from pressures to exercise a restraining influence on expanding competence. National Parliaments, as the losers in this pernicious process, may be expected to blow the whistle. And yet national executives dominate Parliaments most of the time in most of the Member States. So one needs to be careful in identifying what fresh critical thinking national Parliaments may be able realistically to contribute, and what they may not.[46] In any event, national Parliaments are likely to be tempted to voice concerns about matters of substance, extending beyond subsidiarity (which anyway itself lacks firm definitions), and this may generate new and thoroughly unhelpful antagonisms. But it is worth trying; and it *is* already being tried despite the demise of the Treaty establishing a Constitution and in advance of the entry into force of the Lisbon Treaty.[47]

Generally, however, the point of greater involvement by national Parliaments is not to inject radical change but rather to nudge the system in the direction of a more critical approach to EU lawmaking. The principal place for addressing the problems of competence creep must lie in the institutional culture of the EU, nourished by input from national political culture. In fact there is here a mix of constitutionally distinct phenomena at stake in this debate about competence. It covers fixing the scope of legislative competence 'proper' (which is Article 5(1) EC); the directions given by the

[46] For a helpfully nuanced discussion see K Auel, 'Democratic Accountability and National Parliaments: Redefining the Impact of Parliamentary Scrutiny in EU Affairs' (2007) 13 *European Law Journal* 487. For a sceptical view of the value of national Parliaments in this area see P Kiiver, *The National Parliaments in the European Union—a Critical View on EU Constitution-Building* (The Hague, Kluwer Law International, 2006).

[47] Commission Report on Better Lawmaking 2006, COM (2007) 286, 6 June 2007, pp 8–9; see also the (short) report of the Conference of Community and European Affairs Committees of Parliaments of the European Union (COSAC), [2007] OJ C/206/7, s 2.

subsidiarity and proportionality principles on when a legislative competence should be exercised (Articles 5(2) and 5(3) EC); and, more broadly, the exhortations to regulate 'better', which embrace concern for clarity, simplification and so on. That is: there is competence creep and legislative creep and there is plain bad legislating. Part of this concerns the need for a hard look at whether a relevant EU institution possesses not simply an appropriate legal mandate to fulfil a particular task, but also adequate material and human resources and basic expertise.[48] Seen at a general level, all these issues can be grouped together as reflecting a concern that the EU identify its allocated tasks with more precision and discharge them with more care. This is the quest for 'Better Lawmaking'.[49] Poor lawmaking—doing a bad job—is itself damaging to legitimacy, as the Commission argued with vigour in its 2001 White Paper on Governance.[50]

V CONCLUSION

One can convincingly reflect that the depiction of the sovereign state as the dominant paradigm in international law and international relations is a relatively recent development and that history does not teach us that this is natural or normal. That layers of authority overlap is not a new phenomenon, it is an old one.[51] One can develop a convincing (I think) case that the legitimacy of States is in several respects under real and growing pressure as economic and technological changes weaken the significance of political borders, and one can (I think) demonstrate that the EU is in important respects a solution to these problems, not a cause (albeit that defining the proper limits of its role remains a properly contested issue). In this sense, one should not overstate the 'competence problem'. Flexibility in competence allocation promotes legitimacy in the sense of effective problem-solving. But care needs to be taken to curtail illegitimate excess, and institutional reform offers the most promising route to incubating a more critical culture in EU lawmaking.

[48] Sport offers a good example—for the argument that due institutional restraint characterises the 2007 White Paper COM (2007) 391, 11 July 2007, see S Weatherill, 'The White Paper on Sport as an Exercise on Better Regulation' [2008] *International Sports Law Journal* 3.

[49] So the Commission's (usually rather perfunctory) annual reports on Better Lawmaking, issued pursuant to Article 9 of the Protocol on the application of the principles of subsidiarity and proportionality, cover not just subsidiarity and proportionality but also improvements in the regulatory environment, eg 14th report covering 2006, COM (2007) 286, 6 June 2007. Such concerns are pervasive in Europe today: see S Weatherill (ed), *Better Regulation* (Oxford, Hart Publishing, 2007).

[50] COM (2001) 428.

[51] For an elegantly written recent sketch see K Schiemann, 'Europe and the loss of sovereignty' (2007) 56 *I CLQ* 475.

3

Article 308 EC as the Outer Limit of Expressly Conferred Community Competence

ALAN DASHWOOD*

I INTRODUCTION

ARTICLE 308 EC PROVIDES:

> If action by the Community should prove necessary to attain, in the course of operation of the common market, one of the objectives of the Community and this Treaty has not provided the necessary powers, the Council shall, acting unanimously on a proposal from the Commission and after consulting the European Parliament, take the appropriate measures.

The Article has to be reconciled with the principle of conferral,[1] which is expressed, rather ineptly, by the first paragraph of Article 5 EC:

> The Community shall act within the limits of the powers conferred upon it by this Treaty and of the objectives assigned to it therein.[2]

A corollary of the principle of conferral is that the Community does not have general law-making competence to carry out the tasks and activities

* An earlier version of this paper was presented as written evidence to the House of Commons European Scrutiny Committee: see 'Article 308 of the EC Treaty', Twenty-ninth Report of Session 2006/07, HC 41–xxix.

[1] Other descriptions are 'the principle of the attribution of powers' and 'the principle of conferred powers'.

[2] The drafting of Article 5(2) of the TEU, as amended by the Treaty of Lisbon, would be more robust: 'Under the principle of conferral, the Union shall act within the limits of the competences conferred on it by the Member States in the Constitution to attain the objectives set out in the Constitution. Competences not conferred upon the Union in the Constitution remain with the Member States'. This corresponds to Article I-12 of the Treaty establishing a Constitution for Europe.

identified by Articles 2–4 EC. Where action by the Community is contemplated in a given field, it is normally necessary to identify a specific legal basis authorising the institutions to adopt measures of the kind in question.

Article 308 was evidently intended to provide a degree of flexibility in a system based on the specific conferral of powers, without undermining that system. It allows subsidiary powers to be created for the Community institutions in certain cases where a specific legal basis is lacking. There would be an unbearable tension between Article 308 and the principle of conferral, if the action that can be taken under the Article were not subject to definable limits. Those limits have to be sought in the oddly drafted requirement that the Community action which is contemplated must have proved itself necessary in order to attain, in the course of the operation of the common market, one of the objectives of the Community.

II THE CONCEPT OF 'THE COMMON MARKET'

I believe there is an historical explanation for the reference to 'the course of operation of the common market' in Article 308.

The present Article 2 EC contains a list of socio-economic objectives (a harmonious, balanced and sustainable development of economic activities and so on), which it is said to be the task of the Community to promote 'by establishing a common market *and* an economic and monetary union *and* by implementing common policies or activities referred to in Article 3 and 4'.[3] That description of the several means to be employed by the Community in performing its task, dates from the Maastricht Treaty. The original version of Article 2 referred to only two such means: 'establishing a common market and progressively approximating the economic policies of Member States'. This suggests that 'common market' was understood by the authors of the primordial EEC Treaty as a term of art, covering all the aspects of the Community's 'task' other than the progressive approximation of national economic policies.

At the time, this special usage did not place an intolerable strain on language, since the activity of the Community was essentially focused on the creation of the common market mechanism, to replicate the conditions of a single national market in the economic relations between the Member States. The mechanism was conceived in a sophisticated way as comprising not only the four basic principles of free movement (for goods, persons, services and capital) together with rules on competition, but also a variety of flanking measures, including the power to approximate national legislation, and the power to develop a common commercial policy representing the common market's external aspect. As for the common policies on

[3] Emphasis added.

agriculture and transport, these could be seen as special market regimes adapted to the conditions of economic sectors in which a higher than normal degree of interventionism might be found necessary. Even the provisions of the Treaty Title on social policy were, at that time, very much oriented towards addressing problems liable to arise as a result of the removal of the barriers protecting Member States' national markets: for instance, the then Article 119 EEC (now, after amendment, Article 141 EC) on equal pay for men and women was initially regarded as a means of levelling the playing field between Member States with more or less progressive employment legislation. This highly articulated mechanism, to be constructed by the Community institutions using the powers provided by the Treaty, was juxtaposed in Article 2 EEC with the complementary method of pursuing Community objectives through the harmonisation of Member States' economic policies.

III ARTICLE 308 AND THE COMMON MARKET CONCEPT

On that analysis of the common market concept, the drafting of Article 308 (then Article 235 EEC) originally made perfect sense. The Article could be seen as supplementing the tool kit provided by the Treaty for constructing the mechanism central to the performance of the Community's task. Because co-extensive with the common market in the special sense of Article 2, the power conferred on the Council was broad in scope but fairly clearly demarcated. It could not be regarded as circumventing the principle of conferral, because any supplementary legal bases created by the Council must be integral to a market mechanism of the very special kind envisaged by the Treaty.

The logic of Article 308 has been undermined by the great extension of the range of Community competences, more particularly since Maastricht, which is reflected in the changed drafting of Article 2 and in the dropping of the word 'Economic' from the title of the EC Treaty. The common market is no longer the concept unifying the different mechanisms, policies and actions through which the Community pursues its multifarious objectives. Indeed, for most practical purposes it has been displaced by the new concept of 'the internal market', which was introduced by the Single European Act, though the relationship between the two concepts remains controversial. These developments raise questions about Article 308, to which no easy answer is possible. Should the reference to the common market be taken in the broad sense of the former Article 2 EEC or as a synonym for the internal market? On either reading, now that the Community's competences are so much wider, it seems odd that the particular set of activities more or less directly related to the establishment and functioning of the single market should be singled out for special treatment. A fairly convincing case can be made that Article 308 ought to be interpreted in an 'evolutionary' way, reflecting the change in the nature of the Community; at this time of day, it should be understood as authorising the creation of supplementary powers perceived as necessary not just for the purposes of the common market (whatever that now means) but over the whole range of policy areas in which the Treaty allows action to be taken by the Community. To return to the metaphor that was used earlier: a bigger and more complex mechanism requires a tool kit capable of remedying deficiencies in all, not just some, of its working parts. For convenience, I shall refer to this as 'the whole Treaty thesis' of the scope of Article 308.

IV CASE LAW ON ARTICLE 308

Opinion 2/94,[4] delivered by the Court of Justice on 28 March 1996, is the leading post-Maastricht authority on Article 308. In that Opinion, the Court ruled that, under the law as it stood at the time (and still does), the Community had no competence, including under Article 308, to accede to the European Convention for the Protection of Human Rights and Fundamental Freedoms.

In the key paragraph of the judgment for present purposes, the Court said, with reference to Article 308:

> That provision. being an integral part of an institutional system based on the principle of conferred powers, cannot serve as a basis for widening the scope of Community powers beyond the general framework created by the provisions of the Treaty as a whole and, in particular, by those that define the tasks and the activities of the Community. On any view, Article [308] cannot be used as a basis for the adoption of provisions whose effect would, in substance, be to amend the Treaty without following the procedure which it provides for that purpose.[5]

Two points can be made in the light of that passage. First, the Court insists that Article 308 be interpreted and applied consistently with the principle of conferred powers. This may seem obvious, but the view had been held in the past by some of those advising the Community institutions that Article 308 provided a means of making minor Treaty amendments (*la petite revision*). Secondly, there is no mention in the cited paragraph of its being a condition of recourse to Article 308 that the necessity of creating

[4] [1996] ECR I-1759.

[5] At paragraph 31. The German Bundesvervassungsgericht takes a similar view. It was indicated in the famous *Brunner* ruling on ratification of the Maastricht Treaty that a measure based on Article 308 that exceeded the scope of the democratic authorisation given in respect of the transfer of competences to the Community would not be considered binding in Germany: see [1994] 1 CMLR 57.

supplementary powers must have become apparent 'in the course of the operation of the common market'. The reference to 'the general framework created by the provisions of the Treaty as a whole and, in particular, those that define the tasks and the activities of the Community' suggests rather that the Court was implicitly embracing the whole Treaty thesis of the scope of the Article.

Recently, the scope of Article 308 was considered by the Court of First Instance in the *Yusuf* and *Kadi* cases, which at the time of writing, were on appeal to the Court of Justice.[6] The cases concern Regulation (EC) No 881/2002 freezing the assets of certain named individuals believed to be associated with international terrorism.[7] A special mechanism is provided for by Article 60 and Article 301 EC making it possible for the necessary legal steps to be taken under the EC Treaty, in order to implement a decision of the Union's common foreign and security policy (CFSP) imposing financial or economic sanctions on a third country. Since those Articles do not explicitly authorise so-called 'smart sanctions' aimed at individuals, Regulation 881/2002 was given Article 308 as an additional legal basis. In holding that this was a proper use of Article 308, the Court of First Instance (CFI) made no attempt to establish any connection with 'the course of the operation of the common market', which I take as a further indication of the acceptance by the European judicature of the whole Treaty thesis. I shall return in a moment to the issue of whether the CFI was right to regard Article 308 together with Articles 60 and 301 as a necessary and sufficient legal basis for imposing smart sanctions on Messrs Yusuf and Kadi, among others.

V LEGISLATIVE PRACTICE

In broad terms, legislative practice in relation to Article 308 can be placed under two headings—supplementing the areas of authorised Community activity and supplementing the powers conferred by specific legal bases.

The most notable examples of practice of the former kind belong to the pre-Maastricht period. The then Article 235 EEC was the legal basis for the measures establishing the Community's regional policy and environmental policy, as well as for the early development of a framework of protection against sex discrimination in the fields of employment and of social security provision. In my opinion, recourse to Article 308 in relation to such matters could reasonably be regarded as filling a gap in the powers

[6] Case T-306/01, *Yusuf v Council and Commission* [2005] ECR II-3533 and Case T-315/01, *Kadi v Council and Commission* [2005] ECR II-3649; on appeal as, respectively, Case 415/05P and Case 402/05P. Judgment in the two appeals was given on 3 September 2008.

[7] [2002] OJ L/139/9.

necessary to establish a common market reflecting the evolution of socio-economic values since the 1950s, when the EC Treaty was drafted. Less justifiable was the use of the Article to authorise external relations activity not remotely connected with the common market, such as development aid, humanitarian and emergency aid and economic cooperation with countries other than developing countries under programmes like PHARE and TACIS. Those various external initiatives were, presumably, regarded by the Member States as so redolent of motherhood and apple pie that it would have been churlish to contest their legality.

All the Community activities referred to in the previous paragraph are now the subject of specific legal bases, inserted into the EC Treaty by the series of amending Treaties that began with the Single European Act. In my view, there can no longer be any legal justification—nor, indeed, any political excuse—for using Article 308 to open up new policy areas for action by the Community. An egregious example of a recent attempt to do so was the Commission's 2004 proposal for a Regulation, based on Article 308, to establish an 'Instrument for Stability'.[8] The general thrust of the proposed Instrument was defined in Article 1, first paragraph as being to 'finance measures to promote peace and stability and assure the safety and security of the civilian population in third countries and territories . . .'. This was correctly regarded by the Council as a misuse of Article 308, which would have trespassed upon the territory of the CFSP. In the event, the proposal was completely redrafted, to give it the character of a measure ancillary to the Community's policy on cooperation with developing countries (Articles 177 to 181 EC) and with other third countries (Article 181a EC).[9]

However, I believe Article 308 can still perform a useful and constitutionally proper function by allowing the powers of the institutions under specific legal bases to be supplemented, where this proves necessary in order to attain the Community objective for which the power in question has been conferred.

An example would be the creation of new intellectual property forms, such as the Community trade mark. The Community-wide protection, which the trade mark gives, contributes to the smooth functioning of the internal (common) market. However, this could not have been achieved under the general legal basis for internal market legislation, Article 95 EC, which only provides for the adoption of measures to approximate (harmonise) national legislation. Basing the Community Trade Mark Regulation[10]

[8] COM(2004) 630 final.

[9] Reg (EC) 1717/2006 of the European Parliament and of the Council of 15 November 2006 establishing an Instrument for Stability, [2006] OJ L327/1.

[10] Reg 40/94, [1994] OJ L11/36.

on Article 308 can thus be seen as fully orthodox, even on a narrow construction of the Article.

VI THE LEGAL BASIS ISSUE IN *YUSUF* AND *KADI*

What then of the use that was made of Article 308 in the adoption of the Regulation at issue in *Yusuf* and *Kadi*?[11]

I agree with the CFI that a triple legal basis was *necessary* for the adoption of Regulation 881/2002, because neither Articles 60 and 301 together, nor Article 308 on its own, could have done the job.[12] The wording of Articles 60 and 301 cannot be stretched to cover the imposition of 'smart sanctions' against individuals and entities having no necessary connection with a third country's regime or with its territory; and Article 308 cannot be read as giving the institutions carte blanche to create supplementary powers for the Community in respect of matters that fall within the domain of the CFSP.

The combination of the three Articles is a different matter. It provides a *sufficient* legal basis, because the power under Article 308 to supplement the Community's specifically conferred competences is harnessed to provisions with the unique function of supplying a mechanism of economic and financial coercion under the EC Treaty, to help achieve foreign policy and security objectives of the Treaty of European Union (TEU).

The particular mechanism expressly provided by Articles 60 and 301 takes the form of the interruption of economic and financial relations with third countries, where this is called for under a CFSP joint action or common position. However, developing United Nations practice has shown the mechanism to be inadequate for achieving vital objectives of foreign and security policy, which the Union shares with other international actors. Recourse to Article 308, to allow measures of economic coercion against individuals, therefore, passes the test in paragraph 31 of Opinion 2/94: it cannot be said to widen the scope of Community powers beyond the general framework created by the provisions of the Treaty as a whole, because an existing mechanism is being enhanced, so that it can continue to fulfil its purpose effectively.

The textual issue, that Article 308 speaks of action proving necessary to attain 'one of the objectives of the *Community*'[13] was explained by the CFI

[11] See n 6, above.

[12] The opposite view was taken by AG Poiares Maduro in his Opinion of 16 January 2008: see paras 11–16. The Learned Advocate General fails to address the crucial issue considered by the CFI at paragraph 96 in *Kadi*. In its judgment of 3 September 2008, the Court of Justice approved the triple legal basis, on the grounds that are suggested below as an alternative to the 'bridge-building' analysis of the CFI.

[13] Emphasis added.

in the light of the bridge-building function of Articles 60 and 301. Since they have that wholly special function, the principle of consistency in Article 3 of the TEU calls for an interpretation of Article 308 enabling it to be used, in this sole instance, for action deemed necessary to attain a CFSP objective.

I find that reasoning persuasive, though it does place considerable strain on the wording of Article 308. In my view, it is possible, and perhaps preferable, to regard the action provided for by the Regulation as contributing to the attainment of an objective of the Community itself, in addition to those identified by Articles 2 and 3 EC, namely the objective of providing effective means of implementing, by way of coercive economic measures, acts adopted under the competence conferred upon the Union by Title V TEU. That instrumental objective must be understood to have evolved in parallel with the CFSP objectives that it serves, in accordance with the principle of consistency. It falls to be distinguished from the ulterior, CFSP objective of safeguarding international peace and security, which of course belongs to the Union.[14]

For completeness, it may be added that, although the CFI did not see fit to consider whether the measures in question had proved to be necessary 'in the course of operation of the common market', arguably that condition was, in fact, satisfied, since the freezing of assets involves the exercise of Community powers connected with the functioning of the common market.[15]

So I am satisfied that recourse to Article 308 to supplement Articles 60 and 301 as the legal basis for Regulation 881/2002 was perfectly orthodox. However, once the Treaty of Lisbon (TL) enters into force, there will be no further need for this expedient. As has happened in the past where the creation of subsidiary powers pursuant to Article 308 has proved necessary, and this has been followed by the establishment of a specific legal basis relating to the activity in question, Article 215(1) Treaty on the Functioning of the European Union (TFEU), corresponding to the present Article 301 EC, is to be reinforced by a paragraph (2) that provides for the adoption of restrictive measures against natural or legal persons and groups or non-State entities.

VII ARTICLE 308 AS AMENDED BY THE TREATY OF LISBON

The TL would insert into the re-named Treaty on the Functioning of the Union (TFEU) a new Article 352 broadly corresponding to the 'flexibility clause' contained in Article I-18 of the Treaty establishing a Constitution

[14] *Cf* paras 224 to 227 of the Court's judgment in Joined Cases C-402/05P and C-415/05P.
[15] *Ibid*, paras 228 to 231.

for Europe. This refers to action by the Union's proving to be necessary 'within the framework of the policies defined by the Treaties, to attain one of the objectives set out in the Treaties', thus effectively adopting the whole Treaty thesis. The creation of subsidiary powers would, however, be subjected to express conditions not found in the present Article 308 EC. Paragraph (2) of Article 352 TFEU requires the Commission to draw the attention of national parliaments to any proposal based upon the Article, which will give them the opportunity of activating the new subsidiarity mechanism;[16] while paragraph (3) prohibits the use of the Article for adopting harmonisation measures in cases where this is excluded by the Treaties. Finally, paragraph (4) affords specific protection to the CFSP, to prevent the power conferred by Article 342 from being used to circumvent the particularity of the arrangements applicable under chapter 2 of Title V TEU, as amended by the TL. It provides that Article 342 cannot serve as a basis for attaining objectives that belong to the CFSP; and also that acts adopted under the Article must respect the principle enshrined in the new Article 40 TEU, offering protection to the Union's CFSP competence and to its external TFEU competences, against each other.

VIII CONCLUSION

To summarise the main points of the foregoing discussion:

- The drafting of Article 308 EC harks back to the time when the establishment of the common market, including a full range of flanking policies designed to make it a practical reality, was the central project of the European Community.
- The Court of Justice has emphasised that Article 308 must be applied consistently with the principle of conferred powers. It may not be used to amend the EC Treaty, even in a minor way.
- Nevertheless, the European Courts have recognised that Article 308 is available to supplement the powers specifically conferred on the institutions of the Community across the whole range of its activities, not merely those connected with the establishment and functioning of the common market ('the whole Treaty thesis').
- The loose practice of the pre-Maastricht era, in which Article 308 was used to extend Community competence into fields that were not logically connected with the common market project, is no longer acceptable. There remains a role for Article 308 in allowing powers specifically attributed to the Community institutions by the EC Treaty to be supplemented, where this is demonstrably necessary to ensure the

[16] See Protocol on the Application of the Principles of Subsidiarity and Proportionality.

attainment of the objective for which the power in question was conferred. However, that role has become ever more limited, as specific legal bases have proliferated: for example the new legal basis in Article 215(2) TFEU for restrictive measures against individuals, groups or entities not connected with the territory of a particular third country.

— In adopting the whole Treaty thesis, the new Article 342 TFEU to be introduced by the T L is consistent with the case law on the scope of Article 308. Moreover, some further conditions will be imposed, clarifying the limits of the power conferred by the Article.

In conclusion, I would contend that the tension between Article 308 EC (and the future Article 342 TFEU) and the principle of conferral, which is real in theory, has been successfully resolved in practice. The Article, in both its present and its future forms, can be seen to fulfil the function of setting the outer limit of the Community's expressly conferred competence.

4

Which Limits? Control of Powers in an Integrated Legal System

HERWIG CH HOFMANN

I INTRODUCTION

THIS CHAPTER RECONSIDERS the specific conditions for delimiting powers within the EU's highly integrated legal system. It looks at the context for limiting and controlling the exercise of public powers by the European Union and Community. It argues that the specific context for defining limits and control of the exercise of powers in the EU arises from the fact that neither the Member States of the EU nor the EU itself, can be seen as distinct unitary actors. Instead, EU law is part of Member State law and all levels of the Member State executives actively participate in the creation and implementation of EU law. Thus, the understanding of Member States being distinct entities from the EU, and the EU being a supranational body superimposed over the Member States in a quasi-federal two-level system, does not, or at least does no longer, correspond with the legal and practical reality. This has consequences for a realistic understanding of the limits for the exercise of public powers within the European Union.

This paper will develop and illustrate this theme in two steps. First, it turns to the evolutionary development of constitutional principles both for solving conflicts between European and Member State law and for delimiting the powers granted to the European level.[1] These include the principles of supremacy and direct effect,[2] the principle of mutual recogni-

[1] Some authors propose an understanding of Community law existing entirely of conflicts rules. See C Joerges, M Everson, Re-conceptualising Europeanisation as a public law of collisions', in HCH Hofmann and A Türk (eds), *EU Administrative Governance* (Cheltenham, Edward Elgar Publishing, 2006), 512–40.

[2] Case 26/62 *Van Gend en Loos* [1962] ECR 1, paras 10, 12, 13; Case 6/64 *Costa v ENEL* [1964] ECR 585, para 3. Supremacy and direct effect can exist irrespective of the nature of the law which could be either primary treaty law, derived secondary law or individual decisions of an administrative nature.

tion, the principle of subsidiarity,[3] the principle of conferral[4] as well as the proportionality principle.[5] This part of the chapter shows how the evolution of these constitutional principles has led to the EU becoming an integrated legal system requiring a specific framework for establishing limits of the exercise of public power therein.[6]

The second part of the chapter, traces some examples of a modern understanding of the problems arising in the context of an integrated legal system in the case law of the European Court of Justice (ECJ). That part discusses the requirements of forms of limiting and controlling the exercise of public power on the European level in the EU's integrated system.

II THE EVOLUTION OF THE RULES AND PRINCIPLES OF CONFLICT AND DELIMITATION OF POWERS

The evolution of the rules and principles of conflict and for delimitation between the European and the Member States' powers has gone hand in hand with an increasing integration of the legal systems involved. Understanding this evolution requires a review of the development of the principles of supremacy, mutual recognition, and subsidiarity in their legal and historic contexts of vertical integration followed by horizontal integration producing the specific conditions for the exercise of public powers in networks.[7]

A From Supremacy and Direct Effect to Mutual Recognition

The first step in the development of the 'new legal order' arose in the context of the interpretation of the relationship between Community law and the law of the Member States—a question left open by the texts of the Treaties of Paris and Rome. *Costa v ENEL*[8] is known as the starting point

[3] Outlined in Art 5(2) EC and the Protocol attached to the Treaty of Amsterdam on subsidiarity and proportionality.

[4] Enshrined in Arts 5(1) and 7(1) EC, establishing the cases in which powers have been delegated to the European level and defining in what manner and by which institution they may be exercised.

[5] Developed by the case law of the ECJ, also referred to in Art 5(3) EC being a tool for 'fine-tuning' the exercise of powers.

[6] The consequences of this development towards an integrated legal system on the EU Member States being 'disaggregated state' (see A-M Slaughter, *A New World Order* (Princeton, Princeton University Press, 2004), 12–15) will not be the subject of the discussion in this chapter.

[7] The description is taken from a chapter by the author to be published this year in a forthcoming book on the 50th anniversary of the EC Treaty, Loic Azoulaï and Miguel Maduro (eds) *The Past and Future of EU Law* (Oxford, Hart Publishing, 2009).

[8] Case 6/64 *Costa v ENEL* [1964] ECR 585.

in the development of Community-specific conflicts-rules establishing the principles of primacy or supremacy of Community law:[9] Community law had become 'an integral part of' the legal order 'applicable in the territory of each of the Member States'[10] obliging them to set aside any conflicting provision of national law 'which might prevent Community rules from having full force and effect.'[11]

Through the process of such integration Member States gradually opened themselves to the exercise of public power from outside of their territory through a system of shared sovereignty.[12] Initially, the main effect of the principle of primacy was to establish a rule for vertical conflicts between Community and national law. Therefore, the vertical nature of this conflicts rule makes it seem, at first sight, that a hierarchical relationship between EU/EC law and Member State law had been created. This however would be a simplistic and incomplete reading. The principle of primacy or supremacy developed over time into a far less hierarchic and more network oriented structure.

The development towards a network structure began with the 'horizontal' opening of Member States' legal systems. The latter arose under the obligation of the Member States to mutually recognise the legal acts of other Member States, especially where this was necessary to allow for the exercise of fundamental freedoms within the EC.[13] Mutual recognition, required by Community law, led to the trans-territorial effect of the law of

[9] *Ibid*, para 13. In the case the ECJ famously established that Community law, 'stemming from the Treaty' was 'an independent source of law' which could not 'be overridden by domestic legal provisions, however, framed.' The principles established in *Costa v ENEL* were confirmed and further developed in the case law of the ECJ, for example in Case 106/77 *Amministrazione delle Finanze dello Stato v Simmenthal SpA* (*Simmenthal II*) [1978] ECR 629.

[10] 'Any recognition that national legislative measures which encroach upon the field within which the Community exercises its legislative power or which are otherwise incompatible with the provisions of Community law . . . would amount to a corresponding denial of the effectiveness of obligations undertaken unconditionally and irrevocably by Member States ... and would thus imperil the very foundations of the Community' (*ibid*, para 17).

[11] Case 106/77 *Simmenthal II* [1978] ECR 629, para 22.

[12] It is, however, important to recall that European law was acceptable to Member States inter alia because it was not completely alien to the national systems. In European integration, States allowed public power to be exercised also from outside of their legal systems under the condition of being able to participate in its creation and implementation. Member States' executives had become key figures in agenda setting and the legislative procedures as well as the creation of common rules for implementation. Member States were accepting EC law only because they were fully integrated into the legislative and implementing process (JHH Weiler, 'The transformation of Europe', 100 *Yale Law Journal* [1991] 2403–83 at 2413–23).

[13] This horizontal opening is most closely associated with Case 120/78 *Rewe Central AG (Cassis de Dijon)* [1979] ECR 649, which required Member States to mutually accept each others' legislative and administrative decisions in the absence of harmonising legislation from the European level (paras 8, 14).

one Member State in the territory of another Member State.[14] Thereby, Member States opened their territory and their legal systems to the application of public power not only in the vertical dimension from the Community level, but also horizontally from other Member States.[15] The integration of Community law into national law and the horizontal opening of Member States led, in the process of deepening and widening European integration, to the development of additional and more sophisticated tools not to solve conflicts of application but instead to create rules to prevent them, through, for example, the principle of subsidiarity.[16]

B The Failure and Success of the Principle of Subsidiarity

Subsidiarity was initially designed as a kind of meta-principle for the vertical distribution of legislative powers between the European and the national levels.[17] As such, however, in legal terms it did not prove to be very effective. The ECJ never declared a measure to be void due to the violation of the subsidiarity principle. From this point of view, subsidiarity

[14] The *Simmenthal* cases powerfully demonstrate this. The *Simmenthal* saga straddles both the horizontal and the vertical aspect of supremacy. In Case 35/76 *Simmenthal I* [1976] ECR 1871, the underlying question was whether, in order to allow for the exercise of the free movement of goods, the Italian authorities were obliged to horizontally recognise a veterinary certificate issued by the French authorities. EC law therefore required in a 'horizontal conflicts' case, that the law of France should have effect in Italy. After the ECJ in a preliminary ruling had affirmed this, *Simmenthal II* was a case about the consequences of such a ruling on Italian law. The local judge, the Pretore de Susa, needed to know whether he had the right to set aside Italian law which had been found to be incompatible with EC law (*Simmenthal II* above n 11, para 3).

[15] Horizontal effect can also mean an effect of law applied between private parties. The horizontal effect due to the primacy of EU/EC law arises not only between states but also between individuals. A national measure might, for example, be inapplicable in the relationship between individuals of one or several Member States if it is incompatible with Community law in substance. It may also be inapplicable if it violated procedural rules laid down by Community law for the adoption of national provisions. See C-441/93 *Pafitis* [1996] ECR I-1347, C-194/94 *CIA Security International* [1996] ECR I-2201, paras 45–54; C-443/98 *Unilever Italia* [2000] ECR I-7535, paras 31–52 and C-159/00 *Sapod Audic* [2002] ECR I-5031, paras 48–52. See for limitations of this rule, C-226/97 *Lemmens* [1998] ECR I-3711, para 35.

[16] Subsidiarity was designed to add an additional level of control for the exercise of public power in the EU. Art 5(2) EC.

[17] The ECJ rarely entered into an in-depth debate over the merits of subsidiarity related arguments—mainly due to respect for the legislative discretion of the Community legislator. This made subsidiarity a legally rather weak tool. See, eg C-84/94 *Working Time Directive* [1996] ECR I-5755; C-233/94 *Deposit Guarantee Schemes* [1997] ECR I-2405; C- 376/98 *Germany v EP and Council (tobacco advertising)* [2000] ECR I-8419; C-377/98 *Biotechnological Inventions* [2001] ECR I-7079. A more thorough analysis was only undertaken in C-154/04 *Alliance for Natural Health of 12 July 2005*, paras 101–106, albeit with the result that harmonisation under Art 95 could be best achieved under EC law and could not sufficiently be achieved under national law.

did not play a very important role in the distribution of legislative competences between the European and the national levels.

However practically, the invocation of the principle of subsidiarity influenced to a great degree the distribution of powers between legislation and implementation. Historically, the extraordinary development of new and experimental forms of exercising public power goes hand in hand with the focus on subsidiarity in policy debates.[18] The question was whether instead of wholesale legislative harmonisation, it was possible to find new, cooperative and sovereignty-preserving means of sharing policies both on the European as well as the national levels.[19] The emergence of subsidiarity as a constitutional principle in the EU thus goes hand in hand with the development of the current system of decentralised yet cooperative administrative structures. These forms of cooperation have mostly taken the form of executive networks with participants from the Member States, the Community institutions and private parties.[20]

The impact of this development becomes clearer when taking a step back and looking at the emergence of the integrated executive. In the EU-specific system of integration, executive activity goes beyond implementing activity. It also expands to administrative cooperation in agenda setting[21] and policy making.[22] It is most visible in the implementing phase, institutions' activities range from single case decisions and preparatory acts thereof, to

[18] Since Subsidiarity entered the EC Treaty under the Single European Act in the area of environmental law and under the Treaty of Maastricht as a generally applicable principle, several generations of agency foundations have taken place. Equally, during this phase, the phenomenon of comitology was addressed in a more systematic way; first by the reformulation of what is now Arts 202 and 211 EC and secondly by the 1987, 1999 and 2006 comitology decisions (Council Decision of 17 July 2006 amending Decision 1999/468/EC laying down the procedures for the exercise of implementing powers conferred on the Commission, [2006] OJ L200/11; Council Decision of 28 June 1999 laying down the procedures for the exercise of implementing powers conferred on the Commission, [1999] OJ L184/23; Council Decision of 13 July 1987 laying down the procedures for the exercise of implementing powers conferred on the Commission, [1987] OJ L/197/33).

[19] See, eg the cases C-66/04 *UK v Parliament and Council (smoke flavourings)* [2005] ECR I-10553; Case C-217/04 *UK v Parliament and Council (ENISA)* [2006] ECR I-3771 which will be discussed in greater detail later in this paper.

[20] See for further details the contributions to Hofmann and Türk (n 1 above) and M Egeberg, 'Europe's Executive Branch of Governments in the Melting Pot: An Overview' in M Egeberg (ed), *Multilevel Union Administration* (London, Palgrave, 2006) 1–16.

[21] In the phase of agenda setting, national administrations can play a central role in shaping the Commission's policy initiatives. This takes place mainly through expert groups which are generally composed of national civil servants, but also independent experts. These groups are used to test ideas, build coalitions of experts, and pre-determine policy incentives later to be formally presented by the Commission as initiative.

[22] The presence of the national executive actors in the EU's decision-making process is mostly felt within the Council working parties supporting COREPER. Here, the national civil servants have to balance their national mandate against the need to reach a consensus in pursuance of EU tasks. Such interaction, albeit to a lesser extent, also exists through the 'Open Method of Coordination.'

acts of administrative rule-making and the amendment of specific provisions in legislation where so authorised. In many policy areas, the development of the integration of EU and national administrative proceedings has led to 'composite proceedings' to which both national and EU administrations contribute. Diverse structures undertake implementation decisions and administrative rule-making in the various policy areas. Amongst these developments are comitology committee procedures,[23] in certain policy areas expanded to what is now known as the 'Lamfalussy' procedures.[24] Agencies and their administrative networks play an ever increasing role. Implementing networks may also include private parties acting as recipients of limited delegation. Administrative networks, that have been created and adapted to the needs of each policy area, integrate the supranational and national administrative bodies within structures designed to conduct joint or coordinated action.[25] Structures of integrating executive branches of the Member States and the EU operate in large parts beyond the institutions and procedures established by the founding treaties. They have developed in an evolutionary way differing at each stage of the policy cycle and in each policy area.[26]

C Which Place for the Principle of Conferral?

Despite these transformations, EU/EC law remains often understood as a two-level legal system in which the EU/EC legal order has been superimposed

[23] For a discussion of this development, see eg F Bergström *Comitology: Delegation of Powers in the European Union and the Committee System*, (Oxford, Oxford University Press, 2005); K St C Bradley, The European Parliament and Comitology, 'On the Road to Nowhere?', 3 *European Law Journal* [1997], 230–54; K St C Bradley, 'Institutional Aspects of Comitology: Scenes from the Cutting Room Floor', in C Joerges and E Vos (eds) *EU Committees: Social Regulation, Law and Politics* (Oxford, Hart Publishing, 1999), 71–93; G Schusterschitz and S Kotz 'The Comitology Reform of 2006. Increasing the Powers of the European Parliament Without Changing the Treaties', [2007] *European Constitutional Law Review*, 68–90; M Szapiro, 'Comitologie: rétrospective et prospective après la réforme de 2006' [2006] *Revue du droit de l'Union européenne*, no 3, 545–86, 567–8; AE Töller and HCH Hofmann, 'Democracy and the reform of Comitology', in M Andenas, and A Türk (eds) *Delegated legislation and the Role of Committees in the EC* (The Hague, Kluwer 2000), 25–50; AE Töller, *Komitologie* (Opladen, Leske & Buderich, 2005).

[24] See, eg R Lastra, The Governance Structure for Financial Regulation and Supervision in Europe, 10 *Columbia Journal of European Law* (2004), 49; N Moloney, 'The Lamfalussy Legislative Model: A New Era for the EC Securities and Investment Services Regime', 52 *ICLQ* (2003) 509–20. Beatrice Vaccari, 'Le processus Lamfalussy: une réussite pour la comitologie et un exemple de bonne gouvernance européenne (2005) *Revue du droit de l'Union Européenne*, 803–22.

[25] In practice, these forms of cooperation consist of obligations of different intensity. They range from obligations to exchange information either on an ad hoc or on a permanent basis to network structures which have been developed to include forms of implementation such as individually binding decisions.

[26] See with more detail HCH Hofmann and A Türk(n 1 above).

on the Member States' legal systems. One of the central principles of law, drawing a limit between the powers of the Member States and the powers of the EU/EC, the principle of conferral, at first sight seems firmly rooted in this original understanding of the relationship between Member State and EU law. Conferral remains central to the creation of the legal system, in which Member States have conferred a limited amount of more or less well circumscribed powers to the EU. But a brief review of the evolution of rules and principles of conflicts and delimitation of powers, shows that a *quasi-federal* understanding of a two-level structure no longer reflects the whole picture in the understanding of limits to Community and Union powers. As a consequence of the evolution of the EU legal system, with complex vertical, horizontal and composite relationships of the actors within it, there is no longer always a clear distinction between the exercise of public powers between the European and the national levels.

The inter-relatedness of the levels reduces the explanatory value of a two-dimensional delegation model and with it the limiting powers of the principle of conferral. This has consequences not only for our understanding of the role of the EU/EC and the Member States and the limitation of their respective powers, but also for the analysis of key aspects of controlling the exercise of public powers such as accountability. Therefore, although the principle of conferral remains the basis of the rule of law and the control of ultra vires activity, for the delimitation of EU/EC law, conferral needs to be understood in the context of an integrated legal system. This creates obligations for the Member States, the limitations of which can only be described in general terms. This results from several factors.

First, the outer limits of the conferred powers cannot be exhaustively derived from an analysis of the legislative and administrative powers conferred on the EU/EC legal system by the Member States. The effect of such conferral goes further, by integrating general principles of Community law and fundamental rights as protected under Community law into both substantive and procedural law of the Member States. The ECJ has developed its case law requiring the application of general principles and fundamental rights as protected under the Community legal order when Member States act within the sphere of European law.[27] Member States act in the sphere of European law either when implementing EU or EC acts such as regulations,

[27] This approach has been included in Art 51(1) of the Charter of Fundamental Rights of the European Union and will become a Treaty provision with the entry into force of the Treaty of Lisbon. Under Article 52(7) of the Charter 'The explanations drawn up as a way of providing guidance in the interpretation of this Charter shall be given due regard by the courts of the Union and of the Member States.' The explanations to Article 51 make reference to *inter alia* the case *ERT* by stating that 'As regards the Member States, it follows unambiguously from the case law of the Court of Justice that the requirement to respect fundamental rights defined in a Union context is only binding on the Member States when

directives or decisions[28] or when Member States' legislative or administrative activity results in a limitation of a fundamental freedom.[29]

Secondly, when implementing, Member States are under an obligation to ensure the observance of the principles of equivalence and effectiveness of Community law, principles which are developed from the obligation of loyal cooperation under Article 10 EC. The equivalent and effectively enforceable principles include EU/EC general principles and fundamental rights. In the sphere of European law, Member States are obliged to provide for effective implementation and enforcement including dissuasive sanctions for violations of these principles and rights.[30] Member States are also bound by the principle of effectiveness obliging them to provide for procedures which make effective enforcement practically possible by non-application of rules which make enforcement 'excessively difficult'.[31] Further, the Member State provisions have to provide a 'real deterrent effect' against violation of Community law provisions.[32] In cases of conflict between the principles of effectiveness and of equivalence, effectiveness takes precedence. Consequently, Member States cannot be excused by proving that national rules are not effectively implemented either.[33]

they act in the context of Community law (judgment of 13 July 1989, Case 5/88 Wachauf [1989] ECR 2609; judgment of 18 June 1991, ERT [1991] ECR I-2925).'

[28] See as seminal case Case C-5/88 *Wachauf* [1989] ECR I-2609, para 19.

[29] C-260/89 *ERT-AE v DEP* [1991] ECR I-2925, para 43.

[30] Case 14/83 *Von Colsen and Kamann* [1984] ECR I-1891, para 28. In the leading case *Greek Maize* the ECJ held that Member States must 'ensure in particular that infringements of Community law are penalized under conditions, both procedural and substantive, which are analogous to those applicable to infringements of national law of a similar nature and importance and which, in any event, make the penalty effective, proportionate and dissuasive. Moreover, the national authorities must proceed, with respect to infringements of Community law, with the same diligence as that which they bring to bear in implementing corresponding national laws'. Case 68/88 *Commission v Greece (Greek Maize)* [1989] ECR I-2965, paras 24, 25. See with this respect also: Case C-326/88 *Hansen* [1990] ECR I-2911, para 17; Case C-7/90 *Vandevenne and others* [1991] ECR I-4371, para 11; Case C-29/95 *Pastoors and Trans-Cap* [1997] ECR I-285, para 24; Case C-177/95 *Ebony Maritime* [1997] ECR I-1111, paras 35–37; Joined Cases C-387/02, C-391/02 and C-403/02 *Berlusconi* [2005] ECR I-3565 para 65.

[31] See, eg Case C-261/95 *Palmisani* [1997] ECR I-4025, para 27; Case C-326/96 *Levez* [1998] ECR I-7835, para 18; Case C-453/99 *Courage v Crehan* [2001] ECR I-6297, para 29; Case C-255/00 *Grundig Italiana* [2002] ECR I-8003, para 33; Case 199/82 *San Giorgio* [1983] ECR 3595, paras 17, 18.

[32] Case C-180/95 *Draehmpael* [1997] ECR I-2195, paras 24, 25; Case C-271/91 *Marshall II* [1993] ECR I-4367, paras 24–26; Case 14/83 *Von Colson and Kamann* [1983] ECR 1891, para 23. These obligations exist also when Member States opt for non-enforcement. The Court of Justice held that the 'apprehension of internal difficulties cannot justify a failure by a Member State to apply Community law correctly'. Instead, 'it is for the Member State concerned, unless it can show that action on its part would have consequences for public order with which it could not cope by using the means at its disposal, to adopt all appropriate measures to guarantee the full scope and effect of Community law'. (Case C-265/95 *Commission v France (Spanish Strawberries)* [1997] ECR I-6959, para 52).

[33] JH Jans, R de Lange, S Prechal and R JGM Widdershoven, *Europeanisation of Public Law* (Groningen, Europa Law Publishing, 2007), 212.

The result of this evolution can first be observed to be an opening of the Member States to the exercise of public power from outside of their territory, be this from the European level or from other Member States. Secondly, at the same time, Member States' branches of government are involved in the creation, implementation and adjudication of European law. Member State and EU structures are thus not only subject to EU/EC law, they also jointly create and implement it. This is now a central notion to EU/EC law of being an integral part of Member State law. Therefore, the relationship between EU/EC law and the law of the Member States can not be described in two-level terms. The legal orders are highly integrated and such integration is driven by constitutional principles of law. That has a necessary influence on the possibilities of the control of the exercise of public power within such an integrated structure and the control of ultra vires activities.

D The Multiple Roles of the Principle of Proportionality

The principle of proportionality has been developed in the case law of the ECJ as the main instrument to control the exercise of powers conferred on the European level. It is a principle for delimitation developed within the network-nature of the European legal system. The principle of proportionality is a fine-tuning instrument to delimit the extent of public powers. This factor, however, also makes the exact borderlines of the principle of conferral difficult to define in single cases. Proportionality can be used in basically three different contexts. Proportionality is, first, used to delimit the exercise of both Community powers vis-à-vis Member State powers and, secondly, vis-à-vis individual rights. Thirdly, proportionality is also a principle to analyse the degree of justification of limitations of Member State legislative and regulatory activity when limiting the exercise of Community fundamental freedoms. The principle of proportionality is therefore applied not only to the question of legislative powers but also to the issue of the distribution and application of implementing powers. It is a principle which is both used to analyse whether the *forum* for decision-making is right as well as for reviewing the *substance* of a specific measure. Not by accident, it seems, has the principle of proportionality (and the underlying balancing of interests) developed such a prominence in the case law of the ECJ when reviewing the limitations of the exercise of powers—both legislative and administrative in nature. Also it is not surprising that proportionality review is currently undertaken with differing intensity in different contexts. Although generally, proportionality-control as exercised by the ECJ is undertaken from the outset by a fairly standard three-step procedure,[34] so far, measurers of a more administrative nature are submitted to a stricter level of review from the point of view of the proportionality principle[35] than cases of measures of a more legislative nature.[36] In the latter, the Court generally applies a rather 'soft' level of review granting wide (legislative) discretion.[37] Review of discretion in administrative single-case implementing decisions has so far been stricter. Given the importance of cooperative administrative procedures in all phases of the policy cycle and the importance of procedural rights therein, it might be advisable for the ECJ to harden the level of proportionality-review throughout its review of types of measures including legislative action. One of the

[34] The principle of proportionality is referred to in almost every case which applies to a review of measures (well defined eg Case C-189/01 *Jippes* [2001] ECR I-5689, paras 80–101; see also C-331/88 *Fedesa and Others* [1990] ECR I-4023). The ECJ has adopted a three-level test (levels two and three are often addressed together): first, measures may 'not exceed the limits of what is appropriate and necessary in order to attain the objectives legitimately pursued by the legislation in question'. Secondly, 'when there is a choice between several appropriate measures recourse must be had to the least onerous', and thirdly, 'the disadvantages caused must not be disproportionate to the aims pursued'.

[35] An example for a more thorough approach for review of regulatory decision-making exists with respect to measures of administrative nature. In *William Hinton* (C-30/00, *William Hinton & Sons Lda v Fazenda Pública* [2001] ECR I-7511, paras 59–61 (on the interpretation of Arts 1, 2 and 5 of Reg 1697/79 on the post-clearance recovery of import duties) with reference to Case 265/87 *Schräder v Hauptzollamt Gronau* [1989] ECR 2237, para 21, and Case C-295/94 *Hüpeden* [1996] ECR I-3375, para 14) the application of the principle of proportionality was much more directed by a hard-look style review. The Court found that by virtue of the principle of proportionality, 'measures imposing financial charges on traders are lawful provided that the measures are appropriate and necessary for meeting the objectives legitimately pursued by the legislation in question, it being understood that, when there is a choice between several appropriate measures, the least onerous measure must be used and the charges imposed must not be disproportionate to the aims pursued. 'In so far as the exportation of surplus stocks is less onerous than payment of the levy, the principle of proportionality requires that a trader should have a genuine opportunity to export his stock before the expiry of the period prescribed for it.'

[36] An example for the exercise of a rather 'soft' approach to proportionality review in legislative matters is the *Working Time Directive* case. As to political discretion, it was found that 'the Council must be allowed a wide discretion in an area which, as here, involves the legislature in making social political choices and requires it to carry out complex assessments . . . Judicial review of the exercise of that discretion must therefore be limited to examining whether it has been vitiated by manifest error of misuse of powers, or whether the institution concerned has manifestly exceeded the limits of its discretion.' As to the test whether the means were suitable to purpose under the proportionality test the Court held that 'the measures on the organisation of working time which form the subject matter of the directive ... contribute directly to the improvement of health and safety protection for workers within the meaning of Art 118a, and cannot therefore be regarded as unsuited to the purpose of achieving the objective pursued.' With respect to the least onerous measure test, the Court decided with equally limited or non-existent information that 'the objective of harmonizing national legislation on the health and safety of workers, which maintaining the improvements made, could not be achieved by measures less restrictive than those that are the subject-matter of the directive, the Council did not commit any manifest error'. Case C-84/94 *Working Time Directive* [1996] ECR I-5755, at 5811.

[37] See, eg C-233/94, *Deposit Guarantee Schemes*, [1997] ECR I-2405; C-331/88 *Fedesa* [1990] ECR I-4023 para 14; Case C-189/01 *Jippes* [2001] ECR I-5689, of 12 July 2001 paras 80–101.

tools to do so would be to improve the scope of the information available to be taken into account for judicial review. Enforceable procedural rules for impact assessment for legislation and administrative rule-making can make a significant contribution to obtaining the necessary information for an effective use of power-limiting principles such as proportionality.[38] A minimum version of this approach has recently been called on by Advocate General Sharpston in a case concerning a Spanish support scheme for cotton producers. She referred to the obligation of the institutions to explore the element of a decision fully, prior to taking a decision by undertaking an 'impact study'. This obligation is linked to the principle of proportionality in so far as it imposes 'an obligation on Community institutions at least to satisfy themselves that the proposed measures are prima facie adequate to attain the legitimate aims pursued.'[39] The ECJ could thus protect procedural rights in regulatory impact assessment as essential participatory rights. It could then use results of regulatory impact assessment procedures as relevant information for balancing within all three steps of the proportionality test: First, the capability of a measure to contribute to reaching a legitimate policy goal; secondly, the review whether the least onerous measure vis-à-vis the Member States' prerogatives and individual rights has been chosen; thirdly the overall balancing for exclusion of extreme cases of imbalance between means and objectives. These steps might enhance a flexible approach to limitations of powers, adapted to the network structure of the EU. Proportionality thus has an inherent quality important to delimit powers in an evolutionary network-structure like the evolving European legal and political system. It is capable of

[38] Both legislative and regulatory impact assessment can be both an *ex ante* and *ex post* review given the often cyclical nature of the policy cycle developments. The US-model of the notice and comment procedure is an example for a form of use of this genre of tools for sub-legislative rule-making. In general, the tool of impact assessments, especially their use *ex ante* for regulatory activity (or *ex post* prior to reform) can enhance various goals including institutional control and cross-level checks and balances. An in-depth discussion of the needs of development of the tool of regulatory impact assessment in the EU would go beyond the possibilities of this brief paper. The original introduction of the EU scheme of impact assessment was based on a Commission communication (Communication on Impact Assessment, COM(2002) 276 final 1–19), expanded upon in particular by a Commission Staff Working Paper (Impact Assessment: Next Steps—In Support of Competitiveness and Sustainable Development, SEC(2004) 1377 1–15) and the Commission, Impact Assessment Guidelines (SEC(2005) 791) together with detailed annexes (European Commission, Annexes to Impact Assessment Guidelines (SEC(2005) 791) (2005) 1–51) updated in 2006. For complete material see: http://ec.europa.eu/governance/impact/docs_en.htm and discussion eg at GC Rowe, 'Tools for the control of political and administrative agents: impact assessment and administrative governance in the European Union', in HCH Hofmann, A Türk n 1 above) 448–511.

[39] Opinion of Advocate General Sharpston in Case C-310/04 *Spain v Council* [2006] ECR I-7285, paras 80, 94. The violation of the duty to care by the institutions was so severe that they were criticised as appearing arbitrary. The ECJ followed the AG, however explicitly referring to an impact study but instead to the duty of care which requires the Commission to collect and to take into account all relevant information prior to taking a discretionary decision (Case C-310/04 *Spain v Council* [2006] ECR I-7285, para 133.

being applied to balance the exercise of powers of different actors within the highly integrated network structure of the EU/EC legal system.

In summary, the EU's specific system of delimiting the powers of the European vis-à-vis the Member State level developed in phases starting with a vertical followed by a horizontal integration of the legal orders, through supremacy, direct effect and mutual recognition. The principle of subsidiarity which was originally designed to be a soft and adaptable principle to delimit competencies and protect against overreach of powers conferred to the European level, has fostered the development of an integrated legal system. Compliance with the principle of conferral therefore is not only a question of black or white but also a question of degree. In the proportionality review, issues of degree are taken into account when considering the limitation and control of the exercise of public powers in the EU. Although dealing with the limits of powers originally conferred, it governs by defining a balancing exercise, looking at, inter alia: regulatory goals; alternative regulatory approaches; and the impact of these various solutions on the rights of actors within the network.

III INTEGRATION IN COURT – *SMOKE FLAVOURINGS* AND *ENISA*

The theoretic considerations made above in the first part of this chapter, have not remained confined to academic debate. They arise increasingly in real life disputes before the ECJ. Two case studies might illustrate this and serve as examples for the way in which the nature of European integration has changed over time.

The two cases I would like to briefly discuss here as examples for this change of nature and perception of integration are *smoke flavourings*[40] and *ENISA*.[41] They both raised fundamental questions regarding the understanding of the division of competence between the European Community and its Member States under Article 95 EC.[42] They are particularly interesting in the context of the legal developments discussed in this contribution, since they do not only concern the question of the extent of

[40] See n 19 above.

[41] See n 19 above.

[42] Comments in the literature on these two judgements have included worries that they might 'inflame the perennial tensions underlying the division of competence between the Community and the Member States' and have the 'potential to enliven concerns about the magnitude of the Community's competence'. Kathleen Gutman, Case note Case 66/04, *Smoke Flavourings*; Case C-436/03, *SCE*; and Case C-217/04, *ENISA*, 13 *Columbia Journal of European Law* (2006/2007) 147–87, at p 182. For further critical reviews of the cases, especially with respect to the principle of conferral see A Epiney, 'Anmerkung zu' C-217/04, *Neue Verwaltungsrechts Zeitschrift* 2007, 1012–23; M Ludwigs, 'Artikel 95 als allgemeine Kompetenz zur Regelung des Binnenmarktes oder als "begrenzte Einzelermächtigung"?', 2006 *Europäische Zeitschrift für Wirtschaftsrecht*, 417.

the power to issue legislative harmonising measures.[43] Instead, both situations concern the use of European agencies, and in *smoke flavourings*, also a comitology procedure as means to reduce the 'hard' legislative approach to harmonisation and achieve legislative goals through the use of forms of integrated administration.

In both cases, *ENISA* and *smoke flavourings,* the UK essentially contested the legality of the measures. Article 95 EC, the UK government argued, did not confer general regulatory powers in the area of the internal market to the Community. Article 95 EC merely intended to confer powers for the improvement of the conditions for the establishment and functioning of the single market, by means of measures of harmonisation of national law directed towards the Member States. In *smoke flavourings*, the UK argued that the creation of multiple-step regulatory procedures failed to harmonise national law directly and was thus illegal under Article 95 EC.[44] In *ENISA,* the UK argued that the creation of an agency to improve the conditions of exchange of information within the single market could not be regarded as measures addressed at harmonising Member State law and was thus not within the limits of the powers conferred onto the Community under Article 95 EC.

When looking at these arguments more closely, the UK argued basically from an understanding of the Community legal system based on a traditional two-level legal system within the model of executive federalism. Under this model, the Community is in charge of legislating and the Member States having the right to implement through legislative and administrative means. The Court's judgements in *smoke flavourings* and *ENISA* are noteworthy because they implicitly reject a simplistic two-level model of executive federalism for the EU. Despite basing its analysis on the content of powers conferred to the Community under Article 95 EC, the ECJ acknowledges that the relationship between the Community and the Member States is more complex. In *smoke flavourings* the ECJ held that Article 95 EC conferred:

> on the Community legislature a discretion, depending on the general context and the specific circumstances of the matter to be harmonised, as regards the harmonisation technique most appropriate for achieving the desired result, in particular in fields which are characterised by complex technical features.[45]

[43] This was eg,the case in Case C-376/00 *Germany v Parliament and Council (tobacco advertising)* [2000] ECR I-8419. See also Advocate General Fennelly's discussion of the extent of powers as well as the principles of subsidiarity and proportionality in this case.

[44] The UK acknowledged that establishing a detailed decision-making procedure with a regulatory committee procedure assisting and supervising the Commission whose decisions are prepared with input from the European Food Safety Agency established a procedure which could result in harmonisation of national law. That, according to the argument was too far removed to be acceptable under Art 95 EC.

[45] *smoke flavourings* (n19) paras 45, 46.

It continued to find that:

> the mechanism for implementing those elements must be designed in such a way that it leads to a harmonisation within the meaning of Article 95 EC. That is the case where the Community legislature establishes the detailed rules for making decisions at each stage of such an authorisation procedure, and determines and circumscribes precisely the powers of the Commission as the body which has to take the final decision.[46]

Advocate General Kokott had stressed this latter point by entering into a more detailed analysis of the principles of proportionality and subsidiarity. With respect to the relationship between Member State and Community competences, she found that 'everything suggests that the solution chosen is, of the various conceivable regulatory models, the most appropriate for achieving its aim'.[47] She reached this conclusion by comparing different regulatory approaches. On one hand was the regulation's multi-step procedure for establishing a list of marketable smoke flavouring food additives on the European level, including the comitology regulatory procedure for decision-making in combination with scientific analysis prepared by the European agency. This procedure with its forms of highly integrated administrative structures she compared to two different, in a sense more traditional, notions. One is legislation on the European level and implementation on the Member State level with subsequent obligation of the Member States for mutual recognition of each others' administrative decisions. That she found would subsequently lead to conflicts between Member States to the disadvantage of the single market. The other model she compared is the model 'the United Kingdom ultimately recommends'. That:

> would restrict the competences of the Member States just as much as the solution chosen, and would at the same time make the procedure for the authorisation of smoke flavourings considerably clumsier and if anything reduce the rights of participation of manufacturers.[48]

With the latter reference to the rights and interests of private parties, in this case the manufacturers, she widens the circle of rights to be taken into account in the choice of the regulatory approaches. This is an important aspect of a more modern integrated approach to the division of powers and, in my view, it must be added, the necessary procedures for the control and supervision of the exercise of these powers. An integrated legal system, might be in effect both preserving sovereignty of the Member States and increasing legitimacy by including non-state actors in decision-making and thus broadening the amount of interests taken into account in decision-making.

[46] *Ibid*, para 49.
[47] Opinion of Advocate General Kokott in *smoke flavourings ibid*, paras 44–8.
[48] Opinion of Advocate General Kokott in *ibid*, para 47.

In the *ENISA* case, the UK contested the choice of Article 95 EC not for establishing a procedure to create a list of authorised food additives. Instead, it turned against the use of Article 95 EC as the legal basis for a regulation establishing an agency, the European Network and Information Security Agency.[49] The ECJ rejected that reasoning by arguing first, that the addressees of measures under Article 95 EC are not exclusively the Member States. Instead:

> the legislature may deem it necessary to provide for the establishment of a Community body responsible for contributing to the implementation of a process of harmonisation in situations where, in order to facilitate the uniform implementation and application of acts based on that provision, the adoption of non-binding supporting and framework measures seems appropriate.[50]

This is the case as long as the tasks conferred on such a body are 'closely linked to the subject matter of approximation of laws'. With this rather broad understanding of the principle of conferral the Court elaborates that the rights of the Member States will be protected through a proportionality-style review. When the creation of an administrative structure such as an agency with the duty to collect information and suggest solutions to Member States is less intrusive on Member States' prerogatives than whole-scale detailed harmonisation measures, limitations of conferral are not overstepped.

> Such is the case in particular where the Community body thus established provides services to national authorities and/or operators which affect the homogenous implementation of harmonising instruments and which are likely to facilitate their application.[51]

Despite not explicitly referring to the principles of subsidiarity and proportionality, in *ENISA* the ECJ nevertheless analysed the values contained in the principles in its analysis of whether the agency could legally have been created on the basis of Article 95 EC. It found that the creation of the agency was not an isolated measure but needs to be seen within the regulatory context which included a framework directive and many specific directives attempting to establish the conditions for an internal market in electronic communications. Technological factors which needed to be taken into account in such regulatory activity were complex and developing rapidly. In this way, the establishment of an agency providing technical advice at the request of the Commission and the Member States

[49] Regulation EC 460/2004 of the European Parliament and Council of 10 March 2004, [2004] OJ L77/1. The UK argued that Art 308 EC, requiring unanimity in the Council, would have been the correct legal basis for such a measure.

[50] *ENISA* see n 19, paras 43–5.

[51] *Ibid*, paras 43–5.

might not only facilitate the implementation of the various directives in the area, but also made a real contribution to the achievement of the single market.[52]

Thereby the ECJ essentially followed the European Parliament's and the Commission's arguments that establishing an agency for advice of national bodies who remain free to exercise their discretion and adopt different measures than the ones proposed, is a means of 'low-intensity approximation'.[53] What the Parliament here describes as 'low intensity' is essentially applying an approach of administrative cooperation in order to achieve technically sound solutions in an area of complex technical approaches whilst at the same time devising a sovereignty-preserving measure.[54]

In my view, the result of these two examples is innovative in so far as the ECJ interprets EU law in a manner which is open to the requirements and the realities of an integrated legal system. It does not maintain a traditional, federal–constitutional style two-level model. It is open for alternative regulatory models and experimental structures in order to give effect to the principles of subsidiarity and proportionality. It has been observed that 'as a result, these judgements may help to demonstrate that the expansion of the scope of Article 95 need not necessarily lead to the curtailment of the principles of subsidiarity and proportionality, but in fact may contribute to their fulfilment'.[55] The cases show that despite the decreasing role which subsidiarity-type considerations have had in the case law of the ECJ with respect to legislative competencies, subsidiarity-type considerations nevertheless play an eminent role in the ECJ's evaluation of overall regulatory strategies. This evaluation, however, goes beyond an executive federalism type understanding and uses the level of implementation as the grounds for fine-tuning this balancing exercise. It is thus necessary to shift the attention to understand the real value and implications of subsidiarity for the debate, from legislative to administrative fora.

The consequences for European law and its analysis are considerable. It requires a shift from a predominantly constitutional understanding of the legal system and the instruments on offer for the delimitation of EU law towards developing a toolbox for control of powers including many more concepts developed in administrative law. These issues have been mentioned

[52] *Ibid*, paras 60–66. It needs to be added that in *ENISA*, the ECJ did not agree with AG Kokott's conclusions. AG Kokott had argued that Art 95 EC was not the correct legal basis for measures which are not closely related to the approximation of national law. In this way, she argued, it was immaterial whether the measure finally adopted 'had less of an effect on national competences than a genuinely approximating measure' (Opinion of AG Kokott, para 39).

[53] *ENISA*(n 19 above), paras 25, 38.

[54] Especially when compared with full-scale detailed regulation for transposition in Member States under a more traditional two-level model.

[55] Kathleen Gutman, Case note, *Smoke Flavourings*; Case C-436/03, *SCE*; and Case C-217/04, *ENISA*, 13 *Columbia Journal of European Law* (2006/2007) 147–87, at 186.

by AG Kokott for example, as rights of participation. However, they also include questions such as access to judicial review of multi-step regulatory procedures, defence rights, rights of access to information rights and data protection—to name just a few. Discussing the details of these issues is beyond the scope of this short contribution. These are, however, important themes of EU (administrative) law of the future.

IV CONTROL OF POWERS IN AN INTEGRATED LEGAL SYSTEM

This chapter has argued that the European legal system does not lend itself to establishing clear limits between the levels of the Member States and of the EU/EC legal system. Its reality is marked by the prevalence of cooperative procedures in agenda setting, decision making and implementation. It is characterised by the close links established between the different players—public and private, European and national—therein.[56] This development was in part sparked by, in part influenced by, the evolution of the rules and principles on conflicts which have led over time to a complex integrated composite structure rather than a neat separation of Member States on one hand and the EU on the other. Accordingly, when thinking about limits to public powers, traditional multi-level parameters such as the principle of conferral alone will not be able to draw effective limitations to the exercise of powers. This results not least from the difficulty of distinguishing legislative and implementing measures on the European level and the intense cooperation of administrative actors from both the EU and the Member States. These factors need to be taken into account in a search for limits to the exercise of public powers in the unique legal system of the EU/EC. This chapter has been about the options for the control of the exercise of public power in view of the changing nature of integration. Conferral, and with it a more straight-forward ultra vires test, is losing ground as means of the control of the exercise of public power on the European level. Integrated forms and structures are becoming more important. Subsidiarity and proportionality are principles applied for fine-tuning more sovereignty-preserving approaches. These approaches often contain regulatory solutions which cannot be captured in classic constitutional law notions. They imply a shift in focus from classical constitutional law concepts towards principles established in administrative law. Such principle-based approach to finding limits has to be designed

[56] See for a convincing summary Deirdre Curtin, 'European Legal Integration: Paradise Lost?', in D Curtin, A Klip, J Smits, J MacCahey (eds) *European Integration and Law* (Antwerp, Intersentia, 2006) 1–56 at 44.

to take diverse interest public and private alike into account and allow for participation and judicial protection within a complex integrated legal system.

5

Citizenship and Enlargement: The Outer Limits of EU Political Citizenship

JO SHAW*

I INTRODUCTION

WHEN 10 NEW MEMBER States joined the European Union in 2004, followed by a further two in 2007, this brought about a substantial increase in the population of the EU. It has also seen an increase in the numbers of EU citizens resident in other Member States to around nine million persons.[1] This translates to just below 2 per cent of the total population of the Member States. This represents something of an increase in recent years from the historically stable level of 1.5 per cent,[2] an increase which is doubtless attributable to the specific effects of those recent enlargements on labour mobility, as a result of wage differentials between new and old Member States, and higher rates of unemployment in some of the new Member States. These are incentives to labour mobility which are likely to dissipate over the longer term.

In terms of political citizenship, the most obvious impact of moving the outer territorial limits of the Euro-polity in order to encompass these additional states has been to widen the range of opportunities for EU

* Jo Shaw's email address is jo.shaw@ed.ac.uk.

[1] The figures provided in the latest Commission Report on EU Citizenship relate to January 2006, and thus predate the most recent (2007) enlargement. As of that date, there were estimated to be around 8.2m EU citizens resident in another Member State. Since then Romania and Bulgaria have joined the EU, and there are almost 0.5m Romanians in Spain alone, and large numbers in Italy. Allowing for some subsequent increase in the free movement of other new Member State nationals as the transitional barriers have gradually been removed, I have therefore made an estimate of 9m. See Commission Staff Working Document, Annex to the Fifth Report from the Commission on Citizenship of the Union, SEC(2008) 197, 15 February 2008.

[2] *Migration News*, July 2005, vol 11 No 3, http://migration.ucdavis.edu/mn/more.php?id=3117_0_4_0.

citizens to exercise their political rights under Article 19 EC. This affects both the territorial scope and the personal scope of political participation rights. There are 12 additional Member States in which European Parliament elections now take place, with EU citizens having both the right to stand for election and the right to vote on the basis of residence, not nationality (Article 19(2) EC); and 12 additional Member States in which resident EU citizens are entitled to stand for election and vote in local elections under the same conditions as nationals (Article 19(1) EC). In addition, nationals of the post-2004 and post-2007 Member States now reside in the other Member States *as EU citizens*, and thus can exercise citizenship rights, including electoral rights under Article 19 where previously they were treated as third country nationals. For the 2004 European Parliament elections, the Commission estimated that there were an additional one million EU citizens enfranchised as a result of the May 2004 enlargement across the then 25 Member States.[3]

However, the impact of enlargement can be viewed other than through the prism of demography and the territorial expansion of the EU. The concept of 'outer limits' can also have a specifically political meaning. Thus enlargement means bringing new political systems and political cultures into the EU, resulting in changes which impact not only upon the *new* Member States, but also upon the *existing* ones, and upon the political system and culture of the EU and its institutions. The changes wrought by enlargement involve iterative and two-way processes. For example, there are ongoing political realignments within the European Parliament as an institution as a result of enlargement, as the political cleavages between left and right, and between mainstream Christian Democrats, Liberals and Social Democrats, which have dominated the Parliament's politics for decades, are reworked. New political groupings have emerged and existing political groupings have changed in subtle ways, as a result of the impact of MEPs from Central and Eastern European states.

Enlargement also impacts upon political citizenship by forcing us to reconsider a number of settled assumptions about the framework within which rights for non-nationals typically operate. It is widely accepted that systems of local electoral rights for all non-nationals which developed at the *national* level, in states such as the Netherlands and Denmark, did so in large measure as one response to challenges posed by post-war labour migration and consequently the presence of large populations of foreign-born residents in the territory of many of the Western and Northern European states. The granting of electoral rights was seen as an integration measure, and occurred in combination with a dominant liberal political culture in which social democratic parties frequently took the leading role

[3] Commission Press Release, IP/04/126, 29 January 2004.

in pushing for legal change. More generally, even in states which do not have electoral rights for non-nationals above and beyond those mandated by EU law, debates about the political engagement of non-nationals more generally as a dimension of integration of immigrants and their descendants, are common. For example, so-called foreigners' councils can now be found at different levels of national and subnational government in many parts of France, Germany and Italy.

In contrast, the 'new' Member States have generally not, or not yet, become fully engaged in the global migration system as states of immigration. On the contrary, they have hitherto commonly been states of emigration, transit states, and/or states where there are specific regional migration issues in play. On the other hand, many of these states have national minorities resulting from the break-up of former empires or states. In the case of the Soviet Union and Yugoslavia, minorities created within newly independent states frequently do not have the national citizenship of the host state. In these very particular circumstances, which differ sharply from those present in most old Member States, it is inevitable that debates about the political participation of non-nationals (or 'alien suffrage' as it is sometimes termed) will resonate very differently.

The primary objective of this paper is to investigate this resonance in more detail, in order to enhance our understanding of the wider impact of enlargement on political citizenship in the European context and to suggest another way of looking at the concept of 'outer limits'.[4] Specifically, it will look at how the Baltic states (Estonia, Latvia and Lithuania) have addressed the issue of the political participation and integration of the large ethnic Russian minorities within their borders and at how Slovenia has dealt with the issue of citizenship definition and political participation, given its history as a border land state, situated at the cusp of many empires, states and blocs which have come and gone over the centuries.[5] The common element in both these cases is that where substantial populations of non-nationals exist in these states, they have been brought into being not by a process of *migration* (or at least not *transnational* migration), but rather because a state border has moved (or disappeared; or been created), in the recent and/or the more distant past. In both cases, these have turned groups who have moved previously *within* states (or empires) into transnational minority groups, many of whom may lack the citizenship of the host state. As a baseline, of course, all of the states under scrutiny have been obliged to implement Article 19 EC, and the

[4] This paper draws upon J Shaw, *The Transformation of Citizenship in the European Union: Electoral Rights and the Restructuring of Political Space*, (Cambridge, Cambridge University Press, 2007) especially ch 10.

[5] A Gosar, 'The Shatter Belt and the European Core: A Geopolitical Discussion of the Untypical Case of Slovenia', (2001) 52 *GeoJournal* 107 at 114.

implementing directives, since joining the EU in 2004.[6] However, it is national law measures on the political participation of non-nationals and wider questions about the treatment of non-nationals rather than the practical implementation of these EU law measures which are the focus of this paper.

In a more general context, this investigation provides a case study through which it is possible to track changes within the institutions of citizenship at the national and the European levels, highlighting in particular the extent to which the different sites and levels at which rights are granted under EU law and national law are increasingly becoming intermingled and indistinguishable.[7] The paper thus elaborates upon the assumption that a multi-level and pluralistic system of citizenship combining different local/regional, national, supranational and international sources of law and rights is emerging within the European political space.[8]

In that context, it is sometimes hard to mark the outer limits of EU political citizenship with any degree of certainty. It is often argued that the role of the Member States as the gatekeepers of EU citizenship, determining access to Union citizenship by reference to the limits of nationality laws at the Member State level (Article 17 EC), implicitly 'nationalises' EU citizenship. Conversely, however, it is also possible to see how aspects of national citizenship have themselves become 'Europeanised'. The boundaries of national citizenship are no longer as sharply delineated as they once were, largely as a result of the impact of EU law, but also because of other supranational and international legal orders such as the Council of Europe, the European Convention on Human Rights and Fundamental Freedoms (ECHR) and other human rights systems. In addition, the institutions of the national state have come under stress from 'below', through claims for local/regional autonomy and even secession. These pressures have often had as much impact in terms of challenging the hegemony of the national state as have the pressures stemming from supranational and international forms of integration. This is a more general argument, one which need not be confined to the new Member States and the effects of enlargement alone, since some of the issues of democratisation and political and economic modernisation prevalent in the post-2004 and post-2007 Member States still resonate, albeit in a much more attenuated fashion, with

[6] Council Directive 93/109/EC lays down detailed arrangements for the exercise of the right to vote and stand as a candidate in elections to the European Parliament for citizens of the Union residing in a Member State of which they are not nationals, [1993] OJ L329/34; Council Directive 94/80/EC lays down detailed arrangements for the exercise of the right to vote and stand as a candidate in municipal elections by citizens of the Union residing in a Member State of which they are not nationals, [1994] OJ L368/38.

[7] This more general question also underpins my wider investigation of political rights for non-nationals in the European political space: see Shaw, above n 4.

[8] S Besson and A Utzinger, 'Towards European Citizenship', (2008) *The Journal of Social Philosophy* 185; G Delanty, 'European Citizenship: A Critical Reassessment', (2007) 11 *Citizenship Studies* 63.

some of the so-called 'old' Member States (for example, Spain, Portugal, Greece and even Ireland).

However, the specific benefit of looking closely at the impact and the limits of EU political citizenship in some of the post-2004 Member States is that we can thereby understand better the interplay between emerging practices of transnational political citizenship, including the granting of rights under EU law as well as national law, and notions of national sovereignty, especially where it has been relatively recently (re-)gained. We can also identify some more diffuse impacts of European integration upon the national polity ideas which are rather distinctive features of many of the Central and Eastern European states.[9] The examples given will focus in particular on the consequences of polity formation and re-formation, bearing in mind that many of these states have created or re-created concepts of national citizenship during the past 20 years, in some cases more than once. Through this investigation we will come to see how enlargement has re-articulated in rather complex ways a distinct notion of the outer limits of European political citizenship.

II THE CONTEXT OF THE DISCUSSION

It is important to put this discussion in a broader context. National 're-awakenings', political and economic transition, integration into international and European organisations, and the status and protection of so-called national minorities are all important challenges which frame the discussion of political citizenship in the post-2004 Member States.

Since the beginning of the twentieth century, Central and Eastern Europe has been directly affected by the rise, decline and/or dissolution of successive 'empires': the Ottoman Empire, the Austro-Hungarian Empire, the German Reich and its forerunners, and the Soviet Union and its forerunner the Russian Empire. A number of forms of national self-expression have contributed to and been unleashed by these changes, and considerable geo-political instability has been experienced in the region, although there have also been important new opportunities for economic prosperity and political freedom. The most important structural effects have included the creation of new states, with new citizenship and nationality regimes as well as new governance structures, and the creation of diasporas and minorities separated from their so-called 'kin-states'.[10] In addition, the break-up of the Soviet Union and the end of the cold war

[9] M Jachtenfuchs, T Diez and S Jung, 'Which Europe? Conflicting Models of a Legitimate Europea Political Order', (1998) 4 *European Journal of Political Research* 409.

[10] J Tóth, 'Connections of Kin-Minorities to the Kin-State in the Extended Schengen Zone', (2003) 5 *European Journal of Migration and Law* 201.

contributed directly to the dissolution of two federal states, Czechoslovakia and the SFRY (Yugoslavia),[11] the former peacefully and the latter with considerable bloodshed. Of the eight Central and Eastern European countries which acceded to the EU in 2004, all bar Poland and Hungary were 'new' states, constructed or reconstructed since 1989. Each of the six 'new' states, with the exception of the Czech Republic, has significant issues arising around minority groups within its borders: Russians (especially, but also Poles, Belarussians, Ukrainians and others) in the Baltic states; Hungarians in Slovakia; citizens of other former Yugoslav republics in Slovenia. More generally, and outwith the system of states as such, a number of Central and Eastern European states have substantial populations of Roma, who experience high levels of discrimination and social exclusion and segregation. Some of these minority groups may have the national citizenship of the host state; others may lack it. Most members of such 'national' groups, whether they have the national citizenship or not, will perceive themselves as part of an ethnic minority group in the host state, and will probably experience certain problems, notably social, economic and political exclusion, as a consequence.

In many of the cases arising in Central and Eastern Europe, in the post-2004 Member States, it is not being an alien, that is lacking of national membership or citizenship, which is the problem, but rather the issue of the rights of national minorities within host states, and the role of national and international laws in the protection of the rights and interests of such groups once defined as 'minorities', whether by the host state or by the state of origin.

In the context of these transformations, supranational and international organisations have played a central role in structuring transition. A number of external pressures have driven the speedy economic and political transformation and modernisation processes which have occurred within these states since 1989, and these have included the possibilities of acceding to a number of supranational and international organisations. Central amongst these organisations, of course, is the EU, which has long had an explicit enlargement policy, but accession to other organisations such as the Council of Europe and NATO, which perform rather different types of functions as international organisations in the European sphere, has also proved to be of considerable importance for the foreign policy goals of these states. All of this has reinforced the break with the pre-1989 past, but at the same time has raised questions about how the post-1989 period relates back to earlier periods of history, such as the years leading up to 1914, or those following the 1919 peace settlement, which instituted

[11] In order to avoid confusion arising with other manifestations of 'Yugoslavia', the state which was created after the Second World War and existed until it disintegrated in the wars in the 1990s is referred to as the Socialist Federal Republic of Yugoslavia, or SFRY, in this paper.

substantial boundary re-alignments across Europe. In some cases, the post-1989 reawakening has also created the space for certain types of nationalist sentiment to be given political expression, both through the medium of elections bringing to power populist and nationalist groups and parties, and also through the medium of undemocratic activity including violence. There has, of course, been a substantial amount of ethnic conflict in South Eastern Europe since 1989, much of it historically related to earlier conflicts. However, the process of 'joining Europe', in the formal sense of acceding to the EU, the Council of Europe and NATO, has often involved accepting outside scrutiny of internal processes, although this has obviously been of a very different type to that imposed during the period of Soviet domination of Central and Eastern Europe.

Those processes of adjustment, and scrutiny, continue both for the new post-2004 and post-2007 Member States (Romania and Bulgaria), for the next tranche of potential members (candidate countries Croatia and Turkey, with which accession negotiations started in late 2005, and Macedonia, with which they have not yet started), and for the other potential candidate countries identified by the EU in South Eastern Europe (Albania, Bosnia, Serbia, Montenegro and, most recently, Kosovo). These latter states are linked to the EU through a set of stabilisation and association processes and structures. Consequently, it becomes a question of intense interest to the EU and the other Member States how many Macedonians take on Bulgarian national citizenship,[12] or how many Moldovans acquire Romanian national citizenship.[13] For here are two pairs of states straddling the outer boundaries of the EU where substantial numbers of citizens of the state outside the EU are able to qualify, through historical connections, for citizenship of the EU Member State, and thus for EU citizenship. Equally, from the perspective of the states in the 'border regions' of the EU, the requirement to implement the Schengen *acquis* from the moment of enlargement, including the imposition of visa requirements on the citizens of states where there are close historical connections or many co-ethnics, can cause severe destabilisation of relations between

[12] 'For Dream Jobs in Europe, the Line forms in Bulgaria', *New York Times*, 23 July 2006. It is also reported that, in addition to the many Macedonians entitled to Bulgarian nationality, there may be up to 300,000 Moldovans and many Ukrainians who are also qualified through historic connections.

[13] On the intertwining of Moldovan and Romanian nationality, see C Iordachi, 'Dual Citizenship and Policies towards Kin-Minorities in East-Central Europe: A Comparison between Hungary, Romania and the Republic of Moldova', in Z Kántor, B Majtényi, O Ieda, B Vizi and I Halász (eds) *The Hungarian Status Law Syndrome: A Nation Building and/or Minority Protection*, (Sapporo, Savic Research Center, Hokkaido University, 2004) and I Culic, 'Eluding Exit and Entry Controls: Romanian and Moldovan Immigrants in the European Union', (2008) 22 *East European Politics and Societies* 145–70; on Moldova as a challenge after the 2007 enlargement, see E Berg and P Ehin, 'What Kind of Border Regime is in the making?', (2006) 41 *Cooperation and Conflict* 53 at 64.

states.[14] To put it another way, there can be inherent tensions 'between the "re-nationalization" of history in Central and Southeast Europe and the process of European integration'.[15] The pressure put on Bulgaria and Romania to restrict access to citizenship in respect of non-resident 'co-ethnics' in the run-up to the 2007 enlargement can be contrasted with earlier efforts made in the 1990s by the European Commission to pressure Latvia and Estonia in particular to adopt more generous access to citizenship policies in respect of *resident* Russians, in particular to avoid the problem of statelessness in the Baltic states.[16] However, as we shall see later, the three Baltic states have taken rather different approaches to both the citizenship and the electoral rights issues since independence.[17] In sum, there are many new sites of, and styles of, transnational politics in the post-1989 world.

III STATE RE-FORMATION AND ELECTORAL RIGHTS: THE CASE OF THE BALTIC STATES

Figures provided by the European Commission indicated that in 2004 there were around 5,000 'Community voters'[18] in Estonia, 3,500 in Latvia and 1,000 in Lithuania.[19] At the same time, in each of those three states, especially Estonia and Latvia, there are much larger numbers of third country nationals, mainly with Russian nationality, or stateless persons. In all three states, there are high barriers to becoming a national citizen for a resident non-national, including strict language tests, but Lithuania differs from the other two states in that it had a relatively open approach to accessing national citizenship on independence, allowing all permanent residents to apply to become citizens. This accounts for it now having a lower percentage of third country nationals. Since independence in the early 1990s, two of the three states have instituted local electoral rights for third country nationals: Estonia (1992) and Lithuania (2002). Latvia is the exception in refusing to accord local electoral rights to its non-national minorities, and it has coupled this with an exceptionally restrictive set of

[14] Tóth, above n 10; A Tchorbadjiyska, 'Bulgarian Experiences with Visa Policy in the Accession Process: A Story of Visa Lists, Citizenship and Limitations on Citizens' Rights', *Regio: A Review of Studies on Minorities, Politics, Society* 2007/1, 88.

[15] C Iordachi, '"Entangled Histories": Re-thinking the History of Central and Southeastern Europe from a Relational Perspective', *Regio: A Review of Studies on Minorities, Politics, Society*, 2004, 113 at 114.

[16] N Gelazis, 'The European Union and the Statelessness Problem in the Baltic States' (2004) 6 *European Journal of Migration and Law* 225.

[17] R Kalvaitis, 'Citizenship and National Identity in the Baltic States' (1998) 16 *Boston University International Law Journal* 231.

[18] That is EU citizens of voting age who are not nationals of the host state.

[19] Commission Press Release, IP/04/126, 29 January 2004.

rules on acquiring national citizenship. This section looks at these issues in more detail, in order to tease out the differences between the three states, in particular in the way in which tensions between national polity ideas have been negotiated in the context of aspirations to join the EU and become 'part of Europe'.

In March 2005, local elections were held in Latvia at which EU citizens were able to vote, but not the large population of non-citizen ethnic Russians. The controversies surrounding the scope of the electorate in these elections, and the large number of disenfranchised 'aliens' in Latvia, attracted attention in the Western European media.[20] Latvia has refused to grant electoral rights to third country nationals even though the citizenship regime established after Latvian independence excluded most non-ethnic Latvians from obtaining citizenship, because a principle of 'inherited citizenship' was applied restricting citizenship acquisition to those who had been citizens of Latvia in 1940 or their descendants.[21] Ethnic Russians form nearly 30 per cent of the total resident population of around 2.3 million, many having moved to Latvia with Soviet encouragement or indeed compulsion during the post second world war period of industrialisation. Equally, nearly 23 per cent of that population have neither Latvian nationality, nor indeed that of any other state.[22] Many of these 'non-citizens' (that is, in practice, the ethnic Russians referred to above) are effectively stateless and have to travel on 'non-citizen' passports and need visas to visit almost all EU Member States apart from Estonia, Lithuania and Denmark.[23] They find it hard to access Latvian nationality, because of a combination of residence requirements and challenging language and history tests.[24] August 2006, Latvia tightened its arrangements still further, introducing a rule refusing citizenship definitively to anyone who had failed the Latvian language test three times.[25] Only around 11,000 persons are naturalized per year. In total, since 1995, that amounts to just over 100,000 people. Meanwhile, there remain over 400,000 non-citizens in

[20] A Roxburgh, 'Latvia bars its Russian minority from voting', *Sunday Herald*, 13 March 2005; A Roxburgh, 'Citizenship Row divides Latvia', *BBC News*, 25 March 2005, http://news.bbc.co.uk/1/hi/world/europe/4371345.stm.

[21] See K Krūma, 'Checks and balances in Latvian nationality policies: National agendas and international frameworks', in R Bauböck, B Perchinig and W Sievers (eds), *Citizenship Policies in the New Europe*, (Amsterdam, Amsterdam University Press, 2007) 63–88.

[22] The Office of the Citizenship and the Migration Affairs and the European Migration Network, *Public Annual Report 2003 on Statistics on Migration, Asylum and Return*, Riga, March 2006; *The People of Latvia*, Latvian Institute Fact Sheet, October 2005, No 13.

[23] Mark Mardell, 'Stateless in Latvia', *BBC News*, 4 October 2007, http://www.bbc.co.uk/blogs/thereporters/markmardell/2007/10/stateless.html.

[24] T Heleniak, 'Latvia Looks West, But Legacy of Soviets Remains', *Migration Information Source*, February 2006, http://www.migrationinformation.net.

[25] 'Latvia tightens citizenship laws', *BBC News*, 9 August 2006, http://news.bbc.co.uk/1/hi/world/europe/4776511.stm.

Latvia.[26] Even after acquiring Latvian citizenship, non-ethnic Latvian citizens regularly face language discrimination in both the educational and political domains.[27] The Latvian government resists international pressure to extend electoral rights to third country nationals, insisting that the non-citizen problem stems largely from ethnic Russians bearing an attachment to the former Soviet Union, and that the problem of political rights should be solved by the process of naturalisation and assimilation to Latvian culture. Moreover, they argue that to grant political rights in advance of naturalisation would undermine the motivation of non-citizens to apply for naturalisation, and thus to go through the process of integration.[28]

In the accession process, this issue was raised on a number of occasions by various EU institutions, but to no avail. For example, just before enlargement happened in 2004, the European Parliament report on the comprehensive monitoring report of the European Commission on the state of preparedness for EU membership of all the 10 states which acceded on 1 May 2004 commented that:

> the naturalisation process of the non-citizen part of society remains too slow; [the Parliament] therefore invites the Latvian authorities to promote the naturalisation process and considers that minimum language requirements for elderly people may contribute to it; encourages the Latvian authorities to overcome the existing split in society and to favour the genuine integration of 'non-citizens' ensuring an equal competitive chance in education and labour; proposes that the Latvian authorities envisage the possibility of allowing non-citizens who are long-time inhabitants to take part in local self-government elections.[29]

This was not taken further, and now the opportunity has been lost. After accession, the EU institutions lose all purchase upon the conduct of new Member States, since there is nothing in the current state of EU law to oblige any Member State to enact electoral rights for third country nationals.[30]

[26] 'More than 97,000 persons obtain citizenship by naturalization', *Baltic News Service* 26 July 2005, http://www.mfa.gov.lv/en/news/Newsletters/CurrentLatvia/2005/July/618. See also the official presentation of Latvian Citizenship by the Ministry of Foreign Affairs, 26 March 2008, http://www.mfa.gov.lv/en/policy/4641/4642/4651/.

[27] C Taube, 'Latvia: Political Participation of Linguistic Minorities', (2003) 3 *International Journal of Constitutional Law* 511–40.

[28] Union "For Human Rights Law in Latvia", 'International Recommendations on Voting Rights for Latvian Non-citizens', Background information, available from http://www.zapchel.lv.

[29] Para 74 of the European Parliament Resolution P5_TA(2004)0180 of 11 March 2004 on the comprehensive monitoring report of the European Commission on the state of preparedness for EU membership of the Czech Republic, Estonia, Cyprus, Latvia, Lithuania, Hungary, Malta, Poland, Slovenia and Slovakia, based on the Report A5–0111/2004, 25 February 2004.

[30] See Shaw, above n 4, ch 7 for more details.

In marked contrast to Latvia, both Estonia and Lithuania have proved open to the argument that the right to participate in local elections for such groups of non-citizens could be a useful political element in dealing with the ongoing consequences of the break-up of the Soviet Union and the (re-)creation of the Baltic states.[31] However, in terms of their approach to the re-establishment of citizenship in conjunction with independence from the Soviet Union, the two states took markedly different approaches: the 'zero-option' (Lithuania) and the 'reference back' option (Estonia).[32]

Lithuania adopted a 'zero-option' approach to citizenship in its 1989 law on citizenship, offering citizenship to all residents as of the date of independence, with two years prior residence, providing they opted for this within a period of two years (that is by 1991). The boundaries of the polity were thus not drawn on ethnic grounds. Well over 90 per cent of those residents who were not ethnic Lithuanians chose to become Lithuanian citizens. On the other hand, Lithuania is relatively homogeneous, compared to the other Baltic states. The April 2001 census showed that more than 83 per cent of the population was Lithuanian in terms of ethnic origin, with only 6.7 per cent Poles, 6.3 per cent Russians and there were much smaller groups of other ethnicities such as Belarussians and Ukrainians. By 2006 around 99 per cent of the population of Lithuania held Lithuanian citizenship,[33] and citizenship acquisition since the expiry of the two year period of grace for permanent residents had become as difficult as it is in the other Baltic states, requiring 10 years of residence and the passing of language tests.[34]

Estonia, while allowing permanent residents to participate in the independence referendum of 1990 and in certain early elections for the Supreme Council (which was the successor body of the Estonian Supreme Soviet), opted in its 1992 citizenship law for a solution in which only those who had been citizens of Estonia on 16 June 1940, and their descendants, could be citizens. This is essentially an identical approach to that taken in Latvia. In turn, political participation was initially strictly limited to Estonian citizens, and that included both the right to vote and the right to

[31] See further S Day and J Shaw, 'The Boundaries of Suffrage and External Conditionality: Estonia as an Applicant Member State of the EU' (2003) 9 *European Public Law* 211–36 and M Smith and J Shaw, 'Changing Polities and Electoral Rights: Lithuania's Accession to the EU' in P Shah and W Menski, (eds), *Migration, Diasporas and Legal Systems in Europe*, (London, Routledge-Cavendish, 2006) 145–63. Some parts of this section draw directly upon these texts. I am grateful to Dr Stephen Day for carrying out the case study and the interviews in Estonia and to Dr Melanie Smith for doing likewise in Lithuania.

[32] See K Krūma, 'Lithuanian nationality: trump card to independence and its current challenges' in Bauböck *et al*, above n 21, 89–110; P Järve, 'Estonian citizenship: between ethnic preferences and democratic obligations', in Bauböck *et al*, above n 21, 43–62.

[33] Migration Department under the Ministry of the Interior of the Republic of Lithuania, Migration Annual 2004, at 13, available from http://www.migracija.lt/.

[34] Smith and Shaw, above n 31 at 158.

be a member of a political party. However, in terms of the figures for ethnic minorities, Estonia is much more similar to Latvia than it is to Lithuania, with 65 per cent of the population being ethnic Estonians, 28 per cent Russians, plus much smaller groups of other ethnicities such as Ukrainians. The 2000 census[35] found that around 80 per cent of residents were Estonians by national citizenship, and only about 6 per cent were Russians, but a quite large figure of nearly 13 per cent were dual nationals (Estonian plus one other).

It is worth noting that neither Lithuania nor Estonia (nor indeed Latvia) is currently 'restocking' its proportion of foreign-born or non-citizen residents at a high rate, because neither is experiencing substantial levels of inward migration. Indeed all three (although particularly Latvia and Lithuania) are experiencing continued emigration in particular to the UK and Ireland since accession to the EU in 2004, and all have a downward demographic trend with low birth rates and an ageing population.[36] These three states also share the challenge of building a modern democratic polity after 50 years of Soviet domination, not to mention unstable political histories through centuries before that, and Latvia and Estonia in particular have had to deal with the consequences of substantial inward migration of Russians during the period of rapid (and forced) industrialisation after the second world war. Consequently, Russians tend to be predominantly located in all three states in the urban areas, or in the vicinity of major items of infrastructure, such as nuclear power stations. Thus as newly (re-)established states, the Baltic states had to deal with issues of instability, from both an internal and an external perspective. They have adopted quite different trajectories, especially in the internal sphere. In the external sphere, all three opted for collective security, seeking membership of the Council of Europe, the EU and NATO, and were in due course successful in all cases. Internally, stability has been sought in very different ways.

The dynamics of regime change in Estonia and the subsequent impact this had on defining the boundary of the suffrage, began with intense interactions between two bodies: the Supreme Council (formerly the Supreme Soviet) and the Congress of Estonia. The former was dominated by the reformist/pragmatic Popular Front (which included Russian and Estonian intellectuals who emerged out of the Communist Party of Estonia) while the latter emerged from the independence movement, which was dominated by the Estonian Citizens' Committees. Crucially for what was to come, the Citizens' Committees were associated with members of Estonia's indigenous cultural elite. According to Taupio Raun:

35 Results are available from http://www.stat.ee.

36 R Munz, 'Europe: Population and Migration in 2005', *Migration Information Source*, 1 June 2006, available from http://www.migrationinformation.org.

> the competition between the Popular Front and the Citizens' Committees during 1989 already revealed the basic fault line in Estonian politics between what may be called the *fundamentalists*, who argued on the basis of principle and demanded the strict return to the status quo before Soviet rule, and the *pragmatists*, who proceeded from the concrete situation confronting them and were willing to make compromises in a less than ideal world (emphasis in original).[37]

In both cases the desire was freedom from the Soviet yoke but in the latter case this had an added dimension, namely one that equated ethnic Russians with an illegal and unconstitutional occupying force that was associated with the 'Russification' of Estonia. The Congress of Estonia politicised a golden past that advocated the restoration of the pre-war Estonian State based upon the Estonian language, Estonian culture and the 1938 Constitution as the most effective method with which to galvanise support. This had the effect of rendering non-ethnic Estonians unfit for the task of rebuilding the Estonian nation. Supporters of the Congress expected that large numbers of Russians would return to the motherland. The fact that only a small number did so posed a significant problem—what exactly should be done with them?

The right to vote for the Supreme Council had been given to *all permanent residents*, and the right to stand, to those of 10 years permanent residency including members of the Red Army. The Congress of Estonia restricted its electorate to Estonian citizens (based on pre-1940 residency) and those ethnic Russians who had signed the independence charter.[38] Although it was the de facto legislature, the Supreme Council found that its legitimacy was constantly under challenge. The Estonian Congress argued that its legal status was undermined by the inclusive nature of the 1990 franchise and that it therefore lacked the legitimacy to introduce new legislation. In these circumstances, the idea of re-adopting the more inclusive citizenship law of 1920, or the proposal to adopt a 'zero-option' formula of citizenship as in Lithuania were dropped in the face of national political realities. This came in the face of opposition from Russia which believed that the 1991 Treaty of Intergovernmental Relations, which acknowledged Estonian independence, ensured recognition of the civil and political rights of the Russian minority.[39] What emerged ultimately was a situation whereby:

[37] R Raun, 'Democratization and political development in Estonia 1987–1996', in K Dawisha and B Parrott (eds), *The Consolidation of Democracy in East-Central Europe* (Cambridge, Cambridge University Press, 1997) 334–74 at 347.

[38] R Kionka, 'Estonia: A Difficult Transition' *RFE/RL Research Report*, Vol 2, No 1, 1 January 1993, 89–91 at 90.

[39] Interview with representatives of the Russian Embassy in Tallinn, July 2000. Relations with Russia continue to remain problematic, not least over retired military personnel.

> From the Estonian point of view, the citizenship laws were a hard-won compromise between two seemingly conflicting goals. First, lawmakers had sought to assure the survival of the Estonian nation by limiting citizenship to those who understood the country's language and culture. Second, the Supreme Council intended the laws to integrate those who had settled in Estonia under Soviet rule and thus to ensure a stable and loyal population.[40]

These developments were to have an immediate effect upon the nature of the franchise and in turn the polity. While 1,144,309 people had been eligible to participate in Estonia's 1990 Independence Referendum, those eligible to vote in the Constitutional Referendum on 28 June 1992 numbered just 689,319. This was because the 1992 Citizenship Law stipulated that only those who were citizens on 16 June 1940 (regardless of their ethnicity), and their descendants, were automatically deemed citizens. The definition of a citizen became the basis for deciding who was to be entitled to the full array of political rights. In addition, only citizens had the right to be a member of a political party, which under the 1994 Political Parties Act, was defined as 'a voluntary association of *Estonian citizens*'.[41] Despite the fact that this restriction was clearly not in accordance with EU law, the Estonian government was not quick to make changes.[42] This notion of a 'national' politics clearly conforms to a desire to secure internal stability by restricting participation in the political arena.

The changed nature of the franchise was also to have a significant impact upon the outcome of the 1992 election. According to Vello Pettai:

> the ethnic Estonian share of the electorate went from an approximate figure of 65 per cent in 1990 to well over 90 per cent in 1992. Not surprisingly, the first Estonian parliament elected in 1992, was 100 per cent Estonian.[43]

As the title of Pettai's (1997) article aptly put it, there was '*Political Stability through Disenfranchisement*'. According to Graham Smith, Estonia now constituted what he called an 'ethnic democracy' that is a situation whereby the titular nation constructs an institutional architecture that consolidates its political dominance.[44]

[40] Kionka, above n 38 at 90.

[41] Emphasis added. Section 1(1) of the Political Parties Act of June 1994, as amended most recently in March 2002. This Act and all subsequent Estonian legislation cited in this paper can be found in English on the website of the Estonian Legal Language Centre, which is a State Agency administered by the State Chancellery: http://www.legaltext.ee/indexen.htm.

[42] *Opinion of the EU Network of Independent Experts on Fundamental Rights regarding the Participation of EU Citizens in the Political Parties of the Member State of Residence*, CFR-CDF Opinion 1/2005, March 2005, at 13.

[43] V Pettai, 'Political Stability through Disenfranchisement', *Transition*, Vol 3, No 6, 4 April 1997, 21–3 at 20.

[44] G Smith, 'The Ethnic Democracy Thesis and the Citizenship Question in Estonia and Latvia', (1996) 24 *Nationalities Papers* 199–216.

The complete disenfranchisement of the Russian-speaking minority was, according to Kalle Liebert, averted by 'a compromise between political parties and western states, although most of the parties were supportive of this'.[45] The right to vote (but not to stand) in local elections for non-citizens with *permanent residency* status was enshrined, from the outset, in Article 156 of the 1992 Estonian Constitution which provides:

> In elections to local government councils, persons who reside permanently in the territory of the local government and have attained eighteen years of age have the right to vote, under conditions prescribed by law.

Amendments to Section 3 of the Local Government Council Election Act introduced in 1999 lay down in more detail the application of this principle by stipulating that an alien has the right to vote in local elections:

— if he or she has attained 18 years of age by the election day;
— if he or she resides permanently in the territory of the local government;
— if he or she resides in Estonia on the basis of a permanent residence permit;
— if he or she has resided legally in the territory of the corresponding local government for at least five years by 1 January of the election year; and
— if he or she has not been divested of his or her active legal capacity by a court.

Actually putting this right into practice proved to be less straightforward than inserting it into the Constitution. Article 156 was first nominally applied in the local elections held in October 1993. Yet at the time, no legislation had yet been passed to enable non-citizens to register as 'permanent residents'. *Thus there were simply no voters to take advantage of the right to vote.* Indeed, between 1992 and the summer of 1993, non-citizens had no legal status whatsoever in Estonian law. This situation was eventually rectified by the adoption of the highly controversial 1993 Aliens Law which declared that all those living in Estonia without Estonian citizenship would have to apply for residency status—however long they had been resident.[46] It was a decision that caused considerable international consternation. The Estonian President called for national calm while at the same time seeking the opinions of the Organization for Security and Co-operation in Europe (OSCE) and the Council of Europe. The Council

[45] Interview with Kalle Liebert (former judicial counsellor to the citizenship and immigration department), Tallinn, 13 July 2000.

[46] This was to be divided into two categories: permanent residence and temporary residence. The resulting outcome was that Russian-speaking non-citizens were now classified as aliens regardless of whether they had been born in Estonia or how long they had lived there. It also meant that in strict legal terms the state could expel them.

of Europe's panel of experts duly found that 'it was wrong to equate the status of those already resident in Estonia with that of non-citizens not currently resident there'.[47] From Russia's point of view, this was not only an attempt to persuade Russians to leave, but it was the 'first time in history that a state set about forcing its own people to get citizenship of another state'.[48]

Yet in the minds of many of the Estonian political class the existence of a range of civil and social rights had a significant influence upon the nature of the debate concerning the boundaries of suffrage. Some have argued, for example, that the fact that the Estonian Constitution guarantees a range of civil and social rights, such as the right of peaceful assembly (Article 47) and the right to form non-profitmaking undertakings and unions (Article 48), in some way compensated for the absence of *full* political rights.[49] This is explicitly stated in the 1998 Estonian Human Development Report, which states that:

> activities that rely on economic and cultural interests form quite a substantial counterbalance to political alienation among the aliens which accompanies certain restrictions on the non-citizens' political rights. Yet the participation of non-citizens in local elections integrates non-natives into Estonian society on a wider socio-political level. The alien's passport guarantees for local stateless permanent residents Estonian statehood. All these levels of cohesion expedite the acquisition of political citizenship.[50]

The backlog of permanent residency applications continued to delay the effective implementation of Article 156. Indeed, it was not until 1997, that an amendment to the Aliens Law (section 6(2)) provided temporary resident holders with the right to vote at the local level. The amendment enfranchised some 280,000 people. Interestingly, until 2000, those with permanent resident status only accounted for approximately 12 per cent of the overall number of non-citizens.[51] Moreover, residency status is not the only obstacle to political participation. Non-Estonians continue to be denied the right to stand for election, and the language law provisions also

[47] Quoted in A Sheehy, 'The Estonian Law on Aliens' *Radio Free Europe/Radio Liberty* Vol 2, No 38, 24 September 1993.

[48] Interview with representatives from the Russian Embassy, Tallinn, July 2000.

[49] The government report entitled *Integrating Estonia 1997–2000* highlighted the importance of civil society in the following terms: 'the civilizing influence of civil society is expressed in the fact it is founded on democratic norms and values, it increases ... interest and participation', see *Integrating Estonia 1997–2000*, Report of the Government of Estonia, Tallinn, June 2000, p 52.

[50] See the Estonian Human Development Report 1998, at 48. This and additional reports can befound at http://hdr.undp.org/en/reports/.

[51] At this stage with Russians accounting for 90.8% of legal aliens, 311,259 had temporary residence permits compared to only 11,728 with permanent residence permits. Changes were introduced in 1997 to enable those who had applied for a temporary residence permit prior to 12 July 1995 to apply for a permanent residence permit from 12 July 1998.

continued to have exclusionary effects on Russian-speaking Estonian citizens, notwithstanding international pressure.[52]

In sum, one of Estonia's big issues since its independence from the Soviet Union in the August coup of 1991 has been that of defining the polity, and hence of defining the suffrage. Although the reasons for excluding Russians from the citizenry, and hence from the suffrage, were understandable in the early years of Estonian independence, the exclusionary arguments in favour have become increasingly hard to sustain both in the face of external political pressure from the OSCE and from the EU, and in the light of greater internal political maturity and experience with democratic practices and the rule of law. Internally, Estonia wished to avoid a 'one country, two societies' scenario. Externally, it found itself more pressured by international norms and organisations than would have been a more established liberal state, both in the form of OSCE recommendations and in terms of the pressure to conform to the *acquis communautaire* and the 'EU mainstream' prior to accession being contemplated. In this sense, there may be a positive synergy between the need to take steps internally with a view to settling the status of the substantial Russian minority, and the need to take steps in view of accession to settle the status of those who would become Estonia's 'second country nationals', that is other EU citizens. Estonia's economic success since the late 1990s is also likely to contribute positively to an integration of the Estonian and Russian communities, both those amongst the latter who have acquired Estonian citizenship, and those who have not. This could contribute to a distinct Estonian-Russian identity.[53]

The story in relation to Lithuania is very different. Having opted for the inclusion in terms of citizenship norms in 1989, it was in no hurry to enact the electoral legislation which would grant rights to the remaining small number of non-nationals. When independence was initially established (1990–93), the number of immigrants from the Commonwealth of Independent States (CIS) declined from 12,031 to 2,302, while the number of emigrants to CIS, mostly to Russia, Belarus and Ukraine, increased: in 1992, emigration to CIS reached its peak and stood at 26,948. Those ethnic minorities who chose not to exercise the right to obtain Lithuanian citizenship in this period left Lithuania to return to their 'home' state. This left behind extremely small numbers of non-citizens resident in Lithuania

[52] See Day and Shaw, above n 31 at 226–30; N Maveety, and A Grosskopf, '"Constrained" Constitutional Courts as Conduits for Democratic Consolidation' (2004) 38 *Law and Society Review* 463–88; J Hughes, '"Exit" in Deeply Divided Societies: Regimes of Discrimination in Estonia and Latvia and the Potential for Russophone Migration' (2005) 43 *Journal of Common Market Studies* 739–62.

[53] I Kotjuh, 'Varjus loojad', an article in the Estonian newspaper on 8 August 2006, abstracted in English by euro-topics, http://www.eurotopics.net/en/presseschau/archiv/aehnliche/archiv_article/ARTICLE6253.

(regardless of their ethnic heritage). By 2000 Lithuania had more emigration to other foreign countries than immigration: 1,190 against 389.[54] This process has continued, and in 2004, when Lithuania joined the EU, the emigration figure had risen to 15,165 with a net migration figure of minus 9,612.[55]

Furthermore it is possible that economic considerations were relevant when choosing the 'zero-option' route. In order to develop the economic progress of Lithuania as an annexed territory within the Soviet Union, a number of specialists (for instance in industry, and in particular in atomic energy) had been moved there by the Soviet Union in order to develop the region's economy. A number of highly skilled workers were therefore not of Lithuanian ethnic descent. Any long-term perspective on the economic stability and development of Lithuania might wish to encourage such highly skilled workers to remain there, rather than to return to the Soviet Union (or to go elsewhere such as the United States). Encouraging these highly skilled residents to stay would be all the more difficult if those persons, who were of non-ethnic Lithuanian descent, felt that they might be discriminated against, or lacked the ability effectively to access the same rights as were guaranteed to ethnic Lithuanians. A third factor which, like the pursuit of NATO and EU membership, has been high on the foreign policy agenda of the independent Lithuanian state is that of good neighbourly relations.[56] Stabilising relations with its neighbouring states, particularly its previously occupying neighbours Poland and Russia,[57] was an obvious concern given the historical instability of Lithuania's borders. According ethnic Poles and Russians the choice as to which citizenship they would prefer was definitely a move in the right direction and reassured the neighbouring states that their 'ethnic' citizens would not be

[54] Council of Europe, *Framework Convention for the Protection of National Minorities*, State Report submitted by Lithuania, October 2001 ACFC/SR(2001)/007, at 12.

[55] Net migration means the difference between the total number of persons arriving and total number of persons departing. Department of Statistics to the Government of the Republic of Lithuania (Statistics Lithuania).

[56] 'To enable Lithuanians residing abroad and Lithuanian nationals who have left their country lately to develop their ethnic and cultural identity, to maintain contacts with the Motherland, to participate in developing economic and cultural co-operation between Lithuania and foreign states': 'Programme of the Government of Lithuania 2001–2004' under Foreign Policy Objectives, Economic and Cultural Diplomacy http://www.lrv.lt/engl/vyr-programos_en/en_12_programa.html.

[57] Sergey Mironov, Chairman of the Council of Federation of the Federal Assembly of the Russian Federation, on a state visit to meet the Lithuanian President Rolandas Paksas, stated that 'positive bilateral trends can be mainly accounted for by Lithuania's liberal "zero-option" citizenship law, when the citizens could choose themselves, which country's citizenship they wanted to have'. Source: http://mironov.info/Events/63.html, June 2003.

discriminated against. This certainly eased tensions,[58] although there have been some difficulties since that time.[59]

At the same time as the citizenship law, a law that protected the cultural development of national minorities was also introduced.[60] Again this pointed towards a new state which is tolerant of, and indeed which even embraces, a variety of ethnic and cultural heritages. The point was to insulate the ethnic Russians and Poles resident in Lithuania from connecting the choice of Lithuanian citizenship with the obliteration of their cultural identity. This law was the first of its kind in Central and Eastern Europe and the Lithuanian government also set up a Department of National Minorities and Lithuanians Living Abroad, responsible for formulating policies on ethnic harmony, whose task was to assist in the preservation of the cultural identity of national minorities. At such a pivotal time in the formation of a new state, when all residents had a two-year window to choose their citizenship, the Lithuanian state authorities were thus adopting relatively inclusive policies, certainly in comparison to the other Baltic states. It should be reiterated that at the time of independence, the acquisition and holding of national citizenship was the gateway to accessing all rights in Lithuania. Laws relating to minority protection thus focus on protecting the cultural heritage of those who are already Lithuanian *citizens*. The key difference was that at the time of independence it was relatively easy to become a Lithuanian citizen. Subsequently, several new citizenship laws have been introduced, mainly aimed at new arrivals acquiring Lithuanian citizenship, which are decidedly less liberal and inclusive. The most recent prescribed a qualifying period of 10 years permanent residence in Lithuania and knowledge of the language and constitution.[61]

It was only when the time came for Lithuania to comply with the European *acquis* on EU citizens' right to vote and stand as candidates in local elections, that Article 119 of the Lithuanian Constitution relating to

[58] The United Nations Committee on the Elimination of Racial Discrimination has commented that the decision to adopt the 'zero-option' approach on citizenship has 'led to the construction of a more stable society' United Nations, Concluding Observations of the Committee on the Elimination of Racial Discrimination CERD/C/60/CO/8 March 2002.

[59] In 1994 the government suspended the operation of a local council in a predominantly Polish region, accusing it of deliberately blocking reform. This caused considerable tensions which were alleviated by subsequent elections.

[60] Law on Ethnic Minorities 23 November 1989.

[61] Law on Citizenship 17 September 2002, No IX – 1079. This law amended the previous law to ensure those ethnic Lithuanians or those of previous Lithuanian citizenship who left Lithuania after the 1940 German invasion and Russian annexation were able to reclaim their original Lithuanian citizenship, regardless of whether they had acquired a new citizenship in the interim. Originally such persons did not have the right, once they had acquired citizenship of another country, to retain Lithuanian citizenship. Chapter III Arts 17 and 18.

local government was amended to make this possible, and a legal framework enacted which applied to both EU citizens and third country nationals. The constitutional amendment in June 2002 allowed the introduction of further legislation[62] which extends beyond the basic requirements of EU law as it entitles *all* third country nationals the right to vote and stand as a candidate in municipal elections. This will be applied for the first time in local elections in December 2007.

The situation in Lithuania is not, however, without its problems for EU citizens and third country nationals. Whilst all persons are constitutionally guaranteed freedom of expression, thought, conscience and religion (Articles 25–27), only Lithuanian citizens are allowed to form political parties and associations (Article 35). This restriction is elaborated further in the law relating to political parties.[63] While this conditionality does not prevent a non-Lithuanian citizen from standing as a candidate for a municipal council (or in the case of EU citizens the European Parliament) and being elected, in practice parties have hitherto had a monopoly over the nomination of candidates for election.[64] Thus this restriction seems likely to be a problem in the future, although this has been denied by officials.[65] The conditionality may therefore be seen as an indirect hindrance to the inclusion of non-Lithuanian citizens into the political society of Lithuanian (and European) politics and may produce knock-on effects relating to the ability to raise funds to finance electoral campaigns without the financial support of a political party. This is not a restriction based on ethnicity, but on citizenship. Despite accession to the EU, the law in Lithuania regarding political parties remains unchanged, despite mounting pressure within the EU to grant the right to join and found political parties to EU citizens (if not to third country nationals).[66] An amendment to the existing law was tabled in the Lithuanian Parliament in January 2005[67] which envisaged the right of all permanent residents to join political parties, but this was revoked shortly after its introduction. In Lithuania, there are a number of political parties established within national minorities such as the Election Action of the Lithuanian Poles (established in 1994), the Union of Lithuanian Russians (established in 1995) and the Alliance of Lithuanian Citizens (established in 1996). Indeed, representatives of both the Polish and Russian communities have been prominent in national

[62] Law on Elections to Municipal Councils 19 September 2002.

[63] Law on Political Parties 23 March 2004.

[64] R Zukauskiene, *Active Civic Participation of Immigrants in Lithuania*, Country Report prepared for the European research project POLITIS, Oldenburg 2005, http://www.uni-oldenburg.de/politis-europe/download/Lithuania.pdf at 30.

[65] Interview with Zenonas Vaigauskas, Chairman, Central Electoral Committee 28 April 2004.

[66] See the Network of Experts on Fundamental Rights Opinion, above n 42.

[67] Draft Law on the amendment of the Law on Political Parties draft law No. XP-220, 21 January 2005.

politics, in particular at the elections to the Seimas (the national Parliament) in 2000 and 2004. However, again these are confined to citizens.

IV SLOVENIA AND THE CASE OF THE 'ERASED'

Slovenia is another of the states of Central and Eastern Europe amongst the group which acceded to the EU in May 2004 which has already enacted local electoral rights for all non-nationals.[68] Article 43(3) of the Slovenian Constitution provides that: 'The law may provide in which cases and under what conditions aliens have the right to vote.' Amendments to the Law on Local Elections in 2002 made provision for third country nationals, as well as EU citizens, to vote and stand for election in local elections, with the proviso that only a Slovene national is eligible to hold the office of elected head of the executive body of a local government (mayor). Since the EU directive on local elections, which is said by officials in the Ministry of Interior to constitute the inspiration for the legislation,[69] entails provisions for such opt-outs, the Slovene legislature adopted the position that municipal executive functions (mayor) are part of the national competences which are transferred to the local level, that they can have national security functions, and that they can thus be reserved to nationals. The legislation was applied for the first time in 2002, even in advance of EU accession, although in practice there have been no reported cases of non-nationals standing for election and the possibility of third country nationals standing for election has since been removed.[70] This 'mainly symbolic gesture' is none the less said to show 'the willingness of the country's political elite to follow the most advanced European practice in this field'.[71]

There is little more, therefore, that can be said directly about the electoral rights themselves. They should, however, be placed in a wider context of minority protection and citizenship issues, which relate to Slovenia's status as a new state under international law as a consequence of

[68] The others are Hungary and Slovakia; in the Czech Republic, the reciprocity principle, allowing the enactment of electoral rights for non-nationals on condition of reciprocity by other states, has been adopted but not yet acted upon. See Shaw, above n 4 especially ch 3 and a Study on *Trends in the Eu-27 Regarding Participation of Third-Country Nationals in the Host Country's Political Life* prepared for the European Parliament Directorate General for Internal Policies of the Union by the Centre for European Policy Studies, July 2007, Document PE.378.303.

[69] Interview with Ministry Official, December 2003.

[70] S Andreev, *Active Civic Participation of Immigrants in Slovenia*, Country Report prepared for the European research project POLITIS, Oldenburg 2005, http://www.uni-oldenburg.de/politis-europe/download/Slovenia.pdf at 23.

[71] S Andreev, 'Making Slovenian Citizens: The Problem of the Former Yugoslav Citizens and Asylum Seekers Living in Slovenia', (2003) 4 *Southeast European Politics* 1–24 at 17.

its secession from the SFRY in 1991 and its creation of new governing norms of the polity, including a law on national citizenship.

As regards minority rights protection, it should be noted that Slovenia has adopted a number of measures which reflect its commitment to the protection of minority rights, based on Articles 64 and 65 of the Constitution which guarantee the status and special rights of the autochthonous Italian and Hungarian national communities and the Roma community in Slovenia. The former groups enjoy special representation at the national and local levels, through their recognition as self-governing communities, and the latter have special representation at the local level.[72] This protection, especially for the former groups, is a little anomalous, as Hungarians only represent 0.4 per cent of the population, and Italians as little as 0.16 per cent. However, they are long standing historic minorities, and their status can be addressed without need for controversial engagement with the effects of the break-up of the former SFRY, but rather by reference to the historic continuities from the Austro-Hungarian empire, of which Slovenia was once part. In contrast, no special measures have been taken—other than conceivably the provisions on electoral rights for non-nationals—to protect the status of other ethnic groups from the other former SFRY within Slovenia, whether they have national citizenship or not. These groups are rather larger than the autochthonous groups: Croats make up 2.7 per cent of the population, Serbs 2.4 per cent and Bosnians 1.3 per cent.[73]

The initial definition of national citizenship in Slovenia was based in substantial measure on the only reference point which it had as a new state, namely the 'republican' citizenship which existed within the SFRY.[74] It did not have a legacy citizenship, such as that which existed from a prior period of statehood, such as was used in the cases of Estonia and Latvia to define the initial scope of national citizenship, by reference to descent from a historic nation. In addition to those with 'republican' citizenship of Slovenia as a republic within the SFRY, who were presumed to be ethnically Slovenian, it was also possible, for a period of six months after the promulgation of the 1991 Citizenship Act, for others who had been permanent residents of Slovenia, who were actually residing in Slovenia on the day of the independence plebiscite (23 December 1990), to apply to become Slovenian citizens. Such applications did not require proof of linguistic competence, or set other tests of affiliation. The figures cited by

[72] A Petričušić, 'Slovenian legislative system for minority protection', *NoveSSL Revista de Sociolingüística*, Autumn 2004.

[73] European Centre on Racism and Intolerance (ECRI), *Second Report on Slovenia*, December 2002, at 16.

[74] J Zorn, 'Ethnic Citizenship in the Slovenian State', (2005) 9 *Citizenship Studies* 135–52; Andreev, above n 70; F Medved, From civic to ethnic community? The evolution of Slovenian citizenship', in Bauböck *et al*, above n 21.

Jelka Zorn show that 171,000 people (some 8.5 per cent of the population) obtained Slovenian national citizenship by applying during the six month period up to 26 December 1991, but that about 0.9 per cent of Slovenia's population overall (18,305 people) did not succeed in obtaining Slovenian citizenship, either because they did not apply, or because their application was rejected.[75] This group were treated thereafter as foreigners, and their status regulated according to the Aliens Act; this treatment was also given to the war refugees who arrived in Slovenia from this time onwards, who were escaping the conflicts in Croatia, Bosnia and Serbia. However, most controversially for the group of existing residents who became foreigners in their state of residence, in February 1992 they were erased from the Register of Permanent Residents when the Aliens Act began to apply to them, and they were moved to the inactive or dead register, of persons presumed to have died or have emigrated. Consequently, this group came to be known as 'the erased'.

What happened to 'the erased' has been a matter of great controversy within Slovenia since the issue started to come to public attention in the late 1990s, and it reflects both an underlying ethnic definition of citizenship which belied the original approach which appeared to be closer to the 'zero option' of Lithuania than to the ethnic approaches of Latvia or Estonia, and also a worrying element of anti-democratic action, as the measures which were taken with regard to this non-citizen group were undertaken predominantly in secret and without parliamentary scrutiny.[76] Furthermore, notwithstanding a Constitutional Court judgment in 1999,[77] which found that the principles of law-governed state, trust in law and equality were violated by the acts of the state in respect of the erased, no comprehensive changes to the situation of the erased were made. A further 1999 Act on the Regulation of the Status of Citizens of other Successor States of the former SFRY in Slovenia was declared unconstitutional in 2003, not least because it failed to deal with the situation of those who had been deported as a consequence of losing their residence status, and it did not recognise the underlying illegality of the erasure. The issue has been taken up by groups such as the Slovenian Helsinki monitor, the Slovenian Human Rights Ombudsman and latterly Amnesty International, negative international attention has included criticisms in the European Commission against Racism and Intolerance (ECRI) 2002 report on Slovenia,[78] and from 2003 onwards there was substantial public attention on the issue. This was partly because the 2003 Constitutional Court judgment,

[75] Zorn, above n 74 at 136.

[76] Zorn, above n 74; J Dedić, V Jalušič, V and J Zorn, *The Erased: Organized Innocence and the Politics of Exclusion*, Ljubljana: Mirovni inštitut, 2000.

[77] U-I-284/94, 4 February 1999, Official Gazette RS, No 14/99.

[78] ECRI Report, above n 73 at 19–22.

which sought to draw a line under the issue, in fact touched upon some issues which were highly sensitive for both the Slovenian state and, as it turned out, the wider Slovenian public. The judgment included a list of five points for action:

— the state should make a formal apology and recognise its wrongdoing;
— the state should provide a transparent account of what had actually happened and should identify the lines of political and legal responsibility in that respect;
— there should be unconditional retrospective restoration of status;
— general reparations should be granted to all those affected by way of symbolic compensation;
— in addition, where individuals could show specific loss, they should be able to claim additional damages.

The difficulty was that these fundamentally liberal and rule-of-law oriented precepts encountered a negative response amongst both the majority of politicians and within public opinion. There was a deep resistance to the possibility of paying compensation to individuals who might be former officers of the hated Yugoslav federal army, and perhaps persons who opposed Slovenian independence. Many of the group of erased were also Roma, and it has been suggested that the erasure manoeuvre was intended to prevent them becoming Slovenian citizens.[79] A further 'technical law', which had been put forward by the government to deal with the circumstances of a limited group of the erased, was put to a non-binding referendum at the initiative of a group of nationalist politicians in April 2004. Although most politicians and NGOs urged citizens to boycott the vote, the majority view (95 per cent) of those who did vote (on a turnout of 30 per cent) was that the law, and thus in effect the judgment of the Constitutional Court, should be rejected, and in effect the erasure was reinforced. The Amnesty International Annual Report in May 2006 highlighted that by the end of 2005, approximately 6,000 of the erased still did not have a permanent residence permit or, in the alternative, Slovenian citizenship.[80] In October 2007, as Amnesty International reported in its Annual Report 2008, the government presented a draft constitutional law to Parliament intended to resolve the situation of the erased. In fact, in Amnesty's opinion, this law still perpetuated the historical discriminations

[79] D Weissbrod and C Collins, 'The Human Rights of Stateless Persons', (2006) 28 *Human Rights Quarterly* 245–76 at 264.

[80] See the Amnesty International Annual Report 2006, at 231; see also Amnesty International Press Release, 'Restore the Rights of the Erased' AI Index, EUR 68/001/2005, 4 March 2005; Amnesty International's Briefing to the UN Committee on Economic, Social and Cultural Rights on Slovenia, 35th Session, November 2005, http://www.amnesty-eu.org/static/documents/2005/CESCR_briefing_Slovenia_final.pdf.

against this group and Amnesty called for its withdrawal.[81] The issue thus continues to be a significant one in Slovenian political life, and has now come before the European Court of Human Rights with the support of the Open Society Institute.[82] And yet, the case of the erased could not provide a sharper contrast to the case of electoral rights for non-nationals, characterised, as we noted above, as an instance of the Slovenian political elite seeking to position itself at the forefront of European best practice in matters of citizenship and political inclusion. Thus we can see that what at first sight is a policy of inclusion can sometimes be a mask for other policies of exclusion.

V CONCLUSIONS

This paper has concentrated on two sets of cases where new states in Central and Eastern Europe, which acceded to the EU in 2004, have grappled with the intersections between the definition of national citizenship in the post-1989 world, the creation of new minority groups whose treatment has led to scrutiny by international organisations of national state action, and the evolving norms of inclusion which are characterised not only by Article 19 EC but also by the more general, if not yet conclusive, trend towards the extension of local electoral rights to third country nationals. The cases of the Russians (and others) in the Baltic states and the citizens of other Republics of the SFRY in Slovenia have posed challenges both to the internal definition of these new polities, and the norms which underpin their emerging senses of national identity, and their search for international acceptability, especially in the form of accession to the EU. In certain cases, it is arguable that the political conditionality approach adopted prior to accession failed, because states such as Latvia and Slovenia have conspicuously failed to adjust their national legislation in response to concerns that it breached the Copenhagen principles which are supposed to govern enlargement.

It is clear that there is considerable variation even across the small group of states under consideration. One possible provisional conclusion to be drawn from the very different experiences of Estonia, Latvia and Lithuania is that each of the states has experienced the effects of 'Europeanisation'—the 'return' to Europe comprising the search for, and achievement of, international acceptance through membership of bodies such as NATO and the EU—very much through the prism of its own political identity. Moreover, each state has approached the question of Europeanisation by reference to the different domestic constellations of political interests, such

[81] Amnesty International Annual Report 2008, at 268–9.

[82] Application 26826/06 *Makuc and others v Slovenia*.

as the perceived role of, and threat posed by, minorities, both those who have, and those who have not, acquired national citizenship, as well as the specific interests of domestic political elites, including political parties. These variables account for the differing trajectories of the three states, despite their shared heritages and geopolitical situations.

The 'return to Europe' for Slovenia, formerly part of the Austro-Hungarian Empire and historically a borderland state both in geographical and geopolitical terms, has been mediated through its status as much the most stable state to have emerged from the ashes of the SFRY in the 1990s, a state which has been lauded for both its orderly democratic transition and its achievement of economic success. Yet when the case of the erased came to public attention in the late 1990s, it highlighted deep-seated divisions within society in relation to the SFRY heritage (and indeed older divisions within the South Slav area) which Slovenian success in relation to EU membership and other markers of transition had not wholly effaced. On the one hand, Slovenian legislators were capable of moving Slovenia ostensibly to the front rank of European good practice, extending electoral rights in local elections to third country nationals. At the same time, the state organs have remained complicit in what has been widely condemned, internationally, as a major breach of human rights norms by the state, which has effectively denied the personhood of a large group of permanent residents.

This study of the outer limits of political citizenship for non-nationals in the context of an enlarged and exceedingly diverse EU has presented the case for close attention to be paid to the specifics of national constitutional, legal and political conditions when considering the more diffuse effects of accommodation at the national level with the detailed requirements of EU law, such as the electoral rights for non-nationals. A similar point can, unsurprisingly, be made about pre-2004 Member States, where narratives of both political inclusion and exclusion of non-nationals are underpinned by a variety of responses to the increasing demands of political transnationalism in states which have earlier or more recently experienced substantial waves of immigration from third countries. It is important, none the less, to pay specific attention to the EU's still lesser known outer edge, for the reasons of contextual specificity identified at the outset of this paper. The old and the new Member States may apply the same EU laws, but they differ in more than just the length of time during which they have been applying the rules. As I have sought to demonstrate through the cases presented in this paper, constitutional and political culture and relatively undetermined notions such as 'polity ideas' make a difference not only to the practicalities of legal implementation, but also to the quality and ease of the fit between EU and other European norms (for example relating to political liberalism and democratic constitutionalism) and the receiving Member States.

6

European Police Cooperation and its Limits: From Intelligence-led to Coercive Measures?

KONRAD LACHMAYER*

I INTRODUCTION

TRADITIONALLY, POLICING IS considered to lie at the core of state sovereignty and to be an area over which the European Union has no competence and can, and should, have no concern. In practice, given the increasingly transnational nature of crime, the EU has assumed a greater coordinating role. However, this role has been hampered by lack of institutional competence. This has led to the use of a wide range of alternative strategies to overcome some of these Treaty limitations. The Lisbon Treaty—which this chapter refers to—will help address some of the competence issues. This in turn helps to redefine the contours of the outer limits of Community law. However, this chapter does not focus on the human rights and rule of law debate in European police cooperation.

II LIMITING EUROPEAN POLICE COOPERATION? THE UNITED KINGDOM, IRELAND AND DENMARK OPTING OUT FROM THE LISBON TREATY

The Treaty of Lisbon will change European police cooperation crucially. This article integrates the perspective of the Treaty of Lisbon, although it is not clear whether the Treaty will ever enter into force. It is not yet possible fully to predict the dynamics of this further step in the area of freedom,

* Please send comments and remarks to konrad.lachmayer@univie.ac.at; see also http://www.internationalconstitutionallaw.net. I would like to thank Dr Catherine Bernard, who gave me the opportunity to present my ideas in the Centre of European Legal Studies, University of Cambridge and who supported me substantially in improving my manuscript.

security and justice. Three Member States of the EU decided not to follow this major development in European policing. With the Protocol on the position of the United Kingdom and Ireland in respect of the area of freedom, security and justice and the Protocol on the position of Denmark, these three countries are opting out of the activities in the fields of border checks, asylum and immigration policies, judicial cooperation in civil and criminal matters and European police cooperation. As a consequence, none of the provisions of Title V of Part Three of the TFEU (Treaty on the Functioning of the European Union), no measure adopted pursuant to that Title, and no decision of the Court of Justice interpreting any such provision shall be binding upon or applicable in the United Kingdom, Ireland or Denmark; and no such provision, measure or decision shall in any way affect the competences, rights and obligations of those States.[1] These three countries still have the possibility to opt in with regard to particular measures.

These developments raise questions about European police cooperation: Has it already gone too far?; What is European police cooperation for?; Are the EU Member States really interested in a European police cooperation?; What are the limits of a European police cooperation?; and What are the implications for the sovereign powers of the Member States? This article will give some answers to these questions. It focuses on the legal and institutional perspectives, which are important preconditions to the questions of accountability and the rule of law. Thus, the legal framework of police competences in European police cooperation shall be addressed.

III THE IMPORTANCE OF EUROPEAN POLICE COOPERATION

First of all, these questions address the need for European police cooperation in general. I begin by explaining the importance, necessity and inevitability of European police cooperation.

While European police cooperation is one of the main developments in Europe, initially it had nothing to do with the EU and the European integration process. European police cooperation is a reaction to the globalisation of criminality and cross-border crimes.[2] The main challenge to European policing is the globalising of organised crime in its various

[1] See Art 2 of the Protocol on the position of the UK and Ireland in respect of the area of freedom, security and justice and Art 2 of the Protocol on the position of Denmark—Treaty of Lisbon amending the Treaty on European Union and the Treaty establishing the European Community, signed at Lisbon, 13 December 2007, [2007] OJ C/306/1.

[2] Various minor crimes also have cross-border implications. See James Sheptycki, 'Patrolling the New European (In)Security Field; Organisational Dilemmas and Operational Solutions for Policing the Internal Borders of Europe' (2001) 9 *European Journal of Crime, Criminal Law and Criminal Justice* 144–60.

forms—drugs, human trafficking or smuggling of arms—the list of potential transnational crimes is very long. However, of course, the political discussion is dominated by countering terrorism. The role of terrorism in European police cooperation is first of all a political one.[3] Terrorism is an important political argument in the further deepening of European police cooperation.[4] The terrorist attacks in Madrid 2004 and London 2005 showed the significant and dangerous threat Europe is facing. This menace also clears the political way to further police cooperation. While Member States might have a lot of reservations about police cooperation, the terrorist threat underlined the political necessity of a joint effort to fight terrorism.

This problem is not just European but global: no country in the world is able to deal with international criminality alone.[5] Nowadays, the further internationalisation of police cooperation is just a question of time. All the more so, now that technical, economic and social globalisation is bringing peoples together all over the world. More crimes will be committed transnationally; the boundaries of the nation states are not limiting the increased territorial independence of criminal organisations. Police authorities and forces—in order to prevent and pursue crimes—have to cooperate. From this perspective, there are almost no geographical limits for police cooperation.[6]

So, the first stage in the argument is that police cooperation is transnational and international. The second stage is the role for the EU. To establish international police cooperation involves the relevant political institutions on a global and a regional level. For this reason, the EU, as the major political player in Europe, is part of these developments. But police cooperation is of such importance that if the possibilities of the EU are not sufficient, further bilateral and multilateral treaties have to be signed. Police cooperation in Europe is working with, and without, the EU.[7]

[3] Nevertheless, there is also a legal aspect in EU's combating terrorism. See Steve Peers, 'EU responses to terrorism' (2003) 52 *ICLQ* 227–43; Kimmo Nuotio, 'Terrorism as a catalyst for the emergence, harmonization and reform of criminal law' (2006) *Journal of International Criminal Justice* 998–1016, 1008.

[4] See Jan Wouters and Frederic Naert, 'The European Union and "September 11"' (2002–2003) 13 *Indiana International & Comparative Law Review* 719, 726.

[5] Understanding transnational policing in Europe as a multi-level governance, see Hartmut Arden, 'Convergence of Policing Policies and Transnational Policing in Europe', (2001) 9 *European Journal of Crime, Criminal Law and Criminal Justice* 99–112, 108.

[6] See Dilip L Das and Peter C Kratcoski, 'International police co-operation: a world perspective' (1999) 22 *International Journal of Police Strategies & Management* 214–41.

[7] The formal structures of policing are still complex in Europe (and within the EU). See Marc Alain, 'Transnational Police Cooperation in Europe and in North America: Revisiting the Traditional Border between Internal and External Matters, or How Policing is being globalized' (2001) 9 *European Journal of Crime, Criminal Law and Criminal Justice* 113–29, 114.

IV FROM INTERNATIONAL TO SUPRANATIONAL POLICE COOPERATION IN EUROPE

Although European police cooperation is increasing very fast on an EU level, a lot of European police cooperation measures are still organised internationally. To reach the consensus within all the members of the EU seems to be much harder than to organise a 'coalition of the willing'. The multilateral Treaty of Prüm (Prüm Convention)[8] is a good example. The contracting parties of the Treaty are Belgium, Germany, Spain, France, Luxembourg, the Netherlands and Austria. The Prüm Convention includes far-reaching steps towards transnational police cooperation between the contracting parties, not only in the context of broad data exchange but also concerning joint operational actions.[9] It seems that it was much easier to establish an international treaty between EU Member States, which are interested in this cooperation than to convince all the Member States and have a long lasting procedure within the third pillar. The principle of unanimity—especially now with 27 Member States—is obviously an obstacle to further cooperation within the EU.

Since the Prüm Convention was signed as an international treaty, the question arises as to why the contracting parties of the Convention did not use the provisions on enhanced cooperation within the EU Treaty. The formal answer in the context of the Treaty of Prüm is easy. There were only seven contracting parties and for enhanced cooperation under Article 43 EU a minimum of eight Member States is required.[10] The possibility of finding an eighth contracting party was quite strong due to the 2004 enlargement of the EU. Nevertheless, it still seemed easier to organise an independent international treaty than to start European procedures.[11]

Austria, Germany and Spain were the first states to adopt the Prüm Convention at the end of 2006. The early results of the Prüm Convention

[8] Convention between the Kingdom of Belgium, the Federal Republic of Germany, the Kingdom of Spain, the French Republic, the Grand Duchy of Luxembourg, the Kingdom of the Netherlands and the Republic of Austria on the stepping up of cross-border cooperation, particularly in combating terrorism, cross-border crime and illegal migration, signed on 27 May 2005.

[9] See Jacque Ziller, 'Le traite de Prüm Une vraie-fausse coopération renforcée dans l'Espace de sécurité de liberté et de justice', (2006) EUI Working Paper LAW No 2006/32.

[10] See Monica den Boer, 'New Dimensions in EU Police Co-operation: The Hague milestones for what they are worth' in JW de Zwaan and Flora ANJ Goudappel (eds), *Freedom, Security and Justice in the European Union: Implementation of the Hague Programme* (The Hague, TMC Asser Press, 2006) 221–32, 231.

[11] The Prüm can also be understood as a breach of the principle of loyalty regarding Art 10 TEC. See House of Lords, European Union Committee 18th Report of Session 2006–07 'Prüm: an effective weapon against terrorism and crime? Report with Evidence', published 9 May 2007. See also Thierry Balzacq, Didier Bigo, Sergio Carrera and Elspeth Guild, 'The Treaty of Prüm and EC Treaty: Two competing models for EU internal security' in Thierry Balzacq and Sergio Carrera (eds), *Security versus Freedom? A Challenge for Europe's Future* (Aldershot, Ashgate, 2006) 115–36, 118.

were greeted as a success at the Council of the European Union in February 2007.[12] This led to the process of integrating the Prüm Convention into the third pillar of the EU Treaty which was agreed at the council meeting in June 2007.[13] The Prüm Treaty was slightly amended but its main objectives remained (Doc 10232/07).[14] A Prüm Implementing Decision was agreed at the Justice and Home Affairs Council meeting in November 2007 which implemented the Council Decision agreed in June 2007 (the Prüm Decision) and laid down 'the necessary administrative and technical provisions for different forms of cooperation, especially for the automated exchange of DNA data, fingerprinting data and vehicle registration data'.[15]

This two stage strategy can also be observed in other areas of security and justice over the last decades.[16] It started with the Schengen Agreement[17] and the Convention implementing the Schengen Agreement.[18] These multilateral agreements were integrated into the EC Treaty by the Treaty of Amsterdam.[19] Thus, there is a tradition of establishing an international treaty first and integrating it after some time. The interesting

[12] See *2781th Council meeting Justice and Home Affairs in Brussels, February 15, 2007*, Press Release 5922/07 (Press: 16): 'The Treaty has meanwhile entered into force in Austria, Spain and Germany and is expected to be in force in the other original signatory states in the first half of 2007 at the latest. The ratification processes in the countries intending to accede to the Treaty are also well advanced. Already at this early stage, the automatic information exchange has brought about noticeable operational success: For instance, the German authorities matched DNA profiles of open cases against data held by Austrian authorities and found hits in more then 1500 cases. In this context, over 700 open traces from Germany could be attributed to persons known to the Austrian criminal prosecution authorities. Broken down by types of crime, 14 hits in homicide or murder cases, 885 hits in theft cases, and 85 hits in robbery or extortion cases have been found (as at 4 January).'

[13] Furthermore Slovenia, Italy, Finland, Portugal, Bulgaria, Rumania, Greece, Sweden and Estonia decided to join the Prüm Convention.

[14] See the *2807th Council meeting Justice and Home Affairs in Luxemburg, 12–13 June 2007*, Press Release 10267/07 (Press: 125); see also European Parliament Legislative Resolution of 7 June 2007 on the initiative ... on the stepping up of cross-border cooperation, particularly in combating terrorism and cross-border crime (6566/2007 – C6–0079/2007 – 2007/0804(CNS)).

[15] See the *2827th Council meeting Justice and Home Affairs in Brussels, 8–9 November 2007*, Press Release 14617/07 (Press: 253).

[16] See Daniel Thym, 'The political character of supranational differentiation' (2006) 31 *EL Rev* 781, 782.

[17] Agreement between the Governments of the States of the Benelux Economic Union, the Federal Republic of Germany and the French Republic on the gradual abolition of checks at their common borders, see the Schengen acquis as referred to in Art 1(2) of Council Decision (EC) 1999/435 of 20 May 1999 [2000] OJ L239/13.

[18] See Convention implementing the Schengen Agreement of 14 June 1985 between the Governments of the States of the Benelux Economic Union, the Federal Republic of Germany and the French Republic on the gradual abolition of checks at their common borders (see the Schengen acquis as referred to in Art 1(2) of Council Decision (EC) 1999/435 of 20 May 1999 [2000] OJ L239/19); see also Eckhart Wagner, 'The integration of Schengen into the framework of the European Union', (1998) 25(2) *Legal Issues of Economic Integration*, 1–60.

[19] Treaty of Amsterdam amending the Treaty on European Union—Protocol integrating the Schengen acquis into the framework of the European Union, [1997] OJ C/340/93.

aspect of the Prüm Convention was how fast it was possible to start the integration process.

The different efforts to integrate police cooperation further into the framework of the EU will have an impact. But the network of international, multilateral and bilateral treaties remains very important and will be intensified with further police cooperation. Austria, for example, has bilateral treaties with every neighbouring country regarding police cooperation and a lot of bilateral agreements with third states, countries which are not part of the EU.[20], every EU Member State has its own treaty and cooperation network with third countries outside the EU in the field of police data exchange.[21] Regarding these developments, the question remains whether the EU will also start to establish international treaties and agreements with third countries. Will the EU also focus on the external dimension of internal security?[22]

The first example of such an attempt can be seen in the development of the passenger name record data 2007, which is related to the data exchange of flight passenger details with the US[23] and Canada[24]. The European Court of Justice (ECJ) said that the purpose of exchange of flight passenger's personal data was for police and crime prevention purposes.[25]

[20] Treaty between the Austrian Republic and Federal Republic of Germany regarding cross-border cooperation in police and judicial affairs, BGBl III 2005/210; Treaty between the Austrian Republic and the Czech Republic regarding police cooperation BGBl III 2006/121; Treaty between the Austrian Republic and the Republic of Slovakia regarding police cooperation, BGBl 2005/72; Treaty between the Austrian Republic and the Republic of Hungary regarding the prevention and the fight against cross-border crime, BGBl III 2006/99; Treaty between the Austrian Republic and Republic of Slovenia regarding police cooperation, BGBl III 2005/51; Agreement between the Austrian Government and the Italian Government regarding police cooperation, BGBl III 2000/52; Treaty between the Austrian Republic, the Swiss Confederation and the Principality of Liechtenstein regarding the cross-border cooperation of the security and customs authorities BGBl III 2001/120.

[21] For example the international agreements which Europol has already concluded with various countries. See Steve Peers, *EU Justice and Home Affairs* (2nd edn) (Oxford, Oxford University Press, 2006) 558.

[22] See Jörg Monar, 'Anti-terrorism law and policy: the case of the European Union', in VV Ramraj, Michael Hor an Kent Roach (eds), *Global Anti-Terrorism Law and Policy* (Cambridge, Cambridge University Press, 2005) 425–52, 443.

[23] See Council Decision 2007/551/CFSP/JHAof 23 July 2007 on the signing, on behalf of the EU, of an Agreement between the European Union and the United States of America on the processing and transfer of Passenger Name Record (PNR) data by air carriers to the United States Department of Homeland Security (DHS) (2007 PNR Agreement) and the Agreement between the European Union and the United States of America on the processing and transfer of Passenger Name Record (PNR) data by air carriers to the United States Department of Homeland Security (DHS) (2007 PNR Agreement) [2007] OJ L204/16.

[24] Council Decision (EC) 230/2006 of 18 July 2005 on the conclusion of an Agreement between the European Community and the Government of Canada on the processing of API/PNR data and the Agreement between the European Community and the Government of Canada on the processing of Advance Passenger Information and Passenger Name Record data, [2006] OJ L82/14.

[25] Joined Cases C-317/04 and C-318/04 *European Parliament v Council of the European Union* [2006] ECR I-4721.

Although it declared the former agreement void because it was enacted as a harmonisation measure within the first pillar when it should have been adopted under the third pillar, the ECJ makes clear that the EU has legitimately started adding the foreign dimension of internal security into its foreign policy.[26] The ECJ only addressed the question of competences without mentioning the human rights dimension of flight passengers' personal data. As it declared that the agreement had to be implemented within the third pillar, the ECJ did not have jurisdiction over the agreement.

The European police cooperation—only established in recent years—shows clearly that police cooperation has not yet reached its full potential. The combination of European and transnational police cooperation based on international treaties will continue. The attempts of the EU to integrate European police cooperation into its own system are increasing. The necessity of further cooperation will mean that more flexible forms of cooperation are chosen and will build on the already established cooperation within the system of the EU.

V THE OLD AND THE NEW CONCEPT OF EUROPEAN POLICE COOPERATION

A The Developments in the Past[27]

Locating European police cooperation within the third pillar of the EU will be changed dramatically if the Treaty of Lisbon enters into force. In order to understand this shift we have to first consider the contemporary concept and development of the third pillar in European police cooperation.

The creation of the TREVI group in the 1970s[28], the establishment of the European single market and the related measures of the Schengen Agreement[29] and the Schengen Implementation Convention[30] together form the initial phase of European police cooperation. The inclusion of

[26] See Arts 24 and 38 TEU.

[27] See also Neil Walker, 'The pattern of transnational policing' in Tim Newburn (ed), *Handbook of policing* (Cullompton, Willan Publishing, 2003) 111–35.

[28] See, eg John D Occhipinti, *The Politics of EU Police Cooperation: Toward a European FBI?* (Boulder–London, Lynne Rienner Publishers, 2003) 31–3.

[29] Agreement between the Governments of the States of the Benelux Economic Union, the Federal Republic of Germany and the French Republic on the gradual abolition of checks at their common borders, see the Schengen acquis as referred to in Art 1(2) of Council Decision (EC) 1999/435 of 20 May 1999 [2000] OJ L239/13.

[30] See Convention implementing the Schengen Agreement of 14 June 1985 between the Governments of the States of the Benelux Economic Union, the Federal Republic of Germany and the French Republic on the gradual abolition of checks at their common borders (see the Schengen acquis as referred to in Art 1(2) of Council Decision (EC) 1999/435 of 20 May

European police cooperation in the third pillar in Article K.1 No 9 by the Maastricht Treaty was a major step in the European integration process.[31] The establishment of Europol with the Europol Convention institutionalised the growing network of European police. Europol commenced its full activities on 1 July 1999.[32]

At that time the Treaty of Amsterdam made the perspectives of European police cooperation more concrete in various ways.[33] The so-called area of freedom, security and justice was established and integrated European police cooperation into this broader political concept. The Schengen acquis was integrated in the EU[34] and the asylum and visa policies were transferred into the first pillar. Important political agreements in the field of police cooperation started with the Viennese action plan 1998, which placed a special emphasis on the strengthening of Europol in the framework of European police cooperation.[35] The Tampere programme from 1999 provided concrete steps towards the realisation of the area of freedom, security and justice[36] and since then the establishment of European police cooperation has become more realistic. Further institutions such as Eurojust[37], the European Police Chiefs Operational Task Force[38] and the European Police College[39] created the organisational

1999 [2000] OJ L239/19); see also Eckhart Wagner, 'The integration of Schengen into the framework of the European Union', (1998) 25(2) *Legal Issues of Economic Integration* 1–60.

31 Art K.1 No 9 TEU: 'police cooperation for the purposes of preventing and combating terrorism, unlawful drug trafficking and other serious forms of international crime, including if necessary certain aspects of customs cooperation, in connection with the organization of a Union-wide system for exchanging information within a European Police Office (Europol)'.

32 http://www.europol.europa.eu; re the historical developments, see eg Francis R Monaco, 'Europol: The Culmination of European Union's International Police cooperation efforts' (1995–96) 19 *Fordham International Law Journal* 247–308.

33 See Jörg Monar, 'Justice and home affairs in the Treaty of Amsterdam: reform at the price of fragmentation' (1998) 23 *EL Rev*, 320–35.

34 Treaty of Amsterdam amending the Treaty on European Union—Protocol integrating the Schengen acquis into the framework of the European Union, [1997] OJ C/340/93.

35 Council and Commission Action Plan of 3 December 1998 on how best to implement the provisions of the Treaty of Amsterdam on the creation of an area of freedom, security and justice, [1999] OJ C/19/1.

36 The presidency conclusions of the Tampere European Council 15 and 16 October 1999 constitute the Tampere Programme; see http://www.europarl.europa.eu/summits/tam_en.htm.

37 Council Decision 2002/187/JHA of 28 February 2002 setting up Eurojust with a view to reinforcing the fight against serious crime, [2002] OJ L63/1; see also Stephen O'Doherty and Arsha Gosine, 'Eurojust: a new agency for a new era' (2002) 152 *NLJ* 680.

38 The European Police Chiefs Task Force was mentioned in the Tampere Programme, but it was not set up formally. Nevertheless, the European Police Chiefs Task Force held its first meeting in April 2000. See http://ec.europa.eu/justice_home/fsj/police/chief/fsj_police_task_force_en.htm.

39 Council Decision 2000/820/JHA of 22 December 2000 establishing a European Police College (CEPOL) [2000] OJ L336/1; Council Decision 2005/681/JHA of 20 September 2005 establishing the European Police College (CEPOL) and repealing Decision 2000/820/JHA [2005] OJ L256/63.

framework to enhance police cooperation. The enactment of the Council Framework Decision on joint investigation teams[40] was a further step forward.

The Tampere programme lasted five years. After this period the new Hague Programme[41] was agreed on in 2004 covering the years 2005–2010. The main objectives of the Hague programme regarding police cooperation are related to improving the exchange of information, especially within the principle of availability,[42] preventing and combating terrorism[43] and effective combat of cross-border organised crime through intensified practical cooperation between police authorities of Member States and with Europol.[44]

The political and general developments in European police cooperation were always faster than the realisation of its aims. The fate of the constitutional treaty changed the situation by delaying the next step towards full integration of the third pillar. Police cooperation has more time to establish itself but little pressure to do so. The interesting aspect of

[40] Council Framework Decision 2002/465/JHA of 13 June 2002 on joint investigation teams [2002] OJ L162/1.

[41] Annex 1 to the Presidency Conclusions of the Brussels European Council, November 2004 constitutes 'The Hague Programme'. See http://ec.europa.eu/justice_home/news/information_dossiers/the_hague_priorities/index_en.htm. See also Thierry Balzacq and Sergio Carrera, 'The Hague Programme: The Long Road to Freedom, Security and Justice' in Thierry Balzacq and Sergio Carrera (eds) *Security versus Freedom? A Challenge for Europe's Future* (Aldershot, Ashgate, 2006) 1–32; de Zwaan and Goudappel (eds) (n 10 above).

[42] See Part 2.1 of the Hague Programme: 'The European Council is convinced that strengthening freedom, security and justice requires an innovative approach to the cross-border exchange of law-enforcement information. The mere fact that information crosses borders should no longer be relevant. With effect from 1 January 2008 the exchange of such information should be governed by conditions set out below with regard to the principle of availability, which means that, throughout the Union, a law enforcement officer in one Member State who needs information in order to perform his duties can obtain this from another Member State and that the law enforcement agency in the other Member State which holds this information will make it available for the stated purpose, taking into account the requirement of ongoing investigations in that State.'

[43] See Part 2.2 of the Hague Programme: 'As a goal this means that Member States:
- use the powers of their intelligence and security services not only to counter threats to their own security, but also, as the case may be, to protect the internal security of the other Member States;
- bring immediately to the attention of the competent authorities of other Member States any information available to their services which concerns threats to the internal security of these other Member States;
- in cases where persons or goods are under surveillance by security services in connection with terrorist threats, ensure that no gaps occur in their surveillance as a result of their crossing a border.'

[44] See Part 2.3 of the Hague Programme: 'The European Council urges the Member States to enable Europol in cooperation with Eurojust to play a key role in the fight against serious cross-border (organised) crime and terrorism by:
- ratifying and effectively implementing the necessary legal instruments by the end of 2004;
- providing all necessary high quality information to Europol in good time;
- encouraging good cooperation between their competent national authorities and Europol.'

these developments can be seen in transnational cooperation such as in the Prüm Convention. The principle of unanimity made it very difficult to reach consensus regarding the various framework decisions, which are in negotiation, particularly the integration of the Europol Convention[45] and the establishment of data protection in the third pillar.[46] Attempts were made to use the first pillar for some measures such as data exchange with the US and Canada[47] or the Data Retention Directive[48] but the limits to police cooperation within the first pillar were reached very early on.[49]

As shown earlier, the major developments in this field were not taken by the ECJ, due to its lack of competence under the third pillar,[50] but by developments within the European treaties, international treaties and agreements by the Member States. Nevertheless, the ECJ's case law is developing.[51] The most famous decision within the third pillar, the *Pupino* case[52], is related to the concept of Council framework decisions, not European police cooperation. The beginning of a dynamic development of Council framework decision will be ended by the Lisbon Treaty entering into force because those legislative acts will be enacted as directives. The other important decision with regard to police cooperation was the Passenger Name Record Decision, but the crucial statement of the ECJ was related to the competences within the EU[53] and not to data protection in police and criminal cooperation. The Court ruled that the third pillar, not the first, was to be the legal basis for the agreement with the US regarding

[45] Commission (EC), 'Proposal for a Council Decision establishing the European Police Office (Europol)' COM (2006) 0817 final 20 December 2006; see also Opinion of the European Data Protection Supervisor on the Proposal for a Council Decision establishing the European Police Office (Europol)—COM(2006) 817 final, [2007] OJ C/255/13.

[46] Commission (EC), 'Proposal for a Council framework decision on the protection of personal data processed in the framework of police and judicial co-operation in criminal matters' COM (2005) 475 final, 4 October 2005.

[47] See, eg Council Decision (EC) 2004/496 of 17 May 2004 on the conclusion of an Agreement between the European Community and the United States of America on the processing and transfer of PNR data by Air Carriers to the United States Department of Homeland Security, Bureau of Customs and Border Protection and the Agreement between the European Community and the United States of America on the processing and transfer of PNR data by air carriers to the United States Department of Homeland Security, Bureau of Customs and Border Protection [2004] OJ L183/83.

[48] Council Directive (EC) 2006/24 on the retention of data generated or processed in connection with the provision of publicly available electronic communications services or of public communications networks and amending Directive 2002/58/EC, [2006] OJ L105/54.

[49] See ECJ (Grand Chamber) Joined Cases C-317/04 and C-318/04 *European Parliament v Council of the European Union* [2006] ECR I-4721. The data retention directive is also pending with the ECJ.

[50] See Art 35 TEU.

[51] See Vassilis Hatzopoulos, 'With or without you . . . judging politically in the field of Area of Freedom, Security and Justice' (2008) 33 *EL Rev.* 44–65.

[52] See ECJ Case C-105/03 *Criminal proceedings against Maria Pupino* [2005] ECR I-5285.

[53] Joined Cases C-317/04 and C-318/04 *European Parliament v Council of the European Union* [2006] ECR I-4721.

the data exchange of flight passengers. The relevance of the European arrest warrant judgement of the ECJ is again only indirectly related to European police cooperation.[54]

A more dynamic part of the EU's third pillar is the secondary legislation, especially Council framework decisions in the field of crime offences and judicial cooperation,[55] but not directly in the field of European police cooperation. While the framework decisions related to joint investigation teams[56] and the European arrest warrant[57] do affect police cooperation in some ways, the Framework Decision combating terrorism[58] involves mutual recognition in criminal law. This indirectly enhances police cooperation in this field. The harmonisation of criminal law is important and effects policing in so far as it creates a common aim of preventing and prosecuting these crimes. However, the new legal establishment of Europol within the third pillar[59], the framework decision on the use of personal data in judicial and police cooperation[60] and the integration of the Prüm Convention[61] will give a legal basis for police cooperation within the third pillar of the EU.

[54] ECJ (Grand Chamber), *Advocaten voor de Wereld VZW v Leden van de Ministerraad* [2007] ECR I-3633.

[55] See, eg Council Framework Decision 2001/413/JHA of 28 May 2001 combating fraud and counterfeiting of non-cash means of payment [2001] OJ L149/1; Council Framework Decision 2001/500/JHA of 26 June 2001 on money laundering, the identification, tracing, freezing, seizing and confiscation of instrumentalities and the proceeds of crime [2001] OJ L182/1; Council Framework Decision 2002/629/JHA of 19 July 2002 on combating trafficking in human beings [2002] OJ L203/1; Council Framework Decision 2003/568/JHA of 22 July 2003 on combating corruption in the private sector [2003] OJ L192/54. See also Flora ANJ Goudappel, 'Third Pillar Cooperation' in de Zwaan and Goudappel (eds), *Freedom, Security and Justice in the European Union. Implementation of the Hague Programme* (n 10 above) 195–202, 196.

[56] Council Framework Decision 2002/465/JHA of 13 June 2002 on joint investigation teams [2002] OJ L162/1.

[57] Council Framework Decision 2002/584/JHA of 13 June 2002 on the European arrest warrant and the surrender procedures between Member States [2002] OJ L190/1.

[58] Council Framework Decision 2002/475/JHA of 13 June 2002 on combating terrorism [2002] OJ L164/3. See also Commission (EC), 'Proposal for a Council Framework Decision amending Framework Decision 2002/475/JHA on combating terrorism' COM(2007) 650 final, 6 November 2007. See also Steve Peers, 'EU responses to terrorism' (2003) 52 ICLQ 227–243; Jan Wouters / Frederic Naert, 'The European Union and "September 11"' (2002–2003) 13 *Indiana International & Comparative Law Review* 719, 735.

[59] Commission (EC), 'Proposal for a Council Decision establishing the European Police Office (Europol)' COM (2006) 0817 final 20 December 2006.

[60] Commission (EC), 'Proposal for a Council framework decision on the protection of personal data processed in the framework of police and judicial co-operation in criminal matters' COM (2005) 475 final, 4 October 2005.

[61] Initiative of the Kingdom of Belgium, the Republic of Bulgaria, the Federal Republic of Germany, the Kingdom of Spain, the French Republic, the Grand Duchy of Luxembourg, the Kingdom of the Netherlands, the Republic of Austria, the Republic of Slovenia, the Slovak Republic, the Italian Republic, the Republic of Finland, the Portuguese Republic, Romania and the Kingdom of Sweden, with a view to adopting a Council Decision on the stepping up

In conclusion, prior to the Treaty of Lisbon coming into force, there are significant limits on EU competence within the third pillar. Despite this, European police cooperation is working through transnational mutual cooperation, transnational and supranational data exchange, to a limited extent through coordination with and initiative taking by Europol, through to the possibility of participation by Europol in joint investigation teams, and through shared competences of the EU regarding the external dimension of internal security measures (Passenger Name Record (PNR) data exchange). However, the necessity of getting the Member States to agree concrete measures (with regard to data exchange as well as operative action) and finally the requirement of unanimous voting in the third pillar have limited its effectiveness. The initiatives to expand competences are coming from the Member States, especially through European Councils, and from the European Commission, especially its former vice-president Franco Frattini, who was responsible for the EU's policy in the area of freedom, security and justice.[62]

B The Perspectives for the Future

These limitations will be overcome by the Treaty of Lisbon, if the Treaty enters into force and will lead to a further integration of European police cooperation into the revised system of the EU. This means a crucial shift from an international coordinating concept to the integration of policing into the shared competences of the EU within the area of freedom, security and justice (Article 4 [2c] paragraph 2 point j TFEU).

The most important change is the end of the principle of unanimity for the general parts of European police cooperation: the ordinary procedure will become the standard procedure. The individual Member State will not be able to prohibit further legislative developments, because qualified majority will be enough to establish new legislation.[63]

According to Article 87 (69F)(2) TFEU, the EU can establish measures "for the purposes of police cooperation in relation to the prevention,

of cross-border cooperation, particularly in combating terrorism and cross-border crime [2007] OJ C/71/35.

[62] http://ec.europa.eu/commission_barroso/frattini/. 'We have to provide security for our citizens. We should not limit ourselves to use the security provided by others, as we have been doing in the past. We have to be active in building a new security framework, also with a view towards the outside world. Only then will Europe truly represent a space of security and liberty.' Franco Frattini, 'The Hague Programme: Our future investment in democratic stability and democratic security' in de Zwaan and Goudappel (eds), *Freedom, Security and Justice in the European Union: Implementation of the Hague Programme* (n 10 above) 7, 8.

[63] See Jörg Monar, 'Anti-terrorism law and policy: the case of the European Union', in Victor V Ramraj, Michael Hor an Kent Roach (eds), *Global Anti-Terrorism Law and Policy* (Cambridge, Cambridge University Press, 2005) 425, 449.

detection and investigation of criminal offences" under the ordinary legislative procedure, concerning:

— the collection, storage, processing, analysis and exchange of relevant information;
— support for the training of staff, and cooperation on the exchange of staff, on equipment and on research into crime-detection; and
— common investigative techniques in relation to the detection of serious forms of organised crime.

Not only does this provision introduce majority decision making but it also appears to introduce a shift from cooperation to harmonisation. This can perhaps be seen in paragraph (a). Paragraph (c) is even clearer: within the Lisbon Treaty the EU will have the possibility of harmonising 'common investigation techniques'. This compares with the original treaty which provided only for the 'evaluation of techniques'.

Unanimity is, however, retained in two cases. The first relates to the establishment of measures concerning operational cooperation (Article 87 [69F] [3] TFEU). Nevertheless, the unanimity rule comes with a caveat: in case of the absence of unanimity in the Council, a group of at least nine Member States may request that the draft measures be referred to the European Council. In that case, the procedure in the Council shall be suspended. After discussion, and in case of a consensus, the European Council shall, within four months of this suspension, refer the draft back to the Council for adoption. Within the same timeframe, in case of disagreement, and if at least nine Member States wish to establish enhanced cooperation on the basis of the draft measures concerned, they shall notify the European Parliament, the Council and the Commission accordingly.

The second situation where unanimity is retained is Article 89 (69H) TFEU, where the Council must lay down the conditions and limitations under which the competent authorities of the Member States may operate in the territory of another Member State in liaison and in agreement with the authorities of that State.

The dynamic changes introduced by the Lisbon Treaty include a stronger role for the European Commission to initiate new legislation. The European Commission already have the possibility to initiate legislation in the field of police and judicial cooperation in criminal matters. However, there is no initiation monopoly of the European Commission, because every Member State has the same possibility. The Lisbon Treaty will reduce the initiation possibility of the Member States, because only a quarter of the Member States can introduce a legislative proposal. Thus, the position of the European Commission for proposing new legislation enhances (See Article 76 [61 I] TFEU). According to Article 74 (61 G) TFEU, the European Commission will also be integrated into the administrative coordination of police cooperation: 'The Council shall adopt measures to ensure administrative cooperation between the relevant departments of the Member States in the areas covered by this Title, as well as between those departments and the Commission.'[64]

Another effect of the changes introduced by Lisbon is the full involvement of the European Parliament in the area of European police cooperation.[65] Under the ordinary legislative procedure the role of the European Parliament will be equal to the position of the Council of the European Union and so the European Parliament needs not only to be heard but must also accept the proposed legal acts.

Finally, new legal instruments will replace the framework decisions and decisions of the Council as well as the restrictions on them.[66] The establishment of regulations and directives will have different effects in the Member States and a stronger influence on domestic legislation in European police cooperation.

The role of the ECJ and the possible dynamic interpretation of the new provisions may also lead to further integration. After a transitional period of five years the Court of Justice of the European Union will gain its full competence.[67] Then the established European legislative acts will fall under the full jurisdiction of the court.

[64] See already the old provision Art 66 TEC regarding 'Visas, Asylum, Immigration and other policies related to free movement of persons: The Council, acting in accordance with the procedure referred to in Article 67, shall take measures to ensure cooperation between the relevant departments of the administrations of the Member States in the areas covered by this title, as well as between those departments and the Commission.' Thus, the old provision will also be extended to European police cooperation.

[65] The contemporary possibilities of the European Parliament are very poor. See Art 39 TEU: '1. The Council shall consult the European Parliament before adopting any measure referred to in Article 34(2)(b), (c) and (d). The European Parliament shall deliver its opinion within a time limit which the Council may lay down, which shall not be less than three months. In the absence of an opinion within that time limit, the Council may act. 2. The Presidency and the Commission shall regularly inform the European Parliament of discussions in the areas covered by this title. 3. The European Parliament may ask questions of the Council or make recommendations to it. Each year, it shall hold a debate on the progress made in the areas referred to in this title.'

[66] See Art 34 (2b) TEU: 'Framework decisions shall be binding upon the Member States as to the result to be achieved but shall leave to the national authorities the choice of form and methods. They shall not entail direct effect;' and Art 34 (2) TEU in general: 'Unless they provide otherwise, conventions shall, once adopted by at least half of the Member States, enter into force for those Member States. Measures implementing conventions shall be adopted within the Council by a majority of two thirds of the Contracting Parties.'

[67] But there is still a transitional period of five years for some old provisions. See Art 10 (1–3) of the Protocol of transitional provisions: '1. As a transitional measure, and with respect to acts of the Union in the field of police cooperation and judicial cooperation in criminal matters which have been adopted before the entry into force of the Treaty of Lisbon, the powers of the institutions shall be the following at the date of entry into force of that Treaty: the powers of the Commission under Article 226 of the Treaty on the Functioning of the European Union shall not be applicable and the powers of the Court of Justice of the European Union under Title VI of the Treaty on European Union, in the version in force

C How is the Treaty of Lisbon Limiting European Police Cooperation?

Given the extensive changes introduced by the Lisbon Treaty in the field of police cooperation, this raises the question of what are the institutional limits of European police cooperation. Is there anything else left for the Member States regarding police legislation other than to give effect to European requirements? Three special provisions in the treaty are aimed at preserving the strong position of the Member States. These provisions relate to subsidiarity and proportionality, national security and the maintenance of law and order.

First, the special principle of subsidiarity in respect of judicial cooperation in criminal matters and police cooperation in Article 69 (61B) TFEU guarantees that national parliaments will ensure that the proposals and legislative initiatives comply with the principle of subsidiarity, in accordance with the formal and strict arrangements laid down by the Protocol on the application of the principles of subsidiarity and proportionality.[68] The explicit reiteration of the principle of subsidiarity shows the concern of the Member States. Nevertheless, given the importance and necessity of

before the entry into force of the Treaty of Lisbon, shall remain the same, including where they have been accepted under Article 35(2) of the said Treaty on European Union.
2. The amendment of an act referred to in paragraph 1 shall entail the applicability of the powers of the institutions referred to in that paragraph as set out in the Treaties with respect to the amended act for those Member States to which that amended act shall apply.
3. In any case, the transitional measure mentioned in paragraph 1 shall cease to have effect five years after the date of entry into force of the Treaty of Lisbon.'

[68] See Art 5(3b) TEU: 'Under the principle of subsidiarity, in areas which do not fall within its exclusive competence, the Union shall act only if and insofar as the objectives of the proposed action cannot be sufficiently achieved by the Member States, either at central level or at regional and local level, but can rather, by reason of the scale or effects of the proposed action, be better achieved at Union level.' Regarding the Protocol on the Application of principles of subsidiarity and proportionality a strict procedure shall protect this principle of subsidiarity: any draft legislative acts shall be shall be justified with regard to the principles of subsidiarity and proportionality and forwarded to national Parliaments. Any national Parliament (or chamber of a national Parliament), within eight weeks, may send a reasoned opinion stating why it considers that the draft in question does not comply with the principle of subsidiarity. Where reasoned opinions on a draft legislative act's non-compliance with the principle of subsidiarity represent at least one quarter of all the votes allocated to the national Parliaments the draft must be reviewed. Furthermore, under the ordinary legislative procedure, where reasoned opinions on the non-compliance of a proposal for a legislative act with the principle of subsidiarity represent at least a simple majority of the votes allocated to the national Parliaments, the proposal must be reviewed. If the Commission chooses to maintain the proposal, it will have, in a reasoned opinion, to justify why it considers that the proposal complies with the principle of subsidiarity. Before concluding the first reading, the European Parliament and the Council shall consider the compatibility with the principle of subsidiarity, and if, by a majority of 55% of the members of the Council or a majority of the votes cast in the European Parliament, the legislator is of the opinion that the proposal is not compatible with the principle of subsidiarity, the legislative proposal shall not be given further consideration. See also Gavin Barrett, '"The king is dead, long live the king": the recasting by the Treaty of Lisbon of the provisions of the Constitutional Treaty concerning national parliaments' (2008) 33 *EL Rev.* 66–84.

European police cooperation dealing with cross-border crimes and terrorism, this is usually not sufficiently achieved by the Member States on their own. And, if 'by reason of the scale or effects of the proposed action' means that Member States cannot act alone; these issues can be achieved better on a European level. Thus the substantive possibilities of the principle of subsidiarity are in practice rather narrow. There will be discussions about the principle of subsidiarity regarding the area of freedom, security and justice, but again there is only a small margin for discussion. Thus the value of the principle of subsidiarity will be very limited in preventing a further integration process in the field of police cooperation. Only with regard to minor and local crimes will the principle of subsidiarity be a useful limit in the field of European police cooperation. The question of the cross-border dimension of major crimes is not relevant because data collections do not distinguish between local and cross-border crimes. Thus, local major crimes, such as murder, will also be part of European police cooperation.

The second provision, which deals with national security, is now placed very prominently in Article 4 (3a)(1) TEU:

> The Union shall respect the equality of Member States before the Treaties as well as their national identities, inherent in their fundamental structures, political and constitutional, inclusive of regional and local self-government. It shall respect their essential State functions, including ensuring the territorial integrity of the State, maintaining law and order and safeguarding national security. In particular, national security remains the sole responsibility of each Member State.

Thus, national security is a matter for the Member States. What is the meaning of this provision, given the purpose and objectives of European police cooperation? European police cooperation is certainly not only about guaranteeing individual security but national security as well. Take combating terrorism as an example: a major objective of European police cooperation is national security.[69] Moreover, intelligence services are already coordinating their activities on a European level.[70] It appears that the only effect of this provision is that there will not be European legislation directly regulating the intelligence services; however indirect consequences for national security through European police cooperation will fall within EU law.

One consequence of declaring national security the sole responsibility of the Member States is that Article 73 (61 F) TFEU gives Member States the possibility of organising forms of cooperation and coordination between

[69] See Nicolas Grief, 'EU law and security' (2007) 32 *EL Rev*. 752, 764–5.

[70] See the Situation Centre at the Council, see Willy Bruggeman, 'A vision on future police cooperation with special focus on Europol', de Zwaan Goudappel (eds), *Freedom, Security and Justice in the European Union: Implementation of the Hague Programme* (n 10 above) 203, 215.

themselves and under their responsibility as they deem appropriate between the competent departments of their administrations responsible for safeguarding national security. Again, the need for cooperation is obvious. The Member States may create international treaties as they did to supplement the original EU activities in the field of police cooperation. But, it is doubtful whether it is possible to exclude the institutions of the EU from this cooperation.

The third provision in Article 72 (61 E) TFEU was transferred, unchanged, from the old provisions of Article 33 TEU and Article 64 TEC. It states: 'This Title shall not affect the exercise of the responsibilities incumbent upon Member States with regard to the maintenance of law and order and the safeguarding of internal security.'[71] The value of this provision is related to the general understanding of the Member States of the EU as sovereign. It prohibits the legislator and possibly the ECJ from extending police cooperation in a way which takes over responsibility for general law and order. Nevertheless it is quite clear that European police cooperation will (in a positive sense) have an effect on the maintenance of internal security and it shall not interfere with the interests of the Member States (in a negative sense).[72] The problems with regard to the allocation of competences are not related to the purpose of this provision.

In conclusion, the approach of European police cooperation shifted from an international towards a more supranational concept. This crucial shift in competences is not limited by the provisions of the TEU or TFEU. Although the limits seem to be concretised with the principle of subsidiarity and in substance, with national security and the maintenance of law and order, the proposed limits are very general and leave a broad field for the further developments of European police cooperation. Moreover, the concept of European police cooperation within the EU will be more flexible within the ordinary legislative procedure and will therefore give the possibility of further cooperation.

To date there have been two main fields of European police cooperation: one is related to data exchange and data processing, the other is dealing with operational actions and measures. The particular developments in these fields, to which we now turn, show the limits of competences within European police cooperation in more detail.

[71] This provision also resembles Art 4 TEU, which states that the EU It shall respect the essential State functions, including maintaining law and order and safeguarding national security.

[72] 'The most convincing interpretation of Art 33 is therefore that it simply confirms that the implementation of EU policing measures is left to the Member States' authorities, particularly as regards coercive measures'. Peers (n 21 above) 505.

VI INTELLIGENCE-LED POLICING

Traditional policing is related to operative action and coercive measures. Police forces respond to imminent danger or prohibit crimes. While, in the past, intelligence- and information-based policing was not very important, this has now changed.[73] Collecting information and data on crimes, criminals and criminal organisations has been one of the major trends in policing over the last 10 years and is seen as important in preventing and solving crimes.[74] The reason for a strengthening of intelligence-led measures is obviously related to the digitalised world. In traditional policing, data exchange was relevant to alerts on persons and property and fingerprints of suspects. However, in a digitalised world the technical possibilities are endless: video surveillance, DNA data or internet control are just three prominent examples of the use of data in police work. Yet a problem arising from these developments is the erosion of the border between intelligence services and police authorities.

While at domestic level, policing has moved from operational measures to greater use of intelligence-led measures, in the EU the reverse is true. The EU started its police cooperation mainly with the exchange of information and is now additionally trying to establish deeper cooperation with regard to operational measures, which does not mean that the importance of intelligence measures is decreasing. Various reasons can explain this development. From an organisational point of view, it is easier to share information than share manpower. From a political viewpoint, the use of force is a central part of state sovereignty. Information is not seen as being that integral to state powers. As shown below, the Member States of the EU have a reservation against a European use of force. In the field of data-related police cooperation the importance of the EU is increasing. From a police perspective, the mutual trust to share information can be established more easily than persuading different police officers to work together in operative action. Furthermore, data-sharing at EU level builds on other networks of information exchange on a transnational and international level, such as Interpol. These developments on intelligence-led policing create enormous problems of legal protection, privacy and control

[73] See James Sheptycki, 'Patrolling the New European (In)Security Field; Organisational Dilemmas and Operational Solutions for Policing the Internal Borders of Europe' (2001) 9 *European Journal of Crime, Criminal Law and Criminal Justice* 144–60, 146: 'Information technology is the motor of organisational change in contemporary policing.'

[74] See Nick Tilley, 'Community policing, problem-oriented policing and intelligence-led policing', in Tim Newburn (ed), *Handbook of Policing* (Cullompton, Willan Publishing, 2003) 311–39. An even further going understanding of intelligence means any information that is related to 'a crime that for a variety of reasons cannot be used in court'. See Paul Swallow, 'Proactive terrorist investigations and the use of intelligence' (2003) 10 *Journal of Financial Crime* 378.

as the legal framework of the EU does not focus on the rule of law questions with regard to police cooperation.

In this growing field of intelligence-based policing the role of the EU is growing in importance. The merging of information from all Member States creates a huge pool of data, which can be used for the purposes of the EU's area of freedom, security and justice. Different steps and institutions have been necessary to improve the EU's data exchange as a major part of European police cooperation. At the European level itself, the European agency Europol is the most famous part of police cooperation.[75] The European Police Office was founded by the Europol Convention 1995[76] and started its full activities on 1 July 1999.[77] According to Article 3 of the Europol Convention, Europol's major tasks are related to the exchange of information.[78] So the main focus of European police cooperation has been data exchange and data analysis. Europol started as the European equivalent of Interpol but managed to improve and is now established with an independent role in the international network of police cooperation. Europol is more than just an instrument for collecting data on suspects;[79] it can also establish working groups to undertake specific analysis of that data.[80] Nevertheless, the full capacity of Europol has still to be developed.[81]

The process of intelligence-led policing is not limited to the European Police Office. The broad approach towards data accumulation can be seen elsewhere. For example, the Schengen Information System (SIS), as a part of the Schengen Agreement, legitimises the collection of police data in the context of the freedom of movement.[82] The growing importance of border safety and border control has led to the establishment of the agency

[75] Peers,(n 21 above) 536, 551.

[76] Convention based on Art K.3 of the Treaty on European Union, on the establishment of a European Police Office (Europol Convention) [2005] OJ C/316/2.

[77] See http://www.europol.europa.eu/index.asp?page=facts. The European Drugs Unit had already started its activities in 1994.

[78] See Art 3: 'Tasks
1. In the framework of its objective pursuant to Art 2(1), Europol shall have the following principal tasks:
(1) to facilitate the exchange of information between the Member States; (2) to obtain, collate and analyse information and intelligence; (3) to notify the competent authorities of the Member States without delay via the national units referred to in Art 4 of information concerning them and of any connections identified between criminal offences; (4) to aid investigations in the Member States by forwarding all relevant information to the national units; (5) to maintain a computerised system of collected information containing data in accordance with Arts 8, 10 and 11 ...'.

[79] Art 8 Europol Convention.

[80] See Art 10 Europol Convention.

[81] See Paul Swallow, 'Proactive terrorist investigations and the use of intelligence' (2003) *Journal of Financial Crime*, 378, 380s.

[82] See Madeleine Colvin, 'The Schengen Information System: a human rights audit' (2001) *European Human Rights Law Review* 271–9.

Frontex[83] and the Information System Visa Information Systems (VIS)[84]. In general, the policing of travellers and migrants includes many possibilities for data collection. The EU agreement with the US regarding fight passenger data is a good example.[85] All passengers who want to fly to the US, have to accept that 19 different categories of data will be collected and may be used by the US Department of Homeland Security for seven years.[86] The proposal to introduce a similar system in Europe has already been made by the European Commission.[87]

The Data Retention Directive 2006/24/EC [2006] OJ L105/54, is another measure which impacts on European police cooperation. Although the directive was introduced as a harmonisation measure, the purpose of the data retention is obvious.[88] The scope of the directive is very broad as the categories of data to be retained are manifold[89] and the retention

[83] Council Reg (EC) 2007/2004 establishing a European Agency for the Management of Operational Cooperation at the External Borders of the Member States of the European Union [2004] OJ L349/1.

[84] See the *2807th Council meeting Justice and Home Affairs in Luxemburg, 12–13 June 2007*, Press Release 10267/07 (Press: 125).

[85] See again the Council Decision 2007/551/CFSP/JHA of 23 July 2007 on the signing, on behalf of the European Union, of an Agreement between the European Union and the United States of America on the processing and transfer of Passenger Name Record (PNR) data by air carriers to the United States Department of Homeland Security (DHS) (2007 PNR Agreement) and the Agreement between the European Union and the United States of America on the processing and transfer of Passenger Name Record (PNR) data by air carriers to the United States Department of Homeland Security (DHS) (2007 PNR Agreement) [2007] OJ L204/16.

[86] The types of EU PNR collected are the following: '1. PNR record locator code; 2. Date of reservation/issue of ticket; 3. Date(s) of intended travel; 4. Name(s); 5. Available frequent flier and benefit information (ie free tickets, upgrades, etc); 6. Other names on PNR, including number of travellers on PNR; 7. All available contact information (including originator information); 8. All available payment/billing information (not including other transaction details linked to a credit card or account and not connected to the travel transaction); 9. Travel itinerary for specific PNR; 10. Travel agency/travel agent; 11. Code share information; 12. Split/divided information; 13. Travel status of passenger (including confirmations and check-in status); 14. Ticketing information, including ticket number, one-way tickets and Automated Ticket Fare Quote; 15. All baggage information; 16. Seat information, including seat number; 17. General remarks including OSI, SSI and SSR information; 18. Any collected APIS (Advanced Passenger Information System) information; 19. All historical changes to the PNR listed in numbers 1 to 18'.

[87] Commission (EC), 'Proposal for a Council framework decision on the use of Passenger Name Record (PNR) for law enforcement purposes' COM (2007) 654 final, 6 November 2007.

[88] See Art 1 Council Directive (EC) 2006/24 on the retention of data generated or processed in connection with the provision of publicly available electronic communications services or of public communications networks and amending Directive 2002/58/EC [2006] OJ L105/54: 'Subject matter and scope. 1. This Directive aims to harmonise Member States' provisions concerning the obligations of the providers of publicly available electronic communications services or of public communications networks with respect to the retention of certain data which are generated or processed by them, in order to ensure that the data are available for the purpose of the investigation, detection and prosecution of serious crime, as defined by each Member State in its national law.'

[89] See Art 5 of the Data Retention Directive.

period is 'not less than six months and not more than two years from the date of the communication'.[90] Its effects on the general human rights situation are dramatic.

Another problematic development results from the Framework Decision 2006/960/JHA of 18 December 2006 on simplifying the exchange of information and intelligence between law enforcement authorities of the Member States. Article 1 defines the objective of the framework decision to 'establish the rules under which Member States' law enforcement authorities may exchange existing information and intelligence effectively and expeditiously for the purpose of conducting criminal investigations or criminal intelligence operations'.[91] This general purpose legitimises broad data exchange.

Finally, the Treaty of Prüm proposes various possibilities of data exchange, especially automated data exchange regarding searching and comparing of DNA profiles[92], searching of fingerprint data[93] and searching of vehicle registration data.[94] Additionally, the contracting parties supply each other with personal data for major (especially sport) events[95] and information in order to prevent terrorist offences.[96]

The intelligence-based policing initiatives within the EU are very broad and not just limited to formal EU law. Informal networks and bodies complement official institutional and functional structures.[97] The European police task force and the situation centre at the Council are prominent examples.[98] While the European police task force is a meeting of the 'heads of the various law-enforcement agencies across the EU, to

[90] Art 6 of the Data Retention Directive.

[91] The definition of 'criminal intelligence operations' in Art 2 of this Directive emphasises the broad approach: 'a procedural stage, not yet having reached the stage of a criminal investigation, within which a competent law enforcement authority is entitled by national law to collect, process and analyse information about crime or criminal activities with a view to establishing whether concrete criminal acts have been committed or may be committed in the future'.

[92] See Art 3,4 Prüm Convention.

[93] See Art 9 Prüm Convention.

[94] See Art 12 Prüm Convention.

[95] See Art 14 Prüm Convention.

[96] Art 16 Prüm Convention. See also Thierry Balzacq, Didier Bigo, Sergio Carrera and Elspeth Guild, 'The Treaty of Prüm and EC Treaty: Two competing models for EU internal security', Thierry Balzacq and Sergio Carrera (eds), *Security versus Freedom? A Challenge for Europe's Future* (Aldershot, Ashgate, 2006) 115–36, 120–23.

[97] 'Well running police co-operation often rests on informal co-operation and personal networks. As in organized crime, never underestimate the importance of personal contacts and networks in the police. Many of these interpersonal networks can be described as loose and flexible. They often consist of police officers that have met at international conferences and meetings and have got acquainted.' Paul Larsson, 'International police co-operation: a Norwegian perspective' (2006) 13 *Journal of Financial Crime* 456, 458.

[98] See Bruggeman,(n 70 above) 203, 215.

exchange information and assist with the development of more spontaneous interaction and closer cooperation',[99] the situation centre is providing the Council with high quality information received from the Member States, such as diplomatic reporting and information from external intelligence services.[100]

The developments outlined above on the extension of data collection and exchange show that the limits of European police cooperation in the field of intelligence-based policing have not yet been reached.[101] This is especially worrying from a human rights point of view.

The debates about the integration of the Europol Convention into the scheme of the third pillar are expected to be finished in June 2008.[102] This step will help Europol to establish its position in a growing network of European intelligence agencies. The next generation of the Schengen Information System, SIS II, will give various new possibilities for data merging.[103] The newly established Visa Information Systems will be connected to the SIS II database. The integration of the Prüm Convention into the third pillar will extend the possibilities of the Treaty to all Member States of the EU. Further initiatives by the Member States or the European Commission are the so-called 'Check the web' Initiative,[104] controlling internet websites, or the Draft Framework Decisions on data protection and on the exchange of information under the principle of availability.[105] The Treaty of Lisbon will make it easier to realise new intelligence-based projects of police cooperation in Europe as the principle of unanimity will not be applied and the ordinary legislative procedures will suffice.

In conclusion, we can see from projects which are already under way that there is an intensive data collection and data exchange process going on in the EU without the necessary degree of proportionality. The new projects described above show steps to intensify this cooperation. So what is left for the Member States? The approval of data exchange is still necessary if most of the data is coming from the Member States. However,

[99] See http://ec.europa.eu/justice_home/fsj/police/chief/fsj_police_task_force_en.htm.

[100] See the 7th Report of the Committee on the European Union of the House of Lords, app 5, http://www.parliament.the-stationery-office.co.uk/pa/ld200203/ldselect/ldeucom/53/5313.htm.

[101] Thierry Balzacq and Sergio Carrera, 'The Hague Programme: The Long Road to Freedom, Security and Justice', in Thierry Balzacq and Sergio Carrera (eds), *Security versus Freedom? A Challenge for Europe's Future* (Aldershot, Ashgate, 2006) 1, 18–20.

[102] See the *2838th Council meeting Justice and Home Affairs in Brussels, 6–7 December 2007*, Press Release 15966/07 (Press:275).

[103] See Steve Peers, 'The Schengen Information System and EC Immigration and Asylum Law' in de Zwaan and Goudappel (eds), *Freedom, Security and Justice in the European Union. Implementation of the Hague Programme* (n 10 above) 172, 182.

[104] Art 36 Committee Note of 29 May 2007, 8457/3/07, REV 3 http://register.consilium.europa.eu/pdf/en/07/st08/st08457-re03.en07.pdf.

[105] Commission (EC), 'Proposal for a Council framework decision on the exchange of information under the principle of availability' COM (2005) 490, 12 October 2005.

the EU started collecting its own data years ago. There appear to be no limits in practice to the EU's competence to act. Most serious crimes have cross-border implications and this will intensify data exchange. The growing automation of data exchange will also have an impact on a deepening of intelligence cooperation in Europe. Finally, the counter-terrorism activities of the EU will give the necessary legitimation for further steps. The limits to intelligence-based police cooperation can be seen only in respect of minor crimes.

VII THE USE OF FORCE/COERCIVE POWERS AND THE LIMITS OF THE EUROPEAN UNION

The state monopoly on coercive measures taken against its citizens is not only part of the general constitutional setting but goes to the fundamental European understanding of the state. These ideas date back to the social treaty of Thomas Hobbes[106] and the concept of sovereignty of Jean Bodin.[107] In the (German) Theory of the State (*Staatsrechtslehre*), Georg Jellinek in particular (State authority, 'Staatsgewalt'),[108] should be mentioned.[109] This understanding of the state is at stake if the other Member States or the authorities of the EU, like Europol, use coercive powers in a Member State.[110]

Thus, the use of coercive measures by the EU or another Member State of the EU is a sensitive question.[111] It is not only a question of how far a sovereign state can accept other entities acting in its territory, but also a question of 'statehood' of the EU. As the EU will gain considerable legislative power in the field of police cooperation with the Lisbon Treaty, the concession of it being able to use coercive measures would mean

[106] Thomas Hobbes, Elementa Philosophica De Cive, 1647, caput IV, 3.

[107] Jean Bodin, Six Books of the Commonwealth (*Les Six Livres de la République*), 1576, I. 8.

[108] Georg Jellinek *Allgemeine Staatslehre* (3rd edn), (Darmstadt, Wissenschaftliche Buchgesellschaft 1959) 394, 406, 408ff, 427, 429ff, 435, 475, 482.

[109] Loader and Walker especially emphasing Max Weber; .see Ian Loader and Neil Walker, *Civilizing Security* (Cambridge, Cambridge University Press, 2007) 26.

[110] See Hartmut Arden, 'Convergence of Policing Policies and Transnational Policing in Europe' (2001) 9 *European Journal of Crime, Criminal Law and Criminal Justice* 99, 111–12.

[111] See Neil Walker, 'In Search of the Area of Freedom, Security and Justice: A Constitutional Odyssey', in Neil Walker (ed), *Europe's Area of Freedom, Security and Justice* (Oxford, Oxford University Press, 2004) 1–37 (19); Stephen Skinner, 'The third pillar Treaty provisions on police cooperation: Has the EU bitten off more than it can chew?' (2002) 8 *Columbia Journal of European Law* 203, 206.

adding another piece of the puzzle in the 'United States of Europe', which the Member States—and the EU citizens—obviously do not want.[112]

The initial point concerning coercive measures can be seen in the Implementing Convention of the Schengen Agreement.[113] It allowed hot pursuit[114] and cross-border observation[115] between the contracting parties in the case of imminent danger.[116] In the case of hot pursuit, the use of coercive power is restricted to stopping the suspect in exceptional cases and detaining the person until the competent domestic authority arrives.[117] Law enforcement bodies from other Member States are not allowed to enter private buildings or other places not accessible to the public.[118] However, legitimate self-defence is not restricted and this is important as pursuing officers are allowed to wear their service weapons.[119]

Article K.2(2a) of the Treaty of Amsterdam provided the legal basis for operational actions of joint investigation teams.[120] The European Council held in Tampere in October 1999 called for joint investigation teams, as foreseen in the Amsterdam Treaty, to be set up without delay. As a first step they were to combat trafficking in drugs and human beings as well as terrorism.[121] The Council Framework Decision on joint investigation teams[122] implemented this aim. Article 1 of the Framework Decision explains the concept of a joint investigation team: 'By mutual agreement, the competent authorities of two or more Member States may set up a joint investigation team for a specific purpose and a limited period ... to carry

[112] See also Neil Walker, 'The pattern of transnational policing', in Tim Newburn (ed.), *Handbook of policing* (Cullompton, Willan Publishing, 2003) 111, 131.

[113] See Convention implementing the Schengen Agreement of 14 June 1985 between the Governments of the States of the Benelux Economic Union, the Federal Republic of Germany and the French Republic on the gradual abolition of checks at their common borders (see the Schengen acquis as referred to in Art 1(2) of Council Decision (EC) 1999/435 of 20 May 1999 [2000] OJ L239/19).

[114] Art 41 of the Convention Implementing the Schengen Agreement.

[115] Art 40 of the Convention Implementing the Schengen Agreement.

[116] See also Peers, (n 21 above) 529ss.

[117] See Art 41(2) (b) Convention Implementing the Schengen Agreement: 'If no request to cease the hot pursuit is made and if the competent local authorities are unable to intervene quickly enough, the pursuing officers may detain the person pursued until the officers of the Contracting Party in whose territory the pursuit is taking place, who must be informed immediately, are able to establish the person's identity or make an arrest.'

[118] See Art 41(5)(c) Implementing Convention of the Schengen Agreement.

[119] Art. 41(5)(e) Implementing Convention of the Schengen Agreement.

[120] Art K.2 (2) TEU in the version of the Amsterdam Treaty: 'The Council shall promote co-operation through Europol and shall in particular, within a period of five years after the date of entry into force of the Treaty of Amsterdam: (a) enable Europol to facilitate and support the preparation, and to encourage the coordination and carrying out, of specific investigative actions by the competent authorities of the Member States, including operational actions of joint teams comprising representatives of Europol in a support capacity.'

[121] See presidency conclusions of the Tampere European Council 15 and 16 October 1999, 'IX. Stepping up co-operation against crime'; see also Occhipinti,(n 28 above) 79.

[122] Council Framework Decision 2002/465/JHA of 13 June 2002 on joint investigation teams [2002] OJ L162/1.

out criminal investigations in one or more of the Member States.' Under the leadership of the Member State, in which the investigation takes place, team members of other states can be entrusted by the leader of the team to take certain investigative measures. The competent authorities of the hosting Member State have to approve the measure.[123] Thus, it depends on the agreement between the Member States as to which kind of coercive powers can be enforced by an officer of another Member State.[124]

Although there were no clear provisions by which investigative measures can be enforced by other Member States, the purpose of the Framework Decision was still quite clear: 'criminal investigations'. The Treaty of Prüm takes the next step concerning the use of force by police officers from other Member States. Chapter 5 on 'Other forms of cooperation' (Articles 24–26) makes broad provision for joint operations. Article 24 of the Prüm Convention is quite clear about the extension of the concept: 'In order to step up police cooperation, the competent authorities ... in maintaining public order and security and preventing criminal offences, introduce joint patrols and other joint operations in which designated officers ... participate in operations within a Contracting Party's territory.'[125] Thus, the objectives for establishing police cooperation are no longer restricted.

Regarding the use of coercive powers the concept of the Prüm Convention is very clear and broad:

> Each contracting party may, as a host State, in compliance with its own national law, with the seconding State's consent, confer sovereign powers on other Contracting Parties' officers involved in joint operations or, in so far as the host State's law permits, allow other Contracting Parties' officers to exercise their sovereign powers in accordance with the seconding State's law. Such sovereign powers may be exercised only under the guidance and, as a rule, in the presence of officers from the host State.[126]

[123] The joint investigation team has the following structure: The leader of the team shall be a representative of the competent authority participating in criminal investigations from the Member State in which the team operates. The team shall carry out its operations in accordance with the law of the Member State in which it operates. The members of the team shall carry out their tasks under the team leader, taking into account the conditions set by their own authorities in the agreement on setting up the team. The Seconded members, these are the members of the joint investigation team from another state than the Member State of the joint investigation team in which the team operates, shall be entitled to be present when investigative measures are taken in the Member State of operation. Seconded members of the joint investigation team may, in accordance with the law of the Member State where the team operates, be entrusted by the leader of the team with the task taking certain investigative measures where this has been approved by the competent authorities of the Member State of operation and the seconding Member State. See also José Antonio Farah Lopes de Lima, 'Europol as the Director and Coordinator of the Joint Investigation Teams' (2006–2007) 9 *Cambridge Yearbook of European Legal Studies*314–28.

[124] See in detail Conny Rijken and Gert Vermeulen (eds), *Joint Investigation teams in the European Union. From Theory to Practice* (The Hague, TMC Asser Press, 2006).

[125] Art 24 (1) Prüm Convention.

[126] Art 24 Abs 2 Prüm Convention.

Thus sovereign powers are a broad term. Furthermore, the Treaty also allows the exercising of specific police powers established in the police Acts of the seconding state in the host state—of course under the restriction that the host state's law permits such a concept. The general provisions in Article 28 of the Prüm Convention supplement the general concept, which governs the use of arms, ammunition and equipment:

> Officers from a Contracting Party who are involved in a joint operation within another Contracting Party's territory may wear their own national uniforms there. They may carry such arms, ammunition and equipment as they are allowed to under the seconding State's national law.

Paragraph 2 provides

> The arms, ammunition and equipment listed in Annex 2 [these are authorised firearms, pepper sprays and tear gas] may be used only in legitimate defence of officers themselves or of others. The host State's officer in actual charge of the operation may in individual cases, in compliance with national law, give permission for arms, ammunition and equipment to be used for purposes going beyond that specified in the first sentence. The use of arms, ammunition and equipment shall be governed by the host State's law.

Thus, with the Treaty of Prüm a general concept of the transnational use of force is made. The basic principles of the operative measures are determined by the establishment of a joint agreement between the members of the specific joint operation and the leadership of the hosting state.[127]

With the integration of the Prüm Convention into the EU this concept of joint operations will be transferred into the third pillar and with the Treaty of Lisbon into the general part of EU law. This means that the EU will give a general framework to the transnational use of force in police cooperation. Presuming the agreement in the particular joint operation, the integration of other police forces in special or difficult cases can be a standard procedure.

The Treaty of Lisbon is adopting the existing developments regarding the use of force in European police cooperation. The possibilities regarding operative measures are extended. On an institutional basis a new standing committee is to be set up, which is to ensure that 'operational cooperation on internal security is promoted and strengthened within the Union'.[128] Article 88 (69G) TFEU defines Europol's mission as 'to support and strengthen action by the Member States' police authorities and other law

[127] See Art 44 Prüm Convention and Art 14 of the Implementing Agreement to the Prüm Convention.

[128] Art 71 (61 D) TFEU. See Cyrille Fijnaut, 'The Hague Programme and Police Cooperation between the Member States of the EU' in de Zwaan Goudappel (eds), *Freedom, Security and Justice in the European Union. Implementation of the Hague Programme* (n 10 above) 233, 235, 241.

enforcement services and their mutual cooperation in preventing and combating serious crime affecting two or more Member States, terrorism and forms of crime which affect a common interest covered by a Union policy'.

Only a vestigial element of the principle of unanimity remains in Article 87 (69F)(3) TFEU on the establishment of measures concerning operational cooperation. Nevertheless, in case of the absence of unanimity in the Council, a group of at least nine Member States may request the establishment of 'enhanced cooperation on the basis of the draft measures concerned, they shall notify the European Parliament, the Council and the Commission accordingly'.

The use of coercive measures within the police cooperation between the Member States is on the way to being well established, but what about the officers at Europol itself? The Treaty of Lisbon makes it quite clear: the last sentence of Article 88 (69G) TFEU states: 'The application of coercive measures shall be the exclusive responsibility of the competent national authorities.' Nevertheless, Europol has become increasingly important in operational measures in recent years. After the enactment of the Council Framework Decision on Joint Investigation Teams the Europol Convention was adopted and included the possibility that Europol officers could join these joint investigation teams.[129]

The Lisbon Treaty goes further: according to Article 88 (69G) TFEU, the European Parliament and Council are to determine Europol's structure, operation, field of action and tasks. These tasks also include:

> 'the coordination, organisation and implementation of investigative and operational action carried out jointly with the Member States' competent authorities or in the context of joint investigative teams, where appropriate in liaison with Eurojust [..] Any operational action by Europol must be carried out in liaison and in agreement with the authorities of the Member State or States whose territory is concerned.

And, as already mentioned, 'the application of coercive measures shall be the exclusive responsibility of the competent national authorities'. This means that Europol can play a much more active role than before. Europol can lead investigations, not only from the perspective of coordination but also from an operational perspective. Full participation is possible; the only restriction is that Europol officers are not allowed to use coercive measures, of course, with the exception of self-defence. The aspect of self-defence might be the starting point for further developments. If Europol officers can participate fully in operative action it may be necessary to

[129] Annette Herz, 'The role of Europol and Eurojust in Joint Investigation Teams' in Rijken and Vermeulen (eds), *Joint Investigation teams in the European Union. From Theory to Practice* (n 124 above) 159, 165.

support them with better equipment. Thus, the borders between a strict prohibition on the use of force and the necessity of coercive measures in operational action will be weakened.

We have not yet arrived at the point of a European police force. However, the speed of change is fast and the level of cooperation reached in the Prüm Convention seemed impossible only a few years ago. The integration of police cooperation into the first pillar involves a dynamic which cannot yet be anticipated.[130] However, the Member States will be the promoter of the antecedent developments. The rapid border intervention teams provides a good example of the speed of change. They were established in the context of Frontex, the European agency for the management of operational cooperation at the external borders of the Member States of the EU.[131] These intervention teams are composed of domestic border guards (the rRapid Pool).[132] So the Member States are building up intervention forces under the leadership of a European agency. Putting this development together with the cooperation already established between special police forces in Europe, then a possible concept of a European special police force becomes clear.

In November 2007 the Council Decision on the improvement of cooperation between the special intervention units of the Member States of the EU in crisis situations[133] was adopted. This is already a substantial step within European police cooperation towards a joint counter-terrorist action unit or force. The Council Decision is based on the informal Atlas network,[134] which brings European special intervention units together, especially in the field of joint training and communication exchange. A member can 'ask to be assisted by a special intervention unit of another Member State with a view to dealing with a crisis situation.[135] A Member

[130] The increasing cooperation between Europol and Eurojust could also be seen as a possible starting point for further developments. See Art 85 (69D) TFEU 'Eurojust's mission shall be to support and strengthen coordination and cooperation between national investigating and prosecuting authorities in relation to serious crime affecting two or more Member States or requiring a prosecution on common bases, on the basis of operations conducted and information supplied by the Member States' authorities and by Europol.'

[131] Council Reg (EC) 863/2007 of 11 July 2007 establishing a mechanism for the creation of Rapid Border Intervention Teams and amending Council Regulation (EC) 2007/2004 as regards that mechanism and regulating the tasks and powers of guest officers [2007] OJ L199/30.

[132] See Art 4 Reg (EC) 863/2007.

[133] See the Initiative of the Republic of Austria with a view to adopting a Council Decision on the improvement of cooperation between the special intervention units of the Member States of the European Union in crisis situations [2006] OJ C/321/45; see also the *2827th Council meeting Justice and Home Affairs in Brussels, 8–9 November 2007*, Press Release 14617/07 (Press:253).

[134] See also Ludo Block, 'Europe's Emerging Counter-Terrorism Elite: The ATLAS Network' (2007) *5 Terrorism Monitor* 5, 10–12.

[135] The definition of crisis-situation is very general; see Art 2 No 2 of the initiated Council Decision [2006] OJ C/321/45: '"crisis situation" shall mean any man-made situation in a

State may accept or refuse such a request or may propose a different kind of assistance.' The rules are quite general and allow flexible interactions:

> In the case of action on the territory of the requesting Member State, officers of the assisting special intervention unit shall: (a) be authorised to act in a supporting capacity on the territory of the requesting Member State; (b) operate under the responsibility and direction of the requesting Member State and in accordance with the law of the requesting Member State; (c) operate within the limits of their powers under their national law.[136]

Taking both provisions together, a joint intervention force can be built up very quickly. The step towards a European special intervention unit is not far away any more. The only thing missing is giving Europol the status of a permanent headquarter with competences to lead the operations.

The creation of European agencies has already shown that the EU is not only focusing on legislation. From the very beginning, the European Commission had executive powers. As the legislative powers were elaborated over the decades the system of executive powers in the EU has been differentiated. The transnational use of force will be the paradigm example of mutual cooperation between the Member States. A supranational use of force will still be connected to the Member States. The old concept of a state monopoly on the use of force never existed in a pure form. The development of a supranational concept of the use of force came along with the changed legislative landscape. Still the limits on the use of coercive powers in the EU is and will be that European officers itself are not allowed to use force on their own.

VIII ARE THERE ANY LIMITS LEFT?

The description of limits on cooperation of the EU with the Member States and the development of the limits within European police cooperation shows a dynamic picture where the ECJ has no significant role. Thus, are there any limits left on the competences of the EU? The answer can be given by reference to the principle of subsidiarity. There are criminal matters of small and local impact. These will remain in the competence of the Member States, simply because Member States can do it better. Nevertheless, in all crimes which have an organised or cross-border element, the EU is potentially involved. The reason for this is evident. The Member States cannot adequately deal with such crimes alone. Thus, European police cooperation at EU level raises legislative issues, like creating institutional structures, harmonising conditions and providing

Member State presenting a serious direct physical threat to persons or institutions in that Member State, in particular hostage-taking, hijacking and similar incidents.'

[136] Art 3 of the initiated Council Decision [2006] OJ C/321/45.

cooperation. European police cooperation in cross-border crime will also deal with enforcement, data exchange and joint operative action as well as joint action/investigative teams. The European police cooperation will get information and coordination from the European Police Office, Europol.

This is a clear development within the limits of the subsidiarity principle. The legislative aspect is quite predictable. The EU will increase its fundamental impact on the Member State legislation in the field policing by institutionalising, harmonising and establishing mutual recognition.

The big question on limits in European police cooperation remains the enforcement question: 'European police vs police cooperation'. Can Europol investigate on its own, receiving its own data? Can Europol have its own police force without the involvement of the authorities of the Member States? Should Europol have the possibility of using force on its own?[137] A possible answer could be: 'In principle, no'. This is not the European way. The concept of the EU is different. The enforcement is up to the Member States. Europol might get some coordinative leading competence and would then have to work together with national police forces. There might be a European police unit, but consisting of Member States' specialised units. The European police will remain based on cooperation in the next decades.

To avoid 'European statehood', European police cooperation will lead to a European level creation of checks and balances between the Member States and the Union. The one will not act without the other. The more European police cooperation is institutionalised, the more active the use of force (because of the need in practice) will be possible. At the moment, the Member States have to get used to foreign units from other Member States in their countries first.

The final question on the limits of a European police cooperation is not related to competence but to the rule of law.[138] The big challenge will not be the allocation of powers within European police cooperation but to ensure adequate legal protection. To create an area of freedom, security and justice, it is not enough to enable European police cooperation; there must also be legal provisions, judicial protection and the effective application of human rights.[139] The speed of developments in European police cooperation has not been matched by the rule of law within the third pillar.

[137] See, eg Bruggeman,(n 70 above) 203–20 (219s); Peers(n 21 above) 562.

[138] See Sionaidh Douglas-Scott, 'The rule of law in the European Union—putting the security into the area of freedom, security and justice' (2004) 29 *EL Rev.* 219–42.

[139] See, eg Susie Alegre and Marisa Leaf, 'Criminal law and fundamental rights in the European Union: moving towards closer cooperation' (2003) *European Human Rights Law Review* 325, 332.

7

Expanding the Frontiers of Union Citizenship by Dismantling the Territorial Boundaries of the National Welfare States?

MICHAEL DOUGAN*

I INTRODUCTION

WELFARE LAW IS one of those intriguing fields where EU regulatory power is relatively weak, and such binding secondary measures as do exist focus not on the harmonisation of national laws but on their coordination, yet the Member State's duty to respect the free movement obligations derived from the Treaty itself manages to exert an increasingly profound influence on the exercise of domestic competence and the character of national welfare provision. Clearly, lying at the outer limits of Community competence is emphatically *not* the same as nestling safe within some core of Member State sovereignty. This chapter will illustrate that proposition by examining the impact of Union citizenship on the spatial identity of the national welfare states.

It need hardly be recalled that, in a world of limited resources, there is an inherent need for each state to establish the criteria for membership of, and exclusion from, its welfare society; or that, in Western Europe, two of the fundamental criteria traditionally used to identify the welfare-ins from the welfare-outs are nationality and territoriality.[1] The limitation of certain

* This paper is based on the law as it stood on 1 February 2008. It draws upon presentations at the Universities of Oxford, Cambridge and Birmingham, and at the EUSA Biennial Conference (Montreal). I am very grateful to participants for their useful discussions and suggestions. I am particularly indebted to Eleanor Spaventa, Derrick Wyatt and Terri Givens for their invaluable comments on earlier drafts.

[1] Especially in the case of non-contributory benefits and services paid for out of general taxation. See further, eg G Vonk, 'Migration, Social Security and the Law: Some European Dilemmas' [2002] *European Journal of Social Security* 315; M Dougan and E Spaventa,

social rights to own nationals reflects the close interrelationship between the welfare state and the nation state—whereby the community of interests derived from shared national identity provides much of the moral force required to justify the redistribution of wealth through social security and other welfare benefits. That same sense of community underlies the traditional restriction of certain social rights to those resident within the domestic territory: citizens who chose to go abroad, and no longer share in the national community—or for that matter, pay taxes to the national exchequer, or submit themselves to supervision by the national authorities—forfeit the expectation of welfare support from their country of origin. As Halfmann has observed:

> the concepts of equality and solidarity associated with the modern welfare state cannot be understood without the original restriction of welfare state policies to the members of the nation.... welfare policies are meant to impose a territorial criterion on the politics of inclusion in the political system [including] the attempts of the nation state to restrict the welfare state benefits to its citizens or to demand the consumption of the benefits on the state territory.[2]

Community law has, quite consciously, set out to deconstruct these twin criteria of nationality and territoriality—originally only in the case of economic migration by workers and self-employed persons, but increasingly also in the case of economically inactive persons by virtue of their status as Union citizens. Most legal scholarship has focused on the challenge by Community law to the Member State's criterion of nationality: there is an extensive body of legislation, case law and literature on the residency and equal treatment rights of migrant Community nationals within their host state, including the issues surrounding access to and the consequences of drawing upon welfare benefits and other forms of public support.[3] From that *acquis*, it is clear that, under Community law, an economic contribution to the host society must be recognised, in principle, as a valid ticket for entry into the national solidaristic community.[4] More

'Wish You Weren't Here ... New Models of Social Solidarity in the European Union' in M Dougan and E Spaventa (eds), *Social Welfare and EU Law* (Oxford, Hart Publishing, 2005); M Ferrera, 'Towards an "Open" Social Citizenship? The New Boundaries of Welfare in the European Union' in G de Búrca (ed), *EU Law and the Welfare State* (Oxford, Oxford University Press, 2005); H Verschueren, 'European (Internal) Migration as an Instrument for Defining the Boundaries of National Solidarity Systems' (2007) 9 *European Journal of Migration and Law* 307.

[2] J Halfmann, 'Welfare State and Territory' in M Bommes and A Geddes (eds), *Immigration and Welfare: Challenging the Borders of the Welfare State* (London, Routledge, 2000) 41.

[3] See further, eg A P van der Mei, *Free Movement of Persons within the European Community: Cross-Border Access to Public Benefits* (Oxford, Hart Publishing, 2003).

[4] As regards resident migrant workers, any effective and genuine economic activity entitles the claimant to seek equal treatment in the field of social benefits: see, eg Case 249/83 *Hoeckx* [1985] ECR 973; Case C-237/94 *O'Flynn* [1996] ECR I-2617; *cf* Case 53/81 *Levin*

recently, as regards economically inactive migrants, Union citizenship, combined with a tangible shared experience between the individual and his/her host society, has become another legitimate gateway into membership of the domestic welfare community.[5] On all fronts, the nationality threshold has been rolled back to a greater extent than ever before.

The question of how far the Treaty free movement provisions in general, and Union citizenship in particular, might challenge the territoriality criterion for membership of the national welfare society has been rather less well explored. If anything, it has been suggested that, thanks to the emphasis on migrant integration into the host society through evidence of shared experience such as previous and continuing residence, the territorial basis of the national welfare states actually emerges all the stronger.[6] This paper argues otherwise. We begin by summarising briefly the treatment of national territorial restrictions under the Community secondary legislation governing cross-border social security coordination, then outlining in general terms the impact on territoriality of the primary Treaty provisions. The latter includes not only the rather limited opportunities for greater exportation provided by the general principle of non-discrimination on grounds of nationality, but also the more far-reaching implications of the case law on non-discriminatory barriers to movement, which has now been extended to catch refusals to export by the competent domestic authorities. Against that background, it will be argued that the Court has launched a conceptual transformation in the territorial identity of the national welfare state. However, the full implications of this new legal framework remain to be worked out; to that end, subsequent sections will explore two of the main normative arguments that Community law should actively promote the greater exportation of national welfare benefits, and conversely, consider another group of factors which might persuade the Court to adopt a more restrained attitude towards exportation.

[1982] ECR 1035; Case 139/85 *Kempf* [1986] ECR 1741. However, as regards non-resident frontier workers, the Court seems to accept that the host state may require the claimant to demonstrate a sufficiently substantial economic activity within its territory, before granting access to certain social benefits: see Case C-213/05 *Geven* (Judgment of 18 July 2007); *cf* Case C-212/05 *Hartmann* (Judgment of 18 July 2007).

[5] As regards residency, consider, eg Case C-184/99 *Grzelczyk* [2001] ECR I-6193; Case C-413/99 *Baumbast* [2002] ECR I-7091. As regards equal treatment, consider, eg Case C-184/99 *Grzelczyk* [2001] ECR I-6193; Case C-138/02 *Collins* [2004] ECR I-2703; Case C-209/03 *Bidar* [2005] ECR I-2119. See now the detailed provisions on residency and equal treatment contained in Directive 2004/38 [2004] OJ L158/77.

[6] See further, eg G Davies, 'Any Place I Hang My Hat? Or: Residence is the New Nationality' (2005) 11 *European Law Journal* 43; A P van der Mei, 'Union Citizenship and the "De-Nationalisation" of the Territorial Welfare State' (2005) 7 *European Journal of Migration and Law* 203.

II NATIONAL TERRITORIAL RESTRICTIONS: AN OUTLINE OF THE MAIN COMMUNITY LAW PRINCIPLES

A The Community Coordination Regime

Territoriality may well be fundamental to the national welfare state, but it has never been absolute: well before the signing of the Treaty of Rome, international agreements provided the framework for the limited exportation of benefits between various European countries.[7] Nevertheless, Community law—in particular, through the social security coordination regime originally contained in Regulation 3,[8] now Regulation 1408/71[9] and shortly to be Regulation 883/2004[10]—has progressively developed the idea that a Member State cannot cease to pay social security benefits to its own workers and self-employed persons who decide to move to another country in pursuit of an economic activity.[11] However, there are two categories of cases in which exportation pursuant to the coordination regime is limited or precluded altogether.

The first concerns situations excluded from the scope of the coordination regime. In particular, Regulation 1408/71 is limited in its personal scope: it covers (primarily) persons insured under a national social security system either as a worker, a self-employed person or a student; it excludes persons insured under other types of social security scheme, or not insured at all.[12] Moreover, Regulation 1408/71 is also limited in its material scope: it covers only social security benefits provided for by legislation and linked to one of the enumerated contingencies; it excludes (for example) social assistance payments, war benefits, supplementary social security schemes such as occupational pensions, and social security benefits not linked to one of the listed social risks.[13] To a certain extent, this problem will be ameliorated by the entry into force of Regulation 883/2004: the personal scope of the coordination system will be extended to cover all persons insured under a national social security scheme; the material scope will be

[7] See further, eg F Pennings, *Introduction to European Social Security Law* (The Hague, Kluwer Law International, 2001) ch 2; V Paskalia, *Free Movement, Social Security and Gender in the EU* (Oxford, Hart Publishing, 2007) ch 1.

[8] OJ 30 of 16 December 1958.

[9] Last consolidated text published at [1997] OJ L28/1.

[10] [2004] OJ L200/1.

[11] See further, eg R Cornelissen, 'The Principle of Territoriality and the Community Regulations on Social Security' (1996) 33 *Common Market Law Review* 439; DS Martinsen, 'Social Security Regulation in the EU: The De-Territorialisation of Welfare?' in G de Búrca (ed), *EU Law and the Welfare State* (see n 1 above).

[12] For example, Case C-411/98 *Ferlini* [2000] ECR I-8081. See further Pennings, (n 7 above) ch 6.

[13] For example, Case C-249/83 *Hoeckx* [1985] ECR 973; Case C-386/02 *Baldinger* [2004] ECR I-8411. See further Pennings (n 7 above) ch 7.

amended so as also to catch early retirement payments and paternity benefits.[14] However, although a broader range of situations will thus soon be able to benefit from the principle of exportation, the new Regulation will still not cover everyone entitled to welfare support, and certainly not every type of welfare benefit offered by the Member States.

Secondly, as regards situations covered by the coordination regime, it is well known that Regulation 1408/71 provides for the exportation of numerous benefits between Member States. For example, under Article 10, old age cash benefits, invalidity benefits, pensions for accidents at work and occupational diseases and death grants shall not be subject to any reduction or withdrawal by reason of the fact that the recipient resides in another Member State.[15] However, in respect of certain other benefits, the coordination system itself imposes various limitations on the principle of exportation. Consider the relatively restrictive system applicable to unemployment benefits: exportation to the host state is limited to a period of three months, and subject to strict procedural conditions, including a forfeiture rule whereby the claimant will lose all further entitlement to benefits in the home country if he or she fails to return within that three month period.[16] Another illustration concerns special non-contributory cash benefits, which are not subject to the principle of exportation at all, entitlement being explicitly restricted to the claimant's state of habitual residence.[17] Such specific limitations on the exportation of benefits as contained in Regulation 1408/71 will be carried over (with certain minor amendments) into Regulation 883/2004.[18]

B The Primary Treaty Provisions

Viewed in isolation, the Community coordination regime thus offers extensive but hardly comprehensive opportunities for the exportation of welfare benefits across the Member States. In recent years, however, the legal framework for addressing the territorial basis of the national welfare

[14] See further, eg F Pennings, 'Inclusion and Exclusion of Persons and Benefits in the New Coordination Regulation' in M Dougan and E Spaventa (eds), *Social Welfare and EU Law* (Oxford, Hart Publishing, 2005).

[15] See also provisions such as Art 73 Reg 1408/71 on family benefits (eg Cases C-245/94 and C-312/94 *Hoever and Zachow* [1996] ECR I-4895; Case C-333/00 *Maaheimo* [2002] ECR I-10087); and Art 19(1)(b) Reg 1408/71 on cash sickness benefits (eg Case C-160/96 *Molenaar* [1998] ECR I-880; Case C-215/99 *Jauch* [2001] ECR I-1901).

[16] See Art 69 Reg 1408/71. For example, Case C-215/00 *Rydergård* [2002] ECR I-1817; Case 41/79 *Testa* [1980] ECR 1979.

[17] See Art 10a Reg 1408/71. Eg Case C-20/96 *Snares* [1997] ECR I-6057; Case C-154/05 *Kersbergen-Lap* [2006] ECR I-6249. For these purposes, habitual residence is defined by Community criteria, eg Case C-90/97 *Swaddling* [1999] ECR I-1075.

[18] See further, eg F Pennings, 'Inclusion and Exclusion of Persons and Benefits in the New Coordination Regulation' (see n 14 above).

states has changed radically: qualifications to the possibility of exportation, whether domestic or Community in origin, are now exposed to increasing judicial scrutiny. The legal basis for this heightened review is the Treaty itself, under which territorial restrictions are treated as either a breach of the principle of equal treatment on grounds of nationality or a non-discriminatory barrier to the free movement of persons.

(i) Equal Treatment on Grounds of Nationality

The Court has long been prepared to overcome certain of the limitations on the scope of application of the coordination regime, in particular, by permitting claimants residing *within* the host state to rely instead on the general Treaty provisions guaranteeing equal treatment in the sphere of social security. Thus, an individual falling outside the personal scope of Regulation 1408/71 may still be able to claim welfare benefits as a migrant worker relying on Article 7(2) Regulation 1612/68,[19] Article 39 EC and/or Article 12 EC;[20] or as a migrant Union citizen relying on Articles 18 and 12 EC.[21] Similarly, certain benefits falling outside the material scope of the Regulation might still be claimed under other legal bases by migrant workers,[22] and migrant Union citizens.[23] However, while the Treaty free movement provisions have proved adept at overcoming nationality barriers for the benefit of migrants unable to rely on Regulation 1408/71, the principle of equal treatment seems less capable of addressing the territorial barriers facing claimants residing *outside* the relevant Member State—certainly as compared to the principle of exportation contained in the coordination regime proper.

To be more precise, the prohibition of discrimination on grounds of nationality may lead to recognition of a limited right to export welfare benefits in two specific categories of situation.[24] The first concerns frontier workers: a claimant employed in Member State A but living in Member State B may challenge Member State A's refusal to pay welfare benefits on the grounds of non-residence, since such a refusal amounts to indirect discrimination against migrant workers which must be objectively justified.[25] In *Geven*, for example, a Dutch claimant living in the Netherlands

[19] For example, Case C-310/91 *Schmid* [1993] ECR I-3011 (prior to the decision in Case C-308/93 *Cabanis-Issarte* [1996] ECR I-2097).

[20] For example, Case C-411/98 *Ferlini* [2000] ECR I-8081.

[21] For example, Case C-85/96 *María Martínez Sala* [1998] ECR I-2691.

[22] For example, Case C-249/83 *Hoeckx* [1985] ECR 973; Case C-43/99 *Leclere* [2001] ECR I-4265.

[23] For example, Case C-184/99 *Grzelczyk* [2001] ECR I-6193.

[24] Besides the specific rules on educational support for the children of migrant workers resulting from Art 12 Reg 1612/68: see, eg Case C-308/89 *di Leo* [1990] ECR I-4185; Case C-7/94 *Lubor Gaal* [1995] ECR I-1031.

[25] For example, Case C-337/97 *Meeusen* [1999] ECR I-3289.

but working in Germany and who fell outside the personal scope of Regulation 1408/71 was nevertheless able to rely on Article 7(2) Regulation 1612/68 to challenge Germany's refusal to pay child-raising allowances to non-resident workers who were engaged in only 'minor employment'.[26] The second situation concerns ex-workers: such individuals may challenge a refusal by their former host state to continue providing social advantages even after ceasing their economic activity and transferring residence from the territory, provided the relevant benefit can be considered intrinsically linked to the claimant's previous contract of employment (for example, as with a special statutory redundancy payment).[27] Beyond those two situations, however, the Court has held that the general principle of equal treatment provided for under the Treaty guarantees equal access to social advantages only whilst the claimant is pursing an effective economic activity within the territory of the relevant state; it does not transmute into a general right to export social advantages from that territory, after the claimant has ceased to qualify as a worker or self-employed person there.[28]

More recently, the question has arisen whether the same principles can be extended beyond cases falling outside the scope of application of Regulation 1408/71, so as to benefit even individuals whose situation falls within the coordination regime—permitting such claimants effectively to ignore the territorial restrictions sanctioned by the Community legislature itself, by relying directly on other provisions of Community law prohibiting discrimination on grounds of nationality, albeit still in only limited categories of situation, that is either as frontier workers claiming indirect discrimination by their state of employment, or as ex-workers seeking the payment of benefits intrinsically linked to their former contract of employment

The Court established, in cases such as *Commission v Luxembourg*, that the same situation can indeed fall within the scope of both Regulation 1408/71 and Regulation 1612/68.[29] However, Advocate General Geelhoed has argued that, where the two measures might otherwise reach different results on the same facts, Article 42(2) Regulation 1612/68 expressly provides that Regulation 1408/71 should take precedence.[30] The Court managed to avoid adopting a firm stance on this issue in cases such as

[26] Case C-213/05 *Geven* (Judgment of 18 July 2007). See also Case C-212/05 *Hartmann* (Judgment of 18 July 2007).

[27] For example, Case C-57/96 *Meints* [1997] ECR I-6689.

[28] For example, Case C-43/99 *Leclere* [2001] ECR I-4265; Case C-33/99 *Fahmi* [2001] ECR I-2415.

[29] Case C-111/91 *Commission v Luxembourg* [1993] ECR I-817.

[30] Case C-213/05 *Geven* (Opinion of 28 September 2006; Judgment of 18 July 2007), paras 30–1 Opinion; Case C-212/05 *Hartmann* (Opinion of 28 September; Judgment of 18 July 2007), para 50 Opinion.

Leclere,[31] but the ruling in *Collins* did suggest that a migrant Union citizen seeking employment within another Member State could rely on Article 39(2) EC so as to challenge a 'habitual residence' test for access to benefits, even though the payment in question was a special non-contributory [cash] benefit and the residency requirement was authorised under Regulation 1408/71.[32] That approach was extended beyond challenges to the competent state's nationality restrictions by resident claimants, so as also to cover challenges to its territoriality restrictions by non-resident citizens, in the more recent case of *Hendrix*: just because a Dutch benefit for disabled young people was listed as a special non-contributory [cash] benefit under Regulation 1408/71, and under the coordination regime could thus be reserved by the competent state to individuals living within its territory, did not prevent a frontier worker from claiming that national legislation implementing the disputed residency requirement nevertheless amounted to indirect discrimination in breach of Article 7(2) Regulation 1612/68 and Article 39(2) EC which had to be objectively justified.[33]

(ii) Non-discriminatory Barriers to Movement

The principle of equal treatment on grounds of nationality can therefore generate a right to exportation—albeit in favour of relatively limited categories of claimants—both as regards situations falling outside the scope of the coordination regime (as in *Geven*) and even in respect of benefits subject to certain restrictive provisions under Regulation 1408/71 itself (as in *Hendrix*). However, the same is now true of a potentially far wider range of national territorial limitations, thanks to the case law on non-discriminatory barriers to movement.[34]

It will be recalled that, in the early 1990s, the Court in rulings such as *Terhoeve* adopted an expansive interpretation of the Treaty provisions on the economic migration of workers and self-employed persons so as to create the new principle that Member States may not penalise their own nationals for having exercised their right to free movement across the EU, by providing less favourable treatment than that afforded to their own

[31] Case C-43/99 *Leclere* [2001] ECR I-4265.

[32] Case C-138/02 *Collins* [2004] ECR I-2703. See further, eg M Dougan, 'The Court Helps Those Who Help Themselves ... The Legal Status of Migrant Workseekers Under Community Law in the Light of the *Collins* Judgment' [2005] *European Journal of Social Security* 7.

[33] Case C-287/05 *Hendrix* (Judgment of 11 September 2007).

[34] We need not get involved, for present purposes, in the debate about whether such case law is better seen as discrimination, though on grounds of movement rather than nationality. See further, eg E Spaventa, 'Seeing the Wood Despite the Trees? On the Scope of Union Citizenship and Its Constitutional Effects' (2008) 45 *CML Rev* 13.

nationals who chose to remain at home.[35] The same principle was then extended to Article 18 EC, in the context of the free movement of Union citizens for non-economic purposes, by the ruling in *Elsen*.[36] Even though it is now likely that a claimant such as *Elsen* would be treated as a frontier worker under Article 39 EC,[37] the principle that non-discriminatory barriers to movement are caught by Article 18 EC is well-established in the case law.[38]

For present purposes, the barrier to movement principle raised two inter-linked questions. First, would a Member State's refusal to permit the exportation of welfare benefits from its territory also be caught by the *Terheove/Elsen* case law? After all, territorial welfare restrictions clearly reward those who chose to remain in the home state, and have the potential to dissuade others from exercising their right to free movement abroad. In principle, they seem to fall squarely within the economy of the *Terhoeve/Elsen* jurisprudence. Secondly, could such a refusal to permit the exportation of welfare benefits be challenged even where it is specifically sanctioned by Community legislation: either in a negative sense, because the situation is excluded from the scope of the coordination regime; or in a positive sense, based on the restrictive provisions contained in Regulation 1408/71 (for example) as regards unemployment benefits or special non-contributory cash benefits?

The Court has now delivered a sufficient critical mass of case law to enable us to construct at least partial answers to these questions: not only the relatively well-known health care rulings such as *Peerbooms* and *Müller-Fauré*;[39] but also more recent—though equally important—judgments such as *Tas-Hagen* and *De Cuyper*.[40] Thus, in *Tas-Hagen*, a Dutch national living in Spain successfully relied on Article 18 EC so as to

[35] Case C-18/95 *Terhoeve* [1999] ECR I-345. Also, eg Case C-19/92 *Kraus* [1993] ECR I-1663; Case C-302/98 *Sehrer* [2000] ECR I-4585; Case C-109/04 *Kranemann* [2005] ECR I-2421. *Cf* Case C-190/98 *Graf* [2000] ECR I-493. For critical discussion of the case law, see E Spaventa, *Free Movement of Persons in the European Union: Barriers to Movement in their Constitutional Context* (The Hague, Kluwer Law International, 2007).

[36] Case C-135/99 *Elsen* [2000] ECR I-10409.

[37] *Cf* Case C-213/05 *Geven* (Judgment of 18 July 2007); Case C-212/05 *Hartmann* (Judgment of 18 July 2007); Case C-287/05 *Hendrix* (see n 33 above).

[38] For example, Case C-224/98 *D'Hoop* [2002] ECR I-6191; Case C-364/01 *Barbier* [2003] ECR I-15013; Case C-224/02 *Pusa* [2004] ECR I-5763; Case C-345/05 *Commission v Portugal* [2006] ECR I-10633; Case C-520/04 *Turpeinen* [2006] ECR I-10685; Case C-522/04 *Commission v Belgium* (Judgment of 5 July 2007); Case C-76/05 *Schwarz and Gootjes-Schwarz* (Judgment of 11 September 2007); Case C-318/05 *Commission v Germany* (Judgment of 11 September 2007); Case C-152/05 *Commission v Germany* (Judgment of 17 January 2008). *Cf* Case C-386/02 *Baldinger* [2004] ECR I-8411; Case C-403/03 *Schempp* [2005] ECR I-6421.

[39] Case C-157/99 *Peerbooms* [2001] ECR I-5473; Case C-385/99 *Müller-Fauré* [2003] ECR I-4509.

[40] Case C-192/05 *Tas-Hagen* [2006] ECR I-10451; Case C-406/04 *De Cuyper* [2006] ECR I-6947.

challenge Dutch rules restricting applications for a civilian war benefit to those resident within the domestic territory. That was despite the fact that such benefits fall altogether outside the material scope of the Community coordination regime. Similarly, in *De Cuyper*, a Belgian citizen invoked his rights *qua* Union citizen to claim that Belgium could not terminate unemployment benefits on the sole grounds that he had changed habitual residence to France. This time, the Court conducted its assessment under the primary Treaty provisions notwithstanding the fact that the situation fell within the scope of, and appeared fully congruent with, Regulation 1408/71.

(iii) The Significance of the Case Law on National Territorial Restrictions

Rulings such as *Geven* and *Hendrix*, *Peerbooms* and *Müller-Fauré,* and *Tas-Hagen* and *De Cuyper* will be explored in greater detail in the analysis to follow. For now, suffice to say that these cases share in common the Court's basic finding that the Member State's refusal to export welfare benefits, even outside those situations where exportation is positively required by Regulation 1408/71, indeed constitutes a breach of the Union citizen's free movement rights which must be scrutinised to ensure it is genuinely necessary to protect some legitimate public interest. In fact, one might argue that the fundamental importance of these rulings lies less in their final outcome than in the conceptual framework laid down by the Court for assessing territorial welfare restrictions.

Before, Community law took for granted that national welfare systems are territorially bound and naturally entitled to restrict the payment of benefits to those resident within the Member State. Regulation 1408/71 merely created certain exceptions to that territoriality principle for the benefit of certain classes of migrant individuals. But beyond those exceptions, Member States could not be called upon to explain or justify their refusal to extend the territorial scope of their welfare responsibilities across their own frontiers. Now, however, Community law takes as its starting point the idea that *any* refusal by the Member State to export its own social security benefits constitutes a prima facie breach of the Union citizen's free movement rights which must be scrutinised to ensure it is genuinely necessary in the public interest. To that extent, cases such as *Geven* and *Hendrix*, *Peerbooms* and *Müller-Fauré*, *Tas-Hagen* and *De Cuyper* signal a dramatic change in one of the conceptual foundations of the European welfare state: the exportation of benefits is no longer to be treated as some sort of privilege generously bestowed by the Community legislature upon its subjects; rather, the territoriality of the national social security systems is presumed to be a limitation on the full economic and social integration of Union citizens within the broader European Union.

Moreover, as with all situations brought within the scope of the Treaty free movement provisions, the underlying effect of the Court's case law is to reshape the entire policy and decision making system applicable to the territoriality of the national welfare state. Choices about exportation are no longer left alone to the Member State to determine, according to its own framework of economic and social values, negotiated through its own democratic political processes. Such choices are now exposed to scrutiny and possible change by the Community, according to the framework of values judged legitimate under Community law, and where the final decision rests with the judges rather than any politicians.[41]

This conceptual (r)evolution has a profound transformative effect on the relationship between the individual citizen and the Member State, as well as their respective relationships with the Community itself. Regulation 1408/71 embodied the idea of a 'welfare contract' between Member States, that is to compromise the territoriality of their own welfare states, but to do so only on their own terms. By contrast, the ECJ's case law frees exportation from this 'welfare contract' between Member States and empowers the individual to become an active participant in the cross-border welfare system, through the medium of Community law, Union citizenship and judicial review. A similar phenomenon has already been identified, through rulings such as *Grzelczyk* and *Baumbast*, as regards relations between a migrant and his or her host state;[42] cases like *Geven* and *Hendrix*, *Peerbooms* and *Müller-Fauré, Tas-Hagen* and *De Cuyper* represent a parallel development in terms of relations between a migrant and his/her country of origin. By these combined means, Union citizenship becomes constitutive of a new dimension to the welfare relationship between individual and state, and arguably of a new welfare relationship between the individual and the Union. The latter may not have the power to tax and spend, and therefore no welfare system of its own; but the Union now plays a decisive role in organising the welfare rights between individuals and national authorities, and creating new rights to supranational welfare support.

The difficulty is that, although the basic thrust of the Court's case law can now be identified, a number of crucial questions remain unanswered, of which two are particularly relevant and will be addressed in the following sections: the potential normative basis for the Court's case law; and how far the transformative effects of that case law might actually reach in practice.

[41] See further the detailed critical analysis in E Spaventa, (n 35 above).

[42] Case C-184/99 *Grzelczyk* [2001] ECR I-6193; Case C-413/99 *Baumbast* [2002] ECR I-7091. See further, eg M Dougan and E Spaventa, 'Educating Rudy and the (Non-)English Patient: A Double Bill on Residency Rights Under Article 18 EC' (2003) 28 *EL Rev* 699.

III POSSIBLE NORMATIVE BASES FOR PROMOTING EXPORTATION

On what strength does the Court feel entitled to challenge the regulatory compromise hammered out through long years of difficult negotiations between the Community's political institutions, venture so far into a field so closely associated with national sovereignty, and actively reshape the welfare relationship between individuals and their own Member States?

It is possible to identify two (neither intrinsically related, nor mutually exclusive) normative bases by which to justify the Court's transformation of the legal approach to the territoriality of national welfare states, and indeed, to press Community law to offer greater possibilities for exportation than those set out in Regulation 1408/71 alone. The first might be described as 'passive': it argues that, if and when the Court promotes greater exportation, it is merely reflecting, at a Community level, more fundamental changes taking place within the Member States themselves, in particular, through the increasing 'consumerisation' of the post-war European welfare systems. The second explanation is more 'active' in nature: it interprets the barrier to movement case law as an opportunity for the Court to fulfill specifically Community objectives, in particular, overcoming the criticism that free movement for Union citizens is inherently biased in favour of the economically active and/or financially independent individual at the expense of more vulnerable members of society.

A Reflecting the Changing Character of European Welfare States?

The first possible normative basis for the Court's exportation case law can usefully be illustrated by reference to academic work which explores the changing character of the welfare state in Britain.[43]

For several decades, the primacy of the post-war Keynesian welfare settlement was taken for granted, and so too several of the assumptions which it generated. First, the organisation of a vast apparatus of social provision by the central government through the construction of a universal and homogenous welfare state focused attention on the idea of national social solidarity as the moral cornerstone of social provision. Secondly, the construction of the national welfare state also created a special sphere of

[43] The following analysis draws upon the written version of J Harrington, 'Medical Law and the Changing NHS: A Study in Rhetoric' (inaugural lecture delivered at the University of Liverpool on 5 March 2007). On territoriality, see further, eg B Jessop, *The Future of the Capitalist State* (Cambridge, Polity Press, 2002); M Berezin and M Schain (eds), *Europe Without Borders: Remapping Territory, Citizenship and Identity in a Transnational Age* (Baltimore, John Hopkins University Press, 2003); N Brenner, *New State Spaces: Urban Governance and the Rescaling of Statehood* (Oxford, Oxford University Press, 2004). On British welfare state reforms more generally, see also, eg N Harris (ed), *Social Security Law in Context* (Oxford, Oxford University Press, 2000).

social provision which was seen as distinct and separate from the market and competitive forces. Thirdly, the post-war Keynesian welfare settlement provoked a marked reluctance on the part of national judges to question what they regarded as essentially political choices about how to marshal (often scarce or at least finite) domestic welfare resources.

Slowly, however, commentators have identified the emergence of a much more complex conception of the territorial nature of the welfare state. First, there is a recognition that local and supranational spaces also have a legitimate role to play in social provision for individuals over and above, or indeed instead of, the responsibilities traditionally exercised by their central national government. Whether through the devolution of greater welfare powers to local authorities, charities and other non-governmental organisations, or through the influence of membership of the European Union and its extensive rights to free movement and equal treatment, the bonds of social solidarity which citizens might be expected to display towards each other have grown more multi-layered and spatially diverse. Secondly, many commentators also note the increasing tendency to see the state as a 'provider' of welfare services, and conversely to view welfare recipients as 'consumers'. To some extent, this is reflected in changes to benefits systems which express the public role not so much in terms of the 'nanny state' as in terms of the 'enabling state': benefits should act less as a basic safety net against poverty (or more critically, as a trap into welfare dependency), and more as a means to empower and motivate individuals to realise their personal economic and social potential.[44] To another extent, the same process can be seen at work with the ever greater influence of market ideas such as competition between welfare providers, and choice for individuals (even if this seldom gives way to the outright privatisation of welfare provision).[45] Thirdly, many commentators question whether the judges might now have a greater role to perform in ensuring that political choices about the allocation of welfare resources are conducted within the same framework of public law principles as any other branch of national administration, or (where appropriate) the same body of private law principles as any other form of market participation by the public authorities.

Although such trends may be most evident in countries such as the United Kingdom, there is evidence of similar developments across other Member States of the EU as they struggle to cope with similar challenges to

[44] To borrow the phrasing used by N Gilbert, 'The Modern Welfare State: The Changing Context of Social Protection' (written version of paper presented at *The Social Contract in the Modern Welfare Sate: Historical and Theoretical Perspectives* (University of Oxford) 18–20 April 2007).

[45] Though it may imply an expanded role for the private sector in welfare delivery: see the German legislation at issue in Case C-208/05 *ITC Innovative Technology Center* [2007] ECR I-181.

the funding, organisation and delivery of their welfare systems: for example, social changes in fields such as labour market participation, population aging, divorce rates and single parent families; the recognition of a broader range of social risks and the costs of new medical treatments; the economic and budgetary pressures posed by greater global competition; and a more widespread faith in the supposed ability of market forces to play a constructive role in public services. Even if important structural differences remain, the flavour of reform in many countries is now familiar: promoting work rather than protecting labour; selective targeting of support rather than universal entitlement; emphasis on the social obligations of citizens rather than the social right to welfare; and expanding the use of the private sector rather than purely public administration for the delivery of welfare services.[46]

Against that background, it is arguable that the sort of legal deterritorialisation of the welfare state evident in case law such as *Geven* and *Hendrix*, *Peerbooms* and *Müller-Fauré*, and *Tas-Hagen* and *De Cuyper*, is primarily reflecting, and only modestly contributing to, much more fundamental realignments in the grand design of the national welfare states of Western Europe. In particular, it is possible that the Court is merely linking up and fulfilling the expectations which individual citizens have been encouraged to hold as a matter both of national welfare rights and Community free movement policy. In the first place, the individual feels increasingly that he or she is a consumer of welfare services provided by the state, less in its paternal capacity as cradle-to-grave carer and protector, and more in its capacity as enabler and facilitator. In the second place, the individual feels increasingly that he or she is the beneficiary of a right to move and reside across the EU territory, not only in the sphere of economic activity related to the Single Market, but to whatever personal end and in whatever capacity seems appropriate. Why should the enabling welfare state be entitled to restrict the citizen's rights to free movement, by denying him or her access to the continued (cross-border) consumption of welfare

[46] See further, eg M Roche and R van Berkel (eds), *European Citizenship and Social Exclusion* (Aldershot, Ashgate, 1997); D Hine and H Kassim (eds), *Beyond the Market: the EU and National Social Policy* (London, Routledge, 1998); M Ferrera and M Rhodes (eds), *Recasting European Welfare States* (London, Frank Cass Publishers, 2000); S Kuhnle (ed), *Survival of the European Welfare State* (London, Routledge, 2000); J van Vugt and J Peet (eds), *Social Security and Solidarity in the European Union* (Heidelberg, Physica-Verlag, 2000); P Pierson (ed), *The New Politics of the Welfare State* (Oxford, Oxford University Press, 2001); M Kleinman, *A European Welfare State?* (Basingstoke, Palgrave, 2002). Despite its relatively weak competences in this field, the EU may nevertheless play an active role in these structural reforms, especially through the Lisbon Strategy and the OMC as regards modernising social protection. See further, eg N Bernard, 'Between a Rock and a Soft Place: Internal Market versus Open Coordination in EU Social Welfare Law' in M Dougan and E Spaventa (eds), *Social Welfare and EU Law* (see n 1 above); J Zeitlin, 'Social Europe and Experimentalist Governance: Towards a New Constitutional Compromise' in G de Búrca (ed), *EU Law and the Welfare State* (see n 1 above).

support?[47] Or at least, why should the Community courts feel unable to scrutinise such restrictions so as to ensure that they can be objectively justified by the public interest?[48]

B Making the Free Movement Rights of Union Citizens more Universal?

The other possible normative basis for the recent exportation case law argues that the Court's role should be more proactive—consciously using the concept of barriers to movement as an effective means to realise certain substantive Community policy objectives upon which the Court itself chooses to place legal value. In particular, it is arguable that the Court should treat its exportation case law as an important ingredient in the broader process of making Union citizenship a more universally meaningful legal status.

Every federal entity which seeks to offer generalised rights to free movement for its citizens must grapple with the problem of local resistance to the possibility of 'benefit tourism' by migrants from other constituent territories. The range of legal responses available to address this problem depends in no small part upon the competences conferred upon the central authority. For example, in Canada, the federal government offers budgetary transfers to the provinces and territories in respect of various social assistance programmes, on condition (inter alia) that benefits are available to all Canadian citizens and permanent residents without any qualifying conditions requiring a minimum period of residency within the competent local territory.[49] However, since such options are not available to the EU in its current state of development, the Community has been forced to find an alternative response to the problem of free movement for the economically inactive.

That response has centred around the rights to free movement and equal treatment of economically inactive Union citizens within their host society pursuant to Articles 18 and 12 EC. In particular, the inevitable compromise between (on the one hand) the desire to offer meaningful benefits to Union citizens regardless of their economic or financial status and (on the other hand) the need to respect the Member State's limited willingness and

[47] For some interesting empirical insights into the attitudes of migrants towards welfare entitlement vis-à-vis their home and host states, see K Coldron and L Ackers, '(Ab)using European Citizenship? EU Retired Migrants and the Exercise of Healthcare Rights' in M Dougan and H Stalford (eds), *Special Issue: The Impact of Migration on Healthcare Systems in the European Union* (2007) 14 *Maastricht Journal of European and Comparative Law* 239.

[48] *Cf* in the context of the health care case law, M Flear, 'Developing Euro-Biocitizens through Migration for Healthcare Services' in M Dougan and H Stalford, *ibid*.

[49] Originally under the Canada Assistance Act, now schemes such as the Canada Social Transfer. I am very grateful to Derek Hum for drawing my attention to this point.

ability to pay for the upkeep of foreign nationals who might otherwise present an unreasonable burden upon its public finances, has gradually manifested itself in the task of identifying a 'real link' between migrant Union citizens and their host society. The closer the bond between the individual claimant and the Member State, the more secure will be the claimant's right to reside within the territory, free from the fear of expulsion on economic or financial grounds;[50] and the more extensive his or her right to equal treatment within the host society, as regards welfare and other social benefits.[51]

Union citizenship, combined with a tangible shared experience between the individual migrant and his or her host society, has therefore become a legitimate gateway into membership of the national solidaristic community.[52] Viewed in isolation, however, the converse of this particular legal regime is that many economically inactive migrants enjoy only limited and insecure rights under Community law—providing the basis for the widespread critique that Union citizenship, even despite the considerable efforts of the Court and the Community legislature, remains inherently exclusionary.[53] Yet viewed in conjunction with the exportation case law, perhaps a different picture might begin to emerge: Community law in fact imposes obligations upon the home state to provide welfare support in respect of its own nationals who chose to exercise their rights to free movement elsewhere in the EU, helping the migrant to move closer to the point at which he or she can instead claim to be assimilated into the welfare system of the host state.[54]

In other words, the Court could make two discrete legal tools—the barriers to movement principle as a means of challenging the territorial limitations of the home state, and the right to equal treatment as a means of overcoming the nationality limitations of the host state—work together to enhance the practical value of Union citizenship for a broader category

[50] For example, Case C-413/99 *Baumbast* [2002] ECR I-7091. See now the right to permanent residency contained in Directive 2004/38 [2004] OJ L158/77.

[51] For example, Case C-184/99 *Grzelczyk* [2001] ECR I-6193; Case C-138/02 *Collins* [2004] ECR I-2703; Case C-209/03 *Bidar* [2005] ECR I-2119. Again, see now the right to permanent residency contained in Directive 2004/38 [2004] OJ L158/77.

[52] See further, eg C Barnard, 'EU Citizenship and the Principle of Solidarity' in M Dougan and E Spaventa (eds), *Social Welfare and EU Law* (see n 1 above); S Giubboni, 'Free Movement of Persons and European Solidarity' (2007) 13 *European Law Journal* 360. *Cf* A Somek, 'Solidarity Decomposed: Being and Time in European Citizenship' (2007) 32 *EL Rev* 787.

[53] See, eg M Dougan, 'The Court Helps Those Who Help Themselves... The Legal Status of Migrant Workseekers Under Community Law in the Light of the *Collins* Judgment' (n 32 above).

[54] Consider the Court's observations in Cases C-396/05, C-419/05 and C-450/05 *Habelt* (Judgment of 18 December 2007), para 82.

of its potential beneficiaries than either of those legal tools could hope to achieve on its own.[55]

On its face, it might sound rather contradictory for any normative argument to admit that a Member State is entitled to insist that qualification for welfare support depends upon the claimant demonstrating a 'real link' to its society, including the requirement of a minimum period of residence within the national territory; then to deny that the same Member State can still expect evidence of a 'real link' to its society, on the basis of continuing residency, to the detriment of claimants who chose to move elsewhere within the EU. After all, if the idea of a 'real link' is the centrepiece of the legal regime on the migration rights of EU citizens, surely that should argue *against* greater exportation of welfare benefits by individuals who have voluntarily quit the domestic territory, and whose connection to the national community has thereby presumably become more tenuous.[56]

However, the normative contradiction is only apparent: membership of the national welfare society must indeed be earned, particularly when it comes to migrant Union citizens who cannot claim affiliation on the basis of nationality or economic contribution; but equally, one might argue, membership of the national welfare society should not automatically be deemed forfeit as soon as an individual decides to leave the territory.[57] In other words, there is a distinction between the 'real link' as a legitimate connecting factor for migrants with their host society, and as a valid severing factor for migrants vis-à-vis their home state. That distinction creates a useful space within which Community law can pursue its own policy objectives, in particular, the desire that the general right to free movement may be enjoyed in a meaningful way by all Union citizens regardless of their economic or financial status. To that end, the barrier to movement case law under the primary Treaty provisions can be used (in effect) to manufacture a transitional period during which migrants may continue to expect support from their home society, whilst attempting to establish meaningful connections with another country.

[55] See, in particular, academic debate about how best to finance cross-border educational mobility, eg A-P van der Mei, 'EU Law and Education: Promotion of Student Mobility versus Protection of Education Systems' in M Dougan and E Spaventa (n 1 above); M Dougan, 'Fees, Grants, Loans and Dole Cheques: Who Covers the Costs of Migrant Education within the EU?' (2005) 42 *CML Rev* 943; H Verschueren, 'European (Internal) Migration as an Instrument for Defining the Boundaries of National Solidarity Systems' (2007) 9 *European Journal of Migration and Law* 307.

[56] *Cf* G Davies, 'Any Place I Hang My Hat? Or: Residence is the New Nationality' (2005) 11 *European LawJournal* 43: the logic of the equal treatment case law is not only to view the resident migrant as an own national, but also to treat the non-resident own national as a foreigner.

[57] Not least since Dir 2004/38 grants all Union citizens an unconditional right to free movement in another Member State for up to three months: see Art 6.

IV LIMITS TO THE POSSIBILITY OF EXPORTATION

It is, therefore, possible to postulate a convincing normative basis for the Court's exportation case law: the Court is (or should be) projecting the changing expectations of individuals vis-à-vis their own national welfare states into the framework of EU law; and/or linking those expectations up with Union citizenship in an attempt to overcome the otherwise inherently exclusionary nature of the free movement rights created by Article 18 EC.

In practice, however, the situation is much more nuanced than these potential normative bases might imply: the actual outcomes of the decided cases hint at various additional factors which constrain the Court's room for manoeuvre or influence its reasoning; consideration of such factors is essential for constructing a more accurate picture of the judicial attitude towards the relationship between Community law and national territorial restrictions. Two main issues arise. The first concerns the proper role to be performed by Regulation 1408/71: to what degree must application of the coordination regime now give way to an analysis under the primary Treaty provisions? The second issue concerns the process of objective justification, as regards those territorial restrictions which will indeed fall to be assessed directly under the Treaty: what range of factors will the Court take into account, for the purposes of assessing the legality of a Member State's refusal to export?

In each case, it will be argued that key aspects of rulings such as *Grzelczyk* and *Baumbast* concerning relations between migrants and their host state are now being adapted by the Court so as to help govern relations between migrants and their home state. Thus, in the first place, it seems that the provisions of Regulation 1408/71 purporting to restrict exportation are increasingly amenable to a form of indirect judicial review, as regards their application by the national authorities, intended to guarantee that the Community legislature itself does not unduly prejudice the Union citizen's free movement rights. In the second place, for the purposes of assessing the proportionality of territorial welfare restrictions, the Court appears to accept the principle that benefits expressing a 'real link' with the domestic solidaristic community can indeed be territorially limited—provided that the national authorities avoid imposing discriminatory or arbitrary restrictions on exportation, and possibly also that the personal circumstances of the individual claimant are taken into account before the cross-border payment of benefits is terminated.[58]

[58] On the development of 'indirect judicial review' and the 'personal circumstances' assessment, see further: M Dougan, 'The Constitutional Dimension to the Case Law on Union Citizenship' (2006) 31 *EL Rev* 613; E Spaventa, 'Seeing the Wood Despite the Trees? On the Scope of Union Citizenship and Its Constitutional Effects' (2008) 45 *CML Rev* 13.

A The Proper Role of the Coordination Regime Contained in Regulation 1408/71

When it adopted the coordination regime, one may safely assume that the Community legislature believed itself to have established the ceiling for how much of the national welfare systems the Member States were prepared to export between their territories. Yet cases like *Tas-Hagen* and *De Cuyper* suggest that the Court uses the Treaty free movement provisions to treat the coordination regime, not as the ceiling it was intended to be, but merely as a floor—the bare minimum of exportation which individuals are entitled to expect under Community law, waiting to be supplemented by whatever additional rights to extra-territorial welfare support the Court chooses to divine directly from Union citizenship.

In this regard, the interaction between Regulation 1408/71 and the primary Treaty provisions in fact plays itself out in two quite distinct contexts, giving rise to quite distinct legal problems, depending on whether the Member State's refusal to export benefits falls into a situation deliberately excluded from the scope of the coordination regime, or whether the alleged barrier to movement arises in a situation already subject to regulatory intervention by the Community legislature in the form of Regulation 1408/71.

Consider, in the first place, a benefit (such as war benefits or student financial assistance) falling outside the scope of Regulation 1408/71. Exportation pursuant to the primary Treaty provisions may well lead the claimant to enjoy welfare support from the country of origin in circumstances where, due to the lack of a 'real link', he or she would be unlikely to qualify for equivalent welfare support from the host society, or at least to do so without endangering his or her underlying right to residence by becoming an 'unreasonable burden'—and would thus render more meaningful the exercise of the Union citizen's right to free movement in circumstances where he or she would otherwise risk 'falling between' national solidarity systems. But such exportation would also contradict the conscious decision of the Community legislature *not* to provide for the cross-border coordination of those benefits.

Consider, in the second place, benefits such as special non-contributory cash benefits falling within the scope of Regulation 1408/71. In this case, exportation could lead a claimant to enjoy welfare support from his or her country of origin in circumstances where, due to the operation of the coordination regime, responsibility for the provision of benefits is meant to fall solely upon the host society from the moment the claimant takes up residence within its territory.[59] Of course, that allocation of welfare

[59] See, in particular, the non-discrimination/aggregation rules laid down in Art 10a Reg 1408/71. See further, eg AP van der Mei, 'Regulation 1408/71 and Coordination of Special Non-Contributory Benefits' (2002) 27 *EL Rev* 551.

responsibilities between Member States can sometimes give rise to harsh consequences. For example, the host state may not offer benefits comparable to those received by the claimant in his or her country of origin, or which are subject to the precise obligations as regards qualification for special non-contributory cash benefits imposed by the coordination regime. In such cases, the loss of existing benefits will not be compensated by the acquisition of any new rights—and could deprive the claimant of any means of satisfying the host state that he or she possesses the sufficient financial resources required to qualify for residency.[60] Furthermore, it has not yet been clarified in the case law whether the act of claiming special non-contributory cash benefits within the host state, even though pursuant to Regulation 1408/71, may nonetheless render the claimant an 'unreasonable burden' upon the public finances, whose entire right to residency within the Member State is then liable to be revoked.[61] But such harsh consequences are the result of deliberate political choices expressly embodied in the coordination regime.[62] It is therefore even more striking in this situation that the normative arguments in favour of promoting greater exportation of national welfare benefits must be balanced against an important counter-consideration: the constitutional tension between the Court of Justice and the Community legislature over ultimate responsibility for the Community's emergent welfare law.

(i) Situations Falling Outside the Coordination Regime

How has the Court resolved this tension in its extant case law? To begin with, it seems clear that the Court no longer feels bound by the negative sense in which Regulation 1408/71 was intended to limit the scope for exportation: the fact that a particular claimant or benefit falls outside the personal or material scope of the coordination regime is no bar to an examination of the possibility that exportation should nevertheless be carried out in accordance with the primary Treaty provisions themselves.

The prime example of this phenomenon is *Tas-Hagen*.[63] Here, a Dutch claimant who suffered ill health as a result of injuries sustained during the Second World War gave up work and moved to Spain. From there, she applied for a welfare benefit payable to civilian victims of war-time ill treatment, but her application was rejected on the grounds that, under

[60] In accordance with Art 7 Dir 2004/38.

[61] Consider, eg Case C-20/96 *Snares* [1997] ECR I-6057, para 52. Note, however, that in H Verschueren, 'European (Internal) Migration as an Instrument for Defining the Boundaries of National Solidarity Systems' (2007) 9 *European Journal of Migration and Law* 307 the author argues strongly against any such possibility.

[62] As has sometimes been acknowledged by the ECJ: see, eg Case C-20/96 *Snares* [1997] ECR I-6057, para 46.

[63] Case C-192/05 *Tas-Hagen* [2006] ECR I-10451.

Dutch law, the benefit was only payable to persons actually resident in the national territory at the time the application was made. As a war benefit, one may assume that the dispute fell altogether outside the material scope of Regulation 1408/71.[64] Nevertheless, the Court held that the claimant was a Union citizen who had exercised her right to move to another Member State under Article 18 EC, the Dutch rules created a barrier to movement by treating her less favourably than own nationals who chose to remain within the national territory, and (as we shall see further below) those rules could not be objectively justified. The Court has since made similar findings in respect of financial support for students, which again falls outside the material scope of Regulation 1408/71;[65] and also as regards claimants whose particular insurance status brings them outside the personal scope of the coordination regime.[66]

As regards situations falling outside the scope of Regulation 1408/71, it thus appears that the role of the coordination regime is no longer decisive; everything depends on the identification of a barrier to movement and the process of objective justification. There are problems, however, with this approach. In the first place, one must assume that the relevant individuals/benefits were excluded from the personal/material scope of Regulation 1408/71 for a reason. Even if that reason is not entirely satisfactory, it nevertheless represents a conscious policy choice by the Community legislature to limit the prospects for exportation.[67] Against that background, the Court in cases such as *Tas-Hagen* can call upon certain normative arguments in favour of promoting the more widespread exportation of domestic welfare benefits, but it is clearly doing so in the face of choices determined by the political institutions.

In the second place, rulings such as *Tas-Hagen* create the potential for a peculiar reversal of Community law's approach to national territorial restrictions.[68] Where a given benefit has been totally excluded from the coordination system, the Court seems to feel that its path is clear to proceed with full judicial scrutiny of the relevant domestic restrictions—but that puts pressure on the Court to adopt a similarly probing approach towards benefits included within the scope of application of Regulation 1408/71 and in respect of which one assumes the individual is surely not

[64] Art 4(4) Reg 1408/71. *Cf* the case law on war benefits for ex-military personnel, eg Case 9/78 *Gillard* [1978] ECR 1661; Case 207/78 *Even* [1979] ECR 2019; Case C-386/02 *Baldinger* [2004] ECR I-8411.

[65] Cases C-11–12/06 *Morgan* (Judgment of 23 October 2007).

[66] Case C-213/05 *Geven* (Judgment of 18 July 2007); Case C-212/05 *Hartmann* (Judgment of 18 July 2007).

[67] For example, consider the criticism of the continued exclusion of war benefits from Reg 883/2004 by F Pennings, 'Inclusion and Exclusion of Persons and Benefits in the New Coordination Regulation (see n 14 above).

[68] A point also noted by M Cousins, 'Citizenship, Residence and Social Security' (2007) 32 *EL Rev* 386, 393.

intended to enjoy a lesser degree of protection under Community law. After all, why should situations consciously excluded from Regulation 1408/71 be rewarded with a more forceful presumption in favour of exportation than benefits subject to the coordination regime at least to some extent? Consistency favours the argument that, if there is to be full judicial scrutiny of territorial restrictions in cases like *Tas-Hagen*, then that should apply also to territorial restrictions sanctioned by Regulation 1408/71—even if this implies creating possibilities for exportation in contradiction to the express provisions of the coordination regime. How far does the case law support that view?

(ii) Situations Falling within the Coordination Regime

The Court sometimes treats Regulation 1408/71 and the provisions on Union citizenship as virtually inter-changeable. Consider the dispute in *Gaumain-Cerri*.[69] German care allowance was provided to help cover the costs arising from a person's reliance upon third party carers; in addition, insurance funds would pay old age pension contributions on behalf of those third party carers, provided the latter actually resided within the national territory. The Court held that the payment of old age pension contributions on behalf of carers constitutes a sickness benefit falling within the material scope of the coordination regime. As Advocate General Tizzano demonstrated in his Opinion, the provisions of Regulation 1408/71 could in principle have been invoked so as to preclude the German residence requirement.[70] However, the Court considered it unnecessary to reach any finding as to the position under Regulation 1408/71: Germany's refusal to pay old age pension contributions on behalf of the carers put them at a disadvantage, for having exercised their right to move and reside in another Member State, as compared to the treatment of German nationals who chose to remain within the domestic territory. In the absence of any objective justification for this difference in treatment, it was to be considered incompatible with the Treaty provisions on Union citizenship.

The sort of inter-changeability at work in *Gaumain-Cerri* might not seem too objectionable where the Regulation and the Treaty would indeed reach the same result—but what about situations where the two systems come into potential conflict, for example, as with the specific restrictions on exportation which Regulation 1408/71 expressly sanctions the competent state to impose upon unemployment benefits and special non-contributory cash benefits?

[69] Cases C-502/01 and C-31/02 *Gaumain-Cerri* [2004] ECR I-6483.

[70] Cases C-502/01 and C-31/02 *Gaumain-Cerri* [2004] ECR I-6483, especially paras 101–106 Opinion.

At one extreme, the Court has occasionally found specific territorial restrictions contained in Regulation 1408/71 to be incompatible with the competences conferred upon the Community legislature under Article 42 EC. For example, in *Habelt*, coordination rules derogating from the general principle that old age pensions should be exportable under Article 10 Regulation 1408/71, by permitting Germany to recognise certain contributions only where the claimant was actually resident within the national territory, were found to be ultra vires.[71] In such cases, the validity of the coordination rules is directly negated. At the other extreme, the Court has sometimes treated Regulation 1408/71 as a *lex specialis* laying down definitive rules for those situations falling within its scope of application, including the imposition of territorial restrictions, as regards which further consideration of the dispute pursuant to the primary Treaty provisions would be inappropriate. This approach underpins several recent rulings concerning the classification (and consequent non-exportability) of special non-contributory [cash] benefits. For example, *Kersbergen-Lap* concerned a Dutch decision to cease the payment of an incapacity benefit for disabled young people to certain claimants who had relocated to other Member States. The Court held that the invalidity benefit had been correctly listed as a special non-contributory [cash] benefit, entitling the Netherlands to restrict its payment to within the national territory.[72] Such rulings might appear to suggest that the normative arguments in favour of greater exportation, as well as concerns about consistency between the treatment of situations falling outside and inside the scope of the coordination regime, must give way to judicial deference towards the unequivocal policy choices of the Community legislature.

However, invalidity rulings such as *Habelt* are exceptional, while further investigation reveals that *lex specialis* judgments such as *Kersbergen-Lap* do not accurately reflect the true relationship between the coordination regime and the primary Treaty provisions. Other lines of case law demonstrate that the Court is indeed prepared to open up possibilities for exportation, with the potential to contradict the outcomes envisaged by Regulation 1408/71, though without directly impugning the latter's legality.

(a) A Parallel Relationship between Regulation and Treaty   On some occasions, the Court treats Regulation 1408/71 and the primary Treaty provisions as separate but parallel legal regimes, each capable of applying independently to the same dispute, and each capable of producing a

[71] Cases C-396/05, C-419/05 and C-450/05 *Habelt* (Judgment of 18 December 2007).

[72] Case C-154/05 *Kersbergen-Lap* [2006] ECR I-6249. See also, eg Case C-160/02 *Skalka* [2004] ECR I-5613.

different final outcome, though without amounting to a direct clash of norms. This approach is best illustrated by the health care case law.

As is well known, the Court held in *Peerbooms* that, where a Member State is prepared to pay for hospital treatment within its own territory under more favourable conditions than it is prepared to pay for hospital treatment in another territory, this constitutes a barrier to movement under Article 49 EC, since it dissuades insured persons from seeking out hospital services from providers established in other Member States. A requirement of prior authorisation, before sickness funds are prepared to assume the costs of hospital treatment provided in another Member State, can be objectively justified, though the conditions for granting or withholding such prior authorisation are subject to judicial scrutiny under Community law, to ensure that they comply with the principle of proportionality.[73] By contrast, in *Müller-Fauré*, the Court held that the requirement of prior authorisation for non-hospital treatment in another Member State could not be justified at all. There was no evidence that patients would seek treatment from foreign doctors in such large numbers as to endanger the planning and functioning of the national health care system.[74]

Reaction to the health care case law has been very mixed.[75] For present purposes, most pertinent is discussion surrounding the Court's use of the Treaty provisions on the free movement of services so as to encourage the exportation of health insurance between the Member States, even though Article 22 Regulation 1408/71 already contains specific provisions for coordinating the grant by the competent national authorities of prior authorisation for patients to receive medical treatment in another Member State.[76] As regards non-hospital treatment, the Court seemed to have set out deliberately to undermine the regime created by the Community legislature, by permitting claimants effectively to bypass Regulation 1408/71 and seek reimbursement directly under the Treaty, without having to fulfil the conditions for prior authorisation set out in Article 22. As regards hospital treatment, the situation might seem even more peculiar:

[73] Case C-157/99 *Peerbooms* [2001] ECR I-5473.

[74] Case C-385/99 *Müller-Fauré* [2003] ECR I-4509.

[75] For example, contrast A Kaczorowska, 'A Review of the Creation by the European Court of Justice of the Right to Effective and Speedy Medical Treatment and its Outcomes' (2006) 12 *European Law Journal* 345; with C Newdick, 'Citizenship, Free Movement and Health Care: Cementing Individual Rights by Corroding Social Solidarity' (2006) 43 *CML Rev* 1645.

[76] See further, eg A P van der Mei, 'Cross-Border Access to Health Care within the European Union: Some Reflections on *Geraerts-Smits and Peerbooms* and *Vanbraekel*' (2002) 9 *Maastricht Journal of European and Comparative Law* 189; V Hatzopoulous, 'Killing National Health and Insurance Systems But Healing Patients? The European Market for Health Care Services After the Judgments of the ECJ in *Vanbraekel* and *Peerbooms*' (2002) 39 *CML Rev* 683; V Hatzopoulos, 'Health Law and Policy: The Impact of the EU' in G de Búrca (ed), *EU Law and the Welfare State* (see n 1 above).

the ruling in *Watts* clarified that the substantive conditions under which the competent national authorities must grant prior authorisation to receive hospital care in another Member State are the same under Article 22 Regulation 1408/71 as they are for Article 49 EC.[77] The latter development begs the question: what is the point of having a 'new' system of reimbursement under Article 49 EC at all, when the 'old' coordination system established by Regulation 1408/71 could do the job just as well?

In fact, the two systems do remain distinct and wily patients will be expected to negotiate the best deal possible from their national health care system using a complex interplay between the Treaty and the Regulation. For example, the Regulation continues to offer distinct advantages to patients who travel from a relatively limited sickness insurance system to a relatively generous one, since it requires the home state to cover the cost of treatment as if the patient were insured in the host state (whereas Article 49 EC would tie the claimant to the levels of cover available in the home state). Conversely, the Treaty can usefully be called into operation where the patient moves from a relatively munificent sickness insurance system to a more restricted one, since the patient can then rely on Article 49 EC to benefit from the full extent of cover provided by the home state.[78] And of course, the Treaty clearly offers more than the Regulation when it comes to extramural treatment, as in *Müller-Fauré*, where Article 49 EC precludes any requirement of prior authorisation being imposed by the home state as a precondition for reimbursement.

The health care case law therefore shows how the Regulation and the Treaty can co-exist, each offering its own regime for the exportation of welfare benefits, which do not directly conflict but rather interact with each other. On the one hand, this approach might possess the advantage of promoting greater exportation, in accordance with the normative arguments in its favour, but without provoking outright constitutional confrontation between the Court and the Community legislature. On the other hand, the health care case law also illustrates the disadvantages of this approach: the interaction between the Regulation and the Treaty becomes increasingly complex, and there is potential for reaching contradictory outcomes in practice, depending on which legal route is given priority by the claimant. The end result is that, while it might be going too far to accuse the Court of using the primary Treaty provisions to drive a coach and horses through the regulatory choices of the Community legislature, the case law under Article 49 EC has surely upset the model of cross-border health care envisaged under Regulation 1408/71.[79]

[77] Case C-372/04 *Watts* [2006] ECR I-4325.

[78] Case C-368/98 *Vanbraekel* [2001] ECR I-5363.

[79] See further, eg M Cousins, 'Patient Mobility and National Health Systems' (2007) 34 *Legal Issues of Economic Integration* 183.

(b) A Hierarchical Relationship Between Regulation and Treaty On other occasions, however, the Court adopts a very different approach: treating the primary Treaty rules as hierarchically superior to Regulation 1408/71, so that just because a refusal to export appears congruent with the provisions of the coordination regime does not per se shield the Member State from judicial scrutiny for having infringed the Union citizen's right to free movement; but then permitting the provisions of Regulation 1408/71 to act as the primary framework for judicial review during the subsequent process of objective justification, so that compliance with Community secondary legislation creates at least a strong presumption in favour of upholding the national territorial restrictions. Two main cases can be interpreted as illustrating this approach: *De Cuyper* (decided as a barrier to movement case under Article 18 EC);[80] and *Hendrix* (decided as an indirect discrimination case under Article 39 EC).[81]

The claimant in *De Cuyper* was a Belgian national in receipt of unemployment benefits who had declared to the national authorities that he was living alone in Belgium; but during a routine enquiry, the Belgian authorities discovered that the claimant had actually moved to France and decided to terminate payments. The Court observed that the claimant had exercised his right under Article 18 EC to move and reside in another Member State. However, that right is not unconditional: it must be exercised subject to the limitations and conditions imposed by the Treaty, and the measures adopted to give it effect, including Regulation 1408/71. The latter obliges the competent state to pay unemployment benefits to those resident in another Member State only in limited circumstances, none of which applied to this particular case. Nevertheless, Belgium's refusal to export the benefits disadvantaged De Cuyper for having exercised his Treaty right to move to France, and as such had to be objectively justified by a valid public interest objective and the principle of proportionality.

The key to the Court's approach in *De Cuyper* is that Regulation 1408/71 is treated as Community secondary legislation regulating exercise of the Union citizen's rights to free movement of the sort referred to explicitly in Article 18 EC. At one extreme, the existence of a hierarchical relationship between the Regulation and the Treaty does not imply that coordination rules (explicitly or implicitly) restricting the possibilities for exportation are somehow rendered invalid. At the other extreme, however, nor is Regulation 1408/71 to be treated simply as a *lex specialis* establishing definitive rules on the exportation of benefits, regardless of the overarching requirements imposed by Union citizenship. Rather, *De Cuyper* should be seen as a concrete manifestation of the general principle

[80] Case C-406/04 *De Cuyper* [2006] ECR I-6947.
[81] Case C-287/05 *Hendrix* (see n 33 above).

established in *Baumbast*: legislation adopted by the Community legislature to regulate the exercise of free movement rights must itself be treated as a restriction on the Union citizen's right to move and reside under Article 18 EC, which Member States are obliged to apply in accordance with the principle of proportionality.[82]

Viewed in that light, the Court's analysis of the Belgian rules in *De Cuyper* was not simply an example of objective justification under the primary Treaty provisions, conducted independently of the provisions of Regulation 1408/71; it was actually an assessment of how far application of the coordination regime could be considered necessary for the protection of the Member State's legitimate interests, and thus amounted to indirect judicial review of Regulation 1408/71 itself. This interpretation makes *De Cuyper* fundamentally different from rulings such as *Peerbooms* and *Müller-Fauré*: even if in both types of situation the final outcome of the dispute depends upon its assessment under the primary Treaty provisions and the principle of proportionality, under the hierarchical approach established in *De Cuyper*, Regulation 1408/71 is far from irrelevant to the process of objective justification; the *Baumbast* jurisprudence implies rather that Regulation 1408/71 acts as an important reference point for gauging the Community's basic policy stance on territoriality, and thus defines the general framework for judicial review of the Member State's refusal to export.

That difference in interpretation might help to explain some of the adverse academic reaction to the ruling in *De Cuyper*. The imperative requirement recognised by the Court for the purposes of objectively justifying Belgium's refusal to export the claimant's unemployment benefits to France was the administrative need to monitor the financial and family situation of unemployed persons, to ensure that their situation has not changed in a way relevant to payment or calculation of their benefits. The Court continued to find that a residency requirement was indeed a proportionate method of ensuring effective monitoring of the claimant's position—since it permitted national inspectors to carry out the necessary spot checks in an unexpected manner. The Court's proportionality assessment here might seem disappointingly weak: the aim of avoiding errors in the calculation and payment of benefits could have been achieved in a manner less detrimental to free movement simply by insisting upon greater liaison between the relevant national authorities.[83] Such a critique is persuasive if *De Cupyer* is treated as a case of simple objective justification under the primary Treaty provisions, for which purposes Regulation

[82] Case C-413/99 *Baumbast* [2002] ECR I-7091. Though not a *complete* manifestation, as the following analysis will demonstrate.

[83] Contrast with the ruling in Case C-40/05 *Lyyski* [2007] ECR I-99. Further, eg M Cousins, 'Citizenship, Residence and Social Security' (2007) 32 *EL Rev* 386.

1408/71 is inapplicable and irrelevant, as in *Peerbooms* or *Müller-Fauré*. However, the criticism is less convincing if *De Cuyper* is interpreted as a case where Community secondary legislation regulated exercise of the claimant's hierarchically superior free movement rights, as in *Baumbast*: Belgium's refusal to export the claimant's unemployment benefits, even though in accordance with Regulation 1408/71, still amounted to a barrier to movement under the primary Treaty provisions, but judicial review was limited to an assessment of whether the provisions of the coordination regime had been applied to the claimant in an inappropriate manner.

In that regard, *De Cuyper* itself was not really a suitable case for fully integrating Regulation 1408/71 with the broader case law on Union citizenship post-*Baumbast*, that is by obliging the national authorities to apply the restrictive provisions contained in the coordination regime in accordance with the principle of proportionality. After all, the claimant's situation was not marginal, in the sense of falling just beyond the possibilities for exportation permitted under Regulation 1408/71 itself: he very obviously failed to comply with the requirements set out by the Community legislature; furthermore, there was no compelling ground on which to argue that enforcement of the coordination rules at their face value would adversely affect the Union citizen's free movement rights in a manner which clearly outweighed any danger to the Member State's legitimate interests.[84]

What the Court started but could not quite finish in *De Cuyper*, it brought closer to full fruition in *Hendrix*. The case concerned the same Dutch incapacity benefit for disabled young people as had previously been found, in *Kersbergen-Lap*, to have been correctly listed as a special non-contributory [cash] benefit under Regulation 1408/71. The claimant in *Hendrix* was a disabled Dutch national living and working in the Netherlands whose employer was permitted to pay him less than the minimum wage; the claimant was then paid incapacity benefit so as to bring his income up to the standard level. However, when the claimant moved residence to Belgium, his incapacity benefit was terminated in accordance with the non-exportation provisions of Regulation 1408/71. The Court held that the residency requirement for entitlement to the disputed benefit constituted indirect discrimination against the claimant *qua* frontier worker contrary to Article 7(2) Regulation 1612/68. Moreover, the mere fact that the Dutch legislation was fully congruent with the Community coordination regime did not shield it from further scrutiny: Regulation 1408/71 must be interpreted in the light of the objectives of Article 42 EC, its legal basis under the Treaty, which is to contribute to the greatest

[84] *Cf* AG Geelhoed in Case C-406/04 *De Cuyper* [2006] ECR I-6947, especially at paras 112–18 Opinion.

possible freedom of movement for migrant workers; for its part, Article 7(2) Regulation 1612/68 merely gives specific expression to the general principle of equal treatment for migrant workers enshrined in Article 39(2) EC. Against that background, any residency requirement for the disputed benefit could only be enforced if it was objectively justified—taking into account not only the legitimate interests of the Member State, as reflected in the residency provisions of Regulation 1408/71, but also the particular circumstances of the individual claimant, which (as we shall see further below) clearly argued in favour of permitting exportation in this case.

Hendrix can obviously be distinguished from *De Cuyper* in terms of the applicable legal basis and the precise reasoning employed by the Court. But the idea behind both rulings is essentially the same, that is the existence of a hierarchical relationship between the primary Treaty provisions and Regulation 1408/71, which does not render the latter invalid, but does require objective justification of the disputed restriction, albeit taking into account the choices expressed by the Community legislature. In fact, if and when another case like *Hendrix* arises, but the claimant cannot be treated as a frontier worker, simply as a migrant Union citizen, the Court would surely adapt its approach to match that in *De Cuyper*: the provisions on special non-contributory cash benefits under Regulation 1408/71 act as a limitation or condition on exercise of the right to free movement under Article 18 EC whose restrictive effects must still be objectively justified.[85] For those purposes, moreover, *Hendrix* confirms what *De Cuyper* could not, that is that this hierarchical relationship, and its consequent proportionality assessment, does indeed open up the possibility of exportation despite the black letter of the coordination regime.

Read together, therefore, *Hendrix* just as much as *De Cuyper*, even if neither says so explicitly, extend the *Baumbast* technique of using the primary Treaty provisions to conduct an indirect judicial review of restrictive Community secondary legislation, so as to help solve the problem of national territorial restrictions sanctioned by Regulation 1408/71.

(c) Parallel or Hierarchical: When and Why One or the Other? The Court thus employs at least two distinct legal devices—one based on a parallel, the other on a hierarchical relationship—for negotiating between the coordination regime and the primary Treaty provisions. The question arises: does the Court also employ any coherent criteria for choosing between these approaches?

[85] After all, Art 39 EC is itself a specific expression of the Union citizen's rights under Art 18 EC: see Case C-287/05 *Hendrix* (see n 33 above), paras 59–62.

One answer might be that the Court's choice is determined by the near-accident of legal basis. The parallel approach in *Peerbooms* flowed from the Court's finding that medical services received by the claimant abroad were remunerated for the purposes of Article 49 EC, and the Member State's refusal to reimburse their costs amounted to a barrier to the free movement of services. Having triggered Article 49 EC as the applicable legal basis, the exportation provisions of Regulation 1408/71 could really only apply in parallel, since Article 49 EC contains no obvious mechanism for cross-referencing its operation to that of the coordination regime. By contrast, in the absence of anything comparable to a remunerated service, the default legal basis for analysing a case like *De Cuyper* was Article 18 EC itself—and that Treaty provision does contain a clear and explicit mechanism for coordinating its operation with that of secondary legislation such as Regulation 1408/71. Similarly, once the Court decided that the transfer of residence in *Hendrix* was to be treated as a case of frontier work rather than economically inactive migration, the relationship between Articles 39 and 42 EC again pointed to a hierarchically inferior status for the latter's implementing legislation (Regulation 1408/71).[86]

Not everyone will find that explanation convincing. After all, it would not have been beyond the Court's ingenuity to adopt a similar approach, in cases like *Peerbooms*, to the relationship between Articles 49 and 42 EC as it had in *Hendrix*: Regulation 1408/71 sets out the rules on cross-border health care, but those rules must be interpreted in the light of the Treaty's objective of promoting the free movement not only of workers but also of services. Alternatively, the Court could even have treated *Peerbooms* in the same way as *De Cuyper*: Regulation 1408/71 is to be considered as legislation limiting or conditioning the exercise of the Union citizen's right to free movement under Article 18 EC, which can be construed as including a right to move for the purposes of receiving health care.[87] In either case, any refusal of prior authorisation, even if prima facie in accordance with the coordination regime, could be treated as a restriction which must be scrutinised for its proportionality.

Such scepticism suggests that, far from being some mere accident of legal basis, the Court's use of a parallel approach in rulings such as *Peerbooms* was designed, quite consciously, to achieve certain policy goals which could not have been so easily realised under a hierarchical approach of the

[86] Consider, by analogy, the Court's division of its analysis in Case C-76/05 *Schwarz and Gootjes-Schwarz* (Judgment of 11 September 2007) and Case C-318/05 *Commission v Germany* (Judgment of 11 September 2007) between those situations caught by Art 49 EC (where it was possible to identify a remunerated service) and those reserved to Art 18 EC (where the Union citizen was migrating for purely non-economic purposes). See further, eg G Davies, 'Welfare as a Service' (2002) 29 *Legal Issues of Economic Integration* 27.

[87] See further, eg E Spaventa, 'Public Services and European Law: Looking for Boundaries' (2002–2003) 5 *Cambridge Yearbook of European Legal Studies* 271.

sort employed in *De Cuyper* and *Hendrix*. Consider, for example, the objective of broadening patient choice, in particular, as regards their available treatment providers. After all, Regulation 1408/71 depends on a system of administrative cooperation between the competent national authorities of various Member States: prior authorisation will often be granted, under Article 22 of the coordination regime, to receive treatment abroad at certain pre-designated institutions.[88] For various reasons relating (for example) to language, culture, family and social networks, and available treatment options, the foreign institutions chosen by the competent Member State might not tally well with the preferences of the particular patient. Treating Regulation 1408/71 as hierarchically inferior to the primary Treaty provisions would have enabled the Court to deal with substantive problems associated with the criteria for granting or refusing prior authorisation (such as the relevance of national waiting lists), but this approach would not have been so effective at broadening the range of medical providers actually available to patients (even assuming they had received prior authorisation). Treating Regulation 1408/71 instead as parallel to the primary Treaty provisions permitted the Court to respect the system of administrative cooperation established under the coordination regime, while at the same time opening up much wider possibilities for patients to seek medical treatment, in principle still at their home state's expense, with health care providers established anywhere in the Union.[89] Since such considerations will rarely be applicable to cash payments such as unemployment or incapacity benefits, of the sort involved in *De Cuyper* and *Hendrix*, the Court was left in those rulings to structure the relationship between Regulation 1408/71 and the primary Treaty provisions in a different manner.

Whatever the true explanation for the parallel model employed by the Court in its health care case law, it is arguable that the hierarchical approach of *De Cuyper* and *Hendrix* is ultimately more satisfactory as a methodology for solving the problem of territorial welfare restrictions imposed by the Community legislature itself. In the first place, the *De Cuyper/Hendrix* approach involves greater deference towards the basic policy choices embodied in Regulation 1408/71, and thus strikes a better balance between the normative arguments favouring greater exportation for the benefit of migrant Union citizens and the constitutional argument for respecting the regulatory competences of the Community legislature. After all, every time the Court orders exportation despite the terms of

[88] See, eg T Hervey, 'New Governance Responses to Healthcare Migration in the EU: The EU Guidelines on Block Purchasing' in M Dougan and H Stalford (eds), *Special Issue: The Impact of Migration on Healthcare Systems in the European Union* (2007) 14 MJ 303.

[89] See, eg J Montgomery, 'Impact of European Union Law on English Healthcare Law' in M Dougan and E Spaventa (eds), *Social Welfare and EU Law* (see n 1 above).

Regulation 1408/71, it is taking away from the political institutions of the Union and Member States alike some part of their power to decide on important questions of public expenditure and social solidarity. Against that background, the parallel approach of *Peerbooms* is perhaps more of a brazen challenge to the institutional balance of competences than the hierarchical one of *De Cuyper/Hendrix*. The latter line of case law may not be immune from such constitutional criticisms,[90] but it can at least mount an effective defence against them.[91]

In the second place, adopting the hierarchical approach as standard practice would contribute to the emergence of a more coherent doctrinal framework for dealing with the legal implications of Union citizenship. Whether considering the host state's behaviour towards migrants in fields such as residency and equal treatment (as in *Grzelczyk* and *Baumbast*), or the home state's relations with its own nationals who relocate abroad, the primary Treaty right to free movement is always the starting point for analysis; it is within this fundamental legal context that any relevant Community secondary legislation must be taken into consideration. In particular, a Member State's refusal to export its own welfare benefits always breaches the Union citizen's right to free movement under Article 18 EC and must be justified in accordance with a legitimate public interest and the principle of proportionality (as in *Tas-Hagen*). That is true even where such domestic restrictions find their basis in Regulation 1408/71, since all Community secondary legislation limiting or conditioning the Union citizen's rights under Article 18 EC must itself be interpreted so as to facilitate free movement, and to this end, must be applied by the Member States in a proportionate manner (as in *De Cuyper* or *Hendrix*).

B Factors Relevant to the Objective Justification Process

Previous sections discussed the Court's approach to exportation in the light of the limited scope and/or limitative provisions of Regulation 1408/71. As regards those situations where operation of the coordination regime must indeed be supplemented by scrutiny under the primary Treaty provisions, the next question concerns the Court's approach to objectively justifying the relevant national territorial restrictions.

There are indications in the case law that such judicial review should be relatively 'light touch'. As regards situations falling within the scope of Regulation 1408/71, we have already seen how the *De Cuyper/Hendrix*

[90] *Cf* K Hailbronner, 'Union Citizenship and Access to Social Benefits' (2005) 42 *CML Rev* 1245.

[91] *Cf* M Dougan, 'The Constitutional Dimension to the Case Law on Union Citizenship' (2006) 31 *EL Rev* 613.

case law suggests that a restriction on exportation imposed by the Community legislature itself should be given due judicial deference—though still subject to the limits imposed by the primary Treaty provisions and the demands of Union citizenship. Similarly, as regards situations falling outside the scope of the coordination regime, the Court suggested in *Tas-Hagen* that Member States should be given a wide margin of discretion to determine the appropriate degree of connection between claimants of benefits and the society which funds them—but again, still complying with the limits imposed by Community law.[92] Yet all that merely begs the question: what limits does Community law actually impose, and what range of factors will influence that choice?

Here again, it will be argued that some useful lessons can be drawn from the case law already developed by the Court to regulate relations between migrant Union citizens and their host state. For those purposes, we have already noted how the concept of the 'real link' has assumed a position of central importance in determining the extent of a claimant's residency and equal treatment rights.[93] To be more precise, it seems possible to identify two quite distinct enquiries, often subsumed into the single 'real link' catchphrase, arising from a migrant's claim to benefits within his/her host state. In the first place, the idea of a 'real link' may refer to the relationship between a Member State and its system of welfare provision: it seeks to identify whether a given benefit expresses a fundamental relationship of solidarity between the members of the relevant society. If such a relationship (what we shall term a 'solidaristic real link') exists, then we can assume that access to the relevant benefit may be restricted to individuals who are entitled to be considered members of that society.[94]

In the second place, the idea of a 'real link' may then refer to the relationship between the relevant society and any given claimant: in this context, it seeks to determine whether the claimant has demonstrated a sufficient degree of connection to the relevant society as to be considered one of its members. If such a relationship (what we shall term a 'membership real link') exists, then we can assume that the claimant is entitled to access the relevant benefit. The anatomy of the 'membership real link' has occupied much attention in the case law on Union citizenship. In particular, one of the factors identified by the Court as a legitimate indicator of a 'membership real link' is proof that the claimant has resided within the

[92] Case C-192/05 *Tas-Hagen* [2006] ECR I-10451, para 36.

[93] See, eg Case C-224/98 *D'Hoop* [2002] ECR I-6191; Case C-138/02 *Collins* [2004] ECR I-2703, Case C-209/03 *Bidar* [2005] ECR I-2119; Case C-258/04 *Ioannidis* [2005] ECR I-8275.

[94] See further, on the solidaristic character or otherwise of various publicly funded benefits, M Dougan and E Spaventa, 'Wish You Weren't Here ... New Models of Social Solidarity in the European Union' in M Dougan and E Spaventa (eds), *Social Welfare and EU Law* (see n 1 above).

domestic territory for a certain period of time.[95] However, the Court has also held that Member States must be prepared to take into consideration the personal circumstances of the claimant in a broader sense. This might mean that an individual can demonstrate a sufficient connection to the relevant society other than through those generic factors (such as a certain period of residency) recognised under national law.[96]

The language of the 'real link' (or something equivalent) has already been extended by the Court beyond the treatment of migrants by their host state, so as to also cover the relationship between migrants and their home state.[97] In the latter context, we shall see that the concept of the 'real link'—in both its solidaristic and membership guises—can assist with the problem of reconciling the normative arguments in favour of promoting greater exportation of national welfare benefits with those counter-considerations favouring continued respect for the historic geographical boundaries of the domestic welfare states.[98]

(i) Identifying a 'Solidaristic Real Link'

Although the Court does not often explore in detail the nature of the 'solidaristic real link' between benefit and society, it is nevertheless a crucial part of the objective justification process. Indeed, it is arguable that the degree to which the relevant benefit is linked to the specific economic and social environment of the competent Member State exercises a crucial influence on the Court's approach: the stronger the relationship between a given welfare benefit and the domestic system of social solidarity, the weaker the force of the argument for severing the cord connecting payment of benefits to residence within the national territory.

At one extreme, consider benefits funded at least in part by the claimant's own contributions. Such benefits have a more proprietary (or 'consumer') character than non-contributory benefits funded directly from the public purse, and the argument in favour of using the primary Treaty

[95] Consider, eg Case C-184/99 *Grzelczyk* [2001] ECR I-6193; Case C-413/99 *Baumbast* [2002] ECR I-7091; Case C-456/02 *Trojani* [2004] ECR I-7573; Case C-209/03 *Bidar* [2005] ECR I-2119.

[96] Consider, eg Case C-224/98 *D'Hoop* [2002] ECR I-6191; Case C-138/02 *Collins* [2004] ECR I-2703.

[97] See the Opinions and rulings in Case C-192/05 *Tas-Hagen* [2006] ECR I-10451; Case C-213/05 *Geven* (Judgment of 18 July 2007); Case C-212/05 *Hartmann* (Judgment of 18 July 2007); Case C-287/05 *Hendrix* (see n 33 above); Cases C-11–12/06 *Morgan* (Judgment of 23 October 2007).

[98] This is not to deny the serious definitional problems bedevilling the 'real link' as both concept and case law: see, eg S O'Leary, 'Solidarity and Citizenship Rights in the Charter of Fundamental Rights of the European Union' in G de Búrca (ed), *EU Law and the Welfare State* (see n 1 above); A Somek, 'Solidarity Decomposed: Being and Time in European Citizenship' (2007) 32 *EL Rev* 787.

provisions to increase the possibilities of exportation is accordingly more persuasive.[99] Such an approach might assist, for example, with the problem of supplementary social security schemes such as occupational pensions. Those schemes are excluded from the material scope of Regulation 1408/71, since they are not 'legislative' in nature.[100] Other Community measures have sought to ameliorate some of the hardships caused by this exclusion of occupational pensions from the coordination regime,[101] though the Commission has recently shied away from proposals for stronger Community action to promote the exportability of occupational pensions between Member States.[102] Yet, based on the reasonable assumption that the principle of non-discriminatory barriers to movement in breach of the primary Treaty provisions extends beyond purely public behaviour, so as also to catch the activities of economic operators such as pension schemes, it is arguable that the Court should find such restrictions to constitute a breach of Article 18 EC and, for the purposes of objective justification, emphasise the contractual nature of contributory benefits as a factor overriding any (largely administrative) desire on the part of the schemes themselves to impose territorial restrictions on making payments.[103]

At the other extreme, consider those benefits which are intended to manifest a given society's collective concern for its disadvantaged members. Such benefits have an important moral connection to the home society: the construction of an abstract societal willingness to redistribute wealth, so as to subsidise the living standards or social well-being of other individuals, is intimately linked to an equally abstract sense of shared membership of the

[99] *Cf* rulings where the Court has found that contributory benefits were wrongly categorised as special non-contributory [cash] benefits and thereby improperly excluded from the possibility of exportation under Reg 1408/71, eg Case C-215/99 *Jauch* [2001] ECR I-1901; though *cf* Case C-265/05 *Naranjo* [2007] ECR I-347. Bear in mind, however, that ordinary social security benefits are not excluded from the possibility of exportation under Reg 1408/71 simply because they are non-contributory in character, eg Case C-78/91 *Hughes* [1992] ECR I-4839.

[100] See Arts 4(1) and 1(j) Reg 1408/71.

[101] In particular, Directive 98/49 on safeguarding the supplementary pension rights of employed and self-employed persons moving within the Community [1998] OJ L209/46.

[102] Contrast Commission proposal for a directive on improving the portability of supplementary pension rights, COM(2005) 507 Final; with the amended proposal for a directive on minimum requirements for enhancing worker mobility by improving the acquisition and preservation of supplementary pension rights, COM(2007) 603 Final.

[103] On the applicability of the free movement of persons provisions to private parties, consider Case 36/74 *Walrave and Koch* [1974] ECR 1405; Case C-415/93 *Bosman* [1995] ECR I-4921; Case C-281/98 *Angonese* [2000] ECR I-4139; Case C-411/98 *Ferlini* [2000] ECR I-8081; Case C-438/05 *Viking Line* (Judgment of 11 December 2007); Case C-341/05 *Laval* (Judgment of 18 December 2007). Discrimination by purely private operators was caught by Art 39 EC in *Angonese*, but the ECJ has not yet made clear whether such operators are also prohibited from creating non-discriminatory barriers. However, it is arguable that major pension schemes are in a position comparable to trades union, whose non-discriminatory barriers were caught by Arts 43 and 49 EC in *Viking Line* and *Laval*.

national community—including recognition of its territorial boundaries, effectively excluding those who chose to relocate abroad. Such benefits also presuppose a significant financial connection with the territory of the competent state, based on the need to balance revenue raised through general taxation against expenditure on universal solidarity benefits, so as to avoid the assumption of potentially unidentifiable and/or unlimited responsibilities—a risk exacerbated by the prospect of exportation by migrant individuals. Practical considerations may also be highly pertinent, particularly where levels of benefits are calculated by reference to the cost and standard of living of the home society, so that their exportation could result in inadequately low, or inappropriately high, payments in other Member States.

Well before the evolution of the barrier to movement case law under the primary Treaty provisions and its extension to the territorial restriction of domestic welfare benefits, such considerations were recognised as legitimate public interest concerns by the Court of Justice in various rulings relating to the interpretation of Regulation 1408/71. For example, in *Lenoir*, the Court drew a distinction between periodic cash child benefits calculated exclusively by reference to the number and age of the relevant family members, and school expenses allowances closely linked with the social environment and therefore with the place where the persons concerned reside: whereas grant of the former benefits continues to be justified wherever the recipient and his or her family reside, the latter benefits could be excluded from the scope of the exportation provisions on family benefits contained in Regulation 1408/71.[104] Similarly, when called upon to determine how far 'hybrid benefits'—simultaneously providing supplementary payments to insured persons whose social security benefits are inadequate to meet their needs, and subsistence support to individuals falling altogether outside the social security system—should fall within the scope of Regulation 1408/71, the Court took into account the risk that their wholesale exportation could lead to the break-up of the relevant national schemes: only claimants who established a previous connection to the social security system of the competent state could rely on the Regulation to challenge domestic territorial restrictions.[105] Then, after the introduction of special non-contributory [cash] benefits, the Court accepted that the Community legislature was entitled to resolve this policy dilemma by the alternative expedient of excluding the possibility of exportation altogether, and expecting claimants to seek such benefits from

[104] Case 313/86 *Lenoir* [1988] ECR 5391.

[105] For example, Case 24/74 *Biason* [1974] ECR 999; Case 139/82 *Piscitello* [1983] ECR 1427; Case C-356/89 *Newton* [1991] ECR I-3017.

and under the conditions laid down by their country of habitual residence.[106] In particular, the Court affirmed that 'a condition of residence in the [competent state] may legitimately be required for the grant of benefits closely linked with the social environment'.[107] The importance of that link has since been expressly incorporated into the statutory definition of special non-contributory cash benefits.[108]

Various strands of case law on the interpretation of Regulation 1408/71 therefore evinced the Court's sensitivity towards the problems posed by freeing universal solidarity benefits from their existing territorial boundaries. Against that background, it is unsurprising to find that the Court continues to adopt a similar approach towards the exportation of solidarity benefits within the new legal context demanded by the primary Treaty provisions. In *Hendrix*, for example, the Court held that the Dutch incapacity benefit for disabled young people is closely linked to the socio-economic situation of the Netherlands, since it is based on the Dutch minimum wage and standard of living. Together with the fact that the disputed territorial limitation had been expressly sanctioned by the Community legislature, under Regulation 1408/71, this could (in principle) justify the imposition of the Dutch residency requirement.[109] Indeed, in its recent ruling in *Habelt*, the Court specifically contrasted the situation of benefits such as special non-contributory [cash] benefits which are closely linked to the social environment of the competent state with that of ordinary social security benefits.[110] In the former case, territorial limitations may well be justified, whereas in the latter situation, the imposition of a residency requirement would not serve a legitimate public interest objective.[111]

Such judgments highlight the importance of identifying in each case a 'solidaristic real link'. However, this process of objectively justifying territorial barriers to movement taking into account the existence and strength of the connection between benefit and society presents a significant task: the need to undertake a detailed assessment of any given benefit scheme, including its social purpose, applicable qualifying criteria, chosen

[106] Though without having to prove any previous connection to the competent social security system. For example, Case C-20/96 *Snares* [1997] ECR I-6057; Case C-160/02 *Skalka* [2004] ECR I-5613.

[107] Case C-43/99 *Leclere* [2001] ECR I-4265, para 32.

[108] See Art 4(2a) Reg 1408/71 as amended by Reg 647/2005 [2005] OJ L117/1. Note, however, that the precise list of special non-contributory cash benefits contained in the revised Annex IIa is disputed: see Case C-299/05 *Commission v Parliament and Council* (Opinion of 3 May 2007; Judgment pending).

[109] Case C-287/05 *Hendrix* (see n 33 above), para 55.

[110] That is those falling within the scope of Art 4(1) Reg 1408/71.

[111] Cases C-396/05, C-419/05 and C-450/05 *Habelt* (Judgment of 18 December 2007), paras 81–2. Consider also the Court's strict attitude towards the disputed territorial restrictions in Cases C-502/01 and C-31/02 *Gaumain-Cerri* [2004] ECR I-6483.

method of funding, and indeed its perception within the relevant society. With that task comes the inevitable danger that the proper classification of particular benefits will ultimately depend upon drawing rather fine distinctions and invite the making of essentially subjective choices.

Consider, for example, benefits which are essentially compensatory in nature, that is whereby qualification is not dependent on the payment of contributions, or even the demonstration of need, but arises from a recognition by the state that the individual has suffered prejudice to his or her rights or interests, on behalf or as a result of the general good, in respect of which society effectively owes to the claimant a moral debt, settled through the provision of particular forms of public support. That is arguably the case with war benefits for ex-military personnel provided in respect of the individual's service to and suffering on behalf of the state in times of national emergency.[112] In such situations, it is difficult to see why the Member State's obligation to compensate individuals for hardships endured should be conditioned upon the claimant's current status as a resident or non-resident of the domestic territory, or at least to accept that such territorial restrictions should override the normative argument in favour of facilitating greater welfare exportation by Union citizens exercising their rights to free movement under the Treaty. Nevertheless, Advocate General Kokott in *Tas-Hagen* argued that support for ex-military personnel is essentially different from *civilian* war benefits: the latter are not paid in respect of hardship suffered through military service rendered to the country, and are to be considered instead an expression of social solidarity, having the character of non-contributory benefits intended to improve living conditions and compensate for loss of income resulting from war disabilities.[113] The Court agreed: it was legitimate for the Dutch legislature to limit its obligation to pay civilian war benefits to those victims who had links with the population of the Netherlands during and after the Second World War—on which basis it was possible *in principle* to justify the imposition of some sort of residency requirement.[114]

Moreover, there are other benefits which cannot be described as solidaristic in the same sense as universal welfare provision, but which nevertheless fulfil national policy objectives inherently linked to the domestic territory. For example, a childbirth or child-raising benefit may be specifically intended to increase the national birth rate, in pursuit of the entirely legitimate goal of countering the negative effects of demographic change. It would make little sense, one might argue, for Community law to insist

[112] As acknowledged by the ECJ, eg in Case 9/78 *Gillard* [1978] ECR 1661, para 13; Case 207/78 *Even* [1979] ECR 2019, paras 12 and 23; Case C-386/02 *Baldinger* [2004] ECR I-8411, paras 17 and 20.

[113] Case C-192/05 *Tas-Hagen* [2006] ECR I-10451, especially at paras 57–60 Opinion.

[114] Case C-192/05 *Tas-Hagen* [2006] ECR I-10451, especially at paras 34–5.

upon the exportation of such benefits by a claimant who exits the domestic territory, and whose reproductive achievements will thus no longer contribute to fulfilment of the relevant imperative requirement.[115]

There is evidence in the case law that the Court is open to the idea a 'real link' which is not solidaristic in nature, but territorial nonetheless (what we might refer to as a 'territorial real link'). For example, *Peerbooms* recognised that the need to ensure the effective and efficient organisation and long-term planning of the complex infrastructures required for the delivery of hospital treatment can, in principle, justify the imposition of prior authorisation requirements which act as a barrier to cross-border movement. Indeed, 'if insured persons were at liberty, regardless of the circumstances, to use the services of hospitals with which their sickness insurance fund had no contractual arrangements ... all the planning which goes into the contractual system in an effort to guarantee a rationalised, stable, balanced and accessible supply of hospital services would be jeopardised at a stroke'.[116] Similarly, preserving the financial balance of the national social security system may be recognised as a legitimate imperative requirement.[117] For example, the Court in *Morgan* recognised the risk that students claiming financial assistance for studies outside their home state could impose an unreasonable burden capable of having adverse consequences for the overall level of educational assistance that that Member State could afford—thereby justifying the imposition of qualifying criteria designed to ensure a sufficient degree of integration with the relevant society.[118] Or again, consider the Belgian unemployment benefits under dispute in *De Cuyper*, which seem to have been awarded to the claimant at least partially on a contributory rather than a purely solidaristic basis: payments could be territorially limited in accordance with the imperative requirement of monitoring the employment and family situation of unemployed persons for changes which might affect entitlement to or the level of benefits.[119]

[115] *Cf* AG Geelhoed in Case C-213/05 *Geven* (Opinion of 28 September 2006; Judgment of 18 July 2007), para 29 Opinion; Case C-212/05 *Hartmann* (Opinion of 28 September 2006; Judgment of 18 July 2007), para 69 Opinion.

[116] Case C-157/99 *Peerbooms* [2001] ECR I-5473, para 81.

[117] See, eg Cases C-396/05, C-419/05 and C-450/05 *Habelt* (Judgment of 18 December 2007), para 83.

[118] Cases C-11–12/06 *Morgan* (Judgment of 23 October 2007), paras 43–4. Compare with the ruling on migrant–host state relations in Case C-209/03 *Bidar* [2005] ECR I-2119; though contrast with the assessments made in Case C-76/05 *Schwarz and Gootjes-Schwarz* (Judgment of 11 September 2007) and Case C-318/05 *Commission v Germany* (Judgment of 11 September 2007).

[119] Case C-406/04 *De Cuyper* [2006] ECR I-6947. Note also the observations made by AG Geelhoed, at paras 54–65 and 85 Opinion, concerning the relationship between unemployment benefits and national labour market policies.

(ii) Identifying a 'Membership Real Link'

Having established the existence of a 'solidaristic (or territorial) real link' which justifies the Member State in restricting its benefits to an identifiable welfare community, it is then necessary to examine the individual claimant's ability to demonstrate fulfilment of a 'membership real link' to that welfare community conferring a right of access to the relevant benefits. As rulings such as *Hendrix* and *Tas-Hagen* make clear, the imposition of a general residency requirement can, in principle, be considered an appropriate membership criterion—even though its prima facie effect is to exclude from benefit entitlement those who have migrated from the national territory. Nevertheless, there are at least two situations where it is arguable that the Court will still intervene on behalf of individual claimants, using further analysis under the principle of proportionality to swing the pendulum back towards the normative arguments favouring greater exportation.

First, there are those cases where the Member State has accepted the principle of exportation for the relevant benefits, and the individual's primary complaint is that the exact conditions for exportation are discriminatory or arbitrary in nature. Such an approach should already be familiar to Community lawyers from other fields of free movement law: for example, the case law on the Member State's competence to regulate or even prohibit the provision of gambling services.[120] In those situations, generally categorised by complex social choices and significantly conditioned by the cultural context of each Member State, the Court has tended to leave the national authorities a relatively wide margin of appreciation; but the principle of proportionality can still lead to the disapplication of specific national restrictions where there is evidence of discrimination or inconsistency.[121]

Further support can be garnered from the exportation case law itself. In particular, the Court in the health care case law was able to draw upon the long experience acquired through the operation of Regulation 1408/71 to provide a direct Community model for its own exportation case law; the focus of judicial review had less to do with the principle of deterritorialisation itself than with the precise conditions for granting prior authorisation to seek hospital treatment in another Member State (for example) in defining concepts such as what constitutes 'undue delay' in the provision of treatment at a contracted institution.[122] The ruling in *Tas-Hagen* fits the

[120] For example, Case C-275/92 *Schindler* [1994] ECR I-1039; Case C-124/97 *Läärä (Cotswold Microsystems)* [1999] ECR I-6067.

[121] See, in particular, Case C-67/98 *Zenatti* [1999] ECR I-7289; Case C-243/01 *Gambelli* [2003] ECR I-13031; Cases C-338/04, C-359/04 and C-360/04 *Placanica* [2007] ECR I-1891.

[122] For example, Case C-157/99 *Peerbooms* [2001] ECR I-5473; Case C-385/99 *Müller-Fauré* [2003] ECR I-4509; Case C-372/04 *Watts* [2006] ECR I-4325.

same pattern. Despite the Member State's wide margin of discretion when it comes to ensuring the existence of a link between claimants of civilian war benefit and Dutch society, the chosen territoriality requirement was considered disproportionate to its objective: the mere date on which the application for benefit was made does not say anything meaningful about the claimant's actual degree of integration into Dutch society, and could lead to persons who are in comparable situations being treated in practice very differently.[123] After all, the Dutch legislation permitted the exportation of civilian war benefit by those claimants who had already qualified for payment and subsequently chose to move to another Member State.[124]

Secondly, there are those situations where, even though the Member State is entitled to insist on a 'membership real link', and a general residency requirement is acknowledged to be an appropriate means of demonstrating it, the claimant nevertheless argues that residency is not the *only* criterion which the Member State should be obliged to take into consideration. Other factors—such as a continuing contribution or connection to the home society—should also be capable of constituting the desired bond between claimant and benefit.

In this regard, consider the ruling in *Geven*.[125] Germany offered child-raising allowance to claimants who were ordinarily resident within the national territory, and to those resident in another Member State but employed in Germany on a more than minor basis. The Dutch claimant was resident in the Netherlands and working in Germany, but only on a minor basis, and was thus denied the child-raising benefit—a situation found to constitute indirect discrimination on grounds of nationality against frontier workers contrary to Article 7(2) Regulation 1612/68. The Court accepted that Germany was entitled to expect a 'real link' between claimant and benefit, but seemed to place significance on the fact that national law did not treat residency as the sole criterion for demonstrating such a 'real link', instead taking into account the non-resident claimant's economic contribution. Expressly reserving its opinion as to whether a 'real link' could have objectively justified a national rule based exclusively on residency, the Court held that Germany was entitled to exclude from entitlement to benefits frontier workers who failed to demonstrate a sufficiently substantial contribution to the national labour market. The converse question is whether Germany would have been *obliged* as a matter of Community law to recognise a substantial economic contribution to its society by a non-resident claimant, as a legitimate ground for

[123] Case C-192/05 *Tas-Hagen* [2006] ECR I-10451, paras 37–9.
[124] See AG Kokott in Case C-192/05 *Tas-Hagen* [2006] ECR I-10451, para 65 Opinion.
[125] Case C-213/05 *Geven* (Judgment of 18 July 2007). See also Case C-212/05 *Hartmann* (Judgment of 18 July 2007).

claiming membership of its welfare society and therefore access to the child-raising allowance.

This issue arose again in *Hendrix*.[126] As we have seen, the claimant's Dutch incapacity benefit was terminated when he moved residence to Belgium while continuing to work in the Netherlands. The Court accepted that, in principle, the Member State was entitled to impose a residency requirement for enjoyment of the incapacity benefit. However, '[i]t is also necessary that the application of such a condition does not entail an infringement of the [claimant's free movement rights] which goes beyond what is required to achieve the legitimate objective pursued by the national legislation'.[127] In particular, the Court instructed the national judge to take into account the fact that the claimant maintained close economic and social links to the Netherlands as his country of origin. On its face, therefore, *Hendrix* might appear to support the contention that claimants must indeed be capable of demonstrating a 'membership real link', even without maintaining residency within the home state, based on continuing economic and/or social bonds with the relevant society. Again, however, the ruling is not unambiguous. Dutch law expressly provided for waiver of the residency requirement in cases where it would cause an 'unacceptable degree of unfairness'.[128] The Court's instructions to the national judge were aimed at identifying whether such unfairness was established, in this particular case, in accordance with the applicable domestic legislation. It is unclear whether, in the absence of any such express waiver clause, the Court would nevertheless have insisted that the Netherlands permit exportation of the incapacity benefit in the light of the claimant's personal circumstances, so as to ensure a fair balance between the Member State's legitimate interests and effective exercise of the Union citizen's free movement rights.

Further support for the 'personal circumstances' approach to the proportionality assessment can be found in the ruling in *Morgan*.[129] As we have seen, the Court found that Germany was entitled to restrict the exportation of student financial support to claimants who demonstrated a certain degree of integration with the relevant society. For these purposes, however, the Court held that it would be disproportionate for the Member State to enforce a generalised requirement that the claimants had already completed at least one year of their course in Germany, and intended to continue the same training abroad, without taking into consideration the fact that these particular individuals had been raised in Germany and completed their secondary schooling there. Again, however, the ruling

[126] Case C-287/05 *Hendrix* (Judgment of 11 September 2007).
[127] *Ibid*, para 56.
[128] *Ibid*, paras 17 and 57.
[129] Cases C-11–12/06 *Morgan* (Judgment of 23 October 2007).

cannot be seen as unequivocal. As with *Tas-Hagen*, the Member State had already accepted the principle of exportation, and the Court's primary finding was that the precise conditions laid down under German law were arbitrary in character. It is unclear whether the Court would have scrutinised the German rules with the same rigour if the Member State had imposed an absolute territorial bar on its system of student finance.[130]

With that caveat in mind, *Morgan* is nevertheless significant because the Court did clearly instruct the Member State to take into account the claimant's individual circumstances. Moreover, *Morgan* goes further than *Hendrix* in so far as the factors identified by the Court did not relate to an economic contribution to the home society, but consisted of purely social and personal connections. On the one hand, that was perhaps understandable given the nature of the benefit at issue in *Morgan* itself: while hardly impossible, it would certainly be rather difficult to make access to financial assistance for full-time education abroad conditional upon an actual economic contribution to the home society. The Court may thus have been hinting that different considerations will apply to different components of the domestic welfare system, so that the possibility of exporting other types of benefit might still presuppose, as relevant 'personal circumstances', evidence of employed or self-employed activity within the home society—thus limiting judicial review to frontier workers in an equivalent position to *Geven* or *Hendrix*. On the other hand, *Morgan* could be taken as evidence that, when deciding whether to maintain or set aside a prima facie territorial bar on the payment of welfare support, Member States will be obliged *in all cases* to give appropriate weight to both economic and non-economic links with the national community. In this regard, the outcome in *De Cuyper* might suggest that the Member State is entitled to expect something above and beyond the basic bond of shared nationality which most migrants could assert vis-à-vis their country of origin. Certainly, the case law still seems some way off endorsing the more generous approach advocated by our previous normative arguments in favour of greater exportation, that is that while membership of the national welfare community must be earned, it should not be so easily forfeited, creating a legitimate space for Community law to insist that the 'membership real link' between claimant and society must continue for at least a certain period after any transfer of residency, pending the individual's meaningful integration into another Member State.[131]

[130] Consider, in particular, *ibid*, para 28.

[131] *Cf* E Spaventa, 'Seeing the Wood Despite the Trees? On the Scope of Union Citizenship and Its Constitutional Effects' (2008) 45 *CML Rev* 13, who rejects the proposition that the 'personal circumstances' approach evident in the case law on migrant–host state relations applies also to the assessment of barriers to movement imposed by the claimant's home state.

In short: the Court will be called upon in future cases to clarify a crucial aspect of its exportation case law: whether the emphasis of objective justification should lie on identifying a 'solidaristic (or territorial) real link' between the relevant benefit and the specific economic and social environment of the competent state which implies that territoriality should act as the sole criterion relevant to judicial review; or instead on looking for a 'membership real link' between the relevant society and the individual Union citizen which would open the door to the examination of other factors capable of establishing the desired degree of connection, and could lead to exportation even in cases where domestic territorial restrictions are justifiable in principle.

For the Court to adopt the 'personal circumstances' approach to the proportionality assessment as standard practice in cases of territorial welfare restrictions could give rise to certain problems—the most obvious relating to legal certainty.[132] For example, Advocate General Kokott in *Hendrix* warned against imposing any obligation upon the national authorities to undertake a detailed proportionality assessment in every individual dispute, arguing that that would be incompatible with the needs of mass administration based on clear criteria and expeditious decision-making. Residency may be a blunt tool which fails to take into account all factors relevant to a given case, but it nevertheless satisfies the general requirement to demonstrate a real link with the competent state.[133]

Nevertheless, for the Court to adopt the 'personal circumstances' test would have the merit (once again) of contributing to the emergence of a more coherent doctrinal framework for dealing with the legal implications of Union citizenship. After all, cases like *Grzelczyk* and *Baumbast* established the principle that, pursuant to the demands of Union citizenship, national authorities should not apply legislative blunt tools, but must indeed undertake individual administrative evaluations.[134] If that is true for decisions about residency or equal treatment within the migrant's host state, why should it not also be true for decisions adopted by the home state adversely affecting the Union citizen's right to free movement?

[132] See further, eg M Dougan, 'The Constitutional Dimension to the Case Law on Union Citizenship' (2006) 31 *EL Rev* 613; H Verschueren, 'European (Internal) Migration as an Instrument for Defining the Boundaries of National Solidarity Systems' (2007) 9 *European Journal of Migration and Law* 307.

[133] Case C-287/05 *Hendrix* (see n 33 above), especially paras 70–73 Opinion.

[134] See further, eg M Dougan and E Spaventa, 'Educating Rudy and the (Non-)English Patient: A Double Bill on Residency Rights Under Article 18 EC' (2003) 28 *EL Rev* 699.

V ASSESSMENT AND CONCLUSIONS

From an early stage in the Community's development, social rights in Western Europe were increasingly seen as less statist and more cosmopolitan in character: not necessarily linked to one's nationality or to territoriality, but increasingly enjoyed also on the basis of one's economic contribution and even despite one's economic mobility. With the introduction of Union citizenship, the relationship between free movement and the forging of a common European identity has become more ambitious, but also more controversial, as Community law proves increasingly capable of deconstructing the Member State's thresholds for membership of its national welfare community even in the case of non-economic migration.[135]

As regards domestic conceptions of nationality, the Community legislative and judicial authorities seem to have hammered out a basic legal framework, centred around the idea of a 'real link' between migrant and host society which is strong enough to justify his or her assimilation into the national solidaristic community. However, as regards domestic conceptions of territoriality, the position seems less settled doctrinally and less secure conceptually. The underlying question is: how far should Community law open up possibilities for exportation which go beyond those offered by the coordination system contained in Regulation 1408/71?

One possible answer is perhaps summed up by the comments of Advocate General Geelhoed in *Hartmann*. When someone decides to move to another Member State in exercise of their Treaty rights, it is not guaranteed that this move will be financially neutral. Every decision to move to another Member State implies that individuals will simultaneously experience certain advantages and disadvantages thanks to differences in national legislation in the field of social security. It is for the Union citizen to weigh up those benefits and inconveniences, but he or she cannot assume that all existing rights to social protection vis-à-vis his or her country of origin will be maintained. Even if Member States are required not to impose restrictions on own nationals wishing to move elsewhere in the Union, they are not obliged to grant such individuals a bonus for leaving.[136] Such an approach implies that exportation under Community law should mean Regulation 1408/71 and no more.

[135] See further, eg M Bommes and A Geddes (eds), *Immigration and Welfare: Challenging the Borders of the Welfare State* (London, Routledge, 2000); M Berezin and M Schain (eds), *Europe Without Borders: Remapping Territory, Citizenship and Identity in a Transnational Age* (Baltimore, John Hopkins University Press, 2003); F Mayer and J Palmowski, 'European Identities and the EU–The Ties that Bind the Peoples of Europe' (2004) 42 *Journal of Common Market Studies* 573.

[136] Case C-212/05 *Hartmann* (Opinion of 28 September 2006; Judgment of 18 July 2007), para 86 Opinion.

However, the Court seems willing to offer a more ambitious legal response. Having accepted the logic of applying the barrier to movement case law to the field of welfare benefits, the adverse impact of domestic territorial restrictions is no longer simply the result of mere differences in Member State legislation, but constitutes precisely a limitation on own nationals wishing to move elsewhere in the Union, and thus a prima facie breach of the primary Treaty provisions. Nevertheless, the Court has hardly launched a full frontal assault on the criterion of territoriality as a valid threshold criterion for membership of the national solidaristic community. Rather, this paper has argued that the Court is grappling with a host of difficult legal and policy questions. On the one hand, there is the potential normative basis upon which Community law now redefines the territorial space of the national welfare states and should favour greater exportation: one passive, that Community law merely reflects changes in the welfare states themselves; the other active, that the Court should make free movement for Union citizens more universal. On the other hand, there are a series of factors which rather argue against greater exportation, for example: the constitutional relationship between the coordination system already established by the Community legislature through Regulation 1408/71 and the potential for judicial scrutiny under the primary Treaty provisions; and the variables considered relevant to objective justification of a Member State's refusal to permit the exportation of welfare benefits by its own nationals, such as the strength of the social solidarity system or other national policy objectives underpinning the relevant benefit, or the extent of judicial review over the choice of territoriality as a legitimate connecting factor between claimant and competent state.

The complexity of the interaction between such overlapping and potentially contradictory considerations sometimes makes it difficult to comprehend the Court's legal approach—as well as the outcomes of the decided rulings, or the likely direction of future cases—in terms which are entirely structured, coherent and consistent.

Nevertheless, this paper has argued that, looking beyond the confusion on the surface, the case law on national territorial restrictions both draws upon and contributes to the continuing evolution of the broader legal framework governing migrant Union citizens. Two main principles, originally established by the Court in *Grzelczyk* and *Baumbast* but increasingly applicable to all questions of residency, equal treatment and non-discriminatory barriers to movement, can perhaps help make better sense of the case law on the welfare relationship between migrants and their country of origin. First, Community secondary legislation purporting to restrict the opportunities for free movement may nevertheless be amenable to a form of indirect judicial review intended to guarantee that it does not unduly prejudice the Union citizen's rights. Secondly, even where it is legitimate in principle for the Member State to expect a 'real link' between claimant and community, evidenced through generalised criteria such as residency, the national authorities must nevertheless give due consideration to the personal circumstances of each individual.

In any case, our analysis stands as a vivid illustration of two points. On the one hand, drawing upon such familiar tools as equal treatment and barriers to movement, what penetrating strength Community law now stands able to exert in a field which, only a few years ago, most people assumed lay truly at the outer limit of the Treaty. On the other hand, with what sensitivity and restraint Community law must exercise its theoretical power, precisely in an area able to illuminate, in a most unflattering light, the Union's perilously fragile mandate to act. Pursuing the logic of the primary Treaty provisions to the farthest ends of Community competence might end up prompting the question: is the Union trying to run before it can walk?

8

The Outer Limits of EU Citizenship: Displacing Economic Free Movement Rights?

NIAMH NIC SHUIBHNE*

I INTRODUCTION

FRAMING THE LEGAL limits of European Union citizenship is a work in the course of being defined though a process involving multiple actors. EU citizenship would not exist without the Member States; and it would be meaningless if their nationals (and their lawyers, courts and tribunals) had not engaged with its possibilities. Through decades of case law on workers (Article 39 EC), establishment (Article 43 EC) and services (Article 49 EC), the Court of Justice developed a substantive framework for the realisation of personal movement rights. Its interpretative approach seemed expansive almost by default, emphasising the rights of the individual, usually at the expense of national regulatory autonomy. Since the judgment in *Martínez Sala*,[1] Article 18 EC has been used as a distinct source of additional rights; in developing the contours of these additional rights the Court of Justice's role in the legal development of citizenship is clear. The enactment of Directive 2004/38[2] marked a disruption, however, in institutional ownership. This legislation aims to capture and demarcate the rights—and the limits—of EU citizenship law. The Directive was certainly inspired by and strives primarily to codify the Court's jurisprudence. It also breaks down boundaries between the traditional Treaty freedoms, pulling together in one place the rights conferred by different free movement provisions as they apply to (natural)

* Thanks to Graeme Laurie and Dimitra Nassimpian, and to Mina Andreeva for research assistance.

[1] Case C-85/96 *Martínez Sala v Freistaat Bayern* [1998] ECR I-2691.

[2] Dir 2004/38/EC on the right of citizens of the Union and their family members to move and reside freely within the territory of the Member States, [2004] OJ L229/35.

persons—to EU citizens. The coverage of the Directive is very comprehensive;[3] and this should in theory leave the Court with a residual and less innovative interpretative function. In reality, though, this seems unlikely to happen.

This contribution is sited at the outer limits of EU citizenship law, tracking questions that remain still to be worked through about the reach of citizenship rights, and about the relationship between citizenship and free movement law more generally. To explain the central premise of the chapter more fully, the following model suggests a typology that can be used in thinking about the limits of EU citizenship:

Normative Limits: Normative limits describe the conceptual fundamentals of citizenship as an idea and as a status. These limits concern the potential of political entities to generate a meaningful citizenship and associated rights.[4] This is an especially important question within the discipline of political science; but it is one with which legal science must engage too, since normative limits necessarily overlap with and inform what is legally possible and/or legitimate. While the normative limits of (EU) citizenship are by no means settled or resolved, it will be assumed for present purposes that the EU is, at least, a citizenship-*capable* polity.

Inner Limits: This term is used here to denote the State space into which EU citizenship should not intrude. Article 17 EC makes it very clear that EU citizenship is a *complementary* citizenship. The national spaces normally affected by it are primarily legal or regulatory ones (for example, the curbing of a State's immigration competence in respect of other States' nationals). But we know too that Community law can pierce all kinds of political, social, economic and cultural contexts. The boundaries of the inner limits are patrolled by a range of legal devices: the ability of States to derogate from Treaty freedoms, the principle of proportionality, the wholly

[3] Dir 2004/38 amends Arts 10 and 11 of Reg 1612/68 (Sp Ed [1968] OJ L257/2, p 475), and repeals and replaces: Dir 64/221/EEC (Sp Ed [1968] OJ 850/64, 117, public policy, public security or public health); Dir 68/360 (Sp Ed [1968] OJ L257/13, 485, abolition of restrictions on movement and residence within the Community for workers of Member States and their families); Dir 73/148 ([1973] OJ L172/14, abolition of restrictions on movement and residence for establishment and the provision of services); Dir 72/194/EEC (Sp Ed [1972] OJ L121/32, 474, extension of Dir 64/221 to those resident in the territory of a Member State after having been employed there); Dir 75/34/EEC ([1975] OJ L14/10, right to remain in the territory of another Member State after having pursued therein an activity in a self-employed capacity); Dir 75/35/EEC ([1975] OJ L14/14, extending the scope of Dir 64/221 those resident in the territory of another Member State after having pursued an activity in a self-employed capacity); Dir 90/364 ([1990] OJ L180/26, general right of residence); Dir 90/365 ([1990] OJ L180/28, right of residence for retired persons); Dir 93/96 ([1993] OJ L317/59, right of residence for students). Reg 1251/70 ([1970] OJ L142/24, right of workers to remain in the territory of a Member State after having been employed in that State) was repealed separately by Commission Reg 635/2006, [2006] OJ L112/9.

[4] Thus, the contribution to EU citizenship effected by electoral rights will not be addressed in this chapter; see instead the contribution to this volume by J Shaw.

internal rule and so on.[5] It is worth noting that the 'size' of preserved national spaces was already deeply eroded by free movement law in general, long before the watershed of Maastricht. But it is also true that national competence has been chiselled down more radically by the evolving legal demands of EU citizenship. This is compounded by an intensifying requirement that Member States 'must none the less exercise that competence consistently with Community law', enabling the Court of Justice to undertake executive, principle-oriented reviews of subject matter that is openly admitted to be outwith the scope of the Treaty in a substantive sense. Examples of this being applied to supposedly reserved competences in the field of citizenship include the assignation of nationality, regulation of direct taxation and determining the content and organisation of education systems.[6]

Outer Limits: So what does that leave us with? The outer limits of EU citizenship are for present purposes legal or interpretative limits; they represent the boundaries prescribed by the 'wording and general scheme'[7] of both the Treaty and legal interpretations of the Treaty. It must be stressed that there is inevitable overlap with questions described above as 'inner limits', since the extent to which EU citizenship can spread through Member State legal space is inevitably connected with settling the proper domains of Community law per se. But this chapter concentrates principally on assessing the coherence of citizenship rights within and against the scope and logic of the Community legal framework within or against itself. Since they are the most legally developed citizenship rights, most of the analysis focuses on the rights to move and reside conferred by Article 18 EC (although more limited discussion of other citizenship rights is included where relevant). The basic premise is that there *are* limits to the development of EU citizenship in an interpretative sense. The outer limits might be transcended politically through an agreed revision of the normative parameters of EU citizenship. But in the absence of this, and working with what we have, the development of citizenship rights should not be thought of as a boundless enterprise. The analysis also raises questions about who (in an institutional sense) does and/or should, locate the outer limits of EU citizenship.

To evaluate these ideas further, the chapter is divided into two main parts: first, the relationship between EU citizenship and free movement law

[5] For in-depth analysis of these issues, see the contributions to this volume by C Barnard and M Dougan.

[6] Respectively, Case C-369/90 *Micheletti and others v Delegación del Gobierno en Cantabria* [1992] ECR I-4239, para 10; Case 520/04 *Turpeinin* [2006] ECR I-10685, para 11; Joined Cases C-11/06 and C-12/06 *Morgan v Bezirksregierung Köln*; *Bucher v Landrat des Kreises Düren* [2007] ECR I-9161, para 24.

[7] To borrow from Case 26/62 *Van Gend en Loos v Nederlandse Administratie der Belastingen* [1963] ECR 1.

more generally, to outline the extent to which the limits to citizenship law are the same as—but also different from—the outer limits of free movement law; secondly, specific limits imposed on EU citizenship rights by the exercise of economic activity.

II CITIZENSHIP RIGHTS AND FREE MOVEMENT RIGHTS: UNPACKING THE INTERPRETATIVE LIMITS

Several provisions of the EC Treaty confer (personal) free movement rights. The material content of EU citizenship law is strongly grounded in principles developed within the other (traditional or original, for present purposes) free movement provisions, but clearly extends the scope of application of those principles too. This section explores the relationship between them and also the relationship between the limits to them.

A Citizenship and Free Movement: The Same or Different?

On one view, Article 18 EC is the residual source of free movement rights. The Court of Justice has always held, and continues to affirm, that Articles 39 (workers), 43 (establishment) and 49 (services) EC constitute specific expressions of free movement rights and therefore, where possible, should be used in preference to the more generic rights associated with EU citizenship. This view did not dissolve after the profile of citizenship was more confidently worked out in *Martínez Sala*; rather, it is an interpretative rule still and consistently applied.[8] Looking at citizenship jurisprudence as a narrative, however, an evolution in the idea of citizenship as a residual source of free movement rights can be traced. In the first phase of Article 18 EC case law, submissions based solely on Article 18 EC tended to be very tersely dismissed, usually in a brief paragraph outlining the irrelevance of citizenship (given that the question had been resolved on the basis of workers, services or establishment, as appropriate),[9] or even ignoring the citizenship dimension altogether.[10] In the second phase, the specific freedoms and EU citizenship exhibit a more fluid or blended relationship

[8] See recently, eg (relating to Art 49 EC), Case C-76/05 *Schwarz and Gootjes-Schwarz v Finanzamt Bergisch Gladbach*, judgment of 11 September 2007, not yet reported, paras 34–5; the same idea is expressed more convolutedly in Case C-318/05 *Commission v Germany* [2007] ECR I-6957, paras 32–7.

[9] For example, Case C-348/96 *Criminal Proceedings against Donatella Calfa* [1999] ECR I-11, para 30.

[10] Notwithstanding the well-known Opinion of Advocate General Jacobs on the nature of citizenship, the judgment in Case C-168/91 *Konstantinidis v Stadt Altensteig—Standesamt and Landratsamt Calw-Ordnungsamt* [1993] ECR I-1191 provides a good example of this (see in particular, paras 10–11).

than is usually the case; in *Bickel and Franz*, for example, it's not quite clear where services end and citizenship begins.[11] It was increasingly recognised in this transitional phase that there is an inter-changeability at play, with citizenship and the traditional free movement rights often meaning (and conferring) the same thing. This corresponds with the tentative beginnings of citizenship actually meaning something in a substantive legal sense. The judgment in *Martínez Sala* marks the beginning of a third phase, a distinct turning point in and after which Article 18 EC was found to generate meaningful rights above and beyond those grounded in more specific free movement provisions. As that substantive contribution grows over time, the distinction between the original free movement rights and those generated by Article 18 EC is stretched but also more defined. Article 18 EC remains the legal basis of last resort for the resolution of free movement disputes, with the Court still insisting that specific free movement provisions be used where possible. What has changed in the third phase is the willingness and frequency with which the Court *does* go on to find a material contribution through the application of citizenship. This happens because other Treaty provisions could not provide the same benefits. Rephrased in the language of limits, rights generated by Article 18 EC *only* make it easier to see the outer limits of the specific free movement provisions, rather than the other way around. The objective of the following sections is to define or locate the point(s) of departure more precisely.

B The Evolution of Movement

One angle on outer limits could look conceptually at the idea of movement and then track how this is translated into legal effect. Movement is necessary to trigger free movement rights, but to bring about the application of EC law to different factual situations, substantive Community rights can be grounded in all kinds or types of movement. Case law examples suggest a thread that clearly links the case law before and after citizenship—in summary, free movement law was already on an expansive trajectory, but citizenship can add a firmer basis and even accentuate legitimacy in cases where free movement seemed artificially or even wrongly distended.[12] Some of the less obvious types of movement include:

[11] Case C-274/96 *Criminal proceedings against Bickel and Franz* [1998] ECR I-7637.

[12] See E Spaventa, 'From *Gebhard* to *Carpenter*: Towards a (non-)economic European constitution', (2004) 41 *CML Rev* 743, 768.

past movement,[13] future (including potential) movement,[14] the movement of others,[15] and movement deliberately undertaken so that Community rights could be invoked.[16] Even the notion of 'passport movement' (that is where holding a passport from one State is in itself a sufficient trigger for Community rights to be attached to a situation involving one of the other States[17]) is not really an innovation that could only come about through the status of EU citizenship: these situations do remove any curiosity about the *purpose* of the citizen's movement, but it should be remembered that this was also possible under the traditional framework through Directive 90/364. The fact remains that some sort of movement *must* occur if the protection of internal market law is to be activated.[18] In thinking about the scale of that variability, real questions fall to be answered about the shrinking core of purely internal matters that can, in a comparative sense, lead to reverse discrimination against home State nationals. That question—an 'inner' limit for present purposes—is explored elsewhere.[19] What citizenship can offer is a firmer basis and even accentuated legitimacy in cases where free movement seemed artificially or even wrongly distended.[20] In other words, the device of EU citizenship has been used more effectively by the Court in cases where under the traditional four

[13] Case C-370/90 *R v Immigration Appeal Tribunal and Singh*, ex p *Secretary of State for the Home Department* [1992] ECR I-4265 (establishment); Case C-224/98 *D'Hoop v Office national de l'emploi* [2002] ECR I-6191 (citizenship).

[14] Although the Court rejected the possibility that purely hypothetical movement could be used to invoke the protection of citizenship (Case C-299/95 *Kremzow v Austria* [1997] ECR I-2629), other decisions protect an as-yet-to-be exercised right to move (eg, *Calfa* (services), in the context of expulsion *for life* from Greece on the basis of criminal convictions); Case C-148/02 *Garcia Avello v Belgium* [2003] ECR I-11613, para 36 in particular (citizenship, on the inconvenience 'liable to be caused' by different States' rules on surnames). Advocate General Sharpston has discussed the distinction between 'purely hypothetical' and 'potential' (Case C-212/06 *Government of the French Community and Walloon Government v Flemish Community*, judgment of 1 April 2008, not yet reported; Opinion delivered on 28 June 2007, see from para 64 onwards in particular).

[15] Case C-255/99 *Humer* [2002] I-1205 (movement of the worker's dependent child); Case C-403/03 *Schempp v Finanzamt München V* [2005] ECR I-6421 (movement of the EU citizen's former spouse, see paras 21–2 in particular).

[16] It is a well established principle that deliberately taking advantage of Community rights by moving with that express intent does not constitute an abuse of Community law (see eg, Case C-109/01 *Secretary of State for the Home Department v Akrich* [2003] ECR I-9607, paras 55–7, free movement of workers).

[17] Case C-138/02 *Collins v Secretary of State for Work and Pensions* [2004] ECR I-2703; Case C-200/02 *Zhu and Chen v Secretary of State for the Home Department* [2004] ECR I-9925.

[18] Problems caused by the requirement of movement are addressed N. Nic Shuibhne, 'Free movement of persons and the wholly internal rule: Time to move on ?', (2002) 39 *CMLRev* 731; E. Spaventa, 'Seeing the wood despite the trees? On the scope of Union citizenship and its constitutional effects', (2008) 45 *CMLRev* 13.

[19] See again, the references *ibid*.

[20] See E Spaventa, 'From *Gebhard* to *Carpenter*: Towards a (non-)economic European constitution', (2004) 41 *CML Rev* 743, 768.

freedoms the movement link would appear quite tenuous. This reflects a more deliberate (more coherent and therefore also more palatable) shift into the 'general' movement accommodated very well by citizenship rights.[21] The difficulty with cases where the link seems tenuous (as opposed to minimal or marginal, on which more below) is that they cement a fundamental disconnect between the *nature* of the movement and the *substance* of the rights being claimed through that exercise of movement. Again, this is something that evolved over time and began long before citizenship.[22] It means that there is not necessarily a *relative* connection between the extent of the movement undertaken and the extent of the rights protected by Community law in turn, as illustrated by the decision in *Carpenter* where temporary and sporadic service provision in other States (nature of movement) was still strong enough to secure spousal home State residence (substance of rights claimed) against the express intentions of the home State.[23] *Carpenter* probably marked the high watermark of this disconnect, since no formal link between Mr Carpenter's service provision in other Member States and his (third country national) wife's residence in his home State (the UK) was required to be shown. The invocation of factors inherently connected to his humanity, as a service provider, did not seem very coherently worked out, however; a more general problem is that this approach wasn't very consistently applied in the reasoning of the Court.[24] Thus, a nascent or *de facto* citizenship arguably explains the outcome in cases like *Cowan*; and even after the Treaty codification of 'actual' EU citizenship, its undercurrent might help to rationalise cases such as *Carpenter*, or perhaps the

[21] See, eg, *Chen* paras 21–3. The Court reasoned that '[Directive 73/148] cannot in any event serve as a basis for a right of residence of indefinite duration of the kind with which the main proceedings are concerned' (which confirms one half of the decision in Case C-60/00 *Carpenter v Secretary of State for the Home Department* [2002] ECR I-6279; see further below). The Court did not address in *Chen*, however, whether that right could stem from Art 49 EC—since it was able to use Art 18 EC in this case, it basically didn't have to. In *Government of the French Community and Walloon Government v Flemish Community*, the Court again insisted that the wholly internal rule sets a limit to free movement law which citizenship does *not* breach, recalling that '[t]he Court has on several occasions held that citizenship of the Union is not intended to extend the material scope of the Treaty to internal situations which have no link with Community law' (para 39).

[22] This separation of personal and material Treaty scope is illustrated very well in *Martínez Sala*, but had been established before then through case law on the receipt of services (Case 186/87 *Cowan v Trésor Public* [1989] ECR 195).

[23] Case C-60/00 *Carpenter v Secretary of State for the Home Department* [2002] ECR I-6279.

[24] The judgment in Case C-257/00 *Givane v Secretary of State for the Home Department* [2003] ECR I-345 is a noted example of a less family-friendly approach to proportionate analysis of legislative limitations on free movement rights; here, the Court (contrary to its Advocate General) refused to apply a more lenient, rights-infused interpretation of Reg 1251/70 to establish residence rights in the host State for a deceased worker's (third country national) widow and children.

extension of horizontal effect to Article 39 EC in *Angonese*.[25] We can try to represent this visually—the 'traditional' four freedoms, on the one hand, form a shape of four equal parts; but an alternative model looks more like a linear spectrum of activity with citizenship at one end not far from free movement of workers, free movement of goods at the other (capital normally quite close to that point also), establishment and services cropping up more chaotically in many places in between. In other words, maybe divisions *within* the freedoms are becoming more critical than any divisions *across* them. Decisions like *Carpenter* distort the services-quarter of the four freedom model but may find a niche on the linear spectrum, since the premise of the judgment is far closer to citizenship than to services (though truthfully, in the absence of a general human rights mandate for the EC, it is difficult to find any basis for that particular decision at all). The personal/economic splintering that this reasoning suggests is examined in more depth in Section III below.

C Substantive Limitations and Conditions

Alongside rights of movement and residence for EU citizens, Article 18 EC plainly refers to 'limitations and conditions laid down in this Treaty *and by the measures adopted to give it effect*' (emphasis added). We have seen that citizenship and free movement law overlap to a considerable degree. The idea (discussed in more detail below) that there is also a discrete substantive content to free movement rights under Article 18 has also been introduced. The limitations and conditions drawn from the Treaty are typically taken to mean the express Treaty derogations linked to the specific free movement provisions. Considering whether limitations were also laid down by secondary legislation,[26] it had been suggested that the fundamental nature of citizenship should trump the limits imposed by (hierarchically inferior, in a normative sense) pre-existing residence directives.[27] Those measures prescribed that anyone exercising general movement and residence rights had to demonstrate both sufficient economic resources and comprehensive medical insurance.[28] In *Baumbast*, the Court sought to resolve any ambiguity about the applicability of these limitations

[25] Case C-281/98 *Angonese v Cassa di Risparmio di Bolzano* [2000] ECR I-4139.

[26] Over and above the legislative expansion of public health, policy and security (detailed originally in Dir 64/221 and now in Dir 2004/38; see generally N Nic Shuibhne, 'Derogating from the free movement of persons: When can EU citizens be deported?' (2005–6) 8 *Cambridge Yearbook of European Legal Studies* 187).

[27] See eg, the arguments submitted by Portugal in Case C-184/99 *Grzelczyk v Centre public d'aide sociale d'Ottignies-Louvain-la-Neuve* [2001] ECR I-6193, which are outlined by Advocate General Alber at paras 51–2 of his Opinion.

[28] Dirs 90/364, 90/365 and 93/96; these conditions can now be found in Art 7 of Dir 2004/38 (which should be read with Arts 14 and 24).

to rights derived from Article 18 EC, but not altogether successfully.[29] The judgment contains the first clear signal that Article 18 confers directly effective rights to free movement and residence on EU citizens.[30] But it also confirmed explicitly, and for the first time, that the resources and medical insurance conditions can, as Article 18 EC signposts, limit the *exercise*—as opposed to the existence[31]—of those rights.[32]

The application of those limitations is tempered by principles of Community law, notably proportionality (another critical point in the *Baumbast* case). While this interpretative method could well have evolved for the residence directives independently, the application of a primary Treaty right does move things onto a different and normatively higher plane, perhaps best described as a constitutional one.[33] That understanding of things helps us to rationalise why proportionate economic insufficiency or not-fully comprehensive medical insurance might mark the outer limits of free movement law as traditionally understood, but not those of EU citizenship.

It might have been legally cleaner and bolder in *Baumbast*, or before, to start from scratch, to abandon the limitations prescribed by the residence directives since they were designed for a right to move and reside which was premised more narrowly on what is now Article 308 EC, before EU citizenship was ever included in the Treaty. But it would have been, politically, stupid. In terms of organic legitimacy, derived from State acquiescence with regard to the evolution of Community rights, O'Leary has remarked that for the citizenship case law, '[t]here [is], after all, no equivalent in the field of the free movement of persons of the Barber protocol which Member States had annexed to the TEU in 1992 to limit the effects of a judgment of the Court on equal pay and pensions'.[34] Had the critical (from the perspective of State interests, concerns and even fears) conditions on economic resources and medical insurance been trampled more overtly by the Court than they were, we might well have seen such a reactionary protocol and not just secondary re-codification of the conditions in something like Directive 2004/38.

[29] Case C-413/99 *Baumbast and R v Secretary of State for the Home Department* [2002] ECR I-7091.

[30] *Baumbast*, paras 81 and 84.

[31] See S O'Leary, 'Developing an ever closer union between the peoples of Europe? A reappraisal of the case-law of the Court of Justice on the free movement of persons and EU citizenship', Edinburgh Mitchell Working Papers, No 6/2008, at http://www.law.ed.ac.uk/mitchellworkingpapers/papers.aspx, p 13.

[32] *Baumbast*, para 85.

[33] In this vein, see M Dougan, 'The Constitutional dimension to the case law on Union citizenship', (2006) 31 *EL Rev* 613; E Spaventa, 'Seeing the wood despite the trees? On the scope of Union citizenship and its constitutional effects' (2008) 45 *CML Rev* 13.

[34] O'Leary, (n 31) p. 9.

Exploring the citizenship/free movement linkages further, it is worth remembering that while the original Treaty provisions conferring free movement rights are drafted in a way that presumes an occupational context or intention, more *personal* movement rights emerged relatively soon through secondary legislation. For example, as well as the extensive rights for Community workers and their families detailed in Regulation 1612/68, Directive 73/148 arguably created brand new rights by addressing service receipt as well as service provision (endorsed a decade later by the Court).[35] What tends to mark the specific/general free movement boundary, however, is the question of economic self-sufficiency—where the economic dimension is passive (not engaging in economic activity but having sufficient financial resources) or negative (seeking to claim benefits from the host State) rather than a more active or positive contribution by the mover (as would have been the case within contributory free movement traditionally). But this is not an absolute line either; for example, access to social benefits was attached to free movement of workers where the remuneration earned through employment did not in itself save the worker from financial dependence on the host State.[36] The citizenship case law has taken things considerably further though; finding ways to provide host State means in certain circumstances for those who do not come within work, services or establishment at all and who do not properly meet the economic resources/comprehensive medical insurance criteria.[37] The case law on maintenance grants for students is an especially good example, with the Court expressly drawing from the introduction of citizenship rights to overturn its own more limited free movement case law from the 1980s.[38]

Is it arguable that, even without Article 18 EC, the humanising momentum long influencing other free movement provisions might have taken things to the same legal place? The application of proportionality further

[35] Joined Cases 286/82 and 26/83 *Luisi and Carbone v Ministero del Tesoro* [1984] ECR 377.

[36] Case law on part-time workers provides good examples of this; see Case 53/81 *Levin v Staatssecretaris van Justitie* [1982] ECR 1035 and Case 344/87 *Bettray v Staatssecretaris van Justitie* [1989] ECR 1621, para 15. Although the Court went on to consider the application of EU citizenship in the second part of its judgment, the discussion of the first question in Case C-456/02 *Trojani v Centre public d'aide sociale de Bruxelles (CPAS)* [2004] ECR I 7573 related to Art 39 EC and confirms the foundational case law.

[37] As well as *Martínez Sala* and *Trojani*, other case law examples include *Grzelczyk* (insufficient resources) and *Baumbast* (non-comprehensive medical insurance).

[38] See Case C-209/03 *Bidar v London Borough of Ealing; Secretary of State for Education and Skills* [2005] ECR I-2119, paras 38–9 (confirming para 35 of *Grzelczyk* to reverse Case 39/86 *Lair v Universität Hannover* [1988] ECR 3161). In *Grzelczyk* the grant applied for by the student was a general social security benefit and not a specific student maintenance grant; thus the Court has only since *Bidar* expressly overturned both *Lair* and Case 197/86 *Brown v Secretary of State for Scotland* [1988] ECR 3205. In *Morgan* and *Bucher*, citizenship reasoning was extended to support a claim for a study grant from the applicants' home State in respect of attending educational establishments in other States.

to refine the 'comprehensive' medical insurance condition in *Baumbast* was certainly facilitated by EU citizenship, but it was not necessarily dependent on it.[39] The significance of reading free movement rights through the lens of fundamental rights has had decisive effect outwith citizenship also.[40] Even the vocabulary of citizenship appeared in judgments before the word appeared in the Treaty.[41] The tricky question of national budgetary autonomy has been affected by developments in the field of healthcare, for example, as well as education; but the case law on medical services has related to Article 49 and not Article 18 EC. A free movement framework attached to the internal market can thus deliver very human results. But those rights are ultimately more fragile if they stay only in secondary legislation, recalling the constitutionalisation point above. In other words, the humanising trend within free movement law was undoubtedly a necessary prerequisite for the successful progression of EU citizenship, but probably not sufficient on its own to deliver the substance of it.

D Interpretative Limits or Unstoppable Force?

If decisions at the limits of free movement law tend now to be rationalised through more confident recourse to Article 18 EC and the material input of citizenship, the theme of outer limits still forces the question about where *that* whole track of case law must and should stop.[42] We have seen that the impetus of citizenship either takes the material scope of free movement law further than the traditional freedoms could have done, or possibly rationalises some of the more dubious developments in that line of case law—and it should be remembered that economic movement case law is not static just because of the advent of citizenship. This drive to take things further can also be seen in thinking about interpretative scope that is in the interpretation of and/or departure beyond key Community legal principles.

[39] See *Baumbast*, para 91, where the Court states that 'those limitations and conditions must be applied in compliance with the limits imposed by Community law and in accordance with the general principles of that law, in particular the principle of proportionality'—without an express supporting reference to the law or principles of EU citizenship.

[40] See again, *Carpenter*; and more ambiguously, Case C-109/01 *Secretary of State for the Home Department v Akrich* [2003] ECR I-9607 (the Court did not find that Mr Akrich, the third country national spouse of a Community worker, came within the scope of free movement rights but nonetheless included a (standalone?) reference to the importance of resolving his immigration situation with due regard for family rights, see para 58 in particular).

[41] See Case 143/87 *Stanton and SA belge d'assurances "L'Étoile 1905" v Institut national d'assurances sociales pour travailleurs indépendants (Inasti)* [1988] ECR 3877, para 13; confirmed in *Singh*, para 16.

[42] It may be recalled that concerns about national budgetary and social autonomy are conceptualised here as *inner* limits, centred on the identification and preservation of properly delimited State space; see the contribution to this volume by M Dougan.

Examples of this are beginning to stack up. In *Morgan and Bucher*, Advocate General Ruiz-Jarabo Colomer traces the severance of Article 18 EC from Article 12 EC and the principle of non-discrimination. This fits with jurisprudence on non-discriminatory obstacles to free movement more generally,[43] but it does nonetheless make the 'original' judgment in *Martínez Sala* (which was premised on their *combination*) seem almost backward or passé.[44] Even more strikingly, the functional step taken in that case to locate child-raising allowances within the material scope of Community law is also being progressively consigned to legal history: Advocate General Kokott in *Tas-Hagen and Tas* remarked that: 'Union citizens can assert their right to free movement even if the matter concerned or the benefit claimed is not governed by Community law.'[45] And in the recent German cases on tax relief for school fees and study grants,[46] in which German nationals wished to avail themselves of financial benefits from their home State authorities in respect of attending educational institutions established in other States, the tenor of the judgments and their findings in substance seemed arguably to cross into promoting, encouraging, or even rewarding free movement and not just facilitating it.[47]

It does make sense that the general approach to interpreting restrictions on free movement law—that is that while the scope of the freedom and restrictions on it are interpreted broadly, the scope of competing derogations and justifications is set as narrowly as possible—has been transposed to citizenship law also. But citizenship is increasingly felt to add a more acute incentive for the inflation of Community law, more like knock-over than spill-over. Interestingly, apart from the chronically replicated rationale that EU citizenship is 'destined to be the fundamental status of nationals of the Member States',[48] this has been most explicit in the sphere of *inner*

[43] For example, on workers, Case C-415/93 *Union Royale Belge des Societes de Football Association ASBL v Jean-Marc Bosman* [1995] ECR I-4921 and Case C-190/98 *Graf v Filmoser Maschinenbau GmbH* [2000] ECR I-493; on establishment, Case C-19/92 *Kraus v Land Baden-Württemberg* [1993] ECR I-1663.

[44] *Morgan and Bucher*, Opinion of Advocate General Ruiz-Jarabo Colomer, para 67; confirmed by the judgment of the Court, para 28. See further on this, Editorial Comments, 'Two-speed European citizenship: Can the Lisbon Treaty help close the gap?', (2008) 45 *CML Review* 1, 1–2.

[45] Case C-192/05 *Tas-Hagen and Tas v Raadskamer WUBO van de Pensioen- en Uitkeringsraad* [2006] ECR I-10451, para 33 of the Opinion; the Advocate General cites *García Avello*, para 25 in support (where the Court found that '[a]lthough, as Community law stands at present, the rules governing a person's surname are matters coming within the competence of the Member States, the latter must none the less, when exercising that competence, comply with Community law').

[46] *Schwarz*, *Commission v Germany*; *Morgan and Bucher* respectively.

[47] See further, N Nic Shuibhne, Case Comment (on the three judgments collectively), (2008) 45 *CML Rev* 771.

[48] First conceived in *Grzelczyk*, para 31, and now repeated in almost all judgments invoking citizenship rights.

limits. In the context of deportation, for example, the Court found that 'a *particularly restrictive interpretation* of the derogations from [Article 39 EC] is required by virtue of a person's status as a citizen of the Union' (also illustrating the free movement/citizenship inter-relationship).[49] Similarly, Advocate General Sharpston has suggested that the citizenship provisions offer '[a]n additional impetus' for resolving the complexities of reverse discrimination.[50] If the purpose of the Treaty provisions on EU citizenship is to secure the strongest rights possible for those persons who hold that status, then the interpretative development of citizenship law is certainly good work in progress. Against this momentum, which seems entirely about expanding rather than curtailing free movement law, locating the *outer* limits of citizenship law is very difficult.

(i) Remoteness

A potentially restraining interpretative principle lurking around the limits of free movement law in general—the concept of remoteness—might prove useful in locating the outer limits of citizenship also. Within free movement law, the concept of remoteness is applied in a *qualitative* sense (as distinct from the quantitative assessments made when conducting *de minimis* analysis in competition law).[51] The language used to signal a qualitative remoteness assessment in free movement law describes the alleged obstacle to or restriction on movement rights as too 'uncertain', 'indirect', 'tenuous' or 'insignificant'.[52] That analysis is neither submitted nor engaged with systematically in the restriction/justification/proportionality template of free movement interpretation, however; the remoteness question is simply not asked in most cases.

We can see the beginnings of a similar trend in the case law on citizenship. In just one judgment to date, *Morgan and Bucher*, the Court

[49] Joined Cases C-482/01 and C-493/01 *Orfanopoulos and Oliveri v Land Baden-Württemberg* [2004] ECR I-5257, para 65 (emphasis added).

[50] Case C-212/06 *Government of the French Community and Walloon Government v Flemish Community*, para 133 of the Opinion; but see n 21 above for the Court's position.

[51] The Court has recently confirmed the distinction between qualitative remoteness and *de minimis* (*ibid*, para 52 of the judgment), citing in support Case C-49/89 *Corsica Ferries France v Direction générale des douanes françaises* [1989] ECR 4441, para 8; and Case C-169/98 *Commission v France* [2000] ECR I-1049, para 46.

[52] Examples include: Case C-159/90 *SPUC v Grogan* [1991] ECR I-4685, para 24 (services; 'too tenuous'); Case C-20/03 *Criminal proceedings against Burmanjer* [2005] ECR I-4133, para 31 (goods; 'too insignificant and uncertain'); *Graf*, para 25 (workers; 'too uncertain and indirect'). See A Arnull, *The European Union and its Court of Justice*, (2nd edn) (Oxford, Oxford University Press, 2006), 491, where he traces the application of remoteness in its various formulations across the four freedoms; see also C Barnard, 'Employment rights, free movement under the EC Treaty, and the Services Directive', Edinburgh Mitchell Working Papers No 5/2008, available at http://www.law.ed.ac.uk/mitchellworkingpapers/papers.aspx, pp 8–9.

refuted a submission that the restrictive effects of the criteria governing study grants in Germany were 'too uncertain or too insignificant' to constitute a restriction on free movement and residence rights.[53] Advocates General have also been reluctant to engage with questions of remoteness.[54] Advocate General Poiares Maduro did raise the remoteness issue in the context of citizenship (albeit in his Opinion in *Marks & Spencer*, which was not a citizenship case):

> In an internal market 'characterised by the abolition, as between Member States, of obstacles to the free movement of goods, persons, services and capital', the Member States are no longer at liberty to ignore the constraints imposed by those matters on the definition and application of their national policies. In that context the task of the Court is not to engage in challenging every rule of State origin having an *indirect or wholly uncertain effect* on the exercise of the freedoms of movement. It is not for it to review the political choices made by the Member States. Judicial review of measures likely to prohibit, impede or render less attractive the exercise of the freedoms of movement rather seeks to ensure that those choices take account of the impact which they may have on transnational situations. The policies adopted must not result in less favourable treatment being accorded to transnational situations than to purely national situations. Such, it seems to me, must be the objective and the context of the review. Only that interpretation is such as to reconcile the principle of respect for State competences and the safeguarding of *the objective of establishing an internal market in which the rights of European citizens are protected.*[55]

This holistic vision of a market infused with citizenship is returned to in Part III below. The application of remoteness that it encourages remains sporadic and so perhaps still experimental. A key question that possibly holds back more systematic incorporation of the test is whether it would in fact enhance legal certainty, or simply add an unwelcome and confusing layer of subjective analysis to the Court's interpretative function.[56] The point about citizenship, outer limits and remoteness thus remains itself uncertain; but—as the extract above also demonstrates—this, at least, is a puzzle that it is not unique to citizenship law. These issues also add a

[53] *Morgan and Bucher*, para 32.

[54] A rare example can be found in *Schempp*, para 14 of the Opinion of Advocate General Geelhoed, where he outlines (though subsequently refutes) one of the arguments submitted ie 'the link to the right to move freely to another Member State is extremely tenuous, as it is not Mr Schempp, but his former wife, who has exercised her right to move under Article 18(1) EC'.

[55] Case C-446/03 *Marks & Spencer plc v Halsley (Her Majesty Inspector of Taxes)* [2005] ECR I-10837, para 37 of the Opinion (emphasis added).

[56] In her recent Opinion in Case C-142/05 *Åklagaren v Mickelsson and Roos* (pending; opinion delivered on 14 December 2006), Advocate General Kokott (drawing analogies between selling arrangements and rules regulating the use of products for the purposes of applying Art 28 EC) rejects the uncertainties of the remoteness criteria (paras 46–7), but then ventures into debatable quantitative analysis in discussing 'marginal' product use (paras 67–72).

sharper edge to the debate about convergence of free movement law[57]—again, picked up in Part III below; but while it was even difficult to know if like was being compared with like when looking at the traditional four freedoms, adding the 'fifth freedom'[58] of citizenship to that mix makes it more complicated still.

E Development through the Judicial Process

Reflection on interpretative limits forces consideration also of the particular influence of the Court of Justice on the development of citizenship law. The Court's constitutionalisation of free movement law through citizenship was noted above. But rather than seeing EU citizens as being swept along in some uncontrollable jurisprudential force, it is worth remembering that most of the case law on citizenship could not have happened without the active participation of persons involved in free movement disputes pursuing (or at least, tolerating) an Article 234 EC reference to Luxembourg. Moreover, the inherent randomness with which these references materialise mostly explains the incremental construction of the substance of citizenship rights.

There is a potentially serious tension, however, between judicial and legislative shaping of Article 18 EC.[59] In particular, clear points of difference between Directive 2004/38 and the concurrent case law of the Court have already been identified.[60] This suggests the formative actors of citizenship are not acting with a shared vision and reinforces the feeling that citizenship is taking on a character that is not being properly managed or contained. When the Court took a leap of faith in *Martínez Sala*, arguably against the intentions of the majority of the States (who thought they had designed a less ambitious, more rhetorical form of transnational personality), the greater good of securing individual rights arguably justified the means. It is difficult to feel sympathy for the Member States when they had themselves chosen the very word 'citizenship'—with its centuries of meaning and effect.[61] But against the backdrop of a communal institutional exercise like the drafting and enactment of Directive 2004/38,

[57] Seeeg, C Barnard, 'Fitting the remaining pieces into the goods and persons jigsaw?', (2001) 26 *EL Rev* 35.

[58] *CML Rev* Editorial Comments, (n 43) 1.

[59] Discussing institutional influences on the shaping of citizenship law more generally, see D Kostakopoulou, 'Ideas, norms and European citizenship: Explaining institutional change', (2005) 68 *Modern Law Review* 233.

[60] For example, relating to Art 24 of the Directive, see Nic Shuibhne, (n 26) (student grants); M Dougan 'Free movement: The workseeker as citizen', (2001) 4 *Cambridge Yearbook of European Legal Studies* 93 (job-seeker's allowances).

[61] As O'Leary (n 31) remarks, '[w]hile the rights conferred by that status were expressly subject to limitations and conditions, the Member States must have reflected on what the political, never mind the legal and constitutional, resonance of the establishment of this status would be' (p 9).

the question arises as to whether the Court (and indeed, the Community's constitutional order more generally) is really ready for steadfast adherence to the ideology of *Les Verts*[62]—will the Court actually strike down the more limiting provisions of the Directive if challenges as to their compatibility unfold in future case law? Or will proportionality be again summoned to rewrite (or at least recast) the Directive's words? It also remains to be seen whether the enlarged Court of Justice with 27 judges, bearing in mind too the multiple chambers that result from this structure, can retain consistency across its judgments. The Court may resist charges against it of possessing a 'vision' for integration that goes in any way beyond the 'ever closer union' set down by the Treaty itself; but perhaps better a *shared* vision of citizenship law than a confused one or none at all.

As well as problems of judgment/legislation coherence, there are also questions about coherence among judgments/other judgments. This point is well illustrated by an odd dynamic at play just now in case law on the free movement of workers, where some of the restrictions and conditions that make sense in the economically inactive citizenship context are being transplanted into economic free movement rights—not just limiting but actually reversing a more inclusive approach long established in the case law on the free movement of workers (discussed further in Part III below). This example raises broader questions about the role of citizenship in the sphere of economic activity. In other words, while most attention to date has focused on exploring the limits of citizenship within the domain of economic *insufficiency*, the converse question is less frequently addressed: do (any) distinct citizenship rights still apply where economic resources are not problematic, and where the exercise of movement is trade-oriented rather than person(ally)-oriented?

III CITIZENSHIP AND ECONOMIC ACTIVITY: PERSONAL AND FUNCTIONAL LIMITS

> [C]itizenship of the Union has no bearing on the free movement of goods.[63]

[62] In Case 294/83 *Parti écologiste "Les Verts" v European Parliament* [1986] ECR 1339, the Court characterised the EC as 'a Community based on the rule of law, inasmuch as neither its Member States *nor its institutions* can avoid a review of the question whether the measures adopted by them are in conformity with the basic constitutional charter, the Treaty' (para 23, emphasis added). Commenting on the judgment, Lenaerts has remarked that '[t]he Court thus recognised that the Treaties establishing the European Communities perform the function of a constitution in a composite legal order, which means that the institutions of this legal order as well as its component entities see their political decision-making process constrained by the rules laid down in the Treaties' (K Lenaerts, 'Fundamental Rights to be included in a Community Catalogue', (1991) 16 *EL Rev* 367, 367).

[63] P Oliver and S Enchelmaier, 'Free movement of goods: Recent developments in the case law', (2007) 44 *CML Rev* 649, 660.

> [I]t would be neither satisfactory nor true to the development of the case-law to reduce freedom of movement to a mere standard of promotion of trade between Member States. It is important that the freedoms of movement fit into the broader framework of the objectives of the internal market and European citizenship. At present, the freedoms of movement must be understood to be one of the essential elements of the 'fundamental status of nationals of the Member States'. They represent the cross-border dimension of the economic and social status conferred on European citizens.[64]

These extracts capture a question about the interpretative limits of EU citizenship which is the inverse of the issues explored in Part II above. Rather than examining how citizenship expands free movement law, this section considers what happens the other way around, that is, how free movement law is constrained by citizenship. The remainder of the chapter explores restrictiveness within free movement law, either where citizenship cannot be applied or where citizenship *is* applied but in a *limiting* way. We have seen how citizenship adds material rights to free movement law, primarily where the subjects are not economically active. Interestingly, these outer limits of citizenship tend to coalesce precisely because there *is* economic activity.

A Rights and/or Freedoms? (and Whether It Matters)

A first question asks, to what extent are citizenship rights now ring-fenced within Articles 17–22 EC? Shaw talks about 'the gradual accretion of policy competences and the step-by-step policy-making work of the Court and the other institutions in the fields of social policy, free movement of persons, education and vocational training, and cultural policy as expressions of European citizenship and associated rights'.[65] In tracing the history of EU citizenship these policy steps were clearly crucial, pre-dating the Treaty codification of citizenship and generating a powerful corpus of rights which protected the person, or more typically the mover. To what extent have these policy steps been subsumed by formal EU citizenship? And/or, to what extent can broader policy issues be accommodated within formal EU citizenship?

The first Spanish memorandum on citizenship, which fed the pre-Maastricht debates, 'located the adoption of new policies in the area of social relations, health, education, culture, protection of the environment

[64] Joined Cases C-158/04 and C-159/04 *Alfa Vita Vassilopoulos AE and Carrefour Marinopoulos AE v Elliniko Dimosio and Nomarchiaki Aftodioikisi Ioanninon* [2006] ECR I-8135, Opinion of Advocate General Poaires Maduro, para 40.

[65] J Shaw, 'Citizenship of the union: Towards post-national membership?', Jean Monnet Working Paper no 6/97, available at http://www.jeanmonnetprogram.org/papers/97/97–06-.html, Part III, p 4.

and consumers, within the *dynamic content of citizenship*', while admitting that the realisation of this depended on 'the model of political union which had yet to emerge'.[66] We now know that Treaty provisions dealing expressly with these policy questions *did* emerge, but that Community competence in respect of them is very limited in most cases. This means that a merging with EU citizenship broadens not just the scope of citizenship but also potentially broadens the competence to act in these policy areas too. Is this, as Spaventa depicts, a way of looking at protection of 'the citizen *qua citizen*, rather than simply *qua mover*'?[67] After all, Article 17(2) EC speaks of 'the rights conferred by this Treaty', not just *that* part of the Treaty. The 'wider citizenship' question may also reflect the legislation/jurisprudence tension discussed in Part II above, recalling the saturation of education policy with citizenship (in a way that seemed to go further, at least for a while, than Directive 2004/28). What the Court has done in the field of education greatly surpasses what would have been possible legislatively using Article 149 EC on its own.

Until Maastricht, the four freedoms were described in the EEC Treaty as the 'foundations of the Community' and not just (as at present) four among many Community tasks and activities (Articles 2 and 3 EC). The Treaty of Rome bestowed 'rights' to move in respect of work and establishment only. The provision of services was a 'freedom'; and there were no 'rights' to import or export goods, or to effect transfers of capital. Even early secondary legislation did not replicate the Treaty pattern but instead used the language of rights very liberally—although, unlike the rights enjoyed by workers that are detailed throughout Regulation 1612/68, Directive 73/148 was concerned only with rights of entry and residence, thereby facilitating establishment and service provision but not casting the exercise of these activities as rights in themselves.[68]

The wording of the citizenship provisions transformed and unified the language of movement rights in the Treaty by collating the specific expressions of free movement in one provision, as they apply to personal movement at least. Directive 2004/38 is also firmly rooted in the 'rights' associated with movement and residence in other States. This makes for a more seamless understanding of freedom of movement, given that the Treaty and implementing secondary legislation are now mostly in linguistic sync. But the fundamental human/trade dichotomy obviously remains. For example, in Directive 2004/38, the word 'services' appears only once (and

[66] S O'Leary, *The Evolving Concept of Community Citizenship: From the Free Movement of Persons to Union Citizenship*, (The Hague, Kluwer Law International, 1996), p. 26 (emphasis added).

[67] Spaventa (n 12) 744.

[68] Thus mirroring, for workers, Dir 68/360/EEC on the abolition of restrictions on movement and residence within the Community for workers of Member States and their families, rather than Reg 1612/68.

only then in a footnote, in respect of repealing Directive 73/148). We can assume that an EU citizen has a 'primary and individual right'[69] to move and reside freely to provide or receive a service; but others (for example, corporations or third country nationals established in one State providing services in another) have the 'freedom' so to do—does this matter? Does citizenship enhance the former set of rights within the context of economic activity beyond the standards of protection that the latter can expect?

The Constitutional Treaty would have reshuffled the four freedoms: for the first time, the rules on persons would have preceded those on services, goods and capital.[70] But through the Lisbon Treaty, things would stay the same. It would be dangerous to read too much into either of these decisions; but they do suggest some debate among States about free movement in the EU and the meaning of citizenship in that framework. The inclusion of rights to move and reside—for EU citizens—in the Charter of Fundamental rights does remain, however; reflecting the manifestation of citizenship and constitutionalisation. White observes that the Charter too 'seek[s] to divide Community law on workers, establishment, and services into two streams, one of which is primarily concerned with personal rights for the individual, and the other of which is primarily concerned with regulating the market to secure access to the business environment of other Member States'.[71]

A 'fundamental' right to move was developed initially through freedom of movement for workers.[72] The references to 'workers' evolved gradually into the general idea of 'persons'.[73] Things are less settled when the discussion turns to a more general (fundamental) right to *trade*, as expressed via the free movement of goods, for example, or providing and receiving services.[74] Oliver and Roth find a number of references which

[69] Recital 1 to the Preamble of Directive 2004/38; see also, Recital 11 ('the fundamental and personal right of residence').

[70] See Arts I-4 and III-130(2), and Arts III-133 onwards of the Treaty establishing a Constitution for Europe, [2004] OJ C/310/1.

[71] RCA White, *Workers, Establishment and Services in the European Union*, (Oxford, Oxford University Press, 2004), 130.

[72] See, eg, Case 152/82 *Forcheri v Belgium* [1983] ECR 2323, para 11 ('the right to free movement ... constitutes a fundamental right of workers and their families'), Case 222/86 *UNECTEF v Heylens* [1987] ECR 4097, para 14 ('free access to employment is a fundamental right') and *Bosman*, para 129 ('the fundamental right of free access to employment which the Treaty confers individually on each worker').

[73] See, eg, Case C-416/96 *Nour Eddline El-Yassini v Secretary of State for Home Department* [1999] ECR I-1209, para 45 ('the fundamental right of persons to move freely within the Community'); *cf* the more nuanced phrasing in Case C-441/02 *Commission v Germany* [2006] ECR I-3449, para 34 ('the fundamental *principle* of freedom of movement for persons', emphasis added).

[74] For an example of the more limited view, see A von Bogdandy, 'The European Union as a human rights organisation? Human rights and the core of the European Union', (2000) 37 *CML Rev* 1307, 1326. *Cf* S Douglas-Scott, *Constitutional Law of the European Union*, (Harlow, Longman, 2002), 435: 'the European Court has named specific Treaty items as

stop short of fundamental rights terminology,[75] but do point to one instance where the Court described the free movement of goods as a 'fundamental right'.[76] They emphasise also the general tenor of the pivotal decision in *Keck*, 'recasting the scope of Article 28 to bring it back within its proper limits' and dispelling the notion of Article 28 as encompassing a general right to trade unhindered.[77]

Rights are realised not through language, of course,[78] but through their exercise; and when their exercise is challenged or restricted in some way, the Court needs then to determine the extent, scope—and priority—of their content and application. The examples above show that the right to move was conceptualised as a fundamental 'something' very early within the case law, but commentary is somewhat divided on whether the intended application was philosophically equivalent to a fundamental *human* right. The argument has been made that attributing the character of 'fundamental right' to economic freedoms sourced in the EC Treaty denigrates the substance of 'true' fundamental rights at a normative level.[79] Craig and de Búrca summarise a related charge, that 'the Court has manipulated the rhetorical force of the language of rights, while in reality merely advancing the commercial goals of the common market, being biased towards "market rights" instead of protecting values which are genuinely fundamental to the human condition.'[80] This critique has been responded to using an argument of priority within an overall rights framework, which must be driven by the allocation of weighting or

fundamental rights: namely, non-discrimination on grounds of nationality in Art 12 EC and the four fundamental freedoms of goods, services, persons and capital'. In support, she cites Case 240/83 *Procureur de la République v ADBHU* [1985] ECR 520, para 9: '[i]t should be borne in mind that the principles of free movement of goods and freedom of competition, together with freedom of trade as a fundamental right [etc]'.

[75] P Oliver and W-H Roth, 'The internal market and the four freedoms', (2004) 41 *CML Rev* 407, finding descriptions of the free movement of goods as eg 'one of the fundamental principles in the Treaty' (Case C-265/95 *Commission v France* [1997] ECR I-6959, para 27).

[76] Case C-228/98 *Dounias v Minister for Economic Affairs* [2000] ECR I-577, para 64.

[77] Oliver and Roth (n 75) 409, discussing Joined Cases C-267–8/91 *Keck and Mithouard* [1993] ECR I-6097; the authors note the pre-*Keck* plea in this vein delivered by Advocate General Tesauro in Case C-292/92 *Hünermund v Landesapothekerkammer Baden-Württemberg* [1993] ECR I-6787, para 1 of the Opinion, which they consider, judging from the tone of the judgment in *Keck*, not to have fallen on deaf ears.

[78] As Oliver and Roth observe, 'it is naïve to construct an entire theory on the basis of one word occurring in an isolated judgment, especially as its use may simply be attributable to a translation error; but where a term is used consistently in a series of judgments, that cannot go unheeded' (see n 75 above, 408).

[79] See especially, J Coppel and A O'Neill, 'The European Court of Justice: Taking rights seriously?', (1992) 29 *CML Rev* 669, 689–91; see also, DR Phelan, 'Right to life of the unborn v promotion of trade in services: The ECJ and the normative shaping of the European Union', (1992) 55 *Modern Law Review* 670, 677. In a related vein, see Douglas-Scott (n 74) 435, who argues in favour of some 'definitional refinement'.

[80] P Craig and G de Búrca, *EU Law: Text, Cases and Materials*, (4th edn) (Oxford, Oxford University Press, 2007), 419.

balance—not all rights are equal, and when conflicts arise even 'fundamental' rights require in most instances to be balanced against each other.[81]

Perhaps less expectedly, however, it is also suggested that classification of the economic freedoms as fundamental rights could devalue *their* status rather than the other way around; the argument that Treaty freedoms might be unduly limited by (other) competing fundamental rights is closely related to this.[82] A perceived downgrading of the freedoms can also be effected if, irrespective of their status as fundamental rights or otherwise, their importance in the balancing mix is diminished—in other words, the increasing strength of fundamental rights in a general sense and their capacity to limit or override the economic freedoms, which is not universally heralded as an absolute good thing. The different recent outcomes in *Omega* and *Laval* (where respect for nationally construed fundamental rights was very evident in *Omega*, but economic Treaty rights took precedence in *Laval*) suggest that this debate is by no means resolved.[83] The Charter offers one answer for personal movement and residence rights at least. White translates this to constitutional language for EU citizens and thereby suggests the different (lesser, in constitutional terms) freedoms enjoyed by legal persons:

> a justification can be found in the distinction the EC Treaty now makes between individuals and business entities as artificial legal persons. Though not wholly free from doubt, the language of Part Two of the EC Treaty on citizenship of the Union would appear to be limited to people and does not extend to business entities with legal personality. Consequently, people have the constitutional right to move whereas businesses have a lesser Community right to move under the free movement provisions of the Treaty.[84]

But he goes on to play down the legal significance we might read into this:

> The constitutional right to free movement which flows from citizenship of the Union also explains the expansive approach being taken by the Court when it is called upon to deal with issues of personal movement and of the rights which citizens enjoy in every Member State. Separation of this line of case law from that which is essentially concerned with the regulation of interferences with the exercise of the four freedoms through State measures and cognate measures of

[81] See JHH Weiler and NJS Lockhart, '"Taking Rights Seriously" seriously: The European Court of Justice and its fundamental rights jurisprudence', (1995) 32 *CML Rev* 51 and 579, 593–5, who challenge the rights denigration argument as an '... unjustified leap from a lexical equivalence to normative equivalence'.

[82] See, eg, the Editorial Comments on *Carpenter*, 'Freedoms unlimited?', (2003) 40 *CML Rev* 537.

[83] Case C-36/02 *Omega Spielhallen- und Automatenaufstellungs-GmbH v Oberbürgermeisterin der Bundesstadt Bonn* [2004] ECR I-9609; Case C-341/05 *Laval un Partneri Ltd v Svenska Byggnadsarbetareförbundet, Svenska Eyggnadsarbetareförbundets avd 1, Byggettan, Svenska Elektrikerförbundet* [2007] ECR I-11767.

[84] White (n 71) 260–61.

> regulation reveals greater coherence in the case law than some of the literature might suggest. It is certainly possible to posit an argument that the case law taken as a whole, when dealing with interferences with the four freedoms, is broadly consistent and does not make distinctions which are unsustainable. It is in the nature of the case law that anomalies will arise which do not fit the model which academic commentators synthesize from the raw material of the Court's judgments. That reflects both the nature of courts and the serendipity which brings particular disputes to courts in the first place.[85]

This hypothesis—principally 'that the case law taken as a whole ... is broadly consistent and does not make distinctions which are unsustainable' will be examined in more detail in the following sections looking, first, at limits based on the concept of nationality (as it is applied to both natural and legal persons) and, secondly, at 'functional' limits rooted in the purpose of the movement being exercised.

B Limits to 'Nationality'

The ideas suggested by Advocate General Maduro in *Alfa Vita* (cited at the beginning of this section) reflect a new kind of convergence, where the constitutional status of citizenship, the shield attached by Advocate General Jacobs in *Konstantinidis* to the *civis europeus*,[86] performs a function also in the domain of trade. Maduro continued in *Alfa Vita*:

> such a harmonisation of the systems of free movement seems to me to be essential in the light of the requirements of genuine Union citizenship. It would be desirable for the same system to be applied *to all the citizens of the Union wishing to use their freedom of movement or freedom to move services, goods or capital* as well as their freedom to reside or to set up the seat of their activities in the Community. Accordingly, any measure liable to impede or make less attractive the exercise of these fundamental freedoms should be held to be contrary to the Treaty.[87]

We saw above, thinking of examples such as *Martínez Sala*, *Trojani* and *Bidar*, that EU citizens not participating in economic activity can still come within the scope of the Treaty. This provokes the opposite question: can persons still be citizens when they *are* engaging in economic activity? Commenting on Advocate General Maduro's stance in *Alfa Vita*, however, Oliver and Enchelmaier argue that '[i]f taken at face value, his apparent suggestion that citizenship of the Union is to be seen as central to all four

[85] *Ibid*, 266.
[86] *Konstantinidis*, para 46 of the Opinion.
[87] *Alfa Vita*, para 51 of the Opinion (emphasis added).

freedoms, including goods, would lead to retrograde consequences, since it overlooks the position of third country nationals'.[88]

The concept of nationality in Community law is supposedly interchangeable as between natural and legal persons. We saw at the outset that the Court handles the free movement rights of State nationals participating in cross-border economic activity via the specific expressions of those rights in Articles 39, 43 and 49. So, for rights in that vein, even when it *is* a person (a worker, for example), the citizenship provisions are usually superfluous anyway. The recent decision in *FKP Scorpio* evokes an interesting scenario, however, realising Oliver and Enchelmaier's concerns to some extent.[89] In this case, the recipient of services had a registered office in Germany and thus, via Article 48EC, was a 'national of a Member State'; the provider was established in another Member State but trading as a (presumed third country national) natural person. Since no legislation on provision of services by third country nationals has been adopted through Article 49 EC, the Court confirmed that the Treaty per se 'does not extend the benefit of [the services] provisions to providers of services who are nationals of non-member countries, even if they are established within the Community and an intra-Community provision of services is concerned'.[90] The decision limits the scope of the *economic* freedom to provide/receive services. Almost all of the pieces of the services jigsaw were in place—two Member States and a service crossing from one to the other, but here the nationality criterion defeated the claim. Had the provider been a legal person established in the providing State, then the nationality of the person(s) 'behind' that entity would have been completely irrelevant. But the decision also reduces the scope of Treaty protection for service *recipients*, arguably devaluing the market space in which personal and economic movement supposedly coexist. Advocate General Léger grounded his contrasting Opinion in the applicant's service receipt rights (notwithstanding the applicant's status as a legal person) and in the movement of the service itself; and, strikingly, he did so drawing support from case law on *personal* service receipt:

> this is a case in which the recipient of services, who it is agreed *is a national of a Member State*, is seeking to enjoy rights under the Treaty rules on freedom to provide services in the context of the relationship he has with a service provider whose nationality is not known by the national court. In such a situation, I am of the view that the nationality of the service provider is irrelevant as regards the rights enjoyed by the recipient of the services.[91]

[88] Oliver and Enchelmaier (n 63) 677.

[89] Case C-290/04 *FKP Scorpio Konzertproduktionen GmbH v Finanzamt Hamburg-Eimsbüttel* [2006] ECR I-9461.

[90] *FKP Scorpio*, para 68.

[91] *FKP Scorpio*, paras 117–18 of the Opinion (emphasis added).

As well as jurisprudence on tourists and service receipt, for example, the Advocate General drew also from case law on Article 48 EC which gives effect to the Treaty's instruction that natural and legal persons should be treated in the same way for the purposes of freedom of establishment. The classic decision in *Centros* exemplifies the consequences of this approach.[92] Indeed, the high threshold applied in *Centros* for determining an abuse of Community law came from personal free movement (in *Singh*) and after *Centros* worked its way subsequently back into personal movement (in *Akrich*). In terms of limits grounded in nationality, these cases show (1) that although the concept of nationality is applied interchangeably in principle, 'legal' service recipients have not been conferred with rights comparable to natural service recipients; but (2) this confirms the general expansion of personal free movement through citizenship, rather than confirming any outer limits on citizenship itself—unless, the *FKP Scorpio* analysis would be followed for an EU citizen who received services from a third country national established in another State and was similarly deprived of Community protection on the grounds that economic activity was being exercised. This is not a nationality limit, however, but a functional one (on which, more below).

As a final point, it is worth noting that there is a possibility through which free movement rights could be extended to third country nationals on a more unilateral basis, by States rather than by the Community. In the context of voting rights, the Court of Justice has recently found that:

> while citizenship of the Union is destined to be the fundamental status of nationals of the Member States, enabling those who find themselves in the same situation to receive the same treatment in law irrespective of their nationality, subject to such exceptions as are expressly provided for ... that statement does not necessarily mean that the rights recognised by the Treaty are limited to citizens of the Union.[93]

Could the Member States extend citizenship rights other than voting rights to persons 'other than their own nationals or citizens of the Union resident in their territory'?[94] If so, this would accentuate even further the personal/trade fracture heightened by citizenship law. In the same case, Advocate General Tizzano suggested that '[Article 17 EC] may indeed approve the grant to [citizens of the Union] of a series of rights specified elsewhere (in particular in Articles 18 to 21 EC) but that does not in fact imply that only citizens of the Union can enjoy those rights'.[95]

[92] Case C-212/97 *Centros Ltd v Erhvervs-og Selskabsstyrelsen* [1999] ECR I-1459.
[93] Case C-145/04 *Spain v UK* [2006] ECR I-7917, para 74.
[94] *Ibid*, para 78.
[95] *Ibid*, para 90 of the Opinion.

C Functional Limits

It was noted earlier that case law on the free movement of workers is currently seeing the application of restrictions and conditions relevant otherwise to citizenship rights developed for economically inactive persons. O'Leary has recently charted this in detail, looking especially at frontier workers and the application of *D'Hoop* and *Collins* type 'genuine links' so that the Court can determine when/whether benefits can be claimed from States of work and/or residence.[96] She expresses apposite concern at this rather odd and disconcerting instance of citizenship imposing *new* limits on the economic freedoms. This also adds to the impression that there is some element of incompatibility between citizenship and economic activity; and calls into question White's hope that the citizenship/free movement case law remains 'broadly consistent and does not make distinctions which are unsustainable'. In the course of her analysis, O'Leary refers to the Opinion of Advocate-General Geelhoed in *Hartmann*:

> The rights which are connected with each category of free movement differ, although in the course of the years a certain degree of convergence has been attained in the interpretation of the Treaty provisions on workers, establishment and services and there is greater homogeneity in the manner in which these provisions are applied. The Treaty provisions on citizenship, by contrast, remain a distinct category and the rights which may be derived from this status, though evolving, are restricted by comparison to those which flow from the economic freedoms. In order to determine which Treaty provision, and therefore which legal regime, is applicable to a given situation, it is still essential to establish, in an objective sense, the reason for which the person concerned exercises his right to move to another Member State. This constitutes the connecting factor with this or that Treaty provision on free movement.[97]

This is a different free movement model than that sketched by Advocate General Maduro in *Alfa Vita*. It finds outer limits of citizenship in very functional terms, but in doing so it contrasts with the primary 'fundamental status' more usually ascribed to citizenship rights. It is unusual to find a suggestion that citizenship rights are the ones subordinate to rights stemming from economic activity—and somewhat ironic to find that view

[96] O'Leary (n 31) p 16 onwards, where she demonstrates that 'concepts designed specifically with reference to freely moving, economically inactive EU citizens are being transposed to those economically active EU migrants whose rights predate the establishment of EU citizenship, derive from the original Treaty of Rome and have been safeguarded to date by an abundant and seemingly unassailable line of jurisprudence'. O'Leary discusses in detail Case C-212/05 *Hartmann v Freistaat Bayern* [2007] ECR I-6303; Case C-213/05 *Geven v Land Nordrhein-Westfalen* [2007] ECR I-6347; and Case C-287/05 *Hendrix v Raad van Bestuur van het Uitvoeringsinstituut Werknemersverzekeringen*, not yet reported, judgment of 11 September 2007.

[97] *Hartmann*, para 34 of the Opinion, see O'Leary (n 31) 18.

in the context of then *limiting* access to benefits under Article 39 EC by using the 'real link' principle applied under Article 18 EC.

There are cases outwith free movement where the severability of natural/legal 'nationality' at play in *FKP Scorpio* is also evident but, additionally, where overlap between the rights of citizens and economic actors is more directly eschewed on a functional basis. The starting point comes from Advocate General Alber in *Parma Ham*.[98] In the context of the translation of Community documents, he observed that '[a] right cannot ... be derived from [Article 290 EC] whereby all Community law measures must necessarily be available in every official language'.[99] Interestingly, he then drew an analogy between citizens and their rights under Article 21 EC,[100] and the 'economic operators' in the case at hand, who were seeking information from the Commission in a language other than that in which a product specification had been registered (a translation of the specification from its original language thus being sought also); he even suggested that a solution in that vein would 'perhaps comes closest to meeting the requirement of legal certainty'.[101] But taking into account the fact that judicial protection of the product specification would be sought in the national courts (of the Member State of product origin), the Advocate General went on to find that 'a business concerned with placing foreign goods on the market, such as Asda or Hygrade, will generally have the linguistic knowledge necessary for importing the goods or otherwise has available to it appropriate means of overcoming the associated language difficulties. It can therefore also be expected to overcome the obstacles resulting from the fact that the specification is available in the original language only.'[102]

[98] Case C-108/01 *Consorzio del Prosciutto di Parma, Salumificio S. Rita SpA v Asda Stores Ltd and Hygrade Foods Ltd* [2003] ECR I-5121.

[99] *Ibid*, para 135; Art 290 EC provides that '[t]he rules governing the languages of the institutions of the Community shall, without prejudice to the provisions contained in the Statute of the Court of Justice, be determined by the Council, acting unanimously'. The key measure adopted on this basis, setting out rules governing the use of the EU official languages, is Reg 1/58, OJ 1952–1958 English Special Edition p 59.

[100] Art 21 EC provides inter alia that '[e]very citizen of the Union may write to any of the institutions or bodies referred to in this Article or in Art 7 in one of the languages mentioned in Article 314 and have an answer in the same language.' Art 314 EC establishes, in effect, the 21 EU official languages, and the equal authenticity of the texts of the EC Treaty in each one of those 21 language versions.

[101] *Parma Ham*, para 138 of the Opinion.

[102] *Ibid*, para 141. While the Advocate General did refer to Arts 4 and 5 of Reg 1/58 (which relate to the publication of regulations/other documents of general application and the Official Journal respectively), he did not consider the scope of Art 3, which provides that '[d]ocuments which an institution of the Community sends to a Member State or to a person subject to the jurisdiction of a Member State shall be drafted in the language of such State'. There is no comparable discussion in the judgment of the Court of Justice, which hinges more on the broader notion of 'adequate publicity' of the protected designations (see paras 87–99 of the judgment).

This presumption in favour of the linguistic capacity and resources of economic operators emerges again in the series of *Kik* cases, all relating to the rules operated by the Office for Harmonisation in the Internal Market (Trade Marks and Designs) (OHIM) which restrict the number of languages in which Community trade mark applications can be made.[103] Picking up on the ideas in *Parma Ham*, Advocate General Jacobs distinguished clearly between 'the rights of citizens of the Union acting *as such*' (emphasis added) and 'the professional activities of a trade mark agent'.[104] But what are the outer limits to the meaning of 'as such'? The judgment of the Court was based initially on a different approach—excluding the application of Article 21 EC because OHIM was not an institution within the scope of Article 7 EC.[105] But the Court went on to observe that '[a]ccount must also be taken of the fact that the Community trade mark was created for the benefit not of all citizens, but of economic operators, and that economic operators are not under any obligation to make use of it'.[106] This is not the same point that Advocate General Jacobs made about Article 21 EC, but it does pick up the citizen/economic operator distinction and suggests that the application of a different standard of language rights for both can be justified. On one view, we are back in the legitimate personal/trade divide. But there is a very basic factual difference between the situations in *Parma Ham* and *Kik*—given that the economic operator in the latter case was also an EU citizen (as opposed to Asda, which patently is not). Even though the application of Regulation 1/58 was ruled out by the Court, the distinction between 'citizens' and 'economic operators' runs directly contrary to its principles, which offer no such distinction at all. Furthermore, trade mark specialisation does not imply linguistic specialisation. Thus the rights conferred by Article 21 EC were arguably precluded in a formalist more than functional sense. There are questions of wider significance underlying this approach. First, as is the case for Article 18 EC, Article 21 EC also finds replication in the Charter of Fundamental rights—but possibly strengthened by a prohibition on discrimination on grounds of language which is contained in the 'equality' rather than 'citizenship' title.[107] This argues against the rigid personal/trade method. Secondly, the reasoning applied in *Kik* could mark an outer limit to the

[103] See in particular, the final appeal, Case C-361/01 P *Kik v OHIM* [2003] ECR I-8283; for analysis of the *Kik* cases, see the Case Comment by N Nic Shuibhne, (2004) 41 *CML Rev* 1093.

[104] *Ibid*, para 17 of the Opinion.

[105] *Ibid*, para 83 of the Judgment.

[106] *Ibid*, para 88.

[107] See Arts 21(1) (prohibition of discrimination on grounds including language) and 41(4) (communications with the institutions); see also Art 22 (respect for cultural, religious and linguistic diversity).

personal/material scope separation, as first applied to citizenship in *Martínez Sala*. Enabling Ms Kik to invoke Article 21 EC through her personal status as an EU citizen but in her material capacity as an economic operator, would certainly have taken that methodology a step further, but is it really such an inconceivable step?

The message emanating from cases like *FKP Scorpio* and *Kik* is that when formal economic activity is undertaken (with the most likely point of departure being incorporation as a legal person, as distinct from the economic activity inherently involved in work or services, or non-incorporated establishment, although this is not yet clear), then the rights offered by citizenship are not applicable. And interestingly, picking up the discussion above on rights/freedoms and whether it matters, Article 16 of the Charter of Fundamental Rights talks about the *freedom*, but not a right, to conduct a business. This does mark an outer limit beyond which the rights distinct to citizenship cannot be applied. The legal framework that networks interchangeable personal/trade principles, thinking of cases like *Centros*, is thus able to go only 'so far' in functional as well as personal/national terms.

Recent case law is arguably delivering what a meaningful Union citizenship should probably be doing anyway—changing things; challenging the economic moorings of the traditional freedoms; taking them somewhere else in some (human) cases, —*but*—this means leaving behind quite deliberately the 'non-human' business of establishment and goods and services as something *else*—making the 'fifth freedom' hypothesis an attractive idea, but is it one still reconcilable with the internal market definition in Article 14 EC? The problems with how this has been achieved to date also run both ways—a 'humanising' restriction on economic activity (for example, frontier workers and 'real link' case law), but also potentially arbitrary cut-off points that distinguish material economic activity too starkly from personal scope (*Kik* and *FKP Scorpio*).

IV CONCLUDING REMARKS

The interpretation of EU citizenship as a legal concept has been mostly about nudging the outer limits of the status further outwards. Article 18 EC suggests that the limits to the movement and residence rights of citizenship law come from the Treaty itself and from legislation adopted to give effect to it. But even here, the impact of restrictive criteria, such as the economic resources/comprehensive medical insurance conditions, has been softened by an interpretation drawing from general principles of Community law including proportionality and respect for fundamental rights. Some caution should be exercised so that the outer limits of citizenship are not pushed relentlessly outwards, however; especially remembering the fine balance between outer *interpretative limits* and inner (State space) limits. As examples discussed throughout this chapter have shown, there is also a danger that the coherence of citizenship law (and also, the coherence of its relationship to free movement law more generally) is problematic. This demonstrates that more concentrated reflection is needed on *institutional limits* internal to the Court (and its structure); and also, externally, in terms of the legally formative relationship between the Court and the legislative institutions in shaping the content of citizenship.

The strongest indicator of outer limits comes when citizenship is posited 'against' *economic activity*. It is not that expansive case law like *Centros* is trying to provoke a return to the pre-*Keck* days of disdain (so clearly reflected in the judgment itself) for unfettered rights to exercise economic activity. Rather, the conceptual relationship between citizenship and economic free movement rights needs still to be resolved—we have seen divergent recent views on this from different Advocates General, reflecting similar discourse within academic opinion. Some concerns about coherence were identified in this context also; recalling White's point that differences should be 'consistent and sustainable', arbitrary interpretative distinctions should be avoided and more careful working out of the personal and functional scope of citizenship and economic rights respectively is therefore needed. The idea of *remoteness* may assist in determining the outer scope of the citizenship provisions to some extent, but the application of this principle has not yet been worked systematically into the Court's interpretative methodology.

None of this calls into question the fundamentally good objective of securing meaningful content and effect for EU citizenship law. But outer legal limits exist; locating them demands consistency and applying them demands, ultimately, that they be respected as well as acknowledged.

9

The Outer Limits of Article 28 EC: Purely Internal Situations and the Development of the Court's Approach through the Years

ALINA TRYFONIDOU*

I INTRODUCTION

THE CENTRAL OBJECTIVE of the E(E)C Treaty has always been the establishment of a common market. For a single market to be built, freedom of movement of goods, services, persons and capital between the States that form part of that market must be safeguarded. To this end, the E(E)C Treaty includes a number of provisions (the so-called 'fundamental freedoms') which prohibit the imposition of obstacles to the free movement of products and factors of production between the Member States.

The establishment of a customs union in 1968 formed the basis for the construction of a common market in goods in the E(E)C. Following this first successful step, the focus of the activities of the Community institutions was placed on ensuring that the process of creating a single market in goods would not be sabotaged by Member State authorities which, wishing to protect national production, would raise non-tariff obstacles to the free movement of goods. Therefore, from the early 1970s onwards, the emphasis was put on the removal of Member State measures that, although not falling within the scope of the customs duties provisions, were, nonetheless, equally restrictive of inter-state trade. The principal Treaty provision that has been employed for this purpose is Article 28 EC which proscribes the imposition of quantitative restrictions on imports and

* I would like to thank Dr Catherine Barnard for her invaluable comments on an earlier draft of this article.

measures having equivalent effect—a prohibition that is capable of catching a much broader array of national measures than the customs duties provisions, and which can outlaw the imposition of both direct and indirect obstacles[1] to the free movement of goods.[2]

Although in the EC, as in other supranational organisations, the need to define the boundaries of the scope of each level of governance (that is national and supranational) accurately has always existed, a definite line between the two levels of governance has never been drawn by the drafters of the various Treaties. Rather, this delicate and politically charged issue was left to the Court of Justice which, through its case law, would, inter alia, have to specify the limits to the ambit of the various Treaty Articles.[3]

The emphasis placed on the construction of a common market in goods in the first decades of the Community's existence, meant that the interpretation of Article 28 EC and the delimitation of its scope would occupy a major part of the Court's time and resources, at least until the mid-1990s. More specifically, through a line of case law starting in the early 1970s (*Dassonville*[4] and *Cassis de Dijon*[5]), proceeding through to the late 1970s and 1980s (the purely internal situations case law) and culminating in 1993 (*Keck*),[6] the Court of Justice sketched the inner and outer boundaries of the scope of application of Article 28 EC, the two latter groups of cases being, mainly, a response to the lame attempts of traders to avoid the application of restrictive provisions of national law, in instances where this was not necessary for safeguarding the uninhibited pursuit of *inter-state* trade.[7]

In this paper, I will argue that the purely internal rule has been one of the principal ways that the European Court of Justice (ECJ) has traditionally drawn a line between EC and Member State competence. The aim of this paper is twofold: first, to provide an account of how the Court has, in different phases of the Community's development, dealt with purely internal situations and, in particular, to provide an analysis of how the Court's approach in finding a link with EC has developed through the

[1] Case 8/74, *Procureur du Roi v Dassonville* [1974] ECR 837, para 5.

[2] Another provision which shares the same aim, ie the establishment of a common market in goods, is Art 29 EC which is the equivalent to Art 28 EC, but with regard to the exportation of goods from one Member State to another.

[3] It should be noted, however, that the Treaty does not leave us entirely in the dark as to the limits placed on Community competence. The reference to inter-state trade in the wording used in the EC Treaty provisions on free movement and the prohibition on customs duties, suggests that only situations that involve an effect on inter-state trade can fall within the scope of those provisions.

[4] Above n 1.

[5] Case 120/78, *Rewe–Zentrale AG v Bundesmonopolverwaltung für Branntwein*, [1979] ECR 649.

[6] Joined Cases C-267/91 and C-268/91, *Criminal proceedings against Bernard Keck and Daniel Mithouard* [1993] ECR I-6097.

[7] This was explicitly mentioned by the Court in para 14 of its ruling in *Keck*, *ibid*.

years (Section II); and secondly, to offer, in parallel, an exegesis of how the Court seems, now, to be in the early stages of a process through which it aims to address the problems caused by the application of the purely internal situations doctrine (Section III). I will argue that, although the Court has managed to respond successfully to one of the key problems caused by the application of its traditional approach to purely internal situations (that is the failure, in some instances, to reflect economic reality), the Community institutions need to put more effort into dealing effectively with the other major problem arising from the application of the purely internal rule (the reverse discrimination conundrum).

II THE TRADITIONAL APPROACH DEVELOPED BY THE COURT FOR DETERMINING WHETHER A SITUATION IS PURELY INTERNAL TO A MEMBER STATE

The purely internal rule was first established and defined in a case concerning the free movement of workers—*Saunders*[8]—where the Court held that Article 39 EC was inapplicable since 'the provisions of the Treaty on freedom of movement for workers cannot ... be applied to situations which are wholly internal to a Member State, in other words, where there is no factor connecting them to any of the situations envisaged by Community law'.[9] The Court subsequently applied the same rationale in the context of the other fundamental freedoms, and thus it was established early on that the purely internal situations doctrine is one of the ways to draw the external boundaries of, inter alia, Article 28 EC.[10]

Although the Court of Justice has never provided an exact definition of the all-important notion of 'purely internal situation', it has, nonetheless, consistently followed a simple approach in deciding whether a situation falls within the four corners of Article 28 EC, making the existence *and* impediment of the inter-state movement of the goods involved in the facts before the Court,[11] the decisive issue. More specifically, the Court has (implicitly) applied a two-limb test in determining whether a situation

[8] Case 175/78, *R v Saunders* [1979] ECR 1129. Note that simple reference to the notion of 'wholly internal' situations was, for the first time, made by the Court one month before the judgment in *Saunders* was delivered in Case 115/78 *Knoors v Secretary of State for Economic Affairs*, [1979] ECR 399.

[9] *Ibid*, para 11

[10] See Joined Cases 314–316/81 and 83/82 *Procureur de la République and Comite national de defense contre l'alcoolisme v Alex Waterkeyn and others* [1982] ECR 4337, para 11.

[11] The insistence of the traditional approach on the need to prove that the inter-state movement of the specific goods that are involved in the facts before the Court is impeded was expressly stated in the Opinion of Advocate General Cosmas in Case C-36/94 *Belgapom v ITM and Vocarex* [1995] ECR I-2647, para 14: 'the connecting factor bringing a given situation within the ambit of Article 30 [now Article 28] of the Treaty should be sought in the

qualifies for EC protection: first, the contested measure must have been applied to goods that are imported from other Member States (*existence* of inter-state movement); and, secondly, the application of the contested measure must have been capable of impeding the importation of those goods, as a result of imposing requirements which make it less (or even not) attractive to market them in the territory of that State (*impediment* of inter-state movement). This is the so-called 'traditional approach'[12] of the Court in finding a link with EC law and is still applied as the default approach.

Under this approach the first, and sometimes only, question that is asked is whether the facts of the case involve goods that have moved between Member States in the process of an economic activity (that is, goods that have been imported *in order to be put on the market in that State*). If the specific goods that are involved in the facts of the case have moved—or are *definitely*[13] going to move—between two or more Member States, and the contested national measure is capable of impeding that movement, the situation falls within the scope of Article 28 EC. Conversely, if the goods that are involved in the facts of the case have remained confined within the territory of one and the same Member State, the situation immediately qualifies as purely internal and this signifies the end of the enquiry as to a possible violation of Article 28 EC.[14]

The origins of this approach can be traced back to the case of *Waterkeyn.*[15] There, the Court of Justice explained that when a national measure is caught by Article 28 EC, EC law requires the measure to become inapplicable only to goods that are imported from other Member States; the measure can continue to be applied to goods produced in that State and put directly on its market (that is goods that are in a purely internal situation). Based on this, the Court in *Waterkeyn* made it clear

provenance *of the goods allegedly affected in the specific case*, by a given national measure' (emphasis added).

[12] For other authors employing this term see P Oliver and S Enchelmaier, 'Free movement of goods: recent developments in the case law', (2007) 44 *CML Rev* 649, at 650.

[13] This has been expressly established by the Court in a number of free movement of persons and services cases. See, among others, Case 180/83 *Moser v Land Baden-Württemberg* [1984] ECR 2539, para 18; Case C-41/90 *Höfner and Elser v Mactroton GmbH* [1991], ECR I-1979, para 39. Although there is no express pronouncement regarding this issue in the context of Art 28 EC, this requirement appears to have been implicit in the recent Case C-293/02 *Jersey Produce Marketing Organisation Ltd v States of Jersey and Jersey Potato Export Marketing Board* [2005] ECR I-9543, in the context of Art 29 EC.

[14] The approach that has traditionally been followed by the Court in finding a link with EC law has been characterised by D'Oliveira as a 'geographical' approach—see JHUD'Oliveira, 'Is Reverse discrimination still permissible under the Single European Act?' in *Forty years on: The Evolution of Postwar Private International Law in Europe: symposium in celebration of the 40th anniversary of the Centre of Foreign Law and Private International Law, University of Amsterdam, on 27 October 1998* (Deventer, Kluwer, 1990) 73–5.

[15] Above n 10.

that its previous ruling in *Commission v France*,[16] according to which French legislation which restricted the advertising of alcoholic beverages violated Article 28 EC, meant that that legislation should no longer be applied in situations that involved *imported* beverages[17]—however, the legislation could continue being applied to French beverages that were in a purely internal situation.

The Court's traditional approach has the benefit of simplicity which explains why the Court has stuck to it for such a long time and still continues to apply it as the default approach. It is always readily apparent whether a situation involves goods that have moved between Member States and thus the Court, or national courts, can easily and quickly filter out any situations that do not, on the face of it, seem capable of involving an impediment to the free movement of products. Moreover, in deciding whether the goods that form the subject-matter of the case are in a situation which presents a sufficient link with EC law, the Court does not need to have recourse to hypothetical issues and detailed assessments.

These advantages were particularly pertinent during the period in which the Court's traditional approach was shaped—a time when the Court was having to lay the foundations of the common market since the Community legislature was in a state of operational limbo. The Court therefore had to allocate its limited resources in a balanced way so as to be able to give the necessary guidance in as many areas of EC law as possible. Accordingly, a simple method for deciding which situations fell within the scope of EC law was most desirable.

Yet the traditional approach suffers from two important disadvantages which have become increasingly pronounced with the passage of time and the formal completion of the internal market project in 1993. And it is to an explanation of these disadvantages that we now turn.

A The Failure, in Some Instances, to Reflect the Economic Realities of a Case

The first disadvantage of the Court's traditional approach is its insistence on the existence of inter-state movement on the specific facts of the case before the Court. This may lead to decisions that are very far removed from the economic realities of a case, decisions that fail to take into account that even when a measure is, on the facts of the case, applied to situations that do not actually involve an inter-state element, it may, however, *potentially* impede the importation of goods from other Member States. A perfect example of this is a situation which involves the

[16] Case 152/78 *Commission v France* [1980] ECR 2299.
[17] Above n 10, para 11.

application of rules which require public authorities or bodies to reserve a proportion of a public supply contract to producers located within a particular region of national territory. If such a rule is challenged by a producer of goods who is established in another region of the same State, the facts of the case do not involve inter-state movement and thus, under the traditional approach, fall outside the scope of EC law. However, it may also be the case that the authorities and public bodies which have to comply with the rules may have been interested in being supplied, not only with goods from other regions of the State, but also with goods from other Member States. Therefore, in such a situation, just because the case happens to be brought before a court by a national producer of goods and thus there is no inter-state movement on the facts before the Court, this does not mean that the application of the measure to the relevant public bodies does not also have an effect on inter-state trade.[18]

In other words, the traditional approach has, on occasion, proved to be myopic by failing to recognise that the application of a national measure to situations that, on the face of it, do not involve an inter-state element, can, nonetheless, have a substantially negative impact on inter-state trade. As O'Keeffe and Bavasso put it, 'The existence of a cross-border element is still a useful tool to determine if Community rules should come into play .... However, one should not overstate the benefits of this approach. One could easily imagine a transnational case with little impact on the common market and [an] internal matter with a major effect on the common market.'[19] Accordingly, although the requirement of the existence of inter-state movement on the facts before the Court is useful in straightforward factual situations where it is clear that there is no effect on the construction of the internal market, in more complicated cases, the presence or absence of an inter-state element should not be conclusive as to whether the situation before the Court actually involves an impediment to the free movement of goods.

[18] For such a situation see Case C-21/88 *Du Pont de Nemours Italiana SpA v Unità sanitaria locale No 2 di Carrara* [1990] ECR I-889. In that case, although the contested Italian measure was challenged by an Italian company, the Court did not discuss the possibility of this being a purely internal situation. The fact that the Italian company, as plaintiff, was supported by a German company (Du Pont de Nemours Deutschland GmbH) may have made it easier for the Court to accept in its judgment that there was an impact on the inter-state movement of goods. In any event, this factor appears now to be of merely academic interest since in recent years the Court has accepted in its public procurement case law in the area of the free movement of services, that there may be an effect on inter-state trade even in cases which do not involve the exercise of inter-state movement—for such case law see n 43 below.

[19] D O'Keeffe and A Bavasso, 'Four freedoms, one market and national competence: in search of a dividing line' in D O'Keeffe and A Bavasso, *Liber Amicorum in Honour of Lord Slynn of Hadley: Judicial Review in European Union Law* (The Hague/London/Boston, Kluwer, 2000), at 554–5.

This argument is further strengthened by the fact that, following the completion of the internal market which, according to Article 14(2) EC, is an area 'without internal frontiers', it seems increasingly irrelevant to attach so much importance to the crossing of internal (inter-state) frontiers as the deciding factor as to whether a situation falls within the scope of EC law.[20] This view is supported by the Court's new approach to a link with EC law in the sister area of customs duties. In a line of cases starting in 1994[21] (that is one year after the expiry of the 1992 project deadline), the Court said that the imposition of customs duties and charges having equivalent effect by a Member State, can fall within the scope of the customs duties provisions of the Treaty and thus be prohibited, even when the contested dues are imposed on goods that have solely moved within the territory of a *single* Member State (that is where the goods cross regional as well as national frontiers). The Court has rehearsed several arguments in support of this revolutionary approach. However, the most practically sound argument is that, following the formal completion of the internal market in 1993, all frontier controls on goods moving within the internal market have been abolished and, therefore, it is now very difficult to distinguish between goods that have crossed inter-state frontiers and goods that have merely moved within the territory of a single Member State.[22]

B Reverse Discrimination

Another problem emerging as a result of the application of the purely internal rule is reverse discrimination. It arises as a result of the fact that, in purely internal situations, Member States are free to apply a more restrictive regime to their own goods than the one applicable by virtue of EC law to situations that fall within the scope of Community law.[23] This form of discrimination is termed 'reverse' since it is exercised by a Member State against some[24] of its *own* products. It should be highlighted that this

[20] See D'Oliveira, (n 14) 84. See also K Mortelmans, 'Towards convergence in the application of the rules on free movement and on competition?', (2001) 38 *CML Rev* 613, at 631.

[21] Joined Cases C-363/93, C-407/93, C-409/93 and C-411/93 *René Lancry SA v Direction Générale des Douanes* [1994] ECR I-3957; Joined Cases C-485/93 and C-486/93 *Maria Simitzi v Dimos Kos* [1995] ECR I-2655; Case C-72/03 *Carbonati Apuani Srl v Comune di Carrara* [2004] ECR I-8027; *Jersey Potatoes* (n 13).

[22] P Oliver and W-H Roth, 'The internal market and the four freedoms', (2004) 41 *CML Rev* 407, at 431.

[23] For an excellent explanation of the emergence of reverse discrimination in the context of Art 28 EC see M Poiares Maduro, *We the Court: The European Court of Justice and the European Economic Constitution* (Oxford, Hart Publishing, 1998), 154–9.

[24] Products produced in its territory *and* which are in a purely internal situation. It should be noted that products of Member State A which are exported to Member State B and then re-imported to Member State A are no longer considered to be in a purely internal situation,

problem does not only emerge from the application of the Court's traditional approach in determining whether a situation is purely internal; it is a problem which emerges as a result of the fact that purely internal situations (whatever way is used in determining whether a situation qualifies as such) cannot benefit from EC law protection.

A well known example of reverse discrimination is the *3 Glocken* case.[25] There, the Court of Justice held[26] that Article 28 EC prohibited the application to imported pasta products of Italian legislation which allowed only pasta that was made exclusively from durum wheat to be marketed in Italy. This had as a consequence that Italy could, following the Court's judgment, impose its restrictive legislation only on pasta produced within its territory. The practical result of the case was that Italian pasta might have to compete within the same market (that is the Italian market) with pasta that was produced in other Member States by using cheaper raw materials (common or mixed wheat). Therefore, Italian producers of pasta might[27]—as a result of this (reverse) discrimination—suffer a competitive disadvantage without this being a result of their own choice, since they would be required by the impugned legislation to use more expensive raw materials in the production of their pasta.

see Case 229/83 *Association des Centres disributeurs Édouard Leclerc and others v SARL "Au blé vert" and others* [1985] ECR 1 para 26.

[25] Case 407/85 *3 Glocken GmbH and Gertraud Kritzinger v USL Centro-Sud and Provincia autonoma di Bolzano* [1988] ECR 4233. See, also, Case 178/84 *Commission v Germany (German Beer)* [1987] ECR 1227; Case 286/81 *Oosthoek's Uitgeversmaatschappij BV* [1982] ECR 4575 para 9.

[26] *3 Glocken, ibid*, para 25.

[27] It should be noted, however, that as opposed to giving rise to a competitive disadvantage, the use of better quality, and thus more expensive, raw materials may, in reality, provide a competitive advantage. This argument is particularly pertinent in the case of Italian pasta, since Italians know that their domestic pasta tastes good because it is made from durum wheat and, thus, the lower price of (lower quality) imported pasta does not seem to be capable of switching demand towards the latter. This is, also, evident from the Court's judgment in *3 Glocken*: '[…] trends in the export markets demonstrate that competition based on quality operates in favour of durum wheat. The statistics supplied to the Court show a steady increase in the market share held by pasta products made exclusively from durum wheat in other Member States in which they already face competition from pasta made from common wheat or from a mixture of common wheat and durum wheat' (para 27 of the judgment in *3 Glocken, ibid*). For an argument that a requirement for the use of better quality raw materials for national products may not give rise to a competitive disadvantage but may actually create an obstacle to the importation of goods from other Member States see G Davies, *Nationality Discrimination in the European Internal Market* (The Hague/London/New York, Kluwer, 2003) 133. In my view, the question of whether there is a competitive advantage as a result of reverse discrimination requires an examination of (a) the exact requirements imposed by the legislation (ie whether the legislation requires national producers to use raw materials which are of better quality and thus more expensive, or whether the legislation requires the use of, simply, more burdensome production procedures) and (b) the basis of competition on the relevant market (ie whether competition is based on price or quality).

As a result of the competitive disadvantage often suffered by traders in purely internal situations, reverse discrimination has been challenged as differential treatment that is contrary to EC law. The Court of Justice, however, made it clear in its case law that reverse discrimination is not contrary to Article 28 EC, read in conjunction with Article 12 EC, since it is not a difference in treatment that impedes the free movement of goods between Member States.[28]

In the remaining parts of this article I will explore how the Court has, in recent years, attempted to address the problems caused by the application of the purely internal rule. 1993 was a landmark year for the internal market, being the year which signalled its formal completion and—at least on paper—the removal of inter-state frontiers. It will be suggested that this seismic development can be seen as the most important driving force behind the Court's (unspoken) determination to tackle the problems caused by the application of the purely internal rule.

III THE COURT'S NEW APPROACH IN FINDING A LINK WITH EC LAW: RESPONDING TO THE NEED TO REFLECT THE ECONOMIC REALITIES OF A CASE IN A GENUINE INTERNAL MARKET

The 1980s was the decade in which the real difficulties caused by the development of the law on the free movement of goods came to the fore. After the initial enthusiasm, in pro-European circles, with *Dassonville* and *Cassis de Dijon* which were considered a panacea for the difficulties caused by the Eurosclerosis of the 1970s, the first clouds on the horizon started to appear.[29] In particular, there was a general feeling that in some instances the Court had gone too far in the opposite direction and was now becoming too interventionist, by including within the scope of Article 28 EC national measures that seemed to have no impact on the free movement of goods, over and above that which is inherent in every market regulation regime.

The completion of the internal market in 1993 has had important implications for the Court's overall approach in Article 28 cases. In a genuine, mature, internal market which no longer aims merely at opening

[28] See Case 98/86 *Criminal proceedings against Arthur Mathot* [1987] ECR 809 para 7; Case 355/85 *Driancourt v Cognet* [1986] ECR 3231 para 11; Joined cases 80 and 159/85 *Nederlandse Bakkerij Stichting and Others v Edah BV* [1986] ECR 3359 para 18. For a more recent case confirming this see Case C-14/00 *Commission v Italy (Chocolate)* [2003] ECR I-513 paras 71–3.

[29] For literature criticising the case law of the Court in the area of the free movement of goods before *Keck* see D Chalmers, 'Free Movement of goods within the European Community: An unhealthy addiction to Scotch Whisky?', (1993) 42 *ICLQ* 269; J Steiner, 'Drawing the line: Uses and abuses of Article 30 EEC', (1992) 29 *CML Rev* 749; E White, 'In search of the limits to Article 30 of the EEC Treaty', (1989) 26 *CML Rev* 235.

inter-state frontiers but also places importance on other values such as cultural diversity and experimentation, Article 28 EC should only catch those national measures which have a real impact on the inter-state movement of goods. States should remain free to regulate the production and marketing of goods in their territory according to national preferences and values, as long as the regulatory diversity which emerges does not impede inter-state trade. This diversity allows regulatory competition to flourish and thus gives leeway to the Member States to experiment for the best regulatory package. It is only in cases where the application of national rules is not, in reality, neutral in its effects upon entrepreneurs competing within the same national market and thus this system of regulatory competition fails, that the EC should intervene. Therefore, Article 28 EC must only be deployed for striking down national measures which make it harder for imported goods to access (and/or be marketed in) the national market and, thus, have a negative impact on inter-state trade. The requirement that the Community must only intervene in cases which involve a real negative impact on the achievement of its aims which cannot be remedied by the Member States themselves, is enshrined in Article 5 EC and, more specifically, is incarnated in the principles of attributed competence and subsidiarity, the latter being formally recognised by the Treaty of Maastricht in 1993.

The *Keck*[30] case can be seen as a response by the Court to the need to delimit the scope of Article 28 EC in such a way as to respect the principle of subsidiarity, by automatically excluding from the scope of that provision any situations which are obviously harmless to the aim of opening-up (and keeping open) State frontiers and ensuring that goods are free to move between Member States.[31] According to Barnard, *Keck* has 'refocused the emphasis of the enquiry away from "has there been an impact on trade in general" to whether there has been a sufficient impact on cross-border trade'.[32] *Keck* was thus the Court's reaction to the failure of its early case law to reflect, in some instances, the economic realities of a case by *including* within the scope of Article 28 situations that were not sufficiently connected to the aim of that provision.

The major disadvantage of the Court's traditional approach to purely internal situations has been its failure to reflect the economic realities of a case. In this context, however, this failure was due to the fact that the Court's traditional approach automatically excluded from the scope of

[30] Above n 6.

[31] For an author advocating a broadly similar view see J Weiler, 'The Constitution of the Common Market Place: Text and Context in the Evolution of the Free Movement of Goods', in P Craig and G De Búrca, *The Evolution of EU Law* (Oxford, Oxford University Press, 1999) 371–2.

[32] C Barnard, 'Fitting the remaining pieces into the goods and persons jigsaw' (2001) 26 *EL Rev* 35, at 42.

Article 28 EC situations that might, on further examination, prove to be sufficiently harmful to the attainment of the aim of that provision.

Accordingly, once the dust from the *Keck* ruling settled, the Court turned its attention towards the difficulties caused by the application of its traditional approach to purely internal situations. As will be explained in the subsequent part of this section, the Court, in some of its purely internal situations case law from the late 1990s onwards, decided to follow the tide and refine its traditional approach in such a way as to be able to reflect the economic realities of a case. More specifically, in its (relatively) recent jurisprudence, the Court has expressly recognised that it is wrong *automatically* to exclude a situation from the scope of Article 28 EC, *merely* because it involves the application of a measure to goods that are in a purely internal situation. The application of a measure to such goods can, at the same time, have a sufficiently negative impact on the inter-state movement of *other* goods and thus, in certain instances, Article 28 EC requires a national measure to be disapplied even to goods that are in a purely internal situation.

Consequently, *Keck* and the Court's recent jurisprudence on purely internal situations, share the underlying connecting theme of the need to delimit the scope of Article 28 EC in such a way as to *include* within it all rules that are capable of sufficiently impeding the inter-state movement of goods whilst *excluding* from the scope of that provision any rules that are incapable of having such an effect.[33]

The first case where the Court's new approach in finding a link with EC law was employed is *Pistre*.[34] In that case, the question was whether Article 28 EC precluded French legislation which allowed the description 'mountain' to be used *only* in relation to products prepared on national territory from domestic raw materials, after the producer had obtained an authorisation from the French authorities. Hence, the contested legislation

[33] See A Tryfonidou, 'Was *Keck* a half-baked solution after all?' (2007) 34(2) *Legal Issues of Economic Integration* 167. It should be noted that the factual background in *Keck* seems to have involved, in reality, a purely internal situation: it involved the application of rules regulating the marketing of goods. Such rules are, by nature, incapable of impeding the inter-state movement of goods as they (usually) impose an equal burden on imported and domestic goods; moreover, whereas it is for the home State to regulate the production of goods, the regulation of the marketing of goods (ie a subsequent stage in the trading process) should be left to the host State (ie the State in which the goods are marketed) which can apply its rules to all goods marketed within its territory, whether they are also produced there or not. Therefore, some commentators have been of the view that the *Keck* ruling reinforces the purely internal rule—see C Barnard, *ibid*, n 57. See also G Davies, *EU Internal Market Law* (London, Cavendish, 2003) 172.

[34] Joined Cases C-321/94, C-322/94, C-323/94 and C-324/94 *Criminal proceedings against Pistre* [1997] ECR I-2343.

was, in effect, discriminatory against goods imported from other Member States, since it reserved use of the description 'mountain' for national products.[35]

The question referred to the Court arose from criminal proceedings brought against Pistre and others (who were French nationals) for selling, in France, French cooked meat products under a label on which appeared the description 'mountain', despite the fact that the sellers had not obtained the authorisation required by the contested legislation. The Court accepted that the facts from which the question arose did not involve goods that had moved between Member States, however, in its view, this could not be conclusive as to whether the situation was purely internal to France:

> [W]hilst the application of a national measure having no actual link to the importation of goods does not fall within the ambit of Article 30 [now 28] of the Treaty, Article 30 [now 28] cannot be considered inapplicable simply because all the facts of the specific case before the national court are confined to a single Member State. In such a situation, the application of the national measure may also have effects on the free movement of goods between Member States, in particular when the measure in question facilitates the marketing of goods of domestic origin to the detriment of imported goods. In such circumstances, the application of the measure, even if restricted to domestic producers, in itself creates and maintains a difference of treatment between those two categories of goods, hindering, at least potentially, intra-Community trade.[36]

The legislation in *Pistre* was held to be in violation of Article 28 EC because, even when it was solely applied to domestic goods, it nevertheless had the effect of (potentially) inhibiting the importation of 'mountain' goods from other Member States. Since the impugned legislation did not allow, under any circumstances, the use of the designation 'mountain' on products imported from other Member States, this meant that imported products that could demonstrate the qualities associated by the consumer with products coming from mountain areas would not be able to bear that label of quality and would thus be sold as normal products. By allowing the use of a label of quality only on the packaging of meat products that were manufactured within French territory, the contested legislation improved the position of domestic mountain products in the eyes of the French consumer, thereby raising an invisible obstacle to the importation of such products from other Member States.[37]

The innovation in *Pistre* lies in the fact that, although the specific goods to which the contested legislation was applied were not imported products and thus the application of the contested legislation did not impede the

[35] *Ibid*, para 49.
[36] *Ibid*, para 45.
[37] For an excellent explanation see G Davies, (above n 33) 169–72.

inter-state movement of those specific goods, nonetheless, the Court did not consider this factor to be sufficient in itself for qualifying the situation as purely internal. The Court, contrary to its traditional approach, did not interrupt its inquiry as soon as it found that the specific facts of the case did not involve an impediment to the free movement of the goods involved. Rather, in order to reflect economic reality, the Court moved on with its analysis and, after finding that it was obvious that the contested legislation, even when applied to domestic goods, was such as to impede the importation of goods from other Member States (though, it was not possible to specify exactly which 'mountain' products from other Member States would be affected),[38] held that the situation was not a purely internal one.

Despite the various criticisms of *Pistre*,[39] the Court adopted the same mode of reasoning a few years later in the case of *PreussenElektra*,[40] illustrating that the Court's 'new' approach[41] was here to stay. At issue in *PreussenElektra* was the compatibility with Article 28 EC of German legislation which required electricity supply undertakings to purchase the electricity produced from renewable energy sources in their area of supply, in order to satisfy their needs in such electricity. The interveners in the main proceedings and the German government had argued before the Court that the issue was a purely internal one, pointing out that the plaintiff and the defendant were both German and no other kind of cross-border element was present on the facts of the case. The Court, however, noted that:

> an obligation placed on traders in a Member State to obtain a certain percentage of their supplies of a given product from a national supplier limits to that extent the possibility of importing the same product by preventing those traders from obtaining supplies in respect of part of their needs from traders situated in other Member States'.[42]

Therefore, the application of the contested legislation to national suppliers of electricity had, at the same time, an effect on the free movement of

[38] The need to identify a *specific* trader or product that will be negatively affected by a contested measure was firstly dispensed with in the area of the free movement of services, see V Hatzopoulos and TU Do, 'The case law of the ECJ concerning the free provision of services: 2000–2005', (2006) 43 *CML Rev* 923, at 925–6.

[39] See, eg, P Oliver, *Free Movement of Goods in the European Community* (London, Sweet & Maxwell, 2003) 146–54; Oliver and Enchelmaier (n 12) 6578.

[40] Case C-379/98 *PreussenElektra AG v Schleswag AG* [2001] ECR I-2099.

[41] It should be noted that the Court's 'new' approach is not 'revolutionary' in the sense that it has established an entirely novel principle—the fact that Art 28 EC includes within its ambit Member State measures that may have a merely *potential* negative impact on the importation of goods from other Member States was accepted by the Court in *Dassonville* (see para 5 of the judgment, above n 1) in 1974, some five years before the birth of the purely internal rule.

[42] Above n 40, para 70.

goods (electricity produced from renewable energy sources) from other Member States.

As with *Pistre*, the Court therefore accepted that there can be an effect on inter-state trade, and thus a violation of Article 28 EC, even if the national legislation is applied to undertakings/traders that are established in that Member State and the specific facts from which a question arises do not involve inter-state movement. On the facts of the case, it was not possible to show that a specific trader from another Member State had been harmed. And yet, the effect on inter-state trade was so direct and immediate that Article 28 EC should apply. Even though it applied only to national traders, the German legislation had the effect of discriminating against electricity produced in other Member States and was thus per se capable of hindering the free movement of goods—it was as if the contested legislation directly prohibited the importation of green electricity from other Member States.

Thus, under the new approach, the question to be asked is whether the contested measure is capable of having an (actual or potential) effect on intra-Community trade—something which can be proved even when national legislation applies to goods that have been confined within the territory of a single Member State.[43] From a European integration perspective, the Court must be applauded for the new—and more mature—approach adopted in *Pistre* and *PreussenElektra*. The ECJ was correct to find an effect on inter-state trade even when the impugned legislation apparently applied only to domestic goods. The pieces of legislation that were contested in both cases were, by nature, only applicable to domestic goods so one, at first sight, could conclude that it would be impossible for such legislation to have any negative impact on inter-state trade. This, after all, may have been the aim of the astute drafters of the legislation—the rules may have been deliberately drafted so as to apply only to goods within the territory of a single Member State. Therefore, in this way, under the traditional approach, the legislation would have fallen outside the scope of EC law. Yet, under the new, economic reality based approach the Court looked behind the law to consider its effect on inter-state trade.

The Court's new approach has parallels with the test used in EC competition law for determining whether a situation should be assessed

[43] This approach seems to have been followed, also, in the context of Art 29 EC—see *Jersey Potatoes*, (above n 13); and in the context of Art 49 EC, and, in particular, the public procurement case law (though, it could be argued that in this context the Court was merely applying the principles established in its public procurement legislation, to situations that fell outside the scope of those legislative measures)—see, eg, Case C-458/03 *Parking Brixen GmbH v Gemeinde Brixen and Stadtwerke Brixen AG* [2005] ECR I-8612, para 55. For a strong criticism of the application of the Court's new approach in the context of Art 29 EC see A Dawes, 'Importing and exporting poor reasoning: worrying trends in relation to the case law on the free movement of goods', (2007) 8(8) *German Law Journal* 761, at 770–72.

under EC competition law or under national competition provisions.[44] In competition law cases, it has been held that even if the parties to an agreement operate in the same Member State and the agreement takes place wholly within that Member State, the agreement may nonetheless fall within the scope of Article 81 EC, provided that an effect on inter-state trade can be proved.[45] Similarly, the Court has held that there is no need for the involvement of two or more Member States, for a situation to fall within the scope of Article 82 EC—'when the holder of a dominant position obstructs access to the market by competitors, it makes no difference whether such conduct is confined to a single Member State as long as it is capable of affecting patterns of trade and competition in the common market'.[46] Poiares Maduro—in an article written before his appointment as an Advocate General—had already advocated convergence between the two fields.[47]

The real challenge now facing the Court is to ensure that economic reality is actually taken into account, when making an assessment as to whether a situation falls within the scope of EC law. Useful lessons can be learned from the Court's competition law jurisprudence. In particular, account should be taken of the 'economic and legal conditions'[48] of the relevant (product and geographic) market to determine whether the application of the measure can, indeed, have an effect on the free movement of goods. Only in this way will the Court's new approach reflect the view that the internal market is a mature market, the rules of which apply only to situations that involve a real impediment to the achievement of one of its aims.[49] A failure by the Court to take into account the economic and legal context in which a challenged measure is applied,

[44] For a commentary on possible convergence between the fundamental freedoms and competition law in relation to internal situations/requirement of an effect on inter-state trade, see K Mortelmans, (above n 20) at 630–32.

[45] See, eg, Case 246/86 *SC Belasco and others v Commission* [1989] ECR 2117, para 33; Joined Cases T-202, 204 and 207/98, *Tate & Lyle plc and others v Commission* [2001] ECR II-2035 para 79. This is also reflected, and further explained, in paras 77–92 of the Commission's Notice on the effect on trade concept contained in Arts 81 and 82 of the Treaty, [2004] OJ C/101/81.

[46] See para 103 of the judgment in Case 322/81 *Michelin v Commission* [1983] ECR 3461. See also, more recently, Joined Cases C-94/04 and C-202/04 *Cipolla v Portolese* and *Macrino and Capodarte v Meloni* [2006] ECR I-11421 para 45. For further explanation of this see paras 93–9 of the Commission's Notice on the effect on trade concept, *ibid*.

[47] M Poiares Maduro, 'The Scope of European Remedies. The Case of Purely Internal Situations and Reverse Discrimination' in Kilpatrick, Novitz and Skidmore (eds), *The Future of European Remedies* (Oxford, Hart Publishing, 2000), 122 (n 28).

[48] This phrase can be found in a number of competition law cases. See, eg, para 13 of Case 22/71 *Béguelin Import Co v S.A.G.L. Import Export* [1971] ECR 949.

[49] One could argue that in this way the Court is moving towards the 'juridical' approach explained and advocated by D'Oliveira, in establishing whether a situation should fall within the scope of EC law—see D'Oliveira (above n 14) at 73–4.

questions the rationale, and puts into danger the effectiveness of the new approach.[50]

IV THE COURT'S INDIRECT CONTRIBUTION TO THE RESOLUTION OF THE REVERSE DISCRIMINATION CONUNDRUM—*GUIMONT* AND *DZODZI*

The failure to reflect the economic realities of the case before the Court was not the only problem caused by the application of the traditional approach to the purely internal rule. As we have already seen, another, equally important, concern is that the application of the purely internal rule often gives rise to reverse discrimination. And although, as we saw in the previous section of the paper, the Court has provided an appropriate solution to the former problem, through its innovative approach in *Pistre*, the Community and, in particular, the Court of Justice, have up until now, been broadly unresponsive to the latter.[51]

[50] The Court seems to have attempted to use its new approach to finding a link with Art 28 EC in Case C-254/98 *Schutzverband gegen unlauteren Wettbewerb v TK-Heimdienst Sass GmbH* [2000] ECR I-151 which involved an action brought by an Austrian trading company against Austrian legislation which was alleged to be contrary to Art 28 EC. However, it should be noted that in that case the Court was, with respect, wrong to find that the contested legislation was contrary to Art 28 EC, since the nature of the affected products was such as to confine the relevant geographic market within the territory of each Member State (and, in fact, even more narrowly to small areas within each Member State) and thus the economic realities of the case meant that the contested measure could never have a negative impact on inter-state trade, simply because there was no inter-state trade in the goods that were affected by the contested legislation. For an explanation of this see para 12 of the Opinion of Advocate General La Pergola in *TK-Heimdienst*.

[51] It should be noted, however, that in a trilogy of customs duties cases (*Lancry*, above n 21; *Simitzi* above n 21; and *Carbonati Apuani*, above n 21) the Court of Justice seems to have extended the application of the customs duties provisions to goods that have not crossed inter-state frontiers, in order to prevent the emergence of reverse discrimination. This view was expressed by Advocates General Léger and Poiares Maduro in *Jersey Potatoes* (above n 13) and *Carbonati Apuani*, respectively. It also appears to be implicit in some of the judgments of the Court (see, eg, para 30 of *Lancry*). Moreover, it becomes rather more clear from the fact that the Court in the more recent case of *Jersey Potatoes* followed a different mode of reasoning since in that case reverse discrimination would not arise as a result of the Court delivering a judgment excluding goods in a purely internal situation from the scope of application of the customs duties provisions—for an explanation of this see A Tryfonidou, annotation of *Jersey Potatoes*, (2006) 43 *CML Rev* 1727. It should be noted that very recently Advocate General Sharpston has suggested that the *Lancry* reasoning should be applied, also, in the context of the free movement of persons, and, in order to prevent the emergence of reverse discrimination, the scope of application of EC law should be extended to cover the situation of persons who are (according to the Court's traditional approach) considered to be in a purely internal situation by virtue of the fact that they have not exercised inter-state movement—see paras 112–57 of the Opinion of Advocate General Sharpston in Case C-212/06 *Government of the French Community and Walloon Government v Flemish Government* Judgment of 1 April 2008, not yet reported. The Court in its judgment, however, rejected the suggestion of the Advocate General and confirmed its traditional approach according to which the free movement of persons provisions of the Treaty only apply to

Reverse discrimination has always been attacked by traders and economic actors for giving rise to invidious results, both in the area of trade (in the form of competitive distortions) and when affecting the daily lives of Member State nationals (whether as economic actors or, simply, as human beings). The Court's formal response to those complaints is to point out that it is up to the Member States, if they so wish, to provide a remedy to persons and traders who have suffered reverse discrimination.[52]

Many Member States have followed the Court's suggestion and provided a solution to certain instances of reverse discrimination. This has been done in two ways.

First, Member States have drafted legislation providing that the EC rules in a particular area should, as a matter of national law, be extended to purely internal situations (this is called 'voluntary adoption', 'spontaneous harmonisation' or '*renvoi*'). For instance, Belgium has made legislation according to which the same rights of family reunification that are granted by EC law to migrant economic actors should, as a matter of Belgian law, be granted to Belgians in purely internal situations. The rationale behind this legislative move has, obviously, been the desire of the Belgian government to avoid the unfortunate results caused by reverse discrimination in the area of family reunification.[53]

Secondly, in some Member States a remedy to the problem of reverse discrimination has been provided judicially, with their Constitutional courts ruling that instances of reverse discrimination are contrary to the principle of equality enshrined in their Constitution and thus should be corrected as a matter of national constitutional law.[54] And since the Community cannot be required by Member States to level down its standards to match those established at national level, in such instances, Member States are required by their constitutional principle of equality to amend their rules to match those of the Community.

situations which are not confined within a single Member State and which present a connection with the situations envisaged by Community law—see para 33 of the judgment.

[52] Case C-132/93 *Steen v Deutsche Bundespost (No 2)* [1994] ECR I-2715 paras 8–10; Joined Cases C-64 and 65/96 *Uecker and Jacquet v Land Nordrhein-Westfalen* [1997] ECR I-3171, para 23.

[53] See Joined Cases 297/88 and 197/89 *Dzodzi v Belgian State* [1990] ECR I-3763.

[54] For an explanation of how the Italian Constitutional Court ruled in Decision 30 December 1997, No 443, *Riv dir Internaz* (1998) that reverse discrimination is prohibited by the Italian Constitution (and, in particular, the principle of equality enshrined in it) see A Adinolfi, 'The Judicial application of Community law in Italy (1981–1997)', (1998) 35 *CML Rev* 1313, at 1325–1327. See also footnote 11 of the Opinion of Advocate General Poiares Maduro in *Cipolla* (above n 46); para 36 of the Opinion of Advocate General Ruiz-Jarabo Colomer in Case C-451/03 *Servizi Ausiliari Dottori Commercialisti Srl v Giuseppe Calafiori* [2006] ECR I-2941. This was also mentioned by the Commission in its 'Sixteenth Annual Report on Monitoring the Application of Community Law' COM (99) 301 final, [1999] OJ C/354/1, 190.

The above solutions to the reverse discrimination conundrum are provided by the legal systems of some of the Union's Member States. Nonetheless, the Court of Justice does have an indirect role to play in the process of applying both these solutions. Starting with 'spontaneous harmonisation', in its so-called *Dzodzi*-jurisprudence[55] the Court has accepted that it has jurisdiction to reply to a question referred for a preliminary ruling and which has arisen in a case the facts of which are purely internal to a Member State, if the national court's aim in making the reference has been to obtain an interpretation of EC law, which it will then apply to the facts of the case, being required by national legislation to treat purely internal situations in the same way as situations that fall within the scope of EC law.[56] More recently the Court of Justice has initiated another line of case law, the so-called *Guimont*-jurisprudence,[57] according to which the Court has jurisdiction to reply to a question referred by a national court, where the latter, in order to prevent the emergence of reverse discrimination, is required by national law to treat purely internal situations in the same way as situations falling within the scope of EC law. Accordingly, if national law requires instances of reverse discrimination to be corrected, the Court of Justice is more than willing to contribute, indirectly, to this process, by elucidating the meaning of the EC provision that the national court is required to apply to the purely internal situation in question.

There has been an animated discussion between commentators and members of the Court of Justice for,[58] and against,[59] the Court's more open

[55] There is an abundant body of case law in this area. See, among others, *Dzodzi*, (above n 53) paras 31–43; Case C-231/89 *Gmurzynska-Bsher* [1990] ECR I-4003, paras 15–26; Case C-130/95 *Giloy* [1997] ECR I-4291; Case C-28/95 *Leur-Bloem* [1997] ECR I-4161 paras 24–34; Case C-1/99 *Kofisa Italia Srl v Ministero delle Finanze* [2001] ECR I-207 paras 20–33; Case C-3/04 *Poseidon Chartering BV v Marianne Zeeschip VOF and others* [2006] ECR I-2505; Case C-170/03 *Staatssecretaris van Financiën v Feron* [2005] ECR I-2299, para 11.

[56] For an explanation see SL Kaleda, 'Extension of the preliminary rulings procedure outside the scope of Community law: "The Dzodzi line of cases"', European Integration online Papers (EIoP), Vol 4, No 11, 19 October 2000 available at http://eiop.or.at/eiop/texte/2000–011a.htm; C Barnard and E Sharpston, 'The changing face of article 177 references', (1997) 34 *CML Rev* 1113, at 1128–33.

[57] Case C-448/98 *Criminal proceedings against Guimont* [2000] ECR I-10663; Case C-510/99 *Tridon v Fédération départementale des cahsseurs de l'Isère* [2001] ECR I-7777 and Case 298/87 *Proceedings for a compulsory reconstruction against Smanor SA* [1988] ECR 4489 (goods); Joined Cases C-515/99, C-519/99 to C-524/99 and C-526/99 to C-540/99 *Reisch and Others* [2002] ECR I-2157 and Case C-300/01; *Salzmann* [2003] ECR I-4899 (capital); Case C-6/01 *Anomar v Estado português* [2003] ECR I-8621; *Cipolla* (above n 46) and *Calafiori* (above n 54) (services); Case C-250/03 *Mauri v Ministero della Giustizia, Commissione per gli esami di avvocato presso la Corte d'appello di Milano* [2005] ECR I-1267 (establishment).

[58] See, eg, G Davies, (above n 27) 138–9.

[59] See the Joined Opinion of Advocate General Jacobs in *Leur-Bloem* and *Giloy*, (above n 55); C Ritter, 'Purely Internal situations, reverse discrimination, Guimont, Dzodzi and Article

approach[60] to the delimitation of its jurisdiction in cases such as *Dzodzi* and *Guimont*. And although it is beyond the scope of this paper to rehearse these arguments, I would like to suggest that the Court's approach in these cases has been correct. Reverse discrimination is a difference in treatment that is a direct corollary of one of the most important principles of the EC legal system (the purely internal situations doctrine) and which has persisted for the last three decades. Since two of the ways in which reverse discrimination can be remedied are 'spontaneous harmonisation' as well as the use of the Member States' Constitutional Articles on equality, it seems worthwhile for the Court of Justice to use its resources to facilitate national courts to apply those solutions in the most effective way. Consequently, when a national court is requesting an interpretation of a provision of Community law to remedy instances of reverse discrimination, this should be considered sufficient to enable, and perhaps even require, the Court of Justice to exercise its jurisdiction.

Having seen how the Court, through the extension of the scope of its preliminary rulings jurisdiction, has, indirectly, contributed to the resolution of the problem of reverse discrimination, we should now turn to explore the question of whether, and if yes, how a *direct* solution to the reverse discrimination conundrum can be provided at EC level.

V THE FUTURE: POSSIBLE EC SOLUTIONS TO THE PROBLEM OF REVERSE DISCRIMINATION IN THE AREA OF TRADE

In order to decide what is the best way to resolve a problem, the actual origins of the problem must be traced. And some[61] have rightly argued that reverse discrimination should be viewed as an EC problem, as it would not have emerged but for the existence and (limited scope of) application of EC law, and not (as the ECJ presents it) as a problem caused by the Member States choosing to practise discrimination against their own nationals and traders. And, because reverse discrimination is an EC problem, it is the EC itself that should provide the solution(s).

As we have already seen, some Member States have provided solutions to the reverse discrimination conundrum. Nonetheless, despite the various advantages offered by these solutions (such as the maintenance—where

234', (2006) 31(5) *EL Rev* 690 (for a strong criticism of the Court's *Guimont* jurisprudence); paras 17–53 of the Opinion of Advocate General Ruiz-Jarabo Colomer in *Kofisa Italia* (above n 55)

[60] It has traditionally been implicit in the Court's purely internal situations case law that whenever a case involves a situation that is wholly internal to a Member State, not only is EC law inapplicable (as a matter of substance), but also, the Court of Justice does not have jurisdiction to give a reply to the questions referred by the national court.

[61] See, eg, Poiares Maduro (above n 47).

appropriate—of cultural diversity and experimentation and the avoidance of complete uniformity imposed 'from above'), instances of reverse discrimination persist.

'Spontaneous harmonisation' is merely a random way of removing the most disturbing instances of reverse discrimination, such as those in the area of family reunification (see, for example, *Dzodzi*). Furthermore, and more importantly, both of the solutions provided at national level give rise to further instances of inequality since, as a result of their application, there is no longer merely a difference in treatment between persons who fall within the scope of EC law and persons that are not entitled to EC law protection as a result of the fact that they have not contributed to the internal market. Now, there is also a difference in treatment between persons who happen to be nationals of a Member State that has resorted to the above methods for addressing the problems caused by reverse discrimination, and persons who are nationals of a Member State which has preferred to continue applying its more restrictive laws in purely internal situations.

Accordingly, although the Member States themselves can, in some instances, deliver a response to the reverse discrimination conundrum, nonetheless, gaps still persist in the protection from reverse discrimination, this being most notable in Member States which appear reluctant to give up their own standards for the sake of preventing the emergence of reverse discrimination.

It is my contention that those gaps should be filled by actions of the Community institutions. In other words, instances of reverse discrimination that persist despite the fact that national authorities increasingly have recourse to the various solutions available at national level should, now, be remedied at EC level. EC law should be interpreted in such a way as to include within its scope instances of reverse discrimination and the Community institutions should work together to provide appropriate solutions to the reverse discrimination conundrum.

A careful reading of the provisions of the EC Treaty offers the basis for the resolution of the problem of reverse discrimination. Article 14(2) EC defines the internal market as an 'area without internal frontiers in which the free movement of goods, persons, services and capital *is ensured in accordance with the provisions of this Treaty*' (emphasis added). The italicised words above point to the need to ensure that the internal market is not merely a market where products and factors of production move from one Member State to another uninhibited, *without any other considerations coming to play*. Following the completion of the internal market, the emphasis has been placed on ensuring that the internal market is a market which functions properly.[62] The internal market that the signatories to the Single European Act intended to construct by the deadline they set in Article 14(1) EC was to be, not only a single market, but, according to Article 14(2) EC, a single, properly-functioning, market which operates in harmony with the broader aims and aspirations of the Community. Accordingly, whenever EC law requires the removal of inter-state frontiers so that goods can move uninhibited from one Member State to another in the process of establishing and maintaining an internal market, this should be done in a way that will accord with other aims and goals of the Community which have to be promoted in a properly-functioning market. This argument becomes more tangible if Article 14(2) of the Treaty is read in conjunction with Article 3 EC which provides a list of the activities of the Community. This list includes aims/activities such as a contribution to the attainment of a high level of health protection (see Article 3(1)(p) EC); a contribution to the strengthening of consumer protection (see Article 3(1)(t) EC); and, more importantly for our purposes, the need to maintain a system ensuring that competition in the internal market is not distorted (see Article 3(1)(g) EC). Hence, any danger to the protection and achievement of the aims/activities that are included in the Article 3 list *which arises as a side-effect of the process of establishing and maintaining an internal market*, falls within the scope of EC law and is contrary to Article 14(2) read in conjunction with Article 3.[63]

The preceding analysis can be transplanted to the discussion on the issue of reverse discrimination, for illustrating that this difference in treatment falls within the scope of EC law and is capable of being found to amount to a violation of the Treaty. As has been explained in previous parts of this paper, as a result of the exercise of reverse discrimination against producers of goods that are in a purely internal situation, competitive distortions may emerge. Traders whose situation falls outside the scope of EC law, because their products are marketed in their own Member State, may have to comply with a different, more restrictive, production regime than the one applicable to traders whose products cross inter-state frontiers. Yet the mere existence of different rules for the production of products in different Member States is not, in itself, sufficient in order to rule that a situation is contrary to Community law.[64] The problem with reverse discrimination is

[62] See para 148 of the Opinion of Advocate General Geelhoed in Case C-391/01 *The Queen v Secretary of State for Health, ex parte British American Tobacco (Investments) Ltd and others* [2002] ECR I-11453.

[63] For another author advocating this view see G Davies, 'Can selling arrangements be harmonized', (2005) 30(3) *EL Rev* 371, at 380.

[64] This is 'harmonisation discrimination' which the Court of Justice has clearly held not to be prohibited by EC law—see Case 126/82 *Smit Transport BV v Commissie Grensoverschrijdend Beroepsgoederenvervoer* [1983] ECR 73 para 27; Case 14/68 *Walt-Wilhelm et al v Bundeskartellamt* [1969] ECR 1, para 13.

that products that comply with different rules have to compete within the same market (the market of the Member State where the reversely discriminated products originate). And this inequality of treatment appears to be improper in a properly-functioning market not because it is unfair but, more significantly, because it does not enable the market to function properly.

Moreover, it is obvious that reverse discrimination is a direct result of the process of establishing an internal market—in other words, it comes about as a side-effect of the process of opening-up national frontiers and the EC regime governing the free movement of goods. Since the Treaty rules on free movement govern only the situation of products that are involved in inter-state trade, national legislation which is restrictive of trade and is applicable to both imported and domestic products becomes inapplicable, as a result of the operation of EC law, only to imported products, whilst it continues being applicable to traders whose situation is purely internal. Furthermore, the fact that the Community legislature often resorts to the methods of partial[65] or minimum[66] harmonisation (with a 'market access' clause) when making legislation, means that the situations that will be held to fall outside the scope of such legislation will be governed by the (often more restrictive) national legal regime.

Following the above analysis, it becomes obvious that reverse discrimination is a difference in treatment that is capable of falling within the scope of EC law and, if unjustifiable, can be found to be contrary to EC law since it impedes the Community's now all-important aim of ensuring that the internal market is functioning smoothly by ensuring, inter alia, that competition in the internal market is not distorted.

The above conclusion, however, begs the question of what are the actual routes to a solution that are available to the Community institutions, once it is formally recognised that reverse discrimination falls within the scope of EC law and thus should be remedied at EC level.

First, the Court of Justice can make use of a combination of Treaty Articles to require any national measures, the application of which gives rise to reverse discrimination, to become inapplicable in purely internal situations. These provisions will be Article 14(2) EC read in conjunction with Article 3(1)(g) EC, and Article 10 EC which requires Member States to, inter alia, abstain from any measure which could jeopardize the

[65] For an excellent explanation see the Opinion of Advocate General Tesauro in Case C-63/89 *Les Assurances du Crédit SA and Compagnie Belge d'Assurance Crédit SA v Council and Commission* [1991] ECR I-1799.

[66] See Case C-11/92 *The Queen v Secretary of State for Health, ex parte Gallaher Ltd, Imperial Tobacco Ltd and Rothmans International Tobacco (UK) Ltd* [1993] ECR 3545. For an explanation see S Weatherill, 'Regulating the Internal Market: Result orientation in the Court of Justice', (1994) 19(1) *EL Rev* 55; C Barnard, *The Substantive Law of the EU: The Four Freedoms* (Oxford, Oxford University Press, 2007), 600–604.

attainment of the objectives of the Treaty. Since, following the completion of the internal market, one of the main aims of the Treaty is to maintain a properly-functioning market in which there will be a system ensuring that conditions of competition in the market are not distorted, any Member State measure which unjustifiably and appreciably distorts the conditions of competition should be found to fall within the scope of EC law. In this way, instances of reverse discrimination that cannot be justified on some reasonable ground, will be found contrary to EC law and thus Member States will be obliged, as a matter of EC law, not to apply those measures in purely internal situations.

Secondly, the Community legislature itself can provide a solution to the reverse discrimination conundrum through making use of Article 95 EC as its legal basis. In formal terms, Article 95 EC will be able to be used for making legislation specifically for remedying instances of reverse discrimination. This is due to the fact that Article 95 EC gives competence to the Community legislature to make legislation having as its object, inter alia, the functioning of the internal market. The Court of Justice has stressed in its case law that the term 'functioning' of the internal market gives competence to the Community legislature to make legislation for remedying any instances of an appreciable distortion of the conditions of competition in the internal market.[67] And since reverse discrimination can give rise to a distortion of the conditions of competition, the Community legislature appears to have the competence to promulgate legislation for remedying such instances, whenever the distortions are appreciable.[68]

Yet, in practical terms, it seems unlikely that the Community legislature will resort to the above solution. This is because this solution presents the important disadvantage that the EC will be promulgating legislation that is explicitly targeted at purely internal situations (that is EC legislation that extends the application of EC rules to products confined within their State of origin), this being almost certainly likely to cause the fervent objection of the Member States. Moreover, this solution goes against important principles that have always been valued in the European internal market, such as the principle of subsidiarity; competition among rules which promotes experimentation and innovation; and the fact that the overall responsibility for regulating national markets should rest with the Member States.

[67] C-300/89 *Commission v Council (titanium dioxide)* [1991] ECR I-2867 para 15; Case C-376/98 *Germany v Parliament and Council (Tobacco Advertising I)* [2000] ECR I-8419 para 106; Case C-350/92 *Spain v Council* [1995] ECR I-1985 para 32; para 80 of the Opinion of Advocate General Léger in Case C-380/03 *Germany v Parliament and Council* (Directive 2003/33) (*Tobacco Advertising II*) [2006] ECR I-11573.

[68] A similar view appears to have been advocated by Davies—see G Davies, (above n 33) 154–5.

In practical terms, it appears much more likely that the Community legislature will continue drafting legislation at EC level under Article 95 EC for regulating the production and marketing of goods and, where necessary, the Court of Justice will interpret that legislation in such a way as to avoid the emergence of reverse discrimination. In other words, the Court will read EC legislation as covering purely internal situations, when this will be necessary for avoiding the emergence of unjustifiable instances of reverse discrimination. In fact, this may also have been the intent of the Community legislature when making legislation since, according to Poiares Maduro, '[i]n reality, Directives allowing States to impose higher requirements on their nationals (and thus creating reverse discrimination) are an exception. The rule is normally that the requirements apply to both imported and domestic products with those conforming to those requirements benefiting from a market access clause.'[69]

The Court seems to have (implicitly) followed this approach in some of its recent case law on the scope of application of legislative measures the legal basis of which is Article 95 EC. The first case where this approach was followed was *Österreichischer Rundfunk*.[70] At issue in that case was the compatibility with Community law of Austrian legislation which required entities which were subject to control by the Austrian Court of Audit, to inform the latter about the proceeds of their employees whose annual salaries were higher than a certain level. Once that information was received by the Court of Audit, it would be published in a report. More specifically, the question was whether the said legislation was compatible with Directive 95/46/EC,[71] which requires Member States to protect the right to privacy of persons with respect to the processing of personal data, its aim being to ensure that the increased movement of information as a result of the establishment of the internal market does not have a negative impact on the protection of fundamental human rights. One of the preliminary issues that arose before the Court of Justice, was whether the situation was purely internal to Austria, since the dispute concerned the compatibility with EC law (and, in particular, Directive 95/46) of the

[69] M Poiares Maduro, (n 23) 135. For an example of secondary legislation which may apply, partly, to purely internal situations and in this way reverse discrimination will not emerge see Chapter III ('Freedom of establishment for providers') of Directive 2006/123/EC on services in the internal market, [2006] OJ L376/36. For an excellent discussion of the issue as to whether Chapter III of the Services Directive is intended to apply not merely to cross-border, but also to purely internal, situations see C Barnard, 'Unravelling the Services Directive', (2008) 45 *CML Rev* 323. See also, G Davies, 'The Services Directive: extending the country of origin principle and reforming public administration', (2007) 32(2) *EL Rev* 232, 241–3.

[70] Case C-465/00 *Rechnungshof v Österreichischer Rundfunk* [2003] ECR I-4989—annotated by Classen, (2004) 41 *CML Rev* 1377. See, also, C Barnard, (above n 66) 578.

[71] Dir 95/46/EC on the protection of individuals with regard to the processing of personal data and on the free movement of such data, [1995] OJ L281/31.

above Austrian legislation when applied to information about Austrian employees of Austrian bodies in Austria; and, if this was answered in the affirmative, whether the situation fell outside the scope of application of the Directive. The Court of Justice, contrary to the suggestion of the Advocate General, held that the situation fell within the scope of the 1995 Directive. It reasoned as follows:

> [R]ecourse to Article 100a of the Treaty as legal basis does not presuppose the existence of an actual link with free movement between Member States in every situation referred to by the measure founded on that basis ... to justify recourse to Article 100a of the Treaty as the legal basis, what matters is that the measure adopted on that basis must actually be intended to improve the conditions for the establishment and functioning of the internal market.
>
> In those circumstances, the applicability of Directive 95/46 cannot depend on whether the specific situations at issue in the main proceedings have a sufficient link with the exercise of the fundamental freedoms guaranteed by the Treaty, in particular, in those cases, the freedom of movement of workers.[72]

This reasoning was confirmed soon afterwards in the *Lindqvist* case[73] and, more recently, in the free movement of goods case *Germany v Parliament and Council* (*Tobacco Advertising II*).[74] In my view, in the above three cases the Court's main aim was to prevent the emergence of reverse discrimination. In *Österreichischer Rundfunk*, reverse discrimination in the enjoyment of fundamental rights protection (in particular, the right to privacy) might arise as a result of the partial application of the said Directive. If, for example, a Member State does not impede in any way the free movement of information when this is necessary to respect the right to privacy of individuals, a citizen of that Member State in a purely internal situation claiming that the circulation of information concerning his person would violate his right to privacy, would not have any remedy under EC law. More importantly, he would be in a worse position than that of a person from another Member State coming to the former's State, since the latter would have a remedy through the use of Directive 95/46. Therefore, the above cases can be used to support the argument that the Court may now be of the view that, in order to prevent the emergence of reverse discrimination, it can, and perhaps must, interpret EC secondary legislation as including within its scope purely internal situations.

One could, moreover, argue that the Community legislature can indeed play, and, in fact, already plays, an important role in the resolution of the reverse discrimination conundrum, albeit one which is more subtle than that suggested above. It could be argued that the mere making of

72 Above n 70, paras 41–2.
73 Case C-101/01 *Criminal proceedings against Bodil Lindqvist* [2003] ECR I-12971.
74 Above n 67, para 80.

legislation by the Community legislature could be considered as indirectly contributing to the resolution of the reverse discrimination conundrum, since national legislatures usually emulate the actions of the Community legislature, in order to enable their traders to compete effectively within a trans-national market.

This can be explained in the following terms. Reverse discrimination is, in most instances, an *unintended* consequence of the existence of two overlapping spheres of legal competence—the EC and the national. Therefore, under normal circumstances, Member States are eager to remove any disturbing instances of reverse discrimination, being aware of the negative repercussions that this difference in treatment may have on the competitiveness of their products. Moreover, in practical terms, it is highly unlikely that Member States will make (or maintain) two pieces of legislation, one implementing the Community measure for products that fall within the scope of EC law; and another, imposing stricter standards for domestic products. Hence, whenever the Community legislature regulates the conditions for production and marketing of certain products, it is highly probable that the national legislation that will be made for incorporating those standards into national law will be held, by the national authorities, to apply *both* to situations that involve inter-state trade *and* to purely internal situations, thereby transplanting the Community-prescribed standards into purely internal situations.[75] In this way, reverse discrimination against products that fall within a category for which standards have been provided by the Community (EC law, however, requiring those standards to be imposed only on inter-state situations) will no longer emerge, this being another instance of 'spontaneous harmonisation' the seeds of which in this instance, however, are sown by the actions of the Community legislature.

VI CONCLUSION

This paper has had as its aim to present how the approach of the Court of Justice to purely internal situations has developed through the years, together with the overall development of the internal market.

It has been seen that the application of the purely internal rule has given rise to two main problems—the one (that is failure to reflect the economic realities of a case) emerging from the myopic approach followed by the Court traditionally in determining whether a situation qualifies as purely

[75] For an author advocating the view that EC harmonisation may have a spillover effect into, inter alia, purely internal situations see S Weatherill, 'Harmonisation: How Much, How Little?', (2005) *European Business Law Review* 533.

internal; the other (that is reverse discrimination), emerging from the mere application of the purely internal rule.

1993 was a landmark year for the internal market. It was the year which signalled the formal completion of the internal market, this development heralding the beginning of a new era in internal market affairs. This landmark development can be seen as an important driving force behind the Court's (unspoken) determination to tackle the problems caused by the application of the purely internal rule/the traditional approach used in finding a link with EC law.

In response to the need to reflect the economic realities of the case (that is the first problem) and to ensure that, in a genuine internal market, Article 28 EC catches all national measures which have a real impact on the inter-state movement of goods, the Court has recently refined its approach used in finding a link with EC law. Now, it appears that the important question is not whether the application of the contested national measure to the goods involved in the facts before the Court is capable of impeding the inter-state movement of *those* goods, but whether the application of the contested national measure on the facts before the Court is capable of impeding the inter-state movement of goods in general. As underlined in the main analysis, the success of this new approach largely depends on whether the Court will be able to effectively analyse the legal and economic context in which the contested measure is applied, before making its assessment as to whether the measure should be caught by Article 28 EC.

The difficulty lies in the second problem (reverse discrimination), however, since the Court has failed to provide a direct solution to this problem, preferring to leave it up to the Member States to decide whether they will afford a remedy in instances of reverse discrimination. It has been suggested that the completion of the internal market and the emphasis now placed on ensuring that the established market functions properly, has important implications for the reverse discrimination conundrum. Reverse discrimination has no place in a genuine, properly-functioning, market. Reverse discrimination is a difference in treatment that is contrary to the, now dominant, aim of ensuring that the internal market is functioning properly (since it distorts the conditions of competition) *and* falls within the ambit of EC law since it emerges as a side effect of the establishment of the internal market. Hence, any remaining unjustifiable instances of reverse discrimination should be tackled at EC level, either judicially (through the use of a combination of Treaty Articles outlawing unjustifiable instances of reverse discrimination), or, where appropriate, legislatively.

10

Economic Activity as a Limit to Community Law

OKEOGHENE ODUDU*

I INTRODUCTION

CERTAIN TREATY PROVISIONS cannot be applied unless there is economic activity.[1] According to the Commission, 'the freedom to provide services, the right of establishment, the competition and State aid rules of the Treaty *only apply to economic activities*'.[2] The need for economic activity limits Community law, and preserves for Member States a greater degree of autonomy over that which can be said to be non-economic, prompting Advocate General Poiares Maduro to write that:

> [i]n seeking to determine whether an activity carried on by the State or a State entity is of an *economic nature*, the Court is entering dangerous territory, since it must find a balance between the need to protect undistorted competition on the common market and respect for the powers of the Member States.[3]

* This essay develops themes considered in Odudu 'The Meaning of Undertaking within Article 81 EC' 7 *Cambridge Yearbook of European Legal Studies* (2006), 211–241 and 'Annotation of Case C–369/04, Hutchison 3G UK Ltd and Others v Commissioners of Customs and Excise [2007] ECR–I 5247 and C–284/04, T-Mobile Austria GmbH and Others v. Republik Österreich [2007] ECR–I 5189' (2008) 45 *CML Rev* 1269–77.

[1] Case T-313/02 *David Meca-Medina and Igor Majcen v Commission* [2004] ECR II-3291, [37] and [41], Case C-519/04 P *David Meca-Medina and Igor Majcen v Commission* [2006] ECR I-6991, [22] and [25], AG Opinion [18]; Case C-309/99 *JCJ Wouters and Others v Algemene Raad van de Nederlandse Orde van Advocaten* [2002] ECR I-1577 [57]; Case C-369/04 *Hutchison 3G UK Ltd and Others v Commissioners of Customs and Excise* [2007] ECR-I 5247, [28]; and Case C-284/04 *T-Mobile Austria GmbH and Others v Republik Österreich* [2007] ECR-I 5189, [34].

[2] Green Paper on Services of General Interest COM (2003) 270 final, [43], (emphasis added). Also Communication from the Commission: Services of General Interest in Europe [1996] OJ C/281/3, [18]; Communication from the Commission—Services of General Interest in Europe [2001] OJ C/17/4, [28]; Report to the Laeken European Council: Services of General Interest COM/2001/598/FINAL [30].

[3] See, the Opinion of Advocate General Poiares Maduro in Case T-319/99 *Federación Nacional de Empresas de Instrumentación Científica, Médica, Técnica y Dental (Fenin) v Commission* [2003] ECR II-357 para 26.

Owing to the importance of the concept '[t]he question of how to distinguish economic and non-economic [activities] has often been raised'.[4] However, as Buendia Sierra notes, 'the Court's attempts to lay down substantive criteria as regards the concept of economic activity have not produced particularly fortunate results'[5] so that 'it is fair to ask whether the Court of Justice has not lost its way in its attempts to define economic activities'.[6] Whilst the Commission take the view that a definition 'cannot be given *a priori* and requires a case-by-case analysis,'[7] the purpose of this essay is to consider how the existence of economic activity is determined.

Section II considers the definition of economic activity and demonstrates that the Treaty does not contain a single definition. The differences and consequences of difference are also considered. Section III shows that Treaty provisions seemingly limited to economic activity may also be applied to non-economic activity. However, it is argued that the different types of activity are subject to different treatment.

II DEFINITIONS OF ECONOMIC ACTIVITY

Economic activity is used to determine the scope of various Community provisions. As an example, Articles 39, 43, and 49 EC can apply only when there is economic activity.[8] Article 39 EC, which confers rights on workers, applies when a person '*performs services* for and under the direction of another person in return for which he *receives remuneration*'.[9] Article 43 EC, which confers the right of establishment, applies when a service is provided outside any relationship of subordination in return for remuneration.[10] Article 49 EC, which confers the right to provide services, applies to services 'normally provided for *remuneration*'.[11] Similarly,

[4] Communication from The Commission to The European Parliament, The Council, The European Economic And Social Committee and The Committee of The Regions Accompanying the Communication on 'A single market for 21st century Europe' Services of general interest, including social services of general interest: a new European commitment [20.11.2007] COM(2007) 725 Final, p 5.

[5] Buendia Sierra *Exclusive Rights and State Monopolies under EC Law: Article 86 (Former Article 90) of the EC Treaty* (Oxford: Oxford University Press, 1999), [1.182].

[6] *Ibid*, [1.170].

[7] Communication from The Commission, (see above n 4) p 5.

[8] Case 36/74 *Walrave* [1974] ECR 1405 [4]; Case 13/76 *Donà v Mantero* [1976] ECR 1333 [12]; Case C-196/87 *Steymann* [1988] ECR 6159 [9]; Case C-221/89 *Factortame* [1991] ECR I-3905 [21]; Case C-415/93 *Bosman* [1995] ECR I-4353 [73]; Case C-51/96 *Deliège* [2000] ECR I-2549 [41].

[9] Case 66/85 *Lawrie-Blum v Land Baden-Wurttemberg* [1986] ECR 2121, para 17, (emphasis added).

[10] Case C-268/99 *Aldona Malgorzata Jany and Others v Staatssecretaris Van Justitie* [2001] ECR I-8615, [71].

[11] Art 50 EC (emphasis added).

Articles 81 and 82 EC can only be applied to undertakings.[12] The Court of Justice in *Höfner* defines undertakings as 'every entity engaged in an *economic activity*, regardless of the legal status of the entity and the way in which it is financed'.[13] Consequently, absent economic activity the competition provisions do not apply. It is not only Treaty provisions that are restricted to economic activity, so, for example, under Article 2(1) of the Sixth Directive on VAT, the supply of goods or services by a taxable person is subject to value added tax.[14] Article 4(1) of the Sixth Directive defines 'taxable person' as 'any person who independently carries out in any place any *economic activity*'.[15] Consequently, Article 2(1) does not apply unless there is economic activity.

When the need for economic activity is used to limit the application of a Community law provision, one view is that a universal conception of economic activity can be relied on to determine the extent of the limit, regardless of the provision of Community law the concept is required to limit. Such an approach is taken in *Meca-Medina and Majcen* by the Court of First Instance and by the Commission in its early thinking on the matter.[16] However, whilst drawing attention to the virtues of a single

[12] Case C-67/96 *Albany International BV v Stichting Bedrijfspensioenfonds Textielindustrie* [1999] ECR I-5751, AG Opinion para 206.

[13] Case C-41/1990 *Klaus Höfner and Fritz Elser v Macrotron GmbH* [1991] ECR I 1979, para 21, (emphasis added). In Case 118/85 *Commission v Italian Republic* [1987] ECR 2599, 2610, Advocate General Mischo considered that whether a body is to be considered an undertaking turns on 'the industrial and commercial nature of the activity'. Undertaking is defined in Art 80 ECSC as 'any undertaking engaged in production in the coal or the steel industry within the territories referred to ... and also ... any undertaking or agency regularly engaged in distribution other than sale to domestic consumers or small craft industries'. Undertaking is defined in Art 196 Euratom as 'any undertaking or institution which pursues all or any of the activities in the territories of Member States within the field specified ... whatever its public or private legal status'. Undertaking is defined in the Art 1 of Protocol 22 EEA as 'any entity carrying out activities of a commercial or economic nature'. The term is used in Arts 27, 43, 76, 81, 82, 86, 87, 101–103, 105, 110, 131, 132, 137, 157, 163, 164, 167, 171, 267 and 287. It is also used in some of the Treaty Protocols. It is generally accepted that the concept of 'undertaking' for the purposes of Arts 81 and 82 EC is the same and that this concept is also shared with that used in Arts 86, 87 and 88 EC. On the first point see Joined Cases T-68/89, T-77/89 and T-78/89 *Società Italiana Vetro SpA, Fabbrica Pisana SpA and PPG Vernante Pennitalia SpA v Commission* [1992] ECR II-1403 [358]; Case 118/85, *Commission v Italian Republic* (above), AG Opinion p 2613; and Sierra (see n 5 above) [1.103]. On the second point see Case C-222/04 *Ministero dell'Economia e delle Finanze v Cassa di Risparmio di Firenze SpA and Others* [2006] ECR I-289 [107]–[113], AG Opinion [72]–[93]; and Sierra (above) [1.103]. However, Bartosch 'Social Housing and European State Aid Control' 28 *European Competition Law Review* (2007), 563–70, 566, considers the definition of economic activity under the state aid rules differ from the definition used under the competition rules.

[14] Sixth Council Dir 77/388/EEC of 17 May 1977 on the harmonisation of the laws of the Member States relating to turnover taxes–Common system of value added tax: uniform basis of assessment [1977] OJ L145/1.

[15] *Ibid* (emphasis added).

[16] Case T-313/02 (see n 1 above), para 42; Communication from the Commission–Services of General Interest in Europe (see n 2 above), [29]; and Non-Paper: Services of

conception of economic activity, Advocate General Poiares Maduro cautions that 'the scope of freedom of competition and that of the freedom to provide services are not identical'.[17] Advocate General Kokott has also expressed the view that Community law contains 'differing concepts of economic activity'.[18] The existence of different conceptions of economic activity is confirmed by the Court of Justice in *Meca-Medina and Majcen*, ruling that the Treaty does not contain a single set of criteria used to determine whether an activity is economic.[19] Tellingly, since late 2007 the Commission has been more careful not to conflate the concept of economic activity for the purpose of free movement with the concept of economic activity for the purpose of competition.[20] How does the conception of economic activity used for the purpose of limiting Community competition differ from the conception of economic activity used for the purpose of limiting the free movement of workers, establishment and services provision? The contours of the two approaches are considered in Sections A and B below. Differences between the two approaches are considered in Sections C and D below. The existence of two definitions of economic activity is clear, so that the limits of Community law are different under each provision; less clear is whether the differing limits are consciously developed, applied consistently, or rigorously adhered to.

A The Free Movement of Workers, Establishment, and Services Approach

The concept of economic activity used to define the scope of the free movement of workers, establishment and services provisions has two elements. The first element of economic activity is that there must be the

General Economic Interest and State Aid 12 November 2002 available online at http://europa.eu.int/comm/competition/state_aid/others/1759_sieg_en.pdf, 29–31. Further, Case C-41/1990 (see n 13 above) AG Opinion [19]–[20], and [40]; Odudu, *The Boundaries of EC Competition Law: The Scope of Article 81* (Oxford: Oxford University Press, 2006), 27 and Sloane 'Crossed Wires in Luxembourg: Hutchinson 3G & the Competition Test in VAT' 895 *The Tax Journal* (2007), 5–7, 6.

[17] Case C-205/03 P *Federación Española De Empresas De Tecnología Sanitaria (Fenin) v Commission* [2006] ECR I-6295, AG Opinion para 51. However in Case C-281/06 *Hans-Dieter Jundt and Hedwig Jundt v Finanzamt Offenburg* [2007] ECR not yet reported, AG Opinion [11] note 6 AG Maduro relies on the competition law conceptions to clarify the free-movement conception.

[18] Cases C-284/04 (see n 1 above) AG Opinion [61].

[19] Case C-519/04 P (see n 1 above) para 33.

[20] Communication from the Commission to the European Parliament (see n 4 above) 725 final, [2.1].

demand or supply of services to the market; the second element is that there must be remuneration.

(i) Supply or Demand of Services

In *Jany* the Court of Justice took the view that a service exists when 'the provider satisfies a request by the beneficiary ... without producing or transferring material goods'.[21] Article 50 EC gives a number of examples, so that services include activities of an industrial character; activities of a commercial character; activities of craftsmen; and activities of the professions. Persons are engaged in economic activity not only when they supply services but also when they demand services.[22]

(ii) Remuneration

It is clear that 'the activity must not be provided for nothing'.[23] However, activity can be economic even if the provider does not profit from (or intend to profit from) the provision of the service.[24] In order for the supply or demand of services to constitute economic activity it is simply necessary that there is remuneration.[25] In *Humbel* the Court defined remuneration as 'consideration for the service in question ... normally agreed upon between the provider and the recipient of the service'.[26] It is not necessary for the consideration to be provided by the service recipient.[27] And the character of payment is not altered by subsequent reimbursement (in whole or in part) by a third party.[28] However, the method of financing is central to the

[21] Case C-268/99 (see n 10 above) [48]. Also Case C-97/98 *Jagerskiold v Gustafsson* [1999] ECR I-7319, Advocate General Fennelly [20] taking the view that goods are tangible whilst services are intangible.

[22] Joined Cases 286/82 and 26/83 *Graziana Luisi and Giuseppe Carbone v Ministero Del Tesoro* [1984] 377, [10] and Case C-350/96 *Clean-Car Autoservice* [1998] ECR I-2521, [19]–[25].

[23] Case C-281/06 (see n 18 above) [32].

[24] Case C-281/06 (see n 18 above) [32]–[34], [AG Opinion [11]–[12] and Case C-157/99 *Smits and Peerbooms* [2001] ECR I-5473 [50]–[52]. On irrelevance of profit in the Art 50 EC conception of economic activity see Davies 'Welfare as a Service' 29 *Legal Issues of Economic Integration* (2002), 27–40, 29–30.

[25] Joined Cases C-286/82 and 26/83 (see n 23 above) [9]; Case C-205/84 *Commission v Germany* [1986] ECR 3755 [18]; Case C-159/90 *Grogan* [1991] ECR I-4685 [17]; Case C-20/92 *Hubbard* [1993] ECR I-3777 [13]; and Case C-158/96 *Kohll* [1998] ECR I 1931 [29].

[26] Case 263/86 *Humbel* [1988] ECR 5365 [17]. Also Case C-196/87 (see n 8 above) [12]; Case C-157/99 (see n 25 above) [58]; Case C-136/00 *Danner* [2002] ECR I-8147 [26]; Case C-355/00 *Freskot* [2003] ECR I-5263 [55]; and Case C-422/01 *Skandia and Ramstedt* [2003] ECR I-6817 [23]; Case C-76/05 *Schwarz and Gootjes-Schwarz* [2007] ECR not yet reported [38]; and Case C-318/05 *Commission* v *Germany* [2007] ECR not yet reported [67].

[27] Case 352/85 *Bond van Adverteerders v Netherlands* [1988] ECR 2085 [16]; Case C-157/99 (see n 25 above): [55]–[59]; and Case C-318/05 *ibid* [70].

[28] Case C-157/99 (see n 25 above) [58].

characterisation of the activity so that remuneration is present when the supply or demand is 'financed essentially by private funds'[29] and is absent when the supply or demand is 'financed entirely or mainly by public funds'.[30]

B The Competition Law Approach

The concept of economic activity used to define the scope of the competition provisions has two elements.[31] The first element is that there must be an *offer* of goods or services to the market; the second element is that there must be the potential to make profit from the offer of goods or services without state intervention.[32]

(i) Offer of Goods or Services

Under the free movement of workers, establishment and services approach both the offer (supply) and demand of good or services are included in the conception of economic activity. However, from *Commission v Italy* onwards it is clear that, for competition law purposes, economic activity requires the *offer* of goods or services on the market.[33] Here the Court of Justice ruled that by offering goods to the market (the manufacture and sale of tobacco) the Amministrazione Autonoma dei Monopoli di Stato was engaged in economic activity and thus an undertaking, even though it had no legal status separate from that of the state.[34]

Offering goods or services is a necessary element of the concept of economic activity used in Community competition law.[35] On a number of occasions the Court of Justice has ruled that an entity is not engaged in

[29] Case C-318/05 *Commission v Germany* [2007] ECR I-6957 [69], citations omitted.

[30] *Ibid,* [68], citations omitted.

[31] In Odudu (see n 17 above) 23–56, three elements of economic activity are identified; here the third element there identified is treated as part of the second.

[32] See Case 1006/2/1/01 *Bettercare Group Limited v the Director General of Fair Trading* [2002] CAT 7, paras 71–103, Sierra (see n 5 above) para 1.148–1.213,Drijber 'Joined Cases C-264/01, C-306/01, C-354/01 and C-355/01, Aok Bundesverband AO, Judgment of the Full Court 16 March 2004, not yet reported' 42 *CML Rev* (2005), 523–33, 528.

[33] Case 118/85 (see n 13 above) para 7, Case C-343/95 *Diego Cali & Figli Srl v Servizi Ecologici Porto di Genova Spa (Sepg)* [1997] ECR I-1547, para 16, Case C-35/96 *Commission v Italian Republic* [1998] ECR I-2599 [36]; Joined Cases C-180/98 to C-184/98 *Pavel Pavlov v Stichting Pensioenfonds Medische Specialisten* [2000] ECR I-6451, para 75, Case C-475/99 *Ambulanz Glöckner v Landkreis Südwestpfalz* [2001] ECR I-8089, para 19, Case C-218/00 (see n 42 above) para 23, AG Opinion para 38, Case T-319/99 (see n 3 above) para 36.

[34] Case 118/85 (see n 13 above) para 3, 7.

[35] Case T-155/04 *Selex Sistemi Integrati Spa v Commission* [2006] ECR II-4797, [50], [61], and [87] and Commission Staff Working Document–Frequently Asked Questions in Relation with Commission Decision of 28 November 2005 on the Application of Article 86(2) of the EC Treaty to State Aid in the Form of Public Service Compensation Granted to

economic activity on the grounds that they are not offering goods or services to the market.[36] As a first example, in *FENIN*, the Court distinguished the demand or receipt of goods or services from the supply or offer of goods and services, finding that an entity was not engaged in economic activity 'simply because it is a purchaser in a given market'.[37] As a second example, regulating the provision of goods and services is distinguished from the offer of goods or services. In *Bodson*, French law required regional authorities to regulate the provision of various aspects of funeral services.[38] Some regional authorities achieved their regulatory objectives by requiring those offering the service to be licensed; both Advocate General Vilaça and the Court considered that the licensing authority was not engaged in economic activity even though fees were charged in order to obtain a licence.[39]

(ii) Potential to Make Profit from the Offer of Goods or Services without State Intervention

Under the free movement of workers, establishment and services approach the next stage would be to consider whether the offer of goods or services is remunerated. However, whilst remuneration is a necessary element of economic activity under Articles 39, 43, and 49 EC, for the purpose of Articles 81 and 82 EC 'the absence of remuneration ... cannot by itself exclude the possibility that the activity in question is economic in nature'.[40] The central issue under Articles 81 and 82 EC is whether the potential to

Certain Undertakings Entrusted with the Operation of Services of General Economic Interest, and of the Community Framework for State Aid in the Form of Public Service Compensation Accompanying Document to the Communication On "Services of General Interest, Including Social Services of General Interest: A New European Commitment" SEC(2007) 1516 final, [2.2] treats this as a sufficient condition.

[36] Case T-155/04 *ibid.*

[37] Case T-319/99 (see n 3 above) para 37, (emphasis added), upheld in Case C-205/03 (see n 18 above) and applied generally in Case T-155/04 (see n 36 above) [65]–[67]. The Court does not restrict the excluded use to consumption, and so it may be more accurate to use the term dissipation.

[38] The regulated aspects were the carriage of the body after it has been placed in the coffin, the provision of hearses, coffins and external hangings of the house of the deceased, conveyances for mourners, the equipment and staff needed for burial and exhumation and cremation.

[39] Case 30/87 *Bodson v Pompes Funèbres des Régions Libérées SA* [1988] ECR 2479, para 18, AG Opinion para 94. Also Case 5/79 *Procureur General v Hans Buys* [1979] ECR 3203, para 30 and Sierra (see n 5 above), para [1.187], though this seems to be rejected in Case C 309/99 (see n 1 above), para 58, and Shaw 'A Healthy Monopoly for a Dying Trade? ' 13 *EL Rev* (1988), 422–6, 423. In C-369/04 (see n 1 above) [36] and Case C-284/04 (see n 1 above) [42] the Court clarified (for the purpose of the Sixth VAT Directive) that regulation can only be treated as non-economic to the extent that it 'cannot constitute participation in that market by the competent national authority'. This adopts a distinction drawn in Case C-205/03 (see n 18 above) AG Opinion [13]–[15] and Sierra (see n 5 above), [1.144]

[40] Case T-155/04 (see n 36 above) [77].

make a profit without state intervention exists. This condition is clearly expressed by Advocate General Jacobs in *AOK* reporting that '[i]n assessing whether an activity is economic in character, the basic test appears ... to be whether it *could*, at least in principle, be carried on by a private undertaking in order to make profits'.[41] The juridical basis of this element lies in the Court of Justice finding in *Höfner* that activity is economic when it 'has not always been, and is not necessarily, carried out by public entities'.[42] It is not necessary actually to make profit, nor is it necessary to have a profit-making motive.[43]

C Profit-making Potential Compared with Remuneration as the Central Criterion

In order to constitute economic activity the supply of goods or services requires remuneration for the purpose of the internal market rules or the potential to make profit for the purpose of the competition rules. The difference between the two conditions is illustrated by considering activities that are remunerated (thus economic for the purpose of free movement of workers, establishment and services) but from which it is not possible to profit (hence non-economic for the purpose of the competition rules).[44] The existence of such cases is acknowledged by Advocate General Maduro writing that '[t]here is nothing to prevent a transaction involving an exchange being classified as the provision of services [that is, economic

[41] Joined Cases C-264/01, C-306/01, C-354/01 and C-355/01 *AOK Bundesverband v Ichthyol-Gesellschaft Cordes* [2003] ECR I 2493, AG Opinion para 27, (emphasis added), citations omitted. The potential to make profit is explicitly used by numerous Advocates General, in particular in Joined Cases C-159/91 and C-160/91 *Christian Poucet v Assurances Generales De France (Agf) and Caisse Mutuelle Regionale du Languedoc-Roussillon (Camulrac) and Daniel Pistre v Caisse Autonome Nationale de Compensation de L Assurance Vieillesse des Artisans (Cancava)* [1993] ECR I-637, AG Opinion paras 7–8, Case C-364/92 *Sat Fluggesellschaft Mbh v Eurocontrol* [1994] ECR I-43, AG Opinion para 9, Case C-244/94 *Fédération Française des Sociétés D'assurance v Ministère de L'agriculture et de la Pêche* [1995] ECR I-4013, AG Opinion para 11, Case C-343/95 (see n 34 above) AG Opinion para 32, Case C-67/96 (see n 12 above) AG Opinion para 311, Case T-128/98 *Aéroports de Paris* [2000] ECR II-3929, para 124, Case C-218/00 *Cisal di Battistello Venanzio & Co v Istituto Nazionale Per L'assicurazione Contro Gli Infortuni Sul Lavoro (Inail)* [2002] ECR I-691, AG Opinion para 38.

[42] Case C-41/1990 (see n 13 above) para 22. The sentiment is more clearly expressed in Case T-155/04 (see n 36 above) [88]–[89].

[43] Joined Cases 209 to 215 and 218/78 *Van Landewyck* v *Commission* [1980] ECR 3125, para 88; Case C-244/94 *Fédération Française des Sociétés D'assurance v Ministère de L'agriculture et de la Pêche* [1995] ECR I-4013, para 21; and Non-Paper: Services of General Economic Interest and State Aid (see n 17 above).

[44] The converse enquiry could also be made.

activity], even where the parties to the exchange are not undertakings [that is, not engaged in economic activity] for the purposes of competition law'.[45]

(i) Public goods

In *Diego Calì* the protection of the environment at the oil port of Genoa-Multedo was the responsibility of Consorzio Autonomo del Porto (CAP), a public body.[46] CAP delegated the task of monitoring and enforcing safety procedures designed to prevent oil spillages to Servizi Ecologici Porto di Genova (SEPG), a private entity. SEPG sent Diego Calì, a port user, a bill for approximately €4,500 as a contribution to the cost of monitoring and enforcement.[47] Diego Calì refused to pay, arguing that it would be an abuse of a dominant position contrary to Article 82 EC for the port to impose compulsory charges for services it had neither requested nor received.[48]

Considered under the free movement of workers, establishment and services approach, SEPG is engaged in economic activity since there is remuneration. However, the competition approach instead considers whether there is the potential to make profit. For some goods and services the producer cannot prevent non-purchasers from enjoying the benefits of the good or service—that is, the good or service is non-excludable.[49] Since they can benefit without paying, individuals do not have an incentive to pay for consumption.[50] Consequently, private producers have no incentive to manufacture the goods because it is impossible to profit from a good which non-payers cannot be prevented from enjoying.[51] When the Government makes payment compulsory, usually through a system of general

[45] Case C-205/03 (see n 18 above) AG Opinion para 51.

[46] Information on Genoa port services is available from http://www.informare.it/news/forum/capoc1uk.htm.

[47] Case C-343/95 (see n 34 above) [11].

[48] Case C-343/95 *ibid* [13].

[49] Stiglitz *Economics of the Public Sector* (3rd ed) (London: WW Norton, 2000), 128–9, Stiglitz and Driffill *Economics* (London: WW Norton, 2000), 124, Case and Fair *Principles of Economics* 5th edn (Upper Saddle River, New Jersey: Prentice Hall, 1999) 388. In addition to non excludability 'public goods' are non-rivalrous in consumption, meaning that, once produced, an infinite number of consumers can enjoy the good without increased production cost or diminished enjoyment by other consumers. Stiglitz *Economics of the Public Sector* 3rd edn (London: WW Norton, 2000) 128–9; Carlton and Perloff *Modern Industrial Organization* 3rd edn (Harlow: Addison-Wesley, 2000) 82, and Case and Fair *Principles of Economics* 5th edn (Upper Saddle River, New Jersey: Prentice Hall, 1999) 387–8. Stiglitz and Driffill *Economics* (London: WW Norton, 2000) 126 point out that few goods are *pure* public goods, but instead exhibit the two characteristics to a greater or lesser extent.

[50] Stiglitz *Economics of the Public Sector* (*ibid*) 130–46.

[51] This is a classic example of the free-rider problem: Groves and Ledyard 'Optimal Allocation of Public Goods: A Solution to The "Free Rider" Problem' 45 *Econometrica* (1977) 783–810; Case and Fair *Principles of Economics* (5th edn) (Prentice Hall, 1999) 392.

taxation, this solves the problem of non-excludability and non-excludable goods are termed public goods.[52] The task assigned to SEPG is recognised as non-excludable since 'the surveillance has to be exercised regardless [of] whether the fees owed by any particular vessel have been paid'.[53] Thus Advocate General Cosmas explicitly recognises that 'the activity of SEPG cannot conceivably be carried out within a competitive system'.[54] The ability to levy the compulsory charge for the provision of the non-excludable good derives from the taxation powers of the CAP, a public body exercising imperium.[55] Consequently, the activity 'is not of an economic nature justifying the application of the Treaty rules on competition'.[56]

(ii) Solidarity

In *Poucet and Pistre*, French law made sickness and maternity insurance compulsory for the self employed. The task of collecting contributions was entrusted to regional mutual societies. The regional mutual societies were obliged to deposit funds in an account at Banque de France. The funds on account were managed by the National Sickness and Maternity Fund for the Self-employed. The regional mutual societies were also responsible for drawing on the account to pay out benefits to the insured.[57] Christian Poucet challenged court orders to pay contributions to Caisse Mutuelle Régionale du Languedoc-Roussillon, a regional fund, on the ground that compulsory payment was an abuse of a dominant position contrary to Article 82 EC.

Considered under the free movement of workers, establishment and services approach, the regional mutual fund is engaged in economic activity since there is remuneration.[58] However, even though there is 'economic activity for the purposes of Article 49 EC, it does not necessarily follow from that that the organisations which carry on that activity are [engaged in economic activity for the purposes of] competition law'.[59] The competition approach requires us to consider whether there is the potential

[52] Stiglitz and Driffill *Economics* (WW Norton, 2000) 126–7, Stiglitz *Economics of the Public Sector* (see n 51 above) 129–35, and Case and Fair *ibid* 289.

[53] Case C-343/95 (n 34 above) AG Opinion para 49.

[54] Case C-343/95 *ibid,* AG Opinion para 49.

[55] AG Opinion *ibid*, paras 52–4.

[56] *Ibid*, para 23.

[57] Joined Cases C-159/91 and C-160/91 (see n 42 above).

[58] Compare with Case C-158/96 *Kohll* [1998] ECR I-1931; Case C-368/98 *Abdon Vanbraekel and Others* [2001] ECR I-5363; Case C-157/99 (see n 25 above); Case C-385/99 *Muller Faure and van Riet* [2003] ECR I-4509; Case C-56/01 *Patricia Inizan* [2003] ECR I-12403; Case C-8/04 *Leichtle* [2004] ECR I-2641; and Case C-372/04 *Watts* [2006] ECR I-4324.

[59] Case C-205/03 (see n 18 above) AG Opinion para 51.

to make profit. And it has been recognised that it is impossible to profit from 'the redistribution of income between those who are better off and those who, in view of their resources ... would be deprived'[60] or as Advocate General Fennelly put it 'the *inherently uncommercial* act of involuntary subsidization of one social group by another'.[61] Instead the limits of altruism are overcome by making payments compulsory and Advocate General Poiares Maduro expresses the view that economic activity does not exist for competition law purposes to the extent that the principles of solidarity predominate.[62] Consequently, 'activity ... based on the principle of national solidarity and ... entirely non-profit-making ... is not an economic activity and, therefore, the organizations to which it is entrusted are not undertakings within the meaning of Articles [81] and [82] of the Treaty'.[63] Activities organised on the basis of solidarity are inherently unprofitable hence not economic for competition purposes. However, activities governed by the principle of solidarity may be remunerated, hence economic for free movement of workers, establishment and services purposes, so that solidarity cannot prevent the application of these provisions.[64]

D Reasons for Differences in Approach

It is not only in relation to the potential to make profit and remuneration that differences exist. First, whilst the text of both Articles 39 and 49 EC suggest that only the *provider* of services is involved in economic activity, the Court has confirmed that the *recipient* of services is also involved in economic activity.[65] Conversely, whilst Articles 81 and 82 EC are neutral on the issue, the Court has held that only a *provider* of goods or services is engaged in economic activity.[66] Secondly, whilst under the competition approach it is oft-repeated that an activity is economic independently of

[60] Joined Case C-159/91 and C-160/91 (see n 42) para 10, also AG Opinion paras 9–11.

[61] Case C-70/95 *Sodemare SA v Regione Lombardia* [1997] ECR I 3395, AG Opinion para 29, (emphasis added). *Cf* Case C-67/96 (see n 12 above) AG Opinion para 338. Redistribution is seen as the hallmark of solidarity in Case C-70/95, para 29, Case C-218/00(see n 42 above) AG Opinion paras 56, 59–60, and Joined Cases C-264/01, C-306/01, C-354/01 and C-355/01 (see n 42 above) AG Opinion para 32.

[62] Case C-205/03 (see n 18 above) AG Opinion [16].

[63] Joined Case C-159/91 and C-160/91 (see n 42 above) [18]–[19].

[64] Contra Spaventa *Free Movement of Persons in the European Union: Barriers to Movement in Their Constitutional Context* (Alphen aan den Rijn: Kluwer Law International, 2007), 10, note 59 also 50, note 55, and 55 (text accompanying n 67).

[65] See references at n 23 above.

[66] Joined Cases C-180/98 to C-184/98 (see n 34 above) [75], Joined Cases C-264/01, C-306/01, C-354/01 and C-355/01 (n 42 above) AG Opinion para46 . Case T-319/99 (see n 3 above) para 37, (emphasis added), upheld in Case C-205/03 (see n 18 above) and applied generally in Case T-155/04 (see n 36 above) [65]–[67].

'the way in which it is financed'[67] the method of financing is central under the free movement of workers, establishment and services approach.[68] The competition law approach focuses on the nature of the activity, whilst the free movement of workers, establishment and services approach focuses on the way the activity is carried out.[69] As an example, under the free movement approach education financed from the public purse is not economic, since there is no remuneration.[70] However, there is nothing in the nature of the activity of education that means profit cannot be made, so since under the competition law approach there is the potential to profit from education the activity is economic, whether state or privately funded.

It may be argued that the different approaches reflect the differing outcomes of various attempts to either expand or contract the scope of the Treaty provisions and thus expand or contract the autonomy that Member States retain. However, rather than expanding or contacting, it is perhaps more profitable to consider the different approaches as part of an internal process of Community competence allocation. In *Bosman* Advocate General Lenz took the view that a single measure must be compatible with all provisions of Community law, writing that '[n]o reason can be seen why the rules at issue in this case should not be subject both to Article [39] and to EC competition law ... so that in principle both sets of rules may be applicable to a single factual situation'.[71] However, subjecting a single measure to scrutiny under multiple Treaty provisions is not always possible since it may be difficult or impossible for a measure to comply with all Community law simultaneously.[72] The differing definitions of economic

[67] Case C-41/1990(see n 13) para 20. Compare with Oliver 'The Frontiers of the State: Public Authorities and Public Functions under the Human Rights Act' *Public Law* (2000), 476–93, 481–2.

[68] *Cf* Case 263/86 *Humbel* (n 27 above) with Case C-102/92 *Wirth* [1993] ECR I-6447.

[69] Communication from the Commission to the European Parliament (see n 4 above) 725 final, [2.1]

[70] Case 263/86 (see n 27 above).

[71] Case C-415/93 *Asbl v Jean-Marc Bosman, Royal Club Liegeois SA v Jean-Marc Bosman and Others and Uefa v Jean-Marc Bosman* [1995] ECR I-4921 AG Opinion para 253. Also Belhaj and van de Dronden 'Some Room for Competition Does Not Make a Sickness Fund an Undertaking. Is EC Competition Law Applicable to the Heath Care Sector? Joined Cases C-264/01, C-306/01, C-453/01 and C-355/01 Aok' 11 *European Competition Law Review* (2004), 682–7 at 686.

[72] Quinn and MacGowan 'Could Article 30 Impose Obligations on Individuals' 12 *EL Rev* (1987), 163–178, 167–70, van den Bogaert 'Horizontality: The Court Attacks? ' in Barnard and Scott (eds) *The Law of the Single European Market* (Oxford, Hart Publishing, 2002) 123–52, 140, and Weatherill 'Discrimination on Grounds of Nationality in Sport' 9 *Yearbook of European Law* (1989), 55–92, 90–2. At para 138 of the judgment, the Court decided not to deal with the issue, on which see Weatherill 'Case C-415/93, Union Royale Belge Des Societes De Football Association Asbl v Jean-Marc Bosman; Royal Club Liegois SA v Jean-Marc Bosman, SA D'economie Mixte Sportive De L'union Sportive Du Littoral De Dunkerque, Union Royale Belge Des Societes De Football Association Asbl, Union Des Associations Europeennes De Football; Union Des Associations Europeennes De Football v Jean-Marc Bosman, Article 177 Reference by the Cour D'appel, Liege, on the Interpretation

activity could be the outcome of a deliberation over which mutually exclusive Treaty provisions ought to apply to a particular measure, rather than whether Community law applies or national autonomy remains unconstrained. So, for example, whilst the state's purchasing activities are not subject to scrutiny under Articles 81 or 82 EC, they remain subject to scrutiny, under Article 49 EC and the public procurement rules. It may be that the states purchasing would not tolerate scrutiny under all Treaty provisions and that such activities are most appropriately subject to the public procurement and free movement regimes.

Not only can internal allocation of competence be achieved with differing approaches, but it is also true that the question of whether or not economic activity exists is relevant for different purposes under the different provisions. Broadly speaking, the free movement of workers, establishment and services provisions can be described as rights-conferring. A citizen has rights under the provisions when they are engaged in economic activity. However, the rights may be infringed by those not engaged in economic activity. The focus is on the citizen rather than those with obligations to the citizen, a position made clear by the Court of Justice writing that 'the mere fact that a rule is purely sporting [that is, non-economic] in nature does not have the effect of removing from the scope of the Treaty the person engaging in the activity governed by that rule or the body which has laid it down'.[73] Once a person is engaged in economic activity, it is immaterial that the impediment is caused by an entity that is not engaged in economic activity. In contrast, the competition rules can be broadly described as obligation-imposing. An entity has obligations when it is engaged in economic activity, independently of the type of activity in which the rights holder is engaged. Asking whether the Community imposes obligations is not quite the same as asking whether the Community confers rights, and the approaches taken to resolving the question differ as a result.

III NON-ECONOMIC ACTIVITY AND THE TREATY

Not only do the differing concepts of 'economic activity' mean that the different Treaty provisions apply to market conduct in different ways, but the need for 'economic activity' also draws a distinction between economic and non-economic activity. It is important to consider both how the Treaty

of Article 48, 85 and 86 EC. Judgment of the European Court of Justice of 15 December 1995'. 33 *CML Rev* (1996), 991–1033 at 1000–1003, 1018–26, van den Bogaert 'The Court of Justice on the Tatami: Ippon, Waza-Ari or Koka?' 25 *EL Rev* (2000), 554–63 at 557, Weatherill 'Discrimination on Grounds of Nationality in Sport' 9 *Yearbook of European Law* (1989), 55–92 at 60.

[73] Case C-519/04 P (see n 1 above) [27].

applies to non-economic activity and how this differs from the way in which it applies to economic activity. The Treaty citizenship provisions provide the most obvious example of how the Treaty applies to non-economic activity and a comparison of how the economically active national is differently provided for compared to the non-economically active national can be made.[74] However, two less obvious ways in which the Treaty applies to non-economic activity shall be considered. The first is that some Treaty provisions apply to both economic and non-economic activity, so that economic activity is not a pre-condition. Articles 28 and 81 EC are discussed in this context. Second, a tentative argument is made that the substantive assessment that occurs in relation to non-economic activity is different from the substantive assessment that occurs in relation to economic activity. This is true not only in relation to provisions applied to both economic and non-economic activity, but also in relation to provisions which, on the face of it, appear limited to economic activity.

A Provisions applied to both Economic and Non-economic Activity

Article 28 EC applies to goods, which are tangibles '*capable* ... of forming the subject of commercial transactions'.[75] Whilst the Commission identifies the freedom to provide services and the right of establishment as requiring economic activity, it makes no mention of the free movement of goods being limited to the sphere of economic activity.[76] And so it proves to be the case that no transaction need actually occur before Article 28 EC is engaged. The wording of Article 28 EC does not require that goods be moved for a particular objective, and in *Henn and Darby* Advocate General Warner expressed the view that 'Article [28], which is the leading Article on the elimination of quantitative restrictions between Member-States, and which does not itself use the word 'trade', cannot be interpreted as limited to *transactions* by or between traders'.[77] More clearly, in *Commission v Belgium*, Advocate General Jacobs writes that 'objects can benefit from the Treaty provisions concerning the free movement of goods, whether or not they are being transported across national frontiers for the purposes of sale or resale. The principle of the free movement of goods is

[74] See Nic Shuibhne's contribution at ch 8 in this volume.

[75] Case C-2/90 *Commission v Belgium* [1992] ECR I-4431, AG's second opinion, [18], (emphasis added).

[76] Green Paper on Services of General Interest COM(2003) 270 final, [43], (emphasis added). Also Communication from the Commission: Services of General Interest in Europe [1996] OJ C/281/3, [18]; Communication from the Commission–Services of General Interest in Europe (see n 2 above) [28]; Report to the Laeken European Council: Services of General Interest COM/2001/598/FINAL [30].

[77] Case 34/79 *Regina v Maurice Donald Henn and John Frederick Ernest Darby* [1979] 3795, [3827], (emphasis added).

not limited to those goods which are intended to be traded in the Member-State of importation; the principle extends, for instance, to the importation of goods by a private individual for the purposes of personal consumption.'[78] Thus Oliver writes 'it can scarcely be argued today that non-economic movements of goods fall outside the Treaty altogether—and this would be the inevitable result of holding that they are not within the provisions on the free movement of goods'.[79]

It is clear that Article 28 EC applies to both economic and non-economic activity. More controversial is the ability to apply Article 81 EC to non-economic activity. The possibility arises because in addition to undertakings, Article 81 EC also applies to associations of undertakings.[80] An association is an undertaking in its own right when it satisfies the conditions set out in *Höfner* and is thus captured to the extent that it is engaged in economic activity. However, an association may also be captured simply by virtue of the members of the association being undertakings, regardless of the nature of the activities the association is engaged in.[81] In order to determine whether an association is one of undertakings the approach taken is to look not at the association, but at its members.[82] This approach is clear from *Albany*, which considered collective bargaining between trade unions and employers.[83] If employees are undertakings a trade union is an association of *undertakings*. However, if employees are not undertakings then a Trade Union is an association of *employees*, and as such not addressed. The case thus focuses on the employee/employer relationship. Even though employees are engaged in

[78] Case C-2/90 (see n 76 above), AG's second opinion, [15], citing Case 215/87 *Schumacher v Hauptzollamt Frankfurt AM Main Ost* [1989] ECR 617; Case C 362/88 *GB-INNO-BM v Confederation du Commerce Luxembourgeois* [1990] ECR I-667; and Case 34/79 *ibid*, AG Opinion at 3827 .

[79] P Oliver and M Jarvis *Free Movement of Goods in the European Community: Under Articles 28 to 30 of the EC Treaty* (4th edn) (London, Sweet & Maxwell, 2003) [2.31].

[80] A common view is that it is unnecessary to determine whether activity is that of an undertaking or an association of undertakings: Case C-415/93 *Asbl v Jean-Marc Bosman, Royal Club Liegeois SA v Jean-Marc Bosman and Others and Uefa v Jean-Marc Bosman* [1995] ECR I-4921, AG Opinion [258]; Lenaerts, Nuffel *et al Constitutional Law of the European Union* (London, Sweet & Maxwell, 2005), 251, n 866; Wils 'The Undertaking as Subject of EC Competition Law and the Imputation of Infringements to Natural or Legal Persons' 25 *EL Rev* (2000), 99–116, n 2.; and Weatherill 'Discrimination on Grounds of Nationality in Sport' 9 *Yearbook of European Law* (1989), 55–92, 70–71.

[81] Various issues still require elucidation, such as why Community competition law scrutinises non-economic activity; why is it only the non-economic activity of associations of undertakings that falls within the scope of Art 81 EC rather than non-economic activity of all actors; and why is Art 82 EC only addressed to undertakings and not associations of undertakings.

[82] The same approach is taken by the Commission in Joint Selling of the Commercial Rights of the UEFA Champions League [2003] OJ L291/25, [106] See also Robertson 'Professional Rules under the Competition Act 1998' 1 *Competition Law Journal* (2002), 93–100 at 94–5.

[83] Case C-67/96 (see n 12 above).

economic activity under the free movement of workers, establishment and services approach, the employee does not safisfy the competition conception of economic activity, which requires the offer of goods or services and the potential to make profit. This is so, first, because the Treaty has distinguished between goods, services and work, and the employee offers work rather than goods or services[84] and secondly because employees do not bear the financial risk of the enterprise going awry, so are also not in a position to profit.[85] It is because employees are not undertakings in relation to their employers that the trade union is not an association of undertakings but an association of *employees*.[86]

This can be contrasted with *Wouters*, which considered the status of the Netherlands Bar Association, Nederlandse Orde van Advocaten (NOVA), established by statute, composed of all lawyers registered in the Netherlands, and empowered to regulate the legal profession. A question arose as to whether NOVA was an association of undertakings, and as such addressed by the competition rules.[87] Both the Advocate General and the Court of Justice found that the association's members (self-employed lawyers) were engaged in economic activity and thus acting as undertakings within the meaning of Article 81(1) EC.[88] NOVA was thus an *association of undertakings*, by virtue of the activities of its members.[89]

In addition to the requirement that the associations' members be undertakings, analysis of the case law reveals consideration of various institutional factors—composition of the body and criteria for selection as a member of the body, substantive duties and procedural obligations—that have been relied on in order to determine whether the non-economic

[84] See Section IIB(i) above.

[85] Case C-67/96(see n 12 above), AG Opinion [215] and Case C-22/98 *Jean Claude Becu* [2001] ECR I-5665, AG Opinion [53]–[54]. Employees have also been considered to be non-undertakings because all of their conduct is attributable to their employers. See Joined Cases 40/73 to 48/73, 50/73, 54/73 to 56/73, 111/73, 113/73, and 114/73 *Suiker Unie and Others v Commission* [1975] ECR 1663 at para 539. This reasoning is criticised in Nihoul 'Do Workers Constitute Undertakings for the Purpose of the Competition Rules?' (2002) 25 *ELRev* 408–414. On the competition law status of the employee/employer relationship in various jurisdictions see Case C-67/96 (n 12 above), AG Opinion [80]–[111] and Brunn and Hellsten (eds) *Collective Agreement and Competition Law in the EU: The Report of the Colcom-Project* (Copenhagen, DJOEF Publishing, 2001) .

[86] Case C-67/96 (see n 12 above) AG Opinion at para 221.

[87] Case C-309/99 (see n 1 above).

[88] Case C-309/99 (see n 1 above) para 49, Advocate General's Opinion paras 45–55, Vossestein 'Case C-35/99, Arduino, Judgment of 19 February 2000, Full Court; Case C-309/99, Wouters Et Al v Algemene Raad Van De Nederlandse Orde Van Advocaten, Judgment of 19 February 2002, Full Court; not yet reported' 39 *CML Rev* (2002), 841–63, 845–6. Monopolkommission *Cartel Policy Change in the European Union?: On the European Commission's White Paper of 28th April 1999; Special Report by the German Monopolies Commission Pursuant to Sec. 44, Para 1 of the Act against Restraints of Competition (Gwb)* (Baden-Baden: Nomos, 2000) at 30 consider that 'A lawyer is regarded as "an organ of the administration of justice" and not as a profit-maximising entrepreneur.'

[89] Case C-309/99 (see n 1 above), para 71, AG Opinion at para 56–87.

activity of an association of undertakings falls within the scope of the Treaty competition rules.[90] However, it seems clear that the need to be engaged in economic activity is not a condition.[91]

B Different Substantive Obligations

Snell and Andenas recognise that 'from a legal point of view, it would seem that each freedom should be interpreted separately according to the principles valid in that field'.[92] However, they argue that 'goods and services ought to be governed by the same legal principles' since 'there are no good reasons for treating them differently'.[93] Consistent with this, in *Meca-Medina and Majcen* the Court of First Instance express the view that 'the principles extracted from the case-law ... in respect of the freedom of movement of persons and services, *are equally valid* as regards the Treaty provisions relating to competition'.[94] However, since 'economic activity' does not have the same meaning under the various provisions, and some provisions apply to both economic and non-economic activity, it is not clear why this is an acceptable normative proposition.[95] Instead, closer attention must be paid to the nature of the activity, and an appropriate rule applied to that activity. For example, a market access approach can only sensibly be applied when there is a market to access, that is, when there is economic activity. It may also be the case that different justifications are required (and made available) for non-economic activity. This latter proposition can be used to rationalise the approach adopted in *Wouters*, when the Court considers a rule regulating the legal profession that

[90] Similar factors are identified in Cruz, Julio Baquero *Between Competition and Free Movement: The Economic Constitutional Law of the European Community* (Oxford, Hart Publishing, 2002) 154 and Schepel 'Delegation of Regulatory Powers to Private Parties under EC Competition Law: Towards a Procedural Public Interest Test' 39 *CML Rev* (2002), 31–51.

[91] Cases 209–215 and 218/78 *Van Landewyck and Others v Commission* [1980] ECR 3125 [87]–[88], Cases 96–102, 104/82, 105/82, 108/82 and 110/82 *IAZ and Others v Commission* [1983] ECR 3369 [19]–[20] and Cases T-25, 26, 30–2, 34–9, 42–6, 48, 50–71, 87, 88, 103, and 104/95 *Cimenteries CBR SA v Commission* [2000] ECR II-491 [1320], though consider Case C-309/99 (see n 1 above) [57].

[92] Snell and Andenas 'Exploring the Outer Limits: Restrictions on the Free Movement of Goods and Services' in Andenas, Mads and Wulf-Henning Roth (eds) *Services and Free Movement in EU Law* (Oxford, Oxford University Press, 2000) 69–139, 78.

[93] *Ibid*, 69–139, 70.

[94] Case T-313/02 (see n 1 above), para 42, (emphasis added)

[95] Advocate General Capotorti in Case 82/77 *Openbaar Ministerie of the Kingdom of the Netherlands v Jacobus Philippus Van Tiggele* [1978] ECR 25, 47 and van den Bogaert 'Horizontality: The Court Attacks?' in Barnard and Scott (eds) *The Law of the Single European Market* (Oxford, Hart Publishing, 2002) 123–152, 139–43 reject the idea of common principles.

prevents lawyers from entering into partnership with accountants.[96] The non-economic activity of NOVA came within the scope of the Community competition rules because NOVA was an association of undertakings, so the type of activity engaged in by the association was not considered. Wouters claimed the rule prevented the creation of better services tailored to clients operating in complex economic and legal environments, and thus restricted competition.[97] Advocate General Léger and the Court agreed that competition was restricted by the decision of the association of undertakings.[98] However, the restriction of competition was justified by public interest concerns.[99] Such justifications are not available when the competition rules are applied to economic activity.[100]

IV A LIMIT?

On their face, certain Treaty provisions may be invoked only when there is economic activity. It is natural to suppose that closer attention to the definition of economic activity will assist in limiting the Community to areas that properly fall within its competence. The greatest danger is that provisions limited to economic activity may be applied, and the autonomy of the Member States further curtailed, without sufficient consideration being given to the question of whether economic activity exists. Thus, rather than asking whether economic or non-economic activity is involved, the Court at times simply considers whether or not there is discrimination.[101] The Treaty is said to apply when there is discrimination and held not to apply absent discrimination; thus discrimination serves to determine both the scope of the Treaty provisions and the substantive obligation that

[96] The national legal framework is more fully set out in Deards 'Closed Shop Versus One Stop Shop: The Battle Goes On' 27 *EL Rev* (2002), 618–27, 619.

[97] Case C-309/99 (see n 1 above) at para 75–8, 81–4, Advocate General's Opinion para 42, 94.

[98] Case C-309/99 (see n 1 above) at para 86–96, AG Opinion at para 116–33.

[99] Case C-309/99 (see n 1 above) at para 100, AG Opinion at para 43, 84, 95, 113, 173–6.

[100] Schmid 'Diagonal Competence Conflicts between European Competition Law and National Regulation—A Conflict of Laws Reconstruction of the Dispute on Book Price Fixing' 8 *European Review of Public Law* (2000), 155–72 at 166–7, Weatherill and Beaumont *EU Law* (3rd ed) (London: Penguin, 1999) at 521–4, Mortelmans 'Towards Convergence in the Application of the Rules on Free Movement and on Competition? ' 38 *CML Rev* (2001), 613–49 at 642, Cruz *Between Competition and Free Movement: The Economic Constitutional Law of the European Community* (Oxford: Hart Publishing, 2002) at 121–5, Wulf-Henning Roth, reported and analysed in Cruz *Between Competition and Free Movement: The Economic Constitutional Law of the European Community* (Oxford, Hart Publishing, 2002) at 119. *Cf* Robertson 'Professional Rules under the Competition Act 1998' 1 *Competition Law Journal* (2002), 93–100, 98–9, which considers the approach to be of general application.

[101] Green Paper on Services of General Interest COM(2003) 270 final, [32], also [43].

the Treaty imposes.[102] By conflating the jurisdictional and substantive question the limits of Community competence fall to be determined at the justification stage.[103] We must not only be sensitive to the role the concept of economic activity plays in limiting Community competence, but also show appreciation of the role differing conceptions of economic activity play in determining the appropriate Community competence. Absent such an appreciation there is a risk that the limits of particular Treaty privisions are over-extended, for example, that Article 49 EC will be applied whenever there is a potential to make profit, ignoring the need for remuneration requirements or that Article 82 EC will be applied whenever there is remuneration, ignoring the requirement that there must be the potential to make profit from the activity without state intervention. By ignoring the different conceptions the danger is that provisions of Community law will be applied to situations for which they are ill-suited.

[102] Case T-313/02 (see n 1 above), para 49, 55, 62–3.

[103] On the fusion of jurisdictional and justificationary issues see Gyselen 'Case C-67/96, Albany v Stichting Bedrijfspensioenfonds Textielindustrie; Joined Cases C-115–117/97, Brentjens' Handelsonderneming v Stichting Bedrijfspensioenfonds Voor De Handel in Bouwmaterialen; and Case C-219/97, Drijvende Bokken v Stichting Pensioenfonds Voor De Vervoeren Havenbedrijven' 37 *CML Rev* (2000), 425–48, 439. Further discussion of the competence issues raised at the justification stage are considered in ch 12 in this volume.

11

The Outer Limit of the Treaty Free Movement Provisions: Some Reflections on the Significance of Keck, *Remoteness and* Deliège

ELEANOR SPAVENTA*

I INTRODUCTION

IN WRITING A piece on the outer boundaries of the free movement provisions, it is inevitable to be forced to revisit very familiar concepts and case law. This investigation has led to findings that the present author had not anticipated: naively, one could have thought that the outer boundaries of the free movement of goods were a settled affair with the exception of the relationship between the doctrine of 'effect too uncertain and indirect' and the *Keck* selling arrangements. After all, the *Keck* ruling,[1] for all its faults, helped both commentators and national courts to determine when a rule would fall within Article 28 EC: a product requirement is always caught while rules regulating the modalities of sale would in principle, and lacking discrimination, fall outside the scope of that provision. And yet, as noted by Koutrakos,[2] as different situations presented themselves, the Court was forced to 'fine-tune' its approach and more rules have been brought back within the reach of Article 28 EC. On closer scrutiny, this fine-tuning might lead to the conclusion that the effect of the *Keck* ruling has been more limited and less revolutionary than anticipated, and consequently the boundaries of the free movement of goods less defined than one might have thought.

* I am very grateful to Michael Dougan and Catherine Barnard for their comments on an earlier draft. The usual disclaimer applies.

1 Joined Cases C-267/91 and C-268/91 *Keck and Mithouard* [1993] ECR I-6097.

2 P Koutrakos, 'On Groceries, Alcohol and Olive Oil: More on the Free Movement of Goods after *Keck*' (2001) 26 *EL Rev* 391.

On the other hand, one could have thought that the definition of the outer boundaries of the free movement of persons provisions might be more difficult: it is sufficient to recall the *Carpenter* ruling as a reminder of the breadth of these provisions.[3] And yet, exactly because no attempt has so far been made to explicitly exclude a given type of rules from the scope of these provisions, the case law on the free movement of persons appears more internally consistent (which of course does not mean that is not hermeneutically problematic). Thus, almost all rules are caught by the free movement of persons provisions and once we accept the 'discouragement' test as a starting point this should not come as a surprise. There are only a handful of cases in which the Court excluded the relevance of the Treaty in cases concerning the free movement of persons and, by and large, in those cases the claimants were pushing the dicta of the Court beyond reasonable limits. This said, the discouragement test seems to find its physiological limits in relation to tax rules. Higher taxation in another Member State might clearly deter an economic operator from exercising its Treaty rights; and yet, the Court has so far (rightly) resisted the temptation to subject the level of taxation to the proportionality assessment required once a rule is found to fall within the scope of the Treaty free movement provisions.

This contribution will analyse these issues; it will start by introducing the reader to alternative conceptual backgrounds to the *Keck* ruling. It will then turn to a scrutiny of the doctrine of 'effect too uncertain and indirect'; and the case law on selling arrangements. In this respect, it will highlight how the 'refinement' of the Court's approach might signal a change in the very nature of the *Keck* presumption. It will then conclude with a brief analysis of the free movement of persons provisions, focusing on the different approach adopted in relation to tax rules.

II REDEFINING THE BOUNDARIES AFTER *KECK*: POLICY DECISION OR COHERENT HERMENEUTIC CHOICE?

The *Keck* settlement hardly needs repeating: faced with increasing criticism as well as the prospect of an unmanageable case load,[4] the Court decided to exclude, as a matter of principle, some rules from the scope of the

[3] Case C-60/00 *Carpenter v Secretary of State for the Home Department* [2002] ECR I-6279.

[4] For example, AG Van Gerven's Opinion, Case C-145/88 *Torfaen Borough Council v B & Q plc* [1989] ECR I-3851; EL White, 'In Search of the Limits to Article 30 of the EEC Treaty'(1989) 26 *CML Rev* 235; K Mortelmans, 'Article 30 of the EEC Treaty and Legislation Relating to Market Circumstances: Time to Consider a New Definition?' (1991) 28 *CML Rev* 115.

Treaty unless such rules were found to be directly or indirectly discriminatory.[5] As a result, following the *Keck* ruling the test for assessing whether a non-directly discriminatory rule is to be defined as a measure having equivalent effect,[6] and therefore needs to be justified, seems to be—for practical purposes—tripartite.

First, product requirements always fall within the scope of Article 28 EC, without there being any need to prove discrimination or a specific effect on intra-Community trade.[7]

Secondly, selling arrangements fall within the scope of Article 28 EC only insofar as they are directly or indirectly discriminatory,[8] and possibly in the case in which they prevent access to the market of imported goods.[9]

Thirdly, residual rules, that is those rules which are neither product requirements nor *Keck* selling arrangements (such as for instance bans on sale or use;[10] inspections;[11] registration[12] and authorisation requirements;[13] licence requirements;[14] restrictions on transport;[15] and obligations to provide data for statistics[16]) fall within the scope of Article 28 EC if they affect directly or indirectly, actually or potentially intra-Community trade pursuant to the *Dassonville* formula.[17] However, this will not be the case

[5] *Keck and Mithouard* (n 1).

[6] Of course quantitative restrictions (as well as discriminatory measure) always fall within the scope of Art 28 EC.

[7] *Keck and Mithouard* (n 1), para 15.

[8] *Ibid*, para 16.

[9] Case C-405/98 *Konsumentombudsmannen (KO) v Gourmet International Products AB (GIP)*[2001] ECR I-1795.

[10] Case C-293/94 *Criminal proceedings against Brandsma* [1996] ECR I-3159; Case C-400/96 *J Harpegnies* [1998] ECR I-5121; Case C-473/98 *Kemikalieinspektionen v Toolex Alpha AB* [2000] ECR I-5681.

[11] Case C-105/94 *Ditta A Celestini* [1997] ECR I-2971.

[12] Case C-55/99 *Commission v France* [2000] (Registration for reagents) ECR I-1149; Case C-390/99 *Canal Satélite Digital SL v Administracíon General del Estado*, [2002] ECR I-607, where the Court excluded that the *Keck* ruling could apply because of 'the need in certain cases to adapt the products in question to the rules in force in the Member State in which they are marketed' (para 30); to the same effect also Case C-14/02 *ATRAL SA V Belgium* [2003] ECR I-4431.

[13] Case C-120/95 *N Decker v Caisse de Maladie des Employes Privés* [1998] ECR I-1831.

[14] Case C-189/95 *Criminal proceedings against H Franzén* [1997] ECR I-5909; it is not clear whether an obligation to store semen in authorised centres is a selling arrangements or not, *cf* Case C-323/93 *Société Civile Agricole du Centre d'Insémination de la Crespelle v Coopérative d'Elevage et d'Insémination Artificielle du Département de la Mayenne* [1994] ECR I-5077, where the Court unusually refers to Case C-169/91 *Council of the City of Stoke on Trent and Norwich City Council v B & Q plc* [1992] ECR I-6635 (one of the *Sunday trading* cases) rather than to *Keck*.

[15] Case C-350/97 *W Monsees v Unabhängiger Verwaltungssenat fur Kärnten* [1999] ECR I-2921.

[16] Case C-114/96 *René Kieffer and Roman Thill* [1997] ECR I-3629.

[17] Case 8/74 *Procureur du Roi v Dassonville* [1974] ECR 83, para 5 (hereinafter the Dassonville formula).

when the effect of the rule on intra-Community trade is too uncertain and indirect to trigger Article 28 EC.[18]

The landscape of the free movement of goods, and in particular of what exactly is to be considered a measure having equivalent effect to a restriction on imports, is therefore still varied even after the *Keck* ruling. In this respect, while the ruling has introduced a very useful system of presumptions to assess the need for justification of domestic rules (product requirements always fall in, selling arrangements mostly not, and for other rules it depends), it has not done much to clarify the outer boundaries of Article 28 EC, and the rationale underlying the case law.

More specifically, in relation to 'certain selling arrangements', the reasoning in *Keck* carries a presumption that, at first, seemed not rebuttable: such rules are not *as such* capable of either preventing access to the market, or of having an effect on market access different from the impact that such rules would have on access to the market of domestic products.[19] However, the exact significance of this legal presumption introduced by the *Keck* ruling is still unclear. This is all the more so given the existence of the doctrine of 'effect too uncertain and indirect', which also excludes some rules from the scope of Article 28 EC. While this doctrine preceded the *Keck* ruling, and indeed could be seen as the first attempt by the Court to exclude the application of Article 28 EC in certain cases, its survival after *Keck* begs the question as to its relationship with the latter.

In particular, it is unclear whether the presumption that non-discriminatory selling arrangements fall outside the scope of Article 28 EC is aimed at *excluding* rules that would otherwise be capable of affecting actually or potentially, directly or indirectly, intra-Community trade; or rather, whether such rules are excluded because they are *not*, as such, capable of *affecting intra-Community trade*, which is to say that their effect on intra-Community trade is uncertain and indirect if existing at all.[20]

Here, the *Keck* ruling can be interpreted in both ways depending on what one considers to be the scope of application of the Treaty. Thus, those who were unsatisfied by the compromise reached by the Court argued that the focus on the type of rule, rather than on its effect, disregarded the fact that some selling arrangements could have an effect on intra-Community trade regardless of discrimination.[21] This was argued to be the case

[18] For example, Case C-69/88 *H Krantz GmbH & Co v Ontvanger der Directe Belastingen* [1990] ECR I-583; see Section III below.

[19] *Keck and Mithouard*(n 1) para 17.

[20] In which case para 17 of the *Keck* ruling would be nothing more than an explanation—such rules fall outside the scope of Art 28 EC because they do not prevent market access or impede it more than they impede access to the market of domestic goods.

[21] For example, AG Jacobs' Opinion in Case C-412/93 *Leclerc-Siplec* [1995] ECR I-179; L Gormley, 'Reasoning Renounced? The Remarkable Judgement in *Keck & Mithouard*'

especially in relation to some forms of advertising and long-distance selling techniques.[22] In the view of these authors, the a priori exclusion of such rules runs contrary to the aim of Article 28 EC, and to the spirit of the *Dassonille* formula. Viewed in this light then, the *Keck* ruling would have introduced nothing more than a legal presumption,[23] so that *Keck* should be considered nothing more than a policy decision concerning the best level at which regulation should be enacted, a *sui generis* application by the Court of the principle of subsidiarity.[24]

On the other hand, those who welcomed the *Keck* ruling did so in the belief that the aim of the Treaty free movement provisions was merely to prohibit discrimination on grounds of nationality[25] or, in a broader reading,[26] true barriers to intra-Community movement/trade. Interpreted in this way, the Treaty should have no effect on the regulatory autonomy of the Member States, or their ability to decide upon the correct level of market regulation. The only limitation clearly and expressly imposed by the Treaty concerned the need to afford equal treatment to out-of-State economic operators (or not to raise unjustified barriers to intra-Community movement/trade). In this interpretation then, the *Keck* ruling simply rectified the wrong turn taken by the Court during the Sunday trading saga, when rules which did not have discriminatory effects (or any effect at all on intra-Community trade), were brought within the scope of Article 28 EC. Seen in this light, *Keck* would not introduce any presumption; rather, it simply clarifies that, lacking discrimination, certain rules are not per se capable of preventing market access or affect it more than they affect market access for domestic goods. Certain selling arrangements are excluded from the scope of the Treaty not because of a policy decision of sorts, but simply because they do not have an effect on intra-Community

(1994) 5 *European Business Law Review* 63–67, and 'Two Years after Keck' (1996) 19 *Fordham Intlional Law Journal* 866; N Reich, 'The "November Revolution" if the European Court of Justice: *Keck*, *Meng* and *Audi* Revisited' (1994) 31 *CML Rev* 459; D Chalmers, 'Repackaging the Internal Market—The ramifications of the *Keck* judgment' (1994) 19 *EL Rev* 385; S Weatherill, 'After *Keck*: some thoughts on how to clarify the clarification' (1996) 33 *CML Rev* 885; I Higgins, 'The Free and Not so Free Movement of Goods since *Keck*' (1997) 6 *Irish Journal of European Law* 166; C Barnard, 'Fitting the remaining pieces into the goods and persons jigsaw?' (2001) 26 *EL Rev* 35.

[22] See especially AG Jacobs' Opinion in *Leclerc-Siplec ibid*.

[23] See to this effect the Opinion of Advocate General Fennelly in Case C-190/98 *V Graf v Filzmoser Maschinenbau GmbH* [2000] ECR I-493, para 19.

[24] See also AG Tizzano's Opinion in Case C-442/02 *Caixa-Bank* [2004] ECR I-8961, especially paras 59 and ff on the relationship between the allocation of competences in the EC Treaty and the interpretation of the primary free movement provisions; and G Davies, 'Can Selling Arrangements Be Harmonised?' (2005) 30 *EL Rev* 371.

[25] For example, N Bernard, *Multi Level Governance in the European Union* (London, Kluwer Law International, 2002); and J Snell, *Goods and Services in EC Law* (Oxford, Oxford University Press, 2002).

[26] See also AG Poiares Maduro's Opinion in Case C-158/04 *Alfa Vita Vassilopoulos* [2006] ECR I-8135.

trade. As a result, the rationale behind the *Keck* ruling would be the same as the rationale behind the doctrine of 'effect too uncertain and indirect': in both cases the Treaty does not apply because there is no effect on the free movement of goods.

As we shall see in the next sections, both explanations of the *Keck* ruling reflect, at different times, the Court's case law. Thus, it will be argued that in the aftermath of the ruling, the almost mechanical application of the *Keck* presumption might lead to the conclusion that it was best qualified as a policy decision, thus lending support to those who criticised the Court for its lack of hermeneutic consistency. However, in more recent years, following a fine-tuning in the approach to both discrimination and what is to be considered a certain selling arrangement,[27] the nature of the *Keck* ruling might have evolved, so that the focus has shifted back to ascertaining whether the rules under scrutiny affect intra-Community trade.

Before turning to the analysis of the *Keck* case law it is useful to examine the scope of the doctrine of 'effect too uncertain and indirect' since the question as to the rationale underpinning the exclusion of certain selling arrangements from the scope of Article 28 EC is closely linked to the exclusion of certain rules because of the lack of effect on intra-Community trade.

III THE DOCTRINE OF 'EFFECT TOO UNCERTAIN AND INDIRECT'

As mentioned above, the doctrine of 'effect too uncertain and indirect' was first formulated by the Court during the Sunday trading saga, and might be seen as a tentative attempt to curtail the breadth of the *Dassonville* formula. In *Krantz*,[28] to the author's knowledge the first case in which the doctrine was mentioned, the Court examined the compatibility with Article 28 EC of rules which granted tax authorities the power to seize moveable property from the premises of companies in order to recover tax debt. In analysing the issue, Advocate General Darmon argued that *Torfaen* (the first of the *Sunday trading* cases)[29] indicated the presence of a *lower limit* before a measure having equivalent effect on imports could become discernible. Thus, in his opinion, 'the restrictive effects on imports, if inherent in legislation pursuing goals permitted by the Treaty, cannot, unless they are disproportionate, cause a measure to be regarded as a measure having equivalent effect to quantitative restrictions'.[30] He then

[27] See also Koutrakos, (n 2) 391.
[28] *H Krantz GmbH & Co v Ontvanger der Directe Belastingen* (n 18).
[29] Case C-145/88 *Torfaen Borough Council v B & Q plc* [1989] ECR I-3851.
[30] *H Krantz GmbH & Co v Ontvanger der Directe Belastingen* (n 18), Opinion para 16.

found that the rule in question in *Krantz* fell short of that lower limit since its effect on imports could not be substantiated.

The Court followed a slightly different path to reach the same conclusion. It first found that the rules in question applied without distinction and did not seek to control intra-Community trade. It then added:

> *Furthermore*, the possibility that nationals of other Member-States would hesitate to sell goods on instalment terms to purchasers in the Member-State concerned because such goods would be liable to seizure by the collector of taxes if the purchasers failed to discharge their Dutch tax debts is *too uncertain and indirect* to warrant the conclusion that a national provision authorising such seizure is liable to hinder trade between Member-States. (para 11, emphasis added)

Such an approach was repeated in *Baskiciogullari*,[31] where the Court held that a German rule which imposed a duty to provide information on the parties to a contract fell outside the scope of Article 28 EC since its effect was too uncertain and indirect to be liable to hinder trade.

As said above, both cases were decided during the Sunday trading saga; in this respect, Advocate General Tesauro's opinion in *Hünnermund*[32] (the opinion on which the Court based the *Keck* ruling) is interesting since it discusses, however briefly, these two cases in illustrating the confusion, and lack of coherent approach, that had characterised the Court's interpretation of the free movement of goods since the mid-1980s. In proposing what will effectively become the *Keck* test, Mr Tesauro clearly intended to replace the different approaches discernible in the case law with a single (and coherent) test. This notwithstanding, the test suggested by Mr Tesauro focused on the specific measure under consideration—a ban on advertising outside pharmacies—so that, even though Mr Tesauro's reasoning was overall of general application, the test he proposed was not. Viewed in this light, then, it is not altogether surprising that the doctrine of 'effect too uncertain and indirect' survived the *Keck* ruling.[33]

In subsequent case law, the doctrine of 'effect too uncertain and indirect' has been refined. In *Peralta*,[34] the Court suggested that for a rule to fall

[31] Case C-93/92 *Baskiciogullari* [1993] ECR I-5009; here AG Van Gerwen found that the rule fell outside the scope of Art 28 without reference to the effect too uncertain and indirect doctrine.

[32] Case C-292/92 *R Hünermund and others v Landesapothekerkammer Baden-Wurttemberg* [1993] ECR I-6787.

[33] More recently, Advocate General Kokott fell short of suggesting that the doctrine of effect too uncertain and indirect be disposed of because of the difficulties inherent in its application, and that other rules be brought within the *Keck* presumption, Opinion in Case C-142/05 *Åklagaren v Percy Mickelsson and Joakim Roos*, delivered 14 December 2006, case still pending at the time of writing, para 46.

[34] Case C-379/92 *Peralta* [1994] ECR I-3453, para 24; see also Joined Cases C-140 to 142/94 *DIP v Comune di Bassano del Grappa* [1995] ECR I-3257; Case C-96/94 *Centro Servizi Spediporto v Spedizioni Maritima del Golfo Srl* [1995] ECRI-2883; Case C-266/96

outside the scope of Article 28 EC, three conditions need to be met: first of all, absence of discrimination; secondly, the rule should not be intended to regulate trade; and thirdly, the restrictive effects that the rule might have must be too uncertain and indirect to hinder trade between Member States. *Peralta*, albeit not always applied consistently,[35] therefore indicates that the doctrine and the *Keck* exception can be distinguished since the latter applies to non-discriminatory measures which are intended to regulate trade (although not specifically intra-Community trade); whilst the former applies to non-discriminatory measures which do not regulate trade,[36] albeit they might have some very remote effect on it.[37] And in a way, the fact that the doctrine of 'effect too uncertain and indirect' applies only to non-trading rules is entirely in harmony with the *Dassonville* formula that refers to 'trading rules' which actually or potentially restrict intra-Community trade. We shall come back to this point further below.

The ruling in *Semeraro Casa Uno*,[38] seems to support the fact that the 'effect too uncertain and indirect' doctrine applies only to non-trading rules. The case concerned Sunday trading rules and whether they were compatible with both the free movement of goods and the freedom of establishment. The Court found that the rules fell outside the scope of Article 28 EC pursuant to the *Keck* ruling; and that they fell outside the scope of Article 43 EC since they were non-discriminatory; they were not intended to regulate the conditions for establishment; and their effect was

Corsica Ferries France v Gruppo Antichi Ormeggiatori del Porto di Genova and others [1998] ECR I-3949.

[35] See also obiter in Case C-254/98 *TK-Heimdienst* [2000] ECR I-151; however, in Case C-231/03 *Coname* [2005] ECR I-7287, para 20, the Court seems to suggest that a direct award without invitation to tender, considered indirectly discriminatory for lack of transparency, might fall outside the scope if the contract in question would be so modest so that it 'could be reasonably maintained' that out-of-State undertakings would not have an interest, and therefore the effect of the lack of tender procedure would be too uncertain and indirect on the Treaty free movement provisions. It is unclear whether this obiter indicates that rules which might be qualified as indirectly discriminatory might be excluded from the scope of the Treaty pursuant to the uncertain effect doctrine; or whether the negligible economic value of the transaction might altogether exclude discrimination. The latter would be a more coherent approach. A similar confusion is discernible in Case C-20/03 *Burmanjer* [2005] ECR I-4133.

[36] But see *Burmanjer, ibid*, in which the Court seems to suggest that the doctrine of effect too uncertain and indirect might apply also to trading rules.

[37] See also Opinion of AG Fenelly in Case C67/97 *D Bluhme* [1998] ECR I-8033, especially paras 20 and 21 where he considers separately the uncertain effect doctrine, and the *Keck* exception thus also suggesting a different scope of application for the two; and similarly the ECJ's ruling paras 21 and 22 in Case C-134/94 *Esso Española* [1995] ECR I-4223, in relation to rules which imposed upon petroleum traders a duty to supply at least four of the Canary islands; in Case C-44/08 *BASF* [1999] ECR I-6269, the Court, much as it did in *V Graf v Filzmoser Maschinenbau GmbH*(n 23), held that when the effect of a rule depends also on the unforeseeable decisions of economic operators, then the rule's effect is too uncertain and indirect to be considered an obstacle falling within Art 28 EC.

[38] Joined Cases C-418/93 and others *Semeraro Casa Uno Srl v Sindaco del Comune di Ebrusco* [1996] ECR I-2975.

too uncertain and indirect to affect the freedom of establishment. The different approach adopted to scrutinise the same rules signals therefore that selling arrangements and rules the effect of which is too uncertain and indirect are conceptually distinct.

In particular, and as explained by Advocate General La Pergola in *BASF*,[39] in the latter case there is no causal link between rule and alleged restriction and for this reason the *Dassonville* formula, or the other free movement provisions, cannot apply. On the other hand, in relation to selling arrangements there might be an effect on intra-Community trade (for instance the reduction of the total volume of sales) and yet this effect is not relevant for the application of Article 28 EC.

The fact that the doctrine of 'effect too uncertain and indirect' relates (exclusively) to non-trading rules might be further demonstrated by its use in relation to Article 29 EC.[40] As it is well known, the scope of application of Article 29 EC is much narrower than the scope of Article 28 EC since it is limited to a prohibition of measures that restrict patterns of exports by establishing a difference between internal and external trade to the advantage of the former.[41] And yet, the doctrine of 'effect too uncertain and indirect' has found its way in the assessment of alleged restrictions to exports. This is rather surprising since, should the rule be directly discriminatory and advantage domestic trade, then it would fall within the scope of Article 29 EC; but if it is not, by definition it does not fall within the scope of that provision and any reference to the doctrine of 'effect too uncertain and indirect' seems redundant. The fact that the Court still refers to the doctrine of 'effect too uncertain and indirect' then seems to confirm that it is a tool to exclude the application of the free movement provisions in relation to rules which do not regulate trade. It is in relation to those rules that the claimant will need to demonstrate the existence of a causal relationship between rule and alleged barrier; in relation to trading rules, however, the analysis will be exclusively focused on the existence of a barrier (however defined) since causation is taken for granted. Once the barrier is found to exist, there is no need for an investigation as to a causal relationship between that barrier and the situation at issue in the case under investigation.[42] Here,

[39] Opinion Case C-44/08 *BASF* [1999] ECR I-6269, para 18.

[40] Cf, eg Case C-412/97 *ED Srl v I Fenocchio* [1999] ECR I-3845.

[41] Case 237/82 *J Kaas BV et al. V Dutch Government Central Organ Zuivelkontrole* [1984] ECR 483, para 22; more recently see Case C-12/02 *Grilli* [2003] ECR I-11585, especially para 42 in relation to the difference between the scope of Art 28 EC and Art 29 EC.

[42] In this respect see, eg Case C-317/92 *Commission v Germany* (Expiry dates) [1994] ECR I-2039 where the Court dismissed as irrelevant the German Government's contention that rules restricting the expiry dates of certain products to two a year should not fall within the scope of Art 28 EC since the trader was in any event obliged to alter the packaging in order for the information to be given in German.

one way to look at this difference would be to refer back to the *Dassonville* formula mentioned earlier: when assessing the compatibility of trading rules with Article 28 EC the causal connection is taken for granted because even potential barriers to intra-Community trade are caught. The same however does not appear to be true in relation to non-trading rules: whilst a potential effect might be sufficient (there is no authority either way), it still needs to be proven.

IV BACK TO *DASSONVILLE*? THE CASE LAW CERTAIN SELLING ARRANGEMENTS

From the cursory analysis carried out above, it seems that the doctrine of 'effect too uncertain and indirect' and the *Keck* a priori exclusion of some non-discriminatory rules from the scope of Article 28 EC can be kept distinct. Whilst both are tools to exclude the application of Article 28 EC, the former applies to *non-trading* rules which have no causal connection with the alleged barrier; whilst the latter applies to non-discriminatory *trading* rules of a certain type. The significance of this difference will then depend on whether certain selling arrangements are trading rules which lack a sufficient causal connection with the alleged barrier to intra-Community trade; or whether such rules are excluded because of a priori decision as to the appropriate level at which regulation should be enacted (or in certain instances because of an a priori decision as to the merit of the legislation in question). In the former case, the only difference between the doctrine of effect 'too uncertain and indirect' and *Keck* would rest on the type of rule to which the respective doctrines are applied and the two doctrines could be easily merged into one test (albeit they still might be kept separate for ease of convenience). However, if selling arrangements are excluded because of an a priori decision, then the difference between the *Keck* and the *Peralta* doctrine would be of a more substantive nature, in that *Keck* would relate to rules which affect intra-Community trade but are nonetheless excluded from the scope of Article 28 EC, whilst the *Peralta*-type rules would be excluded simply because they do not have an effect on intra-Community trade.

It is therefore necessary to consider the case law on selling arrangements and in particular the extent to which rules regulating the modalities of sales are in practice excluded from the scope of the Treaty. In this respect, we can identify three trends in the case law: first, those cases in which the Court applies almost mechanically the *Keck* formula; secondly, those in which discrimination is used as a flexible tool that can be bent to include selling arrangements without there being the need for the trader to support with any evidence the existence of factual discrimination;[43] thirdly, those cases in which the dividing line between rules which fall within the scope of the *Keck* exception and rules which fall within the standard *Dassonville* formula is not entirely clear.

A The Mechanical Application of the *Keck* Formula

The first line of cases is predominant in the years immediately following the *Keck* judgment. In those cases, the Court applied the *Keck* ruling to exclude, for instance, Sunday trading rules and rules concerning opening hours;[44] rules concerning where and how a product can be sold;[45] and some rules concerning advertisement.[46] Those cases are fairly straightforward: the application of the *Keck* formula is almost mechanical; the assessment of discrimination is purely abstract, if existing at all,[47] and the burden of proof as to the existence of factual discrimination seems to lie with the claimant.[48] Overall, the outcome in these cases is entirely predictable. The lack of any grounded assessment of the effect of the rules at issue on intra-Community trade thus might lend support to the view that, at least at first, the *Keck* ruling was better seen as a policy decision so that certain rules never fell within the scope of Article 28 EC simply because the Court so decided.

B The More Flexible Approach to Discrimination

Less predictable is the second line of cases, where the broad interpretation of the notion of indirect discrimination allows the Court to scrutinise the justification and proportionality of the rules under consideration. Measures which have been found to be indirectly discriminatory include: rules restricting door-to-door sales and sales on rounds of grocery products to traders having an establishment within the district or a bordering district

[43] See Koutrakos, (n 2) 391; also L Prete, 'Of Motorcycles Trailers and Personal Watercrafts: the Battle over *Keck*' (2008) 35 *Legal Issues of Economic Integration* 133.

[44] Case C-401/92 *Tankstation* [1994] ECR I-2199; Case C-69/93 *Punto Casa Spa* [1994] ECR I-2395; *Semeraro Casa Uno Srl v Sindaco del Comune di Ebrusco* and others(n 38).

[45] Case C-391/92 *Commission v Greece* (milk for infants) [1995] ECR I-1621; Case C-387/93 *Banchero* [1995] ECR I-4663; Case C-63/94 *Belgapom* [1995] ECR I-2467; *Burmanjer* (n 35); Case C-441/04 *A Punkt Schmuckhandel* [2006] ECR I-2093.

[46] *R Hünermund and others v Landesapothekerkammer Baden-Wurttemberg* [1993](n 32); *Leclerc-Siplec*(n 21); and, although rather confusing as a ruling, Case C-34/95 *De Agostini* [1997] ECR I-3843; and Case C-71/02 *Karner* [2004] ECR I-3025.

[47] For example Case C-63/94 *Belgapom* [1995] ECR I-2467; *Leclerc-Siplec* (*ibid*)

[48] Case C-34/95 *De Agostini* [1997] ECR I-3843.

of the place where the sale would be carried out (*TK-Heimdienst*);[49] rules prohibiting advertising of alcoholic beverages (*Gourmet*);[50] rules on the packaging of bake-off products (*Morellato*);[51] and rules on a prohibition of internet sales of medicinal products (*DocMorris*).[52]

In these cases the assessment of discrimination seems not always to be based on much hard factual evidence. Rather, very much as it happens with the assessment of discrimination in the case of obstacles to the free movement of persons,[53] it is based on assumptions as to the *likely* effect of the rules under consideration. Such assumptions, however, do not always stand a rigorous scrutiny.[54] Take for instance *TK-Heimdienst*.[55] In that case Advocate General La Pergola found that it was very unlikely that the rules concerning the sale on rounds of grocery products would have an effect on intra-Community trade since there is a 'natural limit' to the areas covered by that form of grocery distribution. On the other hand, the Court relied on purely theoretical reasoning to find that the rules were indirectly discriminatory, therefore relieving the traders from the need to prove any existence of factual discrimination.

Or consider the ruling in *Morellato*.[56] There the issue related to packaging and labelling requirements for bake-off products, that is bakery products which are pre-prepared and undergo only the final stage of baking in the premises where they are sold. The Court found that the rules at issue were not product requirements since they did not entail the need to modify the imported product. Since the rules related to the marketing stage they were to be considered as selling arrangements. The Court then held that there was unjustified factual discrimination. It based its finding on the fact that, since such products were not manufactured in Italy, the rules disadvantaged imported products only, in that they discouraged their imports *or* made the products less attractive to consumers. This broad interpretation of discrimination is at odds with established case law in relation to discriminatory taxation, where the Court has held that when there is no domestic production of goods similar to or in competition with the imported product there cannot be any discrimination;[57] as well as with

[49] Case C-254/98 *Schutzverband gegen unlauteren Wettbewerb v TK-Heimdiest Sass GmbH* [2000] ECR I-2487.

[50] *Konsumentombudsmannen (KO) v Gourmet International Products AB (GIP)* (n 9).

[51] Case C-416/00 *T Morellato v Comune di Padova* (No 2) [2003] ECR I-9343.

[52] Case C-322/01 *Deutscher Apothekerverband eV, 0800 DocMorris NV, Jacque Waterval* [2004] ECR I-4887.

[53] For example Case C-237/94 *O'Flynn v Adjudication Officer* [1996] ECR I-2617.

[54] See also D Wilsher, 'Does *Keck* discrimination make any sense? An assessment of the non-discrimination principle in the European Single Market' (2008) 33 *EL Rev* 3.

[55] *Schutzverband gegen unlauteren Wettbewerb v TK-Heimdiest Sass GmbH* (n 49).

[56] *T Morellato v Comune di Padova* (No 2) (n 51).

[57] Case C-47/88 *Commission v Denmark* (registration duty for cars) [1990] ECR I-4509.

the Court's own finding in the *milk for infants* case.[58] In the latter case, the Commission brought proceedings against Greece in relation to rules which restricted the possibility to sell processed milk for infants to pharmacies. The Court held that the fact that Greece did not produce the goods in question was not relevant in the assessment of discrimination since the applicability of Article 28 EC:

> cannot depend on such a purely fortuitous factual circumstance, which may, moreover, change with the passage of time. If it did, this would have the *illogical* consequence that the same legislation would fall under Article 30 [now 28] in certain Member States but fall outside the scope of that provision in other Member States (para 17, emphasis added).

Whilst it might be argued that the Italian rules in *Morellato* might have had some protectionist effect in that they placed Italian in-store baked bread at an advantage, there is no indication in the ruling that that was the rationale underpinning the Court's reasoning.

Similarly, in *Gourmet* there is little discussion of discrimination: it might be recalled that the rules at issue prohibited the advertising of alcoholic products.[59] In particular, the Swedish Government had submitted evidence to the effect that the sale of whisky and wine, mainly imported, had grown in comparison with the sale of vodka, mainly home-produced. The Court dismissed the evidence by holding that it could not be precluded that in the absence of the legislation at issue the switch in consumers' preferences would have been greater[60] (a *probatio diabolica* if ever there was one).[61] While, again, it could be argued that a prohibition on advertising affects intra-Community trade regardless of discrimination (but then *Keck* should not apply to such rules), the reasoning of the Court, or part thereof, seems more driven by the desire that the rules at issue would be subject to justification, than by a grounded assessment of discrimination.

Even leaving aside the above considerations, the Court's approach to discrimination is not always consistent. Contrast, for instance, *TK-Heimdienst* and *DocMorris*, on the one hand, with *Burmanjer* and *A-Punkt*, on the other. As said above, *TK-Heimdienst* related to rules restricting door-to-door and sales on rounds of groceries to traders having an establishment within the district or a bordering district from where the sale on rounds was to take place;[62] and *DocMorris* concerned rules that

[58] *Commission v Greece* (n 45).

[59] *Konsumentombudsmannen (KO) v Gourmet International Products AB (GIP)*(n 9).

[60] Para 22.

[61] *Cf* AG Tesauro's Opinion in Case C-292/92 *Hünermund and Others v Landesapothekerkammer Baden Württemberg* [1993] ECR I 6787 where he talks about 'probatio diabolica' in relation to a *de minimis* test (para 21). In *Gourmet* the Court also referred to the fact that the evidence did not relate to beer.

[62] *Schutzverband gegen unlauteren Wettbewerb v TK-Heimdiest Sass GmbH* (n 49).

prohibited the internet sale of medicinal products.[63] In both cases the Court found the rules to be indirectly discriminatory: in *TK-Heimdienst*, because of the fact that an establishment requirement is always discriminatory, regardless of the fact that it was very unlikely that out-of-State traders established in places not bordering with Austria would have any interest in travelling hundred of miles to sell their groceries door-to-door. And in *DocMorris*, the rules were found to be discriminatory since:

> for pharmacies not established in Germany, the internet provides a more significant way to gain direct access to the German market. A prohibition which has a greater impact on pharmacies established outside German territory could impede access to the market for products from other Member States more than it impedes access for domestic products (para 74).

On the other hand, in *Burmanjer* a prior authorisation requirement for the itinerant sale of periodicals was found not to be indirectly discriminatory;[64] and in *A-Punkt* the same conclusion was reached in relation to rules prohibiting door-to-door sales of jewellery.[65] If the rationale in *TK-Heimdienst* and *DocMorris* was that the rules were indirectly discriminatory because they placed traders having an establishment in the national territory at an advantage compared to out-of-State traders who are less likely to have already established a presence in the host-State, then such a rationale should have applied a fortiori in the case of *Burmanjer* and *A-Punkt*. In the latter, small economic operators were prevented from effectively broadening their market without incurring significant costs;[66] even though the Court left the assessment as to the existence of discrimination to the national court, it seemed doubtful as to its existence. In *Burmanjer*, the Court dismissed as 'unproven' the submission that rules on itinerant sales of periodicals might affect foreign periodicals more than domestic ones, to then add that even if there were such an effect, it would be 'too insignificant and uncertain' to hinder trade between Member States.[67] It therefore seemed to espouse a *de minimis* approach which fits uncomfortably with its own case law.[68]

Overall, those cases point at a flexible use of factual discrimination, so that certain rules are declared to be indirectly discriminatory regardless of any concrete evidence as to their disparate effect on imported goods.

[63] *Deutscher Apothekerverband eV, 0800 DocMorris NV, Jacque Waterval* (n 52).
[64] *Burmanjer* (n 35).
[65] Case C-441/04 *A-Punkt Schmuckhandel* [2006] ECR I-2093.
[66] See also Commission's submissions as reported in para 22 of the ruling.
[67] *Burmanjer*(n 35) para 31.
[68] For example recently Case C-212/06 *Government of the French Community and Walloon Community v Government of the Flemish Community*, judgment of 1 April 2008, not yet reported, para 52.

Furthermore, a rigorous approach to discrimination should entail a discussion of the appropriate comparator (existing trader or new market entrant?), which is generally lacking in the Court's jurisprudence on selling arrangements. Finally, and as pointed out above, it is unclear why the effect of rules which are similar in kind is judged differently according to the case under consideration. This more flexible approach to discrimination might therefore suggest a considerable relaxation of the 'selling arrangement' exception, so that an increasing number of rules can be brought back within the scope of Article 28 EC and undergo the proportionality scrutiny demanded by the mandatory requirements doctrine.

C The Boundary Between Selling Arrangements and Other Rules

The third strand of case law that deserves attention is that in which the Court is called upon to assess the boundary between rules that fall within the scope of the *Keck* exception, and those which fall outside the 'certain' selling arrangements category that benefit from a narrower application of Article 28 EC. In this respect, while rules which require the modification of the imported product can never be qualified as selling arrangements,[69] in certain cases rules which concern the modalities of sale might be excluded from the *Keck* exception;[70] and in other cases it is more difficult to decide whether the rule does fall within the 'selling arrangement' category.

For instance, juxtapose the case of *Banchero*, on rules which limited the sale of tobacco to authorised licensed retailers,[71] to the case of *Franzén*, on a licensing requirement for the sale of alcoholic products.[72] In the former case the rules were found to be non-discriminatory selling arrangements, whilst in the latter case the rules were found to fall outside the *Keck* exception and were therefore subject to the full force of the *Dassonville* formula. And yet, the rules at issue in the two cases both concerned a licensing requirement whereby the sale of given products was reserved to authorised retailers.

Or compare the rules at issue in the case of *Morellato* with the rules at issue in *Alfa Vita*. As we have seen, in *Morellato*, rules concerning the packaging of bake-off products were found to be selling arrangements; as a

[69] For example Case C-368/95 *Vereinigte Familiapress Zeitungsverlags- und vertriebs GmbH v Heinrich Bauer Verlag* [1997] ECR I-3689; Case C-390/99 *Canal Satélite Digital SL v Administracíon General del Estado* [2002] ECR I-607; Case C-12/00 *Commission v Spain* (chocolate) [2003] ECR I-459.

[70] Other rules by nature do not fall within the product requirements/selling arrangements dichotomy since they do not relate either to the modalities of sale or to the physical characteristics of the products; see above, Section II.

[71] Case C-387/93 *Banchero* [1995] ECR I-4663; see also (pre-*Keck*) C-23/89 *Quietlynn Ltd and BJ Richards v Southend Borough Council* [1990] ECR I-3059.

[72] C-189/95 *Criminal proceedings against H Franzén* [1997] ECR I-5909.

result, the Court had to rely on a broad (and not entirely consistent) finding of discrimination in order to subject the rules to the proportionality assessment.[73] On the other hand, in *Alfa Vita* rules restricting the sale of bread baked on the premises to stores which complied with all the requirements prescribed for bread-making establishments were found not to be selling arrangements since they did not take into consideration the specific nature of bake-off products; they entailed additional costs; and they made the marketing of bake-off products more difficult.[74] In this respect, there seems to be some confusion so that the assessment of the effect of the rule is relevant in determining whether the rule is a certain selling arrangement. In this way, the focus shifts back from assessing the 'type' of rule, to assessing its 'effect'.

It therefore seems that far from having introduced a rigid distinction, the application of the *Keck* ruling will very much depend on the specifics of the case at issue. And yet, in order to understand why certain selling arrangements are excluded from the scope of Article 28 EC, it is important to identify the rationale behind the Court's decisions.

V POSSIBLE EXPLANATIONS FOR THE EXCLUSION OF CERTAIN SELLING ARRANGEMENTS FROM THE SCOPE OF ARTICLE 28 EC

The most obvious explanation for the exclusion of certain selling arrangements from the scope of Article 28 EC is that suggested by the Court in *Keck* itself. Certain rules are excluded from the scope of the Treaty because, provided they are not discriminatory, they neither prevent market access nor impede it more than they impede it for domestic goods. However, and as this might be certainly true for some cases,[75] such an explanation does not help in understanding the different approaches to discrimination, or the reason why some rules which seem similar, and which relate to the way a product can be sold, are classified sometimes as a certain selling arrangement, and sometimes not. For instance, a prohibition on door-to-door sales such as the one at issue in *A-Punkt*, might affect the ability to access the market of out-of-State traders, who do not have an establishment in the territory, more than it affects access of domestic traders. And yet, the rules at issue were found, in principle, not to be discriminatory. On the other hand, a licensing requirement for the sale of alcoholic beverages, such as the one at issue in *Franzén*, does not have a discriminatory effect on market access (as the Court itself held in both

73 *T Morellato v Comune di Padova* (No 2)(n 51).

74 *Alfa Vita Vassilopoulos* (n 26).

75 See especially those analysed in Section IVA above on the mechanical application of the *Keck* ruling.

Franzén and *Banchero*). And yet, the rules at issue in *Franzén* did not benefit from the *Keck* exemption. If the explanation contained in para 17 of *Keck*, according to which non-discriminatory selling arrangements fall outside the scope of Article 28 EC because they do not prevent market access or impede it more than they impede it for domestic products, were always true, then these discrepancies in the case law are difficult to justify.

For this reason, one needs to look at alternative possible explanations: the obvious one is to read *Keck* as a refinement of the *Dassonville* formula, in that it clarifies that a mere reduction in the volume of sales is not, in itself, enough to trigger Article 28 EC; and it introduces a presumption to the effect that certain rules are normally not liable to affect directly or indirectly, actually or potentially intra-Community trade. Thus, some selling arrangements do not affect intra-Community trade in that any effect they have is an effect on trade as a whole and not specifically on trade in goods that have crossed a border. However, some rules concerning selling arrangements might have a specific effect on intra-Community trade, in which case they will be subject to scrutiny by either a broad interpretation of discrimination or by the exclusion of the applicability of the *Keck* presumption. Thus, for instance, the ruling in *TK-Heimdienst* seems consistent with the fact that Community law ill-tolerates any establishment/residence requirement, even though the willingness of out-of-State traders to engage in the commercial practice at issue might be extremely unlikely (if not altogether remote). The ruling in *DocMorris* is fully justified should one consider the effectiveness of internet sales as a means to penetrate foreign markets. The licensing requirement in *Franzén* had an effect on intra-Community trade which the rules in *Banchero* lacked because of the extremely restrictive nature of the rules on the sales of alcoholic beverages in Sweden (as was also the case in *Gourmet*) compared to the non-restrictive effect of the Italian licensing rules on tobacco.[76] The Swedish rules were aimed at discouraging consumption of alcohol; the Italian rules, on the other hand, were aimed at guaranteeing access to tobacco products throughout the national territory, including remote rural communities. Similarly, the rules in *Morellato* and *Alfa Vita* had the effect of making it excessively (and unnecessarily) difficult for a product, bake-off bread, which had traditionally not been sold in Italy and Spain, to be sold in those countries.[77]

[76] See also Case C-438/02 *Hanner* [2005] ECR I-4551, paras 32 and ff, on the distinction between *Franzén* and *Banchero*.

[77] In this respect consider Gormley's argument that the *Sunday trading* cases were simply a misapplication of the *Dassonville* formula, in that Sunday trading rules simply did not affect intra-Community trade; see 'Recent case law on the free movement of goods: some hot potatoes' (1990) 27 *CML Rev* 825.

The focus on the effect on intra-Community trade rather than on the nature of the measure would also explain why rules that might be considered similar from an ontological viewpoint, such as licensing, authorisation or equipment requirements, are de facto treated in a different way depending on the circumstances. And again it would explain the ruling in *Dynamic Medien*.[78] There, the rules at issue prohibited the sale by post of videos, movies and videogames which did not bear an age-limit label corresponding to a classification decision of one of the competent bodies. Advocate General Mengozzi considered the rules to be certain selling arrangements because they concerned modalities of sale; the Court, on the other hand, in order to justify the exclusion of the *Keck* exception, focused also on the double burden that such rules would introduce in relation to those movies which had already undergone a similar scrutiny in the country of origin. However, regardless of the rules of the country of origin, it is clear that such rules affected the possibility of importing movies into Germany in that they required the goods to be subjected to the competent board to assess suitability for given age groups.

This said, the exclusion of the application of Article 28 EC in *Burmanjer* and *A-Punkt* is still puzzling and might lead to the finding that the disparate application of the *Keck* formula indicates that certain rules are to be considered as barriers to intra-Community trade only when their effect is more than minimal. And yet, the Court has so far refused to adopt a *de minimis* approach in relation to the free movement provisions.[79] Furthermore, a *de minimis* approach would fail to explain why some licensing rules have an 'appreciable' effect on trade, whilst rules that restrict consumption of a product to a certain age group would (almost certainly) not.

VI *PERALTA* AND *KECK* V *PERALTA* OR *KECK*?

At the beginning of this analysis we pointed out how the *Keck* ruling could be interpreted in two different ways, either as a decision aimed at excluding some rules from the scope of the Treaty for policy reasons; or, as a decision which merely rectified the mistaken interpretation given to Article 28 EC during the Sunday trading saga according to which a mere reduction in the volume of sales was enough to attract the rules within the ambit of the 'potential' restriction of intra-Community trade pursuant to

[78] Case C-244/06 *Dynamic Medien*, judgment of 14 February 2008, not yet reported.

[79] For example recently Case C-212/06 *Government of the French Community and Walloon Community v Government of the Flemish Community*, judgment of 1 April 2008, not yet reported, para 52.

the *Dassonville* ruling. The choice between the two alternative explanations is important to understand the scope of the Treaty both in order to determine the extent to which the *Keck* presumption is open to rebuttal and to assess the relationship between the remoteness doctrine and the *Keck* ruling.

In this respect, it has been argued that while at the beginning the almost mechanical application of the *Keck* ruling suggested that it was a policy decision, the fine-tuning of its application in more recent years suggests that it is simply a tool to tame the excesses inherent in the broad *Dassonville* formula. Thus, the flexible *ad hoc* approach to discrimination, together with the ease with which the Court excludes certain rules from the 'certain selling arrangements' category, suggests that *Keck* simply introduces a useful system of presumptions as to which rules are more likely to affect intra-Community trade. In this respect, the only certainty after *Keck* seems to be that Sunday trading rules fall outside the scope of Article 28 EC (much as they fall outside the scope of the other free movement provisions).

Thus *Keck*, far from introducing a rigid dichotomy where the test applied to assess the existence of a barrier to intra-Community trade depends on the type of rules at issue, simply introduces a useful and flexible system of presumptions. In this respect, if the crucial factor in the application of Article 28 EC is still the 'effect' on intra-Community trade, then there is a common rationale underlying the case law on remoteness and the *Keck* doctrine. However, the two still differ for two reasons. First of all, the remoteness doctrine applies only to non-trading rules; secondly, it is only in the case of these rules that the claimant has to establish causation. Only if such causation exists will there be a second stage in the investigation to ascertain whether the alleged barrier is a barrier falling within the scope of Article 28 EC. On the other hand, in relation to trading rules causation is presumed exactly because they regulate *trade* and therefore the focus is exclusively on the existence of a barrier. This rather theoretical difference reflects then another presumption, this time in relation to non-trading rules. Those rules, provided they are not discriminatory, do not affect intra-Community trade unless a precise link of causation can be established.[80] An example might be of use to illustrate this point. Take for instance rules on recovery of tax debt at issue in *Krantz*: those rules did not intend to regulate trade; while they might have had a spill-over effect on the ease with which commercial debt could be recovered, in themselves they did not affect trade. For this reason, it would fall upon the claimant to prove that there is a direct link of causation

[80] In this respect see also the ruling in *V Graf v Filzmoser Maschinenbau GmbH* (n 23), and below Section VII.

between the rule at issue, and their ability to enjoy the freedom granted by the Treaty. On the other hand, in relation to trading rules the causal effect is taken for granted and therefore even a purely potential effect on intra-Community trade is sufficient to trigger Article 28 EC. As a result, the trader does not need to prove a specific effect on her situation of the rules at issue. Consider for instance those cases in which the Member State unsuccessfully argued that rules of labelling might in certain instances not have a restrictive effect because of the need for the trader to modify the label to satisfy language requirements.[81] These rules are defined as barriers because they *potentially* affect intra-Community trade and there is no need for the claimant to demonstrate a *specific* effect on her situation. In relation to trading rules causation is presumed and does not need to be proven. On the other hand, in relation to non-trading rules a potential and undemonstrated effect is not enough: the trader must establish causation to bring her situation within the scope of the Treaty.[82]

This said, the rationale behind rules excluded pursuant to the application of the *Keck* presumptions and rules excluded because of the remoteness doctrine is the same: both rules do not have an effect on intra-Community trade relevant for the application of the Treaty. It seems therefore that *Keck* is less revolutionary than it might have appeared at first sight and the rigidity of the *Keck* formula is only apparent: what matters at the end is still whether the rules under scrutiny create a barrier to intra-Community trade. If they do not, they will benefit from the *Keck* exception; but if they do they will be scrutinised either through a broad interpretation of discrimination; or by a limitation of the scope of *Keck* itself.

[81] Case C-317/92 *Commission v Germany* (expiry dates) [1994] ECR I-2039; and to a certain extent Case C-217/99 *Commission v Belgium* (notification numbers) [2000] ECR I-10251.

[82] Seen from another perspective, it is difficult to envisage that the Commission would bring successful proceedings against a non-discriminatory non-trading rule (say a rule of procedure) without demonstrating a precise link between that rule and intra-Community trade.

VII THE OUTER LIMITS OF THE FREE MOVEMENT OF PERSONS[83]

The free movement of persons provisions catch, as well as directly and indirectly discriminatory rules, rules which hinder or discourage movement.[84] The notion of hindrance/discouragement is interpreted in a generous way;[85] and, the intra-Community element necessary to trigger the Treaty has been considerably relaxed.[86] However, notwithstanding this broad interpretation there appears to be *some* limit to the scope of the free movement of persons provisions. The doctrine of 'effect too uncertain and indirect' applies also to the free movement of persons; and in some other cases (notably tax cases, but also social security cases) the interpretation of the free movement provisions seems narrower and limited to an assessment of discrimination. We shall consider these situations in turn.

A The Doctrine of Effect too Uncertain and Indirect and the Ruling in *Deliège*

The rationale underpinning the doctrine of 'effect too uncertain and indirect' is the same regardless of the Treaty freedom invoked. As we have seen above, in order for the doctrine to apply the rules must be non-discriminatory; must not be intended to regulate intra-Community movement or the conditions for the exercise of the relevant Treaty freedom; and there must be no causal connection between the rule and the alleged barrier. Thus, for instance, in the above mentioned ruling of *Semeraro Casa Uno*,[87] the Court found that Sunday trading rules fell outside the scope of Article 43 EC since they applied in the same manner to all relevant traders; their purpose was not to regulate conditions concerning establishment; and their effect on freedom of establishment was too uncertain and indirect to be capable of hindering the Treaty freedom. Similarly, in *Graf* the Court found that in order for non-discriminatory rules to fall within the scope of Article 39 EC, an effect on access to the labour market was necessary.[88] On the facts, that was not the case since the effect of the rules under consideration on free movement depended on a

[83] The doctrine of effect too uncertain and indirect applies also to the free movement of capital; see Case C-282/04 *Commission v Netherlands* (Golden Shares) [2006] ECR I-9141, para 29.

[84] For example Case C-55/94 *Gebhard v Consiglio dell'Ordine degli Avvocati e Procuratori di Milano*[1995] ECR I-4165

[85] For example Case C-60/00 *Carpenter v Secretary of State for the Home Department* (n 3).

[86] For example Case C-35/00 *Freskot* [2003] ECR I-5263.

[87] Joined Cases C-418/93 etc *Semeraro Casa Uno et al* [1996] ECR I-2975, para 32.

[88] *V Graf v Filzmoser Maschinenbau GmbH*(n 23); the *Graf* ruling is probably the clearer indication to date concerning the scope of the free movement of workers, in that it clarifies

'future and hypothetical event' and was therefore too uncertain and indirect to fall within the scope of the Treaty. And, in *Coname*,[89] the Court indicated that a very modest economic interest in relation to a public contract might render Articles 49 and 43 EC inapplicable because undertakings located in other municipalities would have no interest in the contract at issue and therefore the effect of the situation on the Treaty freedoms would be too uncertain and indirect. The ruling in *Coname* is not as straightforward as it might appear since lack of transparency in the award of public contracts is considered to be indirectly discriminatory;[90] however, in theory indirectly discriminatory rules should not benefit form the 'effect to uncertain and indirect' doctrine. Should one not want to dismiss the reference to the remoteness doctrine as a non-conclusive obiter (in the case at issue the economic value of the contract was sufficiently high to trigger the Treaty), then the ruling might indicate the convergence of the 'effect too uncertain and indirect' doctrine into a *de minimis* assessment which however would sit at odds with the ruling in *TK-Heimdienst*, where out-of-state traders would also have had little if any interest in selling groceries door-to-door.

In any event, it should be noted that the doctrine of effect 'too uncertain and indirect' has been applied more seldom in the field of persons, and indeed it is open to debate as to whether it is of any real significance. In particular, it could be queried whether the standard of proof required in order to be able to challenge rules that do not regulate intra-Community movement or the conditions for the exercise of the relevant freedom is any higher than that required to challenge rules regulating movement. Here, consider that in the case of natural persons the factors that might deter movement need not necessarily be linked to the conditions on the exercise of an economic activity. Thus, for instance, the rights of family members might be much more important to the migrant citizen than the need to fulfil an administrative requirement in order to pursue an economic activity. It is not surprising therefore that in these cases there seems no need to prove causation, either because it is given for granted; or simply because the scope of the Treaty free movement of persons provisions is broader.

The other proviso that might exclude the application of the free movement of persons provisions is the '*Deliège* exception';[91] in that case the Court excluded the applicability of Article 49 EC to rules governing the selection of athletes for international tournaments on the grounds that,

that a non-discriminatory barrier, which does not have a specific effect on cross-border movement, is caught only insofar as it has an effect on market access.

[89] Case C-231/03 *Coname* [2005] ECR I-7287.

[90] See also Case C-458/03 *Parking Brixen* [2005] ECR I-8612.

[91] Joined Cases C-51/96 and C-191/97 *C Deliège v Ligue Francophone de Judo et Disciplines Associées ASBL et al* [2000] ECR I-2549.

even though those rules naturally determined a limitation in the number of participants, such a limitation was inherent in the conduct of international high-level sporting events. It is unclear whether the ruling is of relevance beyond the realm of sporting activities and to the author's knowledge it has not been applied again.[92] One could imagine however that a similar reasoning could be used to exclude the application of the free movement of persons provisions in relation to non-discriminatory taxation, to which we shall now turn.

B Non-discriminatory Taxation: A *Keck*-style or a *Deliège*-style Exception?

Article 90 EC prohibits discriminatory and protectionist taxation of foreign goods; otherwise it is for the Member States to decide on the level of taxation of goods within their territory with the possible (and so far theoretical) exception of taxation which is so high as to impede the free movement of goods.[93]

In relation to the free movement of persons there is no provision equivalent to Article 90 EC; for this reason, discriminatory/protectionist taxation falls squarely within the scope of the Treaty free movement provisions. While this fact did not give rise to any problem when the scope of those provisions was limited to a prohibition on discrimination, the matter changed slightly once the Court decided to broaden the scope of the Treaty so as to include all rules which hindered or discouraged movement. It is obvious that high taxation might create a deterrent to movement; and yet, it is also obvious that the decision as to the level of taxation is, by its very nature, a political choice (possibly the 'most' political choice) and that therefore it should not be subject to the proportionality assessment by the Court of Justice.[94] It is therefore not surprising that overall the Court has not engaged in the review of the level of taxation and, indeed, it has made clear that the rights granted by the Treaty do not entail the guarantee that

[92] Although it could be argued that the reasoning in *Deliège* is reminiscent of pre-*Keck* case law on rules the effect of which did not exceed the effects *intrinsic* in trade rules; eg Case 75/81 *JHT Blegsen v Belgium* [1982] ECR 1211

[93] Case C-383/01 *De Danske Billimportører* [2003] ECR I-6065, para 40; the Court clarified that the non applicability of Art 90 EC on discriminatory taxation, does not automatically trigger Art 28 EC, see Joined Cases C-34/01 to C-38/01 *Enirisorse Spa* [2003] ECR I-14243.

[94] See also S Kingston, 'The Boundaries of Sovereignty: the ECJ's Controversial Role Applying Internal Market Law to Direct Tax Measures' (2006–7) 9 *Cambridge Yearbook of European Legal Studies*, 287; and C Barnard 'European Union Law' (2007) *All England Annual Review*, 2008, Lexis Nexis, 179; J Snell, 'Non-discriminatory tax obstacles in Community law' (2007) 56 *ICLQ* 339.

movement will be neutral from a fiscal viewpoint.[95] Rather, the bulk of the case law relating to taxation has focused on the discriminatory effect of the rules governing the way taxation is levied, especially in relation to corporate entities.[96] However, in relation to Article 49 EC, the Court maintains a more ambiguous position which is slightly at odds with what said above. In *De Coster*,[97] the Court qualified a heavy tax on TV satellite dishes as a non-discriminatory obstacle to the free movement of services, thus suggesting that tax rules might be caught by the Treaty regardless of discrimination, and similar dicta can be found in the later cases of *Viacom Outdoor II* and *Mobistar*.[98]

This said, it is open to debate whether this case law is indicative of a change of approach: in *De Coster* the Court did in any event assess the discriminatory effects of the tax in question by pointing out that the tax affected non-domestic broadcasters more than domestic ones, since the latter had unlimited access to the cable network, while the former necessarily had to rely on satellite transmission. In *Viacom Outdoor II* the Court held that a tax on billboard advertising was not caught by Article 49 EC since it was non-discriminatory and its amount was fixed at a level to be considered modest in relation to the value of the services provided. In *Mobistar*, the Court excluded that a non-discriminatory tax on masts and pylon could fall within the scope of the Treaty free movement of services provisions if its only effect was to increase the cost of the service in question.[99] Indeed, some authors have argued that *Viacom Outdoor II* and

[95] Case C-365/02 *Lindorfs* [2004] ECR I-7183, para 34 and see also Case C-403/03 *Schempp* [2005] ECR I-6421. Those cases were decided in relation to Art 18 EC (Union citizenship), but exactly the same approach has been adopted in relation to Art 39 EC in Case C-387/01 *Weigel* [2004] ECR I-9445, para 55.

[96] This is not to say that such case law is not problematic: tax rules are inherently territorial and therefore almost always entail a difference in treatment between residents and non-residents. Thus, a careful assessment of comparability is necessary to ascertain whether the situation of the resident and non-resident are comparable before proceeding to a finding of indirect discrimination and an assessment of the justifications. However, in several rulings the Court has given comparability for granted therefore proceeding directly to the justifications stage; see J Snell, 'Non-discriminatory tax obstacles in Community law' (2007) 56 *ICLQ* 339, at 349 and ff; for a slightly different perspective see S Kingston, 'The Boundaries of Sovereignty: the ECJ's Controversial Role Applying Internal Market Law to Direct Tax Measures' (2006–7) 9 *Cambridge Yearbook of European Legal Studies*, 287; and C Barnard 'European Union Law' (2007) *All England Annual Review*, 2008, Lexis Nexis, 179; Kingston and Barnard point out that a more thorough approach to comparability might be emerging; see, eg Case C-374/04 *Test Claimants in Class IV of the ACT Group Litigation v Commissioners of Inland Revenue* [2006] ECR I-11673, especially para 46.

[97] Case C-17/00 *De Coster* [2001] ECR I-9445; and see also Case C-43/97 *Sandoz* [1999] ECR I-7041 where the very existence of a tax has been defined as an obstacle to the free movement of capital (albeit justified for the part that was not discriminatory) [2005] ECR I-1167.

[98] Case C-134/00 *Viacom Outdoor Srl II* [2005] ECR I-1167, para 36; Joined Cases C-544 and C-545/03 *Mobistar* [2005] ECR I-7723, para 28.

[99] Joined Cases C-544 and C-545/03 *Mobistar* [2005] ECR I-7723, especially para 31.

Mobistar, far from supporting the view of an expansion of the scope of Article 49 EC in the field of non-discriminatory taxation, might signal a retreat so that a more general *Keck*-style exception is being introduced in relation to the free movement of persons.[100] While the present author is not so optimistic about the effect of this case law, it is argued that, despite the general dicta of the Court as to the fact that non-discriminatory taxation might be caught by the Treaty provisions on the free movement of services,[101] taxation de facto if not de jure falls within the scope of the Treaty only in so far as it is directly or indirectly discriminatory. Furthermore, the same can be said in relation to social security rules where, with a few exceptions, the level of social security contribution will not be scrutinised unless there is evidence of discrimination on grounds of nationality or movement.[102]

If that is the case, there are two possible explanations which could provide a justification for the exclusion of certain rules from the scope of the free movement of persons provisions.[103] First, it could be argued that this case law introduces a Keck-style exception.[104] Thus if, in the traditional reading of *Keck*, the latter excludes a certain type of rules (selling arrangements) from the scope of Article 28 EC unless discrimination can be proven or inferred from the rules under scrutiny, a similar rationale might apply to tax rules in the context of the free movement of persons. A policy decision has been made so as to disregard the possible effect on intra-Community movement of tax rules in so far as they determine, in a non-discriminatory way, the level of taxation. Since it is for the Member State to decide upon the level of taxation, the Court is not willing to

[100] See J Meulman and H de Waele, 'A Retreat from Säger? Servicing or Fine-Tuning the Application of Article 49 EC' (2006) 33 *Legal Issues of Economic Integration* 207.

[101] As mentioned above there is the theoretical possibility that if taxation is fixed at such a high level so as to act as a total barrier to the Treaty freedoms it might come under the Court's scrutiny; see n 92 above.

[102] See, eg Case C-18/95 *Terhoeve* [1999] ECR I-345; the extent to which social security rules can be applied to migrant workers depends on whether the worker gains an advantage from affiliation to the social security scheme. When that is not the case the rules are considered indirectly discriminatory.

[103] I have argued elsewhere that if the free movement provisions are understood as granting a right to exercise an economic activity in another Member State then the exclusion of non-discriminatory tax rules from their scope is entirely consistent since non-discriminatory tax rules do not have an effect on the right to exercise an economic activity (albeit they might have an effect on the willingness to do so because of their effect on profit margins); see E Spaventa, *Free Movement of Persons in the European Union—Barriers to Movement in their Constitutional Context* (Amsterdam, Kluwer Law International, 2007).

[104] Some authors have explored the desirability of a more general *Keck*-style exemption, ie not only in relation to tax rules; eg WH Roth, 'The European Court of Justice's Case Law on Freedom to Provide Services: Is *Keck* Relevant?' and JL Da Cruiz Villaça 'On the Application of *Keck* in the Fielf of Free Provision of Services' both in M Andenas and WH Roth (eds) *Services and Free Movement in EU Law* (Oxford, Oxford University Press, 2002); J Meulman and H de Waele, 'A Retreat from Säger? Servicing or Fine-Tuning the Application of Article 49 EC' (2006) 33 *Legal Issues of Economic Integration* 207.

syndicate that choice and therefore excludes such rules from the scope of the Treaty unless discrimination can be proven.

Secondly, it could be argued that the more confined application of the Treaty free movement provisions is justified by a *Deliège* line of reasoning. In this respect, tax rules, by definition, have an impact on the profitability of business; and such an impact is inherent in the very nature of tax rules which are aimed at imposing charges on economic operators to finance public expenditure. In the same way as it is unconceivable to have international tournaments without having rules governing the selection of participants to such competitions, it is unconceivable to have taxation which would not determine expenditure on those who are subject to it. Thus, those rules cannot be considered as a barrier because their effect on intra-Community movement is *inherent* in their aim, an aim which is a priori compatible with Community law.

The *Déliège* line of reasoning differs then from the *Keck*-style reasoning. The latter is a policy decision: tax rules are barriers to intra-Community movement but they are best left to the Member States. The *Déliège* line of reasoning, on the other hand, is conceptual: when the alleged barrier coincides with the very purpose of the rules—be it selecting athletes, or raising funds for the public purse—then, provided the aim in itself is legitimate, any effect that the rule might have on movement is inherent in the rules at issue and therefore cannot be scrutinised. The *Keck*-style reasoning leaves it open for the Court to change its policy; the *Déliège* reasoning defines the boundaries of the free movement provisions and acknowledges that facing a disadvantage, a loss in profit, is not enough to claim that a barrier to intra-Community movement was raised.

VIII CONCLUSIONS

The co-existence of different strands of case law, together with the use of different hermeneutic tools in relation to the same provisions, makes it extremely difficult to identify clear boundaries for the Treaty free movement provisions. Indeed, when the cases are closely scrutinised one might be excused for feeling a slight sense of desperation as to the chaotic picture arising from the Court's jurisprudence. The number of variables influencing the outcome of a case, as well as reasoning which is at times erratic, makes the scholar's job all the more difficult. In this respect, one should accept that it will never be possible to provide an umbrella under which *all* cases can sit comfortably. Furthermore, one should always be aware that the rationale underpinning the interpretation of the free movement provisions is fluid: it evolves as our perception of the problems and aims of the internal market changes with time. This is particularly visible in relation to the free movement of goods. In this respect, it should never be forgotten that the *Keck* ruling was a reaction to a specific problem—that of an excessively broad interpretation of Article 28 EC.

It is, therefore, not surprising that in the aftermath of the *Keck* ruling the main hermeneutic effort was directed at providing a clearer demarcation of the Treaty, so as to relocate the balancing exercise inherent in the proportionality assessment demanded by the mandatory requirements doctrine in the hands of national regulators. The mechanical application of *Keck* can then be properly understood as a policy decision aimed at correcting the imbalances created by the *Sunday trading* interpretation. However, with time, the application of *Keck* becomes more nuanced and the focus seems to shift back to the assessment of the effect on intra-Community trade of the rules under scrutiny. In this way, the rigid system of presumptions which characterised the *Keck* ruling evolves into a flexible system of presumptions which is still useful but not conclusive. Indeed, it could be noted that should one leave aside the *Sunday trading* incident, the pre-*Keck* case law and the post-*Keck* case law are strikingly similar.

In relation to the free movement of persons, and contrary to expectations, it is easier to identify the outer boundaries. Thus, the broader interpretation given to those provisions, as controversial as this might be, gives rise to a jurisprudence which is more internally consistent. The applicability of the Treaty freedoms is excluded only in relation to a handful of situations where it is impossible to establish a causal effect between rule and alleged barrier. And, in cases where the effect of the rule complained about, an effect which is a priori deemed legitimate in the Community system, is inherent in the very aim that the rule seeks to pursue. Taxes inherently inconvenience tax payers: it would be foolhardy to interpret such an inconvenience as a barrier to movement.

12

Derogations, Justifications and the Four Freedoms: Is State Interest Really Protected?

CATHERINE BARNARD

I INTRODUCTION

THE ROLE OF justifications is well known. In the give and take world of *Cassis de Dijon*,[1] justifications are the 'give', the sugar coating for the Member States on what at times can be the bitter pill of market integration. In recent years their number has proliferated as a direct response to the increasingly expansive and dynamic use of the 'restrictions' based approach to free movement. We also know that justifications were introduced to supplement the express derogations found in the Treaty. They, too, were intended to provide room for states to defend crucial national interests.

Yet, as we also know, the derogations and justifications are not necessarily what they seem. While they appear to give states considerable room for manoeuvre and an obvious way of preserving national regulatory autonomy, in practice the Court often says that, on the facts of a particular case, the Member State has failed to make out a justification. And, even where it accepts that the derogation/justification might be made out, the Court has deployed a variety of strategies to limit the possibility of state success. In particular, it has increasingly hemmed the derogations/justifications in with limitations—proportionality, fundamental rights, effective judicial protection, legal certainty—thereby further drawing the teeth on the effective use of derogations/justifications by the Member States. This has marked a significant shift in the balance of power between the European Union (EU) and the Member States.

[1] Case 120/78 *Rewe Zentrale v Bundesmonopolverwaltung für Branntwein* [1979] ECR 649.

For a Court inspired by the goal of market integration, its stance can easily be understood: every derogation/justification successfully invoked by a Member State creates a barrier for traders/migrants/service providers from the other 26 states.[2] Yet, for the defendant Member State, every failed justification is another nail in the coffin of its legislative autonomy and, more generally, for the diversity of national rules. Invariably, it also means a move to deregulation since every unjustified national rule is set aside and only rarely is such a rule reintroduced at the European level. And it may be for this reason that there are signs that national courts are fighting a rearguard action to protect national regulation. If national courts are indeed doing this, then the division of responsibility between the European Court of Justice (ECJ) and the national courts in the context of Article 234 references becomes central to the market integration v maintenance of national regulatory autonomy debate: which court finally decides whether the national rules can be justified on the facts and whether those national rules satisfy the various limitations (proportionality, fundamental rights and so on) determines whether the national rule will be upheld or stuck down. We consider this argument below (Section V). First, however, we shall examine the derogations contained in the Treaty as well as the justifications recognised by the Court (Section II), and the limitations imposed by the Court on their use (Section III). We then examine how the Court has used the derogations/justifications and the proportionality principle over the years, taking as a snapshot cases decided in 1984, 1994 and 2004 (Section IV).

We begin by looking at the substance of the derogations and justifications.

II THE EXPRESS DEROGATIONS AND THE PUBLIC INTEREST JUSTIFICATIONS

A Introduction

According to the orthodoxy, the (general) express derogations are available in respect of any breach of Community law (refusal of entry as well as directly, indirectly and non-discriminatory measures which hinder market access and any measures which create an obstacle to, or restrict, free movement in some way). By contrast, indirectly discriminatory and non-discriminatory measures which hinder free movement, together with measures which restrict free movement or prevent or impede market access, can be saved not only by the express derogations but also by a broader

[2] Or 29 states if the EEA states are included.

category of objective justifications/public interest requirements.[3] While in the context of free movement of workers[4] the language of objective justification is used, in respect of establishment, services and capital, the Court tends to talk about justifications in the 'public' or 'general' interest or 'imperative requirements'.[5] These terms are the functional equivalent of 'objective justifications',[6] which in turn are the persons' equivalent to 'mandatory requirements' in the field of goods.[7] In all cases the Court recognises that there exist certain national interests which are worthy of protection[8] and should take precedence over the free movement provisions.

B The Express Derogations

The express derogations to the four freedoms are so well known that the subject-matter and case law scarcely needs repetition.[9] In summary, each of the main Treaty provisions contains its own set of derogations: the derogations to Articles 28 and 29 on the free movement of goods can be found in Article 30, to the free movement of workers in Article 39(3), to freedom of establishment and free movement of services in Articles 46 and 55, and to free movement of capital in Article 58. There are, of course, differences between the various grounds: the list of derogations for goods is longer than for persons (for example, Article 30 includes public morality and the protection of national treasures possessing artistic, historic or archaeological value), while the free movement of persons contains a specific provision for employment in the public service. The detail of the derogations to freedom of movement of natural persons, including students and persons of independent means, are more fully articulated by the

[3] In some areas, particularly services, there are signs that the Court is prepared to allow directly discriminatory rules to be objectively justified: Joined Cases C-338/04 etc *Placanica* [2007] ECR I-1891.

[4] Case C-237/94 *O'Flynn v Adjudication Officer* [1996] ECR I-2617, para 19.

[5] Case C-76/90 *Säger v Dennemeyer & Co Ltd* [1991] ECR I-4221, para 15; Case C-55/94 *Gebhard* [1996] ECR I-4165, para 37.

[6] This view is supported by the workers case, Case C-195/98 *Österreicher Gewerkschaftsbund v Republik Österreich* [2000] ECR I-10497, para 45, where the Court reported that the Austrian government contends that the restrictions on free movement are '*justified* by overriding reasons of public interest and are consistent with the principle of proportionality', and the services case, Case C-118/96 *Safir v Skattemyndigheten i Dalarnas Län* [1998] ECR I-1897, para 22: 'Article [49] of the Treaty precludes the application of any national legislation which, without objective justification, impedes a provider of services from actually exercising the freedom to provide them'.

[7] In the competition field, see A Albors-LLorens, 'The Role of Objective Justification and Efficiencies in the Application of Article 82 EC' (2007) 44 *CML Rev* 1727.

[8] See Tesauro AG in Case C-118/96 *Safir* [1998] ECR I-1897, para 29. In the context of social rights, see S Giubboni, *Social Rights and Market Freedom in the European Constitution: A Labour Law Perspective* (Cambridge, Cambridge University Press, 2006)

[9] For further detail see C Barnard, *The Substantive Law of the EU: the Four Freedoms* (Oxford, Oxford University Press, 2007), ch 16.

Citizens' Rights Directive 2004/38. Further, while the derogations for goods and persons are exhaustive, the derogations to free movement of capital are potentially open-ended. Yet, at root, certain key principles apply to all the derogations, as the Court noted in *Church of Scientology*[10] where it said that:

— derogations from the fundamental principle of free movement had to be interpreted strictly, so that their scope could not be determined unilaterally by each Member State without any control by the Community institutions;[11]
— derogations could not be misapplied so as, in fact, to serve purely economic ends;[12]
— any person affected by a restrictive measure based on such a derogation had to have access to legal redress;[13] and
— derogations had to be read subject to proportionality[14] and fundamental human rights.[15]

C The Public Interest Justifications

(i) The Public Interest Justifications Recognised by the Court

Given the narrowness of the express derogations and increasing breadth of the scope of Community law, the judicially developed justifications have provided a lifebelt to the Member States. In *Gebhard*,[16] a case on freedom of establishment, the Court elaborated on the requirements necessary for the national rule to satisfy the test of justification. It said that national measures liable to hinder or make less attractive the exercise of fundamental freedoms guaranteed by the Treaty had to fulfil four conditions in order not to breach (in that case) Article 43, namely:

— they had to be applied in a non-discriminatory manner;
— they had to be justified by imperative requirements in the general interest;
— they had to be suitable for securing the attainment of the objective which they pursued; and

[10] Case C-54/99 *Association Eglise de Scientologie de Paris v The Prime Minister* [2000] ECR I-1335, paras 17–18.
[11] Citing Case 36/75 *Rutili v Minister for the Interior* [1975] ECR 1219, paras 26 and 27.
[12] *Ibid*, para 30.
[13] Case 222/86 *Unectef v Heylens and Others* [1987] ECR 4097, paras 14 and 15.
[14] Case 118/75 *Watson and Belmann* [1976] ECR 1185, para 21.
[15] Case C-60/00 *Mary Carpenter v Secretary of State for the Home Department* [2002] ECR I-6279, paras 40–1.
[16] Case C-55/94 [1995] ECR I-4165.

— they could not go beyond what was necessary to attain it.[17]

The operative part of the judgment in *Gebhard* makes clear that this test also applies to the free movement of workers and services.[18]

The Court has recognised a number of public interest grounds. Chalmers et al loosely divide these into four headings.[19] The first concerns essentially the protection of third parties. This heading includes justifications such as:

- guaranteeing the quality of skilled trade work and protecting those who have commissioned such work;[20]
- professional rules intended to protect the recipients of a service;[21]
- protection of intellectual property;[22]
- protection of workers;[23]
- consumer protection;[24]
- social protection of workers in respect of, for example, social security provision;[25]
- protection of children;[26]
- protection of the environment;[27]
- promoting sustainable settlement in a designated area (essentially a regional policy goal) where there has been a decline in population due to harsh climate, vast distances and sparse population;[28]

[17] Para 37.

[18] Para 6.

[19] See also D Chalmers, C Hadjiemmanuil, G Monti and A Tomkins, *EU Law* (Cambridge, Cambridge University Press, 2006), 833–4 on which this section draws.

[20] Case C-58/98 *Josef Corsten* [2000] ECR I-7919, para 38.

[21] Joined Cases 110 and 111/78 *Ministère public v Willy van Wesemael and others* [1979] ECR 35, para 28. In Case C-3/95 *Reisebüro Broede v Sandker* [1996] ECR I 6511, para 38, the Court spelled out this justification more fully: 'the application of professional rules to lawyers, in particular those relating to organisation, qualifications, professional ethics, supervision and liability, ensures that the ultimate consumers of legal services and the sound administration of justice are provided with the necessary guarantees in relation to integrity and experience'.

[22] Case 62/79 *Coditel* [1980] ECR 881 para 15.

[23] Case 279/80 *Criminal Proceedings against Webb* [1981] ECR 3305, para 19; Joined Cases 62–63/81 *Seco v EVI* [1982] ECR 223, para 14; Case C-113/89 *Rush Portuguesa* [1990] ECR I-1417, para 18.

[24] Case 220/83 *Commission v France (Co-insurance)* [1986] ECR 3663, para 20; Case 252/83 *Commission v Denmark (Co-insurance)* [1986] ECR 3713, para 20; Case 205/84 *Commission v Germany (Insurance)* [1986] ECR 3755, para 30; Case 206/84 *Commission v Ireland (Co-insurance)* [1986] ECR 3817, para 20; Case C-180/89 *Commission v Italy (tourist guides)* [1991] ECR I-709, para 20.

[25] Case C-255/04 *Commission v France* [2006] ECR I-5251, para 47.

[26] Case C-244/06 *Dynamic Medien Vertrieb GmbH v Avides Media AG* [2008] ECR I-000, para 42.

[27] Case C-17/00 *François De Coster v Collège des bourgmestre et échevins de Watermael-Boitsfort* [2001] ECR I-9445, paras 36–7; Joined Cases C-151/04 and C-152/04 *Nadin* [2005] ECR I-11203, para 52

[28] Case E-3/05 *EFTA Surveillance Authority v Norway*, judgment of 3 May 2006, para 57.

— road safety;[29] and
— ensuring the adequacy of regular maritime services to, from and between islands.[30]

A second group concerns civil liberties (that is ensuring that the economic freedoms do not compromise the political values which are central to protecting human dignity, autonomy and equality) such as the protection of human dignity[31] or freedom of expression and assembly.[32]

A third group concerns essentially the need to prevent distortions in the market:

— ensuring the balance between sports clubs;[33]
— prevention of social dumping[34] or unfair competition;[35]
— prevention of abuse of free movement of services;[36]
— avoiding disturbances on the labour market;[37] and
— combating illegal employment.[38]

A fourth group relates to the 'preservation of public order' that is 'to supply services that are necessary for the government of its territory'. As Chalmers et al point out, here the Court is not so much concerned to protect certain values or interests per se but, rather, it aims to safeguard the machinery of government that enables such protection. These justifications are particularly intended to be invoked by the state when it is a defendant, not by other types of defendant (for example, trade unions or regulatory bodies). The list of 'public order' justifications includes the *Schindler*[39] justifications for bans on lotteries (for example, preventing gambling and avoiding the lottery from becoming the source of private profit; avoiding the risk of crime or fraud; avoiding the risk of incitement to spend, with damaging individual and social consequences) as elaborated in the subsequent gambling cases to include 'moral, religious and cultural factors'.[40] In

[29] Case C-55/93 *Criminal Proceedings against van Schaik* [1994] ECR I-4837; Joined Cases C-151/04 and C-152/04 *Nadin* [2005] ECR I-11203, para 49

[30] Case C-205/99 *Analir v Administración General del Estado* [2001] ECR I-1271, para 27.

[31] Case C-36/02 *Omega* [2004] ECR I-9609.

[32] See the goods case Case C-112/00 *Schmidberger* [2003] ECR I-5659. The Court tentatively also recognised the right to accommodation in Case C-345/05 *Commission v Portugal (transfer of property)* [2006] ECR I-10633, paras 31.

[33] Case C-415/93 *Bosman* [1995] ECR I-4921, para 106; Case C-176/96 *Lehtonen v FRSB* [2000] ECR I-2681, para 54.

[34] Case C-244/04 *Commission v Germany* [2006] ECR I-885, para 61.

[35] Case C-60/03 *Wolff & Müller v Pereira Félix* [2004] ECR I-9553, para 41.

[36] Case C-244/04 *Commission v Germany* [2006] ECR I-885, para 38.

[37] Case C-445/03 *Commission v Luxembourg* [2004] ECR I-10191, para 38.

[38] Case C-255/04 *Commission v France* [2006] ECR I-5251, para 52.

[39] Case C-275/92 [1994] ECR I-1039, para 60. See also Case C-124/97 *Läärä v Kihlakunnansyyttäjä* [1999] ECR I-6067.

[40] Case C-243/01 *Gambelli* [2003] ECR I-13031, para 63.

these sorts of cases the Court offers states a wide scope for discretion in areas deemed sensitive ideologically or associated with particular risks.[41]

Other situations also fall under the 'preservation of public order' heading, including:

— preserving the systems of administration of justice;[42]
— the coherence of a scheme of taxation;[43]
— the effectiveness of fiscal supervision;[44]
— the need to ensure the effective collection of income tax,[45] and preventing wholly artificial arrangements aimed solely at escaping national tax normally due;[46]
— preserving the financial balance of a social security scheme;[47]
— preventing fraud on the social security system;[48]
— controlling costs, and preventing wastage of financial, technical, and human resources;[49]
— the obligation of solidarity (on the facts of the case between Dutch civilian war victims and the rest of the population of the Netherlands);[50]
— conservation of the national historic and artistic heritage;[51]
— turning to account the archaeological, historical, and artistic heritage of a country and the widest possible dissemination of knowledge of the artistic and cultural heritage of a country;[52] and
— cultural policy.[53]

[41] AG in Case C-145/88 *Torfaen Borough Council v B & Q plc* [1989] ECR 3851, para 102.

[42] Case C-3/95 *Reisebüro Broede v Sandker* [1996] ECR I-611.

[43] Case C-204/90 *Bachmann v Belgian State* [1992] ECR I-249; Case C-300/90 *Commission v Belgium* [1992] ECR I-305; Case C-294/97 *Eurowings Luftverkehrs AG v Finanzamt Dortmund-Unna* [1999] ECR I-7447, para 19.

[44] Case C-55/98 *Skatteministeriet v Bent Vestergaard* [1999] ECR I-7641, para 23. However, a general presumption of tax avoidance/tax fraud is not sufficient to justify a fiscal measure which compromises the objectives of the Treaty: Case C-433/04 *Commission v Belgium* [2006] ECR I-10653, para 35.

[45] Case C-290/04 *FKP Scorpio Konzertproduktionen GmbH v Finanzamt Hamburg-Eimsbüttel* [2006] ECR I-9461, para 35.

[46] Case C-196/04 *Cadbury's Schweppes v Commissioners of the Inland Revenue* [2006] ECR I-7995, para 51.

[47] Case C-158/96 *Kohll* [1998] ECR I-1931, para 41.

[48] Case C-406/04 *De Cuyper v Office national de l'emploi* [2006] ECR I-6947, para 41.

[49] Case C-157/99 *Geraets-Smits and Peerbooms* [2001] ECR I-5473, paras 78–9.

[50] Case C-192/05 *Tas-Hagen v Raadskamer WUBO van de Pensioen- en Uitkeringsrad* [2006] ECR I-10451, paras 34–5.

[51] Case C-180/89 *Commission v Italy* [1991] ECR I-709, para 20.

[52] Case C-154/89 *Commission v France* [1991] ECR I-659, para 17; Case C-198/89 *Commission v Greece* [1991] ECR I-727, para 21.

[53] Case C-288/89 *Gouda* [1991] ECR I-4007, paras 22–3; Case C-353/89 *Commission v Netherlands* [1991] ECR I-4069 and Case C-23/93 *TV10* [1994] ECR I-4795.

The third and fourth category of justifications at times come close to the very type of economic justifications which the Court has rejected in other cases[54] including those where the defendant state has unsuccessfully argued that the national measure is necessary to protect tax revenue[55] and thus the national exchequer.[56]

(ii) Closer Scrutiny of the Justifications offered in Particular Cases

The breadth of the justifications outlined above suggests that Member States can be reassured that their national interests—and their freedom to regulate in such areas[57]—is safe in the Court's hands. However, this reassurance depends on the extent to which the ECJ is actually prepared to accept the justification invoked or whether it merely pays lip-service to the existence of the justification but then finds, on the facts, that the justification does not apply, due to the absence of supporting evidence,[58] or that there is no link between the national measures and the justification invoked.[59] In recent years, the Court has shown an increasing willingness to scrutinise the substance of the justifications raised by the Member States. Two cases from the field of labour law demonstrate this most clearly.

The first is *Viking*[60] which concerned a Finnish company wanting to reflag its vessel, the *Rosella*, under the Estonian flag so that it could man the ship with an Estonian crew to be paid considerably less than the existing Finnish crew. The International Transport Workers' Federation (ITF) told its affiliates to boycott the *Rosella* and to take other solidarity industrial action. Viking therefore sought an injunction in the English High Court, restraining the ITF and the Finnish Seaman's Union (FSU), now also threatening strike action, from breaching Article 43 EC on freedom of establishment. The Court found that the collective action constituted a

[54] Even outside the economic justifications the Court has not been prepared to extend the list indefinitely: eg, Case C-18/95 *Terhoeve* [1999] ECR I-345, para 45, where the Court held that considerations of a purely administrative nature could not make lawful a restriction on the free movement of persons.

[55] Case C-464/02 *Commission v Denmark (company vehicles)* [2005] ECR I-7929, para 45, citing the free movement of capital decision Case C-319/02 *Manninen* [2004] ECR I-7477, para 49.

[56] Case C-109/04 *Kranemann v Land Nordrhein-Westfalen* [2005] ECR I-2421.

[57] *Cf* G Davies, 'Can Selling Arrangements be Harmonised?' (2005) 30 *EL Rev* 370.

[58] Case C-319/06 *Commission v Luxembourg*, judgment of 19 June 2008. para. 51 'It must be remembered that the reasons which may be invoked by a Member State in order to justify a derogation from the principle of freedom to provide services must be accompanied by appropriate evidence or by an analysis of the expediency and proportionality of the restrictive measure adopted by that state, and precise evidence enabling its arguments to be substantiated'

[59] Case C-243/01 *Gambelli* [2003] ECR I-13031, para 63.

[60] Case C-438/05 *Viking Line ABP v The International Transport Workers' Federation, the Finnish Seaman's Union* [2007] ECR I-10779.

restriction on free movement and so breached Article 43. On justification, the Court noted that the right to take collective action for the protection of workers was an overriding reason of public interest provided that jobs or conditions of employment were jeopardised or under serious threat.[61] On the facts, the Court suggested this was unlikely because Viking had given an undertaking that no Finnish workers would be made redundant and so it was unlikely that the justification would be made out. Since the case was subsequently settled, we shall never know the British Court of Appeal's view on this point.

The second case is *Laval*.[62] Laval, a Latvian company, won a contract to refurbish a school in Sweden using its own Latvian workers who earned about 40 per cent less than comparable Swedish workers. The Swedish construction union wanted Laval to apply the Swedish collective agreement but Laval refused, in part because the collective agreement was unclear as to how much Laval would have to pay its workers. There followed a union picket at the school site, a blockade by construction workers, and sympathy industrial action by the electricians unions. The Court said this industrial action also breached Article 49. On justification, it recognised the right to take collective action for the protection of Swedish workers 'against possible social dumping' but found, on the facts, that using collective action to force Laval to sign a collective agreement whose content on central matters such as pay was unclear, could not be justified.

In the past a lot of this analysis might have been conducted through the suitability limb of the proportionality review (see below).[63] Increasingly however, national legislation is being considered—and rejected—at the earlier justification stage, thereby (as in *Laval*) dispensing with the need to consider the proportionality of the rule. This change in approach may be explained by the fact that, in the context of Article 234 references at least, the Court feels on stronger ground to express its views on justification rather than on proportionality which should still be a matter for the national courts to decide. This argument will be considered further below.

[61] This comes close to the sort of economic justifications that the Court has rejected in the context of a state defendant.

[62] Case C-341/05 *Laval un Partneri Ltd v Svenska Byggnadsarbetareförbundet* [2007] ECR I-11767.

[63] For good measure in Case C-225/04 *Comission v France Performing Artists* [2006] ECR I-5251 the Court, having dismissed the French argument that its rules were justified on the grounds of combating concealed employment, added 'the establishment of a system or ex post facto control, together with deterrent penalties to prevent and identify individual instances of the use of bogus amateur or unpaid status, would suffice to combat concealed employment effectively' (para 53). This sounds rather like a proportionality review.

III THE LIMITS ON THE DEROGATIONS AND JUSTIFICATIONS

Even if the court (ECJ or national court) finds that a particular justification has been made out on the facts, the Court of Justice requires that the national rule be scrutinised for its proportionality, its compatibility with fundamental human rights, its legal certainty and its respect of principles of good governance. Each hurdle is a fairly stiff one to jump; collectively they may be insurmountable for a state which has not carefully thought through its law and policy.

A Proportionality

(i) The Substance of the Proportionality Principle

Any justification put forward by the Member State must satisfy the test of proportionality. The principle of proportionality comprises essentially two tests: a test of suitability and a test of necessity.[64] As Tridimas explains,[65] the first (suitability) refers to the relationship between the means and the ends: the means employed by the test must be suitable (or adequate or proportionate). The second test (necessity) is one of weighing competing interests: the Court assesses the adverse consequences that the measure has on an interest worthy of legal protection and determines whether those consequences are justified in view of the importance of the objective pursued. Sometimes this second limb is viewed as having two distinct elements: whether there are other less restrictive means of producing the same result and, even if there are no less restrictive means, the measure does not have an excessive effect on the applicant's interests.[66]

Generally, when the Court is considering the proportionality of national rules it applies the principle strictly. This can be seen in *Bosman*[67] where the Court said that the transfer fee rules were not an adequate means of maintaining financial and competitive balance in the world of football because they neither precluded the richest clubs from securing the services of the best players nor did they prevent the availability of financial resources from being a decisive factor in competitive sport. It also said that

[64] *Cf* P Craig, *EU Administrative Law* (Oxford, Oxford University Press, 2006), 670 who notes that when the applicant contests the legality of a measure by arguing that the burden placed on it by the measure is disproportionate to the benefits secured, the Court will consider a third limb of the test namely the 'stricto sensu' proportionality enquiry.

[65] T Tridimas, 'Proportionality in Community Law: Searching for the Appropriate Standard of Scrutiny', in E Ellis (ed), *The Principle of Proportionality in the Laws of Europe* (Oxford, Hart Publishing, 1999), 68.

[66] See Craig above n 55.

[67] Case C-415/93 *Union Royale Belge des Sociétés de Football Association ASBL v Bosman* [1995] ECR I-4921.

the prospect of receiving transfer fees was neither a decisive factor in encouraging recruitment and training of young players nor an adequate means of financing such activities. For these reasons the Court rejected football's arguments on the basis of suitability. For good measure, it also suggested that the transfer fee rules went beyond what was necessary to attain the objectives. Referring to Advocate General Lenz's opinion, the Court accepted that the same aims could be achieved at least as efficiently by other means which did not impede freedom of movement of workers.[68]

A strict application of the proportionality principle has also meant that consumer protection/public health protection, two of the most frequently invoked justifications in the field of goods, have often not been successful on the facts.[69] In particular, the Court has seen labelling as the cure for many ills, as the *Beer Purity*[70] case shows. According to the German *Biersteuergestez*, the name '*Bier*' could be used for products brewed with only malted barley, hops, yeast and water. The German government attempted to justify restricting the name '*Bier*' on the ground of consumer protection: since Germans linked the name '*Bier*' to products manufactured with only the ingredients listed in the *Biersteuergesetz* they might be misled if the name was applied to products containing other ingredients. The Court rejected these arguments, saying that consumers could be protected 'by means which do not prevent the importation of products which have been lawfully manufactured and marketed in other Member States and, in particular, by the compulsory affixing of suitable labels giving the nature of the product sold'.[71] The Court noted that these labels could even be attached to the casks or the beer taps when beers were sold in draught.[72]

Even in areas where the Court has been generous in the past it has taken an increasingly strict approach to proportionality. This can be seen in the gambling cases following *Schindler*.[73] In that case, the Court did not subject the various justifications put forward by the UK (about the dangers

[68] Para 110.

[69] Unberath and Johnston note in their survey (H Unberath and A Johnston, 'The Double-headed Approach of the ECJ concerning Consumer Protection' (2007) 44 *CML Rev* 1237) that 'To our knowledge, in all but one case [Case C-366/04 *Schwarz v Bürgermeister der Landeshauptstadt Salzburg* [2005] ECR I-10139] between 2001 and 2006 was the Court of the view that the national measure was disproportionate because it was not strictly or at least in every respect necessary to protect public health. This is not simply a coincidence but the result of a remarkably strict handling of the health derogation in Article 30 EC.' See also Weatherill, 'Recent Case Law Concerning the Free Movement of Goods' (1999) 36 *CML Rev* 51.

[70] Case 178/84 *Commission v Germany* [1987] ECR 1227.

[71] See, more recently, Joined Cases C-158/04 and C-159/04 *Alfa Vita Vassilopoulos AE v Elliniko Dimosio* [2006] ECR I-8135, para 25.

[72] Para 36.

[73] Case C-275/92 [1994] ECR I-1039, para 60. See also Case C-124/97 *Läärä v Kihlakunnansyyttäjä* [1999] ECR I-6067.

of gambling) to any scrutiny, a situation made more absurd by the fact that the Court itself noted that the National Lotteries Bill was going through Parliament at the time. The Court also did not require the UK to show a link between the national measures and the justification invoked,[74] nor did it subject those justifications to any proportionality review. Yet, in *Gambelli,*[75] nearly 10 years later, the Court indicated that an Italian law imposing criminal penalties, including imprisonment, on private individuals in Italy who collaborated over the web with a British bookmaker to collect bets, an activity normally reserved to the Italian state monopoly CONI, was disproportionate. The Court said the national court had to consider whether the criminal penalty was disproportionate in the light of the fact that involvement in betting was encouraged in the context of games organised by licensed *national* bodies[76] and that the British supplier was already regulated in the UK.[77]

In the field of posted workers, the Court has also been increasingly rigorous—albeit nuanced—in its application of the justification/proportionality formula. In the first case, *Rush Portuguesa,*[78] the Court allowed host Member States to apply their labour laws to 'posted' workers coming from a third state. It said:

> Community law does not preclude Member States from extending their legislation, or collective labour agreements entered into by both sides of industry, to any person who is employed, even temporarily, within their territory, no matter in which country the employer is established; nor does Community law prohibit Member States from enforcing those rules by appropriate means.[79]

The Court did not scrutinise whether it was necessary, in the name of worker protection, for the host state to apply its rules to temporary migrants, nor did it consider the proportionality of applying all of these rules to posted workers. Yet, four years later in *Vander Elst*[80] the Court considered the justification for the national rule (to obtain work permits for those workers from a national immigration authority and to pay the attendant costs, with the imposition of an administrative fine as the penalty for infringement) and found it disproportionate.

This is the pattern in subsequent cases and, more often than not, the Court finds the host state's rules to be disproportionate. For example, it has said that host state laws requiring the posted worker to have been

[74] Case C-243/01 *Gambelli* [2003] ECR I-13031, para 63.
[75] Case C-243/01 *Gambelli* [2003] ECR I-13031.
[76] Para 72.
[77] Para 73.
[78] Case C-113/89 *Rush Portuguesa v Office national d'immigration* [1990] ECR I-1417.
[79] Para 18.
[80] Case C-43/93 *Vander Elst v Office des migrations internationals* [1994] ECR I-3803.

employed by the service provider for at least six months in the case of Luxembourg[81] (a year in the case of Germany[82]) was not lawful. A requirement for the posted workers to have individual work permits which were granted only where the labour market situation so allowed was also not compatible with the EC law,[83] nor was a requirement for the service provider to provide, for the purposes of obtaining a work permit, a bank guarantee to cover costs in the event of repatriation of the worker at the end of his deployment,[84] nor was a requirement that the work be licensed.[85]

So the overall tenor of the case law points in the direction of a finding that the national measure may be justified but is often not proportionate. This confirms the sense that national regulatory autonomy is being undermined to the benefit of greater market integration. Of course, there continue to be cases that buck this trend. *Schmidberger*[86] is one such example. An environmental association organised a demonstration, blocking a stretch of the Brenner Motorway for 30 hours. The Court, while saying that the authorities' failure to ban this demonstration was capable of breaching Articles 28 and 29 EC read together with Article 10,[87] recognised that the authorities' (in)action was justified on the ground of the fundamental rights of the demonstrators to freedom of expression and freedom of assembly.[88] The Court then engaged in a balancing act to determine whether a fair balance had been struck between the competing interests.[89] Noting that the demonstration took place following a request for authorisation as required by national law and after the Austrian authorities had decided to allow it to go ahead;[90] that the obstacle to free movement was limited (a single event, on a single route, lasting for 30 hours) and that various administrative and supporting measures had been taken by the Austrian authorities to limit the disruption to road traffic, it found that the Austrian government's inaction was compatible with Community law.[91]

[81] Case C-445/03 *Commission v Luxembourg* [2004] ECR I-10191, paras 32–3.
[82] Case C-244/04 *Commission v Germany* [2006] ECR I-885.
[83] Case C-445/03 *Commission v Luxembourg* [2004] ECR I-10191, paras 42–3. See also the earlier case of Case C-43/93 *Vander Elst* [1994] ECR I-3803.
[84] *Ibid*, para 47.
[85] *Ibid*, para 30.
[86] Case C-112/00 *Eugen Schmidberger, Internationale Transporte und Planzüge v Republic of Austria* [2003] ECR I-5659.
[87] Para 64.
[88] Paras 71–3.
[89] Para 81.
[90] Para 84.
[91] Para 94.

(ii) The Proceduralisation of Proportionality

Since the early 1980s, in cases such as *UHT*,[92] the Court has limited the use of the derogations/justifications through the application of the principle of mutual recognition: it has prevented the host State from replicating checks on imported products which have already been carried out by the State of origin. The Court says that such double-checks are disproportionate.[93] In *Biologische Producten*[94] the Court reminded the Member States of their duty 'to assist in bringing about a relaxation of the controls existing in intra-Community trade'.[95] In *Commission v Portugal* the Court went further and said that '[s]trict compliance' with the obligation to cooperate requires 'an active approach' on the part of the authorities in the host state. The Member States must also ensure that the competent approval bodies cooperate with each other to facilitate the procedures to be followed to obtain access to the national market of the host state.[96] As we have seen, a requirement to take into account the level of protection provided by the national system is also a standard requirement in the field of free movement of services but tends to be factored into the question of justification.[97]

This proceduralisation of the proportionality principle has also been emphasised in a number of more recent cases. This can be seen in *Radlberger*[98] concerning the German deposit and return system. The Court accepted that the system, which had a discriminatory effect on importers,[99] could be justified on the grounds of environmental protection, and that the measures were suitable to achieve the environmental objective. However, it said that the German measures were disproportionate to achieving the objective because they did not afford the producers and distributors a transitional period sufficient to enable them to adapt to the requirements of the new system before the new system entered into force.[100] The same

[92] Case 124/81 *Commission v UK* [1983] ECR 203.

[93] Case 132/80 *United Foods* [1981] ECR 995, para 29; Case 188/84 *Commission v France (woodworking machines)* [1986] ECR 419, para 16; Case C-293/93 *Houtwipper* [1994] ECR I-4249, para 19.

[94] Case 272/80 [1981] ECR 3277. See also Case C-292/94 *Criminal Proceedings against Brandsma* [1996] ECR I-2159, Case C-400/96 *Criminal Proceedings against Jean Harpegnies* [1998] ECR I-5121 and Case C-212/03 *Commission v France* [2005] ECR I-4213, paras 42–3

[95] Case 272/80 [1981] ECR 3277, para 14.

[96] Case C-432/03 *Commission v Portugal* [2005] ECR I-9665, para 47.

[97] See also Case C-272/94 *Guiot* [1996] ECR I-1905, para 17. See also Joined Cases C-369/96 and C-376 *Arblade* [1999] ECR I-8453, para 80.

[98] Case C-309/02 *Radlberger Getränkegesellschaft mbH & Co v Land Baden-Württemberg* [2004] ECR I-11763, para 70. See also Case C-463/01 *Commission v Germany (deposit and return)* [2004] ECR I-11705, para 67.

[99] Para 68.

[100] Case C-463/01 *Commission v Germany (deposit and return)* [2004] ECR I-11705, para 79; Case C-309/02 *Radlberger Getränkegesellschaft mbH & Co v Land Baden-Württemberg* [2004] ECR I-11763, para 81.

argument influenced the Court in *Commission v Austria (heavy lorries)*[101] where it found that the Austrian ban on heavy lorries using the A12 in the Tyrol on environmental grounds was disproportionate: a transitional period of only two months for introducing the ban was 'clearly insufficient'.[102] It also said that the Austrian authorities were 'under a duty to examine carefully the possibility of using measures less restrictive of freedom of movement'[103] before adopting a measure 'so radical as a total traffic ban on a section of motorway constituting a vital route of communication between certain Member States'.[104]

The requirement that the procedure comply with the principles of good administration (namely be readily accessible, subject to criteria known in advance and reviewed from time to time, and be completed within a reasonable time[105]) was also emphasised in the healthcare cases, especially *Geraets-Smits and Peerbooms*[106] and *Müller-Fauré and van Riet.*[107] The Court found that a system of prior authorisation for intramural care was in principle 'both necessary and reasonable' on public health grounds in order to guarantee a 'rationalised, stable, balanced and accessible supply of hospital services',[108] provided that the conditions under which the authorisation was granted—both substantively and procedurally—could themselves be justified.[109] In respect of the *procedural* conditions,[110] the Court said that these could be justified provided the procedural system was easily accessible for patients; that the decision whether to grant authorisation was based on objective, non-discriminatory and pre-determined criteria; that the request was dealt with objectively and impartially and within a reasonable time; and that refusals to grant authorisation were capable of being challenged in judicial or quasi-judicial proceedings.[111]

(ii) Fundamental Rights

The discussion so far has emphasised how the Member States' ability to invoke the justifications is curtailed by a rigorous application of the

[101] Case C-320/03 *Commission v Austria (Heavy Lorries)* [2005] ECR I 7929, para 35.
[102] Para 90.
[103] Para 87.
[104] *Ibid.* The authorities also should have ensured there was sufficient rail capacity to allow a transfer from road to rail before implementing such a measure (para 88).
[105] See also Case C-224/02 *Pusa* [2004] ECR I-5763, para 48.
[106] Case C-157/99 [2001] ECR I-5473.
[107] Case C-385/99 *VG Müller-Fauré v Onderlinge Waarborgmaatschappij oz Zorgverzekeringen UA and EEM van Riet v Onderlinge Waarborgmaatschappij oz Zorgverzekeringen UA* [2003] ECR I-4509.
[108] Paras 80–1.
[109] As elaborated by Case C-385/99 *Müller-Fauré* [2003] ECR I-4509, para 66.
[110] On the importance of the procedural requirements, see Case C-205/99 *Analir* [2001] ECR I-1271, paras 37–8.
[111] Para 90.

proportionality principle and an increasing reliance on procedural conditions. Since *ERT*[112] the Court has added a further limitation: the derogations (in that case) and the justifications (in *Familiapress*[113]) had to be 'appraised' in the light of fundamental rights. Inevitably this leads to a balancing act with the principle of proportionality. This can be seen in *Familiapress* concerning the Austrian prohibition on prize competitions in magazines. The Court recognised that the rule might be discriminatory but could be justified by the need to preserve press diversity[114]—by preventing large publishers from driving smaller publishers off the market owing to their ability to offer larger prizes. However, the Court also recognised that the rule could 'detract from freedom of expression', contrary to Article 10 of the European Convention, albeit that Article 10 does permit derogations for the purposes of maintaining press diversity, in so far as they are prescribed by law and are necessary in a democratic society.[115] The Court then said that it was for the national court to determine whether the national law was proportionate to the aim of maintaining press diversity and whether the objective could be attained by measures less restrictive of both intra-Community trade and freedom of expression.[116]

The follow up to this case is instructive. When it returned to the Austrian court, the court issued an injunction suspending sales of the German magazine *Laura* which did contain prize competitions, contrary to the Austrian prohibition, pending the conduct of the necessary market research to see if it was truly the case that prize competitions benefited larger publishers who could offer better prizes. The first court that heard the case considered the Austrian statute to be incompatible with EC law. The court said that the claimant had failed to prove that prize competitions in magazines did have an influence on media plurality in Austria. This view was upheld on appeal. However, the Supreme Court disagreed.[117] It said that it was a task for the court (and not the claimant) to prove an impact on media plurality and that an impact had to be likely and plausible. Since the court had failed to do this, national law was compatible with EC Law.

[112] Case C-260/89 *Elliniki Radiophonia Tiléorassi AE v Dimotiki Etairia Pliroforissis and Sotirios Kouvelas* [1991] ECR I-2925, para 45.

[113] Case C-368/95 [1997] ECR I-3689.

[114] This was a particular problem in Austria where the market share of the largest press group was 55%, whereas in the UK it was 35% and in Germany 24%.

[115] Para 26, citing the judgment of the ECtHR of 24 November 1993 in *Informationsverein Lentia and Others v Austria*, Series A, No 276.

[116] Para 27.

[117] OGH 23 March 1999, 4 Ob 249/98s. Thanks to Konrad Lachmeyer for this information.

(iii) Legal Certainty

Closely allied to the requirement of both the procedural aspect of proportionality and fundamental rights is the principle of legal certainty. This is particularly important in the field of free movement of capital, as the *Association Eglise de Scientologie de Paris* shows. Having outlined the general rules which govern the use of the derogations (discussed above), the Court added that restrictions on free movement of capital also had to be subject to the principle of legal certainty. It said that individuals had to be 'apprised of the extent of their rights and obligations deriving from Article [56] of the Treaty'.[118] Although legal certainty is a general principle of law, only in capital is the requirement so clearly stated.

IV AN EVOLUTIONARY PERSPECTIVE

A Introduction

In the previous two sections I have outlined the basic structure of the ECJ's approach to the derogations and justifications invoked by Member States to defend their national laws. I have suggested that the general trend in the Court's case law is a greater recognition of an ever wider range of justifications but this is matched by closer scrutiny of those justifications and/or the strict application of the proportionality principle and the other limitations. This means that, subject to certain notable exceptions, the Court is finding an increasing number of national laws incompatible with Community law and that, in many instances, state interest is not, in fact, being protected by the justification jurisprudence. In the two previous sections I have drawn on a number of well known cases to illustrate the Court's more recent approach to derogations/justifications/proportionality. In this section I have adopted a more systematic methodology. Using the structure outlined in sections II and III above, I have looked at all the Article 234 references on the four freedoms decided in 2004 (the last year for which there is a complete set of European Court Reports when this chapter was being researched), 1994 and 1984 (I did not go back further than 1984 because the *Cassis de Dijon* decision which first expressly recognised mandatory requirements was handed down only in 1979 and took a while to bed down). In those cases where a breach of the Treaty was established, I looked to see whether the defendant state invoked a derogation or a *Cassis*-style justification if an indistinctly/non-discriminatory measures was at stake, whether the justification was upheld by the ECJ or sent back to the national court to decide, and how the

[118] Para 22.

proportionality principle was applied in each case, if at all, and by which court (ECJ or national court). The results can be found in table 1 below. In the light of this data the following observations can be made.

B Derogations and Justifications

When comparing the cases decided in 1984 with those decided in 2004, the most striking feature is the Court's increasing willingness to scrutinise the derogations and justifications put forward by the defendant (usually state but also other regulatory bodies). In 1984 all the breaches of the Treaty were defended by reference to the express derogations only. By and large the Court accepted the arguments advanced by the Member States, especially concerning public health and public security. There was also little reference to proportionality. By contrast, in 1994 the *Cassis* type justifications were being invoked as frequently as the express derogations, and the Court was recognising an ever wider range of justifications (for example, road safety in *Van Schaik*[119] and cultural policy in *TV10*[120]). Sometimes, the Court found that the justifications were not made out (for example, *Clinique,*[121] *Scholz,*[122] *Halliburton*[123]), in others it accepted the justifications put forward (for example, *TV10, Van Schaik* and (notoriously) *Schindler*).

With public health there were signs in 1994 that the Court was being more rigorous in its requirements of what was necessary before the state could successfully invoke the public health derogation (for example, *Van de Veldt*[124]), although the Court was not always consistent in this (compare *de la Crespelle*[125] and *Ortscheit*[126]). This approach to public health continued in 2004: the Court carried on tightening up on the requirements necessary before a state could successfully invoke the public health derogation (for example, *Greenham and Abel*[127] discussed below). It also rejected more public health claims (for example, *Kohlpharma*[128] and

[119] Case C-55/93 *Criminal Proceedings against van Schaik* [1994] ECR I-4837.

[120] Case C-23/93 *TV10* [1994] ECR I-4795.

[121] Case C-315/92 *Verband Sozialer Wettbewerb ev v Clinique Laboratories SNC* [1994] ECR I-317.

[122] Case C-419/92 *Scholz v Opera Universitaria di Cagliari and Cinzia Porcedda* [1994] ECR I-505.

[123] Case C-1/93 *Halliburton Services BV v Staatssecretaris van Financiën* [1994] ECR I-1137.

[124] Case C-17/93 *Criminal proceedings against Van der Veldt* [1994] ECR I-3537.

[125] Case C-323/93 *Société Civile Agricole du Centre d'Insémination de la Crespelle v Coopérative d'Elevage et d'Insémination Artificielle du Département de la Mayenne* [1994] ECR I-5077.

[126] Case C-320/93 *Ortscheit v Eurim-Pharm* [1994] ECR I-5243.

[127] Case C-95/01 *Greenham and Abel* [2004] ECR I-1333.

[128] Case C-122/02 *Kohlpharma* [2004] ECR I-3369.

Douwe Egberts[129]). However, as in 1994 the Court was not always consistent and there were a number of cases where the Court upheld the public health derogations without much scrutiny (for example, *Schreiber*[130] and *Bacardi France*[131]).

Perhaps the most striking feature of the cases decided in 2004 is that generally the states were much less successful in invoking justifications. This was most obviously the case with justifications concerning taxation. In the 1992 case of *Bachmann*[132] the Court had recognised the 'need to preserve the cohesion of the tax system' as a justification. The case concerned a Belgian law according to which the cost of life insurance premiums could not be deducted from taxable income where the premiums were paid in other Member States. This was because Belgian tax law gave the individual the choice of either having tax deducted on the premiums and then paying tax on future benefits or not having tax deducted on the premiums and then not paying tax on future benefits. If Bachmann was able to deduct tax on premiums paid in Germany, the Belgian authorities would have no way of being able to tax future benefits also payable in Germany.[133] For this reason the Belgian rules were justified, and so did not breach Articles 39 on workers and 49 on services, because there was a 'direct link' between the right to deduct contributions and the taxation of sums payable by insurers under pension and life assurance contracts; and that preserving that link was necessary to safeguard the cohesion of the tax system.[134]

Since *Bachmann* Member States regularly invoked fiscal cohesion as a justification for their tax policies, between 1992 and 2008 but always without success.[135] The Court has insisted that the cohesion defence requires a direct link between the discriminatory tax rule and the compensating tax advantage and this has not been found in subsequent cases.[136] This can be seen very clearly in the tax cases decided in 2004: in *de*

[129] Case C-239/02 *Douwe Egberts* [2004] ECR I-7007.

[130] Case C-443/02 *Schreiber* [2004] ECR I-7275.

[131] Case C-429/02 *Bacardi v Télévision Française 1 SA* [2004] ECR I-6613. See also Case C-262/02 *Commission v France* [2004] ECR I-6569.

[132] Case C-204/90 *Bachmann v Belgian State* [1992] ECR I-249, para 21, and Case C-300/90 *Commission v Belgium* [1992] ECR I-305, para 14.

[133] Para 23.

[134] Paras 21–3.

[135] See, eg, Case C-80/94 *Wielockx v Inspecteur der Directe Belastingen* [1995] ECR I-2493; Case C-107/94 *Asscher v Staatssecretaris van Financiën* [1996] ECR I-3089; Case C-264/96 *Imperial Chemical Industries (ICI) v Colmer* [1998] ECR I-4695.

[136] See M Gammie, 'The Role of the European Court of Justice in the Development of Direct Discrimination in the European Union' (2003) 57 *Bulletin for International Fiscal Documentation* 86, 93. Cf Case C-157/07 Finanzant für Körperschaften III in *Berlin v Krankenheim Ruhesitz am Wannsee-Seniorenheimstatt* GmbH, Judgement of 23 October 2008, para 42.

Laysterie du Saillant,[137] *Wallentin*,[138] *Weidert*,[139] *Lenz*,[140] and *Manninen*[141] the justifications invoked by the states were all unsuccessful. As we also know, there has since been a backlash by the Member States against these decisions and in *Marks & Spencer*,[142] a case decided in 2005, the Court adopted a much more nuanced approach to justifications in tax cases.[143] Yet, the Court still insists on the defendant state establishing a link between the justification and the steps taken by the state. Therefore in *Schwarz*[144] the Court required that the German government show a link between its tax policy (which allowed tax relief for parents whose children went to private school in Germany but not for those educated in other Member States) and the policy decision to subsidise schooling in its own system. Since, on the facts the subsidy went to the parents and not to the schools, the justification was not made out.

The 2004 review also suggests that the Court is suspicious of states invoking the consumer protection justification (for example, *Caixa-Bank*[145]), a concept which the Court has drawn narrowly, taking into account only 'the presumed expectations of an average consumer who is reasonably well-informed and reasonably observant and circumspect'.[146] However, the Court continues to show some deference to the Member States in areas of political sensitivity. The posted workers case law provides one example (*Wollf & Müller*,[147] although this can now be contrasted with *Laval* discussed above). *Omega*[148] concerning the German ban on games involving 'playing at killing' is another example. There the Court upheld the ban on public policy grounds: 'the commercial exploitation of games involving the simulated killing of human beings infringed a fundamental value enshrined in the national [German] constitution, namely human dignity'.[149]

[137] Case C-9/02 *de Lasteyrie du Saillant* [2004] ECR I-2409.

[138] Case C-169/03 *Wallentin* [2004] ECR I-6443.

[139] Case C-242/03 *Ministre des Finances v Weidert and Paulus* [2004] ECR I-7379.

[140] Case C-315/02 *Lenz* [2004] ECR I-7063, para 40.

[141] Case C-319/02 *Manninen* [2004] ECR I-7477, para 29.

[142] Case C-446/03 *Marks & Spencer plc v Halsey (Her Majesty's Inspector of Taxes)* [2005] ECR I-10837.

[143] S Kingston, 'The Boundaries of Sovereignty: The ECJ's Controversial Role Applying Internal Market Law to Direct Tax Measures' (2006–7) 9 *Cambridge Yearbook of European Legal Studies* 287.

[144] Case C-76/05 *Schwarz v Finanzamt Bergisch Gladbach* [2007] ECR I-000, para 71.

[145] Case C-442/02 *Caixa-Bank v Ministère de l'Économie, des Finances and de l'industrie* [2004] ECR I-8961.

[146] Case C-210/96 *Gut Springenheide GmbH v Oberkreisdirektor des Kreises Steinfurt* [1998] ECR I-4657, para 31.

[147] Case C-60/03 *Wolff & Müller* [2004] ECR I-9553.

[148] Case C-36/02 *Omega Spielhallen- und Automatenaufstellungs-GmbH v Oberbürgermeisterin der Bundesstadt Bonn* [2004] ECR I-9609, para 36.

[149] Para 32.

This brief review suggests that where there is a genuine justification at stake, which the host state is able to prove and show that the steps taken actually meet the objective, the Court will accept the derogation/justification (as in, for example, *Radlberger*[150]). More usually, however, the Court demonstrates its suspicions of the justifications invoked.

B Limits on the Derogations/Justifications

(i) Proportionality

In 1984, the question of proportionality was scarcely considered: if the Court of Justice upheld the derogation, it was assumed that the steps taken were proportionate. In 1994 the Court seemed to uphold the proportionality of the national measure in just two cases (*Schindler*[151] and *Van Schaik*) but in neither case was the proportionality of the measure actually expressly discussed. In 2004 the Court upheld the proportionality of the national rule in three cases (*Schreiber*, *Bacardi France* and *Omega*).

In 2004 the national rules were found disproportionate in four cases, sometimes in conjunction with a finding that the steps could not be justified (*de Lasteyrie du Saillant*, *Douwe Egberts*,[152] *Caixa-Bank* and *Van der Elst*). This was in addition to the five tax cases where the Court found that the justifications were not made out (*de Laysterie du Saillant*, *Wallentin*, *Weidert*, *Lenz* and *Manninen*). Further, in five cases the proportionality question was left to the national court (*Collins*,[153] *Leichtle*,[154] *Pusa*,[155] *Wolff*, *Radlberger*[156]). So, in 2004 in somewhere between nine and 13 cases national law was found to contravene Community law. This contrasts with the situation in 1994 where the ECJ found the national rules to be disproportionate in just two cases (*Van der Veldt* and *Van der Elst*). This was in addition to the two cases where the Court found that the justifications were not made out. In two cases in 1994 the proportionality question was left to the national court (*de la Crespelle*, *Ortscheit*). The significance of which court decides the application of the proportionality principle is considered below.

[150] Case C-309/02 *Radlberger Getränkegesellschaft and S Spitz* [2004] ECR I-1176.

[151] Case C-275/92 [1994] ECR I-1039.

[152] Case C-239/02 *Douwe Egberts NV v Westrom Pharma* [2004] ECR I-7007.

[153] Case C-138/02 *Collins v Secretary of State for Work and Pensions* [2004] ECR I-2703.

[154] Case C-8/02 *Leichtle v Bundesanstalt für Arbeit* [2004] ECR I-2641.

[155] Case C-224/02 *Heikki Antero Pusa v Osuuspankkien Keskinainen Vakuutusyhtiö*, [2004] ECR I-5763.

[156] Case C-309/02 *Radlberger Getränkegesellschaft mbH & Co v Land Baden-Württemberg* [2004] ECR I-11763, para 70. See also Case C-463/01 *Commission v Germany (deposit and return)* [2004] ECR I-11705, para 67.

(ii) Proceduralisation of Proportionality

As we have seen, there is an increasing requirement of 'good governance' in the states' approach to the question of proportionality, a point emphasised as early as 1984 in *Heijn*[157] and confirmed more eloquently in *Commission v France*[158] and *Greenham and Abel*,[159] both decided in 2004. Greenham was prosecuted for selling meal replacements food supplements ('Juice Plus + vegetable mixture and Juice Plus + fruit mixture) which had been imported from other Member States where they had been lawfully manufactured and/or marketed. The substance coenzyme Q10 had been added to these products, a nutrient whose addition was not authorised in France for human consumption (although authorised in a number of other Member States), and vitamins in quantities exceeding that of the recommended daily intake. The Court said that the French requirements breached Article 28 but could be justified under Article 30 provided the following conditions were satisfied:

— The national rules had to make provision for a procedure enabling economic operators to have a nutrient included on the national list of authorised substances. The procedure had to be readily accessible and completed within a reasonable time. If the application was turned down, this decision had to be open to challenge before the courts.[160]
— An application to obtain the inclusion of a nutrient on the national list of authorised substances could be refused by the competent national authorities only if such substance posed a genuine risk to public health following a detailed assessment of the risk to public health, using the most reliable scientific data available and the most recent results of international research. The state also had to show that the steps taken were proportionate.[161]

These cases demonstrate a growing emphasis on the need for the state to show that not only are the national restrictions justified on substantive grounds but on procedural grounds too.

(iii) Fundamental Human Rights and Legal Certainty

No cases in the period under review expressly turned on either fundamental human rights or legal certainty as a limitation on a state's ability to

[157] Case C-94/83 *Heijn* [1984] ECR 3263.
[158] Case C-24/00 *Commission v France (nutrients)* [2004] ECR I-1277.
[159] Case C-95/01 *Greenham and Abel* [2004] ECR I-1333.
[160] *Greenham and Abel*, para 35.
[161] *Ibid*, para 36.

invoke a derogation or justification.[162] However, as the criteria in *Commission v France* and *Greenham and Abel* show, the need for the national procedure for authorisation to be accessible and subject to review essentially embody the rights to effective judicial protection and legal certainty.

C Preliminary Conclusions

The cases from 1984, 1994 and 2004 show a remarkable shift by the Court from considerable deference to Member States' regulatory freedom in 1984 (before the 1996 single market programme) to a greater willingness to review Member State justifications in 1994 (two years after the 1992 deadline) and, most recently, a more substantial review of the Member States' justifications in 2004, albeit combined with a recognition of a greater number of justifications. The analysis of these cases supports the thesis that while the Court appears increasingly to be 'giving' to the Member States through the justifications on the one hand, it is, in fact, taking with the other hand through the onerous requirement that Member States have to prove the justification is made out and through the rigorous application of the principle of proportionality, fundamental rights and legal certainty. A preliminary conclusion is that market integration appears, in recent years, to take precedence over national regulatory autonomy.

V DIVISION OF RESPONSIBILITIES BETWEEN THE COURT OF JUSTICE AND THE NATIONAL COURTS

An examination of the cases in the periods under review reveals a further nuance on the market integration v national regulatory autonomy debate. According to the orthodoxy, in the context of an Article 234 reference, there is a division of responsibility between the Court of Justice and national courts: the ECJ gives a ruling on an abstract point of Community law, the national court applies that ruling to the facts. Of course, it is difficult always to distinguish clearly between the interpretation of the law and its application to the facts.[163] In many cases the Court of Justice will give an interpretation on the meaning of a justification in a situation such as the one referred to (for example in *Viking*) and the national court will see if the justification is made out on the facts. Likewise, the ECJ will give an abstract ruling on the meaning of proportionality (for example in

[162] Although *cf Omega* where fundamental rights actually constituted the derogation/justification.

[163] See further Craig above n 64, 711.

Familiapress) but the national court will apply the proportionality principle to the facts. Yet, as we have seen, in 2004 the Court of Justice itself upheld the proportionality of the national rule in three cases and found the national rule disproportionate in four others. This was in addition to the five cases where the Court found that the justifications were not made out. In only five cases was the proportionality question left to the national court.

The fact that the ECJ appears to have trodden on the toes of the national court in 12 cases (3 + 4 + 5) raises the question as to why it is doing so. One explanation is that the Court is acutely sensitive to the outcome in the case: if it feels the case is of considerable importance and/or it is an area over which it wishes to maintain 'maximum control'[164] it will decide the issue of justification and/or proportionality itself. Another explanation is that Court knows that national courts often struggle to apply the proportionality test. As Jarvis notes,[165] national courts have difficulty locating the 'objective' of national legislation which often represents a compromise between several highly charged political and social interests. They also have problems when faced with cases where the restrictive effect on inter-state trade is very small (thus satisfying the 'suitability' limb of the proportionality test) but for which there is no necessity because there are alterative means of achieving the objective in question (thereby failing the 'necessity' test). In these situations the ECJ will decide proportionality for itself and, in more recent years, the Court is more likely than not to find the national rule unlawful.

By contrast, if the ECJ considers the case less important and/or it genuinely does not have sufficient facts to decide the proportionality question, it will refer these matters back to the national court. In 1994, in one (*de la Crespelle*), possibly two (*Ortscheit*) cases, the ECJ referred back the proportionality question to the national court. In 2004 five cases were sent back to the national court (*Collins,*[166] *Leichtle,*[167] *Pusa,*[168] *Wolff, Radlberger*). My sense is that if these key questions are left to the national courts they will generally strive to uphold the national rule. We have already seen this result in *Familiapress* considered above. However, the evidence for such an assertion is harder to come by, for it is often a difficult task to track down the decision (if any) of the national courts.[169] I have

[164] *Ibid.*
[165] *The Application of EC Law by National Courts* (Oxford, Oxford University Press, 1998), 436.
[166] Case C-138/02 *Collins* [2004] ECR I-2703.
[167] Case C-8/02 *Leichtle* [2004] ECR I-2641.
[168] Case C-224/02 *Pusa* [2004] ECR I-5763.
[169] Although see the more comprehensive survey by M Jarvis, *The Application of EC Law by National Courts* (Oxford, Oxford University Press, 1998). See also in a particular sector B Rodger (ed), *Article 234 and Competition Law* (Dordrecht, Kluwer, 2008).

therefore followed through three well known cases, one from the period under review—*Collins*—and two earlier decisions—*De Agostini* and *GIP* to see how the national courts responded to the reference when it returned from the Court of Justice.

Collins, [170] a case decided in 2004, concerned a British rule which said that entitlement to a jobseeker's allowance in the UK was conditional upon a requirement of being habitually resident in the UK. This was found to be indirectly discriminatory against workers under Article 39 EC but the Court of Justice upheld the justification offered by the UK that it was legitimate for the national legislature to wish to ensure a genuine link between an applicant for an allowance and the employment market of the state granting that allowance. However, on the question of proportionality, the Court concluded that while a residence requirement was, in principle, appropriate for the purpose of ensuring such a connection, if it was to be proportionate it could not go beyond what was necessary in order to attain that objective. In recognition of the requirement of good governance observed elsewhere, the Court added the application of the residence requirement by the national authorities had to 'rest on clear criteria known in advance and provision must be made for the possibility of a means of redress of a judicial nature'.[171] The Court concluded:

> In any event, if compliance with the requirement demands a period of residence, the period must not exceed what is necessary in order for the national authorities to be able to satisfy themselves that the person concerned is genuinely seeking work in the employment market of the host Member State.[172]

The question of proportionality went back to the British court and ended up before the Social Security Commissioner who (narrowly) upheld the proportionality of the measure. Collins' appeal to the Court of Appeal on other matters was also unsuccessful.

The national court's approach in the well known case of *De Agostini*[173] also illustrates a willingness to uphold national law. It will be recalled that the case concerned a Swedish ban on television advertising directed at children under 12 and a ban on misleading commercials for skin-care products and detergents. The Court suggested that this ban was a discriminatory certain selling arrangement and so breached Article 28 unless it could be justified and the steps were proportionate. When the case returned to Sweden, the Swedish Market Court[174] concluded that because

[170] Case C-138/02 *Collins v Secretary of State for Work and Pensions* [2004] ECR I-2703.
[171] Para 72.
[172] *Ibid*.
[173] Joined Cases C-34–36/95 *Konsumentombudsmannen (KO) v De Agostini (Svenska) Förlag AB* and *TV-Shop i Sverige AB* [1997] ECR I-3843, noted by J Stuyck (1997) 34 *CML Rev* 1445, 1465.
[174] Marknadsdomstolen 1998:17.

the national provision did not discriminate between products on the ground of nationality, Article 28 EC did not apply. The national court therefore did not need to consider the question of justification and proportionality.[175] De Agostini was also obliged, under the threat of a penalty payment, to terminate the advertising activities in Swedish-based broadcasting.[176]

The approach in *De Agostini* can, however, be contrasted with that in *GIP*.[177] The case concerned a total ban on advertising alcohol on the radio, on television or in magazines. Following *De Agostini* the Court of Justice found the rule to constitute a discriminatory selling arrangement and so breached Article 28. It could, however, be justified on public health grounds, subject to a decision by the national court on the proportionality of the measure. The Swedish Market Court[178] ruled, in accordance with the preliminary ruling asked for by Stockholms Tingsrätt, that the Swedish general ban on the publishing of commercials for alcoholic beverages fell under Article 28 EC but the ban was not proportional with regard to its stated objective (the safeguarding of human health): according to the court's evaluation of the evidence presented to it, an advertising ban had only a marginal influence on the promotion of human health.

VI CONCLUSIONS

While much attention is given to the scope of Community law (whether a particular national rule is, in principle, caught by the Treaty),[179] the number of situations which now fall outside the scope of Community law is, in fact, relatively small and the principle reconciliation between the (EC) demands of market integration and the (domestic) needs of maintaining the integrity of the national system is actually conducted through the application of the justifications and the limitations on those justifications. This has become increasingly important as the Court has extended the range of circumstances in which the justifications will apply (to all of the obstacles/restrictions jurisprudence and even occasionally to cases involving direct

[175] Email correspondence from Professor Per Cramér, Göteborg University, Sweden.

[176] However, as Per Camer points out, the Swedish Market Court's ruling concerned only TV commercials that had been transmitted by a Swedish broadcaster using a surface-based transmission system located on Swedish territory. The court found that it did not have jurisdiction concerning TV commercials transmitted by satellite from Great Britain addressed to a Swedish audience. This finding was based on the transmitting state principle found in the Television Without Frontiers Directive 89/552/EEC. Thus the British based TV3, broadcasting in Swedish, could continue to transmit the TV commercials to a Swedish audience.

[177] Case C-405/98 *Konsumentombudsmannen v Gourmet International Products (GIP)* [2001] ECR I-1795.

[178] Marknadsdomstolen 2003:5.

[179] See the chs 11 and 9 in this volume by Spaventa and Tryfonidou respectively.

discrimination in the field of free movement of services[180]). So does the Court of Justice respect the integrity of the national rules? More often than not the answer appears to be no. Generally speaking, the Court is now much stricter in its scrutiny of the justifications put forward and often tough on the question of proportionality, especially when it decides the proportionality question for itself. When proportionality is left to the national court to decide the ECJ gives increasing amounts of guidance, defining the parameters of the analysis ever more closely, in order to stop the national courts manifesting a nationalistic preference and upholding the integrity of domestic rules. While national courts are meant to be European courts too, in fact, it is still up to the ECJ to preserve the interest of the EU as a whole which, in most cases, means striking down national rules which are an impediment to inter-state movement. In the long run, individuals and corporations benefit more from free movement and an open market than they do from (sentimentally) hanging on to the integrity of their national systems. In the meantime states find an ever increasing number of their national rules to be incompatible with EC law.

Table 1: Article 234 references heard by the ECJ in 1984, 1994 and 2004. Cases listed only where there are breaches of Community law established.[181]

Case Name	Field	Derogation	Justification	Proportionality	Other comments
		1984			
238/82 *Duphar*	Goods	Public health—left to national court to decide			
16/83 *Prantl*	Goods	Public policy and protection of industrial and commercial policy both rejected by ECJ			

[180] Joined Cases C-338/04 etc *Placanica* [2007] ECR I-1891.

[181] I have generally ruled out IP cases, cases concerning mutual recognition of diplomas or other qualifications and driving licence cases. None of these cases have much to say about the subject of justifications/derogations.

177/82 and 178/82 *Van de Haar*	Goods	Not raised			
97/83 *Melkunie*	Goods	Public health—upheld by ECJ		Not raised	
72/83 *Campus Oil*	Goods	Public security upheld by ECJ		Left to national court within guidelines laid down by ECJ	
107/83 *Klopp*	Establishment		(ECJ referred to justifications but they were not directly relevant here)		
94/83 *Heijn*	Goods	Public health upheld by ECJ			Member States obliged to keep prescribed level of pesticides under review
177/83 *Kohl*	Goods	Public policy does not include consumer protection			
1994					
C-315/92 *Clinique*	Goods		Consumer protection—ECJ finds justification is not made out		

C-419/92 *Scholz*	Workers		ECJ says that the employer's conduct is 'unjustified indirect discrimination'		
C-275/92 *Schindler*	Services		All justifications accepted	No proportionality review	
C-1/93 *Halliburton*	Establishment		Justification not accepted by ECJ		
C-17/93 *Van der Veldt*	Goods	ECJ said public health defence not made out because it was based on 'general conjecture' not scientific research		Labelling would have been more proportionate	
C-43/93 *Van der Elst*	Services		Justification appears to be accepted by ECJ	ECJ finds application of national requirements disproportionate	
C-323/93 *Centre d'Insémination de la Crespelle*	Goods	Public health derogation upheld by ECJ		Proportionality(?) and discrimination to be determined by the national court	
C-23/93 *TV10*	Services		ECJ upholds justification based on cultural policy	Not considered by ECJ or referred to; human rights analysis instead; national law upheld	

C-55/93 *Van Schaik*	Services		ECJ upheld road safety justification	No proportionality review but ECJ pointed to the fact that national approach supported by a Directive and was therefore upheld	
C-320/93 *Ortscheit*	Goods	Public health derogation upheld		Proportionality referred to in the judgment but not in the dispositif. May be left to the national court to determine	
2004					
C-95/01 *Greenham and Abel*	Goods	Public health derogation recognised provided defendant state undertook detailed assessment of risk			
C-9/02 de *Lasteyrie du Saillant*	Establishment		Tax justification not made out	ECJ also says that national law is disproportion-ate	
C-138/02 *Collins*	Workers		Justification requiring a connection between persons who claim entitlement to JSA and host state's employment market accepted by ECJ	Proportionality is for national court to decide	

C-8/02 *Leichtle*	Services		Justification accepted in part but no evidence offered	Some aspects for the national court to consider	
C-224/02 *Pusa*	Citizenship		Justification accepted	'governance' proportionality to be applied by the national court	
C-112/02 *Kohl-pharma*	Goods	Public health derogation not made out			
C-482/01 and 493/01 *Orfano-poulos*	Workers/-services	Public policy needed to be shown on case- by-case basis			Subject to funda-mental rights review
C-443/02 *Schreiber*	Goods	Public health accepted by the ECJ		ECJ upholds proportionality of rule with no analysis	
C-239/02 *Douwe Egberts*	Goods	Public health not accepted on the facts		ECJ also finds the rule disproportion-ate	
C-169/03 *Wallentin*	Workers		Justification based on the need to ensure the cohesion of the tax system not made out on the facts		
C-242/03 *Weidert*	Capital		Justification based on the need to ensure the cohesion of the tax system not made out on the facts		

C-315/02 *Lenz*	Capital		Justification based on fact that tax is lower in another Member State is not accepted; justification based on the need to ensure the cohesion of the tax system not made out on the facts		
C-429/02 *Bacardi France*	Services	Public heath derogation accepted by ECJ		ECJ upheld the proportionality of the public health derogation	
C-319/02 *Manninen*	Capital		Justification offered (reduction in tax revenue) not accepted		
C-442/02 *Caixa-Bank*	Establishment		Consumer protection justification not accepted on facts	ECJ also said steps taken were disproportion-ate	
			Justification based on encouraging long-tem saving apparently accepted	ECJ said steps taken were disproportion-ate	

C-60/03 *Wolff & Müller*	Services		Worker protection justification accepted by ECJ	Proportionality for the national court	
C-36/02 *Omega*	Services		Fundamental rights justification accepted by ECJ	ECJ said that national rule was proportionate	
C-309/02 *Radlberger*	Goods		Environ-mental protection justification accepted by ECJ	'good governance' proportionality; guidance offered by the Court; up to the national court to apply it	

13

The Application of EC Law to Defence Industries—Changing Interpretations of Article 296 EC

PANOS KOUTRAKOS

I INTRODUCTION

FOR A LONG time, defence industries were considered to be entirely beyond the reach of EU law. Their function for the organisation of national defence was deemed to place them at the core of national sovereignty, a space much removed from the incrementally developing purview of Community law and the increasingly expanding jurisdiction of the European Court of Justice. The validity of this view was purported to be substantiated by Article 296 EC, a rather obscure provision of the EC Treaty which refers specifically to arms, munitions and war materials.

However, recent developments have questioned this assumption, highlighted its flaws and gradually rendered defence industries at the centre of an increasingly multilayered legislative and political dialogue at EU level. These developments are legal, political and economic in nature and are all interrelated in their implications.

This chapter will tell the story of this gradual shift of the position of defence industries from the margins of European integration to the centre of EU policy-making. In doing so, it will chart this development, explain its significance and set out its constitutional, institutional and political implications for the EU and its Member States.

II THE POSITION ACCORDING TO PRIMARY LAW: ARTICLE 296 EC

The only provision in the EC Treaty referring expressly to defence industries is Article 296 EC. It reads as follows:

> 1. The provisions of this Treaty shall not preclude the application of the following rules:

(a) no Member State shall be obliged to supply information the disclosure of which it considers contrary to the essential interests of its security;

(b) any Member State may take such measures as it considers necessary for the protection of the essential interests of its security which are concerned with the production of or trade in arms, munitions and war material; such measures shall not adversely affect the conditions of competition in the common market regarding products which are not intended for specifically military purposes.

2. The Council may, acting unanimously on a proposal from the Commission, make changes to the list, which it drew up on 15 April 1958, of the products to which the provisions of paragraph 1(b) apply.

In essence, this obscure EC Treaty provision introduces a public security derogation. However, it goes considerably further than the other similar derogations provided in the areas of free movement of goods (Article 30 EC), persons (Article 39(3) EC and Article 46 EC) and capital (Article 48(1)(b) EC) in so far as it authorises the Member States to deviate from the entire body of EC law. It is for this reason that, while the above provisos are exceptional, Article 296 EC has been viewed by the Court of Justice as 'wholly exceptional'.[1] The implications of this definition are twofold: on the one hand, there is no limit to the type of measure which a Member State may adopt and, on the other hand, in adopting such a measure, the State in question may deviate from the entire body of EC law.

The 'wholly exceptional' nature of Article 296 EC is further illustrated by the provision of an extraordinary procedure for judicial review. This is set out in Article 298 EC which reads as follows:

If measures taken in the circumstances referred to in Articles 296 and 297 have the effect of distorting the conditions of competition in the common market, the Commission shall, together with the State concerned, examine how these measures can be adjusted to the rules laid down in the Treaty.

By way of derogation from the procedure laid down in Articles 226 and 227, the Commission or any Member State may bring the matter directly before the Court of Justice if it considers that another Member State is making improper use of the powers provided for in Articles 296 and 297. The Court of Justice shall give its ruling in camera.

[1] Case 222/84 *Marguerite Johnston v Chief Constable of the Royal Ulster Constabulary* [1986] ECR 1651, para 27. See also the Opinion of AG Jacobs in Case C-120/94 *Commission v Greece (FYROM)* ECR I-1513 at para 46. The other such EC provision is Art 297 EC which is remarkably badly drafted: 'Member states shall consult each other with a view to taking together the steps needed to prevent the functioning of the common market being affected by measures which a Member State may be called upon to take in the event of serious internal disturbances affecting the maintenance of law and order, in the event of war, serious international tension constituting a threat of war, or in order to carry out obligations it has accepted for the purpose of maintaining peace and international security'. On the interpretation of this provision, see Koutrakos, 'Is Article 297 EC "a reserve of sovereignty"?' (2000) 37 *CML Rev* 1339.

While badly drafted and wide-ranging both in its content and implications, the 'wholly exceptional clause' of Article 296 EC does not grant Member States a *carte blanche*. This conclusion follows not only from the oft-repeated principle that the exceptional clauses set out in the EC Treaty 'deal with exceptional cases which are clearly defined and which do not lend themselves to any wide interpretation'[2] but also from the wording of the EC Treaty provision itself. First, it is confined to the products which are described in the Article 296(2) EC list. Therefore, the reference in Article 296(1)(b) EC to 'the production of or trade in arms, munitions and war material' was not envisaged as an open-ended category of products. In this vein, it was not envisaged that products which may be of both civil and military application (that is dual-use goods) should be regulated by national measures deviating from the entire body of EC law. This is supported not only by the content of the Article 296(2) EC list but also the reference to the effects that such measures should not have on 'products which are not intended for specifically military purposes' in Article 296(1)(b) EC.

Secondly, national measures deviating from EC law must be deemed 'necessary for the protection of the essential interests of [national] security'. This is quite an emphatic statement that Article 296(b) EC is not merely a public security clause: instead, it should be invoked only when the protection of the core of national sovereignty is at stake.

Thirdly, any reliance upon Article 296 EC should take into account the effects it may have on the status and movement of other products which fall beyond its rather narrow scope. In effect, this provision suggests that national measures deviating from EC law as a whole should not be adopted in a legal vacuum. Instead, Member States are under a duty to consider the implications that such measures may have for the common market.

Fourthly, Article 298(1) EC provides for the involvement of the Commission in cases where reliance upon Article 296 EC by a Member State would lead to distortions of competition. This provision should be interpreted in the light of the duty of loyal cooperation enshrined in Article 10 EC. In other words, a Member State invoking Article 296 EC is under a legal duty to cooperate with the Commission in order to adjust any ensuing distortions of competition to the EC rules.

Finally, any deviation from EC law pursuant to Article 296 EC is subject to the jurisdiction of the Court of Justice. The reference to the 'improper use of the powers provided for in Article ... 296' in Article 298(2) EC refers both to the substantive conditions which need to be met by a

[2] Case 13/68 *Salgoil Salgoil SpA vItalian Ministry for Foreign Trade* [1968] ECR 453, 463, Case 222/84 *Johnston(ibid)*, para 26.

Member State invoking Article 296 EC (namely those regarding its scope of application, the assessment of 'essential interests of security') and the procedural ones (that is the duty to cooperate with the Commission inferred from Article 298(1) EC).

III PREVAILING INTERPRETATIONS OF ARTICLE 296 EC

It follows from the above that, according to a strict reading of Articles 296 and 298 EC, the right of Member States to regulate their defence industries by deviating from the entire scope of the *acquis communautaire* was confined to a specific class of products, should be exercised in accordance with certain principles, and was subject to the jurisdiction of the Court of Justice should its exercise amount to an abuse of power. However, contrary to this interpretation, Article 296 EC was viewed for a long time as rendering defence industries beyond the scope of EC law altogether.[3]

On the one hand, the Member States were only too eager to assume that Article 296 EC applied to the defence products generally, without engaging in any assessment of whether the specific conditions laid down therein were met. A case in point is public procurement: as the Commission points out, the low number of publications in the Official Journal appears to imply that some Member States believe they can apply the derogation automatically.[4] This approach was not challenged directly by the EU institutions for a long time. While none of the latter suggested that armaments were, in principle, beyond the scope of EC law, in practice they shied away from any controversy which would raise the question of the position of defence industries in the EC legal order, the extent to which this should be covered under EC law and the leeway which Member States enjoyed under Article 296 EC. It is noteworthy that, since the establishment of the Community, there has been only one infringement action against a Member State the subject-matter of which was armaments.[5] In the context of specific procedures, such as in the area of state aids, the Commission examined the compatibility of a national measure with Article 296 EC only in terms of whether that measure applied to products intended solely for products of a specifically military nature.[6]

[3] See P Koutrakos, *Trade, Foreign Policy and Defence in EU Constitutional Law* (Oxford, Hart Publishing, 2001) 175–82.

[4] COM (2004) 608 final *Green Paper on Defence Procurement*, p 6.

[5] Case C-414/97 *Commission v Spain* [1999] ECR I-5585. See the analysis in M Trybus, *European Union Law and Defence Integration* (Oxford, Hart Publishing, 2005) 152–4.

[6] See, eg, Decision 1999/763/EC on the measures, implemented and proposed, by the Federal State of Bremen, Germany in favour of Lürssen Maritime Beteiligungen GmbH & Co KG [1999] OJ L301/8.

On the other hand, the fate of the list of products to which Article 296(2) EC refers is indicative of the ambiguity into which the *ratio* of Article 296 EC was shrouded. While it was drawn up, as Council Decision 255/58, in April 1958, it was not published in the Official Journal or in any official document. Over the years, it was published in certain academic publications[7] and it was only in 2001 when it became publicly available by the European Commission in a response to a question at the European Parliament.[8] The list is quite broad.[9] This rather elusive quality of the list appeared to enhance the general view that defence industries were somehow afforded a special kind of protection under EU law.

IV GRADUALLY QUESTIONING OLD ASSUMPTIONS: LEGAL AND ECONOMIC DEVELOPMENTS

In the 1990s, a cautious and distinctly gradual shift developed in relation to the position of Article 296 EC in our EU vocabulary. This was due to a variety of factors. One of them was the case law of the EU Courts. The first judgment on the applicability of Article 296 EC was delivered by the Court of Justice in Case C-414/97 *Commission v Spain*.[10] This was about Spanish legislation exempting from VAT intra-Community imports and acquisitions of arms, munitions and equipment exclusively for military use. The Sixth VAT Directive excluded aircraft and warships. The action against Spain was brought because the relevant Spanish rules also covered an additional range of defence products. The Spanish Government argued that a VAT exemption for armaments constituted a necessary measure for the purposes of guaranteeing the achievement of the essential objectives of its overall strategic plan and, in particular, to ensure the effectiveness of the Spanish armed forces both in national defence and as part of NATO.

The Court of Justice held that, as in other public safety clauses set out in the EC Treaty, 'it is for the Member State which seeks to rely on those

[7] See H Wulf (ed) *Arms Industry Limited* (Oxford, Oxford University Press, 1993) at 214.

[8] Written Question E-1324/01 [2001] OJ C/364E/85.

[9] It covers the following categories, some of which are further divided into subcategories: 1. Portable and automatic firearms. 2. Artillery, and smoke, gas and flame throwing weapons. 3. Ammunition for the weapons at 1 and 2 above. 4. Bombs, torpedoes, rockets and guided missiles. 5. Military fire control equipment. 6. Tanks and specialist fighting vehicles. 7. Toxic or radioactive agents. 9. Warships and their specialist equipment. 10. Aircraft and equipment for military use. 11. Military electronic equipment. 12. Cameras specially designed for military use. 13. Other equipment and material. 14. Specialised parts and items of material included in this list in so far as they are of a military nature. 15. Machines, equipment and items exclusively designed for the study, manufacture, testing and control of arms, munitions and apparatus of an exclusively military nature included in this list.

[10] See n 5 above.

exceptions to furnish evidence that the exemptions in question do not go beyond the limits of such cases'.[11] It went on to point out that:

> Spain has not demonstrated that the exemptions provided for by the Spanish Law are necessary for the protection of the essential interests of its security. It is clear from the preamble to [the relevant national] Law that its principal objective is to determine and allocate the financial resources for the reinforcement and modernization of the Spanish armed forces by laying the economic and financial basis for its overall strategic plan. It follows that the VAT exemptions are not necessary in order to achieve the objective of protecting the essential interests of the security of the Kingdom of Spain.[12]

In addition to the above, the Court reiterated an economic argument, already made by Advocate General Saggio:

> the imposition of VAT on imports and acquisitions of armaments would not compromise that objective since the income from payment of VAT on the transactions in question would flow into the State's coffers apart from a small percentage which would be diverted to the Community as own resources.[13]

The judgment is characterised by a distinct focus on a construction of Article 296 EC which would not render it a *carte blanche* for the Member States. The conditions laid down in that provision were viewed as substantive conditions which needed to be met in a manner about which Member States need to convince the Court of Justice. This appeared to remove defence industries from a twilight zone of EC law and put the onus on the Member States to justify the exceptional status of particular defence industries on a case-by-case basis.

Four years later, in 2003, the Court of First Instance (CFI) delivered a judgment in Case T-26/01 *Fiocchi*.[14] In this case, the applicant, an Italian undertaking operating in the arms and munitions manufacturing and marketing sector, complained to the Commission about subsidies granted by the Spanish government to a Spanish arms production undertaking and enquired about their compatibility with the EC Treaty competition provisions as well as Article 296 EC. The Commission then requested information from the Spanish Government as to the nature and amount of the aid granted. When more than 15 months had passed and the applicant had heard nothing, it brought an action against the Commission for a declaration of failure to act.

[11] Para 22. For the strict interpretation of the exemptions set out in the public procurement measures, see Case C-324/93 *R v Secretary of State for the Home Department, ex parte Evans Medical and MacFarlane Smith Ltd* [1995] ECR I-563 at para 48.

[12] See n 5 above, para 22.

[13] *Ibid*, para 23.

[14] [2003] ECR II-3951.

It is interesting that the Spanish undertaking which received the subsidies in question also produced engines for civil aviation and components for olive oil decanting equipment. This illustrates the type of issues which the Commission needs to explore in cases of alleged use of Article 296 EC. The action was dismissed by the CFI as inadmissible, because the Commission had defined its position and, therefore, there was no failure to act within the meaning of Article 232 EC. Nevertheless, the CFI did engage in an examination of both Articles 296 EC and 298 EC. In relation to the former, it acknowledged the 'particularly wide discretion [conferred on the Member States] in assessing the needs receiving such protection' under Article 296 EC. However, the CFI made it clear that the special protection set out in that provision is limited to the Article 296(2) EC list.[15] The CFI also referred to the bilateral examination which the Commission and the Member State concerned are required to carry out under Article 298 EC and pointed out that the former is under no duty to adopt a decision concerning the measures at issue at the conclusion of the examination; the Commission has no power to address a final decision or directive to the Member State concerned.

In terms of the substance of the dispute, the applicant argued that the subsidies in question benefited the export activities of the company receiving them and, as such, fell beyond the scope of Article 296 EC. This was a point which the Commission pursued with the Spanish authorities and whose explanations appeared to be deemed credible.

Finally, the Court of Justice reinforced the wholly exceptional nature of Article 296 EC in three rulings on the application of sex equality rules in the armed forces. In Case C-273/97 *Sirdar*,[16] Case C-285/98 *Kreil*[17] and Case C-186/01 *Dory*,[18] it ruled that all the EC Treaty exceptional provisions, including Article 296 EC:

> deal with exceptional and clearly defined cases. It is not possible to infer from those articles that there is inherent in the Treaty a general exception covering all measures taken for reasons of public security. To recognise the existence of such an exception, regardless of the specific requirements laid down by the Treaty, might impair the binding nature of Community law and its uniform application.[19]

[15] To that effect, see also the Opinion of AG Jacobs in Case C-367/89 *Richardt et Les Accessoires Scientifiques SNC* [1991] ECR I-4621 at para 30.

[16] [1999] ECR I-7403.

[17] [2000] ECR I-69.

[18] [2003] ECR I-2479.

[19] Case C-273/97 *Sirdar,* (n 16) at para 16, Case C-285/98 *Kreil,* (n17) at para 16 and Case C-186/01 *Dory,* (n 18) at paras 30–31. For a comment, see P Koutrakos, 'How far is far enough? EC law and the organisation of the armed forces after *Dory*', (2003) 66 *Modern Law Review* 759 and M Trybus, *European Union Law and Defence Integration* (Oxford, Hart Publishing, 2005) ch 6.

In addition to the correct interpretation of Article 296 EC stressed by the Court in its case law, another development which questioned the validity of the position of defence industries as entirely beyond the reach of EC law was the change of political and economic climate. Following the end of the Cold War, the defence industries in the Member States suffered from considerable financial and structural problems: fragmentation and divergence of capabilities, excess production capability in certain areas and shortages in others, duplication, short production runs, reduced budgetary resources, and failure to engage in increasingly costly research.[20] This highly fragmented state gave rise to a number of initiatives, originating in both industry and State bodies, to achieve a degree of convergence which would enhance the competitiveness of the European defence industries.

Against this background of economic and structural deterioration, the European Commission took the initiative in the late 1990s and put forward a comprehensive approach to the restructuring and consolidation of the defence industries of the Member States. Based on an assessment of the economic problems and challenges facing their fragmented state in an increasingly globalised market,[21] it adopted a document entitled *Implementing European Union Strategy on Defence Related Industries*.[22] This suggested a detailed set of legal measures which was comprehensive in scope and covered areas such as public procurement, defence and technological development, standardisation and technical harmonisation, competition policy, structural funds, export policies and import duties on military equipment. This document articulated the need for a wide synergy of Community, EU, national and international measures while affirming the link between their subject-matter and the core of national sovereignty.

However, this initiative was not taken up by the Member States. In response to a request by the European Parliament, the Commission returned to the issues raised by the need for the consolidation of the defence industries in 2003. In a document adopted that year, it reiterated the need for a coherent cross-pillar approach to the legal regulation of defence industries with special emphasis on standardisation, intra-Community transfers, competition, procurement, exports of dual-use goods and research.[23]

[20] See, amongst others, A Georgopoulos, 'The European Armaments Policy: A *conditio sine qua non* for the European Security and Defence Policy?' in M Trybus and N White, *European Security Law* (Oxford, Oxford University Press, 2007) 198 at 203–205.

[21] COM(96) 10 final *The Challenges facing the European Defence-Related Industry. A Contribution for Action at European Level*, adopted on 24 January 1996.

[22] COM(97) 583 final, adopted on 12 December 1997.

[23] COM(2003) 113 final *European Defence—Industrial and Market Issues. Towards an EU Defence Equipment Policy* (adopted on 11 March 2003).

V THE RECENT INITIATIVE BY THE COMMISSION: CLARIFYING THE APPLICATION OF ARTICLE 296 EC

In December 2006, the Commission adopted the *Interpretative Communication on the application of Article 296 of the Treaty in the field of defence procurement*.[24] Its objective is 'to prevent possible misinterpretation and misuse of Article 296 EC in the field of defence procurement' and 'give contract awarding authorities some guidance for their assessment whether the use of the exemption is justified'.[25]

Drawing upon the wording of Article 296 EC and the Court's case law on the interpretation of the exceptional clause set out in primary and secondary legislation, the thrust of the Commission's initiative is that 'both the field and the conditions of application of Article 296 EC must be interpreted in a restrictive way'. In relation to the former, and drawing upon the CFI judgment in *Fiocchi*, it is argued that the material scope of Article 296 EC is confined to the Article 296(2) EC list which is 'sufficiently generic to cover recent and future developments', therefore enabling the exceptional clause to cover the procurement of services and works directly related to the goods included in the list, as well as modern, capability-focused acquisition methods.[26] However, it would not cover dual-use goods, for whose procurement security interests may justify the exemption from EC rules only on the basis of the exceptional clause set out in the Public Procurement Directive.[27]

In relation to the conditions of application of Article 296 EC, the Commission acknowledges the wide discretion granted to a Member State in order to determine whether its essential security interests ought to be protected by deviating from EC law. However, this discretion is not unfettered. To that effect, it is argued that any interests other than security ones, such as industrial or economic, cannot justify recourse to Article 296 EC even if they are connected with the production of and trade in arms, munitions and war material.[28] Furthermore, the reference in Article 296 EC to 'essential security interests' is viewed as 'limit[ing] possible exemptions to procurements which are of the highest importance for Member States' military capabilities'.[29]

[24] COM(2006) 779 final, adopted on 7 December 2006. On the area of defence procurement, see M Trybus, *European Defence Procurement Law* (The Hague, Kluwer, 1999).

[25] Page 3.

[26] Page 5.

[27] On the other hand, the Commission argues that the procurement of dual-use goods may be covered by Art 296(1)(a) EC 'if the application of Community rules would oblige a Member State to disclose information prejudicial to the essential interests of its security' (p 6).

[28] To that effect, it is argued that 'indirect non-military offsets which do not serve specific security interests but general economic interests, are not covered by Article 296 EC, even if they are related to a defence procurement contract exempted on the basis of that Article' (p 7).

[29] *Ibid*.

The Commission's Communication, then, refers to the role of the Member States. It states that it is:

> the Member States' prerogative to define their essential security interests and their duty to protect them. The concept of essential security interests gives them flexibility in the choice of measure to protect those interests, but also a special responsibility to respect their Treaty obligations and not to abuse this flexibility'.[30]

This general understanding of the Member States' role is further defined in relation to public procurement. The Commission argues that 'the only way for Member States to reconcile their prerogatives in the field of security with their Treaty obligations is to assess with great care for each procurement contract whether an exemption from Community rules is justified or not. Such *case-by-case assessment* must be particularly rigorous at the borderline of Article 296 EC where the use of the exemption may be controversial'.[31]

The corollary of the above is the careful definition of the role of the Commission. It is described as follows:[32]

> It is not for the Commission to assess Member States' essential security interests, nor which military equipment they procure to protect those interests. However, as guardian of the Treaty, the Commission may verify whether the conditions for exempting procurement contracts on the basis of Article 296 TEC are fulfilled.
>
> In such cases, it is for Member States to provide, *at the Commission's request*, the necessary information and prove that exemption is necessary for the protection of their essential security interests. The Court of Justice has repeatedly stated that "Article 10 EC makes it clear that the Member States are required to cooperate in good faith with the enquiries of the Commission pursuant to Article 226 EC, and to provide the Commission with all the information requested for that purpose" [Case C-82/03 *Commission v Italy*, para 15]. This concerns all investigations carried out by the Commission as guardian of the Treaty, including possible verifications of the applicability of Article 296 EC to defence contracts.
>
> Therefore, when the Commission investigates a defence procurement case, it is for the Member State concerned to furnish evidence that, under the specific conditions of the procurement at issue, application of the Community Directive would undermine the essential interests of its security. General references to the geographical and political situation, history and Alliance commitments are not sufficient in this context.

[30] *Ibid.*

[31] Page 8. The document goes on to mention the particular questions which need to be addressed by the national authorities: 'which essential security interest is concerned? What is the connection between this security interest and the specific procurement decision? Why is the non-application of the Public Procurement Directive in this specific case necessary for the protection of this essential security interest?' (*ibid*).

[32] *Ibid.*

The Commission's initiative does not advocate either the abolition or the revision of Article 296 EC. In the past, such radical solutions had been advocated by the European Parliament[33] which had viewed them as essential to the full application of the *acquis communautaire* to the defence industries.[34] Instead, this wholly exceptional provision appears to carry out an understandable function in the whole context of EC law, namely to ensure that certain activities associated with the core of national sovereignty are not subject to the rules and principles set out in the EC Treaty and articulated by the Court of Justice. It is interesting that, in its effort to justify the retention of Article 296 EC, the Commission actually engages in a creative exercise of adjusting and updating the Article 296(2) EC list: it states that the list should be interpreted in a way which recognises developments in technology since the list was drawn up and the different practices now employed to procure such items, such as 'modern, capability-focused acquisition methods' and the inclusion of contracts for related services and works.[35]

In its document, the Commission draws upon the very limited case law of the EU judiciary time and again. By doing so, not only does it substantiate its approach but it also suggests that its initiative aims to consolidate and clarify the existing position rather than introducing change in a highly sensitive area. The extent to which the Commission draws upon the Court's case law is by no means a novelty. It certainly lacks the direct interaction underpinning its response to the judgment in *Cassis de Dijon* where it underlined the policy ramifications introduced by *Cassis* and where it signalled a shift in the model of regulatory intervention.[36] Neither does it suggest such a direct policy effect as that underpinning the revision of the common rules on exports of dual-use goods where Regulation 1334/2000 abandoned the previous inter pillar regime[37] and introduced new rules exclusively based on the Community legal framework with express reference in its preamble to the judgments in *Werner*[38] and *Leifer*.[39] Instead, the emphasis in the Commission's document on the

[33] See, eg, Resolution A3–0260/92 on the Community's role in the supervision of arms exports and the armaments industry [1992] OJ C/284/138 at 142 and Resolution on the need for European controls on the export or transfer of arms [1995] OJ C/43/89 at 90, Resolution A3–0260/92 [1992] OJ C/284/138 at 142.

[34] The Parliament adopted subsequently a subtler position, asking for the revision of Art 296 EC and even pointing out its potential usefulness in shielding European defence industries from coming under the control of third-country companies: Report A4–76/97.

[35] See n 24 above, p 5.

[36] 'Communication from the Commission regarding the *Cassis de Dijon* judgment', [1980] OJ C/256/2.

[37] [2000] OJ L159/1. The previous regime was established under Reg 3381/94 [1994] OJ L367/1 and Decision 94/942/CFSP [1994] OJ L367/8.

[38] Case C-70/94 [1995] ECR I-3189.

[39] Case C-83/94 [1995] ECR I-3231.

Court's rulings aims to confine Article 296 EC to its proper context by clarifying the conditions under which Member States may invoke it.

Furthermore, the Communication stresses the role of the Member States and the discretion which they enjoy in assessing whether the protection of their security warrants reliance upon Article 296 EC—the prerogative of the Member States to define their essential security interests is acknowledged time and again throughout the document. What the Commission does not do is to bring this point to its natural conclusion and be clearer as to the corollary of the wide discretion enjoyed by the Member States, namely the inherently limited control which the Court of Justice may exercise pursuant to Article 298 EC. In another, albeit related, context, that of exports of dual-use goods, the Court of Justice stressed the discretion enjoyed by national authorities when adopting measures they deem necessary in order to guarantee public security and pointed out that it was the exercise of their discretion in accordance with the principles of necessity and proportionality which was to be determined by national courts.[40] In yet another context, that of Article 297 EC, Advocate General Jacobs stressed the highly subjective nature of the assessment that national authorities are called upon to make and the corresponding paucity of judicially applicable criteria for the exercise of judicial control of high intensity.[41] In this vein, it is suggested that, in terms of the essential interests of national security, the Commission, in the context of Article 298(1) EC, and the Court of Justice, in the context of Article 298(2) EC, would seek to establish only whether the argument put forward by the national Government is unreasonable.[42] This interpretation, which differs from the application of the traditional proportionality test, is consistent with the wording and the general scheme of Articles 296 EC and 298 EC.

Finally, the emphasis on the limited material scope of Article 296(1)(b) EC, the consultation procedure set out in order to address any ensuing distortions of competition under Article 298(1) EC, and the role of the Commission, all point towards the proceduralisation of the exceptional powers set out in Article 296 EC. This approach would allow the Commission to become more involved in cases where national authorities invoke this provision. Indeed, the entire Communication reads like a statement of intent, declaring the Commission's readiness to step into areas of high political sensitivity. This political character of the document should not be underestimated, all the more so as the interpretation put forward is rather stating what, from a legal point of view, has been obvious. This political dimension is also recognised by the Commission which seeks to strike the balance between its more pronounced role and the discretion

[40] See, eg, Case C-367/89 *Richardt,* (n 15 above) at paras 20 and 25.
[41] Note 1 above .
[42] See Koutrakos (n 3 above) at 189–91.

enjoyed by the Member States. For instance, it is stated that 'in evaluating possible infringements, the Commission will take into account the specific sensitivity of the defence sector'.[43]

In the light of the above, the content, emphasis and tone of the Commission's Communication suggest a gradual shift towards the normalisation of the application of Article 296 EC: rather than enabling Member States to approach it as the source of legal ambiguity and political sensitivity, it is to become subject to the Community law mechanisms of interpretation and enforcement, account being taken of the political and economic specificity of the defence industries. This is a significant development not only because of the apparent political sensitivity of the area, but also because of the number of developments and initiatives which have placed the defence industries at the centre of EU legislative and political dialogue. It is within this context, outlined in the following section, that Article 296 EC, and the Commission's recent approach to it need to be assessed.

VI POLICY INITIATIVES WITHIN THE EC LEGAL ORDER AND BEYOND

The Commission's recent expression of intent to enforce a stricter interpretation of Article 296 EC is not an isolated and random measure. Instead, it was designed as part of a wider and concerted host of policy initiatives focused on the rationalisation of the European defence industries.

These initiatives, outlined in advance and in a state of gestation for some time,[44] were formalised and presented in December 2007 as the Commission's 'defence package'. This consists of three measures. The first is a Communication on the competitiveness of the defence industry in which the Commission sets out a number of measures which would strengthen the European defence market.[45] These include common procurement rules, rules on intra-community transfers, the promotion of the use of common standards, the development of an EU system on security of information, the possibility of a common control system of strategic defence assets, and a host of measures aimed at improving overall coordination between national authorities in the process of defence planning and investment.

[43] See n 24 above, p 9.

[44] In March 2003, it adopted a document in which it sought to define the various strands of an effective defence equipment policy (COM(2003) 113 final *Communication on European Defence—Industrial and Market Issues: Towards an EU Defence Equipment Policy*). This deals with issues such as standardisation, intra-Community transfers, competition, procurement, export controls of dual-use goods and research.

[45] COM(207) 764 final (along with the other two documents, this was adopted on 5 December 2007).

The first two of the above measures were further articulated by the Commission in the form of specific legislative proposals adopted on the same date. In the area of defence procurement, a proposal for a Directive on public procurement of arms, munitions, war material, and related works and services was put forward.[46] Following a long period of consultation,[47] this proposal is based on the assumption that the highly fragmented state of the defence markets has serious implications for the European taxpayer, the competitiveness of the European defence industries and the effectiveness of the European Security and Defence. The main objective of this proposal is to introduce transparency and non-discrimination in an area where legal ambiguity and political considerations have imposed national solutions on the basis of considerations often at odds with economic efficiency. A central feature of the proposed Directive is the acknowledgement of the specific requirements of defence procurement: its preamble refers to them 'in terms of complexity, security of information or security of supply'.[48] To that effect, provision is made to allow Member States flexibility in the process of the negotiation of all aspects of the award as well as to impose specific clauses in order to ensure the confidentiality of sensitive information.

The second proposal adopted by the Commission in December 2007 is for a Directive on intra-Community transfers.[49] It targets the existing divergent national licensing regimes and suggests their simplification and harmonisation. Its aim is twofold: on the one hand, to facilitate specialisation and industrial cooperation within the EU, hence, strengthening the European defence industries; on the other hand, to improve security of supply of European defence products for Member States.

In addition to the above, the Commission has also dealt with the area of research and development. In 2004, it produced a document about the need to focus on research and development in the area of security.[50] The main tenet of this proposal is the development of a coherent security research programme at EU level which would be 'capability-driven, targeted at the development of interoperable systems, products and services useful for the protection of European citizens, territory and critical infrastructures as well as for peacekeeping activities' whilst also directly linked to 'the good functioning of such key European services as transport

[46] COM(2007) 766 final.

[47] In September 2004, the Commission had adopted COM(2004) 608 final in which it introduced the idea for a specific EC Directive in the area. The results of the public consultation process were presented in December 2005 in COM(2005) 626 final *Communication on the results of the consultation launched by the Green Paper on Defence Procurement and on the future Commission initiatives.*

[48] See n 46 above, para 25.

[49] COM(2007) 765 final.

[50] COM(2004) 590 final *Security Research: The Next Step.*

and energy supply'.[51] Four different areas are targeted: consultation and cooperation with users, industry and research organisations under the umbrella of a European Security Research Advisory Board; the establishment of a European Security Research Programme implemented as a specific programme with its own set of procedures, rules for participation, contracts and funding arrangements; cooperation with other institutional actors established under the Common Foreign and Security Policy (CFSP) and European Security and Defence Policy (ESDP) framework and especially the European Defence Agency; the establishment of a structure which would ensure the flexible and effective management of the European Security Research Programme. In addition to the above, the Commission also adopted a Green Paper on Defence Procurement.[52]

So far, this section has examined the various initiatives undertaken by the Commission in order to address the status and rationalisation needs of the European defence industries within the Community legal order. However, there is a parallel development seeking to serve similar objectives and originating beyond the Community legal order. This development follows directly from the process of the drafting of the Treaty Establishing a Constitution for Europe. While this Treaty proved to be ill-fated, it is significant in the context of this analysis because it provided for a number of innovations which were in fact taken up by the EU institutions as a matter of policy prior to the protracted death of the Treaty and which are maintained in the Lisbon Treaty.

The Constitutional Treaty provided for the establishment of an agency under the name of European Defence Agency (EDA) which would be specialised in the area of defence capabilities development, research, acquisition and armaments.[53] This was reproduced in the Lisbon Treaty, according to which the Agency:

> shall identify operational requirements, shall promote measures to satisfy those requirements, shall contribute to identifying and, where appropriate, implementing any measure needed to strengthen the industrial and technological base of the defence sector, shall participate in defining a European capabilities and armaments policy, and shall assist the Council in evaluating the improvement of military capabilities.[54]

However, the establishment of this Agency became an issue separate from the fate of the Constitutional Treaty and the Lisbon Treaty. Following a decision by the Thessaloniki European Council in June 2003, the Council set up an intergovernmental agency in the field of defence capabilities

[51] *Ibid* at 4.
[52] COM(2004) 608 final.
[53] Art I-41(3)(2).
[54] Art 28A(3) TEU as amended by the Lisbon Treaty (this reproduces Art I-41(3)(2) of the Constitutional Treaty. Further, see Art 28 D TEU as introduced by the Lisbon Treaty.

pursuant to a Joint Action in July 2004.[55] The objective of the Agency is 'to support the Council and the Member States in their effort to improve the EU's defence capabilities in the field of crisis management and to sustain the ESDP as it stands now and develops in the future' without prejudice to either the competences of the EC or those of the Member States in defence matters.[56] The tasks carried out by the EDA are in the areas of defence capabilities development, armaments cooperation, European Defence technological and industrial base and defence equipment market, and research and technology.

A general assessment of the function and record of the EDA is beyond the scope of this chapter.[57] Instead, it is its more recent initiative in the area of defence procurement which is relevant. In November 2005, the Defence Ministers of all the then participating Member States,[58] agreed a voluntary code on defence procurement. This entered into force on 1 July 2006.[59] This Code applies to contracts worth more than €1m which are covered by Article 296 EC.[60] It sets out to establish a single online portal, provided by the EDA, which would publicise procurement opportunities. It is based on objective award criteria based on the most economically advantageous solution for the particular requirement. Furthermore, it provides for debriefing, whereby all unsuccessful bidders who so request will be given feedback after the contract is awarded. The regime provides for exceptions for reasons of pressing operational urgency, follow-on work or supplementary goods and services, and extraordinary and compelling reasons of national security. An interesting aspect of this regime is its focus, amongst

[55] 2004/551/CFSP [2004] OJ L245/17. See also Council Decision 2003/834/EC creating a team to prepare for the establishment of the agency in the field of defence capabilities development, research, acquisition and armaments [2003] OJ L318/19.

[56] *Ibid*, Arts 2(1), 1(2) and 2(2).

[57] See A Georgopoulos, 'The New European Defence Agency: Major Development or Fig Leaf?' (2005) 14 *Public Procurement Law Review* 103, P Koutrakos, *EU International Relations* (Oxford, Hart Publishing, 2006) 473-5, M Trybus, 'The new European Defence Agency: a contribution to a common European security and defence policy or a challenge to the Community *acquis*?' (2006) 43 *CML Rev* 667.

[58] With the exception of Denmark, which has a permanent opt-out in the area of defence pursuant to Protocol 5 annexed to the Amsterdam Treaty. Currently all the other Member states participate, with the exception of Romania which is currently considering joining this regime.

[59] http://ue.eu.int/ueDocs/cms_Data/docs/pressData/en/misc/87058.pdf.

[60] It excludes nuclear weapons and nuclear propulsion systems, chemical, bacteriological and radiological goods and services, and cryptographic equipment, as well research and technology and collaborative procurements. Contracts which fall beyond the scope of Art 296 EC are covered by the EC public procurement secondary legislation. According to Art 10 of Dir 2004/18/EC on the coordination of procedures for the award of public works contracts, public supply contracts and public service contracts [2004] OJ L134/114, '[t]his Directive shall apply to public contracts awarded by contracting authorities in the field of defence, subject to Article 296 of the Treaty'.

others, on small and medium-sized enterprises and non-traditional supplies. The development of the portal for industry contract opportunities enables them to find sub-contracting opportunities listed in the same place, and, hence, help them in a tangible manner to participate in the developing transnational market.

The objective of this regime is to introduce transparency in defence procurement and increase the competitiveness of defence industries. The EDA considers the regime a success. In the first year of its application, governments advertised nearly 200 contract opportunities worth approximately €10 billion on the European Bulletin Board online portal. In its Report on European Security and Defence Policy, approved by the Council in June 2007, the German Presidency stated that the Agency 'was proving itself a fully effective instrument'[61] and implementation of the Code of Conduct was seen as 'successful'.[62]

VII A MULTILAYERED APPROACH: INCREMENTALLY TOWARDS RELATIVE NORMALISATION

This chapter has highlighted the development of a gradual shift of the legal position of defence industries from a *terra incognita* shrouded by legal ambiguity to a legal space within the Union constitutional order and the Community legal order where it attracts institutional attention both at supranational and intergovernmental level. The combined effect of the initiatives outlined above is the gradual normalisation of the position of defence industries and the growing emphasis on the relevance of EU law to its consolidation and restructuring. This normalisation is facilitated by the emphasis on the economic argument for the reliance upon common formulas. It is noteworthy that a starting point for all the Commission's initiatives is the stagnation and lack of competitiveness of the European defence industries. In an interesting parallel, the Commission recently proposed the imposition of criminal sanctions for serious violations of EC rules on exports of dual-use goods in order to ensure their effective application.[63] Following the judgment in C-176/03 *Commission v Council* (*Environmental Crimes*),[64] it suggested the application of this controversial instrument in an area which had been viewed for a long time to be too sensitive for Community regulation. It remains to be seen whether this

[61] Document 10910/07, at p 19.
[62] *Ibid* at p 20.
[63] COM (2006) 829 final *Proposal for a Council Regulation setting up a Community regime for the control; of exports of dual-use items and technology.*
[64] [2005] ECR I-7879.

proposal will be taken up.[65] It will be recalled that in the area of dual-use goods it was following two judgments of the Court of Justice[66] that the export of such products became subject to the full discipline of EC law. While the analogy with the legal regime of defence industries can only go so far, this is an interesting example of how 'legal normalisation' may occur in areas of acute political sensitivity.

However, it should be stressed that the origins of this gradual shift towards normalisation have been political as well as economic and legal. The development of the ESDP, the emphasis on the Union's security identity in the process of drafting and debating the Constitutional Treaty, the range of operations undertaken by the European Union around the world, all point towards the increasing significance of this policy for the development of the EU. This underlines, inevitably, the significance of its effectiveness which is undermined by the serious problems facing the defence industries. Therefore, a European defence industry riddled with economic problems would always prove to be an inherent limit to the effectiveness and efficiency of the ESDP. This political dimension is central to the recent Commission's initiatives. In the proposed Directive on defence procurement, for instance, the very first recital of the preamble states that '[t]he gradual establishment of a European defence equipment market is essential for strengthening the defence industrial and technological base in Europe and developing the military capabilities required to implement the European Security and Defence Policy'.[67]

It is interesting that one of the main contributions of the process of drafting, negotiating and ratifying the Constitutional Treaty should be to render the ESDP, an intergovernmental policy par excellence, at the very centre of the Union's development and create the momentum for addressing the requirements for its effectiveness. The fate of the Constitutional Treaty did not undermine this momentum as illustrated, at policy level, by the initiatives of supranational as well as intergovernmental actors in this area which had been considered, until recently, alien to any common regulatory initiative imposed from above. In this vein, it is noteworthy that the ESDP is the most popular EU policy: the January 2007 Eurobarometer shows a 75 per cent score of approval for having such a policy (in the UK the figure was 57 per cent; only Sweden and Ireland scored lower). In other words, there is a clear political as well as economic imperative for the rationalisation of the defence industries.

However, precisely because of the political underpinnings of any effort to rationalise the defence industries, the process suggested by the recent

[65] The judgment in Case C-440/05 *Commission v Council (Ship Source Pollution)* [2007] ECR I-9097 does not affect the substance of the Commission's proposal.

[66] Case C-70/94 *Werner*, (n 38) and Case 83/94 *Leifer* (n 39).

[67] Note 46 above at 10.

initiatives outlined in this chapter is bound to be met with caution, be long in its elaboration and not devoid of uncertainties in its application. Put it differently, the process of normalisation suggested above will be inherently relative in its substance and effects. At an institutional level, the developing position of defence industries is addressed on the basis of an approach which is multilayered in its scope and involves a variety of institutional actors. It suggests reliance upon legal as well as voluntary measures and engages the EC and the intergovernmental level of governance for its implementation. While this approach addresses the multifarious dimensions of, and interests underpinning, the regulation of defence industries, it would also give rise to inter-institutional tensions which may slow down the process and hamper its effectiveness. For instance, it will be interesting to see how the Commission's initiative in the area of defence procurement would work along with the EDA Code of Conduct. While their scope of application differs (the former applies to products not covered by Article 296 EC, the latter applies to products within the scope of Article 296 EC), the definition of the dividing line between the two is likely to be less clear cut than the Commission services envisage. The Commission is keen to stress the complementary nature of these initiatives.[68] However, any inter-institutional disputes in this area would be bound to be exacerbated by the political underpinnings of their subject-matter.

In terms of policy-making, for all the activity in the legislative sphere, the political will of the Member States for any substantial progress to be achieved is vital. This is not only in relation to the extent to which the Member States decide to commit themselves to this process, but also, in substantive terms, their willingness to bring about a convergence in their views of procurement policy.[69] Such commitment is essentially political in nature and cannot be forced on the Member States by means of secondary legislation.[70] In this respect, knowing the limits of the function of legal rules is to know how to rely upon them and with which other initiatives to combine them. A related factor which will test the viability of the Commission's proposals is the climate of economic nationalism[71] which appears to be increasingly popular in a number of Member States. Taking

[68] In its document, the Commission states that it 'will ... follow with great interest the development of the Code of Conduct' and points out that this 'kind of intergovernmental initiative would usefully complement the initiatives taken at Community level'. See also Answer to Written Question E-5644/2006.

[69] In the context of the consultation in advance of the Commission's Interpretative Communication on Article 296 EC, UNICE (The Confederation of European Business, renamed in January 2007 Europe Business) pointed out the different fundamental views of procurement policy of the Member State. (November 2006).

[70] To that effect, see the French response to the Commission's Green Paper on Defence Procurement.

[71] The French ex-Prime Minister De Villepin used the term 'economic patriotism': see *Financial Times*, 6 February 2007.

the form of measures preventing the takeover of domestic companies deemed 'national champions' by other EU companies, national governments did not hide their willingness to adopt such tactics in high profile cases in Germany, France, Italy, Spain and Poland last year.[72]

VIII CONCLUSION

This chapter told the story of a policy shift regarding an industry associated with the core of national sovereignty: once shrouded in legal ambiguity, political sensitivity and institutional caution, defence industries are gradually brought towards the centre of the EU constitutional framework and the Community legal order. The central position of their rationalisation for the effective conduct of the ESDP has created a political imperative which neither the Community institutions nor the Member States can afford to ignore. Viewed from this angle, the new interpretation of Article 296 EC suggested by the Commission along with the legislative proposals which it unveiled in December 2007 are welcome.

While the problems which their adoption would face should not be underestimated,[73] the significance of these initiatives should not be ignored. In policy terms, any progress made along the way is bound to be beneficial to the competitiveness of the defence industries as well as the effectiveness of the ESDP. Currently, the defence procurement market accounts for a large share of EU public procurement (it is estimated at about €80 billion out of a combined State defence budget of €170 billion).[74] More generally, the initiatives discussed in this chapter suggest that the momentum build from the process of drafting the Constitutional Treaty regarding the development of the ESDP is not only maintained but also develops a new focus on the practical aspects of that policy which had been overlooked in the past. This development illustrates a shift from the rhetoric about the effective role of the EU as a security and defence actor to the actual requirements for this role to be carried out.

Finally, the pace of the shift outlined in this chapter will be determined pursuant to as many and diverse factors as the policy needs which underpinned its genesis. After all, none of the initiatives discussed and the

[72] Indeed, in the recent financial scandal which hit the bank Société Générale, a number of senior politicians, including the European Affairs Minister, suggested that any foreign takeover attempt should be fought by the State, provoking a stern warning by Commissioner McCreevy: see *International Herald Tribune*, 31 January 2008.

[73] For instance, see *European Voice*, 28 February and 5 March 2008 at p 31 for objections by the French Government. See also *Financial Times*, 5 December 2007 at p 6 for concerns expressed by the industry.

[74] See debate at the European Parliament on 19 June 2007 on Oral Question 0–0022/2007.

measures proposed may be assessed in isolation. They need to be understood as parts of a gradually shifting, constantly evolving, multi-faceted legal and political space. It is their combined effect which would shape the position of defence industries in the Community legal order and the Union framework.

14

National and EC Remedies under the EU Treaty: Limits and the Role of the ECHR

ANGELA WARD*

I INTRODUCTION

Good *laws* are such laws for which good reasons can be given: good *decisions* are such decisions for which good reasons can be given. On the part of a judge whose wish it is that his decisions be good, who thinks them so, and who knows why he thinks them so (it is only in proportion as he knows why he thinks them good that they are likely so to be,) an equally natural object of anxiety will be the communicating the like persuasion to all to whose cognizance it may happen to them to present themselves; and more especially to those from whom a more immediate conformity to them is expected.

Jeremy Bentham 'Of Publicity and Privacy as Applied to Judicature in General and to the Collection of Evidence in Particular' in *Works of Jeremy Bentham* Vol 6 chapter X, 351.

ACCESS TO PUBLIC courts, and its necessary corollary, the availability of effective remedies to correct wrongs found to exist,[1] is a foundation principle of contemporary democratic governance everywhere. As the Court of Human Rights has observed, access to courts is 'one of the features of the common spiritual heritage of the member States of the Council of Europe';[2] it is essential to secure adherence to the rule of law,[3] and to guarantee against the exercise of arbitrary power.[4] It is

* Thanks to the Arts and Humanities Research Board for supporting this research, and for comments from Professor Rosa Greaves, University of Glasgow, Dr Catherine Donnelly, Trinity College Dublin, Dr Catherine Barnard of the University of Cambridge and Professor Judith Resnik of Yale Law School. Any faults remain those of the author.

[1] Application No 22774/93 *Immobiliare Saffi v Italy*, judgment of 28 July 1999.

[2] Application No 4451/70 *Golder v UK*, judgment of 21 February 1975, para 34.

[3] See para 57 of Application No 8225/78 *Ashingdane v UK*, judgment of 28 May 1985, citing paras 34–5 of Application No 4451/70 *Golder v UK*, judgment of 21 February 1975.

[4] Application No 4451/70 *Golder v UK*, judgment of 21 February 1975, para 35.

unsurprising, therefore, that it is reaffirmed in Article 47 of the EU Charter of Fundamental Rights.[5]

Yet, in the European Union (EU) system, the reasons for court involvement in adherence to the rule of law required express justification, at least with respect to the work of national judges in securing compliance by Member States with the rules promulgated by the new *sui generis* polity that the EEC represented. The main reason for this was rooted in constitutional framework established in the original EEC Treaty, but which subsists today. It remains a paradox of judicial review in the EU that the Treaty says almost nothing about judicial remedies to apply before the Member State courts when the compatibility of national rules with EC measures is in issue, and a great deal about the sanctions and procedures applicable when an individual wishes to challenge, before a judicial body, the legality of measures promulgated by the EU institutions. In justifying an expansive role for national courts in the former, the Court of Justice famously resorted to the concept of 'individual rights' which the national court had a duty to protect.[6] The same concept heavily under-pinned the later development of principles which extensively regulated Member State remedies and procedural rules. Individual rights, bolstered by the Article 10 EC duty of good faith and cooperation, have served to legitimate disapplication of national law on many significant occasions.[7]

While Article 234 of the EC Treaty vested national courts with the authority to refer questions to the Court of Justice on interpretation and validity of EC measures, the Treaty was silent on what these courts were bound to do, once a ruling on interpretation and validity had been made. In contrast, the judicial landscape was laid out in detail in the EEC Treaty, with respect to challenge to the legality, under EU administrative law,[8] of measures promulgated by EEC organs. A two month time limit was set under Article 230(5) for the nullity procedure established under Article 230(4); the same time limit applied to the action for failure to act established under Article 232. A test for *locus standi* was included in both

[5] It provides as follows: Everyone whose rights and freedoms guaranteed by the law of the Union are violated has the right to an effective remedy before a tribunal in compliance with the conditions laid down in this Article. Everyone is entitled to a fair and public hearing within a reasonable time by an independent and impartial tribunal previously established by law. Everyone shall have the possibility of being advised, defended and represented. Legal aid shall be made available to those who lack sufficient resources in so far as such aid is necessary to ensure effective access to justice.

[6] Case 26/62 *van Gend en Loos* [1963] ECR I-1.

[7] The best example is found, perhaps, in Court of Justice case law on State liability, which is predicated entirely on the concept of individual rights. See, eg, Case 46/93 and 48/93 *Brasserie du Pêcheur and Factortame III* [1996] ECR I-1029. For a most detailed study see M Dougan *National Remedies Before the Court of Justice* (Oxford, Hart Publishing, 2004).

[8] For a detailed study see T Tridimas, *The General Principles of EU Law* (Oxford, Oxford University Press, 2007).

Articles 230(4) and 232(3), supplying the now infamous threshold of 'direct and individual concern' as the standard to be met before the door of the Community judicature could be opened.[9] Damages were supplied as an express remedy, and indeed evolved into a free-standing procedure, under Articles 235 and 288(2),[10] with provision of a five year limitation period appearing in the rules of procedure. Finally, specific allowance was made for the award of interim relief by the Community judicature, with respect to suspension of EC measures, under Article 243 of the Treaty.

Aside from this, the powers of the Court of Justice to create remedies were stunted, in the sense that Article 231 provided only a power to declare EEC measures void, leaving the institution concerned with a duty, under Article 233, to 'take the necessary measures to comply with the judgment of the Court of Justice'. The Court of Justice has held repeatedly that it has no authority to issue any further remedies, such as compelling orders, going beyond the limits imposed by the EC Treaty, even if this is necessary, on the facts at hand, for timely correction of the wrong in issue.[11] This contrasts markedly with the classically intrusive case law of the Court with respect to Member State remedies and procedures, which patently requires the Member State courts to re-tailor national remedies if they supply inadequate safeguards against violation of Community rules.[12]

This paper will map out the extent to which there is disjuncture, or unevenness, between the remedies available to individuals when they contest the legality of EC rules, as opposed to the failure of Member States to respect the obligations imposed by (lawful) EU measures. Ironically, the crafting, in the original EEC Treaty, of express remedies and procedures to challenge the legality of EEC measures has had a dominantly limiting effect, while the silence of the foundation treaties on national sanctions and procedures has led to a body of case law that has 'grown like Topsy', and which places no clear limits on the extent to which Member State law, including constitutional law, must fall under the imperatives of *effet utile*.[13] The paper will also contend that the scale of the gap in standards of protection in judicial review is such that the case law on Member State remedies and procedural rules goes beyond

[9] See classically A Arnull, 'Private Applicants and the Actions for Annulment since *Codorniu*' (2001) 38 *CML Rev* 7.

[10] The test for *locus standi* under Art 230(4) does not apply under Art 288(2). Private parties are free to bring free-standing actions for damages. See, eg, Case C-63/89 *Assurances du Crédit v Council* [1991] ECR 1799.

[11] For example, Case T-2/04 *Korkmaz v Commission*, [2006] ECR II-32, request for an order suspending pre accession assistance to Turkey; Case T-285/94 *Pfloeschner v Commission* [1995] ECR II-3029, requests for the Commission to calculate a pension correctly; Case T-468/93 *Frinil Frio Naval e Industrial SA v Commission* [1994] ECR II-33, request for a declaration that a sum calculated in a specific manner was owed under the European Social Fund.

[12] See further below.

[13] See Section III A(i) below.

the minimum limits set by Articles 6(1) and 13 of the European Convention on Human Rights (ECHR), while the scheme for challenging the legality of EU measures quite possibly fails to measure up to them. Further, there is little evidence that the Lisbon Treaty will make any major adjustment to the legal scheme in place, aside from altering the test for individual concern under Article 230(4);[14] the Lisbon Treaty does not address the broader remedial problems here discussed.

The paper will then explore the feasibility of resorting to the case law of the Strasbourg court under Articles 6(1) and 13 ECHR to perform two functions; first, to stem the flow of references from national courts on the compatibility with Community law of Member State remedies and procedural rules, and, secondly, to prize open remedial barriers to an effective remedy when challenge to the legality of EC rules is in issue. Suggestion will also be made for reform to the text of Article 230(4), and the insertion of a new remedial provision into the EU Treaty, that would be addressed to both the Community judicature and Member State courts, that might assist in securing the same goal.

But why should this disjuncture in standards of judicial review matter? It matters, I would argue, for at least one key reason. As noted above, the rights of 'individuals' to effective judicial review to enforce their rights has, from the outset, formed a foundation of the constitutional matrix, justifying the enforcement of EC law over conflicting national Member State laws, and propelling the case law on national sanctions and procedures. It has been the touchstone of the reasoning that has secured compliance by national courts with this key plank of the constitutional edifice. If these standards do not apply when the same individuals are wronged by Community misconduct, then this pivotal constitutional plank loosens. As former Advocate General Jacobs has observed, in the context of Article 230(4) standing, while it may be 'too harsh to speak of double standards ... it cannot be denied that the strict rules on standing ... seem increasingly untenable in the light of the Court's case law on the principle of effective judicial protection'.[15] The extent to which this concern pervades other areas of the law on access to courts, remedies and procedural law, will be here considered.

II RIGHT OF ACCESS TO A COURT AND EFFECTIVE REMEDIES UNDER ARTICLES 6(1) AND 13 OF THE ECHR, AND THE ARTICLE 14 PRINCIPLE OF NON-DISCRIMINATION IN A REMEDIAL CONTEXT

The Court of Human Rights in Strasbourg has developed highly evolved principles on the minimum standards to be contained in schemes for

[14] See Section IV A below.

[15] Case C-50/00 P *UPA v Council* [2002] ECR I-6677, para 98.

judicial review for matters affecting 'civil rights and obligations' and 'criminal charges'.[16] States parties are precluded from imposing barriers that impair the 'very essence' of right of access to a court; restrictions must pursue a legitimate aim, and comply with the principle of proportionality.[17] This standard will be breached, for example, when an applicant is prevented in a 'practical manner' from bringing their claim in the domestic courts.[18]

Article 6(1) also prohibits states party from maintaining procedural rules at a level of incoherency such that they fail to afford an 'effective right of access' to courts.[19] Article 6(1) requires schemes of judicial review to be 'sufficiently coherent and clear' so as to afford 'a practical, effective right of access' to courts.[20] Thus, if rules of administrative and constitutional review are of 'such complexity' that they create 'legal uncertainty', then infraction of Article 6 will result.[21] What Article 6(1) imports is a system that achieves a 'fair balance' between the interests of governmental authorities, on the one hand, and, on the other, those of private parties wishing to challenge public measures.[22] Judicial remedies must be 'sufficiently attended by safeguards to prevent a misunderstanding as to the procedures for making use of available remedies'.[23] It is established that 'unreasonable construction of a procedural requirement' by a court can result in breach of right of access to a court;[24] the 'manner in which they are applied' may give rise to breach of Article 6(1).[25]

The requirements of Article 13 ECHR are less onerous, and less detailed, but nonetheless the Court of Human Rights is increasingly placing flesh on its bones.[26] While states parties are not bound to supply a judicial remedy

[16] While there are a core of public functions that do not attract the protection afforded by Art 6(1), such as taxation matters that fall short of imposing criminal penalties (see Application No 44759/98 *Ferrazzini v Italy* judgment of 12 July 2001) there are now a range of administrative functions that are caught by Art 6(1). There are many, therefore, legal disputes concerning EU law that fall within the ambit of 'civil rights and obligations'.

[17] Application 116/1997/900/1112 *Pérez de Rada Cavanilles v Spain*, judgment of 28 October 1998 para 44; Application 62/1997/846/1052–1053 *Tinnelly & Sons Ltd and Others v UK* 10 July 1998, para 72.

[18] Application No 28945/95 *TP and KM v UK*, judgment of 10 May 2001, para 100.

[19] Application No 12964/87 *Geouffre de la Pradelle v France*, judgment of 16 December 1992, para 35.

[20] *Ibid* at para 35.

[21] *Ibid* at para 33.

[22] *Ibid* at para 34.

[23] Application No 21/1995/527/613 *Bellet v France*, judgment of 20 November 1995, para 37.

[24] For example, Application No 23436/03 *Melnyk v Ukraine*, judgment of 28 June 2006, para 23; see also eg, Application No 47273/99 *Běleš v The Czech Republic*, judgment of 12 February 2003, paras 50 and 51.

[25] Application No 51343/99 *Angel Angelov v Bulgaria*, judgment of 15 May 2007, para 36.

[26] '[I]n recent years ... the ECt HR appears to have 'rediscovered' art 13. Whilst the substantive case law as such has not changed, art 13 is being successfully invoked with

to enforce Convention rights,[27] if judicial means are chosen they must ensure 'appropriate relief' and 'adequate redress' for violation of the ECHR.[28] Remedies must be effective both 'in practice and in law'.[29] Further, the scale, or depth, of scrutiny exercised by judicial authorities is also governed by principles that have been elaborated pursuant to Article 13. For example, it has been held, in the context of the Article 8 right to private and family life, that review for irrationality under English administrative law provided insufficient scrutiny to protect that provision.[30]

The Article 14 prohibition on discrimination, on grounds of sex, race, colour, language, religion, political or other opinion, national or social origin, association with a national minority, property, birth, or other status in the enjoyment of Convention rights also extends to remedial discrimination arising in the context of breach of an ECHR substantive right. That means, for example, that it applies to the payment of benefits which a state party chooses to provide 'which fall within the scope of a substantive article'.[31] Such benefits must be payable in compliance with the requirements of Article 14. It equally means that, if there has been discrimination in right of access to a court, then breach of Article 14 will follow.[32] Article 14, like the parallel EU rule on remedies and procedures (the principle of equivalence or non-discrimination) contains a requirement to prove difference of treatment in a comparable or analogous situation as a pre-requisite to showing breach.[33] Objective justification for a difference in treatment with respect to a remedy or a procedure (including assessment for proportionality) forms the final tranch of the exercise necessary to determine whether there as been breach of Article 14 ECHR.[34] As will be shown below, this does not appear to form part of the test for equivalence in EU

increasing frequency, in judgments of increasing detail, so as to encourage the appropriate adaptation of national legal systems to secure the Convention rights within domestic law.' T de la Mare 'The Right to an Effective Remedy' in Lester and Pannick *Human Rights Law and Practice* 2nd edn (London, Lexis Nexis, 2004) para 4.13.2.

[27] Application No 30210/ 96 *Kudla v Poland* 26 October 2000, para 151.

[28] *Ibid* paras 57 and 58.

[29] Application No 45701/199 *Metropolitan Church of Bessaruba and Others v Molodova*, judgment of 27 March 2002, para 137.

[30] Application No 44647/98 *Peck v UK* 28 April 2003; Application No 36022/97 *Hatton v UK* 8 July 2003.

[31] *R (Hooper, Withey, Naylor and Martin) v Secretary of State for Work and Pensions* [2002] EWHC 191 (Admin) at para 17.

[32] For two examples of cases in which this was pleaded that there had been a breach of Art 14 in the context of Art 6(1) see Application 62/1997/846/1052–1053 *Tinelly v UK*, judgment of 10 July 1998, and Application No 6289/73 *Airey v Ireland*, judgment of 9 October 1979.

[33] For example, Case 36–37/1995/542–543/628–629 *Stubbings v UK*, judgment of 24 September 1996. For an example in the EU context see, eg Case C-34/02 *Sante Pasquini v INPS* [2003] ECR I-6515.

[34] For example, Application No 11581/85 *Darby v Sweden*, judgment of 23 October 1990, para 31.

law, at least in the context of review of Member State sanctions and procedural law.

III EU LAW

To what extent, then, can it be said that these standards form part of EU law? Does compliance with them differ depending on whether a dispute concerns an allegation of unlawful conduct by an EU institution, or compliance by a Member State with (lawful) EU rules?

A General Principles Applicable Before the National Courts

(i) Remedies and Access to a Court in EU Law

The first point to note is that, while the Court of Justice has held that Articles 6(1) and 13 form part of the legal principles from which it draws inspiration in implying fundamental rights into the EU legal order,[35] its reliance on these provisions to craft parallel rules for the EU legal order has rather been done in a vacuum. There has been a notable absence of reference to relevant Strasbourg authority when Article 6(1) and 13 issues have arisen.[36] This is not atypical. As one commentator has observed, 'incoherence and conspicuous lack of method' has characterised the manner in which the Luxembourg and Strasbourg courts have relied on each other's case law in all fields.[37]

For example, in the context of Article 6(1), there is no requirement under the EU law equivalent for a litigant to prove that a 'civil right or obligation', or 'criminal charge' has been hindered as a pre requisite for triggering the right to a 'fair and public hearing',[38] including the right of access to a court.[39] Nor does the requirement appear in Article 47 of the

[35] Most notably in Case 222/86 *Johnston v Chief Constable of the RUC* [1986] ECR 1651.

[36] For a notable exception see Case C-276/01 *Steffensen* [2003] ECR I-3735, in which the Court of Justice relied on relevant Strasbourg authority in determining whether there had been a breach of the principle of equality of arms. For a recent detailed study comparing the two systems see S Douglas-Scott 'A Tale of Two Courts: Luxembourg, Strasbourg, and the Growing European Human Rights *aquis*' (2006) 43 *CML Rev* 629.

[37] Douglas-Scott *ibid* at 655–6. For a recent example, however, on extensive reference to Strasbourg case law, to determine the existence and content of any right to family reunification in EU law, see Case C-540/03 *European Parliament v Council* [2006] ECR 5769.

[38] See, eg, AG Alber in Case C-63/01 *Evans* [2003] I-14447; M Dougan above n 7 at 5 . See also text of the EU Charter of Fundamental Rights, Art 47 (n 5).

[39] Paradoxically, in Application No 28541/95 *Pelligrin v France*, judgment of 8 December 1999, consideration was given to the meaning of 'public service' afforded by the Court of

EU Charter. At present, national judges do not examine whether an allegedly obstructive sanction or procedural rule strikes at the 'heart' of right of access to a court. They do not examine whether the impediment pursues a legitimate aim, or whether it complies with the principle of proportionality. Therefore, while it is to be assumed, and is indeed reflected in Opinions of the Advocates General,[40] that the case law on Articles 6(1) and 13 here produced is reflected in EU fundamental rights law and, in principle, applies to review of Member State sanctions and procedures, it is by no means binding on the Luxembourg court, and the specific elements here laid out are yet to be formally adopted in an ECJ judgment.

The context in which the Article 13 ECHR case law has been elaborated merits consideration. Under ECHR law, there is a right to an effective remedy only with respect to violation of the substantive rights contained in the ECHR; Article 13, like Article 14, is not, therefore, a free-standing head of review, and must be attached to a subsisting right appearing in the Convention. In this sense, it translates a little more awkwardly into EU law than the Article 6(1) right of access to a court. Article 6(1) includes a right to full consideration of principles of EU law when they are relevant to a dispute before a state party court,[41] thus setting down a general principle directly relevant to the enforcement of Community law rights. That said, however, it would seem that the 'heart' or 'spirit' of Article 13 is reflected in Community law in the remedial case law on *effet utile*, to which I will now turn.

The seminal *San Giorgio* case of the Court of Justice embedded, in the EU Constitutional matrix, the principle that national remedies and procedural rules that render Community law impossible in practice or excessively difficult to enforce have to be disapplied.[42] This principle evolved not as an offshoot of Articles 6(1) and 13 of the ECHR, but rather under the auspices of the Article 10 duty on Member State courts to secure the full effectiveness of Community law.[43]

This *San Giorgio* rule has resulted, over the years, in disapplication of onerous rules of evidence operative under national law,[44] the setting aside of a defence based on 'excusable error',[45] disapplication of restrictions on

Justice in Case 149/79 *Commission v Belgium* [1980] ECR 3881, to limit the meaning of 'civil right or obligation' under Art 6(1). See Douglas-Scott above n 36 at 642.

40 For example, AG Alber in *Evans* (above n 38) and AG Sharpston in Case C-432/05 *UNIBET (London) and Another v Justitiekanslern* [2007] ECR I-2271.

41 Application No 107/1995/613/701 *Hornsby v Greece*, judgment of 25 February 1997; Application No 36677/97 *Dangeville v France*, judgment of 16 July 2002.

42 Case 199/82 *San Giorgio* [1983] ECR 3595, para 14.

43 See in particular Dougan (n 7 above).

44 *Ibid*.

45 Case C-188/95 *Fantask* [1997] ECR I-6783.

the payment of interest,[46] confusion on whether or not temporal restrictions of various kinds appertaining under national law can survive the imperatives of *effet utile*[47] (and which remain on-going)[48] adjustment to national laws on unjust enrichment,[49] and the setting aside of national fault requirements with respect to claims based on Community law,[50] ultimately culminating in the development of State liability in damages.[51] It has also entailed a clear obligation on national judges to create new remedies, if there is a remedial gap under national law in the sense of no sanction being available,[52] and required specific improvement of remedies, such as the creation of rules that would prevent victimisation of ex-employees who had suffered discrimination under the Equal Treatment Directive, when it was not supplied under national law.[53] It has also been considered in a myriad of other contexts, and recently in a case as to whether national procedural rules regulating the undertakings entitled to participate in market analysis proceedings complied with *effet utile*.[54]

In short, the principle of effectiveness continues to generate questions on the compatibility with Community law of an eclectic range of national sanctions and procedural rules, which are sometimes reviewed by the Court of Justice, and sometimes sent back to the national court for consideration. The main fettering rule has been the obligation on the national judge to assess the national rule in issue by reference to the role of that provision in the procedure, its progress and its special features, viewed as a whole,[55] rather than the principles elaborated by Strasbourg under Articles 6(1) and 13, which have never been relied on to impose limiting effects. Examples of application of *effet utile*, that have been left to national referring courts, after judgment from the Court of Justice, include whether national rules governing costs on Article 234 reference breach render Community law impossible in practice or excessively difficult to

[46] Cases C-397/98 and C-410/98 *Metallgesellshcaft and Others v Commissioners of Inland Revenue* [2001] ECR I-1727; see also Case C-470/04 *Kantoor Almelo* [2006] ECR I-7409. *Cf* however, Case C-66/95 *Sutton* [1997] ECR I-2163.

[47] Section III A(i) below.

[48] See, eg, Case C-2/06 *Willy Kempter AG v Hauptzollamt Hamburg Jonas*, judgment of 14 February 2008.

[49] See, eg, Case C-192–218/95 *Comateb* [1997] ECR I-165.

[50] Case 177/88 *Dekker v Stichting* [1990] ECR I-3941.

[51] Case C-46/93 *Brasserie du Pêcheur and Factortame III* [1996] ECR I-1029.

[52] Established in Case C 213/89 *Factortame No 1* [1990] ECR I 2433. See also, significantly Case C-97/91 *Borelli* [1992] ECR I-6313; Case C-432/05 *UNIBET (LONDON) and Another v Justitiekanslern* [2007] I ECR 2271, paras 40 and 41.

[53] Case C-185/97 *Coote v Granada Hospitality* [1998] ECR I-5199.

[54] Case C-426/05 *Tele 2 Telecommunications GmbH v Telekom-Control-Kommission*, judgment of 21 February 2008.

[55] Eg recently Joined Cases C-222/05, C-223/05, C-224/05, C-225/05 *Van der Weerd and Others v Minister van Landbouw, Natuur en Voedselkwaliteit* [2007] ECR I-4233, para 33, citing Case C-312/93 *Peterbroeck* [1995] ECR I-4 599; C 430 and 431/93 *van Schijndel* [1995] ECR I-4705.

enforce,[56] whether a rule on preclusion of placement of goods on the market pending customs clearance infringed the same,[57] and whether national rules applied to the enforcement of a Directive complied with the Article 6(1) ECHR principle of equality of arms.[58] It is plain, therefore, that the open-ended nature of the *San Giorgio* test has meant that there is, apparently, no end to the types of national procedural rules, and principles concerning sanctions, which potentially fall for review by either the Court of Justice or the national courts for breach of the principle of *effet utile*; the outcome of whether a rule is in compliance with it or not presents as a rather hit and miss affair.

Further, there has been considerable expansion of the scope of *effet utile* in that it now applies to obstructions to effective sanctions that arise in the context of *horizontal* enforcement of Directives between private sector actors.[59] Further, Article 6(1) ECHR has also been applied in the context of a European Framework decision, along with the doctrine of sympathetic interpretation;[60] a jurisprudential tool that has been traditionally confined to the first pillar. This carried the kernel for extension of the remedial case law on *effet utile* to the Police and Judicial Cooperation in Criminal Matters pillar. It has recently been held that, while no direct action lies against EU institutions with respect to Common Positions, the correct route of challenge is via the national courts, and Article 35(1) TEU.[61] In that context, an obligation lies on Member States courts to interpret and apply national procedural rules in a way that enables legal persons to challenge before the national courts Member State measures relating to the drafting or application to them of an act of the EU.[62] This would appear to open the gate to the possibility for the application of *effet utile* rules with respect to Common and Foreign Security Policy measures before Member State courts, albeit by reference to national measures that secure their implementation. This case law offers more to individuals than the principles elaborated by the Court of Human Rights under the case law developed under Articles 6(1) and 13 ECHR.

[56] Case C-472/99 *Clean Car Auto-Service GmBH v Austria* [2001] ECR I-9687.

[57] Case C-228/98 *Dounias v Minister for Economic Affairs* [2000] ECR I-577.

[58] Case C-276/01 *Steffensen* [2003] ECR I-3735.

[59] See notably Case C-185/97(n 53 above); see also Case C-473/00 *Cofidis SA v Jean Louis Fredout* [2002] ECRI-10875.

[60] Case C-105/03 *Maria Pupino* [2005] ECR I-5285. However, it was recently established that no action for damages whatsoever under Title VI of the EU Treaty. Case C-354/04P *Gestoras Pro Amnista and Others v Council* [2007] ECR I-1579, paras 44–8; Case C-355/04P *Segi and Others v Council of the European Union* [2007] ECR I-1657 paras 53–6. For a further example of fundamental rights review and Framework decisions see Case C-303/05 *Advocaten voor de Wereld VZW v Leden van de Ministerraad* [2007] ECR 3633.

[61] Case C-354/04P *Gestoras Pro Amnista and Others v Council* [2007] ECR I-1 579 paras 53–5.

[62] *Ibid* at para 56; Case C-355/04P *Segi and Others v Council of the European Union* [2007] ECR I-1657, para 56.

So, for example, the Court of Human Rights will not interpret national time limits for filing of documents to ascertain their compliance with the Article 6(1) right of access to a court; the interpretative task will be left to the national courts, with the Court of Human Rights ruling on whether the effect of that interpretation complies with Article 6(1).[63] While the Court of Human Rights will find breach of Article 6(1) if there has been an unreasonably rigorous application of a national time limit for lodging documents,[64] it may be slow, in comparison with the Luxembourg Court, to declare a national time limit per se unlawful. It will find violation of Article 6(1) if a state party court has concluded, in error, that documents were filed out of time,[65] but would be reluctant to impugn the time limit itself.

The types of measures that will be considered by the Court of Human Rights to amount to a disproportionate breach of Article 6(1) include those that prevent a judicial determination of the merits of the complaint at hand;[66] but if such a determination occurs, and the applicant has not been prevented in any practical manner from bringing their case before the courts, there will be no violation of the right of access to a court.[67] Overly rigorous application of prescribed rules of statutory procedure will also result in violation of Article 6(1)[68] but, again, rarely the procedure itself. For example, retroactive application of the rules of civil procedure that was unforeseeable will result in violation of Article 6(1),[69] but the procedural rules themselves are less likely to fall foul of Article 6(1).

(ii) The Principle of Equivalence

The second arm of Court of Justice case law on national sanctions and procedural rules is comprised of the principle of equivalence. National sanctions and procedural rules will require disapplication, as a matter of Community law, if they are less favourable than those extended to national claims of a purely domestic nature.[70] That is all that is required. In contrast

[63] Application No 116/1997/900/1112 *Pérez de Rada Cavanilles v Spain*, judgment of 28 October 1998, para 43.

[64] *Ibid* at para 48.

[65] Application No 51343/99 *Angel Angelov v Bulgaria*, judgment of 15 May 2007, para 38.

[66] For example, *Tinelly* (n 32) at para 77.

[67] *TP and KM v UK* above n 18 at para 101.

[68] Application No 47273/99 *Bělěs v The Czech Republic*, judgment of 12 February 2003 paras 48– 52.

[69] Application No 23436/03 *Melnyk v Ukraine*, judgment of 28 March 2006 paras 29 to 31.

[70] For example, Case C-326/97 *Levez v Jennings (Harlow Pools) Ltd* [1998] ECR I-7 835; Case C-261/95 *Palmisani v Istituto Nazionale della Providenza Sociale (INPS)* [1997] ECR I-4025. T Tridimas, *The General Principles of EU Law* (Oxford, Oxford University Press, 2006) 424–7.

with the case law of the Court of Human Rights under Article 14, and indeed the case law of the Court of Justice itself concerning indirect breach of the principle of equal treatment as a general principle of law, objective justification has no operation in the case of sanctions and procedural rules.[71] Even though the Court of Justice has held that the principle of equivalence in Member State remedies and procedural rules is 'simply an expression of the principle of equal treatment',[72] it does not usually, in the remedial cases, go on to consider whether there is objective justification for a difference in treatment with respect to a remedy or a procedure (including assessment for proportionality) although this forms the final tranch of the exercise necessary to determine whether there as been breach of Article 14 ECHR.[73] Objective justification also forms part of the test under EU law for direct infraction of principle of equal treatment, when it is applied as a general principle of EU law.[74]

Rather, the Court of Justice has finessed the rule on equivalence by stressing that, when assessing whether a provision complies with it, account must be taken of its function in the procedure as a whole, as well as its operation and special features before the national court;[75] that is, it has applied the same 'brake' as that which has been formulated with respect to *effet utile*. While the comparative exercise necessarily makes it less open-ended than the principle of effectiveness, the absence of a limiting rule, such as objective justification, renders it equally vulnerable to stretching to the minutiae of national law. It has been held to be applicable to 'all procedural rules governing the treatment of comparable situations, whether administrative or judicial'.[76] It has been considered, for example, in the context of limitation periods,[77] caps on the sums recoverable for breach of equal treatment law,[78] the applicability of the concept of

[71] Tridimas *ibid* at 426 expresses the following view: 'It seems appropriate that the requirement of equivalence should prohibit not only direct but also indirect discrimination against claims based on Community law. Where a procedural rule applies to certain categories of claims, most of which are based on Community law, and a more favourable rule applies to other categories of claim, most of which are based on national law, the first rule may run counter to the requirement of equivalence unless it is objectively justified. There is however no express judicial endorsement of that view and what case law there is may cast doubt on it.'

[72] *Pasquini* (above n 33) at para 70.

[73] For example, Application No 11581/85 *Darby v Sweden*, judgment of 23 October 1990, para 31.

[74] See, eg, Case 170/84 *Bilka-Kaufhaus GmbH v Weber von Hartz* [1986] ECR 1607. Tridimas (above n 8).

[75] *Levez* above n 70 at para 44. Cited in Tridimas (above n 70) at 425.

[76] Case C-34/02 *Sante Pasquini v INPS* [2003] ECR I-6515, para 62.

[77] Case C-261/95 *Palmisani v INPS* [1997] ECR 4025.

[78] *Levez* above n 70. Case C-180/95 *Draehmpaehl* [1997] ECR I-2195.

excusable error,[79] repayment of taxes,[80] payment of interest,[81] and the applicability of the principle of 'good faith'.[82]

B Remedial Principles and General Remedial Powers of the Court of Justice

Reference to both the Strasbourg principles here discussed, and the principles elaborated in the context of Member State remedies and procedural rules, has been conspicuously absent in the interpretation by the Court of Justice in the elaboration of its powers under Articles 231 and 233. There has been a surprising lack of comparison, in the case law, between the standard imposed by the EC Treaty and the rules of procedure of the Court of First Instance and the Court of Justice, and those applicable before Member State courts. A notable exception is found in the Opinion of Advocate General Jacobs in Case C-312/93 *Peterbroeck*.[83] There Advocate General Jacobs, in an Opinion that differed from the findings of the Court of Justice, observed as follows, before concluding that a national time limit on the raising of arguments to an appeal court was compatible with Community law.

> The position is not dissimilar in Community law itself. What constitutes an issue which this Court will examine of its own motion, depends, as in national law, on the nature of the proceedings. In proceedings for the review of the legality of Community measures before this Court or the Court of First Instance, for example under Article 173 or Article 179 of the Treaty, it will be for the parties to define the issues and hence to delimit the scope of the action, but the Court will examine of its own motion whether, for example, the time limits for bringing the action have been observed. (23) However, in actions for compensation brought against the Community under the second paragraph of Article 215 of the Treaty, the Court will not of its own motion raise the issue of time limitation under Article 43 of the Protocol on the Statute of the Court of Justice of the EC where that issue has not been raised by the defendant—that position receiving some support, in cases of non-contractual liability, if one invokes the 'general principles common to the laws of the Member States' referred to in the second paragraph of Article 215. (24) In a reference for a preliminary ruling under Article 177 of the Treaty, on the other hand, the proceedings are not contentious (25) and the Court will in some circumstances raise issues going beyond the

[79] Case C-62/93 *BP Supergas v Greek State* [1995] ECR I-1883: see the Opinion of the AG.
[80] Case C-147/01 *Weber's Wine World* [2003] ECR I-11365.
[81] Case C-222/99 *Riccardo Prisco v Amminstrazione delle Finanze dello Stato* [2002] ECR I-6761
[82] Case C-34/02 *Sante Pasquini v INPS* [2003] ECR I-6515
[83] [1995] ECR I-4599.

observations submitted to the Court, in order to give the national court the fullest guidance on the questions of Community law relevant to that court's decision.[84]

As has already been mentioned, the Community judicature has held steadfastly to the position that the text of Articles 231 and 233 preclude it from using directions and particularised orders, to correct a wrong found to exist. So, for example, it has declined a request for an order suspending pre-accession assistance to Turkey,[85] and an application for an order that a pension should be calculated by reference to the correct formula,[86] and refused to issue a declaration that a sum owed under the European Social Fund be determined in a specific manner.[87] Similarly, the Court of Justice has interpreted Article 288(2) as allowing the Community judicature to issues damages orders only, and no ancillary or other order.[88]

This can lead, I would argue, to violation of *San Giorgio* rule, in that no practical remedy may be available when a declaration that a measure is 'void' fails to cure the wrong which has occurred. This will typically arise when a Community institution has withheld something it was bound by law to supply or do. It might also be viewed as 'excessively difficult' to expect the applicant to wait for the Community institution to decide what action is required before the wrong is corrected. Damages under Article 288(2) may not, in all circumstances, be of great practical utility. The interpretation of Articles 231 and 233 by the Community judicature may also infringe the principle of equivalence. Have litigants before the Community judicature been treated in a manner different from litigants before the national courts? If this discrimination is indirect, is there objective justification for it (even though this need not be shown under the current remedial case law)? At minimum, there are questions that need to be asked about the compliance with Articles 6(1) and 13 of the restrictions on the orders that the Community judicature are empowered to make.

Even by the lighter standards elaborated by Strasbourg, the case law under Article 231 and 233 may breach Articles 6(1) and 13 of the ECHR. If the remedies available are, in some circumstances, ineffectual, does this strike at the heart of the right of access to a court? It is established that effective sanctions form part of the Article 6(1) right of access to a court.[89] What then, is the objective justification for the restriction on the range of orders the Community judicature can issue? Is the restriction proportionate? Has the

[84] *Ibid* at para 38.

[85] Case T-2/04 *Korkmaz v Commission* [2006] ECR II-32.

[86] Case T-285/94 *Pfloeschner v Commission* [1995] ECR II-3029.

[87] Case T-468/93 *Frinil-Frio Naval e Industrial SA v Commission* [1994] ECR II-33.

[88] Case C-63/89 *Assurances du Crédit and Compagnie Belge d'Assurance Crédit v Council and Commission* [1991] ECR 1 799.

[89] *Immobliari Saffi* above n 1.

Community judicature made an overly rigorous interpretation of these provisions, resulting in violation of Article 6(1)? Has Article 13 been breached, due to the failure to provide 'appropriate relief' and 'adequate redress' both 'in practice and in law'?[90]

The specific remedial provisions supplied under the EC Treaty, namely Articles 230(4) (standing; coupled with Article 234 validity), Article 230(5) (time limits), Article 243(interim measures) and Articles 235 and 288(2) damages will be considered below. Here too, with the possible exception of Article 288(2), there is a remedial gap, creating doubts over their compliance with the standards set by both the Luxembourg and Strasbourg courts.

IV SPECIFIC REMEDIAL POWERS IN THE EC TREATY AND GAPS IN REMEDIAL PROTECTION

A The *Locus Standi* Test under Article 230(4)

The question of *locus standi* to challenge the compliance of Member State laws with Community rules is governed by national rules, subject to the principles of effectiveness and non-discrimination. In contrast, a Community standard is supplied under Article 230(4), requiring individuals to meet the notoriously difficult threshold of 'direct and individual concern'.[91] In contemporary times, there has been some relaxation of the classical requirement that the measure impugned affects the individual challenging it in the same way as an addressee.[92] It seems now that there is no requirement to prove that a measure amounts to a disguised decision as a necessary pre-requisite to conferral of standing;[93] if EC legislation guarantees a right to participation in a process, and it has been exercised, then *locus standi* will follow;[94] if there is a special relationship between severe economic effects on a trader, and the measure impugned, then the trader will be taken to be individually concerned by the measure;[95] if EC legislation imposed an obligation on an EU institution to consider the position of the Applicant, and they failed to do so, then standing will be conferred;[96] and breach of the principle of democracy appears to have been given a special status, with standing having been granted for those who

[90] See text to nn 26–9.

[91] For a detailed and classical study see Arnull (above n 9). For a recent case on direct concern see Case C-15/06 P *Regione Siciliana v Commission* [2007] ECR I-2591.

[92] Case 25/62 *Plaumann v Commission* [1963] ECR 95.

[93] For example, Case T-13/99 *Pfizer Animal Health SA v Council* [2002] II-ECR 3305.

[94] For example, Case T-339/00 *Bactria v Commission* [2002] ECR II-2287, para 51.

[95] Case C-309/89 *Cordoniu SA v Council* [1994] ECR I-1853.

[96] See classically Case C-152/88 *Sofrimport v Commission* [1990] ECR I-2477.

have suffered loss as a result of its breach.[97] Yet, even these categories have been difficult to prove,[98] and they have not resulted, in practice, in any significant shift away from the original restrictive test.[99]

So does this rule square with the standard imposed on Member States with respect to sanctions and procedures, and the case law of the Court of Human rights?

The Community judicature is yet to apply the *San Giorgio* rule to the context of the interpretation of Article 230(4). As a result, there has been no principled consideration of whether Article 230(4) renders access to judicial review impossible in practice or excessively difficult.

As far as the Strasbourg case law is concerned, Articles 6(1) and 13 have been referred to in judgments of the Court of Justice when compliance of Article 230 (4) with the Strasbourg standard has been questioned. This occurred perhaps most prominently in the judgment of the Court of First Instance in Case T-177/01 *Jégo Quéré v Commission*[100] where modification to the test for direct and individual concern was suggested by the Court of First Instance, but later rejected by the Court of Justice.[101] There the Court of First Instance observed as follows:

> In that regard, it should be borne in mind that the Court of Justice itself has confirmed that access to the courts is one of the essential elements of a community based on the rule of law and is guaranteed in the legal order based on the EC Treaty, inasmuch as the Treaty established a complete system of legal remedies and procedures designed to permit the Court of Justice to review the legality of acts of the institutions (Case 294/83 *Les Verts v European Parliament* [1986] ECR 1339, paragraph 23). The Court of Justice bases the right to an effective remedy before a court of competent jurisdiction on the constitutional traditions common to the Member States and on Articles 6 and 13 of the ECHR (Case 222/84 *Johnston* [1986] ECR 1651, paragraph 18).
>
> In addition, the right to an effective remedy for everyone whose rights and freedoms guaranteed by the law of the Union are violated has been reaffirmed by Article 47 of the Charter of Fundamental Rights of the European Union proclaimed at Nice on 7 December 2000 (OJ 2000 C 364, p. 1).

[97] Case T-135/96 *UEAPME v Council* [1998] ECR II-2335.

[98] See in particular the *Cordoniu* economic effects exception. For a discussion see A Ward, *Judicial Review and the Rights of Private Parties in EU Law* (Oxford, Oxford University Press, 2007) 305–10.

[99] For an example, however, on conferral of individual concern because the decision appertained to a 'series of identified vessels' (para 48) and because the Commission knew that the decision concerned 'solely the interests and positions of those owners' thus constituting a 'closed group of identified persons' (para 49) see Joined Cases T-218/03– T-240/03 *Boyle v Commission* [2006] ECR II-1699.

[100] [2002] ECR II-2365.

[101] Case C-263/02P [2004] ECR 3425. See also Case C-50/00 *UPA* [2002] ECR I-6677.

> It is therefore necessary to consider whether, in a case such as this, where an individual applicant is contesting the lawfulness of provisions of general application directly affecting its legal situation, the inadmissibility of the action for annulment would deprive the applicant of the right to an effective remedy.[102]

Here too there was a lack of reference to any of the relevant Strasbourg case law in the assessment of whether the traditional test for individual concern precipitated breach of right of access to a court. In finding that it did, the Court of First Instance was particularly mindful of the fact that, in the case at hand, there were no national implementing measures, thus tying off Article 234 review as a possible avenue of redress, and the inadequacy of Article 288(2) damages on the facts at hand.[103] Yet no analysis was made as to whether this struck at the heart of access to a court, whether the restrictions imposed under Article 230(4) pursued a legitimate aim, or whether they were proportionate.

Subsequent to this case, however, both the Court of Justice and the Court of First Instance have consistently come to conclusions contrary to those made in *Jego Quéré*. They have done so on the basis that Article 234 validity review *does* supply adequate means of redress, reminding national courts of their Article 10 duty of loyal cooperation to see to it that effective remedies are available.[104] The availability of Article 288(2) damages has also been underscored.[105] These conclusions have equally been reached in the absence of consideration of Strasbourg case law concerning Articles 6(1) and 13. In the light of the case law, is the view sustainable that Article 234 validity guarantees effective judicial review?

Since the Court of First Instance issued its judgment in *Jégo Quéré*,[106] the case law has edged away from the requirement of the existence of national implementing measures as a pre-requisite to challenge to the validity of Community laws; this no longer appears to be necessary.[107] It has been suggested that this means that national courts are bound to open up new channels of validity review if they do not exist under national law.[108]

102 Above n 100 at paras 41–3.

103 *Ibid* at para 45.

104 For example, *UPA* (above n 15) at paras 40–4; eg Joined Cases T-172/98 and 175/98–177/98 *Salamander AG and Others v European Parliament and Council* [2000] ECR II-2487 para 74; Case T-377/00, T-379/00, T-380/00, T-260/01 and T-272/01; *Philip Morris* [2003] ECR II-1 at paras 120–4. Case C-15/06P *Regione Siciliana v Commission of the European Communities* [2007] above n 91, para 39.

105 Case T-2/04 *Korkmaz v Commission*, [2006] ECR II-32, para 55.

106 Above n 100.

107 Joined Cases C-27 and 122 /00 *R v Secretary of State for the Environment, Transport, and the Regions ex parte Omega Air and Omega Air v Irish Authority* [2002] ECR I-2569; Case C-344/04, *The Queen on the Application of (1) International Air Transport Association and (2) European Low Fares Airline Association v Department of Transport* [2006] ECR I-403.

108 J Temple-Lang 'Actions for Declarations that Community Regulations are Invalid; the Duties of National Courts Under Article 10 EC' (2003) 28 *EL Rev* 102 at 111.

Doubt still might be cast, I would argue, on whether the validity channel is a remedy of practical utility, as is required under both Articles 6(1)[109] and 13 ECHR.[110] In practice, how easy is it to persuade national judges to open up a channel for redress in the absence of a national implementing measure, and thus a lack of direct connection with the judge's own national jurisdiction? Further, the applicant is not entitled to an Article 234 validity reference to the Court of Justice; the applicant must persuade the national judge that there is serious doubt as to the validity of the Community measure concerned.[111] Does this barrier, combined with the restrictions on Article 230(4), render in practice, access to a court so difficult that it strike's at the heart of it? Is there any legitimate aim to support the obstacles in place to securing judicial review of Community measures, and are they proportionate? Article 234 validity is by no means a speedy procedure. Are there problems under Article 6(1) due to the delay inherent in the scheme?[112]

Finding the correct avenue for judicial review of EC measures is further complicated by the so-called *TWD* rule, which precludes an individual from having recourse to Article 234 validity review if they 'without any doubt' could have brought proceedings under Article 230(4).[113] Yet, the Article 230(4) case law is constantly under pressure for change. Does the *TWD* rule create such confusion that it fails to meet the legal certainty requirements, and outlined above,[114] built into Article 6(1)? Is the rule 'sufficiently attended by safeguards to prevent a misunderstanding as to the procedures for making use of available remedies'?[115]

There is one final respect in which the interpretation of Article 230(4) that has been made by the Community judicature might be considered overly rigorous or unreasonable, in breach of the requirements of Article 6(1) ECHR. As I have pointed out elsewhere, the Court of Justice has, from the very beginning of its Article 230(4) case law, categorised measures as 'legislative' in nature, thus attracting the *Plaumann* test for direct and individual concern, when the measures might more realistically be viewed

[109] Above text to nn 17–18.

[110] Above text to nn 25–30.

[111] Case 314/58 *Foto-Frost* [1987] ECR 4199.

[112] But see the judgment of the Court of Human Rights in Application No 163/1996/782/983 *Pafitis and others v Greece*, judgment of 26 February 1998, para 95, Art 234 does not form part of the remedial landscape for which states party to the ECHR can be held responsible under Art 6(1).

[113] Case C-188/92 *TWD Deggnedorf v Germany* [1994] ECR I-833; Case C-441/05 *Roquette Freres v Ministre de l'Agriculture, de l'Alimentation, de la Pêche et de la Ruralité* [2007] ECR I-1993.

[114] Above text to nn 18–25.

[115] Application No 21/1995/527/613 *Bellet v France*, judgment of 20 November 1995.

as administrative.[116] For example, in the *Plaumann* case itself,[117] the measure impugned concerned a Commission Decision addressed to the German Government in which the Commission had refused authorisation for change in the customs duties applicable to clementines. This approach has subsisted,[118] with the Court of First Instance showing only occasional willingness to declare 'direct and individual concern' with respect to Decisions addressed to Member States, but which are plainly targeted at individual traders.[119] It has been suggested that a more realistic assessment of the administrative or normative nature of an EC measure might result if account was taken instead of the procedure through which a measure is promulgated; legislative processes involving the Parliament might be expected to create normative rules properly reviewable under Article 234 validity proceedings, while delegated functions such as the comitology process might be characterised as administrative or executive, and thus apt for review under Article 230(4).[120] The extent to which the Lisbon Treaty might have opened the door for the evolution of the law in the fashion will be considered below.

B Time Limits

There has been no significant alteration to the time limits set with respect to nullity review under Article 230(5) (two months) or Article 288(2) damages claims (five years). The case law of the Court of Justice parallels the Strasbourg 'standard', albeit in the absence of reference to Article 6(1) ECHR or the relevant case law; that is the time limits themselves have not been questioned, and the Court of Justice has avoided overly-rigorous interpretation of them. The time limit can be extended due to unforeseeable circumstances and *force majeur*,[121] excusable error, such as conduct of a Community institution that has caused delay.[122] The same can be said for the interpretation by the Court of Justice of Article 48(2) of the Rules of Procedure of the Court of First Instance. It, in effect, imposes a temporal

[116] Ward, '*Locus Standi* Under Article 230(4) of the EC Treaty: crafting a coherent test for a wobbly polity' (2003) *Yearbook of European Law* (Oxford, Oxford University Press, 2003) 45–78.

[117] Above n 92.

[118] For example, Case T-370/02 *Alpenhain-Camembert-Werk v Commission* [2004] ECR II-2097.

[119] See *Boyle* above n 99.

[120] Ward (see above n 116). See also M Vogt 'Indirect Judicial Protection in EC Law—the case of the plea of illegality' (2006) 3 *EL Rev* 364; H Hofmann 'A Critical Analysis of the new Typology of Acts in the Draft Treaty Establishing a Constitution for Europe' *European Integration Online Papers* vol 7 (2003) No 9.

[121] See Art 45 of the Statute of the Court of Justice; Case T-201/04 *Microsoft Corporation v Commission* [2005] ECR II 1491.

[122] For example, Case C-193/01 *Pistiorlas v Council* [2003] ECR I-4837.

restriction on the raising of arguments, by precluding new arguments after the written phase has closed. This restriction has been reinforced in the case law of the Court of Justice, to the determinant of private parties.[123]

On the other hand, the saga of Court of Justice intervention in national time limits for bringing proceedings, and temporal restrictions on the raising of arguments on appeal, before *national* courts, is well known. The application of the principles of effectiveness and non-discrimination to this area of the law, entirely insulated from the relevant Strasbourg principles under Article 6(1), has created a river of case law. This started with the 1990 *Emmott* case[124] and the 1995 *Peterbroeck* ruling concerning respectively, time limits for bringing proceedings and the raising of new arguments on appeal. The *Emmott* case, at the time it was issued, appeared to require the wholesale disapplication of national time limits, under the imperative of *effet utile*, with respect to unimplemented Directives. While this was pared back in the ensuing decade, to a general principle that reasonable time limits for bringing proceedings will be compatible with the principle of *effet utile*,[125] provided that the Member State had not discouraged the individual concerned from bringing proceedings in good time,[126] the question continues to arise before both the Court of Justice and the national courts,[127] sometimes resulting in disapplication of a temporal rule. So, for example, in Case 225/100 *Grundig Italia*[128] a transitional time limit of three years for bringing proceedings, which had replaced a five year period, was held by the Court of Justice to breach the principle of effectiveness. The Court of Justice reached this conclusion, even though the Advocate General had ruled that it was so clear that the three year time limit was *lawful*, that the whole matter could have been dealt with using Article 104(3) of the Rules of Procedure and the accelerated process it provides.[129]

With regard to temporal restrictions on the raising of new arguments on appeal, this topic recently received illumination in Joined Cases C-222/05 and C-223/05, C-222/04 and C-225/05 *Van der Weerd and Others v Minsiter van Landbouw, Natuuur en Voedselkwaliteit*.[130] There, the applicants had

[123] For example, Case C-227/92P *Hoechst AG v Commission* [1999] ECR I-4443, paras 93–4; *Gestoras Pro Amnistia and Others v Council of the EU* above n 61, paras 29–32.

[124] C-208/90 *Theresa Emmott v Minister for Social Welfare and AG* [1991] ECR I-4269.

[125] See in particular Case C-188/95 *Fantask* [1997] ECR I-6 783.

[126] For example, Case C-231/96 *Edis* [1998] ECR I-4951, para 48.

[127] *Re Time Barred Appeal Against Tax Assessment* [2007] 2 CLMR 10 (German Federal Finance Court); *The Medical House plc v Her Majesty's Commissioners for Revenue and Customs* [2007] 2 CMLR 8, Manchester VAT Tribunal; *The Conde Naste Publications Limited v Commissioners for HM Revenue and Customs* [2007] 2 CMLR 35 (English Court of Appeal).

[128] [2002] ECR I-8003.

[129] Opinion of 14 March 2002, para 32.

[130] [2007] ECR 4233.

wholly failed, within the time frames set under national law, to refer to EC authority relevant to the resolution of the dispute at hand. It was held, in the light of the principles established in Case C-430 and 431/93 *van Schijndel*[131], that provided the parties were given a genuine opportunity to raise a plea based on Community law before a national court, then the national court did not have to do so of its own motion. Of most interest, is that the Court of Justice expressly distinguished past case law in which it had been held that temporal restrictions on the raising of arguments based on EC law breached the principle of effectiveness.

> That result is not called into question by the case law in *Peterbroeck*; Case C-126/97 *Eco Swiss* [1999] ECR I-3055; Joined Cases C-240/98 to C-244/98 *Océano Grupo Editorial and Salvat Editores* [2000] ECR I-4941; Case C-473/00 *Cofidis* [2002] ECR I-10875; and Case C-168/05 *Mostaza Claro* [2006] ECR I-10421.
>
> The case law cited in the previous paragraph is not relevant in the present case. One of those cases can be distinguished by reason of circumstances peculiar to the dispute, which led to the applicant in the main proceedings being deprived of the opportunity to rely effectively on the incompatibility of a domestic provision with Community law (see *Peterbroeck*, paragraph 16 *et seq*). In other cases, the Court's findings are justified by the need to ensure that consumers are given the effective protection which Council Directive 93/13/EEC of 5 April 1993 on unfair terms in consumer contracts (OJ 1993 L 95, p 29) seeks to achieve (see *Océano Grupo Editorial and Salvat Editores*, paragraph 26; *Cofidis*, paragraph 33; and *Mostaza Claro*, paragraph 29). Moreover, that case law cannot be properly invoked in an analysis of an infringement of the principle of effectiveness, since it seeks to determine whether equal treatment is given to pleas based on national law and those based on Community law (see *Eco Swiss*, paragraph 37).[132]

While this represents a welcome attempt at clarification, and deference to national procedural authority, it may not suffice to dispel entirely the legal certainty problems that have occurred in this field. When will 'peculiar' circumstances arise justifying an obligation on national judges to deal with points of Community law of their own motion? When will it be apparent that the purpose underpinning a Directive requires a national judge to do the same? The Court's enigmatic reference to ensuring the observance of the principle of equal treatment in the context of pleas based on EC law as underpinning the 'exceptional' cases is insufficiently reasoned and unconvincing.

Raw statistical results show that legal uncertainty continues to dominate the case law when *effet utile* collides with temporal restrictions. Of 13

[131] [1995] ECR I-4705.
[132] *Ibid* at paras 39–40.

leading cases[133] decided in the last six years concerning the compatibility of temporal restrictions under national law with the principle of effectiveness, six have resulted in judgments against the application of the national restriction,[134] while one of them left a question on this point for the national referring court to decide.[135] I would argue that one way in which this flow of case law, and authority, might be arrested, lies in modification of the *San Giorgio* rule itself, in the light of the minimum requirements on access to a court and remedies set by the case law of the Strasbourg court. In this way, the flow of references on *effet utile* and remedies that continue to go to the Court of Justice[136] might be reduced.

C Interim Relief

Neither Articles 6(1) or 13 of the ECHR have been interpreted by the Strasbourg court as necessarily obliging states parties to ensure the availability of interim relief for alleged breach of a right protected by the ECHR. However, if failure of a state party to supply an interim order led to violation of the general principles elaborated under these articles, then a violation would surely result. Further, the Court of Human Rights has recently held that failure to enforce an interim order can result in breach of substantive rights protected under the Convention (in the case before it, breach of the right to family life).[137] Interim relief is also available, as a

[133] Joined Cases C-240/98–C-244/98 *Océano Grupo Editorial SA v Rocio Murciano Qunitero* [2000] ECR I-4941; Case C-88/99 *Roquette Frères SA v Direction des Services Fiscaux du Pas-de-Calais* [2000] ECR I-10465; Case C-78/98 *Preston* [2000] ECR I-3201; Case C-481/99 *Heininger and Heininger v Bayerishce Hypo-und Vereinsbank AG* [2001] ECR I-9945; Case C-62/00 *Marks & Spencer plc v Commissioners of Customs and Excise* [2000] ECR I-6325; Joined Cases C-216/99 and C-222/99 *Ricardo Prisco Srl v Amministrazione delle Finanze dello Stato* [2002] ECR I-6761; Case C-255/00 *Grundig Italiana SpA v Ministero delle Finanze* [2002] ECR I-8003; Case C-473/00 *Cofidis SA v Jean-Louis Fredout* [2002] ECR I-10875; Case C-327/00 *Santex SpA v Unità Socio Sanitaria Locale n. 42 di Pavia* [2003] ECR I-1877; Case C-125/01 *Peter Pflücke v Bundesanstalt für Arbeit* [2003] ECR I-9375; Case C-234/04 *Rosemarie Kapferer v Schlank & Schick GmbH* [2006] ECR I-2585; Opinion of AG Tizzano of 10 November 2005; *Van der Weerd* above n 130; Case C-2/06 *Willy Kempter AG v Hauptzollamt Hamburg-Jonas*, judgment of 12 February 2008.

[134] Joined Cases C-240/98–C-244/98 *Océano Grupo Editorial SA v Rocio Murciano Qunitero* [2000] ECR I-4941; Case C-78/ 98 *Preston* [2000] ECR I-3201; Case C-62/00 *Marks & Spencer plc v Commissioners of Customs and Excise* [2002] ECR I-6325; Case C-255/00 *Grundig Italiana SpA v Ministero delle Finanze* [2002] ECR I-8003; Case C-473/00 *Cofidis SA v Jean-Louis Fredout*, judgment of 21 November 2002, [2002] ECR I-10875; Case C-327/00 *Santex SpA v Unità Socio Sanitaria Locale n 42 di Pavia* [2003] ECR I-1877.

[135] Case C-125/01 *Pflücke v Bundesanstalt für Arbeit* [2001] ECR I-9375.

[136] For example, Case C-35/05 *Reemtsma Cigarettenfabriken GmbH v Ministero delle Finanze* [2007] ECR I-2425 on reimbursement of taxes and *Tele 2* above n 54, on the right to participate in market analysis proceedings.

[137] Application No 39177/05 *VAM v Serbia*, judgment of 13 June 2007, paras 137–44.

legally enforceable right, to individuals who petition the Court of Human Rights, but whose final judgment is pending.[138]

It is perhaps unsurprising, therefore, that Articles 6(1) and 13 have had no relevance to the elaboration of the rules on interim relief before the Community judicature. The foundation principles governing the award of interim relief in Article 230(4) claims are found in Article 242 and 243 of the EC Treaty, and Articles 104 to 110 of the Rules of Procedure the Court of First Instance.[139] Under Article 104(2) applicants seeking interim orders must state the circumstances giving rise to urgency[140] and the pleas of fact and law that establish a prima facie case for the grant of the order.[141] They must show that serious and irreparable harm will be suffered if the award is not granted.[142] While it is not necessary for it to be absolutely certain that the damage will occur, a sufficient degree of probability being enough, the applicant is none the less required to prove the facts which are considered to found the prospect of such damage.[143] Purely financial damage will not be enough,[144] unless it threatens the survival of the undertaking, and therefore could not be fully compensated in the main action. While it seems that irreparable damage to an ecosystem might justify the issue of an interim order, the threshold is very high; it must 'certainly and imminently' ensue before interim relief will be ordered.[145]

[138] *Mamatkulov and Abdurasulovic*, judgment of 4 February 2005.

[139] See also Art 242 of the EC Treaty and the authority of the Court of Justice to suspend the temporal effects of judgments. See discussion in Joined Cases C-486/01 P – R and C-488/01 P – R *Front National, Jean-Claude Martinez v European Parliament* [2002] ECR I-1843. Similar powers are vested in the Court of First Instance under the second and third paragraphs of Art 39 CS in conjunction with Art 4 of Council Decision 88/591/ECSC, EEC, Euratom of 24 October 1988 establishing a Court of First Instance of the European Communities ([1988] OJ L/319/1) as amended by Decision 93/350/Euratom ECSC EEC of 8 June 1993 ([1993] OJ L/144/21).

[140] For example, Case T-34/02 R *B v Commission* [2002] ECR II-2803, paras 85–102; Case T-198/01 R *Technische Glaswerke Ilmenau GmbH v Commission* [2002] ECR II-2153 paras 96–109; Case T-392/02 R *Solvay Pharmaceuticals BV v Council* [2003] ECR II-1825, paras 104–120; Case C-471/00 P(R) *Commission v Cambridge Healthcare Supplies Ltd* [2001] ECR I-2865 paras 107–28; Case T-367/07R *Dow AgroSciences Ltd v Commission*, judgment of 17 December 2007.

[141] For example, Case T-392/02 R *Solvay Pharmaceuticals BV v Council* [2003] ECR II-1825, paras 70–88; Case T-345/05 R III *V v European Parliament*, judgment of 22 November 2007; Case C-236/07P(R) *Sumitomo Chemical Agro Europe SAS v Commission*, judgment of 23 January 2008.

[142] See, eg, Case C-404/01P(R) *Commission v Euroalliages and others* [2001] ECR I-10367, para 63.

[143] Case C-180/01 P–R *Commission v NALOO* [2001] ECR I-5737, para 53.

[144] For example, Case C-471/00 P(R) *Commission v Cambridge Healthcare Supplies Ltd* [2001] ECR I-2865, para 113.

[145] Case T-37/04 R, *The Autonomous Region of the Azores v Council*, [2004] ECR II-2153, para 153.

All the interests involved will be weighed in the balance before an order is issued, including the Community interest.[146] Economic interests, in the form of loss sustained by a private party will not outweigh the need to protect human health when the latter is reflected in the impugned EC measure.[147] If interim relief is viewed as a disproportionate remedy, in the light of the aim to be achieved, it will be refused.[148] Finally, the applicant must also be able to show, at the interim relief stage, that they have a legal interest in bringing proceedings.[149]

There is one key issue, however, that forms a significant barrier to interim relief before the Court of First Instance, but which does not appertain in proceedings before national courts. In order to obtain an interim order, the party seeking it will have to show that prima facie, they are directly and individually concerned by the measure they are seeking to suspend. Direct and individual concern remains the most tenacious barrier to direct access to the Court of First Instance. The Court of Justice ruled that the same requirement was applicable to proceedings concerning interim relief, even though it is mentioned in neither the Rules of Procedure nor Articles 242 or 243, because 'otherwise, proceedings based on Article 185 would make it possible to obtain de facto the result sought by the main action, while the outcome of the latter remains . . . doubtful'.[150] In the light of all these features, the test for the award of interim relief, as elaborated by the Court of Justice and the Court of First Instance, has proved to be difficult to satisfy, and requests for interim orders are often refused.

The position is quite different when an individual challenges the compatibility of national law with Community measures before national tribunals.

[146] For examples of cases in which these rules have been applied in the context of Art 230(4) challenge to regulations, see Case T-228/95R *S Lehrfeund Ltd v Council and Commission* [1996] ECR II-111 (hereafter referred to as *Lehrfeund*); Case T-168R *Eridania Zuccherifici Nazionali SpA and others v Council* order of the President of the Court of First Instance of [1995] ECR II-2817; Case T-6/95 R *Cantine dei colli Berici coop. arl v Commission* [1995] ECR II-647; Case T-230/97 R *Comafrica SpA and Dole Fresh Fruit Europe Ltd and Co v Commission* [1997] ECR II-1589; Case T-13/99 R *Pfizer Animal Health SA/NV v Council* [1999] ECR II-1961 and Case T-70/99 *Alpharma Inc v Council* [2002] ECR II-3495; Case T-198/01 R *Technische Glaswerke Ilmenau GmbH v Commission* [2002] ECR II-2153 paras 113– 24; Case T-392/02 R *Solvay Pharmaceuticals BV v Council* [2003] ECR II-1825, paras 120–27.

[147] Case T-76/96 R *The National Farmers Union and Others v Commission* [1996] ECR II-815.

[148] Case T-37/04 R *The Autonomous Region of the Azores v Council* [2004] ECR II – 2153, paras 127–138.

[149] For example, Case T-398/02 R *Linea GIG Srl v Commission* [2003] ECR II-1139, para 26; only measures that have binding legal effects such as to bring about a distinct change in the applicants' legal position can attract an application for interim relief. See Case C-521/04 P(R) *Hans Martin Tillack v Commission* [2005] ECR I-3103, paras 15 and 34.

[150] Case 44/75 R *Firma Karl Könecke v Commission* [1975] ECR 637, 640 (a regulation). For directives see, eg, *R Pfizer v Commission* [1987] ECR 1691.

Member State courts are bound to ensure that the remedy of interim relief is 'available' when an individual litigant contests the compatibility of Member State law with Community rules.[151] It was established, after a period of doubt,[152] in the 2007 case of *Unibet*,[153] that the conditions governing the award of interim relief are governed by national law, subject to respect for the principles of effectiveness and equivalence.[154] The conditions described above, which are operative in nullity cases before the Court of Justice, are of no direct relevance, therefore, in compatibility cases before the Court of Justice.

In the context, however, of Article 234 validity review, the national applicable rules are to be analogous to those applicable when an application for interim relief is brought before the Community courts.[155] At paragraph 79 of *Unibet* the Court of Justice observed that it 'is clear from established case law that the suspension of enforcement of a national provision based on a Community regulation in proceedings pending before a national court, whilst it is governed by national procedural law, is in all Member States subject to conditions which are uniform and analogous with the conditions for application for interim relief brought before the Community court'. It is to be assumed, and hoped, however, that this is exclusive of the requirement to prove a prima facie case of direct and individual concern. In other words, a national judge in a validity case must apply principles analogous to those reproduced above,[156] which derive from Articles 242 and 243 of the EC Treaty, while interim relief in compatibility cases is governed, in the ordinary course of events, by national law.

Are rules on the availability of interim relief more or less generous before Member State courts in 'compatibility' cases, than those operative under Article 234 validity review, or in Article 230(4) nullity proceedings? Given the scale of procedural autonomy in the former case, this is difficult to judge. However, the requirement to prove a *prima facie* case of direct and individual concern, at least in nullity proceedings, and the balancing of the 'Community interest' that appertains in both nullity and validity review, makes it tempting to conclude that individuals are better placed to secure an interim order in the context of Member State as opposed to Community wrongdoing.

151 *Factortame No 1* (see above n 52).
152 See Case C-143/88 and 92/89 *Zuckerfabrik* [1991] ECR I-415; Case C-465/93 *Atlanta Fruchthandelsgesellschaft* [1995] ECR I-3761.
153 Above n 40.
154 *Ibid* at para 82.
155 *Ibid* at para 79.
156 Above text nn 138–49.

D Damages

Similarly, neither Articles 6(1) or 13 of the Convention have been interpreted as imposing an obligation on states parties to the ECHR to supply a specific remedy of damages to correct infraction of ECHR rights. What is important is that there is a remedy of some kind in place that allows the right to be enforced.[157] In other words, the payment of compensation may not be necessary to protect against violation. Article 41 of the ECHR provides for awards for compensation against states parties before the Strasbourg court under three broad conditions (i) a proven violation of the Convention (ii) domestic law has not provided for full recovery of any fiscal loss that has occurred and (iii) it is necessary to afford just satisfaction to the injured party. The rules elaborated by the Strasbourg court under Article 41 have aided in the interpretation of national rules on compensation in states parties that have expressly implemented the Convention.[158]

It is unsurprising that the case law elaborated by the Court of Human Rights under Article 41 has had little relevance to either damages against Community institutions under Article 288(2), or in the elaboration of rules on Member State liability. The conditions for the payment of compensation by Community institutions were famously harmonised with those appertaining to Member States by the combined effects of Cases C-46/93 and 48/93 *Brasserie du Pêcheur and Factortame III*,[159] and Case C-352/98 P *Laboratoires Pharmaceutiques Bergarderm SA v Commission.*[160] In both contexts, when the wrongdoer has reduced discretion, 'the mere infringement of Community law may be sufficient to establish the existence of a sufficiently serious breach'.[161] When the wrongdoer has wide discretion, it is necessary to show a manifest and grave breach of a Community rule vesting individuals with rights.[162] In both cases, it is necessary to show a direct causal link between the loss suffered and the damage sustained.[163]

157 See, eg, Application No 10873/84 *Tre Traktörer Aktiebolag v Sweden*, judgment of 7 July 1989, paras 47–9.

158 For example, *R v Secretary of State for the Home Departments ex parte Greenfield* [2005] UKHL 14.

159 [1996] ECR I-1029. For an example of its subsequent application see Case T-333/03 *Masdar UK Ltd v Commission* [2006] ECR II-4377.

160 [2000] ECR I-5291. See in particular T Tridimas, 'Liability for Breach of Community Law Growing Up and Mellowing Down?' (2001) 38 *CML Rev* 301.

161 *Ibid* at para 44.

162 See in particular, *Brasserie du Pêcheur* above n 7.

163 For a recent example of application of the rules see Case C-470/03 *AGM–COS.MET SRL v Suomen Valtio and Another* [2007] ECR I-2 749 including the operation of residual Member State rules, subject to the principles of effectiveness and non-discrimination, see also eg, Case C-524/04 *Test Claimants in the Thin CAP Group Litigation v Commissioners for Inland Revenue* [2007] ECR I-2107.

On the face of it, therefore, there does indeed appear to be parity of remedial treatment, in the context of compensation, irrespective of whether the wrong is grounded in Community or Member State misconduct. To this, however, I would add two caveats.

First, as I have pointed out elsewhere, the Court of Justice, in actions for damages against EU institutions, has tended to categorise the measure concerned as vesting the decision maker with broad discretion, when it might be more comfortably, or logically, categorised as a measure of an administrative nature, or one vesting narrow discretion.[164] This is the same error, I would argue, that has befallen Article 230(4), in the sense that measures are routinely classified as legislative in nature, when they are, in reality, administrative, consequently impacting on the test for standing. Thus, in the *Bergaderm* case itself, the Court of Justice declined to accept the argument of the applicant that a Directive banning the use of an allegedly carcinogenic molecule in sun protection and bronzing products was in fact an individual decision, and that the simple test of breach that applies to non-discretionary measures was the appropriate one to apply. The Court of Justice held that the 'general or individual nature of a measure taken by an institution is not a decisive criterion for identifying the limits of the discretion enjoyed by the institution in question'.[165] This habit, which has shown only sparse sign of attenuation,[166] may mean, in practice, that the rigorous test for payment of compensation may be applied in a Community context in circumstances in which the less rigorous non-discretionary test might be applicable if similar facts arise at national level.

Secondly, there is a requirement under Article 288(2) that all effective domestic remedies are exhausted before recourse is made to Article 288(2). In practical terms, this requires resort to the Article 234 validity process before the national courts.[167] This rule has generated a complex body of case law.[168] However, relatively recently, the Court of First Instance has confirmed that it is not a requirement, under EC law, to have recourse to domestic remedies if it renders the exercise of individual rights 'excessively difficult'.[169] This conclusion was reached without reference to the *San Giorgio* case. While the limitation imposed on the exhaustion of domestic

164 Ward, (see above n 98) 399–402.

165 *Bergaderm* (see above n 160) at para 46.

166 See most notably Case C-472/00P *Commission v Fresh Marine* [2003] ECR I-7 541.

167 See, eg, M de Visser 'The Concept of Concurrent Liability and Its Relationship with the Principle of Effectiveness; A One Way Ticket into Oblivion?' (2004) 11 *Maastricht Journal of European and Comparative Law* 47.

168 For a recent analysis see Ward (above n 98, ch 8).

169 Case T-166/98 *Cantina sociale di Dolianova and others v Commission* [2004] ECR II-3991 para 117. The judgment was successfully appealed to the Court of Justice on 17 July 2008 in Case C-51/05 P *Commission v Cantina Sociale di Dolianova and others* [2008] ECR I-000 on the basis of expiry of the time limit for actions for damages .

rule is welcome, it is at least arguable that it remains a significant practical barrier within the meaning of Article 6(1) ECHR, and may render the scheme for judicial review so complex as to violate the legal certainty requirements built in to Article 6(1).[170] It may also cause inordinate delay.

E Depth of Scrutiny

Finally, as noted above, one of the elements of the case law promulgated under Article 13 of the ECHR on right of access to a court requires that, once the door of access is open under Article 6(1), sufficiently probative scrutiny must follow. If it does not, then breach of Article 13 ensues.[171]

One of the general principles of EU administrative law is that, rather in the fashion of a slide rule, the scale of judicial review decreases with the expansion of the breadth of the discretion enjoyed by the rule maker.[172] While this practice does not, in principle, breach Article 13 ECHR, its untrammelled expansion might raise cause for concern. So, for example, in Case T-306/01 *Yusuf* and Case T-315/01 *Kadi*[173] the Court of First Instance was petitioned by applicants contesting the legality of a Council Regulation implementing UN Security Council anti-terrorist measures freezing their assets. The Court of First Instance held that this was a UN act immune from review in Community courts, save for review under international *jus cogens* principles. Doubt might well be raised as to whether the scale of judicial review proposed by the Court of First Instance meets the probative requirements of Article 13 ECHR.[174]

F Conclusion

The above analysis reveals that there are indeed gaps in remedial protection in all of the areas outlined above. Private litigants face tenacious barriers to the grant of standing against EU institutions (which feeds into the rules on the award of interim relief); are bound almost unwaveringly to comply with time limits set under the EC Treaty and its rules of procedure, and may have lower prospects of success when they claim damages against EU institutions as opposed to Member States.

[170] Above text nn 16–25.

[171] Above text nn 29–30.

[172] For a detailed analysis see Tridimas (above n 8).

[173] *Kadi* [2005] ECR II-3649; *Yusuf* [2005] ECR II-3533.

[174] See also Douglas-Scott above n 37 at 633–4. AG Maduro held, in his Opinion of 16 January 2008, that the Court of First Instance had acted unlawfully in instituting such limited scrutiny. The judgment of the Court of First Instance was set aside by the Court of Justice on 3 Sept 2008 on appeal, in Joined Cases C-402/05 P and C-415/05 P *Kadi and Al Barakaat International Foundation v Council.*

The case law also reveals a will on the part of the Court of Justice toward deference to national procedural autonomy. This is reflected most notably in *Unibet*,[175] and *Van der Weerd*,[176] the former because it established, after some speculation, that ordinary national rules on interim relief will apply to claims based on Community law, and the latter because it held that Member State timetables for the raising of arguments will be disapplied, under the imperative of *effet utile*, only exceptionally. Yet, both judgments lacked the development of new principle that would serve to pare back *effet utile*, and prevent it from catching vast amounts of national procedural rules. How this might be achieved will be considered below.

V SUGGESTIONS FOR REFORM

A The Lisbon Treaty

The Lisbon Treaty makes no suggestion for change that would help ameliorate the problems described in this paper. No remedial provision has been proposed that would cut away at the legal tests of *effet utile* and equivalence for testing the compliance of national remedies and procedural rules with EU law. On the contrary, Article 9 states that 'Member States shall provide remedies sufficient to ensure effective legal protection in the fields covered by Union law', although the term 'effective legal protection' is not defined. However, Article 6 of the Lisbon Treaty fully imports the EU Charter into EU law, giving it 'the same legal values as the Treaties',[177] while fundamental rights as guaranteed by the ECHR, and the constitutional traditions common to the Member States, are cast in Article 6 as general principles of the Union's law. This provides further support for resort to the Strasbourg case law as a means through which *effet utile* might be attenuated.

[175] Above n 40.

[176] Above n 130.

[177] See, however, the UK and Polish opt out: **Article 1**

1. The Charter does not extend the ability of the Court of Justice [in Luxembourg], or any court or tribunal of the United Kingdom, to find that the laws, regulations or administrative provisions, practices or action of the United Kingdom are inconsistent with the fundamental rights, freedoms and principles that it reaffirms.

2. In particular, and for the avoidance of doubt, nothing in [Title IV] of the Charter creates justiciable rights applicable to the United Kingdom except in so far as the United Kingdom has provided for such rights in its national law.

Article 2

To the extent that a provision of the Charter refers to national laws and practices, it shall only apply in the United Kingdom to the extent that the rights or principles that it contains are recognised in the law or practices of the United Kingdom.

The changes proposed to remedial law with respect to challenge to EU rules are meagre. The Article 241 plea of illegality has been re-drafted but not re-cast, as has Article 231, which empowers the Court of Justice to state which of the effects of matters declared void are definitive. A fifth paragraph has been added to Article 230, allowing bodies, offices and agencies of the Union to lay down specific rules for actions brought against them by private parties.

By far the most significant change to sanctions appears in the proposed new Article 230(4). It states as follows:

> Any natural or legal person may, under the conditions laid down in the first or second paragraph, institute proceedings against an act addressed to that person or which is of direct and individual concern to them, and against a regulatory act which is of direct concern to them and does not entail implementing measures.

This change, it would seem, is designed to address the *Jego Quéré* conundrum of individuals having no means of challenging EU measures that do not require national implementation, sometimes obliging them to break the law to get into court. Yet, as noted above, the Court of Justice appears to have gone some way to ameliorating this, by obliging national courts to open up channels for validity review, albeit possibly flawed by the practical difficulties entailed in persuading Member State judges to do so.[178]

Far preferable, I would argue, would be a change to Article 230(4) that reflects the clearer delineation in the hierarchy of norms that the Lisbon Treaty proposes to introduce. A distinction is drawn in the Lisbon Treaty between 'legislative acts' involving the European Parliament (Article 289(3)) and 'non-legislative acts' which do not (Article 290). Article 290(1) states that:

> A legislative act may delegate to the Commission the power to adopt non-legislative acts of general application to supplement or amend certain non-essential elements of the legislative act.

If Article 230(4) were recast to encompass all 'non-legislative acts', leaving Article 234 validity review for challenge to 'legislative acts' then the EU judicial architecture would reflect more accurately the legal traditions common to the Member States, and the exceptional nature of judicial review of normative rules, promulgated via democratic processes with the input of a Parliament, when compared with the function of courts in checking wrongful exercise of power in an administrative or executive context. Yet, at present, the proposed text of Article 230(4) is in no way indexed to the important changes wrought in Articles 289 and 290.

[178] Above text nn 105–15.

Finally, the Lisbon Treaty, unlike the Constitutional Treaty, provides no express supremacy clause securing the primacy of EU measures over Member State laws. There is, however, a provision bolstering the Article 10 EC good faith duty; Article 291(1) states that 'Member States shall adopt all measures of national law necessary to implement legally binding Union acts.' The absence of a supremacy clause remains significant for one key reason. A supremacy clause might have allowed the Court of Justice to ease away from the notion of a Union based on 'individual rights', which national courts had a duty to protect, to support the federal legal construct it has put in place. The cessation of reliance on 'individual rights', in the supremacy context, might have had flow on effects, reducing it as an imperative in cases concerning remedies and procedures, and helping in the development of less intrusive legal doctrines on the remedial plane.

B Draft Provisions

I would suggest the following changes.

First, the two month time limit for nullity review should be removed from the Treaty, and placed in the Rules of Procedure. As a procedural rule, it is ill-suited to a constitutional document, and, like the five year time limit for Article 288(2) damages claims, should be placed with other principles that relate to procedural matters.

With regard to Article 230(4), it might be recast along the following lines.

> Any natural or legal person may, under the same conditions, institute proceedings against any act addressed to that person, and any non legislative act, as defined in Article 290.
>
> Any natural or legal person may, under the same conditions, institute proceedings against any legislative act, as defined in Article 289, before the national courts under the Article 234 validity procedure.
>
> In all cases natural and legal persons must show that their legal interests are engaged.

Articles 231 and 232 might be repealed, and replaced with the following:

> All EU and Member State acts declared unlawful by the Union courts shall be void. The Union Courts shall, if they considers this necessary, state which of the effects of the act which it has declared void shall be considered definitive.
>
> Both the Union courts and the Member State courts shall supply appropriate relief and adequate redress for measures declared unlawful, including the issuing of adequate remedial directions. Any restrictions on sanctions and procedural

rules applying to acts impugned for illegality must pursue a legitimate aim, and be proportionate to that aim. Any difference in treatment must be objectively justified.

Such a provision might have the effect of limiting the import of *effet utile* in the context of compatibility cases before Member State courts, while at the same time expand the remedial powers of the Court of Justice and the Court of First Instance. In the alternative, the same change might be brought about via case law, if the Court of Justice and Court of First Instance could be persuaded to place greater and reliance, or at least draw deeper inspiration from, the Strasbourg jurisprudence in its case law on *effet utile*, and in interpreting Articles 231 and 232. The incorporation of the Charter into the main body of the EU Treaty might provide the impetus required for this to occur.

VI CONCLUSION

Scholars have, over the years, struggled nobly to place Court of Justice case law on national remedies and procedural rules into a coherent and principled paradigm.[179] One study has placed stress on a sectoral approach, and considered the substantive area of the law to which *effet utile* is attached to help make sense of the case law.[180] Similarly, others have suggested that 'Community remedial competence should, so far as possible, be selectively matched to the actual degree of Community substantive competence exercised over any given policy matter'.[181]

This contribution to the debate reflected in this paper has sought to highlight three points. First, there is a factual and practical problem of 'uneveness' in standards of judicial protection in the EU, which is indexed to whether the wrongdoer is a Member State or an EU institution. Secondly, the legal tests presently in place remain too open-ended to diminish, in any significant way, the scope of national rules that might potentially fall under the imperative of *effet utile*. The Court of Justice is yet to formulate a test of sufficient precision to discourage national judges from referring Article 234 questions on national remedies and procedural rules when they are called into question. These references are unnecessary, and clog the important constitutional work that the Court of Justice was established to perform. Thirdly, it has been suggested that both problems might be cured by reference to the minimum standards on access to courts

[179] For example, M Ruffert 'Rights and Remedies in European Community Law: a Comparative View' (1997) 34 *CML Rev* 307.

[180] C Kilpatrick 'Turning Remedies Around: A Sectoral Analysis of the Court of Justice' in G de Burca and J Weiler (eds) *The European Court of Justice* (Oxford, Oxford University Press, 2001).

[181] Dougan, (n 7) 67. See also ch 4.

and remedies that have been formulated in the case law of the Strasbourg court under Articles 6(1) and 13 ECHR.

But perhaps most importantly, the difficulties here analysed cut across the folly warned against in the works of Jeremy Bentham. There is a lack of persuasiveness, or good reasons in the case law of the Court of Justice in this field; and to a degree, I would argue, that renders surprising the lack of significant compliance problems to date. Given the cardinal role of the Member State courts as supporting walls of the constitutional edifice, it is to be hoped that future case law of the Court of Justice on access to courts, remedies and sanctions, will be characterised by more principled legal analysis, whether wrongdoing is embedded in Member State or Union misconduct.

15

Civil Antitrust Remedies Between Community and National Law

ASSIMAKIS P KOMNINOS*

I INTRODUCTION

THE APPLICATION OF EC competition law by civil courts, though not particularly developed, has not been a recent phenomenon. Indeed, the very first preliminary reference made by a national court to Luxembourg under the old Article 177 EEC, which was, according to witnesses, an event that was duly celebrated with champagne at that time in the Grand Duchy, was a competition case where EC competition law arose in the context of private litigation.[1] Of course, the mere *application* of the competition rules by national courts cannot be said to amount to a system of private antitrust *enforcement*. The very term 'enforcement' signifies an instrumental role of private actions in the sense of the private litigants becoming themselves actors in enhancing the overall efficiency and effectiveness of the competition enforcement system. It is only very recently that private antitrust enforcement appears for the first time as a real enforcement mechanism and thus as a meaningful complement to public enforcement.

The road was opened by the *modernisation* and *decentralisation* reforms in the years 1999 to 2004 that have produced a new enforcement system for the twenty-first century. But it has also come as a consequence of ground-breaking rulings by the *Court of Justice*, which has extended the scope of remedies available to individuals by Community law to cover also individual civil liability and has always imposed demanding conditions on national substantive and procedural law, in order to ensure the effectiveness of the Treaty competition rules. The Court of Justice has indeed been particularly bold in this field due to mainly historical

* The usual disclaimer applies.

[1] Case 13/61, *Kledingverkoopbedrijf de Geus en Uitdenbogerd v Robert Bosch GmbH and Maatschappij tot voortzetting van de zaken der Firma Willem van Rijn*, [1962] ECR 45.

reasons: the Community competition rules have long been recognised as having horizontal direct effect and at the same time they have invariably been treated with a high degree of deference as part of the Community's economic constitution, thus enjoying an increased normative value.

It is only in the aftermath of the Court of Justice's important pronouncements that the European Commission decided to go forward with the publication of its Green[2] and White[3] Papers on damages actions. In so doing, the Commission availed itself of an increased degree of legitimacy in an area which is always sensitive due to the inevitable intrusion on what is perceived as the Member States' 'institutional and procedural autonomy'. It would have been very difficult for the Commission to go ahead and propose Community legislative action, if it had not been for the Court of Justice's seminal rulings. This intellectual debt is fully acknowledged in the recent Commission White Paper, which gives much space on the *acquis communautaire*, as established by the Court.

II CIVIL ANTITRUST REMEDIES BETWEEN NATIONAL AND COMMUNITY LAW

At the heart of private antitrust enforcement in Europe lies the question of the relationship between Community and national law. At the current stage of European integration, rights and obligations emanating from Community law are in principle enforced under national law and before national courts. The Community legal order is not a federal one and the Community acts only within the limits of the powers conferred upon it by the EC Treaty. The Community standard is that Community law is enforced primarily by having recourse to national administrative and civil

[2] Commission Green Paper on Damages Actions for Breach of the EC Antitrust Rules, COM(2005) 672 final. The Green Paper, published in December 2005, was accompanied by a Staff Working Paper which set out the various options more discursively: Commission Staff Working Paper, Annex to the Green Paper on Damages Actions for Breach of the EC Antitrust Rules, SEC(2005) 1732.

[3] Commission White Paper on Damages Actions for Breach of the EC Antitrust Rules, COM(2008) 165 final. The White Paper, published in April 2008, summarises the far more developed Staff Working Paper: Commission Staff Working Paper Accompanying the White Paper on Damages Actions for Breach of the EC Antitrust Rules, SEC(2008) 404. The Commission has also published an impressive 600-page long Impact Assessment Study, prepared by the Centre for European Policy Studies, the Erasmus University Rotterdam and the Italian University Luiss Guido Carli: Making Antitrust Damages Actions More Effective in the EU: Welfare Impact and Potential Scenarios, Final Report for the European Commission, 30 March 2008. This is itself usefully summarised in a Commission Impact Assessment Report: Commission Staff Working Document Accompanying the White Paper on Damages Actions for Breach of the EC Antitrust Rules, Impact Assessment, SEC(2008) 405.

law before national administrative authorities (*administration communautaire indirecte*)[4] and national courts (*juges communautaires de droit commun*).[5]

Thus, on the side of *substance*, there is no Community law of contract, tort or unjustified enrichment, or a European Civil Code. Indeed, even if the Community had the power or intention to legislate in such a vast cross-sector area, it would be almost impossible to arrive at a common denominator applicable throughout the EU Member States, taking into account the century-long divisions in the European legal systems. Equally, on the side of *procedure*, there are no Community courts of general jurisdiction that could apply Community law and deal with Community law-based claims. Although it has already been proposed to introduce such courts of general jurisdiction, following the US model of federal circuit

[4] On this Community transformation of national administrative authorities see in general Dubey, 'Administration indirecte et fédéralisme d'exécution en Europe', (2003) 39 *Cahiers de Droit Européen* 87 *ff*. See also Temple Lang, 'The Duties of National Authorities under Community Constitutional Law', (1998) 23 *EL Rev* 109; Kakouris, 'Special Administrative Courts of the Member States and the Court of the European Communities', in Kakouris (ed), *Perspectives, Droit communautaire européen, Théorie générale du droit, Domaine méta-juridique* (Athens/Komotini, Ant. N. Sakkoulas, 1998) 513; Chiti, 'L'organismo di diritto pubblico e la nozione comunitaria di pubblica amministrazione', in *Annuario 1999–2000 dell'Associazione italiana dei professori di diritto amministrativo* (Milan, Giuffrè, 2001) 37–8; Sydow, 'Europäisierte Verwaltungsverfahren', (2005) 45 *Juristische Schulung* 97. See also Case C-453/00, *Kühne & Heitz NV v Productschap voor Pluimvee en Eieren*, [2004] ECR I-837, para 20: 'it is for all the authorities of the Member States to ensure observance of the rules of Community law within the sphere of their competence'.

[5] See inter alia, Ehlermann, 'Ein Plädoyer für die dezentrale Kontrolle der Anwendung des Gemeinschaftsrechts durch die Mitgliedstaaten', in Capotorti, Ehlermann *et al* (eds), *Du droit international au droit de l'intégration, Liber Amicorum Pierre Pescatore* (Baden-Baden, Nomos, 1987) 217 *ff*; O Dubos, *Les juridictions nationales, juge communautaire, Contribution à l'étude des transformations de la fonction juridictionnelle dans les États-membres de l'Union européenne* (Paris, 2001). On this *dédoublement fonctionnel* as to national authorities and courts see in general R Lecourt, *L'Europe des juges* (Brussels, Bruylant, 1976) 8–9; D Simon, *Le système juridique communautaire* (Paris, Presses Universitaires de France, 2001) 163–4, 167; Radermacher, 'Gemeinschaftsrechtliche Staatshaftung für höchstrichterliche Entscheidungen', (2004) 23 *Neue Zeitschrift für Verwaltungsrecht* 1415, 1416; Canivet, 'Les réseaux de juges au sein del'Union européenne : Raisons, nécessités et réalisations', in Idot and Poillot-Peruzzetto (eds), *Internormativité et réseaux d'autorités, L'ordre communautaire et les nouvelles formes de relations (Toulouse, 24 Octobre 2003)*, *Petites Affiches*, 5 October 2004, No 199, 45, 46. See also Case T-51/89, *Tetra Pak Rausing SA v Commission*, [1990] ECR II-309, para 42: 'when applying Article 86 [now 82] ... the national courts are acting as Community courts of general jurisdiction'. *Cf*, however, AG Léger's Opinion in Case C-224/01, *Gerhard Köbler v Austria*, [2003] ECR I-10239, para 66, who sees the *dédoublement fonctionnel* more symbolically than literally: 'That expression must not be understood literally, but symbolically: where a national court is called upon to apply Community law, it is in its capacity as an organ of a Member State, and not as a Community organ, as a result of dual functions.'

courts,[6] the current judicial structure is bound to remain unchanged for some time. Thus national courts act also as 'Community courts' of general jurisdiction (*juges communautaires de droit commun*).[7] They have been conceived as such by the Community, in order to strengthen the efficiency of Community law, since it is taken for granted that Member States and their citizens are far more likely to respect the decisions of their own national courts than those of distant 'international' tribunals.[8]

It is true that in the last 20 years much has changed, and one can now speak of a *positive integration* drive to unify or harmonise rules on remedies and procedures. Thus, there is now, for example, secondary Community legislation on substantive and procedural rules in the areas of consumer protection,[9] unfair commercial practices,[10] public procurement,[11] sex and racial

[6] See, eg, Hawk, 'The Role of the Judge—Working Paper II', in Ehlermann and Laudati (eds), *European Competition Law Annual 1996* (The Hague/Boston/London, Kluwer, 1997) 338–9; Sullivan, 'Antitrust around the World', (2000) *Antitrust Report* 30, 31–2.

[7] See Skouris, 'The Proposals for the Reform of the Community System of Judicial Protection: On the Basis of the Draft Constitution of the European Union', in Frangakis (ed), *The Court of Justice of the European Communities after 50 Years of Operation* (Athens/Komotini, Ant. N. Sakkoulas, 2004) [in Greek], 18, with references to Art I-29(1)(b) of the European Constitution Treaty (now Article 19(1)(b) of the Treaty on European Union, as amended by the Treaty of Lisbon), which stresses that 'Member States shall provide remedies sufficient to ensure effective legal protection in the fields covered by Union law'.

[8] See B Beutler, R Bieber, J Pipkorn, J Streil and JHH Weiler, *L'Unione europea, Istituzioni, ordinamento e politiche* (Bologna, Il Mulino, 2001) 230.

[9] See, eg, Council Dir 85/374/EEC of 25 July 1985 on the Approximation of the Laws, Regulations and Administrative Provisions of the Member States Concerning Liability for Defective Products, [1985] OJ L210/29, as amended by European Parliament and Council Directive 99/34/EC of 10 May 1999, [1999] OJ L141/20; Council Dir 85/577/EEC of 20 December 1985 to Protect the Consumer in Respect of Contracts Negotiated Away from Business Premises, [1985] OJ L372/31; Council Dir 93/13/EEC of 5 April 1993 on Unfair Terms in Consumer Contracts, [1993] OJ L95/2; European Parliament and Council Dir 97/7/EC of 20 May 1997 on the Protection of Consumers in Respect of Distance Contracts, [1997] OJ L144/19; European Parliament and Council Dir 98/27/EC of 19 May 1998 on Injunctions for the Protection of Consumers' Interests, [1998] OJ L166/51; European Parliament and Council Dir 99/44/EC of 25 May 1999 on Certain Aspects of the Sale of Consumer Goods and Associated Guarantees, [1999] OJ L171/12; European Parliament and Council Dir 2002/65/EC of 23 September 2002 Concerning the Distance Marketing of Consumer Financial Services and Amending Council Directive 90/619/EEC and Directives 97/7/EC and 98/27/EC, [2002] OJ L271/16; European Parliament and Council Dir 2008/48/EC of 23 April 2008 on Credit Agreements for Consumers and Repealing Council Directive 87/102/EEC, [2008] OJ L133/66. *Cf* now Commission proposal for a European Parliament and Council Dir on Consumer Rights, COM(2008) 614/3.

[10] European Parliament and Council Dir 2005/29/EC of 11 May 2005 Concerning Unfair Business-to-Consumer Commercial Practices in the Internal Market and Amending Council Directive 84/450/EEC, Directives 97/7/EC, 98/27/EC and 2002/65/EC of the European Parliament and of the Council and Regulation (EC) No 2006/2004 of the European Parliament and of the Council ('Unfair Commercial Practices Directive'), [2005] OJ L149/22. See further Stuyck, Terryn and Van Dyck, 'Confidence through Fairness? The New Directive on Unfair Business-to-Consumer Commercial Practices in the Internal Market', (2006) 43 *CML Rev* 107; Abbamonte, 'The Unfair Commercial Practices Directive and its General Prohibition', in S Weatherill and U Bernitz (eds), *The Regulation of Unfair Commercial*

discrimination,[12] electronic commerce,[13] environmental protection,[14] late payments,[15] and enforcement of intellectual property rights,[16] which indeed manifest a more active stance by the Community legislator. However, with

Practices under EC Directive 2005/29, New Rules and New Techniques (Oxford, Hart Publishing, 2007) 11 *ff*.

[11] See, eg, Council Dir 89/665/EEC of 21 December 1989 on the Co-ordination of the Laws, Regulations and Administrative Provisions Relating to the Application of Review Procedures to the Award of Public Supply and Public Works Contracts, [1989] OJ L395/33; Council Dir 92/13/EEC of 25 February 1992 Coordinating the Laws, Regulations and Administrative Provisions Relating to the Application of Community Rules on the Procurement Procedures of Entities Operating in the Water, Energy, Transport and Telecommunications Sectors, [1992] OJ L76/14; European Parliament and Council Dir 2007/66/EC of 11 December 2007 Amending Council Directives 89/665/EEC and 92/13/EEC with Regard to Improving the Effectiveness of Review Procedures Concerning the Award of Public Contracts, [2007] OJ L335/31. See also Commission Proposal for a Directive Amending Council Directives 89/665/EEC and 92/13/EEC with Regard to Improving the Effectiveness of Review Procedures Concerning the Award of Public Contracts, COM(2006) 195 final. Note that the fact that a contract may fall below the thresholds for the application of the public procurement Dirs does not mean that primary Community law does not impose limits on the national legal orders. Thus individuals are always entitled to effective judicial protection of the rights they derive from the Community legal order, even if secondary Community legislation (ie the remedies Dirs) is not applicable. *Cf* the Commission Interpretative Communication on the Community Law Applicable to Contract Awards not or not Fully Subject to the Provisions of the Public Procurement Directives, [2006] OJ C/179/2, section 2.3.

[12] From among the new generation measures, see, eg, Council Dir 97/80/EC of 15 December 1997 on the Burden of Proof in Cases of Discrimination Based on Sex, [1998] OJ L14/6; Council Dir 2000/43/EC of 29 June 2000 Implementing the Principle of Equal Treatment between Persons irrespective of Racial or Ethnic Origin, [2000] OJ L180/22; Council Dir 2000/78/EC of 27 November 2000 Establishing a General Framework for Equal Treatment in Employment and Occupation, [2000] OJ L303/16; European Parliament and Council Dir 2002/73/EC of 23 September 2002 Amending Council Dir 76/207/EEC on the Implementation of the Principle of Equal Treatment for Men and Women as Regards Access to Employment, Vocational Training and Promotion, and Working Conditions, [2002] OJ L269/15; Council Dir 2004/113/EC of 13 December 2004 Implementing the Principle of Equal Treatment between Men and Women in the Access to and Supply of Goods and Services, [2004] OJ L373/37; European Parliament and Council Dir 2006/54/EC of 5 July 2006 on the Implementation of the Principle of Equal Opportunities and Equal Treatment of Men and Women in Matters of Employment and Occupation (Recast), [2006] OJ L204/23, which repeals Dir 97/80 as of 15 August 2009.

[13] European Parliament and Council Dir 2000/31/EC of 8 June 2000 on Certain Legal Aspects of Information Society Services, in Particular Electronic Commerce, in the Internal Market ('Directive on Electronic Commerce'), [2000] OJ L178/1.

[14] See, eg, European Parliament and Council Dir 2003/35/EC of 26 May 2003 Providing for Public Participation in Respect of the Drawing up of Certain Plans and Programmes Relating to the Environment and Amending with Regard to Public Participation and Access to Justice Council Directives 85/337/EEC and 96/61/EC, [2003] OJ L156/17; European Parliament and Council Dir 2004/35/EC of 21 April 2004 on Environmental Liability with Regard to the Prevention and Remedying of Environmental Damage, [2004] OJ L143/56, as amended by European Parliament and Council Dir 2006/21/EC of 15 March 2006, [2006] OJ L102/15.

[15] European Parliament and Council Dir 2000/35/EC of 29 June 2000 on Combating Late Payment in Commercial Transactions, [2000] OJ L200/35.

[16] European Parliament and Council Dir 2004/48/EC of 29 April 2004 on the Enforcement of Intellectual Property Rights, [2004] OJ L195/16.

very few exceptions,[17] these are sectoral rules applying to very specific areas that are considered important for the attainment of the Community's most basic objectives. This remarkable progress cannot change the basic reality that there are no cross-sector Community rules of civil law dealing with the enforcement of Community law-based rights.

Over-ambitious projects to harmonise or unify national civil rules on contract and tort and national procedural rules have had rather modest results, not least because of the very defensive—if not hostile—attitude of the legal professions in the Member States. The long-standing proposal—or rather, wish—to introduce a European Civil Code has been watered down to proposals to improve the coherence of the existing and future sectoral *acquis*, especially in the area of consumer protection, and to reflect on the desirability of an optional instrument on European contract law, which would provide parties to a contract with a body of rules particularly adapted to cross-border contracts in the internal market.[18] An even more ambitious project to harmonise national civil procedural laws met a rather worse fate and was abandoned.[19] Thus in the area of

[17] See Council Dir 2002/8/EC of 27 January 2003 to Improve Access to Justice in Cross-border Disputes by Establishing Minimum Common Rules Relating to Legal Aid for Such Disputes, [2003] OJ L26/41. This is one of the few exceptional cross-sector legislative measures, though again limited to cross-border matters. *Cf* S Weatherill, *EU Consumer Law and Policy* (Cheltenham, Edward Elgar Publishing, 2005) 240, who in respect of this Directive notes emerging traces of a 'European legal space'. See also European Parliament and Council Dir 2008/52/EC of 21 May 2008 on Certain Aspects of Mediation in Civil and Commercial Matters, [2008] OJ L133/3.

[18] See Commission Communication of 11 July 2001 to the Council and the European Parliament on European Contract Law, COM(2001) 398 final, [2001] OJ C/255/1; Communication from the Commission to the European Parliament and the Council, A More Coherent European Contract Law, An Action Plan, [2003] OJ C/63/1; Council Resolution on 'A More Coherent European Contract Law', [2003] OJ C/246/1; Communication from the Commission to the European Parliament and the Council, European Contract Law and the Revision of the acquis: The Way Forward, COM(2004) 651 final; Commission Green Paper on the Review of the Consumer Acquis, COM(2006) 744 final. See now Commission proposal for a European Parliament and Council Dir on Consumer Rights, COM(2008) 614/3. On the original plans related to the possible introduction of a European Civil Code and the subsequent developments, see Legrand, 'Against a European Civil Code', (1997) 60 *MLR* 44; Basedow, 'The Renascence of Uniform Law: European Contract Law and its Components', (1998) 18 *Legal Studies* 121; Schmid, 'Legitimacy Conditions for a European Civil Code', (2001) 8 *Maastricht Journal of European and Comparative Law* 277; Weatherill, 'European Contract Law: Taking the Heat out of Questions of Competence', (2004) 15 *European Business Law Review* 23. On the constitutional law underpinnings of the development of a 'European contract law' and of a 'European Civil Code' see more generally Remien, 'Europäisches Privatrecht als Verfassungsfrage', (2005) 40 *Europarecht* 699.

[19] On this and other similar projects see, eg, Storme (ed), *Rapprochement du droit judiciaire de l'Union européenne* (Dordrecht/Boston/London, Nijhoff, 1994); Kerameus, 'Procedural Harmonization in Europe', (1995) 43 *American Journal of Comparative Law* 401; Gilles, 'Vereinheitlichung und Angleichung unterschiedlicher nationaler Rechte—Die Europäisierung des Zivilprozeßrechts als ein Beispiel', (2002) 7 *Zeitschrift für Zivilprozessrecht* 3, 8 *ff*; M Dougan, *National Remedies before the Court of Justice, Issues of Harmonisation and Differentiation* (Oxford, Hart Publishing, 2004) 99. This result illustrates

procedural law the Community has preferred to adopt and develop Community instruments applicable to the international (transborder) rather than to the national side of procedures.[20]

Consequently, natural and legal persons relying upon Articles 81 and 82 EC would have no other means to pursue their civil claims but through access to national courts and laws.[21] However, the substantive and procedural conditions of civil antitrust enforcement can be quite different in Europe depending on which national law applies and which national court adjudicates. Inconsistencies and inadequacies in national laws on remedies and procedures are certainly a source of some concern, not just for EC competition law but for Community law in general. In this context, the problem can be identified in three different, albeit interconnected, levels:[22]

First, there is a problem of *effective or adequate judicial protection*, that is, the effective protection of Community rights.[23] This is a principle not only of Community law but also of human rights law. Indeed, effective judicial protection in the access to the courts configuration derives from Articles 6 and 13 of the European Convention on Human Rights.[24] As far as Community law is concerned, as the Court of Justice has recognised, Articles 81 and 82 EC 'tend by their very nature to produce direct effects in

well the fact that harmonisation or 'communitarisation' of procedure is more taboo than harmonisation of substantive laws.

[20] See Council Reg 44/2001 (*Brussels I* Regulation); Council Reg 1206/2001 of 28 May 2001 on Cooperation between the Courts of the Member States in the Taking of Evidence in Civil and Commercial Matters, [2001] OJ L174/1; Council Reg 2201/2003 of 27 November 2003 Concerning Jurisdiction and the Recognition and Enforcement of Judgments in Matrimonial Matters and the Matters of Parental Responsibility, Repealing Regulation 1347/2000 (Brussels II Regulation), [2003] OJ L338/1; European Parliament and Council Reg 805/2004 of 21 April 2004 Creating a European Enforcement Order for Uncontested Claims, [2004] OJ L143/15; European Parliament and Council Reg 1393/2007 of 13 November 2007 on the Service in the Member States of Judicial and Extrajudicial Documents in Civil or Commercial Matters (Service of Documents), [2007] OJ L324/79. See also Council Decision 2001/470/EC of 28 May 2001 Establishing a European Judicial Network in Civil and Commercial Matters, [2001] OJ L174/25.

[21] See, however, below at section IV on the new line of ECJ case law, in particular the *Courage* and *Manfredi* rulings.

[22] See further Komninos, 'New Prospects for Private Enforcement of EC Competition Law: *Courage v Crehan* and the Community Right to Damages', (2002) 39 *CML Rev* 447, 464.

[23] Among the abundant works on this principle central to Community law, see Van Gerven, 'Of Rights and Remedies in the Enforcement of European Community Law before National Courts: From the Communitarization of Domestic Law towards the Europeanization of Community Law', (1997) VIII(1) *Collected Courses of the Academy of European Law* 241, 247 *ff*; T Tridimas, *The General Principles of EC Law* (Oxford, Oxford University Press, 1999) 276 *ff*; Rodrìguez Iglesias, 'Judicial Protection of the Citizen under European Law', in Markesinis (ed), *The Clifford Chance Millennium Lectures, The Coming together of the Common Law and the Civil Law* (Oxford, Hart Publishing, 2000) 195 *ff*.

[24] See among others AD Pliakos, *Le principe général de la protection juridictionnelle efficace en droit communautaire* (Athens/Brussels, Bruylant, 1997) 101 *ff*.

relations between individuals [and] create direct rights in respect of the individuals concerned which the national courts must safeguard'. Failure to afford this safeguard 'would mean depriving individuals of rights which they hold under the Treaty itself'.[25] This is, of course, an old question that transcends the boundaries of EC competition law. Indeed, since the 1980s, the 'Community rights-national remedies' duality has risen to become the central issue in 'second' and 'third generation' Community law, to use a 'classical' expression.[26]

Secondly, there is a problem for the *effectiveness* of the whole system of Community law as such and, more particularly, for the *efficiency* of the Community (competition) rules. There are two facets here. One is Community law-specific and the other is competition law-specific. The first facet of the problem is that when citizens pursue their Community rights before the *juges communautaires de droit commun*, in addition to serving their private interests, they are also instrumental for and indirectly act in the Community interest, becoming 'the principal "guardians" of the legal integrity of Community law in Europe'.[27] The direct effect doctrine was developed partly with this consideration in mind. The second, competition law-specific, facet refers to the 'private attorney-general' role of individuals in antitrust cases. In a mature antitrust system, private enforcement is a necessary complement of public enforcement and by no means inferior or weaker. In such a system private actions and, we should stress, particularly actions for damages, are crucial for the efficiency of the system as a whole.[28]

Thirdly, the disparities and inadequacies of national legal systems offend against the principle of *consistent and uniform application of Community law*.[29] It has been persuasively argued that the requirement of uniform application or enforcement is not 'an all-embracing *principle* which does

[25] Case 127/73, *Belgische Radio en Televisie and Societé Belge des Auteurs, Compositeurs et Editeurs de Musique v SV SABAM and NV Fonior (I)*, [1974] ECR 51, paras 16 and 17.

[26] See Curtin and Mortelmans, 'Application and Enforcement of Community Law by the Member States: Actors in Search of a Third Generation Script', in Curtin and Heukels (eds), *Institutional Dynamics of European Integration, Essays in Honour of Henry G. Schermers*, Vol II (Dordrecht/Boston/London, Nijhoff, 1994). *Cf* also Eilmansberger, 'The Relationship between Rights and Remedies in EC Law: In Search of the Missing Link', (2004) 41 *CML Rev* 1199, 1202 *ff*.

[27] See JHH Weiler, *The Constitution of Europe, 'Do the New Clothes have an Emperor?' and Other Essays on European Integration* (Cambridge, Cambridge University Press, 1999) 20.

[28] On this particular point, see below section IV and the analysis of the ECJ's *Courage* ruling.

[29] On the principle of uniform application of Community law, see Fines, 'L'application uniforme du droit communautaire dans la jurisprudence de la Cour de justice des Communautés européennes', in *Études en l'honneur de Jean-Claude Gautron, Les dynamiques du droit européen en début de siècle* (Paris, Pedone, 2004) 334.

not allow for national principles'.[30] Therefore, national remedial and procedural discrepancies to a certain extent are unavoidable.[31] It is arguable, however, that such discrepancies are particularly regrettable from an EC *competition* law point of view, because they tend to create variations in the costs of enforcing the EC antitrust rules, and thus to unequal conditions of competition among the Member States.[32]

In the decentralised system of EC antitrust enforcement the problem is exacerbated. Competitors and economic actors in general take the likelihood of public or private antitrust action seriously into account in defining their market strategies. In this context, damages have an especially powerful impact on business behaviour. An economic operator's exploitation of its 'immunity' from civil actions in damages in one jurisdiction, as opposed to other jurisdictions where companies are constantly successfully or unsuccessfully defending civil antitrust actions and victims are fully compensated, is hardly compatible with the creation of 'a level playing field for agreements, decisions by associations of undertakings and concerted practices within the internal market', as Regulation 1/2003 propagates.[33]

[30] See Van Gerven, 'Of Rights, Remedies and Procedures', (2000) 37 *CML Rev* 501, 503 (emphasis in the original text). The author goes on to argue that 'although the objective of uniform enforcement of Community law throughout the Community is a fundamental requirement of the Community legal order that must be pursued as much as possible, it is not a Community law principle of the same nature as direct effect, supremacy, or access to a court' (p 522). In the same spirit see Fines, (above n 29) 336.

[31] See AG Reischl's Opinion in Case 61/79, *Amministrazione delle finanze dello Stato v Denkavit italiana Srl*, [1980] ECR 1205, at 1233: 'That the legal position of the individual may … differ in the various Member States is simply a consequence of the implementation of Community law by the Member States, which is accepted by the Community legal system.'

[32] It is interesting to note that this argument in favour of more uniformity has been used not only in the antitrust area itself but also in the EC labour law field, since the principles of equivalence and effectiveness cannot extinguish cost variations in the enforcement of EC labour legal provisions in the different EU Member States. See in this respect Ryan, 'The Private Enforcement of European Union Labour Laws', in Kilpatrick, Novitz and Skidmore (eds), *The Future of Remedies in Europe* (Oxford, Hart Publishing, 2000) 161–2.

[33] Council Reg 1/2003 of 16 December 2002 on the Implementation of the Rules on Competition Laid down in Articles 81 and 82 of the Treaty, [2003] OJ L 1/1, Recital 8. See also Recital 1, which speaks of the necessity for Arts 81 and 82 EC to 'be applied effectively and *uniformly* in the Community' (emphasis added), and the Impact Assessment Form of the September 2000 Regulation proposal, p 56, where reference is made to a 'level playing field for companies in the internal market by ensuring more widespread application of the Community competition rules'. See further Temple Lang, 'Rapport général', in *XVIII congrès FIDE (Stockholm, 3–6 juin 1998)*, Vol II, *Application nationale du droit européen de la concurrence* (Stockholm, FIDE, 1999) 290; Paulis, 'Coherent Application of EC Competition Rules in a System of Parallel Competencies', in Ehlermann and Atanasiu (eds), *European Competition Law Annual 2000: The Modernisation of EC Antitrust Policy* (Oxford, Hart Publishing, 2001) 399, according to whom divergences in the enforcement of the antitrust rules constitute discrimination that can lead to distortions of competition in the market.

III NATIONAL REMEDIAL AND PROCEDURAL AUTONOMY: A NEW APPROACH

The Court of Justice[34] has recognised in a consistent line of judgments, though rarely by name,[35] the 'procedural and institutional autonomy' of the Member States[36] to identify the remedies, courts and procedures that are necessary for the exercise of Community law rights at the national level. The term 'procedural autonomy' creates the incorrect impression that this principle refers only to national rules of civil, administrative or criminal procedure. In fact its scope is much larger and covers all substantive or procedural mechanisms at national level that can be used for the enforcement of Community law. That is why the term 'remedial/ procedural autonomy' is preferable. Besides, it is not always clear in the EU Member States' legal systems where substance stops and procedure begins, or vice versa.[37]

More importantly, however, the Court has also imposed demanding Community limits and safeguards upon that autonomy.[38] These are the

[34] The role of the CFI in this area is virtually non-existent, since these legal issues arise in ECJ preliminary reference cases.

[35] See Case C-201/02, *R ex p Delena Wells v Secretary of State for Transport, Local Government and the Regions*, [2004] ECR I-723. In para 70 of its ruling, the ECJ stresses: 'Under Article 10 EC the competent authorities are obliged to take, within the sphere of their competence, all general or particular measures for remedying the failure to carry out an assessment of the environmental effects of a project as provided for in Article 2(1) of Directive 85/337. The detailed procedural rules applicable in that context are a matter for the domestic legal order of each Member State, *under the principle of procedural autonomy of the Member States*, provided that they are not less favourable than those governing similar domestic situations (principle of equivalence) and that they do not render impossible in practice or excessively difficult the exercise of rights conferred by the Community legal order (principle of effectiveness)' (emphasis added). See also Case C-212/04, *Konstantinos Adeneler et al v Ellinikos Organismos Galaktos (ELOG)*, [2006] ECR I-6057, para 95; Case C-53/04, *Cristiano Marrosu and Gianluca Sardino v Azienda Ospedaliera Ospedale San Martino di Genova e Cliniche Universitarie Convenzionate*, [2006] ECR I-7213, para 52; Case C-180/04, *Andrea Vassallo v Azienda Ospedaliera Ospedale San Martino di Genova e Cliniche Universitarie Convenzionate*, [2006] ECR I-7251, para 37; Case C-1/06, *Bonn Fleisch Ex- und Import GmbH v Hauptzollamt Hamburg-Jonas*, [2007] ECR I-5609, para 41.

[36] On whether a principle of 'national procedural autonomy' really exists, see the provocative article by the late ECJ Judge Kakouris, 'Do the Member States Possess Judicial Procedural "Autonomy"?', (1997) 34 *CML Rev* 1389. According to Kakouris, national remedial and procedural systems are subservient to Community law. Thus, the 'principle' of national procedural autonomy is a descriptive term that does not mean that the Community lacks the power to legislate or regulate such procedural and remedial rules as are necessary for the enforcement of substantive Community rules. Some commentators approach the principle of national procedural autonomy in the context of subsidiarity. See, eg, Gautron, 'Subsidiarité ou neo-subsidiarité', (1998) 8 *Revue des Affaires Européennes / Law and European Affairs* 3, 5–7, speaking of 'judicial subsidiarity'.

[37] See on this question Bergé and Sinopoli, 'Droit des obligations et autonomie procédurale: La distinction fond/procédure sous le double éclairage du droit communautaire et du droit des États membres', *Petites Affiches*, 24 August 2004, No 169, 7, 8–10.

[38] On the remedial and procedural autonomy of Member States and its Community law limits, see, eg, Tridimas, 'Enforcing Community Rights in National Courts: Some Recent

principles of *equality* and *effectiveness*.[39] The first principle means that the enforcement of Community law at the national level should not be submitted to more onerous procedures than the enforcement of comparable national law. The second principle, which is a direct consequence of the principles of direct effect and supremacy,[40] is a much more demanding test. It means that although Community-derived rights will have to count on national substantive and procedural remedies for their enforcement, such remedies still have to be effective and must not render the exercise and enforcement of those rights impossible or unjustifiably onerous. It reflects a more general guiding principle of Community law, that of full and useful effectiveness (*effet utile*).[41] Undoubtedly those two requirements make the national divergences that we described above less burdensome. To all these we must also add the Article 234 EC preliminary reference procedure.

The Court of Justice has, nevertheless, proceeded further than that. Starting with such cases as *Francovich*, *Factortame I* and *Zuckerfabrik Süderdithmarschen*,[42] it has also recognised the existence of certain

Developments', in O'Keeffe and Bavasso (eds), *Liber Amicorum in Honour of Lord Slynn of Hadley*, Vol I, *Judicial Review in European Union Law* (The Hague/London/Boston, Kluwer, 2000) 465 *ff*; Kilpatrick, 'The Future of Remedies in Europe', in Kilpatrick, Novitz and Skidmore (eds), *The Future of Remedies in Europe* (Oxford, Hart Publishing, 2000) 2 *ff*; Jacobs and Deisenhofer, 'Procedural Aspects of the Effective Private Enforcement of EC Competition Rules: A Community Perspective', in Ehlermann and Atanasiu (eds), *European Competition Law Annual 2001: Effective Private Enforcement of EC Antitrust Law* (Oxford, Hart Publishing, 2003) 215 *ff*; Vilaras, 'Réflexions sur le présent et l'avenir de la protection juridictionnelle des particuliers', in Alivizatos, Dimitropoulos *et al* (eds), *Essays in Honour of Georgios I. Kassimatis* (Athens/Brussels/Berlin, Ant. N. Sakkoulas, 2004) 878–9; Mehdi, 'Le revirement jurisprudentiel en droit communautaire', in *L'intégration européenne au XXIe siècle, En hommage à Jacques Bourrinet* (Paris, 2004) 122–3; Dougan, (n 19) 20 *ff*; J-V Louis and T Ronse, *L'ordre juridique de l'Union européenne* (Brussels/Paris, Helbing & Lichtenhahn, 2005) 262 *ff* and 292 *ff*; A Arnull, A Dashwood, M Dougan, M Ross, E Spaventa and D Wyatt, *Wyatt & Dashwood's European Union Law* (London, Sweet & Maxwell, 2006) 208 *ff*

[39] See, eg Case 33/76, *Rewe-Zentralfinanz eG and Rewe-Zentral AG v Landwirtschaftskammer für das Saarland*, [1976] ECR 1989, para 5; Case 45/76, *Comet BV v Produkschap voor Siergewassen*, [1976] ECR 2043, paras 12–13; Case 130/79, *Express Dairy Foods Ltd v Intervention Board for Agricultural Produce*, [1980] ECR 1887, para 12; Case 199/82, *Amministrazione delle Finanze dello Stato v San Giorgio*, [1983] ECR 3595, para 12; Case C-261/95, *Rosalba Palmisani v Istituto Nazionale della Previdenza Sociale (INPS)*, [1997] ECR I-4025, para 27.

[40] See Louis and Ronse, (above n 38) 296.

[41] On the principle of effectiveness (*effet utile*) see inter alia RM D'Sa, *European Community Law and Civil Remedies in England and Wales* (London, Sweet & Maxwell, 1994) 153 *ff*; Pliakos, (n 24) 179 *ff*; Dubos, (n 5) 278 *ff*; Zuleeg, 'Die Wirksamkeit des Europarechts', in Colneric, Edward *et al* (eds), *Une Communauté de droit, Festschrift für Gil Carlos Rodriguez Iglesias* (Berlin, Berliner Wissenschafts-Verlag, 2003) 222 and 228 *ff*; K Lenaerts, D Arts, I Maselis and R Bray, *Procedural Law of the European Union* (London, Sweet & Maxwell, 2006) 83 *ff*.

[42] Joined Cases C-6/90 and C-9/90, *Andrea Francovich et al v Italy*, [1991] ECR I-5357; Case C-213/89, *R v Secretary of State for Transport, ex p Factortame Ltd et al (I)*, [1990] ECR I-2433; Joined Cases 143/88 and C-92/89, *Zuckerfabrik Süderdithmarschen AG v Hauptzollamt Itzehoe* and *Zuckerfabrik Soest GmbH v Hauptzollamt Paderborn*, [1991] ECR I-415.

autonomous Community law remedies for Community law-based rights,[43] and has delegated to national law only the very specific conditions for their exercise, as well as the procedural framework rules, always within the limitations of equality and effectiveness. In doing so, it has been guided by the principle *ubi ius, ibi remedium*, under which a Community law right must be protected through an appropriate corresponding remedy,[44] and has relied upon 'the full effectiveness of Community rules and the effective protection of the rights which they confer' and upon the duties that Article 10 EC imposes on Member States and their judicial organs.[45]

A former Advocate General of the Court of Justice and eminent scholar of Community law has therefore proposed a more global approach to the issue of remedies in Community law, thus stressing the requirement of effective judicial protection which better describes the Court's case law on remedies. Professor Van Gerven speaks of four already existing Community substantive remedies: a general one, to have national measures that conflict with EC law set aside;[46] and three specific ones, compensation, interim relief and restitution.[47] Individual civil liability is integrated in the first limb of these three specific remedies, beside its admittedly much more developed sibling, state liability.[48]

The former Advocate General further makes a distinction between the 'constitutive' and 'executive' elements of remedies. The first pertain to the principle of the remedy as such; the second to its 'content and extent'. The first type of elements must be uniform, since they are entirely connected with the Community 'right' of which individuals avail themselves. The executive elements, on the other hand, may to a certain extent be governed by national law, but only under more substantial Community requirements. For these elements Community law should require an 'adequacy

[43] See, eg, B Hofstötter, *Non-compliance of National Courts, Remedies in European Community Law and Beyond* (The Hague, TMC Asser Press, 2005) 31–3; PP Craig, *EU Administrative Law, Collected Courses of the Academy of European Law*, Vol XVI/1 (Oxford, Oxford University Press, 2006) 791 *ff*.

[44] See, eg, Pliakos, (above n 24) 141 *ff*.

[45] Joined Cases C-46/93 and C-48/93, *Brasserie du Pêcheur SA v Germany* and *R v Secretary of State for Transport, ex p Factortame Ltd et al (Factortame III)*, [1996] ECR I-1029, para 39. On the Art 10 EC legal basis, see in particular Temple Lang, 'The Duties of Cooperation of National Authorities and Courts under Article 10 EC: Two More Reflexions', (2001) 26 *EL Rev* 84, 87.

[46] This general remedy, in our view, encapsulates the duty of national courts to ignore national law that conflicts with directly effective Community law (principles of supremacy and direct effect), and to interpret national law in conformity with Community law.

[47] See Van Gerven, (above n 30) 503. *Cf* also, more recently, Reich, 'Horizontal Liability in EC Law: Hybridization of Remedies for Compensation in Case of Breaches of EC Rights', (2007) 44 *CML Rev* 705.

[48] On the extension of this principle to cover individual civil liability, see section IV below.

test', rather than a mere 'minimum effectiveness' or 'non-impossibility' test which may continue to apply for simple procedural rules.[49]

On the above basis, it is interesting to note that Article I-29(1)(b) of the ill-fated Treaty establishing a Constitution for Europe and now Article 19(1)(b) of the new Treaty on European Union, as amended by the Treaty of Lisbon, totally missed this point and used a rather unsophisticated text, referring to Member States providing 'remedies sufficient to ensure effective legal protection in the fields covered by Union law'.[50] While the intention was clearly to ensure the effective judicial protection of Community-law-based rights,[51] the language used seems to imply that the corresponding remedies[52] are a matter of national law only. Such a reading, however, would not only contradict the case law of the Court of Justice ever since *Factortame I* and *Francovich*, but would not be in accordance with the spirit and system of the new Treaty itself. In any event, this provision, which is a paragraph in the Article dealing with the Court of Justice, should not be considered as a rule on competences. Its aim is to energise the national courts and point to their duties as Community judges of general jurisdiction. It therefore cannot be intended to exclude the possibility for Community law itself to provide for remedies in appropriate cases.

IV THE PARADIGM OF THE RIGHT IN DAMAGES: *COURAGE*

A The Way to *Courage*

The Treaty of Rome did not include a provision on the award of damages to victims of anti-competitive practices, unlike US antitrust law and competition laws in some Member States.

Until 2001, the Court of Justice never had the opportunity to rule on the issue of civil liabilities arising from the violation of EC competition rules, although in some instances it referred to possible damages and other civil claims that private parties could pursue before national courts,[53] but without touching upon the question of the Community or national legal basis.[54]

[49] See Van Gerven, (above n 30) 502–504, 524–6.

[50] The consolidated version of the new Treaty, as amended, appears in [2008] OJ C115/13.

[51] See Skouris, (above n 7) 18.

[52] This is the only time that the Treaties refer to 'remedies'.

[53] This was already implicit in *BRT v SABAM I*, (n 25), paras 16 and 22. Reference should also be made to Case C-242/95, *GT-Link A/S v De Danske Statsbaner*, [1997] ECR I-4349, para 57; Case C-282/95 P, *Guérin Automobiles v Commission*, [1996] ECR I-1503, para 39.

[54] It is noteworthy that the CFI in Case T-24/90, *Automec Srl v Commission (Automec II)*, [1992] ECR II-2223, para 50, had expressed itself in favour of the national law basis of

Outside the area of competition law, however, the Court incrementally imposed severe limits on national institutional and remedial/procedural autonomy, first stressing the Community law requirements of non-discrimination/equality and adequacy/effectiveness, and ultimately recognising the existence, as a matter of Community law, of Community remedies available to individuals. Thus there was an impressive development from the early case law, where it was stated that Community law imposed no duties on national laws and courts to introduce new remedies,[55] to a more proactive approach, notably with rulings dealing with remedies in the fields of social policy and sex discrimination,[56] interim protection[57] and, ultimately, state liability for breaches of EC law.[58] In particular, the Community principle of state liability for breaches of EC law by Member States, established in *Francovich*, increasingly led commentators to argue that a right in damages in cases of EC competition law infringements was a matter of EC and not of national law. It was thought that there was no compelling reason to differentiate between state and individual liability for damage caused by infringements of Community law, since the basis for such liability, which is the principle of *effet utile* or effectiveness of Community law, is not affected by the identity of the perpetrator, that is whether it is the state or individuals.[59]

such claims: 'The other consequences attaching to an infringement of Article [81] of the Treaty [apart from the nullity of Article 81(2)], such as the obligation to make good the damage caused to a third party or a possible obligation to enter into a contract . . . are to be determined under national law.' It is beyond the scope of this study to explain the occasional failures of the CFI to grasp the more general picture of Community law in some of its rulings on competition law. See also below n 93 on the CFI's ruling in *Atlantic Container*, which in our view misread *Courage*.

[55] Case 158/80, *Rewe-Handelsgesellschaft Nord mbH and Rewe-Markt Steffen v Hauptzollamt Kiel (Butter-buying Cruises)*, [1981] ECR 1805.

[56] See, eg, Case 14/83, *Sabine von Colson and Elisabeth Kamann v Land Nordhein-Westfalen*, [1984] ECR 1891; Case C-177/88, *Elisabeth Johanna Pacifica Dekker v Stichting Vormingscentrum voor Jong Volwassenen (VJV-Centrum) Plus*, [1990] ECR I-3941; Case C-271/91, *MH Marshall v Southampton and South West Hampshire Area Health Authority (Marshall II)*, [1993] ECR I-4367. All these cases stressed the principle according to which sanctions for enforcement of Community law must be able to guarantee real and effective judicial protection to the discrimination victim, and must have a real deterrent effect on the employer who has breached the pertinent rules.

[57] See in particular *Factortame I*, (above n 42). See, with regard to this case, VA Christianos, *Overruling of Prior Judgments in the Case Law of the Court of Justice of the European Communities* (Athens/Komotini, Ant. N. Sakkoulas, 1998) [in Greek] 69, speaking in this context of a clear case of departure from the *Butter-buying Cruises* case.

[58] *Francovich*, (n 42); *Brasserie du Pêcheur/Factortame III*, (n 45). See also, for an analysis of this development of the case law, Dougan, (above n 19) 227 *ff*.

[59] For the first attempts to deduce a Community principle of individual civil liability in EC competition law cases from *Francovich*, see Smith, 'The *Francovich* Case: State Liability and the Individual's Right in damages', (1992) 13 *European Competition Law Review* 129, 132; Hoskins, '*Garden Cottage* Revisited: The Availability of Damages in the National Courts for Breaches of the EEC Competition Rules', (1992) 13 *European Competition Law Review* 257, 259.

Meanwhile, a powerful boost to that line of argument was given in 1993 by Advocate General Van Gerven in his Opinion in *Banks*,[60] in which he argued extensively in favour of recognising a Community right to obtain reparation in respect of loss and damage sustained as a result of an undertaking's infringement of the directly effective Community competition rules.[61] The Advocate General considered in his carefully structured Opinion that the general basis established by the Court in *Francovich* also applied to the case of 'breach of a right which an individual derives from an obligation imposed by Community law on another individual'.

> The full effect of Community law would be impaired if the former individual or undertaking did not have the possibility of obtaining reparation from the party who can be held responsible for the breach of Community law—all the more so, evidently, if a directly effective provision of Community law is infringed.[62]

In competition law, in particular, the Advocate General observed that such a Community right in damages would make the Treaty antitrust rules 'more operational', adducing an argument from the US system of antitrust enforcement, where civil suits for damages have played a dominant role.[63] Interestingly enough, he then went on to draw up 'detailed rules governing an action for damages in respect of breach of the rules of Community law' and, more specifically, 'uniform conditions of liability', relying on the Court's case law on the non-contractual liability of the Community (Article 288(2) EC).[64] In *Banks*, however, the Court declined to address all these fundamental issues, because it reached the conclusion that the only set of rules applicable to the facts, Articles 65 and 66 ECSC, did not have direct effect.

Notwithstanding this missed opportunity, advocates of a Community remedy of damages for antitrust violations drew further support from the progressively more elaborate jurisprudence of the Court of Justice on state liability, notably in *Brasserie du Pêcheur/Factortame III*, but also from the Court's shift towards a more remedies-oriented case law, where effective judicial protection acquired a central role, as a complement of or corollary to the fundamental principle of direct effect. In 1999, a groundbreaking monograph written by Clifford Jones persuasively argued in favour of a

[60] Case C-128/92, *HJ Banks & Co Ltd v British Coal Corporation*, [1994] ECR I-1209.

[61] *Banks*, *ibid*, AG's Opinion, paras 37 *ff*

[62] *Ibid*, para 43.

[63] *Ibid*, para 44.

[64] *Ibid*, paras 46 *ff*. According to AG Van Gerven, there were three conditions for liability in damages to arise: damage, a causal connection between the breach and the ensuing damage, and the illegality of the alleged conduct. It should be stressed that at that time the Court had not yet accepted the transposability of the then Art 215(2) EC case law to the liability of Member States, as it did later (*Brasserie du Pêcheur/Factortame III*, (above n 45), para 42), although AG Mischo in *Francovich* had already so suggested (*Francovich*, above n 42, AG's Opinion, para 71).

private enforcement system in Europe, after demolishing many of the misconceptions of European scholars as to the exceptionality and non-transposability of the mature US system of private antitrust enforcement.[65] A point central to that study was the view that there was a right under EC law allowing claims for damages from undertakings which had violated Articles 81 and 82 EC, in the line of the *Francovich* and *Brasserie du Pêcheur/Factortame III* judgments.[66] This monograph was to be quite influential with the Court of Justice.

B *Courage v Crehan*: The Consecration of a Community Right in Damages

The fundamental issue of the Community or national law basis of the right in damages in EC competition law violations was finally addressed by the Court of Justice in its *Courage* ruling of 20 September 2001.[67] There, the Court recognised a right in damages as a matter of Community rather than national law, and stressed the fundamental character of the EC competition rules in the overall system of the Treaty.

The dilemma for the Court was to choose between the 'traditionalist' and the more 'integrationist' approach. It could either consider the whole question of damages in the context of national remedial and procedural autonomy, that is as a question of national law subject to the minimum Community law requirements of equivalence and effectiveness, or proceed to the recognition of a Community right in damages, as Advocate General Van Gerven had previously proposed in *Banks.*

It is noteworthy that the 'traditionalist' approach had basically been represented by continental textbooks and articles, particularly by German and French (competition law-specific) literature. It is no exaggeration to say that the whole issue of the Community or national legal basis for a right in damages had been ignored by the majority of this part of the literature, or at best had been considered in the context of national remedial-procedural autonomy and its Community law limits.[68] On the

[65] CA Jones, *Private Enforcement of Antitrust Law in the EU, UK and USA* (Oxford, Oxford University Press, 1999).

[66] *Ibid*, 72.

[67] Case C-453/99, *Courage Ltd v Bernard Crehan*, [2001] ECR I-6297.

[68] See, eg, A Toffoletto, *Il risarcimento del danno nel sistema delle sanzioni per la violazione della normativa antitrust* (Milan, Giuffrè, 1996) 114–15; Schmidt, in Immenga and Mestmäcker (eds), *EG-Wettbewerbsrecht, Kommentar*, Vol I (Munich, C. H. Beck, 1997), p. 58 *ff*; S Poillot-Peruzzetto and M Luby, *Le droit communautaire appliqué à l'entreprise* (Paris, Dalloz, 1998), 270; M Tavassi and M Scuffi, *Diritto processuale antitrust, Tutela giurisdizionale della concorrenza* (Milan, Giuffrè, 1998) 301; Maitz-Strassnig, 'Rapport autrichien', in *XVIII congrès FIDE (Stockholm, 3–6 juin 1998)*, Vol II, *Application nationale du droit européen de la concurrence* (Stockholm, FIDE, 1999) 31–2; Schröter, in Von der

other hand, English-speaking sources had shown an extreme awareness of and conviction as to the existence of a Community remedy of damages, not only *de lege ferenda*, but also *de lege lata*.[69] This difference of philosophy

Groeben, Thiesing and Ehlermann (eds), *Kommentar zum EU-/EG-Vertrag*, Vol 2/I, *Artikel 85–87 EGV* (Baden-Baden, Nomos, 1999), 2/268 *ff* and 2/767; KL Ritter, DW Braun and F Rawlinson, *European Competition Law: A Practitioner's Guide* (The Hague/London/Boston, Kluwer, 2000) 926; Mestmäcker, 'The EC Commission's Modernization of Competition Policy: A Challenge to the Community's Constitutional Order', (2000) 1 *European Business Organisation Law Review* 401, 421 *ff*; Schröter, in Schröter, Jakob and Mederer (eds), *Kommentar zum Europäischen Wettbewerbsrecht* (Baden-Baden, Nomos, 2003) 309, 327; CP Iliopoulos, *The Enforcement of the European Law of Free Competition in Greece (1981–2005)—The EC Regulation 1/2003 and the Law 3373/2005* (Athens/Komotini, Ant. N. Sakkoulas, 2006) [in Greek] 45. See, however, S Mail-Fouilleul, *Les sanctions de la violation du droit communautaire de la concurrence* (Paris, LGDJ, 2002) 580–82, who seems to accept the Community law basis; C Nowak, *Konkurrentenschutz in der EG, Interdependenz des gemeinschaftsrechtlichen und mitgliedstaalichen Rechtsschutzes von Konkurrenten* (Baden-Baden, Nomos, 1997) 230 *ff*, referring to *Banks* and to the state liability case law of the ECJ and supporting the Community law basis of the right in damages; Weyer, 'Gemeinschaftsrechtliches Verbot und nationale Zivilrechtsfolgen—Eine Untersuchung am Beispiel der Artikel 81, 82 EG-Vertrag', (1999) 7 *Zeitschrift für Europäisches Privatrecht* 424, 437–9, addressing this issue but rejecting the Community basis. Some Austrian commentators appear to be more perceptive of the Community basis of the right in damages (see Stillfried and Stockenhuber, 'Schadenersatz bei Verstoß gegen das Kartellverbot des Art 85 EG-V', (1995) 9 *Wirtschaftsrechtliche Blätter* 301 + 345, 345 *ff*). See also Bastianon, 'Il risarcimento del danno per violazione del diritto antitrust in Inghilterra e in Italia', (1998) 3 *Danno e Responsabilità* 1066, 1067, who, referring to the recent Community case law (though not to AG Van Gerven's Opinion in *Banks*), makes an interesting distinction between recovery of damages (*risarcimento*) and recoverability of damages (*risarcibilità*). According to this author, the latter should rather be a principle of Community law, since its basis lies directly in the rights that EC law confers on individuals.

[69] See, eg, Maitland-Walker, 'Editorial: A Step Closer to a Definitive Ruling on a Right in Damages for Breach of the EC Competition Rules', (1992) 13 *European Competition Law Review* 3; D'Sa, (n 41) 169–74; Shaw, 'Decentralization and Law Enforcement in EC Competition Law', (1995) 15 *Legal Studies* 128, 138 *ff*; Winterstein, 'A Community Right in Damages for Breach of EC Competition Rules?', (1995) 16 *European Competition Law Review* 49; Francis, 'Subsidiarity and Antitrust: The Enforcement of European Competition Law in the National Courts of Member States', (1995) 27 *Law & Policy of International Business* 247, 254, 273; Vaughan, 'EC Competition Law in National Proceedings', in Slynn and Pappas (eds), *Procedural Aspects of EC Competition Law* (Maastricht, EIPA, 1995) 27; C Lewis, *Remedies and the Enforcement of European Community Law* (London, Sweet & Maxwell, 1996) 137–8; Weatherill, 'Public Interest Litigation in EC Competition Law', in Micklitz and Reich (eds), *Public Interest Litigation Before European Courts* (Baden-Baden, Nomos, 1996) 185; Tickle and Tyler, 'Community Competition Law, Recovering Damages in the English Courts: New Era? False Dawn', in Lonbay and Biondi (eds), *Remedies for Breach of EC Law* (Chichester, Wiley, 1997) 137 *ff*; Whish, 'The Enforcement of EC Competition Law in the Domestic Courts of Member States', in Gormley (ed), *Current and Future Perspectives on EC Competition Law, A Tribute to Professor MR Mok* (London/The Hague/Boston, Kluwer, 1997) 81–2; Hiljemark, 'Enforcement of EC Competition Law in National Courts—The Perspective of Judicial Protection', (1997) 17 *Yearbook of European Law* 83, 126 *ff*; Anderson, 'Damages for Breach of Competition Rules', in Andenas and Jacobs (eds), *European Community Law in the English Courts* (Oxford, Oxford University Press, 1998) 185 *ff*; Rodger and MacCulloch, 'Community Competition Law Enforcement, Deregulation and Re-regulation: The Commission, National Authorities and Private Enforcement', (1998) 4 *Columbia Journal of European Law* 579, 599–600; CS Kerse, *EC Antitrust Procedure* (London, Sweet & Maxwell, 1998) 439–41; PM Taylor, *EC and UK Competition*

is not due to the continentals' lack of judgment, but rather to more systemic differences between the common and the civil law worlds.

The facts of *Courage* were rather undistinguished. Breweries in Britain usually own pubs which they lease to tenants, while the latter are under contractual obligations to buy almost all the beer they serve from their landlords. In 1991 Bernard Crehan signed a 20-year lease with Courage Ltd whereby he had to buy a fixed minimum quantity of beer exclusively from Courage, while the brewery undertook to supply the specified quantities at prices shown in the tenant's price list. The rent was initially lower than the market rate and it was subject to a regular upward review, but it never rose above the best open market rate. In 1993 Mr Crehan and other tenants fell into financial arrears, basically blaming this on Courage's supply of beer at lower prices to other non-tied pubs, 'free houses'. In the same year Courage brought an action for the recovery from Mr Crehan of sums for unpaid deliveries of beer. Mr Crehan, alleging the incompatibility with Article 81(1) EC of the clause requiring him to purchase a fixed minimum quantity of beer from Courage, counter-claimed for damages.[70]

There were two specific obstacles to Mr Crehan's success. The first one was that according to earlier case law, Article 81 EC had been interpreted as protecting only third parties, that is competitors or consumers, but not co-contractors, that is parties to the illegal and void agreement.[71] The second issue was that under English law a party to an illegal agreement, as

Law and Compliance: A Practical Guide (London, Sweet & Maxwell, 1999) 267; R Lane, *EC Competition Law* (Dorchester, Longman, 2000) 203–204; PM Roth (ed), *Bellamy & Child European Community Law of Competition* (London, Sweet & Maxwell, 2001) 801–809; Wahl, 'Damages for Infringement of Competition Law', in Wahlgren (ed), *Scandinavian Studies in Law*, Vol 41, *Tort Liability and Insurance* (Stockholm, 2001) 555. See also Green, 'The Treaty of Rome, National Courts, and English Common Law: The Enforcement of European Competition Law after *Milk Marketing Board*', (1989) 48 *Rabels Zeitschrift für Ausländisches und Internationales Privatrecht* 509, whose views at that distant time, before *Francovich* and other cases on remedies had been decided by the ECJ, are very 'modern'.

[70] There is some uncertainty as to the exact nature of Mr Crehan's claim for damages. The question is whether this was a claim in tort (breach of statutory duty) or in restitution. This uncertainty might be accentuated by the fact that the recovery Mr Crehan sought is limited in extent. He basically asked the national court to put him in the condition he would have been in had he not entered into the agreement. He did not, therefore, claim damages for consequential losses or lost profits. In this respect, his claim, albeit in tort, was of a merely restitutionary nature. See on the issue Gyselen, 'Comment from the Point of View of EU Competition Law', in Wouters and Stuyck (eds), *Principles of Proper Conduct for Supranational, State and Private Actors in the European Union: Towards a* Ius Commune, *Essays in Honour of Walter van Gerven* (Antwerp/Groningen/Oxford, Intersentia, 2001) 139. Van Gerven speaks of 'restitutionary damages', which are on the borderline between damages (in tort) and unjustified enrichment (Van Gerven, 'Substantive Remedies for the Private Enforcement of EC Antitrust Rules Before National Courts', in Ehlermann and Atanasiu (eds), *European Competition Law Annual 2001: Effective Private Enforcement of EC Antitrust Law* (Oxford, Hart Publishing, 2003) 60). It seems, however, that the action in this case was, or in any case was stated by the referring national court to be, one in tort (breach for statutory duty).

[71] *Gibbs Mew plc v Gemmell* (CA), [1998] ELR 588.

this was considered to be by the Court of Appeal, could not claim damages from the other party. This was as a result of the strict construction English courts were giving to the *nemo auditur turpitudinem propriam (suam) allegans* or *in pari delicto potior est conditio defendentis* or *ex dolo malo non oritur causa* rule,[72] which in essence meant that Mr Crehan's claim in damages would fail, because he was a co-contractor in an illegal agreement. That seems to explain the link between these two central issues.[73]

The Court of Justice, following the ruling in *Francovich* which had recognised the principle of state liability as a principle of Community law, and also relying on its *Eco Swiss* ruling,[74] stressed the primacy of Article 81 EC in the system of the Treaty, since it 'constitutes a fundamental provision which is essential for the accomplishment of the tasks entrusted to the Community and, in particular, for the functioning of the internal market'.[75] It also stressed, with particular reference to 'the possibility of seeking compensation for loss caused by a contract or by conduct liable to restrict or distort competition', the task of national courts to ensure the full effect (*plein effet*) of Community rules and the protection of individuals' rights conferred by those rules. The full effectiveness (*pleine efficacité*) of the Treaty competition rules and, in particular 'the practical effect [*effet utile*] of the prohibition laid down in Article [81(1)]' would be put at risk if individuals could not claim damages for losses caused by the infringement of those rules. The instrumental character of such liability for the effectiveness of the law as such is more than evident in this passage, exactly as was the case with state liability in *Francovich*.[76] And finally, the Court dispelled any doubt as to its pronouncement:

> Indeed, *the existence* of such a right strengthens the working of the Community competition rules and discourages agreements or practices, which are frequently covert, which are liable to restrict or distort competition. From that point of view, actions for damages before the national courts *can make a significant contribution to the maintenance of effective competition in the Community*.[77]

This last quote makes it clear that the meaning of effectiveness in *Courage* has a double facet.[78] It refers not only to Community law in general, but

[72] See on all these rules, with subtle distinctions, Virgo, 'The Effect of Illegality on Claims for Restitution in English Law', in Swadling (ed), *The Limits of Restitutionary Claims: A Comparative Analysis* (London, BIICL, 1997) 150 *ff*.

[73] See further Komninos, (above n 22) 462–3. The *in pari delicto* defence applies to restitutionary, as well as to tortious claims and has invariably drawn strong criticism.

[74] Case C-126/97, *Eco Swiss China Time Ltd v Benetton International NV*, [1999] ECR I-3055.

[75] *Courage*, (n 67) para 20.

[76] *Ibid*, para 26, very close to the text of para 33 of *Francovich*.

[77] *Ibid*, para 27 (emphasis added), another text that can be read in parallel to para 34 of *Francovich*.

[78] See section II above on these two facets.

also to the specific field of antitrust. This is clear from the Court's use of the term 'significant contribution' to refer to the role of damages claims for the efficiency of antitrust enforcement in Europe, with a view to maintaining effective competition. More authoritative words in favour of private enforcement and the 'private attorney-general' role[79] of the civil litigant could hardly be pronounced.

C *Courage* Seen between Community and National Law

The importance of *Courage* is that it sets out the principle.[80] This has both symbolic and practical consequences. The recognition of a right in damages by the Community judge eliminates a state of uncertainty and gives national courts an important signal.[81] The saga on whether damages can be awarded for violation of the Treaty competition rules has now ended once and for all. Indeed, to use the example of English law, it was a very unfortunate situation to wonder at the end of the 1990s on the existence of a right in damages as such,[82] and always to revisit the *Garden Cottage*[83]

[79] Private antitrust actions, apart from their compensatory function, further the overall deterrent effect of the law. Thus, economic agents themselves become instrumental in implementing the regulatory policy on competition and the general level of compliance with the law is raised. It is for that reason that the private litigant in US antitrust has been called a 'private attorney-general' (J Jerome Franck in *Associated Industries of New York State, Inc v Ickes*, 134 F.2d 694, 704 (2d Cir. 1943)).

[80] See, eg, S Weatherill, *Cases and Materials on EU Law* (Oxford, Oxford University Press, 2003) 606, speaking of the Court's 'anxiety to promote the *effectiveness* of private enforcement'.

[81] See DG Goyder, *EC Competition Law* (Oxford, Oxford University Press, 2003) 560.

[82] See, eg, M Coleman and M Grenfell, *The Competition Act 1998, Law and Practice* (Oxford, Oxford University Press, 1999) 288, who were still writing that 'it is not absolutely certain that third parties *do* in fact have a right in damages in the English courts under Articles 81 and 82'. See also Beard, 'Damages in Competition Law Litigation', in Ward and Smith (eds), *Competition Litigation in the UK* (London, Sweet & Maxwell, 2005) 257–8.

[83] *Garden Cottage Foods Ltd v Milk Marketing Board* (HL), [1983] 2 All ER 770. This case has been traditionally cited in England as the authority providing support—though not as a direct precedent—for the proposition that an infringement of Community competition law gives rise to tort liability. See also *An Bord Bainne Co-operative Ltd (Irish Dairy Board) v Milk Marketing Board* (QB), [1984] 1 CMLR 519; on appeal [1984] 2 CMLR 584; *Bourgoin SA v Ministry of Agriculture, Fisheries and Food* (QB), [1985] 3 All ER 585, on appeal (CA), [1986] 1 CMLR 287. There has also been a long discussion about the relevant and appropriate cause of action in English law for claims based on Arts 81 and 82 EC. There were three main views: one was to rely on 'economic torts' such as conspiracy, inducing breach of contract, wrongful interference with one's business and intimidation; another was to invent a *sui generis* tort involving breach of Community law; another was to categorise breaches of Arts 81 and 82 EC as breaches of statutory duty. For a description of these views see, inter alia, Shaw, 'United Kingdom', in Behrens (ed), *EEC Competition Rules in National Courts*, Vol I, *United Kingdom and Italy* (Baden-Baden, Nomos, 1992) 74–6; C Jones, (n 65) 113 *ff*. This debate has finally ended, and most commentators and courts in England are now aware of the Community law requirements that damages be available to remedy harm caused by the violation of Community competition law. Commentators and courts now categorise

dicta.[84] Although it is true that certain European legal systems have availed themselves of clear legal bases for damages claims in the case of antitrust-related harm,[85] we fail to see how this reality could be an obstacle to the development of Community law, which has its own exigencies and aspirations. It has been rightly pointed out that even if there is no clear gap in the effective judicial protection of Community competition law-based rights in those legal systems, still the recognition of a Community remedy in damages makes a valuable contribution towards the uniformity, consistency and maximum effectiveness–efficiency of the application of EC (competition) law at the national level.[86]

The enunciation of a Community right in damages and, by implication, of a principle of civil liability of individuals for breach of Community law, is a logical consequence of the Court's abundant case law on state liability, and reflects a more general principle of Community law that 'everyone is bound to make good loss or damage arising as a result of his conduct in breach of a legal duty' (*neminem laedere*).[87] That principle is wholly connected with the very nature of the Community and actually reflects the 'dogmatic-developmental history of the Community legal order' (*dogmatische Entwicklungsgeschichte der Gemeinschaftsrechtsordnung*).[88] The

such claims as breaches of statutory duty, but the national legal categorisation of the cause of action is no longer important. See presciently C Jones, (above note 65) 148; Komninos (n 22) 480–81.

[84] This state of uncertainty has been described and castigated by C Jones, (above n 65) 97, 147.

[85] A German commentator, while the Court's judgment was awaited, had emphasised that the 'invention' of a Community right in damages would offer nothing at all in the German context, since German law already provided for appropriate remedies (see Basedow, 'Who Will Protect Competition in Europe? From Central Enforcement to Authority Networks and Private Litigation', in Einhorn (ed), *Liber Amicorum EJ Mestmäcker*, (2001) 2 *European Business Organization Law Review* 443, 461–2). See also Mestmäcker, (above n 68) 426, who, arguing against the thesis of Clifford Jones on the Community nature of the right in damages, considers that 'new Community law remedies for a breach of competition rules are not self-explanatory nor self-executing and do not define themselves'. It is unclear, however, what this highly respected commentator means by this aphorism. He goes on to stress that the only way to provide for such remedies would be through approximation, in other words through a directive.

[86] See Stillfried and Stockenhuber, (above n 68) 350. See also in this sense, Kerse, (above n 69) 440–41.

[87] See Edward and Robinson, 'Is there a Place for Private Law Principles in Community Law?', in Heukels and McDonnell (eds), *The Action for Damages in Community Law* (The Hague/London/Boston, Kluwer, 1997) 341, referring to para 12 of AG Tesauro's Opinion in *Brasserie du Pêcheur/Factortame III*, (n 45). In that passage the AG had reached the conclusion that 'in so far as at least the principle of state liability is part of the tradition of all the legal systems, it must be able to be applied also where the unlawful conduct consists of an infringement of a Community provision' (*ibid*, para 13 of AG's Opinion). The AG had started from the premise that the idea of state liability formed part of a more general principle of non-contractual liability (*neminem laedere*).

[88] See A Metaxas, *State Liability for Violations of Community Law by National Supreme Court Judgments* (Athens/Thessaloniki, Sakkoulas, 2005) [in Greek] 23–4, with further references to German literature.

extension of this principle to the liability of individuals makes it possible to speak of a system of civil liability for Community law infringements,[89] irrespective of their perpetrator. This has not been missed by the Commission, which in its 2004 co-operation Notice lists together the remedy of damages in case of an infringement by an undertaking, referring to *Courage*, and the remedy of damages in case of an infringement by a Member State or an authority which is an emanation of the State, referring to *Francovich*.[90] This is exactly what Advocate General Van Gerven had argued for in *Banks* and what has also been proposed by other authors in the past.[91]

Meanwhile, the Court's approach in *Courage* of recognising this Community law principle in a non-consecrational way, and without, at least at that time, defining specific uniform conditions, created some confusion. While the majority of commentators grasped the fundamental importance of this ruling,[92] others failed to see the basic principle and merely spoke of

[89] See also Drexl, 'Do We Need "Courage" for International Antitrust Law? Choosing between Supranational and International Law Principles of Enforcement', in Drexl (ed), *The Future of Transnational Antitrust—From Comparative to Common Competition Law* (Berne, Staempfli, 2003) 339.

[90] Commission Notice on the Co-operation between the Commission and the Courts of the EU Member States in the Application of Articles 81 and 82 EC, [2004] OJ C 101/54, para 10, fn 26.

[91] See in this sense Edward and Robinson, (n 87) 340 *ff*; W Van Gerven, J Lever and P Larouche, *Common Law of Europe Casebooks: Tort Law* (Oxford, Hart Publishing, 2000) 895. See also Saggio, 'La responsabilità dello stato per violazione del diritto comunitario', (2001) 6 *Danno e Responsabilità* 223, 242, according to whom the exigency of effective judicial protection which to some extent forms the basis for the Community nature of the principle of state liability for violation of EC law must also apply to civil liability of individuals for Community law violations.

[92] See, eg, Nowak, (2001) 12 *Europäische Zeitschrift für Wirtschaftsrecht* 717, who, after underlining the judgment's similarities with *Francovich*, stresses the primary Community law basis of the right in damages, notwithstanding the fact that the Court did not explicitly speak of a Community principle (as in *Francovich*); Klages, (2001) 2 *Revue du Droit de l'Union Européenne* 1003, 1005; Poillot-Peruzzetto, (2002) 12(1) *Contrats-Concurrence-Consommation* 28, 29; Palmieri and Pardolesi, (2002) 125 *Il Foro Italiano*, IV, 76, 77; Jones and Beard, 'Co-contractors, Damages and Article 81: The ECJ Finally Speaks', (2002) 23 *European Competition Law Review* 246, 251 *ff*; Komninos, (n 22) 466 *ff*; Stuyck and Van Dyck, 'EC Competition Rules on Vertical Restrictions and the Realities of a Changing Retail Sector and of National Contract Laws', Paper Presented at the Society of European Contract Law, London Conference (16–17 May 2002), 39–46; Alvizou, 'Individual Tort Liability for Infringements of Community Law', (2002) 29 *Legal Issues of Economic Integration* 177, 184 *ff*; Odudu and Edelman, 'Compensatory Damages for Breach of Article 81', (2002) 27 *EL Rev* 327, 334–6; R Hempel, *Privater Rechtsschutz im Kartellrecht, Eine rechtsvergleichende Analyse* (Baden-Baden, Nomos, 2002) 98–101; Van Gerven, 'The Emergence of a Common European Law in the Area of Tort Law: The EU Contribution', in Fairgrieve, Andenas and Bell (eds), *Tort Liability of Public Authorities in Comparative Perspective* (London, BIICL, 2002) 140–44; S Amadeo, *Norme comunitarie, posizioni giuridiche soggettive e giudizi interni* (Milan, Giuffrè, 2002) 299–303; Kremer, 'Die Haftung Privater für Verstöße gegen Gemeinschaftsrecht', (2003) 38 *Europarecht* 696, 697 *ff*; *idem*, 'Liability for Breach of European Community Law: An Analysis of the New Remedy in the Light of English and German Law', (2003) 22 *Yearbook of European Law* 203, 209*ff*; N Reich, C Goddard and K

national remedies which are adapted by having recourse to the classical minimum effectiveness proviso.[93] Interestingly, this is also the express position of the German *Bundeskartellamt*, which in a 2005 Discussion

Vasiljeva, *Understanding EU Law, Objectives, Principles and Methods of Community Law* (Antwerp/Oxford/New York, Intersentia, 2003) 315 *ff*; Mäsch, 'Private Ansprüche bei Verstößen gegen das europäische Kartellverbot—'Courage' und die Folgen', (2003) 38 *Europarecht* 825; Eilmansberger, (n 26) 1226–7; C Joerges, 'Sur la légitimité d'européaniser le droit privé, Plaidoyer pour une approche procédurale', EUI Working Paper, Law No 2004/4, 21–2, 36, speaking of the creation of a 'new private law that the Member States must incorporate as their "national law"'; Stuyck, 'La place des consommateurs dans le vouveau système d'application des articles 81–82 CE', in Nihoul (ed), *La décentralisation dans l'application du droit de la concurrence, Un rôle accru pour le practicien?* (Brussels/ Louvain-la Neuve, Bruylant, 2004) 208–209, 212; *idem*, 'EC Competition Law after Modernisation: More Than Ever in the Interest of Consumers', (2005) 28 *Journal of Consumer Policy* 1, 16; Reich, 'The *Courage* Doctrine: Encouraging or Discouraging Compensation for Antitrust Injuries?', (2005) 42 *CML Rev* 35, 37–9; B Markesinis, H Unberath and A Johnston, *The German Law of Contract, A Comparative Treatise* (Oxford, Hart Publishing, 2006) 41; C Van Dam, *European Tort Law* (Oxford, Oxford University Press, 2006) 31–7; Lenaerts, Arts, Maselis and Bray, (n 41) 108–15 and 114 in particular; Drake, 'Scope of *Courage* and the Principle of "Individual Liability" for Damages: Further Development of the Principle of Effective Judicial Protection by the Court of Justice', (2006) 31 *EL Rev* 841, 846 *ff*; Temple Lang, 'Commitment Decisions and Settlements with Antitrust Authorities and Private Parties under European Antitrust Law', in Hawk (ed), *International Antitrust Law and Policy 2005, Annual Proceedings of the Fordham Corporate Law Institute* (New York, Juris, 2006) 310–11; D Chalmers, C Hadjiemmanuil, G Monti and A Tomkins, *European Union Law* (Cambridge, Cambridge University Press, 2006) 968–71; Arnull, *et al*, (n 38) 1111–13; M Gray, M Lester, G Darbon, G Facenna, C Brown and E Holmes, *EU Competition Law: Procedures and Remedies* (Richmond, Richmond Law & Tax, 2006) 258; Wachsmann, 'Le développement des actions privées en droit de la concurrence : Un autre point de vue', in Idot and Prieto (eds), *Les entreprises face au nouveau droit des pratiques anticoncurrentielles: Le Règlement 1/2003 modifie-t-il les stratégies contentieuses ?* (Brussels, Bruylant, 2006), 193; Odudu, 'Effective Remedies and Effective Incentives in Community Competition Law', (2006) 5 *Competition Law Journal* 134, 140 *ff*; Norberg, 'Application by National Courts of Articles 81 and 82 of the EC Treaty—Reflections Especially in Light of the Swedish Case', in Baudenbacher, Gulmann *et al* (eds), *Liber Amicorum in Honour of Bo Vesterdorf* (Brussels, Bruyant, 2007) 409; PP Craig and G De Búrca, *EU Law: Text, Cases and Materials* (Oxford, Oxford University Press, 2008) 333 *ff*. See also, in favour of the Community law basis of the right to damages, para 53 of AG Poiares Maduro's Opinion in Case C-438/05, *The International Transport Workers' Federation and The Finnish Seamen's Union v Viking Line ABP and OÜ Viking Line Eesti*, [2007] ECR I-10779, which, referring to *Courage*, clearly speaks of a claim 'based directly' on Community law. See generally AP Komninos, *EC Private Antitrust Enforcement, Decentralised Application of EC Competition Law by National Courts* (Oxford, Hart Publishing, 2008) 170 *ff*.

93 See, eg, Weyer, (2002) 51 *Gewerblicher Rechtsschutz und Urheberrecht: Internationaler Teil* 57, 58; Lettl, 'Der Schadensersatzanspruch gemäß § 823 Abs. 2 BGB i.V. mit Art 81 Abs. 1 EG', (2003) 167 *Zeitschrift für das gesamte Handelsrecht und Wirtschaftsrecht* 473, 477; Weyer, 'Schadenersatzansprüche gegen Private kraft Gemeinschaftsrecht', (2003) 11 *Zeitschrift für Europäishes Privatecht* 318, 323 *ff*; Dougan, (n 19), 378 *ff* and 394; Betlem, 'Torts, a European *ius commune* and the Private Enforcement of Community Law', (2005) 64 *Cambridge Law Journal* 126 142 *ff*; R O'Donoghue and JA Padilla, *The Law and Economics of Article 82 EC* (Oxford, Hart Publishing, 2006) 743, who see the whole case from a procedural autonomy-Community limits angle. See also in this sense Albors-Llorens, '*Courage v Crehan*: Judicial Activism or Consistent Approach?', (2002) 61 *Cambridge Law Journal* 38 40; Tesauro, 'Competition Authorities and Private Rights', in Andenas, Hutchings and Marsden (eds), *Current Competition Law*, Vol II (London, BIICL, 2004) 185, n 3; PJ Slot and

Paper on private actions felt the need to take a position on this debate and sided with the view that considers the right to damages to be subject to national law.[94] Such reluctance to accept the Community-law basis of the civil liability principle should not, however, come as a surprise, since in the past there have even been voices doubting the Community-law basis of the principle of state liability, notwithstanding the Court's much clearer language in *Francovich*.[95]

Courage in this context is similar to restitution cases, where individuals claim recovery of charges for sums levied in violation of Community law by public authorities.[96] Exactly as in *Courage*, in these cases the Court follows a more reserved approach. It has stressed that repayment or restitution of unlawfully levied charges is required and that this right has a Community law basis.[97] But it then delegates the issue and the conditions

A Johnston, *An Introduction to Competition Law* (Oxford, Hart Publishing, 2006) 207, who consider that the Court did not follow AG Van Gerven's *Banks* Opinion and that it confirmed that the right to compensation in EC competition law cases remains a matter of national law. Surprisingly enough, the same approach is followed by the CFI in Case T-395/94, *Atlantic Container Line AB et al v Commission*, [2002] ECR II-875, para 414, where reference is made to para 29 of *Courage*, ie to the *Rewe/Comet* formula on national procedural autonomy and on its two Community provisos, non-discrimination and effectiveness (see above): '... the case-law establishes that the consequences in civil law attaching to an infringement of Article [81] of the Treaty, such as the obligation to make good the damage caused to a third party or a possible obligation to enter into a contract, are to be determined under national law ... [references to para 29 of *Courage* and to para 50 of *Automec II*] ... subject, however, to not undermining the effectiveness of the Treaty'. This reference completely ignores the preceding paragraphs of *Courage* and constitutes in our view a misreading of that fundamental judgment. The language of *Courage*—we should not forget—should be seen in the Art 234 EC context of 'dialogue' between the Community court and the *juges communautaires de droit commun*, and it therefore serves the exigencies of its context, which the CFI—a court in a different context—may have missed.

[94] See Bundeskartellamt, *Private Kartellrechtsdurchsetzung: Stand, Probleme, Perspektiven*, Diskussionspapier für die Sitzung des Arbeitskreises Kartellrecht am 26 September 2005, 6. See also WF Bulst, *Schadensersatzansprüche der Marktgegenseite im Kartellrecht, Zur Schadensabwälzung nach deutschem, europäischem und US-amerikanischem Recht* (Baden-Baden, Nomos, 2006), 187 *ff*; Säcker and Jaecks, in Hirsch, Montag and Säcker (eds), *Münchener Kommentar zum europäischen und deutschen Wettbewerbsrecht (Kartellrecht)*, Vol I, *Europäisches Wettbewerbsrecht* (Munich, C. H. Beck, 2007) 731 *ff*, with detailed argumentation against the Community law basis.

[95] See, eg, Nettesheim, 'Gemeinschaftsrechtliche Vorgaben für das deutsche Staatshaftungsrecht', (1992) 45 DÖV 999.

[96] After the outcome in *Courage*, it would not be difficult to say that under Community law there is also in principle a right of individuals, as against other individuals, to restitution for sums paid in violation of Community law. This is so because the requirement of effective judicial protection should not have a different function in such private disputes. On restitution and Community law, see A Jones, *Restitution and European Community Law* (London, LLP, 2000).

[97] *Cf* eg, *San Giorgio*, (n 39), para 12; Joined Cases C-192/95 to C-218/95, *Société Comateb et al v Directeur Général des Douanes et Droits Indirects*, [1997] ECR I-165, para 20; Case C-188/95, *Fantask A/S e.al. v Industriministeriet (Erhvervministeriet)*, [1997] I-9763, para 38; Joined Cases C-397/98 and C-410/98, *Metallgesellschaft Ltd, Hoechst AG and Hoechst UK Ltd v Commissioners of Inland Revenue and H.M. Attorney General*, [2001] ECR I-1727, paras 82 to 86; Case C-147/01, *Weber's Wine World Handels-GmbH et*

of the *exercise* of the right to restitution to national law, while stressing the Community law requirements of equivalence and effectiveness. In recent years, indeed, the Court has gradually laid down a growing number of uniform conditions, albeit in a negative way, that is by reading national provisions basically through the proviso of effectiveness of Community law.[98]

Furthermore, both in *Francovich* and in *Brasserie du Pêcheur/Factortame III* the Court introduced some flexibility by stressing that the conditions under which liability arises 'depend on the nature of the breach of Community law giving rise to the loss and damage'.[99] In reality, *Courage* is a *Francovich* and not a *Brasserie du Pêcheur/Factortame III* type of case. By this we mean that it was only the first case, setting out the principle. In other words, the Court left open the future possibility of proceeding in an appropriate way to set out the conditions of the remedy in greater detail,[100] either positively by itself defining, to use former Advocate General Van Gerven's scheme,[101] the pertinent 'constitutive conditions'; or negatively, by checking whether the 'executive conditions' governed by national law offend against the principles of equivalence and effectiveness–adequacy. This is certainly a sign that the inter-relationship between Community and national law has reached maturity. It is also a sign of a more 'deliberative', rather than a hierarchical mode of interaction with national courts.[102] As one author

al v Abgabenberufungskommission Wien, [2003] ECR I-11365, para 93: 'Individuals are entitled to obtain repayment of charges levied in a Member State in breach of Community provisions. That right is the consequence and the complement of the rights conferred on individuals by Community provisions as interpreted by the Court. The Member State in question is therefore required, in principle, to repay charges levied in breach of Community law'. That the right of restitution is based directly on Community law is made clear by the following statement of the Court regarding the passing-on defence and the principle that unjust enrichment should be avoided: 'As that exception is a restriction *on a subjective right derived from the Community legal order*, it must be interpreted restrictively' (above para 95, emphasis added). On the Community principle and the national conditions (plus the Community provisos) in such cases see Dougan, 'Cutting your Losses in the Enforcement Deficit: A Community Right to the Recovery of Unlawfully Levied Charges?', (1998) 1 *Cambridge Yearbook of European Legal Studies* 233, 235 *ff*; J Beatson and E Schrage, *Casebooks on the Common Law of Europe, Unjustified Enrichment* (Oxford, Hart Publishing, 2003) 10–11.

[98] According to Van Gerven, (n 30) 517, although the remedy of restitution is in principle a matter of Community law, the Court has nevertheless left a lot of leeway to national law and courts, while imposing limits on the latter when Community requirements make it necessary. Interestingly enough, many recent judgments of the Court provide for increasingly detailed limitations on national procedural autonomy. See, eg, Case C-62/00, *Marks & Spencer plc v Commissioners of Customs & Excise*, [2002] ECR I-6325, para 40 *ff*.

[99] *Francovich*, (n 42), para 38; *Brasserie du Pêcheur/Factortame III*, (n 45), para 38.

[100] See Van Gerven, 'Bringing (Private) Laws Closer to Each Other at the European Level', in Cafaggi (ed), *The Institutional Framework of European Private Law* (Oxford, Oxford University Press, 2006) 54.

[101] See section III above.

[102] On this point of the relationship between the ECJ and national courts, especially in private law cases, see Joerges, 'The Bright and the Dark Side of the Consumer's Access to Justice in the EU', 1(2) (2001) *Global Jurist Topics*, Art 1, 9.

observed, 'since the general principles of the law governing remedies have now been established, the Court can entrust national courts to apply those principles and be more selective with regard to the national rules with which it takes issue'.[103]

V *MANFREDI* AND THE RECENT WHITE PAPER

Indeed, as predicted by commentators,[104] in the recent *Manfredi* ruling,[105] the Court of Justice proceeded to deal further with the 'constitutive' and 'executive' conditions of the Community right in damages.[106] If *Courage* was a *Francovich* type of case, *Manfredi* can be seen as the *Brasserie du Pêcheur/Factortame III* of individual civil liability. This was a preliminary reference case from Italy, where insurance companies had been sued for damages by Italian consumers for prohibited cartel behaviour previously condemned by the Italian competition authority.[107] The European Court of Justice (ECJ) was basically called to decide:

- whether consumers enjoy a right to sue cartel members and claim damages for the harm suffered when there is a causal relationship between the agreement or concerted practice and the harm;
- whether the starting time of the limitation period for bringing an action for damages is the day on which the agreement or concerted practice was put in effect or the day when it came to an end;
- whether a national court should also of its own motion award punitive damages to the injured third party, in order to make the compensable amount higher than the advantage gained by the infringing party and

[103] See Tridimas, 'Judicial Review and the Community Judicature: Towards a New European Constitutionalism?', in Wouters and Stuyck (eds), *Principles of Proper Conduct for Supranational, State and Private Actors in the European Union: Towards a* Ius Commune, *Essays in Honour of Walter van Gerven* (Antwerp, Intersentia, 2001) 77, speaking of 'selective deference' to national remedial and procedural autonomy.

[104] *Cf* Komninos, (above n 22) 478.

[105] Joined Cases C-295/04 to C-298/04, *Vincenzo Manfredi et al v Lloyd Adriatico Assicurazioni SpA et al*, [2006] ECR I-6619.

[106] See also De Smijter and O'Sullivan, 'The *Manfredi* Judgment of the ECJ and How It Relates to the Commission's Initiative on EC Antitrust Damages Actions', (2006–3) *EC Competition Policy Newsletter* 23, 24, according to whom 'the judgment in *Manfredi* has now crystallised—and effectively harmonised—the law on a number of salient points'.

[107] Italian courts had earlier sent similar preliminary references to Luxembourg, but the ECJ had held them to be inadmissible because it thought that the referring courts had not included enough information as to the purpose of and necessity for the references: Case C-425/03, *Provvidenza Regio v AXA Assicurazioni SpA*, Order of 19 October 2004, unpublished; Joined Cases C-438/03, C-439/03, C-509/03 and C-2/04, *Antonio Cannito et al v Fondiaria Assicurazioni SpA et al*, Order of 11 February 2004, [2004] ECR I-1605.

> discourage the adoption of agreements or concerted practices prohibited under Article 81 EC.[108]

The Court, building on *Courage*, and after making it clear that the basis for individual civil liabilities deriving from a violation of Article 81 EC indeed lies in Community law, seems to have followed former Advocate General Van Gerven's scheme of 'constitutive', 'executive' and simple 'procedural' conditions of the Community right in damages. Thus, the Court makes a fundamental distinction between the 'existence' and 'exercise' of the right in damages. That the 'existence' of the right is a matter of Community law is obvious from the fact that the Court solemnly reiterated the most important pronouncements of *Courage*.[109] In this context, it is also clear that the Court proceeded to define, as a matter of Community law, what former Advocate General Van Gerven calls 'constitutive' conditions of the right in damages:

> It follows that any individual can claim compensation for the harm suffered where there is a causal relationship between that harm and an agreement or practice prohibited under Article 81 EC.[110]

In other words, the right in damages is open (a) to 'any individual' as long as there is (b) 'harm', (c) a competition law violation, and (d) a 'causal relationship' between that harm and that violation.[111] In thus defining the Community law constitutive conditions of the right in damages, the Court has produced a broad rule of standing, which includes consumers and

[108] The Court was also called to decide whether the nullity of agreements contrary to Art 81 EC can be relied upon by third parties (its answer was yes), and whether Community law is contrary to a national rule which provides that plaintiffs must bring their actions for damages for infringement of Community and national competition rules before a court other than that which usually has jurisdiction in actions for damages of similar value, thereby involving a considerable increase in costs and time. Another preliminary question sent to Luxembourg in this case related to the applicability of Community law to the anti-competitive conduct.

[109] *Manfredi*, (n 105), paras 60, 61, 63, 89–91, citing paras 25–7 of *Courage*. In particular, para 91 of *Manfredi*, quoting para 27 of *Courage*, stresses that 'the *existence* of such a right strengthens the working of the Community competition rules and discourages agreements or practices, frequently covert, which are liable to restrict or distort competition. From that point of view, actions for damages before the national courts can make a significant contribution to the maintenance of effective competition in the Community' (emphasis added).

[110] *Ibid*, para 61.

[111] *Cf* also the recent ruling in *City Motors* which again refers to the constitutive conditions of the right to damages in the motor vehicle distribution context: Case C-421/05, *City Motors Groep NV v Citroën Belux NV*, [2007] ECR I-653, para 33: 'In the event of a breach by a supplier of the condition for application of the block exemption set out in Article 3(4) of Regulation No 1400/2002, the national court must be in a position to draw all the necessary inferences, in accordance with national law, concerning both the validity of the agreement at issue with regard to Article 81 EC and *compensation for any harm suffered by the distributor where there is a causal relationship between that harm and an agreement or practice prohibited under Article 81 EC*.' (emphasis added)

indirect purchasers, while at the same time omitting the requirement of fault, which means that national rules following more restrictive rules on standing or requiring intention or negligence for an action for damages to be successful are contrary to the constitutive conditions in Community law of the *Courage/Manfredi* right in damages.

To mark the distinction between the existence of the right and its constitutive conditions, governed by Community law, and its exercise and executive conditions, governed by national law, the Court stresses again that 'any individual ... can claim compensation for [harm causally related with an Article 81 EC violation]', but 'in the absence of Community rules governing the matter, it is for the domestic legal system of each Member State to prescribe the detailed rules governing the *exercise* of that right, including those on the application of the concept of 'causal relationship', provided that the principles of equivalence and effectiveness are observed.'[112] We submit that the Court refers here to the 'executive' rules of the Community right in damages. In Van Gerven's scheme these are separate from purely procedural rules, which are again a matter for national law. They are also subject to a higher standard of control under an 'adequacy test', rather than a mere 'minimum effectiveness' or 'non-impossibility' test, which may continue to apply for simple procedural rules.

Indeed, the Court in *Manfredi* makes a clear distinction in its analysis between specific questions pertaining to the causal relationship between harm and antitrust violation and the availability of punitive damages, both seen as 'executive' conditions,[113] and questions on limitation of actions and competent national tribunals, both seen as 'detailed procedural rules'. In addition, the Court seems to share the former Advocate General's conviction that the former affect the very core of the exercise of Community-based rights and should therefore be subject to a more stringent test concerning the Community principle of effectiveness, while the latter can be subject to a more relaxed 'non-impossibility' test.[114] It is thus no surprise that in *Manfredi* the Court uses the 'non-impossibility' language only in the context of mere procedural rules and not in the context of the 'executive' conditions.[115] This means that questions such as causality, nature of harm and damages, and defences, which can be

[112] *Manfredi*, (n 105), paras 63–4, (emphasis added).

[113] *Ibid*, paras 64 and 92 *ff*, as to causal relationship and punitive damages respectively.

[114] *Cf* Case C-255/04, *Commission v France*, [2006] ECR I-5251, para 40, which also makes a clear distinction between conditions affecting the very exercise of a Community right and 'detailed procedural rules governing actions at law'.

[115] *Cf* paras 64 and 92, which refer merely to effectiveness, with paras 71 and 78, which refer to effectiveness seen through the prism of 'rendering practically impossible or excessively difficult the exercise of rights conferred by Community law'.

characterised as 'executive' conditions, will be subject to a more demanding test of effectiveness/adequacy, while questions such as competence of courts, limitation periods and rules on proof, which are more 'procedural' in nature, will be subject to a minimum effectiveness/non-practical impossibility test.

The recent White Paper confirms the above. The White Paper starts from the premise that the right to be compensated for harm caused by an antitrust violation is a right guaranteed by the Treaty itself, as the Court of Justice has stressed in *Courage* and *Manfredi*. This statement itself is an important reminder because the idea that the right to damages finds its basis in Community law is still resisted by some commentators, particularly in the German-speaking theory, who see this purely as a matter of national law. The Commission is now unequivocal: there are many references to '*the establishment under Community law* of a right to compensation', derived '*directly from Community law*' and to the fact that 'this *European law remedy* can as such not be refuted or conditioned by national legislation of any kind'.[116] There is also a clear distinction between the existence of the right, which is a matter of primary Community law, and its exercise which is determined by national legislation but which the White Paper intends harmonising to a certain extent through secondary Community law.[117]

VI THE IMPACT OF *COURAGE/MANFREDI* ON TWO SELECT EC COMPETITION LAW ISSUES: STANDING AND FAULT

Under the *Courage/Manfredi* principle of individual civil liability, while national law can provide for detailed 'executive' rules on the right in damages, these rules cannot go as far as to affect the constitutive conditions of individual civil liability, as set out in *Courage* and *Manfredi*, by adding stricter criteria based on the nature or degree of the infringement or fault. Such restrictive conditions are plainly incompatible with the specific constitutive conditions of the Community right in damages. This is not really a question of national remedial/procedural autonomy, to be dealt with under the Community principle of effectiveness, but rather a direct question of supremacy of Community over national law.[118]

[116] Staff Working Paper, (n 3), paras 308–309, (emphasis added). See also section 1.1 of the White Paper.

[117] Staff Working Paper, (n 3) para 309.

[118] *Cf* Jacobs and Deisenhofer, (above n 38) 216, who make a distinction between substance and procedure. While, according to the authors, national substantive rules are vis-à-vis Community law subject to the principle of supremacy, procedural rules must only comply with the principles of equivalence and effectiveness. In our view, the constitutive conditions of individual civil liability, as defined by Community law itself, would fall under

The recent *Traghetti del Mediterraneo* case, which deals with Member State liability for infringement of Community law by national supreme courts, is indicative of this important difference.[119] There the Court of Justice had to decide on the compatibility with Community law of an Italian rule that limited state liability solely to cases of intentional fault and serious misconduct on the part of courts. Rather than following an approach based on national autonomy-Community law effectiveness, the Court stressed that national law could not interfere with the Community principle established by *Köbler*, according to which the manifest infringement of the applicable Community law by a national supreme court exceptionally leads to state liability for damage caused to individuals by reason of that infringement.[120] Thus according to the Court, 'under no circumstances may [national] criteria impose requirements stricter than that of a manifest infringement of the applicable [Community] law, as set out in paragraphs 53 to 56 of the *Köbler* judgment'.[121] In other words, when Community law itself defines the constitutive conditions of a specific Community right, it is not open to national law to restrict the exercise of that right.[122]

The fact that Community law in the post-*Courage/Manfredi* era *itself* defines the constitutive conditions of the right in damages, has profound consequences for very important questions such as the rules on standing, in particular for indirect purchasers and consumers, and fault.

A Standing

In *Courage*, the Court had no difficulty in finding that Article 81 EC not only protected third-party competitors, in that case third-party beer suppliers foreclosed by a specific network of exclusive beer supply agreements, but could also be relied upon by 'any individual',[123] including co-contracting parties, in that case tenants.[124] *Manfredi*, as we developed above, built on *Courage* and defined in detail the Community law constitutive condition of

those authors' 'substance' definition, and should thus supersede any contrary national rule, pursuant to the principle of supremacy, rather than the principle of effectiveness.

[119] Case C-173/03, *Traghetti del Mediterraneo SpA v Repubblica Italiana*, [2006] ECR I-5177. For a comment, see Tietjen, 'Die Bedeutung der deutschen Richterprivilegien im System des gemeinschaftsrechtlichen Staatshaftungsrecht—Das EuGH-Urtel "*Traghetti del Mediterraneo*"', (2007) 18 *Europäisches Wirtschafts-und Steuerrecht* 15.

[120] *Köbler*, (n 5), paras 53–6.

[121] *Traghetti del Mediterraneo*, (n 119), para 44.

[122] See also Jans, 'State Liability: In Search of a Dividing Line between National and European Law', in Obradovic and Lavranos (eds), *Interface between EU Law and National Law* (Groningen, Europa Law Publishing, 2007) 283 *ff*.

[123] *Courage*, (n 67) para 26.

[124] See Brealey, 'Adopt *Perma Life*, but Follow *Hanover Shoe* to *Illinois*? Who Can Sue for Damages for Breach of EC Competition Law', (2002) 1 *Competition Law Journal* 127, 128.

standing, explicitly recognising that consumers enjoy standing to sue for harm caused to them by anti-competitive conduct.[125] Such a principle can also be adduced from the letter of Article 81(3) EC, which speaks of 'allowing *consumers* a fair share of the resulting benefit'.[126]

Therefore, if the unequivocal words used in *Courage* as to the very existence of a right in damages in Community law for all harmed individuals had rendered redundant[127] any effort to make a distinction, based on the 'protective scope' of Articles 81 and 82 EC, between co-contractors,[128] competitors, consumers, purchasers (direct or indirect)[129] and other third parties, following *Manfredi*, we can now indeed say that such distinctions are incompatible with Community law[130] and, pursuant to the principle of supremacy, should be set aside.[131] The current state of the law is that irrespective of the protective scope of the competition law provisions, all private parties who have been harmed by an anti-competitive practice enjoy a *Community law-based right* in damages.

Under US antitrust law, indirect purchasers, for example traders that have purchased from retailers rather than from the manufacturer cannot recover damages, notwithstanding the fact that the harm may have been passed on to them. In the European context of damages claims, the constitutional status of the Treaty competition provisions and the fact that they form the basis of rights for individuals, mean that the US theories should not be adopted uncritically. This parameter of private EC antitrust enforcement means that compensation of victims of anti-competitive practices cannot be ignored as easily in Europe as in the US.[132] The *a priori* exclusion of indirect purchasers and consumers from the ambit of the

[125] *Manfredi*, (n 105), paras 60, 61, 63. *Cf* AG Mischo's Opinion in *Courage*, (n 67) para 38, stressing that 'the individuals who can benefit from such protection are, of course, primarily third parties, that is to say *consumers* and competitors who are adversely affected by a prohibited agreement' (emphasis added).

[126] Emphasis added.

[127] See Van Gerven, 'Private Enforcement of EC Competition Rules', Paper Presented at the Joint IBA and European Commission Conference on Antitrust Reform in Europe: A Year in Practice (Brussels, 9–11 March 2005) p 8.

[128] Bar cases where a co-contrator bears a significant degree of responsability for the violation of competition law (*Courage*, n 67, para 31). This, however, is not a question of standing or falling under the Community law-defined constitutive conditions of the right in damages, but rather one of contributory fault, falling under the—for the time being—national law-defined executive conditions of the right in damages.

[129] As to the so-called 'indirect purchasers' standing, see below.

[130] See Komninos, (above n 22), 482; Eilmansberger, (above n 26); *idem*, 'The Green Paper on Damages Actions for Breach of the EC Antitrust Rules and Beyond: Reflections on the Utility and Feasibility of Stimulating Private Enforcement through Legislative Action', (2007) 44 *CML Rev* 431, 465.

[131] We stress again that standing referring to the *constitutive* conditions of the Community right to damages, it should be the principle of supremacy rather than of effectiveness that is applicable to this conflict.

[132] See C Jones, (above n 65) 197, who also considers that the ban of the passing-on defence should not be thought as requiring the concomitant denial of standing to indirect

persons who can claim damages would therefore not be compatible with Community law,[133] and in addition, any allocative objectives of EC competition law would be undermined.[134] From the above, it is obvious that as Community law currently stands, it is open to any affected individual to bring a claim for damages on the basis of Articles 81 and 82 EC.

The recent White Paper, indeed, follows that approach and adopts a broad rule of standing, covering also indirect purchasers. It is actually interesting that the White Paper refers to indirect purchasers' standing not as a proposal but rather as part of the already-existing *acquis communautaire.*[135] Thus, in Europe, the solution will be the opposite from the US: both direct and indirect purchasers will have standing to sue, but at the same time the passing-on defence will be available. Allowing the passing-on defence is a logical consequence of the broad rule of standing, otherwise, as the White Paper accepts, there would be a risk of unjust enrichment of those purchasers that passed on the illegal overcharge to their customers and of multiple compensation of the overcharge.[136]

Finally, since difficulties also arise when the indirect purchaser invokes the passing-on of the illegal overcharge as a basis of his claim ('offensive passing-on'), the White Paper proposes the introduction of a rebuttable presumption that the overcharge has indeed been fully passed on to the plaintiff—indirect purchaser. This is intended as an alleviation of the

purchasers. See also Van Dijk and Niels, 'The Economics of Quantifying Damages', (2002) 1 *Competition Law Journal* 69, 74.

133 See C Jones, (above n 65) 186, 195; Temple Lang, (n 33) 292; Brealey, (n 124) 133.

134 See in this sense Toffoletto, (above n 68) 127–9. *Cf* paras 32–3 of AG's Poiares Maduro's Opinion in *International Transport Workers' Federation* (n 92, emphasis added): 'Together with the provisions on competition, the provisions on freedom of movement are part of a coherent set of rules, the purpose of which is described in Article 3 EC. This purpose is to ensure, as between Member States, the free movement of goods, services, persons and capital under conditions of fair competition. The rules on freedom of movement and the rules on competition achieve this purpose principally *by granting rights to market participants.* Essentially, they protect market participants by empowering them to challenge certain impediments to the opportunity to compete on equal terms in the common market. The existence of that opportunity is the crucial element *in the pursuit of allocative efficiency in the Community as a whole.* Without the rules on freedom of movement and competition, it would be impossible to achieve the Community's fundamental aim of having a functioning common market.' *Cf* also the position taken by Norberg, 'Competition Policy of the European Commission: In the Interest of Consumers?', Speech Made at Leuven, 20 June 2003, in http://ec.europa.eu/comm/competition/speeches, p 28, who stresses the importance of damages actions for the interests of consumers.

135 Staff Working Paper, (n 3) paras 33–7. Of course, the broad rule of standing does not affect the necessity of a causal link between the harm and the infringement of Arts 81 and 82 EC. See Staff Working Paper, (above n 3) paras 37 and 205.

136 Staff Working Paper, (n 3) para 210. At the same time, the White Paper stresses that the standard of proof for the passing-on defence should not be lower than the claimant's standard to prove the damage. Under this model, the plaintiff must prove that he has suffered loss, but it is open to the defendant to prove that the plaintiff mitigated the loss by passing on the whole or part of the overcharge to downstream purchasers.

victim's burden of proof, without, however, affecting the main conditions of civil liability: in other words, the plaintiff would still have to prove the infringement, the existence of the initial overcharge and the extent the overcharge caused him harm (including causation).[137]

Where the White Paper may give rise to a discussion as to its compatibility with the *Courage/Manfredi* case law is its proposal to limit the civil liability of successful immunity recipients[138] to claims by their 'direct and indirect contractual partners'. The aim is basically to safeguard the effectiveness of the Leniency Programme, which might have been put at risk as a result of the Commission's drive for an enhanced system of private actions in Europe. According to that proposal, the immunity recipient would be liable only to persons that bought directly from him the products or services in question (direct contractual partners) or those down the supply chain who bought these products or services from the direct contractual partners themselves.[139] Thus, a victim that did not buy cartelised products or services[140] directly or indirectly from him and a harmed competitor, will not be able to claim damages. At the same time, this rule would in effect remove the immunity recipient's joint liability,[141] since, as the Commission, explains in an example, 'where 30% of a victim's total purchases of cartelised products originate from the immunity recipient, the latter would only be liable for 30% of the total harm suffered by this victim due to the overcharge of the cartelised products'.[142]

The question here is whether the limitation of the right of competitors and others not falling under the Commission's definition of 'direct and indirect contractual partners' is at odds with primary Community law, that is, with the Treaty itself and the ECJ rulings in *Courage* and *Manfredi*, which stress that the right to damages should be open to 'any individual'. However, the fact that primary Community law itself provides for a broad rule of standing does not mean to say that the Community legislator cannot make a policy decision and restrict—though not eliminate—the right of some plaintiffs, if that would be beneficial to the effectiveness of the whole system of enforcement.

137 Staff Working Paper, (n 3) para 220.

138 This proposal does not cover the other leniency applicants that did not receive full immunity.

139 Staff Working Paper, (n 3) para 305.

140 An issue is what happens with cartels that do not involve sale of goods or services to contractual partners (eg a boycotting cartel not to sell in a particular market or to a particular client).

141 The White Paper considers that removal of joint liability by itself is not sufficient to effectively limit the immunity recipient's liability (Staff Working Paper, (n 3) para 304). *Cf*, however, para 322 of the Staff Working Paper, where removal of joint liability is surprisingly mentioned as a separate proposed measure. Perhaps the reference in para 322 was left in from a previous draft by mistake.

142 Staff Working Paper, (n 3) n 160.

Indeed, if we look more closely at the proposed solution, we see that in reality the White Paper does not propose to affect the exercise of those persons' right to damages against the other cartel members that did not receive full immunity from fines. Indeed, joint and several liability of these cartel members continues to be the rule, so they would still be jointly and severally liable to pay damages to a potential harmed competitor for the whole of his harm. Thus, in reality what the White Paper proposes is not to totally bar some persons from suing for damages but rather it would make those persons only slightly worse off by increasing their risk in case of the insolvency of all or some of the other cartel members with the exception of the immunity recipient. This is a rather low risk.[143] In fact, irrespective of this White Paper proposal and of what primary Community law dictates, all plaintiffs always bear the risk of all the cartel members' insolvency. So, it seems to us that the proposed solution would most probably not seriously affect the existence of the Community right to damages, while at the same time it would undoubtedly strengthen the effectiveness of one aspect of the Leniency Programme, the race to the authority to be the first undertaking that self-reports, thus ensuring full immunity status.[144] Being second or third would not only mean the loss of full immunity but also exposure to damages liability for the whole of the harm.[145]

Besides, ensuring that the leniency programme remains attractive and thus effective is quite beneficial for private enforcement and potential plaintiffs. First, the plaintiffs become aware of the cartel infringement, which is more effectively exposed to the public authority by the leniency applicants, secondly, the facts are established during the administrative proceedings, thirdly, courts or plaintiffs could under certain circumstances ask for documentary evidence in the hands of the public enforcer, in order to establish the liability and/or the damage, and fourthly, a final public decision, depending on the applicable rules, may have a binding effect on the follow-on civil proceeding or may constitute *prima facie* evidence of the cartel violation.[146]

[143] The cartels that are prosecuted by the Commission under Article 81 EC are likely to concern activity and companies of a certain size and therefore the risk of insolvency of any of these companies is extremely low.

[144] See also Impact Assessment Study, (above n 3) 521.

[145] Note, however, that the Commission does not propose to disallow contribution among the (non-immunity recipient) cartel members.

[146] See also Komninos, 'The EU White Paper for Damages Actions: A First Appraisal', 2/2008 *Concurrences* 84, 89–90.

B Fault

Another basic question that was answered in a definitive way by the *Courage/Manfredi* case law is whether liability for damages for breach of Articles 81 and 82 EC presupposes fault or whether it is strict. The answer to this question is that in principle it is only strict liability that renders the prohibitions of those Articles meaningful.[147] The Treaty rules on competition do not generally require subjective intent to contravene the relevant prohibitions,[148] so civil liability for EC competition law breaches should not be based upon such a condition.

Of course, we must distinguish conceptually between fault in the context of the *anti-competitive conduct* and fault in the context of *civil liability* and *civil damages*. Although interconnected, the two questions are different. The Court of Justice in *Courage* stressed this conceptual difference in the following terms:

> Contrary to the submission of Courage, making a distinction as to the extent of the parties' liability does not conflict with the case-law of the Court to the effect that it does not matter, for the purposes of the application of Article [81] of the Treaty, whether the parties to an agreement are on an equal footing as regards their economic position and function. That case-law concerns the conditions for application of Article [81] of the Treaty while the questions put before the Court in the present case concern certain consequences in civil law of a breach of that provision.[149]

It is the second context that we deal with here, that is, whether culpability should play a role for the establishment of civil liability flowing from a proven antitrust violation, and the answer is that it should not. In all such cases, liability for EC competition law violations is strict. Indeed, the requirement of intention or negligence for the imposition of fines by the Commission or national competition authorities in the context of administrative public

[147] See in this sense Temple Lang, (above n 33) 277; A Jones and B Sufrin, *EC Competition Law, Text, Cases, and Materials* (Oxford, Oxford University Press, 2004) 1219.

[148] With regard to Art 81 EC, the critical factor is the *objective* meaning and purpose of the agreement in its economic context, while the *subjective* intention of the parties is immaterial. Vice versa, an agreement might not have as its object the restriction of competition merely because the parties subjectively aimed at this. In Art 82 EC, again, abuse is an objective concept and the intention of the dominant undertaking is irrelevant. However, exceptionally, intention may play a role in establishing an abuse of dominant position in predatory pricing cases, and in cases where the abuse takes the form of vexatious litigation which is part of a systematic campaign or strategy of the dominant undertaking to intimidate, harass, and exhaust competitors by raising their costs unreasonably. For another recent Art 82 case where intention seems to play an important role as a constituent element of the abuse, see Commission Decision of 15 June 2005 (*AstraZeneca*).

[149] *Courage*, (above n 67) para 35. The Court was of course dealing in that specific case with the issue of the plaintiff's contributory fault but its clear distinction between fault for the establishment of the antitrust violation and fault for the civil liability is of general importance.

enforcement[150] should be distinguished, because such penalties do not aim at compensating the victims of the anti-competitive practices, but rather at punishing and deterring their perpetrators.[151] Civil liability, on the other hand, while also containing deterrence elements, predominantly compensates the harm caused by anti-competitive conduct, and this harm should not be compensated only in cases of the perpetrator's fault.

This differentiates individual civil liability for violation of Community competition law from its older sibling, state liability, which arises only where the Member State has committed a 'sufficiently serious breach' of Community law.[152] There is, however, no compelling reason for accepting such a requirement in individual liability cases. Indeed, as some authors argue, there are inherent features in state liability which justify and necessitate the 'sufficiently serious breach' condition, but that cannot be transposed to individual liability for Community law violations.[153] Such a limitation has been imposed on public policy grounds in order to limit the liability of Member States when acting in their sphere of legislative discretion. On the other hand, when Member States do not enjoy legislative discretion, liability according to the Court of Justice is strict.[154] Therefore, strict liability is more appropriate for all breaches of the Treaty competition rules.[155]

The strict liability principle was indeed recognised by the Court of Justice in *Manfredi*, which enumerated the constitutive conditions of individual civil liability but left the requirement of fault out.[156] This sits in stark contrast to some national laws, such as the German and Swedish Competition Acts, which require intention or negligence for a right in

[150] See Art 23 Reg 1/2003 with regard to fines. The same should also be accepted for periodic penalty payments.

[151] *Cf* Case T-59/02, *Archer Daniels Midland Co v Commission*, [2006] ECR II-3627, para 351: 'In so far as the damages at issue amount to compensation for European Union purchasers, the Court considers that the proceedings at issue and the payments demanded by the Commission, on the one hand, and by the United States authorities on the other clearly do not pursue the same objectives. *Whilst in the first case the Commission seeks to sanction an infringement of competition law* in the Community or the EEA *by means of a fine, in the second case the United States authorities seek to compensate victims of ADM's dealings*' (emphasis added).

[152] *Brasserie du Pêcheur/Factortame III*, (n 45) paras 51, 55 *ff*.

[153] See Saggio, (above n 91) 242; Craig and De Búrca, (above n 92) 1084. See also M Brealey and M Hoskins, *Remedies in EC Law, Law and Practice in the English and EC Courts* (London, Sweet & Maxwell, 1998) 124.

[154] Case C-5/94, *R v Ministry of Agriculture, Fisheries and Food ex p Hedley Lomas (Ireland) Ltd*, [1996] ECR I-2553, para 28.

[155] See in this sense Mail-Fouilleul, (above n 68) 592; Winckler, 'Remedies Available under French Law in the Application of EC Competition Rules', in Ehlermann and Atanasiu (eds), *European Competition Law Annual 2001: Effective Private Enforcement of EC Antitrust Law* (Oxford, Hart Publishing, 2003) 128; Van Gerven, 'Harmonization of Private Law: Do we Need it?', (2004) 41 *CML Rev* 505, 522.

[156] *Manfredi*, (n 105) para 61. See, however, *contra* Eilmansberger, (above n 26) 458, who thinks that *Manfredi* did not touch upon the question of fault.

damages to arise.[157] Some form of fault is also required in Finnish,[158] Austrian,[159] Danish, and Greek law.[160] As explained above, such national provisions ought to be set aside by national courts pursuant to the principle of supremacy.

The White Paper seems to accept the above[161] and, indeed, notes that the rule should be that of strict or objective liability for damages once an infringement of EC antitrust rules has been proven.[162] The Commission also proposes to qualify the strict liability rule by allowing the defendants to exculpate themselves if their breach of the antitrust rules was due to an 'excusable error'.[163] This qualification by no means affects the strict liability rule, which remains a matter of primary Community law, since it is only exceptionally that some form of fault must be required for civil liability to arise, in order to avoid excesses. A useful example is offered by the Defective Products Liability Directive,[164] which introduces the principle of strict liability, but also includes in Article 7 exceptions to the rule under which the producer has the burden to prove certain exonerating facts.[165] This shows that a rule of strict liability can accommodate a relaxation in order to comply with basic notions of fairness or some specified public policy.[166]

[157] S 33(3) GWB; Art 33(1) Swedish Competition Act.

[158] Art 18a(1) Act on Competition Restrictions of 1992, as amended in 2004.

[159] See Eilmansberger and Thyri, 'Austria', in D Cahill (ed), *The Modernisation of EU Competition Law Enforcement in the European Union, FIDE 2004 National Reports* (Cambridge, Cambridge University Press, 2004) 54.

[160] In English law, however, liability for breach of statutory duty is usually strict and absolute.

[161] See, in particular, Staff Working Paper, (above n 3) paras 170–71.

[162] This, of course, does not affect or eliminate the requirement of causation. The causal link between the antitrust infringement and the damage itself must still be proven.

[163] The Commission views 'excusable error' rather restrictively. See Staff Working Paper, (above n 3) para 175 *ff*.

[164] Dir 85/374/EEC, (n 9).

[165] Art 7: 'The producer shall not be liable as a result of this Directive if he proves: (a) that he did not put the product into circulation; or (b) that, having regard to the circumstances, it is probable that the defect which caused the damage did not exist at the time when the product was put into circulation by him or that this defect came into being afterwards; or (c) that the product was neither manufactured by him for sale or any form of distribution for economic purpose nor manufactured or distributed by him in the course of his business; or (d) that the defect is due to compliance of the product with mandatory regulations issued by the public authorities; or (e) that the state of scientific and technical knowledge at the time when he put the product into circulation was not such as to enable the existence of the defect to be discovered; or (f) in the case of a manufacturer of a component, that the defect is attributable to the design of the product in which the component has been fitted or to the instructions given by the manufacturer of the product.'

[166] The public policy concerned here is that to apply an unqualified strict liability rule to a horizontal co-operation agreement whereby the parties genuinely believed that they were acting lawfully or to the conduct of a dominant company that is considered to be abusive for the first time, would risk stifling healthy competition and innovation.

VII CONCLUSION

The Treaty competition rules have offered us a first paradigm of a more active role of Community law in the field of remedies in horizontal relationships between private parties and thus of a corresponding retreat of national remedial/procedural autonomy. That was a judge-made development that opened, indeed, the way to Community legislative action. Why competition law was the first paradigm, can probably be explained historically and normatively.[167] The role of the Court of Justice in the formation through its case law of a 'European private law' is, of course, outside the scope of this chapter,[168] but it suffices to stress here that competition law is by no means the only possible paradigm for such a remarkable development. There is, therefore, no 'outer limit' of Community law that was reached here. Rather, this has to be seen as a step in the long process of ensuring homogeneity and consistency in the broad area of Community law remedies,[169] while ensuring full access to courts for individuals.[170]

[167] See the introduction above.

[168] See, eg, Basedow, 'Grundlagen des europäischen Privatrechts', (2004) 44 *Juristische Schulung* 89, 93–5.

[169] On the exigencies of consistency, harmonisation and homogeneity in the area of remedies for the protection of Community rights, see Van Gerven, 'Toward a Coherent Constitutional System within the European Union', (1996) 2 *European Public Law* 81, 96–8.

[170] See also Arts 6 and 13 ECHR; Art 47 EU Charter of Fundamental Freedoms.

16

Potency and Act of the Principle of Effectiveness: The Development of Competition Law Remedies and Procedures in Community Law

RENATO NAZZINI*

I OVERVIEW

THIS CHAPTER EXAMINES the scope and limits of private law remedies for breach of Article 81 or 82 of the EC Treaty under Community law.[1]

In 2005, the Commission published a Green Paper on actions for damages for breach of the EC antitrust rules, which spurred a wide-ranging debate.[2] A White Paper was published in April 2008.[3] In March

* The author is grateful to Professor Rosa Greaves, Steven Altham, Paolisa Nebia, Ali Nikpay and Oke Odudu. The views expressed are purely personal.

[1] For the evolution of the legal thinking on the right to damages for breach of Community competition law up until the Green Paper on Damages actions (below n 2), see J Temple Lang, 'Community Antitrust Law—Compliance and Enforcement' [1981] *CML Rev* 335; F Jacobs, 'Damages for Breach of Article 86 EEC' [1983] *EL Rev* 353; J Temple Lang, 'EEC Competition Actions in Member States—Claims for Damages, Declarations and Injunctions for Breach of Community Antitrust Law' in BE Hawk (ed), *Annual Proceedings of the Fordham Corporate Law Institute: Antitrust and Trade Policies of the European Economic Community* (New York, Matthew Bender, 1984) 219; F Jacobs, 'Civil Enforcement of EEC Antitrust Law' [1984] *Michigan Law Review* 1364; J Shaw, 'Actions for Damages in the English Courts for Breach of EEC Competition Law' [1985] *ICLQ* 178; J Steiner, 'How to Make the Action Suit the Case: Domestic Remedies for Breach of EEC Law' [1987] *EL Rev* 102; J Maitland-Walker, 'A Step Closer to a Definitive Ruling on a Right in Damages for Breach of EC Competition Rules' [1992] *European Competition Law Review* 3; JHJ Bourgeois, 'EC Competition Law and Member State Courts' in BE Hawk (ed), *Annual Proceedings of the Fordham Corporate Law Institute: Antitrust in a Global Economy* (New York, Kluwer Law and Taxation, 1994) 20; R Whish, 'The Enforcement of EC Competition Law in the Domestic Courts of Member States' [1994] *European Competition Law Review* 61–7; D Good, 'Eurotort with Europrocedure?', in M Hutchings and M Andenas, *Competition Law Yearbook 2002* (London, British Institute of International and Comparative Law, 2003) 345–54; D Vaughan 'Damages in EC Competition Law', *ibid*, 355–64; D Waelbroeck,

2007, the Directorate General for Health and Consumer Protection (DG SANCO) of the Commission launched a comprehensive study, which is not specific to one area of law but includes competition law, in order to evaluate the effectiveness and efficiency of collective redress mechanisms in the European Union (EU), with the aim of assessing whether consumers suffer detriment as a result of the unavailability, ineffectiveness or inefficiency of such mechanisms.[4]

In the UK, increasing the number of well-founded private actions in competition law has been a clearly articulated policy objective at least since the 2001 White Paper 'A World Class Competition Regime'.[5] In 2007, the UK Office of Fair Trading undertook a review of the private actions regime that had been envisaged in the 2001 White Paper and implemented in the Enterprise Act 2002. It published a Discussion Paper[6] and, following a consultation process, a set of recommendations to Government[7] with the aim of improving the effectiveness of the system. A number of other Member States, such as Germany, have introduced specific provisions on private actions in competition law.[8] Other Member States, such as Italy,[9] have introduced collective actions of general application, including but not

'Private Enforcement of Competition Rules and its Limits', *ibid*, 369–82; WPJ Wils, 'Should Private Enforcement Be Encouraged in Europe?' [2003] *World Competition* 473–88; CA Jones, 'Private Antitrust Enforcement in Europe: A Policy Analysis and Reality Check' [2004] *World Competition* 13–24.

[2] Commission Green Paper on Damages actions for breach of the EC antitrust rules, Brussels, 19 December 2005 COM(2005) 672 final (the 'Green Paper on Damages actions') and the Commission Staff Working Paper (Annex to the Green Paper), Brussels, 19 December 2005, SEC(2005) 1732 (the 'Staff Working Paper (Annex to the Green Paper)').

[3] Commission White Paper on Damages actions for breach of the EC antitrust rules, Brussels, 2 April 2008 COM(2008) 165 final (the 'White Paper on Damages actions'), Commission Staff Working Paper accompanying the White Paper on Damages actions for breach of the EC antitrust rules, Brussels, 2 April 2008 SEC(2008) 404 (the 'Staff Working Paper on Damages actions') , and Commission Staff Working Document—Accompanying document to the White Paper on Damages actions for breach of the EC antitrust rules: Impact Assessment, Brussels, 2. April 2008 SEC(2008) 405 (the 'Impact Assessment accompanying the White Paper on Damages actions').

[4] The tender is available on DG SANCO's website. DG SANCO has also consulted on consumer collective redress benchmarks. The consultation is also available on DG SANCO's website.

[5] 'A World Class Competition Regime-Department of Trade and Industry' (cm 5233, July 2001).

[6] 'Private actions in competition law: effective redress for consumers and business' (OFT916, April 2007).

[7] 'Private actions in competition law: effective redress for consumers and business—Recommendations from the Office of Fair Trading' (OFT916resp, November 2007).

[8] *Siebtes Gesetz zur Änderung des Gesetzes gegen Wettbewerbsbeschränkungen*, Federal Law Gazette (*Bundesgesetzblatt*, BGBl) 2005, Part I, 1954–1969, last amended by *Gesetz zur Beschleunigung der Umsetzung von Öffentlich-Privaten Partnerschaften und zur Verbesserung gesetzlicher Rahmenbedingungen für Öffentlich-Private Partnerschaften*, BGBl 2005, Part I, 2676–81.

[9] Legge finanziaria 2008-Legge 24 Dicembre 2007, n 244 (art 2 commi 445–449), in GU n 300 del 28Dicembre 2007 – SO n 285.

limited to competition law. In England and Wales, in parallel with competition-specific initiatives, a wider debate is taking place on the need or desirability of introducing a class action procedure of general application, which would include competition law.[10]

The current legal position is not entirely satisfactory. National rules on remedies and procedure are subject to Community law scrutiny under the doctrine of procedural autonomy.[11] This doctrine requires a functional analysis focusing on whether national rules make the exercise of Community law rights impossible or excessively difficult. However, this test has failed to provide certainty as to the minimum legal standards that must apply in safeguarding Community law rights through the civil process.[12] This is for a number of reasons. First, the European Court of Justice has been ambiguous in the use of the term 'effectiveness' to cover both the principle of full effectiveness of Community law and the principle of effective judicial protection. Secondly, the determination of the content of the right, which is a key element of the analysis, is not given sufficient weight. Thirdly, the case law often does not clearly distinguish between the three different analytical steps of the identification of the legal basis of the right, the determination of its content, and the assessment of national rules on remedies and procedure.

In the competition law field, different civil procedure systems coexist in the EU. A clear analytical framework for the determination of the scope and limits of the Community right to damages for breach of Article 81 or 82 is required. However, reforms in the Member States do not appear to be clearly guided by a coherent Community law rationale. The Commission's initiative to publish the Green Paper has shed little light on the broader theme of the scope and limits of the right to damages and the application of the doctrine of procedural autonomy. The White Paper states that the primary objective of damages actions for breach of Article 81 or 82 is the principle of full compensation but adds that 'improving compensatory justice would therefore *inherently* also produce beneficial effects in terms of *deterrence* of future infringements and greater compliance with EC antitrust rules.'[13] The White Paper is an important step forward but does little to free the current understanding of private remedies in Community

[10] In August 2008, the Civil Justice Council of England and Wales recommended the introduction of a general opt-out class action: *Improving Access to Justice through Collective Actions: A Series of Recommendations to the Lord Chancellor*, available on the website of the Civil Justice Council.

[11] On the meaning and scope of the doctrine of procedural autonomy, see section II below.

[12] A Ward in ch 14 of this volume discusses the uncertainty in the application of the rule that national requirements must not make the exercise of a Community law right impossible or excessively difficult as set out in the seminal *San Giorgio* case. Case 199/82 *Amministrazione delle Finanze dello Stato v SpA San Giorgio* [1983] ECR 3595, para 14.

[13] White Paper on Damages actions (above n 3) 3 (emphasis in the original).

law from the shortcomings of the procedural autonomy approach. This is probably because the White Paper does not fully explore the link between the principle of full compensation and the principle of full effectiveness of Community law. However, these principles, inextricably linked in the jurisprudence of the European Court of Justice, constitute the fundamental structure of the right to damages for breach of Article 81 or 82.[14]

The lack of a coherent rationale for competition law private actions (both at Member State level and at EU level) calls for a closer examination of the legal basis[15] of the right to damages for breach of Community law generally and Article 81 or 82 in particular. The identification of such a legal basis would help clarify the requirements that Community law imposes on Member States based on a functional analysis. This would release Community law remedies from the limits artificially imposed on their coherent development by the doctrine of procedural autonomy. The outer limits of the Treaty in this area could thus be redefined in light of the legal basis and function of the right to damages. In particular, the rationale for the conferral of the right to damages for breach of Article 81 or 82 would shed light on the substantive content of the right.[16] Only by doing this could the further requirements of full effectiveness of Community law[17] and effective judicial protection[18] be meaningfully applied. In other words, only if the content of the right is clear, is it possible to assess whether national remedies and procedures comply with the principle of effectiveness. The principle of effectiveness,[19] comprising both the principle of full effectiveness of Community law and the principle of effective

[14] See section III B (iii) below.

[15] By 'legal basis of the right', it is meant the Treaty provision or principle that confers a particular right. As regards the legal basis of rights that are not expressly recognised by the Treaty or by EC legislation, the identification of the legal basis often involves an interpretation of the relevant Treaty provision in light of a more general principle of Community law. For instance, the right to damages for breach of Art 81 or 82 is based on an interpretation of these provisions in light of the principle of full effectiveness of Community law (see section III B below). What matters in this interpretative process is the principle of full effectiveness rather than the wording of Art 81 or 82. As a consequence, it is possible to say that the principle of full effectiveness of Community law is the legal basis of the right in question although technically the legal basis is Art 81 or 82 interpreted in light of the principle of full effectiveness of Community law. P Craig, *EU Administrative Law* (Oxford, Oxford University Press, 2006) 791–815, convincingly demonstrates that the principle of effectiveness may require the creation of national remedies to protect Community law rights.

[16] By 'content of the right', it is meant the primary benefit conferred on the holder and the corresponding obligations imposed on the defendant.

[17] The principle of full effectiveness of Community law concerns the enforcement of Treaty norms in the public interest: see M Dougan, *National Remedies before the Court of Justice* (Oxford, Hart Publishing, 2004) 38–45.

[18] The principle of effective judicial protection concerns 'the effectiveness of subjective rights enjoyed by individuals under the Treaty as they are enforced against Member States or private parties': *ibid* 27.

[19] The principle of effectiveness is a general principle of Community law: T Tridimas, *The General Principles of EU Law* (2nd edn) (Oxford, Oxford University Press, 2006) 418.

judicial protection, must be applied in light of the content of the right and its function.[20]

The case law suggests that the principle of full effectiveness of Community is a leading theme in the conferral on individuals of a right to damages for breach of Community law. More particularly, the effective enforcement of Articles 81 and 82 is the legal basis of the right to damages for breach of Community competition law and defines the content and function of the right. This functional approach removes artificial constraints on the right to damages that would follow from the application of the traditional procedural autonomy doctrine.[21] However, this approach also means that the right to damages or its exercise may be limited when this is necessary to preserve the full effectiveness of Community law.[22]

This chapter is structured as follows. First, it demonstrates the inadequacy of the doctrine of procedural autonomy in providing a sufficiently clear benchmark to assess the compatibility of national procedures and remedies with Community law. Secondly, it discusses the legal basis of the right to damages for breach of Community law, identifying in the principle of full effectiveness of Community law a leading theme in the development of Community law rights and remedies. In particular, the objective of the right to damages for breach of Article 81 or 82 is the effective enforcement of Community competition law. This objective provides a standard by which it is possible to determine the content of the right and to assess the compatibility of national law with Community law requirements. This chapter goes on to discuss how the principle of full effectiveness of Community law can have both an expansive function (in relation to collective actions) and a limiting function (in relation to the need to protect the integrity of leniency programmes). Finally, conclusions will be drawn.

II THE INADEQUACY OF THE DOCTRINE OF 'PROCEDURAL AUTONOMY'

The doctrine of procedural autonomy[23] does not provide an adequate answer to the problems which arise in defining the content and the limits

[20] By 'function of the right', it is meant the objective for which the right is conferred. As regards rights that are not expressly recognised by the Treaty or by EC legislation, the interpretative process identifying the legal basis of the right often reveals the function of the right, namely the ultimate objective for which the right is conferred.

[21] See section IV A below.

[22] See section IV B below.

[23] Procedural autonomy does not mean that Member States have a reserved area of competence in matters of remedies and procedure: CN Kakouris, 'Do Member States Possess Judicial Procedural "Autonomy"?' [1997] *CML Rev* 1389, rightly points out that national procedures are ancillary to the effective application of Community law. In the absence of Community legislation or case law, national remedies and procedures serve the purpose of achieving effective and uniform protection of Community law rights: W van Gerven, 'Of

of the right to damages for breach of Community competition law. The doctrine of procedural autonomy presupposes the existence of a right. Any assessment of the adequacy of judicial protection of a substantive right is meaningless if the content of the right and its legal basis are not defined. The legal basis of the right, which is determinative of its function and content, must be the starting point of the analysis and not, as is often the case, a vague concept of procedural autonomy somehow combined with the ambiguous use of the principle of effectiveness.

In its classic formulation, the doctrine of procedural autonomy provides that, in the absence of Community rules on the subject,[24] remedies and procedures fall to be determined by the national legal systems of the Member States.[25] This doctrine consists of three elements. The first is that, if the Community has legislated to harmonise the law on the matter in question, procedural autonomy has no role to play. The second element is that national rules cannot make the exercise of Community law rights excessively difficult or impossible.[26] This principle of effectiveness applies to rules of procedure as well as to remedies.[27] The third element is the principle of non-discrimination or equivalence.[28] Judicial protection of Community law rights may not be subject to stricter requirements than those applicable to comparable claims under national law.

In the sphere of competition law remedies, the first rule of national law to fall under scrutiny by the Court of Justice was the English law rule *ex turpi*

Rights, Remedies and Procedures' [2000] *CML Rev* 501, 502–504. Procedural autonomy is not a reserved power of the Member States but rather a term which describes the fact that matters of remedies, evidence and procedure are still largely governed by provisions of national law: S Prechal, 'Community Law in National Courts: The Lessons from *van Schijndel*' [1998] *CML Rev* 681.

[24] Measures harmonising rules on standing and remedies are more and more frequent in Community law. In the area of collective actions Council Directive (EEC) No 13/93 of 5 April 1993 on unfair terms in consumer contracts [1993] OJ L95/29, Art 7(2) makes provision to give standing to 'persons or organizations, having a legitimate interest under national law in protecting consumers' to bring actions on behalf of the consumers before courts or administrative bodies 'for a decision as to whether contractual terms drawn up for general use are unfair, so that they can apply appropriate and effective means to prevent the continued use of such terms'. In competition law, Council Regulation (EC) No 1/2003 of 16 December 2002 on the implementation of the rules on competition laid down in Arts 81 and 82 of the Treaty [2003] OJ L1/1, Art 2, contains rules on the burden of proof in proceedings relating to Art 81 or 82. For other examples see *Wyatt & Dashwood's European Union Law* (5th edn) (London, Sweet & Maxwell, 2006) 232–3.

[25] Case 33/76 *Rewe-Zentralfinanz eG v Landwirtschaftskammer für das Saarland* [1976] ECR 1989; Case 45/76 *Comet BV v Produktschap voor Siergewassen* [1976] ECR 2043.

[26] C 33/76 *Rewe-Zentralfinanz ibid* para 5; Case 45/76 *Comet ibid* para 16.

[27] Joined Cases C-6/90 and 9/90 *Andrea Francovich v Italian Republic* [1991] ECR I-5357; Case C-213/89 *R v Secretary of State for Transport, ex p Factortame Ltd* [1990] ECR I-2433; Case C-453/99 *Courage Ltd v Bernard Crehan* [2001] ECR I-6297.

[28] *Rewe-Zentralfinanz* (n 25) para 5; *Comet* (n 25) para 13; Case C-261/95 *Rosalba Palmisani v Instituto Nazionale della Previdenza Sociale* [1997] ECR I-4025, para 27.

causa non oritur actio.[29] In *Courage Ltd v Bernard Crehan*,[30] the Court held that the effectiveness of the prohibition in Article 81 demanded that there should be no absolute bar to recovery of damages by a party to an anti-competitive agreement. The Court recognised the existence of a right to damages for breach of Article 81 or 82 with no reference to the doctrine of procedural autonomy.[31] The Court relied on the doctrine of procedural autonomy later in the judgment.[32] First, the Court reiterated that the rules on jurisdiction, evidence, and procedure fall within the realm of national law in so far as the principles of effectiveness and equivalence are complied with.[33] It then went on to rule that national law may recognise exceptions to the right to damages under Article 81 within the constraints imposed by Community law. Such exceptions may be imposed to avoid the unjust enrichment of parties to anti-competitive agreements and consistently with the principle that a litigant should not benefit from his own unlawful conduct. As a result, a party who bears significant responsibility for the breach of competition law may be precluded from obtaining damages. This assessment must be carried out in the economic and legal context and taking into account the relative bargaining positions of the parties.[34]

The Court seems to take a two-stage approach. First, it is necessary to determine whether a right exists. Secondly, the national rules are scrutinised under the doctrine of procedural autonomy. However, there is still much confusion in the application of this two-stage analysis and no clear link between the legal basis of the right and its limits. In particular, the Court does not explain why the limits of the right to damages[35] are justified in light of the considerations that led to the recognition of the right.[36] While the conclusions

[29] In English law, a party to an illegal contract cannot recover damages from the other party.

[30] *Courage Ltd v Bernard Crehan* (n 27) paras 19–28. On this case, see AP Komninos, 'New Prospects for Private Enforcement of EC Competition Law: *Courage v Crehan* and the Community Right to Damages' [2002] *CML Rev* 447; G Monti, 'Anticompetitive Agreements: The Innocent Party's Right to Damages' (2002) 27 *EL Rev* 282; T Lettl, 'Der Schadensersatzanspruch gemäß §823 Abs. 2 BGB i.V.m. Art. 81 Abs. 1 EG' (2003) 167 Zeitschrift für das gesamte Handelsrecht und Wirtschaftsrecht 473; W Wurmnest, 'Zivilrechtliche Ausgleichsansprüche von Kartellbeteiligten bei Verstößen gegen das EG-Kartellverbot' (2003) 49 Recht der Internationalen Wirtschaft 896; G Mäsch, 'Private Ansprüche bei Verstößen gegen das europäische Kartellverbot— "Courage" und die Folgen', (2003) 38 *Europarecht* 825.

[31] The Court in *Crehan* (n 27) did not expressly state that a breach of Art 82 may also give rise to a cause of action in damages. However, the reasoning of the Court appears to be equally applicable to Art 82. Therefore, unless the context requires otherwise, we will refer hereinafter to a right to damages for breach of Art 81 or 82 even when discussing specific judgments that only explicitly refer to Art 81.

[32] *Crehan* (n 27) paras 29–35.

[33] *Ibid*, para 29.

[34] *Ibid*, paras 29–35.

[35] *Ibid*, paras 29–35.

[36] *Ibid*, paras 24–8.

of the Court appear reasonable and accord both with common sense and an elementary notion of justice and fairness, the failure to articulate the link between the legal basis, function, and content of the right, on the one hand, and its limits, on the other, creates a gap in the legal reasoning that leads to lack of clarity and predictability in the application of the test.

The point may be illustrated by the judgment of the Court of Justice in *Vincenzo Manfredi v Lloyd Adriatico Assicurazioni SpA*.[37] In that case, the Court ruled that any individual can claim compensation for harm caused to him by an infringement of Article 81[38] but 'in the absence of Community rules governing the matter, it is for the domestic legal system of each Member State to prescribe the detailed rules governing the exercise of that right, including those on the application of the concept of "causal relationship", provided that the principles of equivalence and effectiveness are observed'. The Court's approach may appear to be a straightforward application of the doctrine of procedural autonomy consistent with a distinction between constitutive elements of the right, subject to Community law only, and executive elements, governed by national law subject to the scrutiny of the Court of Justice under the principles of effectiveness and equivalence.[39] The Court's approach to procedural autonomy in *Courage* and *Manfredi* is problematic.

The example of 'causal relationship' in *Manfredi* is particularly illustrative. The concept of 'causal relationship' in and of itself is, as a matter of law, meaningless. It is the 'detailed rules' that determine whether the right and the remedy exist or not. Depending on what exactly is meant by causal relationship, a person has a right to compensation or not. The problem with the distinction between constitutive and executive elements is that it is currently applied in a descriptive way in order to rationalise the case law of the Court of Justice. However, the distinction has the potential to be used in a normative way in order to distinguish between the legal basis and function of the right, on the one hand, and the procedures and remedies available to enforce the right, on the other. Procedures and remedies must be defined so as to be consistent with the legal basis of the right and attain its function. If the legal basis of the right in *Manfredi* is the effective enforcement of Community competition law, the concept of causal relationship must be interpreted so as to attain this objective.

In purely procedural matters, the Court of Justice has taken a similar approach. However, if the existence of the right is not in dispute, the focus

[37] Case C-295/04 *Vincenzo Manfredi v Lloyd Adriatico Assicurazioni SpA* [2006] ECR I-6619.

[38] The *Manfredi* case does not discuss whether a breach of Art 82 gives rise to a cause of action in damages. However, as in *Crehan* (n 27) the reasoning of the Court appears to be equally applicable to Art 82: (see n 31 above).

[39] W van Gerven, 'Of Rights, Remedies and Procedures' (n 23) 502–504, 524–6; A Komninos, ch 15 of this volume.

is exclusively on procedural autonomy. Civil procedural rules should not make the enforcement of rights conferred upon the parties by directly effective Community law excessively difficult or impossible.[40] Similarly, there must be equivalent treatment of claims and defences based on Community competition law and those based on purely domestic law.[41] In the scrutiny of national procedural rules, a key factor is the objective pursued by those rules and their function in ensuring fair and efficient administration of justice.[42] However, the Court has not been able to provide a clear analytical framework for the 'balancing exercise' required in this assessment. This is due, again, to the insufficient weight given to the content of the right as the key element of the test and to ambiguity in the use of the term 'effectiveness'. Furthermore, the application of the principle of equivalence is also often problematic. The identification of the relevant national comparator may be far from straightforward. Once the comparator has been identified, it may be impossible to say which treatment is more favourable because different legal rules may simply reflect different policy decisions attaching different weight to different or the same factors.[43]

The doctrine of procedural autonomy appears inadequate on its own for the purposes of defining the outer limits of EU law with respect to private Community law remedies in general and the right to damages for breach of Article 81 or 82 in particular. This doctrine only provides a framework for assessing whether the protection of the right under national law is effective. However, this assessment depends on two questions: (a) what the function and content of the right is; and (b) whether national procedures and remedies are adequate to the protection of the right in light of its function and content. The doctrine of procedural autonomy does not provide an answer to the first question but only to the second. As a result, the outcome of the procedural autonomy scrutiny is either arbitrary, as in the definition of the limits to the right to damages in the *Crehan* case, or uncertain, as in the non-definition of the concept of 'causal relationship' in the *Manfredi* case.

[40] Joined Cases C-430–431/93 *Jeroen Van Schijndel v Stichting Pensioenfonds voor Fysiotherapeuten* [1995] ECR I-4705. The *Van Schijndel* case can be seen as purely procedural, in the sense that the Court was not asked to determine whether the party had a right, or to define the scope of such a right, but was called upon to rule on purely procedural matters, that is on whether national courts have the duty to raise Community law points ex officio.

[41] *Ibid.*

[42] *Ibid*; Case C-312/93 *Peterbroeck Van Campenhout & Cie SCS v Belgium* [1995] ECR I-4599, para 14; S Prechal, 'Community Law in National Courts: the Lessons from *van Schijndel*' (n 23) 690–93. P Craig, *EU Administrative Law* (n 15) 803–15, approves of this nuanced approach of the Court of Justice, noting that this trend was first identified by G De Búrca, 'National Procedural Rules and Remedies: The Changing Approach of the ECJ', in A Biondi and J Lonbay (eds), *Remedies for Breach of EC Law* (Chichester, Wiley, 1997) ch 4.

[43] For an illustration of this proposition, see section IV B below.

To avoid either arbitrariness or uncertainty, the scrutiny of national rules under the doctrine of procedural autonomy must focus on the content of the right. The content of the right in itself turns on its function, which crucially depends on the legal basis of the right. This framework requires three modifications to the traditional approach to the procedural autonomy scrutiny of national rules. The first modification is that the 'procedural autonomy' scrutiny requires a three-stage analysis. The first stage is the identification of the legal basis the right, which is determinative of its function. The second stage relates to the determination of the content of the right. The third stage focuses on whether national rules on remedies and procedure make the exercise of the right impossible or excessively difficult. Only the third stage is properly a procedural autonomy scrutiny. The second modification is that the term 'effectiveness' must be clarified and deconstructed in its distinct meanings of full effectiveness of Community law and effective judicial protection. The two principles may play different roles in the three stages of the identification of the legal basis of the right, the determination of the content of the right, and the assessment of national rules. The third modification is that the principles of full effectiveness of Community law and effective judicial protection as limits to the procedural autonomy of the Member States must be applied in light of the function and content of the right as determined by its legal basis.

The following section examines the legal basis of private remedies in Community law generally and of the Community law right to damages for breach of Article 81 or 82 in particular.

III THE LEGAL BASIS OF THE RIGHT TO DAMAGES FOR BREACH OF ARTICLE 81 OR 82

A The Right to Damages in the Wider Framework of Community Law

(i) Structure of the Inquiry

In order to define the content of the Community law right to damages for breach of Article 81 or 82 of the Treaty, it is necessary to identify its legal basis. This in turn calls for an answer to the question of why individuals have a right to damages for breach of Article 81 or 82. At a theoretical level, it is possible to say that a right may be the manifestation of the legal protection of an individual interest or an instrument to achieve the effective enforcement of the law in an objective way. While both legal bases may co-exist, it is relevant to identify which one is prevalent, that is whether certain private rights are used predominantly for a public policy objective or whether a public policy objective is also, incidentally, served by the legal protection of individual interests.[44] The centre of gravity of the legal basis of a private right may determine the function of a right and its content.

It is worth clarifying at the outset that Community law does not necessarily recognise different individual rights relying on the same legal basis. It is entirely natural that certain rights, such as fundamental rights,[45] are recognised because a given individual interest is deemed worthy of legal protection. On the other hand, other rights, such as the right to damages for breach of Article 81 or 82,[46] may be recognised because they strengthen the effectiveness of a given Community policy. Nevertheless, it is instructive to examine the case law of the Court of Justice on national remedies more generally as it is illustrative of the analytical framework the Court adopts in recognising individual rights and assessing national rules on remedies and procedure under the principle of effectiveness.

(ii) Direct Effect and Full Effectiveness of Community law

In the *Van Gend en Loos* case,[47] the Court of Justice established the doctrine of direct effect. First, the Court had to justify why an international treaty may confer rights upon individuals. The Court ruled that the Community constitutes a new legal order the subjects of which are not only the Member States but also their nationals. As a consequence, Community law not only imposes obligations on individuals but is also intended to confer rights upon them. These rights may be expressly granted by the Treaty, or may be implied by reason of obligations which the Treaty imposes in a clearly defined way upon individuals as well as upon the Member States and upon the institutions of the Community.

The next question in the *Van Gend en Loos* case was to identify the legal basis for conferring upon individuals the right to rely on Article 25 EC[48] before the national courts. The Court noted the argument that the Treaty

[44] P Nebbia, 'Damages actions for the infringement of EC competition law: compensation or deterrence?' (2008) 33 *EL Rev*, 23, 24–36, notes that private remedies for breach of Community law may pursue a dual function (compensation and deterrence) but 'while compromise may be possible in most cases, in some other cases priorities will need to be set'. The intuition that different possible functions of a right may not necessarily be reconciled appears to be correct. However, in our view, on a functional analysis compensation and deterrence are not mutually exclusive: see section III B (iii) below.

[45] When the Community Courts recognise fundamental rights, it is generally clear that they do so because the right protects an interest which is considered to be in itself worthy of legal recognition as fundamental. See, eg, Case 44/79 *Hauer v Land Rheinland-Pfalz* [1979] ECR 3727, paras 17–18.

[46] See the discussion on the legal basis of the right to damages for breach of Art 81 or 82 in section III B below.

[47] Case 26/62 *NV Algemene Transport- en Expeditie Onderneming van Gend & Loos v Netherlands Inland Revenue Administration* [1963] ECR 1.

[48] Art 25 EC provides: 'Customs duties on imports and exports and charges having equivalent effect shall be prohibited between Member States. This prohibition shall also apply to customs duties of a fiscal nature'.

explicitly provides for a remedy against a Member State for failure to fulfil Community law obligations.[49] However, the Court added that there was a risk that recourse to remedies on the application of the Commission or another Member State would be ineffective if it occurred after the implementation of a national decision taken contrary to the provisions of the Treaty. The Court went on to say that the vigilance of individuals concerned to protect their rights amounts to an effective supervision in addition to the supervision entrusted by Articles 226 and 227 EC to the Commission and the Member States.

If Community law conferred on individuals the right to rely on Article 25 only because it recognised the individual interest in free trade as worthy of legal protection, there would not have been any need for the Court to go further in the *Van Gend en Loos* case. Instead, the Court felt it necessary to explain why the fact that the Treaty provides for remedies against Member States on the application of the Commission or other Member States does not render private rights superfluous. A private right protected as the manifestation of a private interest is capable of being justified by reference to the nature of the protected interest and the system of trade-offs with other interests worthy of protection. Any reference to the 'effective supervision' of Member States' compliance with Community law would be redundant.

The enforcement rationale is even more clearly articulated in cases in which the objective of Community law is plainly not to confer rights on individuals but individual rights are nevertheless recognised by the Court as an instrument to achieve the full effectiveness of Community law.

In *Muñoz and Superior Fruiticola v Frumar Ltd*,[50] the Court of Justice was called upon to decide whether compliance with the provisions of certain regulations on quality standards applicable to fruit and vegetables must be capable of enforcement by means of civil proceedings instituted by a trader against a competitor. The Court decided this question in the affirmative, relying exclusively on an effectiveness rationale. The Court said that the full effectiveness of the rules on quality standards and, in particular, the practical effect of the obligation laid down in the relevant regulations imply that it must be possible to enforce that obligation by means of civil proceedings instituted by a trader against a competitor. The possibility of bringing such proceedings strengthens the practical working

[49] See, now, Arts 226 and 227 EC. Art 226 provides that, if the Commission considers that a Member State has failed to fulfil an obligation under the EC Treaty, it shall deliver a reasoned opinion on the matter after giving the State concerned the opportunity to submit its observations. If the State concerned does not comply with the opinion within the period laid down by the Commission, the latter may bring the matter before the Court of Justice. Art 227 provides for a procedure whereby a Member State may take action with respect to another Member State for failure to fulfil obligations under the EC Treaty.

[50] C-253/00 *Muñoz and Superior Fruiticola v Frumar Ltd* [2002] ECR I-7289.

of the Community rules on quality standards and is in addition to public enforcement mechanisms. In this way, private actions may substantially contribute to ensuring fair trading and transparency of markets in the Community.[51]

In the *Muñoz* case, the Court was exclusively concerned with whether the claimant had a private right of action. The issue of effective judicial protection of an existing right under the doctrine of procedural autonomy did not arise. The full effectiveness of Community law as an enforcement rationale is, therefore, expressed in its purest form.

(iii) The Case Law on State Liability

In other cases, and particularly in State liability cases, the Court of Justice has been more ambiguous in identifying the legal basis for the recognition of a Community law right. This can be explained, however, because in these cases the Court was mainly concerned with a remedy for breach of a primary right which Community law conferred or intended to confer on individuals.

In *Francovich v Italy*, a fundamental case on the liability of the State[52] for non-implementation of directives, the main question was whether the claimant had a remedy in damages against the State for failure to implement a directive which would have conferred a benefit on the claimant. The Court of Justice had no doubt that the claimant had a right to damages. The problem was not whether Community law intended to protect an individual interest. In a *Francovich*-type of case, the individual interest to be protected is the benefit conferred upon individuals by the non-implemented directive. The question was whether the claimant had a remedy against the State if the State had failed to implement the directive thus denying the claimant the benefit of the primary right. The Court said that the full effectiveness of Community rules would be impaired and the protection of the rights which they grant would be weakened if individuals were unable to obtain redress when a Member State infringes their Community law rights. This is particularly indispensable where, in the absence of action by a Member State, individuals cannot enforce before the national courts the rights conferred upon them by Community law.[53]

The 'full effectiveness of the Community rules', as distinct from 'the protection of the rights which they grant', relates to the attainment of the objective of Community law in the field in question. Individual rights are instrumental to the effectiveness of the Community legal order. This is the

[51] *Ibid*, paras 31 and 32.

[52] On State liability see T Tridimas, (n 19) 498–547 (with references to the case law and extensive literature).

[53] *Francovich* (n 27) paras 33 and 34.

same idea to which the Court referred in *Van Gend en Loos* when it spoke about the 'vigilance' of individuals ensuring that Member States comply with Community law.[54]

In *R v Secretary of State for Transport, ex parte Factortame Ltd*,[55] there was no issue as to whether the claimants in the main proceedings had a right under Community law. The only question was whether the national courts should set aside a domestic rule preventing them from granting interim relief. The Court could have simply relied on the principle of effective judicial protection as the exclusive basis for setting aside the national rule. If, because of the need to institute legal proceedings and the inevitable hiatus between the existence of the right, its violation, and a final judgment on the merits, the right is irremediably compromised, then interim relief becomes a necessary remedy to ensure the effective judicial protection of the right. However, the Court still felt the need to rely on the principle of full effectiveness of Community law[56] as well as on effective judicial protection.[57]

Brasserie du Pêcheur SA and Factortame is a further refinement of this approach, whereby the principle of full effectiveness of Community law and the principle of effective judicial protection are inextricably intertwined and yet distinct. The case concerned State liability for breach of directly effective Community law.[58] The main question was, as in the *Factortame* case, not whether Community law was directly effective but whether the individual had a remedy against the State.

Adopting a three-stage framework, the Court first identified the legal basis of the right to damages. It relied on the *Francovich* case to explain that the full effectiveness of Community law would be impaired if individuals were unable to obtain redress when their rights were infringed by a breach of Community law.[59]

In the second stage, relying again on the *Francovich* case,[60] the Court said that State liability rests on two principles: first, the full effectiveness of Community rules and the effective protection of the rights which they confer and, secondly, the obligation to cooperate imposed on Member

[54] *Van Gend en Loos* (n 47).

[55] *R v Secretary of State for Transport, ex parte Factortame Ltd* (n 27).

[56] *Ibid*, paras 18 and 20.

[57] Effective judicial protection is perhaps a concurring ratio: see *ibid*, paras 19 and 21.

[58] Joined cases C-46/93 and C-48/93 *Brasserie du Pêcheur SA v Bundesrepublik Deutschland and R v Secretary of State for Transport, ex parte Factortame Ltd* ECR [1996] I-1029.

[59] *Ibid*, para 20, referring to para 33 of the *Francovich* case (n 27). Paragraph 21 of *Brasserie du Pêcheur SA and Factortame* also refers to an interests-based rationale, emphasising that reliance on directly effective Community law does not secure for individuals the benefit of the rights conferred on them by Community law. Individuals may suffer loss as a result of action or omission on the part of the State. However, the protection of the individual interest is linked to the 'full effectiveness' of Community law.

[60] *Francovich* (n 27).

States by Article 10 of the Treaty.[61] The full effectiveness of Community law and the effective protection of individual rights are seen as a single principle but they are, in fact, two different principles that in certain cases may even conflict with each other.[62] These principles are applied not to identify the legal basis of the right but to determine its function and content. After setting out the three conditions for State liability, the Court said that those conditions satisfy the requirements of the full effectiveness of the rules of Community law and of the effective protection of the rights which those rules confer.[63] This is an important part of the judgment because it demonstrates that the conditions for State liability are not only subject to the principle of effective judicial protection but also to the principle of full effectiveness of Community law. Therefore, the question is not only whether the individual right receives effective judicial protection but also whether national rules impair the effectiveness of the Community legal order. This is arguably because the full effectiveness of Community law is the legal basis of the right.

In the third stage, the Court carried out an assessment of certain rules of German and English law under the principle of supremacy of Community law and under the doctrine of procedural autonomy.[64]

A further example of this approach is *Köbler*,[65] where the Court of Justice ruled that a breach of Community law by a national court of last instance was capable of giving rise to State liability in certain circumstances. The Court stated that, because of the role played by the judiciary in the protection of rights conferred by Community law rules, the full effectiveness of those rules would be called into question and the protection of those rights would be weakened if individuals were precluded from obtaining reparation when their rights are affected by an infringement of Community law attributable to a decision of a court of a Member State adjudicating at last instance.[66] The Court followed *Francovich* and *Brasserie du Pêcheur SA and Factortame* in that it referred to both the full effectiveness of Community law and effective judicial protection. Both principles apply in determining whether limitations on State liability are compatible with Community law.

[61] *Brasserie du Pêcheur SA and Factortame* (n 58) para 39, referring to paras 33 and 34 of the *Francovich* case (n 27).

[62] See section IV B below.

[63] *Brasserie du Pêcheur SA and Factortame* (n 58) para 52.

[64] *Ibid*, paras 67–100. The Court fails to articulate a clear distinction between the application of the doctrine of supremacy of Community law, under which national rules that are incompatible with the content of the right to damages as determined by Community law must be set aside, and the application of the doctrine of procedural autonomy, which considers whether national rules comply with the principles effectiveness (covering both the full effectiveness of Community law and effective judicial protection) and equivalence.

[65] Case C-224/01 *Gerhard Köbler v Republik Österreich* [2003] ECR I-10239.

[66] *Ibid*, para 33.

(iv) Full Effectiveness and Effective Judicial Protection Distinguished

The analysis of the case law on direct effect and State liability shows that the principle of full effectiveness of Community law may be relevant at three different stages. First, it may be used as the legal basis of a Community law right. Secondly, it may used to determine the content and function of the right or the existence or scope of a particular remedy.[67] Thirdly, it may be used to assess whether national rules make the enforcement of the right impossible or excessively difficult.[68] In the second and third stage, the principle of full effectiveness co-exists with the principle of effective judicial protection. The latter principle focuses on the exercise of the individual right while the former considers the individual right as an instrument for the attainment of the objectives of the Community. The principle of effectiveness under the doctrine of procedural autonomy must be understood as covering both the principle of full effectiveness of Community law and the principle of effective judicial protection.[69]

The role of the principle of full effectiveness of Community law outlined above does not mean that the right to damages in Community law has the objective of punishing and deterring perpetrators of public wrongs. It remains a private right the immediate purpose of which is compensation. In the *A.G.M.-COS.MET Srl* case, the Court emphasised that the purpose of State liability under Community law is not deterrence or punishment but compensation for the damage suffered by individuals as a result of breaches of Community law by Member States.[70] As a consequence, a private claimant seeking damages before a national court does not act in a public law capacity. Nor does Community law require that national courts must award multiple or punitive damages designed to achieve a given level of deterrence.

This approach is fully consistent with the legal basis and function of the right being the attainment of the full effectiveness of Community law. Full effectiveness must be understood as the attainment of the objective that the law intends to achieve. If the attainment of the objective is frustrated by a Member State not implementing a directive or an undertaking acting in breach of Article 81 or 82, full compensation ensures that the objective of the law is attained *ex post* by placing the parties in the position in which they would have been but for the infringement of Community law.[71] This

[67] *Brasserie du Pêcheur SA and Factortame* case (n 58) and *Köbler v Republik Österreich* (n 65).

[68] *R v Secretary of State for Transport, ex p Factortame Ltd* (n 27).

[69] M Dougan, (n 17) 26–45.

[70] Case C-470/03 *A.G.M.-COS.MET Srl v Suomen valtio* [2007] ECR I-2749.

[71] Case C-271/91 *M Helen Marshall v Southampton and South-West Hampshire Area Health Authority (No 2)* [1993] ECR I-04367.

has in itself beneficial effects from the point of view of the legal system as a whole and encourages compliance with the law. First, individuals have an incentive to police compliance with Community law.[72] This may in turn trigger public enforcement proceedings. Secondly, if the claimant is successful, the infringement of Community law is neutralised *ex post* so that the legal order is restored.[73] Third, access to effective redress strengthens public confidence in the legal system.

The additional function of punishment and deterrence is distinct from the primary function of private actions and may be more effectively pursued by public authorities. As regards Articles 81 and 82, the European Commission and national competition authorities are entrusted with the enforcement of Community competition law with the primary objective of bringing infringements to an end and punishing and deterring the perpetrators in appropriate cases.[74] However, private actions have an equally important role to play in ensuring the effectiveness of Community competition law, as the Court of Justice has clearly recognised.[75]

B The Legal Basis of the Right to Damages for Breach of Article 81 or 82

(i) The Need for a Competition Specific Enquiry

The legal bases, functions and contents of the right to damages against the State for breach of Community law or of the right to prevent a trader from acting in breach of the provisions of the EC Regulations on quality standards applicable to fruit and vegetables[76] may well be different from the legal basis, function and content of the right to damages for breach of Article 81 or 82. It is, therefore, necessary to narrow the scope of the enquiry to the direct effect of these two provisions.

(ii) The Case Law on the Direct Effect of Articles 81 and 82

The earlier cases recognising the direct effect of Articles 81 and 82 do not articulate the reasons for the conferral of individual rights.

[72] *Van Gend en Loos* (n 47).

[73] For instance, in a competition case, a successful claim may operate a wealth transfer from the defendant to the claimant thus stripping the defendant of supra-competitive profits and remedying the competitive disadvantage a competitor or customer may have suffered.

[74] Council Regulation (EC) No 1/2003 (n 24).

[75] *Crehan* (n 27) and *Manfredi* (n 37).

[76] *Muñoz* (n 50).

In *BRT v SABAM*,[77] the Court ruled on whether the initiation of proceedings by the Commission deprived national courts of their jurisdiction pursuant to Article 9(3) of Regulation 17/62.[78] The Court stated that Article 3 of Regulation 17 did not apply to national courts because their jurisdiction derives from the direct effect of the Treaty provisions. The Court went on to say that the prohibitions in Articles 81(1) and 82 tend by their very nature to produce direct effects in relations between individuals and create direct rights in respect of the individuals concerned which the national courts must safeguard. To deny the national courts' jurisdiction to afford this safeguard would mean depriving individuals of rights which they hold under the Treaty itself.[79] In this case, the Court appears to have relied on the rationale of effective judicial protection as an argument for holding that national court proceedings concerning individual rights can run in parallel with an investigation by the Commission.[80]

Similarly, in *Guérin automobiles v Commission*,[81] the Court of Justice dismissed an appeal brought in an action against the Commission for failure to act on a complaint. The Court held that any undertaking which considers that it has suffered damage as a result of restrictive practices may rely before the national courts on the rights conferred on it by Article 81(1) and Article 82 of the Treaty, which produce direct effect in relations between individuals. Therefore, the appellant's plea relating to the breach of the right to a judicial remedy was held to be unfounded.[82]

In both *BRT v SABAM* and *Guérin*, the Court was not articulating the rationale for the conferral of individual rights on individuals but assumed that individuals had such rights and relied on the principle of effective judicial protection to justify its conclusions relating to a different issue of law.

(iii) The Case Law on the Right to Damages for Breach of Article 81 or 82

When the Court was required to address the core question of whether those who have been harmed by a breach of Article 81(1) have a right to damages, the enforcement rationale becomes more evident.

[77] Case 127/73 *Belgische Radio en Televisie v SV SABAM (BRT v SABAM)* [1974] ECR 51, para 16.
[78] Council Regulation (EEC) 17/62: First Regulation implementing Arts 85 and 86 of the Treaty [1962] JO 13/204, [1959–1962] OJ Spec Ed 87.
[79] *BRT v SABAM* (n 77) paras 16 and 17.
[80] This is subject to the safeguards set out at paras 21–23 of the judgment.
[81] Case C-282/95 P *Guérin automobiles v Commission* [1997] ECR I-1503.
[82] *Ibid*, paras 39–40.

In *Courage v Crehan*, the Court of Justice was called upon to decide whether the English law rule *ex turpi causa non oritur actio* was incompatible with Community law in so far as it prevented a party to an agreement prohibited by Article 81(1) from recovering damages from the other party.[83] The Court said that the full effectiveness of Article 81 of the Treaty and, in particular, the practical effect of the prohibition laid down in Article 81(1) would be put at risk if it were not open to any individual to claim damages for loss caused to him by a contract or by conduct liable to restrict or distort competition. The Court added that the existence of such a right strengthens the working of the Community competition rules and discourages anti-competitive agreements or practices. Finally, the Court said that actions for damages before the national courts can make a significant contribution to the maintenance of effective competition in the Community.[84] The enforcement rationale could not be more clearly articulated.

In the subsequent case of *Vincenzo Manfredi v Lloyd Adriatico Assicurazioni SpA*,[85] the Court repeated almost verbatim paragraphs 26 and 27 of the *Crehan* case.[86] The Court was ruling on whether Article 81 must be interpreted as requiring national courts to award punitive damages, greater than the advantage obtained by the defendant, thereby deterring agreements or concerted practices prohibited under that Article.[87] The question referred by the National Court explicitly linked the award of punitive damages to deterrence. It was, therefore, important for the Court to make it clear that the fact that Community law does not require the award of punitive damages does not mean that the right to damages for loss caused by a breach of Article 81 or 82 is any less important in ensuring the effectiveness of Community competition law.

Although strictly not required to do so, the Court went on to determine the content of the right in light of its function of ensuring the full effectiveness of Community competition law. The Court considered that the effectiveness of Community competition law and the right to seek compensation required that the claimant be entitled to 'full compensation', including actual loss, loss of profit, and interest, but leaving the award of punitive damages to national law subject to the principle of equivalence.[88] In determining the damages recoverable, the Court relied both on the principle of effectiveness and on the right to seek compensation.[89] In doing so, the Court applied a test similar to

[83] *Crehan* (n 27) para 26.
[84] *Ibid*, paras 26 and 27.
[85] *Manfredi* (n 37).
[86] *Ibid*, paras 90 and 91.
[87] *Ibid*, para 83.
[88] *Ibid*, paras 95–100.
[89] *Ibid*, para 95. It would appear that the principle of effectiveness denotes the full effectiveness of Community law and the right to seek compensation denotes effective judicial protection.

that set out in *Brasserie du Pêcheur SA and Factortame*,[90] whereby the remedies available for the protection of the right are determined according to both the requirement of full effectiveness of Community law and the requirement of effective judicial protection.[91]

Applying the three-stage framework proposed in this chapter, it would appear that, in the first stage, the Community right to damages for breach of Article 81 or 82 is recognised based entirely upon the enforcement rationale. In the second stage, the principle of full effectiveness of Community law applies, in conjunction with the principle of effective judicial protection, to determine the content of the right. Finally, in the third stage, under the doctrine of procedural autonomy, the principles of full effectiveness of Community law and effective judicial protection apply to assess whether national rules on remedies and procedure are compatible with Community law.[92] So far, the Court has not had to rule on a trade-off between the principle of full effectiveness of Community law and the principle of effective judicial protection.[93]

Some appear to argue that the objective of the Community law right to damages for breach of the competition provisions is compensation and not the effectiveness of the regime.[94] However, it is necessary to distinguish between the content of the right, on the one hand, and its legal basis and function, on the other. The discussion so far has demonstrated that full compensation as the content of the right is consistent with the objective of ensuring the effective enforcement of Community competition law. Furthermore, the competition law cases of *Crehan* and *Manfredi* clearly articulate in unambiguous language an enforcement rationale for the conferral of the right to damages.

The enforcement rationale which underpins the right to damages for breach of Article 81 or 82 is further demonstrated by the absence of the 'protective purpose' doctrine under Community law. The protective purpose doctrine is well established under German tort law, where the claimant is only entitled to compensation if he suffers harm as a consequence of the violation of a norm the purpose of which was to protect a person in the position of the claimant from the harm in question.[95] The

[90] *Brasserie du Pêcheur SA and Factortame* (n 58) paras 39 and 52.

[91] However, the Court is not adapting the *Francovich* and *Brasserie du Pêcheur SA and Factortame* case law to the conduct of private parties: M Dougan, *National Remedies before the Court of Justice* (n 17) 378; *Wyatt & Dashwood's European Union Law* (n 24) 232.

[92] In the third stage, these principles, often conflated into a single 'principle of effectiveness', co-exist with the weaker principle of equivalence.

[93] See the discussion on the limiting function of the principle in protecting the leniency programmes in section IV B below.

[94] Nebbia, 'Damages actions for the infringement of EC competition law: compensation or deterrence?' (n 44) 35–6.

[95] M Ruffert, 'Rights and Remedies in European Community law: A Comparative View' [1997] *CML Rev* 307, 311–12.

concept is not alien to English tort law where the claimant, to recover damages for breach of statutory duty, must establish that he is within the category of person the statute intended to protect from the harm in question.[96] The Court of Justice in *Manfredi* appears to have rejected, albeit implicitly, the protective purpose doctrine. The Court said that Article 81 must be interpreted as meaning that any individual can rely on the invalidity of an agreement or practice prohibited under that Article and, where there is a causal relationship between the latter and the harm suffered, claim compensation for that harm.[97]

The absence of the protective purpose doctrine in Community competition law is consistent with an enforcement rationale. If the legal basis of the right to damages for breach of Article 81 or 82 were to protect individual interests, it would follow that the claimant would have to prove that he belongs to the category of person that Article 81 or 82 intends to protect and that the harm suffered is of the type that those provisions intend to prevent.

IV THE PRINCIPLE OF EFFECTIVENESS AND ITS IMPLICATIONS FOR COMPETITION LAW REMEDIES AND PROCEDURES

A The Expansive Function of the Principle: Collective Actions

(i) The Problem

The effective enforcement legal basis of the right to damages for breach of Article 81 or 82 indicates that such a right is conferred on individuals to strengthen the enforcement of Articles 81 and 82. Therefore, the right to damages and its enforcement should ensure, as far as possible, that the perpetrator of an infringement of competition law is at risk of being held liable for the whole loss it caused. This is particularly true with respect to standalone actions where the only sanction for the anti-competitive conduct is the private action.[98] It follows that adequate procedural rules must be in place so that those who have been harmed are not deterred from

[96] In English law, a cause of action in tort arises from the breach of a duty imposed by statute if it can be shown that the 'statutory duty was imposed for the protection of a limited class of the public and that Parliament intended to confer on members of that class a private right of action for breach of the duty': *X (minors) v Bedfordshire County Council* [1995] 2 AC 633, 731, (Lord Browne-Wilkinson). On the tort of breach of statutory duty, see *Clerk & Lindsell on Torts* (London, Sweet & Maxwell, 2006) 519–61.

[97] *Manfredi* (n 37) paras 60 and 63, relying, inter alia, on *Crehan* (n 27) para 26.

[98] Standalone actions are actions that relate to instances of alleged anti-competitive behaviour which have not previously been found to be an infringement of Art 81 or 82 by a competition authority.

bringing meritorious cases. The smaller the likely number of claimants bringing proceedings against the perpetrators, the lower the risk of the perpetrator being held liable for the whole loss it caused.

Barriers that deter claimants from bringing proceedings in meritorious cases may be subject to Community law scrutiny under the effectiveness principle.[99] While the Court consistently held that in the absence of Community rules governing the matter, it is for the domestic legal system of each Member State to designate the courts and tribunals having jurisdiction and to lay down the detailed procedural rules governing actions for safeguarding rights which individuals derive directly from Community law, it is also clear that national rules are subject to the principles of full effectiveness of Community law and effective judicial protection.[100]

Barriers to effective redress may be of different types. The funding necessary to start an action, the potential liability in costs to the other party if the claimant is unsuccessful, excessively high court fees, unavailability of evidence, and legal uncertainty may deter claimants from bringing meritorious claims. It is an empirical question, to an extent depending on the facts of individual cases, whether any national rule of procedure infringes the principle of full effectiveness of Community law or effective judicial protection. One particularly problematic area, however, is the availability and regulation of collective actions.[101]

(ii) The Need for Collective Actions in Competition Law

Competition infringements may harm a significant number of individuals so that the individual loss may be relatively small while the aggregate loss to all potential claimants may be large. Both of the national cases that gave rise to the references to the Court of Justice on the right to damages for breach of Article 81(1) are instances in which an infringement of competition law affected a significant number of businesses or consumers in a similar way. In the *Crehan* case, the issues related to the anti-competitive

[99] This includes not only the principle of effective judicial protection but also the need to ensure the effective enforcement of Community law: *Brasserie du Pêcheur SA and Factortame* (n 58) para 52. Effective enforcement and effective judicial protection are often simply two sides of the same coin since access to effective redress ensures the effective enforcement of Community competition law and the effective enforcement of Community competition law is best achieved if those who have suffered harm for a breach of Art 81 or 82 obtain effective redress. If this is the case, no trade-off is required.

[100] *Manfredi* (n 37) para 62; *Palmisani* (n 28) para 27; and *Crehan* (n 27) para 29.

[101] On collective actions, see C Hodges, *Multi-Part Actions* (Oxford, Oxford University Press, 2001) and R Mulheron, *The Class Action in Common Law Legal Systems: A Comparative Perspective* (Oxford, Hart Publishing, 2004).

effects of a 'beer tie' agreement.[102] A significant number of publicans were in the same position as Mr Crehan as they had been lessees of tied houses during the relevant period and claimed to have suffered loss as a result. In the *Manfredi* case, a policy holder claimed damages against the insurers alleging that the insurance premiums of compulsory civil liability insurance relating to accidents caused by motor vehicles had been artificially increased as a result of a cartel among the insurers.[103] A large number of motor vehicle owners in Italy alleged to have been similarly affected.

Dealing with a significant number of similar claims raises issues of efficiency of the civil justice system as well as issues of proportionality and fairness to the defendant. From the perspective of the effective enforcement of Community competition law, the question is whether the Treaty requires that an effective collective action mechanism be in place.

The question can be addressed from two different perspectives. The first is whether the effective enforcement of Community competition law requires that a particular procedure be available to the claimants in certain circumstances. The second is whether the unavailability of a collective redress mechanism means that effective judicial protection of the claimant's right is not safeguarded. The focus on effective enforcement in the case law of the European Court of Justice suggests that the first perspective should prevail but the same conclusion would be achieved from the second perspective so that no trade-off is required in this regard.[104] Effective enforcement is best achieved if all claimants are fully compensated for harm resulting from breaches of Community competition law. Effective redress for individuals equals effective enforcement of Community competition law. The key issue is, therefore, whether the effective enforcement of Articles 81 and 82 may be compromised because of the unavailability of effective collective redress mechanisms under national law.

Generally, systems of civil procedure envisage mechanisms whereby two or more individual claims can be brought together so that common issues may be decided once in a way which binds all the claimants. Obvious

[102] A beer tie agreement is a clause in a contract between a publican and its landlord that obliges the former to purchase almost all of its beer supply from the latter or a company nominated by it at the list price in force from time to time.

[103] The Autorità Garante della Concorrenza e del Mercato had established the infringement in its decision No 8546 (I377) of 28 July 2000 (Bollettino 30/2000 of 14 August 2000).

[104] Some argue that a trade-off may be required if the claimants are at different levels of the supply chain: see Nebbia, 'Damages actions for the infringement of EC competition law: compensation or deterrence?' (n 44) 39. However, identifying the function of the right to damages in the achievement of the full effectiveness of Community law is not incompatible with ensuring that indirect purchasers are compensated. On the contrary, it is possible to devise an effective collective redress mechanism that would achieve consolidation of the claims by different categories of claimant, quantification of the harm caused by the defendant(s), and distribution of damages among the different categories of claimant. The discussion of the passing on defence and the standing of indirect purchasers are outside the scope of this chapter.

principles of judicial economy and avoidance of conflicting judgments make the availability of such a procedure if not necessary then at least highly desirable in any legal system. More recently, however, collective actions have been playing an additional role in modern societies: ensuring access to justice and the effective enforcement of the law.[105]

Today, infringements of the law that give rise to individual causes of action have the potential to affect thousands if not millions of individuals. Given the size of each individual claim relative to the costs of bringing the claim, individual claimants may be effectively deterred from bringing proceedings even if they have a well-founded case. The result may be that, when the perpetrator of an infringement harms a great number of individuals in circumstances in which the individual loss is not sufficiently large to justify the costs and risks of bringing an individual claim, in the absence of an effective collective redress mechanism, the perpetrator will not be held liable for the loss it caused and those who have been harmed will not be compensated. In the case of an infringement of Article 81 or 82, this means that the perpetrator of an infringement of Community competition law will not have to compensate other undertakings or consumers for the loss it caused. The effective enforcement of Community competition law, which is the very reason why individuals have a right to damages for breaches of Article 81 or 82, is impaired. As a result, the unavailability or the specific features of collective redress mechanisms in the Member States may be subject to scrutiny under the doctrine of effectiveness.

The principle of full effectiveness of Community law requires that Member States must provide an effective redress mechanism which ensures that the right to damages of those who have been harmed by competition law infringements is effective in circumstances in which a sufficiently large number of individual claims would in practice be unlikely to be brought. The effectiveness of the right to damages does not only require the theoretical possibility to bring a claim in a way which does not discriminate between remedies and procedures available in comparable national and Community law situations. It also requires that there should not be obstacles making the exercise of the right to damages impossible or excessively difficult in practice. Furthermore, it follows from the above discussion on the legal basis and function of the right to damages that its effectiveness must be assessed, in the first place, against the objective of the effective enforcement of Community competition law.

[105] The objective of ensuring the effective enforcement of the law, however, is not universally accepted: see R Mulheron (n 101) 63–6.

(iii) Collections Actions and the Principle of 'Full Compensation'

Community law seeks to achieve the effective enforcement of its competition rules through the principle of full compensation. In the *Manfredi* case, one of the questions referred to the European Court of Justice was whether Article 81 must be interpreted as requiring national courts to award punitive damages, greater than the advantage obtained by the defendant, thereby deterring agreements or concerted practices prohibited under that Article.[106]

It is interesting to analyse how the Court addressed the question relating to punitive damages. First, it explicitly adopted a deterrence rationale for the right to damages. The Court said that the right to damages for breach of Article 81 or 82 strengthens the working of the Community competition rules and discourages anti-competitive agreements or practices. The Court added that actions for damages before the national courts can make a significant contribution to the maintenance of effective competition in the Community.[107]

The Court then ruled that Community law did not require the award of punitive damages, provided that the principles of equivalence and effectiveness were observed. However, the principle of effectiveness and the right of any individual to seek compensation for loss caused by conduct liable to restrict or distort competition required that injured persons must be able to seek compensation not only for actual loss (*damnum emergens*) but also for loss of profit (*lucrum cessans*) plus interest.[108] As regards the award of interest, the Court in *Manfredi* relied on the case of *Marshall (No 2)*. In that case, the Court said that full compensation for the loss and damage sustained as a result of discriminatory dismissal cannot leave out of account factors which may reduce its value. The award of interest, in accordance with the applicable national rules, must therefore be regarded as an essential component of compensation for the purposes of restoring real equality of treatment.[109]

The function of 'full compensation' in the *Marshall (No 2)* case is to arrive at real equality of opportunity. This must be ensured by measures appropriate to restore such equality when it has not been observed. Those measures, the Court said in *Marshall (No 2)*, 'must be such as to guarantee real and effective judicial protection and have a real deterrent effect on the employer'.[110] Therefore, the Court of Justice held that 'full compensation' is the minimum content of the right and scope of the remedy required by

106 *Manfredi* (n 37) para 83.
107 *Ibid*, para 91.
108 *Ibid*, para 95.
109 *Marshall (No 2)* (n 71) para 31.
110 *Ibid*, para 24.

both the principle of full effectiveness of Community law (which the Court refers to as 'the principle of effectiveness') and the principle of effective judicial protection (which the Court refers to as 'the right of any individual to seek compensation'). Full compensation is fully consistent with an enforcement rationale. The same line of reasoning is adopted in *Manfredi*. The principle of full compensation is instrumental to the effective enforcement of Community competition law.

The principle of full compensation as set out in the *Marshall (No 2)* case has two functions: ensuring that individual claimants obtain full compensation (the 'effective judicial protection' rationale) and requiring that the defendant should be at risk of being held liable for the entire loss it caused (the 'deterrent effect' rationale). The enforcement rationale adopted by the European Court of Justice in the cases of *Crehan* and *Manfredi* would appear to be consistent with the dual function of full compensation. On this analysis, if the anti-competitive practice harms a great number of persons, the full compensation principle requires not only that each individual is fully compensated but that the perpetrator is at risk of having to compensate in full the harm it caused. It follows that if the issuing of individual proceedings is not a viable option in practice, Member States must provide an effective collective redress mechanism which overcomes the barriers to full compensation.

(iv) Opt-out Collective Actions

In the absence of Community measures of harmonisation, the design of the appropriate collective redress mechanism is left to the Member States. The Member States, however, are subject to the principles of full effectiveness of Community law and the principle of effective judicial protection of individual rights. The principle of full effectiveness of Community law requires that a collective redress mechanism should be such that the perpetrator is at risk of having to compensate the full harm it caused.

Collective actions may of two types. Opt-in collective actions are based on the principle that an action may only be brought on behalf of persons who have expressly consented to be represented in the proceedings. Opt-out collective actions are based on the principle that the action may be brought on behalf of an appropriately defined class of affected persons that will all be bound by the outcome of the litigation unless they explicitly opt-out of the action. The default position is that if a member of the class, having being adequately informed of the pending action, does not state its intention not be represented in the action, the action is brought on his behalf.

Opt-in collective actions may fall significantly short of ensuring that full compensation of the anti-competitive harm is achieved. Empirical evidence tends to show that so-called opt-in models tend to achieve very low levels of compensation.[111] If this is true, then the procedure in question may fall short of the principle of full effectiveness of Community law. The perpetrator is not at risk of having to compensate the full harm it caused and the right to damages does not act as a deterrent from engaging in anti-competitive conduct. The reluctance of individual claimants to take active steps to join a prospective or pending action benefits the perpetrators of an infringement of Community competition law. On the other hand, an opt-out collective action maximises the compensation that the perpetrators will ultimately be liable to pay.[112]

Opt-out actions, however, are controversial. Some may argue that opt-out collective actions are not embedded in the legal traditions of the Member States.[113] However, a number of Member States have adopted collective redress systems that either allow or come close to opt-out procedures, including Denmark,[114] Portugal,[115] Spain,[116] the Netherlands,[117] and Norway.[118] In England and Wales, the representative party

[111] See, eg, R Mulheron, 'Reform of Collective Redress in England and Wales: A Perspective of Need. A Research Paper for Submission to the Civil Justice Council of England and Wales', 2008, available on the website of the Civil Justice Council of England and Wales. It is not the purpose of this chapter to set out the empirical evidence for the proposition that opt-in models of collective action tend to achieve lower levels of compensation. This chapter discusses the consequences of this proposition, assumed true, under the principle of effectiveness of Community law.

[112] An opt-out collective redress mechanism may raise issues of compatibility with Art 6 of the ECHR. Those who do not opt-out in the prescribed way are bound by the outcome of the litigation. Assuming that this may be considered a restriction of the right to access to a court, it must be remembered that not all such restrictions are an infringement of the right to a fair trial under ECHR, Art 6. The lawfulness of the restriction will depend on whether it pursues a legitimate aim and whether it is proportionate: *Golder v UK* (1975) EHRR 524 and *Ashingdane v UK* (1985) 7 EHRR 528.

[113] For a judicial *dictum* see *Campos v Kentucky & Indiana Terminal Railroad Co* [1962] 2 Lloyd's Rep 459.

[114] Lov nr 181 28 February 2007 (Act No 181 of 28 February 2007).

[115] See Law No 83/95 of 31 August, Right of Proceeding, Participation and Popular Action; and Law No 24/96 of 31 July, Establishing the Legal System Applicable to Consumer Protection, discussed in Mulheron, (n 111) 97–101.

[116] Ley 1/2000, de 7 de enero, de Enjuiciamiento Civil (BOE núm 7, de 8 de enero del 2000, pp 575–728. Corrección de errores BOE núm 90, de 14–04–2000, p 15278 y BOE núm 180, de 28–07–2001, p 27746) (LEC). See, in particular, LEC, Libro I, Título I, Capítulo 1, Articulo 6 Capacidad para ser parte: Podrán ser parte en los procesos ante los tribunales civiles: . . . 7.º Los grupos de consumidores o usuarios afectados por un hecho dañoso cuando los individuos que lo compongan estén determinados o sean fácilmente determinables. Para demandar en juicio será necesario que el grupo se constituya con la mayoría de los afectados.

[117] Wet van 23 juni 2005 tot wijziging van het Burgerlijk Wetboek en het Wetboek van Burgerlijke Rechtsvordering teneinde de collectieve afwikkeling van massaschades te vergemakkelijken (Wet collectieve afwikkeling massaschade), Staatsblad 2005, 340.

[118] LOV-1915–08–13–6, Act Relating to the Litigation Procedure in Civil Disputes (The Dispute Act), 13 August 1915 no 6. See C Bernt-Hamre, 'Class Actions, Group Litigation and Other Forms of Collective Litigation in the Norwegian Courts' (National Report prepared for the conference 'The Globalisation of Class Actions', Oxford, 12–14 December 2007, available at http://www.law.stanford.edu/display/images/dynamic/events_media/Norway_National_Report.pdf).

action has long been recognised[119] and the Civil Procedure Rules (CPR) provide for group litigation orders.[120]

Furthermore, even if it is accepted that in certain cases individual claims or an opt-in action will equally fail to deliver full compensation, it may be argued that, in such cases, it is for public authorities to ensure that sufficiently dissuasive penalties are imposed on the perpetrators. However, in *Van Gend en Loos*, the Court of Justice rejected this argument and established that the availability of a public enforcement mechanism does not render the role of private actions redundant. First, the Court relied on the principle of effective judicial protection, emphasising that public enforcement may not be sufficiently timely in securing individual rights. Secondly, the Court stated that 'the vigilance of individuals concerned to protect their rights amounts to an effective supervision in addition to the supervision' entrusted to the Commission and the Member States.[121] This principle is confirmed in the subsequent case law. The doctrine of State liability rests upon the assumption that private actions ensure the full effectiveness of Community law[122] even if a public enforcement mechanism is available for exactly the same purpose.[123] Both *Crehan* and *Manfredi* upheld a right to damages for breach of Community law in circumstances in which a public enforcement mechanism was plainly available. Indeed, while in *Crehan* the Commission did not take action with respect to the agreement in dispute in the case, in *Manfredi* the Italian national competition authority had established the infringement of competition law (albeit limited to the Italian equivalent of Article 81) and fined the defendants.[124] Nevertheless, the Court relied on the effectiveness rationale to justify the conferral of the right to damages on any individual who has suffered loss as a result of an infringement of Article 81.[125]

In conclusion, it would appear that Community law requires that an opt-out collective redress mechanism be available in circumstances in which the need for individual proceedings or individual consent to a collective action would not ensure that the defendant is held liable for the full loss it caused. An opt-out collective action would also ensure that individual claimants have a realistic prospect of obtaining full compensation. The proposal in the White Paper on Damages actions that Member

[119] CPR, r 19.6.

[120] CPR, rr 19.10–19.15. Rule 19.12 envisages circumstances in which a judgment or order may bind the parties to a claim which is entered on the group register after the order or judgment was made.

[121] *Van Gend en Loos* (n 47).

[122] *Francovich* (n 27) paras 33–4.

[123] Arts 226–228 of the EC Treaty provide for a mechanism whereby a Member State may be held to account and fined for non-compliance with Community obligations.

[124] *Manfredi* (n 37) para 11.

[125] *Ibid*, paras 60– 61.

States should be able to designate qualified entities 'to bring representative actions for damages on behalf of identified or, in rather restricted cases, identifiable victims (not necessarily their members)'[126] is consistent with this analysis.

B The Limiting Function of the Principle: Protection of the Leniency Programme

The principle of effectiveness of Community law as the legal basis of the right to damages for breach of Community competition law has the potential of moving forward the boundaries of the Treaty well beyond what a traditional reading of the doctrine of procedural autonomy might suggest. However, the same principle may limit the exercise of the right to damages in certain circumstances, namely when private actions may themselves impair the full effectiveness of Community competition law. An area where this may occur is the interaction between leniency programmes and private actions.

Leniency programmes are designed to reward with immunity from fines or with a reduced fine undertakings that reveal to the competition authorities the existence of a cartel or provide useful evidence in the course of an investigation.[127] Leniency programmes are generally seen as an essential tool in the fight against cartels.[128]

The decision of an undertaking to apply for leniency is a complex one. The likelihood of detection and the likely amount of any sanction are the main factors that are taken into account. From the undertaking's point of view, the sanction is not only the fine that may be imposed by a competition authority but also any damages that may be recoverable by those who have been harmed by the infringement.

Any undertaking in receipt of leniency is at risk of being the primary target, and perhaps the sole target, of a private action. The reasons are largely practical. First, a claimant would generally assume that the leniency applicant is likely to have sufficient evidence in his possession that may be obtained through disclosure or a court order relating to specific documents. Secondly, it is tactically very difficult for a leniency applicant to

[126] See White Paper on Damages actions (above n 3) 4 and Staff Working Paper on Damages actions (above n 3) para 52. The quotation is from the latter document.

[127] For an overview of the leniency policy see OECD 'Fighting Hardcore Cartels: Harm, Effective Sanctions, and Leniency Programmes' 2002.

[128] See the Commission Notice on Immunity from fines and reduction of fines in cartel cases [2006] OJ C/298/11, at paras 1–5. As of 1 July 2007, competition authorities in 24 Member States operate a leniency programme. The US Department of Justice, Antitrust Division, operates a Corporate Leniency Policy and a Leniency Policy for Individuals. For an overview of the US system see R Nazzini, *Concurrent Proceedings in Competition Law: Procedure, Evidence and Remedies* (Oxford, Oxford University Press, 2004) 415–17.

dispute its liability in court even if the relevant competition authority has not yet made an infringement decision or, technically, the decision of the competition authority would not bind the court. Finally, if the relevant competition authority has not yet made a decision, the claimant will assume that the leniency applicant is likely to be an addressee of any infringement decision while there may be some uncertainty as regards the other parties. If the leniency applicant is jointly and severally liable with the other cartelists, there is therefore a strong incentive for the claimant to sue the leniency applicant and, possibly, only the leniency applicant[129] for the entire loss.

In the decision to apply for leniency, the likely magnitude of private law liability and the likelihood of being the primary target in any private action could discourage leniency applications in certain circumstances. If this were to happen, fewer cartels would be uncovered. This would undermine the effective enforcement of Community competition law. Ultimately, the level of compensation for cartels may also decrease, as in Europe many private actions in this field are follow-on actions.[130] The principle of effectiveness of Community competition law not only allows but arguably requires that appropriate action be taken in order to preserve the effectiveness of leniency programmes to the extent that they may be compromised by the threat of private litigation. In the absence of Community measures in this area, it is for the Member States to act appropriately as long as the principles of equivalence and effectiveness are observed.

Both the Commission in the White Paper on Damages actions[131] and the UK Office of Fair Trading in its recommendations to the UK Government of November 2007[132] put forward proposals aimed at safeguarding the effectiveness of leniency programmes against the background of increased private litigation. These proposals are complex and require a balancing of different factors based on empirical evidence.[133] One area, however,

[129] If the leniency applicant is solvent and able to satisfy the entire claim, the claimant would not have an incentive to sue the other cartelists as he would be exposed to adverse costs orders in relation to more than one defendant. The costs of the litigation are also likely to be higher the more defendants are jointly sued in the same action.

[130] It is important to note, however, that significant damages may be recovered in cases with no prior public enforcement activity.: see RH Lande and JP Davis, 'Report of American Antitrust Institute's Private Enforcement Project—Benefits from Private Antitrust Enforcement: An Analysis of Forty Cases' (10 December 2007).

[131] White Paper on Damages actions (above n 3) 10 and Staff Working Paper on Damages actions (above n 3) paras 287–302. This option was put forward in the Green Paper on Damages actions (above n 2) option 28.

[132] 'Private actions in competition law: effective redress for consumers and business—Recommendations from the Office of Fair Trading' (above n 7) para 9.5.

[133] Another set of proposals relates to the removal of joint and several liability for the leniency applicant (probably limited to the undertaking that receives full immunity) so that it is only liable for the harm it caused to its direct and indirect purchasers: Green Paper on Damages actions (above n 2) options 29–30; 'Private actions in competition law: effective

appears ripe for consideration, namely the use in civil litigation of leniency documents. Both the Commission and the OFT make proposals in this regard. The aim is to avoid the increased likelihood of private actions and the increased size of potential damages awards in opt-out collective actions having a negative effect on the number and quality of leniency applications. This may occur because, in the context of the leniency programme, the leniency applicant will generally have produced written corporate statements and witness statements that explain in detail the functioning of the cartels and admit its participation in the anti-competitive arrangements. These documents may be discoverable in litigation thus placing the leniency applicant in a substantially worse position than other cartelists merely as a result of the leniency application. The obvious solution would be to exclude documents that only came into existence because of the leniency application from use in civil litigation without the consent of the leniency applicant.[134]

In order to assess this option under the doctrine of procedural autonomy, the key question to be asked is whether this is an adequate measure to preserve the effectiveness of the leniency programme in line with the principles of full effectiveness of Community law and effective judicial protection of the right to damages for breach of Article 81 or 82. This question is of crucial importance because the answer may require a trade-off between the effective enforcement principle and the effective judicial protection principle.

The possibility of disclosure and use in litigation of leniency documents[135] increases the incentives of the claimants to sue the leniency applicant as the primary or only target and constitutes a significant disadvantage for the leniency applicant in the litigation. It has, therefore, the potential to discourage applications for leniency. To exclude the use of leniency documents from use in civil proceedings without the consent of the leniency applicant appears to be an adequate response to the potential risk that private actions pose to the leniency process. The assessment requires a trade-off between the principle of full effectiveness of Community law and the principle of effective judicial protection akin to a proportionality test. The principle of full effectiveness prevails but the

redress for consumers and business—Recommendations from the Office of Fair Trading' (above n 7) paras 9.9–9.10. In the US, see the Antitrust Criminal Penalty Enhancement and Reform Act of 2004 15 USCA § 1 note.

134 White Paper on Damages actions, 10 (n 3) and Staff Working Paper on Damages actions (n 3) paras 287–302; 'Private actions in competition law: effective redress for consumers and business—Recommendations from the Office of Fair Trading' (*ibid*) para 9.5.

135 In legal systems where there is a disclosure process, such documents are disclosable. Even in legal systems where there is no common law disclosure, it is generally possible to apply for a court order requiring a party to produce specified documents. Leniency documents can generally be described in a sufficiently precise manner so that the requirements for an order for production of documents are likely to be satisfied.

interference with the principle of effective judicial protection should be kept to what is necessary to achieve the prevailing objective. If leniency documents are defined as documents that would not have come into existence but for the leniency application, all other evidence, and in particular any contemporaneous documentary evidence of the cartel, is available. The unavailability of leniency documents for use in civil proceedings does not disproportionately restrict the individual right to damages and does not make its exercise impossible or excessively difficult.[136]

Under the doctrine of procedural autonomy, an interesting question would be how to apply the principle of equivalence if leniency applications relating to infringements of national competition law were treated differently from leniency applications relating to infringements of Community competition law or leniency applications to the national competition authority were treated differently from leniency applications to the European Commission. Let us suppose that leniency documents are disclosable as regards leniency programmes relating to national competition law but they are not disclosable in relation to the leniency programme relating to Article 81. Which treatment is more favourable? Clearly, leniency applicants are better off in the latter situation and claimants are better off in the former. Leniency applicants, however, are protected in so far as it is necessary to ensure the effectiveness of the enforcement of Article 81. Measures aimed at ensuring the effective enforcement of Article 81 may limit the modes of exercise of the claimant's right to damages for breach of Article 81. The principle of equivalence in itself does not provide an answer because it is impossible to say, without recourse to the principle of full effectiveness of Community law, which situation is more favourable. This example revels the weakness of the principle of equivalence, whose function is limited to ensuring that clear-cut forms of discrimination between national legal rights and Community law rights are outlawed. The key test relates to the principles of full effectiveness of Community law and effective judicial protection.

Consistently with the analysis in this section, the White Paper on Damages actions proposes that corporate statements should not be disclosable in so far as they relate to Article 81 whether they have been submitted to the European Commission or to national competition authorities.[137] If

[136] Restrictions on the admissibility of evidence may raise a question of compatibility with Art 6 of the EC HR. As in relation to the right to access to court more generally (see above n 112), restrictions on disclosure or admissibility of evidence may be justified if necessary in the public interest provided that the party's right to a fair trial is not denied (see, eg, *Rowe and Davis v UK* (2000) 30 EHRR 1). In civil proceedings, it is unlikely that the inadmissibility of leniency documents, narrowly defined as those documents which would not exist but for the leniency application, might deny the claimant the right to a fair trial.

[137] White Paper on Damages actions (above n 3) 10, and Staff Working Paper on Damages actions (above n 3) paras 288–93.

this proposal is implemented, the difficulties relating to the application of the principle of equivalence will not arise as the matter will be governed by harmonised Community law.

V CONCLUSION

After decades of case law developments on Community law private rights and remedies, the contours of the Community acquis and the criteria under which the compatibility of national rules on remedies and procedure must be assessed remain unclear. This is due to the inadequacy of the doctrine of procedural autonomy in its traditional formulation to provide a robust analytical framework for the understanding of Community law rights and remedies. First, the doctrine of procedural autonomy presupposes the existence of a Community law right. Too little attention is given, in the case law of the Court of Justice, to the legal basis of the right and how the legal basis of the right determines its function and content as well as the existence and scope of the remedy. Secondly, the Court of Justice often uses the term 'effectiveness' ambiguously to cover both the principle of full effectiveness of Community law and the principle of effective judicial protection. These principles are closely linked and often point in the same direction but should be kept distinct. The principle of effective judicial protection presupposes the existence of a right while the principle of full effectiveness of Community law may be the legal basis of the right. More importantly, the principle of full enforcement relates to the attainment of the objective of a Community policy while the principle of effective judicial protection relates to the protection of the individual right. Finally, in some cases, the two principles may be in conflict with each other so that a trade-off is required. Thirdly, the principle of equivalence is often given undue prominence in the application of the doctrine of procedural autonomy. The key test would appear to be whether national rules comply with the principles of full effectiveness of Community law and effective judicial protection. The principle of equivalence has a residual role in ruling out clear-cut forms of discrimination between the treatment of Community law rights and clearly comparable national law rights. The traditional understanding of the doctrine of procedural autonomy has imposed artificial limits on the development of Community law rights and limits such as the refusal of the Court in the *Manfredi* case to address the definition of the concept of 'causal relationship'.

This chapter proposes a three-stage analytical framework for the assessment of whether national rules on remedies and procedure are compatible with Community law. First, the legal basis of the right must be identified as a matter of Community law. The legal basis of a right may include the recognition of an individual interest deemed to be worthy of legal protection or the full effectiveness of Community law as the public interest in the attainment of the objectives of the Community. Secondly, the legal basis of the right, in conjunction with the principle of effective judicial protection, determines function and content of the right under Community law and the existence and scope of the remedy. Thirdly, national rules on remedies and procedure are assessed under the doctrine of procedural autonomy. The key test is whether national law complies with the principles of full effectiveness of Community law and effective judicial protection. The legal basis of the right may determine the relative weight of the two principles. If the legal basis of the right is the effective enforcement of Community law, then the principle of full effectiveness prevails over the principle of effective judicial protection in the assessment of national rules. The principle of equivalence has a residual application.

Community law recognises a right to damages for breach of Article 81 or 82. The legal basis of the right is the effective enforcement of Community competition law. Community competition law is not intended to protect specific individual interests but to pursue a public interest goal.[138] The reason why individual rights are upheld under Community law is that such rights strengthen 'the working of the Community competition rules' and discourage 'agreements or practices, frequently covert, which are liable to restrict or distort competition'. Therefore, 'actions for damages before the national courts can make a significant contribution to the maintenance of effective competition in the Community'.[139] The fact that multiple damages are not a requirement under Community law is not incompatible with this rationale. In the *Manfredi* case, following the previous case of *Marshal (No 2)*, the European Court of Justice held that full compensation is the minimum requirement to achieve the full effectiveness of Community competition law.

The principle of full effectiveness of Community law plays a significant role in the assessment of national rules, both substantive and procedural. In circumstances in which the infringement of the Community competition rules causes harm to a significant number of persons and such persons are unlikely in practice to take active steps to issue individual proceedings or join a collective action, Member States, in the absence of Community law harmonisation, must ensure that an opt-out collective redress mechanism is available.

This conclusion is controversial. Opt-out collective redress mechanisms are still only adopted in a minority of Member States. The conservatism of the legal institutions in many Member States may resonate with the European Court of Justice. The ruling in *Manfredi*, which, on the one

[138] It is controversial what this public interest is or should be: see M Motta, *Competition Policy* (Cambridge, Cambridge University Press, 2004) 17–30; R Nazzini, 'Article 81 EC between time present and time past: a normative critique of "restriction of competition" in EU law' [2006] *CML Rev* 497.

[139] *Manfredi* (n 37) para 91.

hand, adopts an effective enforcement rationale, and, on the other hand, concludes that multiple damages are not required by Community law, may suggest that the Court accepts that complex policy decisions are best left to the political institutions even if the goal is mandated by Community law. It was, therefore, necessary and appropriate for the Commission to take the initiative to propose a Community instrument requiring Member States to introduce an opt-out collective redress mechanism to be activated in circumstances in which individual or opt-in claims would not achieve the full effectiveness of Community law. The White Paper on Damages actions proposes a representative action on behalf of identifiable persons brought by qualified entities designated in advance by the relevant Member State.[140] Whether this solution is technically desirable or unduly timid is outside the scope of this chapter. What this chapter argues, however, is that the introduction of an opt-out collective redress mechanism may be required under Community law and Community harmonisation seems to be the most appropriate way forward.

The effective enforcement rationale for the right to damages may also have a limiting function. Private actions must not jeopardise the effective enforcement of Community competition law. An example where this may occur is in relation to leniency programmes. If there is evidence that the threat of private actions deters leniency applications and, as a result, the detection rate of cartels is likely to decrease, then the individual right to damages may be limited to the extent that it is necessary to protect the effectiveness of the leniency programmes. A measure that may be adopted is the exclusion from use in private litigation of an appropriately defined class of documents that came into existence because of the leniency application. The White Paper on Damages actions proposes that adequate protection against disclosure in private actions for damages should be ensured for corporate statements submitted by a leniency applicant in order to avoid placing the applicant in a less favourable situation than the co-infringers.[141] This solution, while limiting the exercise of the right to damages for breach of Article 81, is not only compatible with Community law but necessary as a result of the trade-off between the principle of full effectiveness of Community law and the principle of effective judicial protection. The former principle prevails because the legal basis of the right to damages for breach of Article 81 or 82 is the full effectiveness of Community law and not only the recognition of an individual interest worthy of legal protection per se.[142]

140 White Paper on Damages actions (n 3) 4.

141 *Ibid*, 10.

142 As explained in section IV B above, in order to be lawful under Community law, the limitation of the right to damages must pursue the objective of ensuring the full effectiveness of Art 81, must be proportionate to this aim, and must be empirically justified.

Index

www.ingramcontent.com/pod-product-compliance
Ingram Content Group UK Ltd.
Pitfield, Milton Keynes, MK11 3LW, UK
UKHW021033041026
15470UKWH00018B/1844/J

9 781841 138602